Handbook of
RESEARCH
DESIGN
and
SOCIAL
MEASUREMENT

A TEXT
AND REFERENCE BOOK
FOR THE SOCIAL
AND BEHAVIORAL SCIENCES

Handbook of
RESEARCH
DESIGN
and
SOCIAL
Fourth Edition
MEASUREMENT

Delbert C. Miller

PROFESSOR OF SOCIOLOGY
AND BUSINESS ADMINISTRATION
INDIANA UNIVERSITY

Longman
New York & London

HANDBOOK OF RESEARCH DESIGN AND SOCIAL MEASUREMENT

Fourth Edition

Longman Inc., 1560 Broadway, New York, N.Y. 10036
Associated companies, branches, and representatives throughout the world.

Developmental Editor: Nicole Benevento
Editorial and Design Supervisor: Frances Althaus
Production Supervisor: Ferne Kawahara
Manufacturing Supervisor: Marion Hess
Interior Design: Pencils Portfolio, Inc.

Library of Congress Cataloging in Publication Data

Miller, Delbert Charles, 1913–
    Handbook of research design and social measurement.

    Includes bibliographies and index.
    1. Social sciences—Research. 2. Sociometry.
I. Title.
H62.M44   1983   302'.072   82–15287
ISBN 0–582–28326–4   AACR2

Manufactured in the United States of America

Printing: 9 8 7 6 5 4 3 2 1   Year: 91 90 89 87 86 85 84 83

Dedication

Social and behavioral scientists compose nearly one-third of all scientists in science and engineering. Social and behavioral scientists are 31.8% of the 343,000 persons who earned doctorate degrees in all fields of science and engineering in the United States from 1936 through 1978. (Psychologists are the largest component at 16.6%.) Other categories include biologists and biochemists, 21.9%; engineers, 15%; chemists, 14.4%; physicists and astronomers, 8.5%; mathematicians and computer scientists, 5.9%.

Social and behavioral scientists are young. They are a young part, collectively, in terms of recency of training. Over half (53.2% of all the social-behavioral scientists received their Ph.D.s since 1970, compared with 45.1% for all fields of science and engineering.

Women social scientists are proportionately greater in number. They are a leading part, relatively, in terms of career opportunities for women. One out of five (20.1%) of the doctorate holders in social and behavioral science are women, compared with 11.2% for all fields of science and engineering.

Almost two-thirds are in education. They are a prominent part of education institutions. Compared to doctorates from all other fields, social and behavioral scientists are more apt to be employed in educational institutions (64.5% vs. 54.3%), less apt to be working in business and industry (12.7% vs. 27.6%), and about equally apt to be working in federal, state, or local government (9.6% vs. 10.5%).

Recognition has been achieved in major scientific bodies. They are now a formally recognized part of the major national science institutions. Since 1973 the Assembly of Behavioral and Social Sciences has been co-equal to the Assemblies of Engineering, Life Sciences, and Mathematical and Physical Sciences in the National Academy of Sciences. In that same period, the number of social and behavioral scientists elected to the National Academy has approximately doubled, and today 149 of the 1313 members are from these disciplines. In 1968 the Public Law that governs the National Science Foundation was amended to explicitly include the social sciences in the authority that directs NSF to initiate and support basic science research.

All sciences, including the social and behavioral, share a common commitment to the scientific method. All sciences, including the social and behavioral, share a commitment to norms regarding evidence, verification, inference, rigor, and so forth. To systemize knowledge, and hence make it useful, every science develops approaches, techniques, and theories appropriate for the phenomena they study. The chemist, biologist, or physicist organizes knowledge at the atomic, molecular, or cellular levels. By contrast, a social or behavioral scientist may analyze the world in terms of personal, group, societal, or cultural levels. Controlled experiments at these levels are more difficult, are sometimes made and more often approximated, or the data are handled in other ways. But commitment to rigorous testing of hypotheses is firmly grounded, and research designs appropriate to the problem are applied.*

* For the data and script I am indebted to Dr. Otto Larsen, director, Division of Social and Economic Sciences, National Science Foundation. A more comprehensive statement will be found in *Footnotes* of the American Sociological Association, March 1981, p. 8.

Acknowledgments

Permission to reprint from the following gratefully acknowledged.

from *Career Patterns of Liberal Arts Graduates* by Robert Calvert, Jr. Copyright © 1973 by The Carroll Press. Reprinted by permission of The Carroll Press, Cranston, Rhode Island.

from *Mail and Telephone Surveys* by Don A. Dillman. Copyright © 1978 by John Wiley and Sons, Inc. Reprinted by permission of John Wiley and Sons, Inc.

from *Concepts, Theory, and Explanation in the Behavioral Sciences* by Gordon J. DiRenzo (ed.). Copyright © 1967 by Random House, Inc. Reprinted by permission of Random House Inc.

from *Surveys by Telephone* (New York: Academic Press, 1979) by Robert M. Groves and Robert L. Kahn. Reprinted by permission of the publisher and Robert M. Groves.

from "Urban Friendships: Qualitative and Quantitative Aspects of Primary-Relations in an Urban Setting," unpublished dissertation by Lea Hagoel. Copyright © 1982 by Lea Hagoel. Reprinted by permission of the author.

from *Process of Stratification* (New York: Academic Press, 1977) by Robert M. Hauser and David L. Featherman. Reprinted by permission of Academic Press and David L. Featherman.

from "Factors Affecting Response Rate to Mailed Questionnaires: A Quantitative Analysis of the Published Literature" by Thomas A. Heberlein and Robert Baumgartner in *American Sociological Review* 43 (August 1978). Reprinted by permission of the American Sociological Association and the authors.

from *Community Power Succession: Atlanta's Policy-Makers Revisited* by Floyd Hunter. Copyright © 1980 by the University of North Carolina Press. Reprinted by permission of the publisher.

from *Organizational Stress: Studies in Role Conflict and Ambiguity* by Robert L. Kahn et al. Copyright © 1964 by John Wiley & Sons, Inc. Reprinted by permission of the publisher.

from *The Conduct of Inquiry* (pp. 30–33) by Abraham Kaplan (Chandler Publishing Co.). Copyright © 1964 by Harper & Row, Publishers, Inc. Reprinted by permission of the publisher.

from *Statistical Analysis for Sociologists: A Student Manual* by Herman J. Loether and Donald G. McTavish. Copyright © 1974 by Allyn and Bacon, Inc. Reprinted by permission of the publisher.

from "Occupational Status Scores: Stability and Change" by Charles B. Nam, John LaRocque, Marty G. Powers, and Joan Holmberg in *Proceedings of the American Statistical Association,* 1975. Reprinted by permission of the American Statistical Association.

from *Handbook of Survey Research* (New York: Academic Press, 1982) by Peter Rossi, James D. Wright, and Andy Anderson (eds.). Reprinted by permission of the publisher and Don A. Dillman.

from *A Methodology for Social Research* (New York: Harper & Row, 1968) by Gideon Sjoberg and Roger Nett. Copyright held by Sjoberg and Nett, and reprinted with their permission.

from *Social Sciences Index* for 1982. Copyright © 1982 by the H. W. Wilson Company. Material reproduced by permission of the publisher.

from "Recording Changes" to "Reliability of Results" (pp. 217–218) in *Say it With Figures,* 4th edition, by Hans Zeisel. Copyright 1947, 1950, 1957 by Harper and Row, Publishers, Inc. Reprinted by permission of the publisher.

Contents

Preface

This revision holds to the book's original purpose. The aim, as before, is to provide a book that will be equally useful as a text for students or a reference book for teachers and professional research workers. As a text the book provides a step-by-step set of instructions for the research training of a student. It begins where every researcher, student or professional, begins—in finding a creative idea, a middle-range theory, and initial hypotheses. It proceeds through design, proposal, collection and analysis of data, and finally writing, reporting, publication, and utilization of research skills.

As a reference work, the book includes every digest of useful knowledge that behavioral science researchers need as a guide to their research requirements. For that reason the contents cover searches of periodicals, useful source books, bibliographies, computer programs, many of the most important scales and sources of scales, sources of funding and publication—and much more. The purpose is to place in the Handbook enough information so that older researchers can find digests of material not taught in the days of their graduate training or information that may be used for review by any researcher.

Besides the standard and often "classic" contents preserved from the previous editions, this Fourth Revised Handbook contains much new material including:

How science is built
The variety of research designs available to behavioral science researchers
Major social periodicals that have been indexed and are available for computer search
Records of return rates from many different mail questionnaires
Instructions for telephone interviewing
Guides for choosing the mail questionnaire, personal interview, or telephone survey
Panel techniques
Human relations area files
Human relations skills in social research
Preparing data for the computer
Computer programs
Dictionary of newer statistical tools and methodological techniques
Updated scales for social status and prestige
New scales for social variables such as friendship, international occupational prestige, job-related tensions in organizations, and community leadership
Updated listing of all scales reported in *American Sociological Review* 1965–80
Review of continuity in sociological research

How a researcher makes a social scale
Models of master scale construction
Complete revision of new funding opportunities, requirements, and limitations
Cost guides for mail questionnaire, telephone survey, and personal interview
New or updated listings of sociological and related-field journals that serve as publication outlets to behavioral scientists
How sociologists get published and how they take rejection
Major publications sponsored by the American Sociological Association and the American Psychological Association, major journals used in political science and public administration, anthropology, education, business, journalism, and mass communication
Applied sociology and policy making
Careers for sociology degree holders in academic and nonacademic markets
Indexes of names and subjects

I am grateful to behavioral science researchers everywhere, especially to the users and contributors to previous editions. There is an intellectual kinship across the social and applied social sciences knit by our common adherence to scientific methods and the methodological and statistical techniques that guide our work. For this reason the book's dedication to all behavioral science researchers seems fitting. The reader is directed to examine the perspective that places behavioral scientists among all contemporary scientists.

I wish to express my indebtedness to Professors Hermon J. Loether of the California State College at Dominguez Hills and Donald G. McTavish of the University of Minnesota, who taught and reviewed the Third Edition. They have provided many valuable suggestions and material for this edition. I am especially grateful for the secretarial services of Susan Platter, Eleanor Schloesser, Cheryl Price, and Judy Bolick in the Department of Sociology at Indiana University. Sociology colleagues have always provided a guiding hand when I sought help, and subtle additions that have resulted from intellectual osmosis are beyond measurement.

Handbook of
RESEARCH
DESIGN
and
SOCIAL
MEASUREMENT

General Description of the Guides to Research Design and Sampling

PART 1 contains guides to accompany the first five steps in the sequence of a planned research proposal. These are (1) selection and definition of a sociological problem, (2) description of the relationship of the problem to a theoretical framework, (3) formulation of working hypotheses, (4) design of the experiment or inquiry, and (5) sampling procedures. The brief treatments of these subjects may be enriched by use of the bibliography placed at the end of part 1.

AN OUTLINE GUIDE FOR THE DESIGN OF A SOCIAL RESEARCH PROBLEM*

Instructions for Use of Guide 1.1

This outline for the design of social research lists the essential considerations in designing a research project. It is recommended that all steps be planned before field or laboratory work is undertaken. Each of the guides in part 1 has been selected to aid in planning the first five steps shown in the outline. Other guides in parts 2, 3, and 4 are available to assist the researcher in most of the steps shown.

I. The Sociological Problem
1. Present a clear, brief statement of the problem with concepts defined where necessary.
2. Show that the problem is limited to bounds amenable to treatment or test.
3. Describe the significance of the problem with reference to one or more of the following criteria:
   a. Is timely.
   b. Relates to a practical problem.
   c. Relates to a wide population.
   d. Relates to an influential or critical population.
   e. Fills a research gap.
   f. Permits generalization to broader principles of social interaction or general theory.
   g. Sharpens the definition of an important concept or relationship.
   h. Has many implications for a wide range of practical problems.
   i. May create or improve an instrument for observing and analyzing data.
   j. Provides an opportunity for gathering data that is restricted by the limited time available for gathering particular data.
   k. Provides the possibility for a fruitful exploration with known techniques.
II. The Theoretical Framework
1. Describe the relationship of the problem to a theoretical framework.
2. Demonstrate the relationship of the problem to previous research.
3. Present alternate hypotheses considered feasible within the framework of the theory.
III. The Hypotheses
1. Clearly state the hypotheses selected for test. (Null and alternate hypothesis should be stated.)
2. Indicate the significance of test hypotheses to the advancement of research and theory.
3. Define concepts or variables (preferably in operational terms).
   a. Independent and dependent variables should be distinguished from each other.
   b. The scale upon which variables are to be measured (quantitative, semi-quantitative, or qualitative) should be specified.
4. Describe possible mistakes and their consequences.
5. Note seriousness of possible mistakes.

---

* Based on Russell L. Ackoff, *The Design of Social Research* (Chicago: University of Chicago, 1953). Adapted by Delbert C. Miller.

IV. Design of the Experiment or Inquiry
    1. Describe ideal design or designs with particular attention to the control of interfering variables.
    2. Describe selected operational design.
        a. Describe stimuli, subjects, environment, and responses with the objects, events, and properties necessary for their specification.
        b. Describe how control of interfering variables is achieved.
    3. Specify statistical tests including dummy tables for each test.
        a. Specify level of confidence desired.

V. Sampling Procedures
    1. Describe experimental and control samples.
        a. Specify the population to which the hypotheses are relevant.
        b. Explain determination of size and type of sample.
    2. Specify method of drawing or selecting sample.
        a. Specify relative importance of Type I Error and Type II Error.
        b. Estimate relative costs of the various sizes and types of samples allowed by the theory.

VI. Methods of Gathering Data
    1. Describe measures of quantitative variables showing reliability and validity when these are known. Describe means of identifying qualitative variables.
    2. Include the following in description of questionnaires or schedules, if these are used.
        a. Approximate number of questions to be asked of each respondent.
        b. Approximate time needed for interview.
        c. The schedule as it has been constructed to this time.
        d. Preliminary testing of interview and results.
    3. Include the following in description of interview procedure, if this is used.
        a. Means of obtaining information, i.e., by direct interview, all or part by mail, telephone, or other means.
        b. Particular characteristics interviewers must have or special training that must be given them.
    4. Describe use to be made of pilot study, pretest, or trial run.
        a. Importance of and means for coping with unavailables, refusals, and response error.

VII. Working Guide
    1. Prepare working guide with time and budget estimates.
        a. Planning.
        b. Pilot Study and Pretests.
        c. Drawing sample.
        d. Preparing observational materials.
        e. Selection and training.
        f. Trial plan.
        g. Revising plans.
        h. Collecting data.
        i. Processing data.
        j. Preparing final report.
    2. Estimate total man-hours and cost.

VIII. Analysis of Results
    1. Specify method of analysis.
        a. Use of tables, calculator, sorter, computer, etc.
        b. Use of graphic techniques.
        c. Specify type of tables to be constructed.

IX. Interpretation of Results
    1. Discuss how conclusions will be fed back into theory.

X. Publication or Reporting Plans
1. Write these according to department and graduate school requirements.
2. Select for journal publication the most significant aspects of the problem in succinct form (probably not more than fifteen typewritten pages double spaced). Follow style and format specified by the journal to which the article will be submitted.

A GENERAL STATEMENT TO GUIDE THE BASIC RESEARCHER IN THE FORMULATION OF RESEARCH PROBLEMS　　*1.2*

Instructions for Use of Guide 1.2

The first step in the design of research is the selection of a fruitful problem. The range of potential topics for social research is as broad as the range of social behavior. This fact does not aid the researcher in making a *choice.* And the choice is the most important step. It becomes a commitment of time, money, and energy. It is not unusual for a researcher to give six months to a year finding the specific problem and formulating it for research study; it may take many years to conduct and publish his research.

The significance of a problem rests upon its probable contribution to knowledge. How can this significance be foreseen for research not yet undertaken and tested? The answer is that this is, to a great extent, an art; but there is little mystery about it. The master researcher knows the research literature and where the cutting edges of current research are. A rich array of theory and methodology is available against which to cast the proposed problem. To this is added a creative imagination, which provides the master contribution.

The student is led through this process during training and can develop mastery by finding a personal path. A progress chart that provides suggestions for maximizing effectiveness in finding a dissertation topic and research design follows:

1. Choosing begins with the first course.
  a. The art of raising questions is cultivated.
  b. The research implications of these questions are explored.
2. Choice of Field. Consider:
  a. your interest.
  b. your capacity.
  c. your potential growth and future career.
  d. ability of professor.
  e. ability to work with professor.
          As you continue course work.
3. Grow through seminars.
  a. Examine carefully how others have tackled research problems.
  b. Initiate small research projects in direction of your interests.
4. Begin discussion and work on a given topic.
  a. *Which* large, unexplored areas of the field should be studied?
  b. Define and delineate specific areas.
  c. Investigate previous research in one or more areas.

    d. Make a review of pertinent theory as it bears upon the specific areas.

    e. Set up hypotheses. Formulate theoretical background. Review all research pertaining.

    f. Feasibility of Testing Hypotheses.

        i. Time required.

        ii. Money required.

        iii. Availability of data.

        iv. Promise of fruitful contribution to general field.

    g. Fix experimental design.

        i. Progress chart with time schedule.

    h. "Pretest" design by setting up dummy tables.

        i. Check scales of measurement, statistics.

    i. Prepare your dissertation proposal by following outline guide 1.1.

It is well to recognize that this plan rests on the assumption that the student is planning for a future career and not simply to "knock out a thesis" (a plan of short-run expediency). From a thesis may emerge published articles that will provide the base for the researcher's reputation in the field and the springboard for future growth and contributions.

For the young researcher seeking to be a master researcher there are no shortcuts to this process except that he or she may perform an important role by replicating some outstanding research models on different populations and in different settings. Social science needs this kind of research badly in acquiring cumulative evidence. The student may utilize secondary data (see part 2.17, Guide to Bodies of Collected Data for the Social Science Researcher: Data References and Data Archives) to enrich research and minimize time and money problems.

A few suggestions of value for selecting important problems may be found in some books now especially written for students.* The final formulation of the problem determines its potential for the growth of knowledge.

A preliminary assessment of the worth of a problem can be gauged by using the suggested criteria for research problems that follows.

Suggested Criteria for Research Problems**

1. A concern with basic concepts and relationships of concepts, as distinguished from local, particularized, or exclusively applied research, to the end that the knowledge produced may be cumulative with that from other studies.

2. The development, refinement, and testing of theoretical formulations. At present the theories appropriate as research guides will be more limited in scope than the comprehensive, speculative systems prominent in the early history of social science.

3. Superior research design, including careful specification of the variables involved and use of the most precise and appropriate methods available.

---

   * Jacqueline P. Wiseman and Marcia S. Aron, *Field Projects for Sociology Students* (Cambridge, Mass.: Schenkman, 1970); Editors of Arco Books, *1000 Ideas for Term Papers for Sociology Students* (New York: Arco, 1970); Shulamit Reinharz, *On Becoming a Social Scientist* (San Francisco: Jossey-Bass, 1979).

   ** From *Report of the Study for the Ford Foundation on Policy and Program* (Detroit: Ford Foundation, November 1949).

4. A probable contribution to methodology by the discovery, development, or refinement of practicable tools, techniques, or methods.
5. Full utilization of relevant concepts, theories, evidence, and techniques from related disciplines.
6. The integration of any single study in a planned program of related research to the end that the results become meaningful in a broad context.
7. Adequate provision to train additional research scientists.
8. Provision, wherever feasible, to repeat or check related research of other persons in order to provide a check on the generality of conclusions. A special aspect of this characteristic would be the repetition of studies in more than one culture group.

Decisions Ahead: Some Alternatives of Sociological Research Design

Even in the choosing of the problem, there must be some evaluation of the total research design. Obviously, no problem, however valuable, is a good choice if the required research cannot be carried out. Some considerations may be classified and used as a preliminary check list.*

Type of Underlying Theory	General theory
	Middle-range theory
	Suppositions
Study Design	Experimental group after
	Experimental group before and after
	Experimental and control group after
	Experimental and control group before and after
	Other (See 1.3 Choice of Study Design)
Access to Organization and Respondents	Requires permission of individual respondents only
	Requires permission of organizational officials
	Requires permission of organizational and labor officials
	Requires permission of organizational and labor officials and respondents
Researcher Control over the Social System to Be Studied	No control
	Partial control
	Complete control
Data for Test of Hypotheses	Case and observational studies only
	Quantitative analysis only
	Quantitative supplemented with case and observational studies
	Other (historical, cross-cultural, etc.)
Type of Datum	Personal (fact predicated about single individual)
	Unit (fact predicated about aggregate of persons)

---

* I am indebted to Matilda White Riley for the idea of "alternatives of sociological research design." See her treatment on the cover page of *Sociological Research: A Case Approach* (New York: Harcourt, Brace & World, 1963).

Temporal Dimension	Cases from a single society at a single period (cross-sectional)
	Cases from a single society at many periods (time series or longitudinal)
	Cases from many societies at a single period (comparative cross-cultural)
	Cases from many societies at different periods (comparative longitudinal)
Sample or Universe to Be Studied	Individual in a role within a group
	Pair of interrelated group members (dyad)
	Primary group (30 or less)
	Secondary group (31 or more)
	Tertiary group (crowd, public, etc.)
	State, nation, or society
Number of Cases	Single or few cases
	Small sample of selected or random cases (under 30)
	Large sample of selected or random cases (31–5000 or more)
Source of Data	New data collected specifically by researcher
	Secondary data to be secured
	Secondary data already in hand
Method of Gathering Data	Direct observation with researcher as observer
	Participant observation with researcher as participant
	Interviewing by personal contact of researcher
	Interviewing by use of assistants or agents
	Mailed questionnaire
	Combined observation and interviewing
	Other
Number of Variables Involved	One
	Two
	More than two
Type of Variables Involved	Nominal
	Ordinal
	Interval
Selection of Scales for Measurement	None available; requires researcher to construct
	Scales available but relatively untested
	Scales of proved utility with high reliability and validity
Character of Distribution of Variables	Normal (allowing for parametric statistics)
	Nonnormal (requiring nonparametric statistics)
Treatment of Data	Hand calculation
	Machine calculation
	Computer
Time Required for Study	Less than one year
	Two years
	More than two years

Funding Required

Personal funds sufficient
Partial support required
Full support required

Availability of Funds

Assured
Local funds available requiring competitive application
National funds available requiring competitive application

In the pages that follow, guides have been provided for many of these design decisions. The choice of a research design is most important because this decision influences greatly all the outcomes of the study.

THE CHOICE OF RESEARCH DESIGN

1.3

Instructions for Use of Guide 1.3

Empirical research in social science proceeds in a variety of settings and contexts. The choice of a design setting for any research project is generally a vital concern of the researcher who seeks to determine the validity of a hypothesis and how best to discover evidence to either accept or reject it. Social phenomena are usually interlaced with numerous variables, and control of variables is difficult at best. What design will best ascertain associations or causal paths among the variables under study? How that question is answered may well determine the future outcome of the study. It will most certainly determine the time and money required for the study.

The guideline "Start Strong" supersedes any other consideration. It specifies that every effort be made to select a design setting with a population in which *large variations* of both independent and dependent variables may be found. And for any research project, *insurance* is important and may be secured by combining case analysis with any other research design. Failure to find statistical relations spurs the need for case study. In the intense probing, especially of *extreme cases at the tails of a distribution,* may be found polarized relationships that suggest new hypotheses, new designs, and new analyses of the data.

Look at the various designs, their characteristics, and prospective outcomes.

Type of research design setting	Central characteristics	Prospective outcomes
1. Descriptive survey a. Cross-sectional study. *Examples:* U.S. decennial census; James A. Davis, *Undergraduate Career Decisions;* Peter M. Blau and O. D. Duncan, *The American Occupational Structure.*	Concerned with information generally obtained by interview or mailed questionnaire. Other sources include official reports or statistics. Occasionally, data banks of other researchers provide appropriate information. Requires an effort to procure 100 percent enumeration of the population under study.	A sizable volume of information that can be classified by type, frequency, and central tendency. Expense of survey will be very large if population is substantial. Final yield: data that may be analyzed for numerous relationships.

Type of research design setting	Central characteristics	Prospective outcomes
b. Longitudinal study. *Example:* Greg J. Duncan and James N. Morgan, eds., *Five Thousand American Families,* vol. 8, *Eleven Years of the Panel Study of Income Dynamics.*	Time series are produced showing social or behavioral changes over varying periods of time.	Standardized data capable of comparative analysis over successive time intervals.
2. Sample survey. *Examples:* Gallup, Harris, and Roper polls of public opinion; Current Population Surveys of the Bureau of the Census; William H. Sewell and Robert M. Hauser, *Education, Occupation, and Earnings.*	Deals with only a fraction of a total population (universe). Sampling methods employed to provide a sample that is an accurate representation of the total population. Test hypotheses may be established. To ensure validity, researcher will utilize techniques for scaling, careful attention to questionnaire wording, inclusion of personal background data, etc.	Data may be analyzed for simple relationships between two variables. Multivariate analysis may involve factor analysis, matrix, and multiple discriminant analysis. Both quantitative and qualitative data analyzed with appropriate parametric or nonparametric statistics.
3. Field studies. *Examples:* Robert and Helen Lynd, *Middletown and Middletown in Transition;* August S. Hollingshead, *Elmtown's Youth;* William F. Whyte, *Street Corner Society;* Phillip E. Hammond, ed., *Sociologists at Work.*	Concerned primarily with processes and patterns under investigation of a single group, family, institution, organization or community. Emphasis is on the social structure i.e., interrelationships of parts of the structure and social interaction taking place. Attempts observations of social interactions or investigates thoroughly the reciprocal perceptions and attitudes of people playing interdependent roles. Direct and participant observation, interview, and scaling techniques employed.	Data gathered enable many hypotheses to be tested that were not amenable to survey data. Greater control achieved by focusing on subgroup of larger population. Sociological products such as processes, patterns, roles, attitudes, and values made available.
4. Case studies of persons. *Examples:* Elizabeth Eddy, *Becoming A Teacher: The Passage to Professional Status;* Irwin O. Smigel, *The Wall Street Lawyer;* W. F. Cottrell, *The Railroader.*	Usually refers to relatively intensive analysis of a single instance of phenomenon being investigated. Investigator interviews individuals or studies life history documents to gain insight into behavior. Attempts to discover unique features and common traits shared by all persons in a given classification. Cases may be grouped by type to discover uniformities.	Data can be assembled to throw light on conditioning relationships and causative factors. Personality and socialization processes can be identified. Concepts can be tested; concepts can be discovered. Cases may be coded and statistical tests applied to classifications providing associations between variables.

Type of research design setting	Central characteristics	Prospective outcomes
5. Combined survey and case study. *Example:* E. W. Burgess and Leonard S. Cottrell, Jr., *Predicting Success or Failure in Marriage;* Alfred C. Kinsey and Associates, *Sexual Behavior in the Human Male* and *Sexual Behavior in the Human Female.*	Survey methodology is combined with study of specific cases to illumine relationships first portrayed in a correlational pattern and then interpreted through case study to display processes and patterns. Cases selected after survey reveals those that are high or low on a criterion variable or those that display significant characteristics.	Relationships accompanied by process and pattern data revealing personal socialization in greater depth. Two data banks assembled: statistical data and case analysis data.
6. Prediction studies. *Examples:* Sheldon and Eleanor Glueck, *Predicting Delinquency and Crime;* Paul Horst, *The Prediction of Personal Adjustment* (see especially Paul Wallin, "The Prediction of Individual Behavior from Case Studies").	Aim is to estimate, in advance of participation, the level of an individual's performance in a given activity. Search is made on a population to find factors to serve as basis of prediction for such outcomes as success or failure in marriage, degree of success on parole, finding potential delinquents at an early age, school success, criminal behavior. A dichotomous dependent variable is always sought: stable marriage vs. broken (divorced) marriage. Law abiding vs. criminal behavior; delinquent vs. nondelinquent boys and girls. Academic achievers vs. nonacademic achievers.	Relationships between a number of factors and a prediction criterion determined. Selected factors weighted (perhaps as few as five or six with highest relationship with the criterion) in the construction of prognostic tables. Prognostic tables utilized to make predictions.
7. Controlled experiments. Major types are laboratory, "natural," and field experiment. a. Laboratory *Example:* Robert Bales, *Personality and Interpersonal Behavior.*	Investigator creates a situation with the exact conditions he wants and in which he controls some and manipulates other variables. He observes and measures effect of manipulation of independent variables on dependent variables in a situation where other relevant factors are held to a minimum.	Relationships found can be considered more precise as a result of control of other "interfering" variables.

Type of research design setting	Central characteristics	Prospective outcomes
b. "Natural" experiments (cross-sectional or ex post facto). *Example:* F. S. Chapin, *Experimental Designs in Social Research;* see Stouffer in this Handbook, pp. 35–39.	Researcher capitalizes on some ongoing changes in normal community setting and studies their effect in an experimental design. A treatment or social program may be given to one group of persons and their personal adjustment compared with a group of persons without such a program. Matching of groups makes the two groups homogeneous when selected factors are held constant by individual or frequency matching.	Discovers and exposes causal complexes under controlled conditions. Statements of greater rigor made possible and increased validity of social treatments or programs demonstrated.
c. Field experiment. *Example:* J. G. Miller, *Experiments in Social Process.*	Involves manipulation of conditions by the experimenter in order to determine causal relations. Maximum variation in the independent and dependent variables are built into structure of design. Experimental and control groups established holding constant factors believed to interfere with relationship under study.	Independent variable (treatment) is capable of wide variation; sensitive or definitive criterion variable is found. Matching data provide strongest possible control. A causal pattern may be inferred with high confidence.

1.4 HOW SCIENCE IS BUILT

Instructions for Use of Guide 1.4

This guide sets forth the canons of science as seen by the behavioral researcher. Treat the guide as a signpost that points the direction and possible difficulties ahead. Call it a digest of the philosophy that a researcher carries in his head, uses in his work, and lives by amid the ups and downs of research life.

The four statements that follow describe (1) the importance of conceptual definition and theory formulation in the construction of scientific knowledge, (2) assumptions underlying the application of the scientific method, (3) dilemmas of the researcher and the distinctiveness of behavioral science, and (4) the researcher's commitment.

IMPORTANCE OF CONCEPTUAL DEFINITION AND THEORY FORMULATION*

Gordon J. DiRenzo

Scientific investigation seeks to explain the phenomena it studies in our world of experience; by establishing general principles with which to explain them, hopefully, science can predict such phenomena. The principles of science are stated ultimately in what are known as theories. To explain the facts of reality, scientists require an organized system of concepts. A "science without concepts" is an impossibility—as unthinkable as any form of rational activity without concepts would be. Yet, to say that concepts are indispensable to science is merely to presuppose or to make possible the problems, namely, the definition and formation of the required scientific elements.

Initially, in scientific inquiry, description of phenomena may be stated in a non-technical vocabulary. The growth of a discipline soon involves the development of a system of speculation, more or less abstract, of concepts and corresponding terminology. Nevertheless, even after decades of definition, and redefinition, many of the fundamental terms in the sciences are far from being distinguished by a universally accepted definition—as much within as outside of particular disciplines. For example, to name just three of the pivotal concepts of the behavioral sciences, there are several denotations for "society," "culture," and "personality." How scientific and technical concepts are introduced and how they function in the scientific process are the central questions here.

Conceptual definition and theory formulation go hand in hand as necessary steps in one unified process of scientific research. The analysis of concepts is but one phase—a fundamental requisite—of that complex process of scientific inquiry which culminates in theory. Concepts, thus, are the irreducible elements of theory or theoretical systems, as the term "theory" has come to be understood more particularly in the behavioral sciences. The more precise and refined conceptual elements, the more precise and refined the theory.

The question to which we are addressing ourselves is a fundamental one for all areas of scientific inquiry.

ASSUMPTIONS UNDERLYING THE APPLICATION OF THE SCIENTIFIC METHOD**

Gideon Sjoberg and Roger Nett

A minimum set of assumptions (often left unstated) which underlie the application of the scientific method are (1) that there exists a definite order of recurrence of events, (2) that knowledge is superior to ignorance, (3) that a communication tie, based upon sense impressions, exists between the scientist

* Reprinted with permission from Gordon J. DiRenzo, *Concepts, Theory, and Explanation in the Behavioral Sciences* (New York: Random House, 1967), p. 66.

** Reprinted with permission from Gideon Sjoberg and Roger Nett, *A Methodology for the Social Researcher* (New York: Harper & Row, 1968), pp. 30–31.

and "external reality" (the so-called "empirical assumption"), and (4) that there are cause-and-effect relationships within the physical and the social orders. Moreover, (5) there are certain "observer" assumptions: (*a*) that the observer is driven to attain knowledge by his desire to ameliorate human conditions, (*b*) that the observer has the capacity to conceptually relate observations and impute meanings to events, and (*c*) that society will sustain the observer in his pursuit of knowledge. These assumptions, which the scientist more or less takes for granted, are in the last analysis largely understandable as "functional fictions." Their usefulness in the acquisition of knowledge is the primary raison d'etre.

The Assumption of Order in the "Natural" World

Science, in so far as it seeks to generalize and predict, depends upon the existence of some degree of order in the physical or social world under study. That which it cannot describe as a manifestation of regularity it must define as some describable departure from regularity. Such reasoning assumes that events are ordered along certain dimensions. To be sure, all systems of knowledge rest upon the assumption of order in the universe, but this may be of greater significance for science than for other systems of knowledge. After all, scientists spend most of their time differentiating among classes of relative uniformity and relating these one to another. Even within a rapidly changing, revolutionary system there is a degree of order. And change itself displays patterns that can be described and analyzed.

The assumption of order leads the social scientist, if he is to remain a scientist, to eschew historicism. Those who advocate the historicist position in its extreme form assume that every cultural system must be studied as a separate entity and that, moreover, no regularities obtain across cultures. Of course, even the historicist admits there is a uniformity of sorts, for he recognizes that each system has its own laws of development.

The notion of order is closely related to the concept of a "natural universe." In our sketch of the history of science, we observed that a major breakthrough occurred when scholars were able to conceive of the physical and social environments in naturalistic terms, that is, as functioning independently of factors in the spiritual realm. This was an essential step in modern man's development of the means to manipulate and positively control aspects of the social and physical spheres.

In light of the evidence, it would be a mistake to confuse scientifically based knowledge with wisdom, as did some of the utopian thinkers of the nineteenth century. Wisdom involves sound ethical direction, the exercise of good taste, and distinguishing the worthwhile from the not so worthwhile.

The scientific method (in the narrow sense) does not tell us how to use empirically verified knowledge other than to further the ends of science; however, by utilizing more of the empirically validated knowledge and less of the unverified and often fiat knowledge of other epistemologies the cause of humanity may be advanced.

DILEMMAS OF THE RESEARCHER AND THE DISTINCTIVENESS OF
BEHAVIORAL SCIENCE*

Abraham Kaplan

Dilemmas

In the conduct of inquiry we are continuously subjected to pulls in opposite
directions: to search for data or to formulate hypotheses, to construct theories
or to perform experiments, to focus on general laws or on individual cases,
to conduct molar studies or molecular ones, to engage in synthesis or in
analysis. It is seldom of much help, in the concrete, to be told that we
must do both. In the constraints of specific problematic situations these are
genuine dilemmas. But they are a species of what have come to be known
as existential dilemmas: not characteristic of some special historical situation
but intrinsic to the pursuit of truth. We do not make a choice of the lesser
of two evils and abide by the unhappy outcome. The problems which the
existential dilemmas pose cannot be solved at all, but only coped with; which
is to say, we learn to live with them. "We need hard workers and empiricism,
not inspiration," it is urged with good reason. But equally good reason can
also be given for the converse. The fact is, we need all we can get. This
state of affairs is in no way peculiar to behavioral science. Its methodology,
as I see it, is no different from that of any other science whatever. If this
identity is contemplated in speaking of "the scientific method," I warmly
approve of the usage.

The Specialty of Behavioral Science

What is distinctive of behavioral science, therefore, is basically its subject-
matter; the techniques that the subject-matter permits or demands are only
derivative. If some single discriminant of this subject-matter is called for, I
believe the most generally applicable one is that suggested by C. W. Morris:
the use of "signs." Behavioral science deals with those processes in which
symbols, or at any rate meanings, play an essential part. Just how broadly
"meaning" is to be construed, and how much of animal behavior it comprises
even in its broadest construction, are questions which need not trouble us
here. There is no doubt that behavioral science spills over into biology however
we choose to circumscribe its limits. But this difficulty is more administrative
(for foundations, librarians, and deans) than methodological.

What is significant here is that the data for behavioral science are not
sheer movements but actions—that is, acts performed in a perspective which
gives them meaning or purpose. Plainly, it is of crucial importance that we
distinguish between the meaning of the act to the actor (or to other people,
including ourselves, reacting with him) and its meaning to us as scientists,
taking the action as subject-matter. I call these, respectively, *act meaning*
and *action meaning*. I shall return to this distinction later; for the present,

---

* Reprinted with permission from Abraham Kaplan, *The Conduct of Inquiry* (San Francisco:
Chandler, 1964), pp. 30–33.

we may note that behavioral science is involved in a double process of interpretation, and it is this which is responsible for such of its techniques as are distinctive. The behavioral scientist must first arrive at an act meaning, that is, construe what conduct a particular piece of behavior represents; and then he must search for the meaning of the interpreted action, its interconnections with other actions or circumstances. He must first see the act of marking a ballot or operating a machine as the action of casting a vote, and then pursue his study of voting behavior.

Now although interpretation for act meanings usually involves special techniques, these are subject to the same methodological norms that govern interpretation for action meanings (and thereby other sciences as well). We interpret speech-acts (in our own language) without any special effort—indeed, usually without any awareness at all of the acts as acts (we do not hear the words, but what is said). Yet every such interpretation is a hypothesis, every reply an experiment—we may, after all, have misunderstood. When it comes to interpreting foreign languages, and in general to interpreting the patterns of another culture, the situation becomes clearer, though it is essentially no different. Some implications of this state of affairs will be explored in connection with the role of "verstehen" in behavioral science. The point I am making here is that the behavioral scientist seeks to understand behavior in just the same sense that the physicist, say, seeks to understand nuclear processes. The difference is not that there are two kinds of understanding but that the behavioral scientist has two different things to understand: for instance, a psychiatrist needs to understand why a patient makes certain noises (to tell his therapist how much he hates him), and why he says the things he does (because he has not yet worked through the transference). Admittedly, we have special ways of understanding noises, because we are ourselves human; but for the same reason, we also have special ways of interpreting light waves, but need quite other techniques for radio waves. The point is that even what we see is not always to be believed. Every technique is subject to validation, and the same norms apply to all of them.

THE RESEARCHER'S COMMITMENT

Delbert C. Miller

I've always felt that many great scientists who have made many valuable contributions were not primarily motivated by curiosity or a great desire to serve humanity, but by an emotional reluctance to accept defeat.—Hans Selye

In the real world a large number of social variables are found to be highly interrelated. Causes and effects are hard to disentangle. In social science itself theories and explanations abound for the same phenomena. Individual biases and ideological differences reside in the very methodological approaches that are advised by various "experts."

So why do young social researchers commit themselves to work with such uncertain, shifting, confusing, and exasperating phenomena? Many students feel the challenge of working in new scientific fields where the origins are only a scant century old. Others just like the social sciences because they address what they consider the most important problems of our time. Some respect the criteria of the scientific method and they respect the mathematical tools that demand intellectual discipline and integrity. All of those who get research "in their blood" find challenge and satisfaction that sustain them through all difficulty.[1]

Committed social researchers never give up! Whatever the outcome researchers have a responsibility both to themselves and to other researchers to search for better ways to handle the data. Researchers seek causal statements. They often seek relationships to fit such generic propositions as: Under conditions A, B, and C, if X were increased (or decreased), then Y can be expected to increase (or decrease) by a determined magnitude. This is commonly expressed in probability terms but the effort is always to increase that probability. Researchers would like "overwhelming results." They attempt replication to affirm findings. With each increase in predictive power, the value of the knowledge and of the discipline increases. When the policy maker demands social science data and finds it indispensable, social science moves forward and research is enhanced. When theory and data intertwine and research strengthens theory, social study becomes social science.

Note

1. Cf. John B. Williamson, *The Research Craft* (Boston: Little, Brown, 1977).

THE BEARING OF SOCIOLOGICAL THEORY ON EMPIRICAL RESEARCH

1.5

Instructions for Use of Guide 1.5

Robert K. Merton describes the bearing of theory on empirical research. He says that the ". . . notion of directed research implies that, in part, empirical inquiry is so organized that if and when empirical discoveries are made, they have direct consequences for a theoretic system." Note the functions of theory that he sets forth. The researcher must often formulate "middle range" or miniature theories that will link hypotheses to a more inclusive theory. Zetterberg has written that miniature theories delineate convenient research problems. "Granted that our ultimate purpose is a general theory and that this general theory will in part be made up by means of miniature theories, experimental evidence supporting a miniature theory will support also the inclusive theory of which the miniature theory is a special case."[1]

Milton Friedman has listed the following criteria for significant theory: "A theory is 'simpler' the less initial knowledge is needed to make a prediction within a given field of phenomena; it is the more 'fruitful' the more precise the resulting prediction, the wider the area within which the theory yields predictions, and the more additional lines for further research it suggests. . . . The only relevant test of the validity of a hypothesis is comparison of prediction with experience."[2]

Notes

1. Hans L. Zetterberg, *On Theory and Verification in Sociology* (New York: Tressler Press, 1954), p. 15.

2. Milton Friedman, "The Methodology of Positive Economics," *Essays in Positive Economics* (Chicago: University of Chicago Press, 1953), p. 10.

EMPIRICAL GENERALIZATIONS IN SOCIOLOGY*

Robert K. Merton

Not infrequently it is said that the object of sociological theory is to arrive at statements of social uniformities. This is an elliptical assertion and hence requires clarification. For there are two types of statements of sociological uniformities that differ significantly in their bearing on theory. The first of these is the empirical generalization: an isolated proposition summarizing observed uniformities of relationships between two or more variables.[1] The sociological literature abounds with such generalizations that have not been assimilated to sociological theory. Thus, Engel's "laws" of consumption may be cited as examples. So, too, the Halbwachs' finding that laborers spend more per adult unit for food than white-collar employees of the same income class.[2] Such generalizations may be of greater or less precision, but this does not affect their logical place in the structure of inquiry. The Groves-Ogburn finding, for a sample of American cities, that "cities with a larger percentage engaged in manufacturing also have, on the average, slightly larger percentages of young persons married" has been expressed in an equation indicating the degree of this relationship. Although propositions of this order are essential in empirical research, a miscellany of such propositions only provides the raw materials for sociology as a discipline. The theoretic task, and the orientation of empirical research toward theory, first begins when the bearing of such uniformities on a set of interrelated propositions is tentatively established. The notion of directed research implies that, in part,[3] empirical inquiry is so organized that if and when empirical uniformities are discovered, they have direct consequences for a theoretic system. Insofar as the research is directed, the rationale of findings is set forth before the findings are obtained.

Sociological Theory

The second type of sociological generalization, the so-called scientific law, differs from the foregoing inasmuch as it is a statement of invariance derivable from a theory. The paucity of such laws in the sociological field perhaps reflects the prevailing bifurcation of theory and empirical research. Despite the many volumes dealing with the history of sociological theory and despite the plethora of empirical investigations, sociologists (including the writer) may discuss the logical criteria of sociological laws without citing a single instance that fully satisfies these criteria.[4]

Approximations to these criteria are not entirely wanting. To exhibit the relations of empirical generalizations to theory and to set forth the functions of theory, it may be useful to examine a familiar case in which such generaliza-

* Reprinted with permission of the publisher from Robert K. Merton, "The Bearing of Sociological Theory on Empirical Research," *Social Theory and Social Structure*, rev. ed. (Glencoe, Ill.: Free Press, 1957), pp. 95–99. Copyright 1949 by The Free Press, copyright 1957 by The Free Press, A Corporation.

tions were incorporated into a body of substantive theory. Thus, it has long been established as a statistical uniformity that, in a variety of populations, Catholics have a lower suicide rate than Protestants.[5] In this form the uniformity posed a theoretical problem. It merely constituted an empirical regularity that would become significant for theory only if it could be derived from a set of other propositions, a task that Durkheim set himself. If we restate his theoretic assumptions in formal fashion, the paradigm of his theoretic analysis becomes clear:

1. Social cohesion provides psychic support to group members subjected to acute stresses and anxieties.
2. Suicide rates are functions of *unrelieved* anxieties and stresses to which persons are subjected.
3. Catholics have greater social cohesion than Protestants.
4. Therefore, lower suicide rates should be anticipated among Catholics than among Protestants.[6]

This case serves to locate the place of empirical generalizations in relation to theory and to illustrate the several functions of theory.

1. It indicates that theoretic pertinence is not inherently present or absent in empirical generalizations but appears when the generalization is conceptualized in abstractions of higher order (Catholicism-social cohesion-relieved anxieties-suicide rate) that are embodied in more general statements of relationships.[7] What was initially taken as an isolated uniformity is restated as a relation, not between religious affiliation and behavior, but between groups with certain conceptualized attributes (social cohesion) and the behavior. The *scope* of the original empirical finding is considerably extended, and several seemingly disparate uniformities are seen to be interrelated (thus differentials in suicide rates between married and single persons can be derived from the same theory).

2. Once having established the theoretic pertinence of a uniformity by deriving it from a set of interrelated propositions, we provide for the *cumulation* both of theory and of research findings. The differentials-in-suicide-rate uniformities add confirmation to the set of propositions from which they— and other uniformities—have been derived. This is a major function of *systematic theory*.

3. Whereas the empirical uniformity did not lend itself to the drawing of diverse consequences, the reformulation gives rise to various consequences in fields of conduct quite remote from that of suicidal behavior. For example, inquiries into obsessive behavior, morbid preoccupations, and other maladaptive behavior have found these also to be related to inadequacies of group cohesion.[8] The conversion of empirical uniformities into theoretic statements thus increases the *fruitfulness* of research through the successive exploration of implications.

4. By providing a rationale, the theory introduces a *ground for prediction* that is more secure than mere empirical extrapolation from previously observed trends. Thus, should independent measures indicate a decrease of social cohesion among Catholics, the theorist would predict a tendency toward increased rates of suicide in this group. The atheoretic empiricist would have no alternative, however, but to predict on the basis of extrapolation.

5. The foregoing list of functions presupposes one further attribute of theory that is not altogether true of the Durkheim formulation and which gives rise to a general problem that has peculiarly beset sociological theory, at least, up to the present. If theory is to be productive, it must be sufficiently *precise* to be *determinate*. Precision is an integral element of the criterion of *testability*. The prevailing pressure toward the utilization of statistical data in sociology, whenever possible, to control and test theoretic inferences has a justifiable basis, when we consider the logical place of precision in disciplined inquiry.

The more precise the inferences (predictions) that can be drawn from a theory, the less the likelihood of *alternative* hypotheses that will be adequate to these predictions. In other words, precise predictions and data serve to reduce the *empirical* bearing upon research of the *logical* fallacy of affirming the consequent.[9] It is well known that verified predictions derived from a theory do not prove or demonstrate that theory; they merely supply a measure of confirmation, for it is always possible that alternative hypotheses drawn from different theoretic systems can also account for the predicted phenomena.[10] But those theories that admit of precise predictions confirmed by observation take on strategic importance since they provide an initial basis for choice between competing hypotheses. In other words, precision enhances the likelihood of approximating a "crucial" observation or experiment.

The internal coherence of a theory has much the same function, for if a variety of empirically confirmed consequences are drawn from one theoretic system, this reduces the likelihood that competing theories can adequately account for the same data. The integrated theory sustains a larger measure of confirmation than is the case with distinct and unrelated hypotheses, thus accumulating a greater weight of evidence.

Both pressures—toward precision and logical coherence—can lead to unproductive activity, particularly in the social sciences. Any procedure can be abused as well as used. A premature insistence on precision at all costs may sterilize imaginative hypotheses. It may lead to a reformulation of the scientific problem in order to permit measurement with, at times, the result that the subsequent materials do not bear on the initial problem in hand.[11] In the search for precision, care must be taken to see that significant problems are not thus inadvertently blotted from view. Similarly, the pressure for logical consistency has at times invited logomachy and sterile theorizing, inasmuch as the assumptions contained in the system of analysis are so far removed from empirical referents or involve such high abstractions as not to permit of empirical inquiry.[12] But warrant for these criteria of inquiry is not vitiated by such abuses.

Notes

1. This usage of the term "empirical" is common, as Dewey notes. In this context, *"empirical* means that the subject-matter of a given proposition which has existential inference, represents merely a set of uniform conjunctions of traits repeatedly observed to exist, without any understanding of *why* the conjunction occurs; without a theory which states its rationale." John Dewey, *Logic: The Theory of Inquiry* (New York: Henry Holt, 1938), p. 305.

2. See a considerable collection of such uniformities summarized by C. C. Zimmerman, *Consumption and Standards of Living* (New York: Van Nostrand, 1936), pp. 55 ff.

3. "In part," if only because it stultifies the possibilities of obtaining fertile new findings to confine researches *wholly* to the test of predetermined hypotheses. Hunches originating in the course of the inquiry that may not have immediately obvious implications for a broader theoretic system may eventuate in the discovery of empirical uniformities that can later be incorporated into a theory. For example, in the sociology of political behavior, it has been recently established that the larger the number of social cross-pressures to which voters are subjected, the less interest they exhibit in a presidential election (P. F. Lazarsfeld, Bernard Berelson, and Hazel Gaudet, *The People's Choice* [New York: Duell, Sloan & Pearce, 1944], pp. 56–64). This finding, which was wholly unanticipated when the research was first formulated, may well initiate new lines of systematic inquiry into political behavior, even though it is not yet integrated into a generalized theory. Fruitful empirical research not only tests theoretically derived hypotheses; it also originates new hypotheses. This might be termed the "serendipity" component of research, i.e., the discovery, by chance or sagacity, of valid results that were not sought for.

4. E.g., see the discussion by George A. Lundberg, "The Concept of Law in the Social Sciences," *Philosophy of Science* 5 (1938): 189–203, which affirms the possibility of such laws without including any case in point. The book by K. D. Har, *Social Laws* (Chapel Hill: University of North Carolina, 1930), does not fulfill the promise implicit in the title. A panel of social scientists discussing the possibility of obtaining social laws finds it difficult to instance cases. Herbert Blumer, *An Appraisal of Thomas and Znaniecki's The Polish Peasant in Europe and America* (New York: Social Science Research Council, 1939), pp. 142–50.

5. It need hardly be said that this statement assumes that education, income, nationality, rural-urban residence, and other factors that might render this finding spurious have been held constant.

6. We need not examine further aspects of this illustration, e.g. (1) the extent of which we have adequately stated the premises implicit in Durkheim's interpretation; (2) the supplementary theoretic analysis that would take these premises not as given but as problematic; (3) the grounds on which the potentially infinite regression of theoretic interpretations is halted at one rather than another point; (4) the problems involved in the introduction of such intervening variables as social cohesion that are not directly measured; (5) the extent to which the premises have been empirically confirmed; (6) the comparatively low order of abstraction represented by this illustration; and (7) the fact that Durkheim derived several empirical generalizations from this same set of hypotheses.

7. Thorstein Veblen has put this with typical cogency: "All this may seem like taking pains about trivialities. But the data with which any scientific inquiry has to do are trivialities in some other bearing than that one in which they are of account." *The Place of Science in Modern Civilization* (New York: Russell & Russell, 1961), p. 42.

8. See, e.g., Elton Mayo, *Human Problems of an Industrial Civilization* (New York: Macmillan, 1933), pp. 113 and passim. The theoretical framework utilized in the studies of industrial morale by Whitehead, Roethlisberger, and Dickson stemmed appreciably from the Durkheim formulations, as the authors testify.

9. The paradigm of "proof through prediction" is, of course, logically fallacious: If *A* (hypothesis), then *B* (prediction).

B is observed.

Therefore, *A* is true.

This is not overdisturbing for scientific research, inasmuch as other than formal criteria are involved.

10. As a case in point, consider that different theorists had predicted war and internecine conflict on a large scale at midcentury. Sorokin and some Marxists, for example, set forth this prediction on the basis of quite distinct theoretic systems. The actual outbreak of large-scale conflicts does not in itself enable us to choose between these schemes of analysis, if only because the observed fact is consistent with both. Only if the predictions had been so *specified,* had been so precise, that the actual occurrences coincided with the one prediction and not with the other, would a determinate test have been instituted.

11. Stuart A. Rice comments on this tendency in public opinion research; see *Eleven Twenty-six: A Decade of Social Science Research,* ed. Louis Wirth (Chicago: University of Chicago, 1940), p. 167.

12. It is this practice to which E. Ronald Walker refers, in the field of economics, as "theoretic blight." *From Economic Theory to Policy* (Chicago: University of Chicago, 1943), chap. 4.

Additional Readings

GREER, SCOTT. *The Logic of Inquiry.* Chicago: Aldine, 1969.

HANSON, N. R. *Patterns of Discovery: An Inquiry into the Conceptual Foundations of Science.* Cambridge, Eng.: Cambridge University, 1958. See chap. 4, "Theories."

HEMPEL, CARL G., and OPPENHEIM, P. "Studies in the Logic of Explanation." *Philosophy of Science* 15 (1948): 135–75.

KAPLAN, ABRAHAM. *The Conduct of Inquiry, Methodology for Behavioral Science.* San Francisco: Chandler, 1964. See chap 8, "Theories."

STEPHENS, WILLIAM N. *Hypotheses and Evidence.* New York: Crowell, 1968.

WESTIE, FRANK R. "Toward Closer Relations between Theory and Research: A Procedure and an Example," *American Sociological Review* 22 (April, 1957): 149–54.

ZETTERBERG, HANS L. *On Theory and Verification in Sociology.* 3rd ed. rev. Totowa, N.J.: Bedminster Press, 1965.

1.6 BRIDGING THE GAP BETWEEN THE LANGUAGES OF THEORY AND RESEARCH*

Hubert M. Blalock, Jr.

1. Owing to the inherent nature of the scientific method, there is a gap between the languages of theory and research. Causal inferences belong on the theoretical level, whereas actual research can only establish covariations and temporal sequences.

2. As a result, we can never actually demonstrate causal laws empirically. This is true even where experimentation is possible. Causal laws are working assumptions of the scientist, involving hypothetical statements of the if-then variety.

3. One admits that causal thinking belongs completely on the theoretical level and that causal laws can never be demonstrated empirically. But this does not mean that it is not helpful to think causally and to develop causal models that have implications that are indirectly testable. In working with these models it will be necessary to make use of a whole series of untestable simplifying assumptions, so that even when a given model yields correct

* Reprinted with permission from Hubert M. Blalock, Jr., *Causal Inferences in Non-experimental Research* (Chapel Hill: University of North Carolina Press, 1961, 1964), pp. 172–73, 6–7, 26.

empirical predictions, this does not mean that its correctness can be demonstrated.

Reality, or at least our perception of reality, admittedly consists of ongoing processes. No two events are ever exactly repeated, nor does any object or organism remain precisely the same from one moment to the next.[1] And yet, if we are ever to understand the nature of the real world, we must act and think as though events are repeated and as if objects do have properties that remain constant for some period of time, however short. Unless we permit ourselves to make such simple types of assumptions, we shall never be able to generalize beyond the simple and unique event.

4. The point we are emphasizing is that no matter how elaborate the design, certain simplifying assumptions must always be made. In particular, we must at some point assume that the effects of confounding factors are negligible. Randomization helps to rule out some of such variables, but the plausibility of this particular kind of simplifying assumption is always a question of degree. We wish to underscore this fact in order to stress the underlying similarity between the logic of making causal inferences on the basis of experimental and nonexperimental designs.

Note

1. This particular point is emphasized in Karl Pearson's classic, *The Grammar of Science,* 1957 ed. (New York: Meridian, 1957), chap. 5.

CRITERIA FOR JUDGING USABLE HYPOTHESES*   *1.7*

Instructions for Use of Guide 1.7

The formulation of usable hypotheses is of central importance. The entire study rests upon the potential significance of the hypotheses. In this guide, William J. Goode and Paul K. Hatt prescribe step-by-step methods for evaluating hypotheses against criteria. Note again the emphasis given to the criterion that a hypothesis should be related to a body of theory. It is also important to anticipate the verification problem. Zetterberg has stated three criteria for the acceptance of a working hypothesis: (1) that the empirical data were found to be arranged in the manner predicted by the working hypothesis; (2) that we have disproved the null hypothesis with a certain probability; and (3) that we have disproved alternate hypotheses to the one tested.

FROM *METHODS IN SOCIAL RESEARCH*

William J. Goode and Paul K. Hatt

1. *The hypotheses must be conceptually clear.* The concepts should be clearly defined, operationally if possible. Moreover, they should be definitions

---

* By permission from William J. Goode and Paul K. Hatt, *Methods in Social Research* (New York: McGraw-Hill, 1952), pp. 68–73. Copyright 1962 by McGraw-Hill Book Company, Inc.

that are commonly accepted and communicable rather than the products of a "private world."

What to do: One simple device for clarifying concepts is to write out a list of the concepts used in the research outline. Then try to define them (*a*) in words, (*b*) in terms of particular operations (index calculations, types of observations, etc.), and (*c*) with reference to other concepts to be found in previous research. Talk over each concept with fellow students and other researchers in the field. It will often be found that supposedly simple concepts contain many meanings. Then it is possible to decide which is the desired referent.

2. *Hypotheses should have empirical referents.* It has also been previously pointed out that scientific concepts must have an ultimate empirical referent. No usable hypothesis can embody moral judgments. Such statements as "criminals are no worse than businessmen," "women should pursue a career," or "capitalists exploit their workers" are no more usable hypotheses than is the familiar proposition that "pigs are well named because they are so dirty" or the classical question, "How many yards of buttermilk are required to make a pair of breeches for a black bull?" In other words, while a hypothesis may involve the study of value judgments, such a goal must be separated from a moral preachment or a plea for acceptance of one's values.

What to do: First, analyze the concepts that express attitudes rather than describe or refer to empirical phenomena. Watch for key words such as "ought," "should," "bad," etc. Then transform the notions into more useful concepts. "Bad parents" is a value term, but the researcher may have a definite description in mind: parents who follow such practices as whimsical and arbitrary authoritarianism, inducing psychic insecurity in the child, failure to give love, etc. "Should" is also a value term, but the student may simply mean, "If women do not pursue a career, we can predict emotional difficulties when the children leave home, or we can predict that the society will not be able to produce as much goods," etc. When, instead, we find that our referent is simply a vague feeling and we cannot define the operations needed to observe it, we should study the problem further and discover what it is that we really wish to investigate.

3. *The hypotheses must be specific.* That is, all the operations and predictions indicated by it should be spelled out. The possibility of actually testing the hypothesis can thus be appraised. Often hypotheses are expressed in such general terms, and with so grandiose a scope, that they are simply not testable. Because of their magnitude, such grand ideas are tempting because they seem impressive and important. It is better for the student to avoid such problems and instead develop his skills upon more tangible notions.

By making all the concepts and operations explicit is meant not only conceptual clarity but a description of any indexes to be used. Thus, to hypothesize that the degree of vertical social mobility is decreasing in the United States requires the use of indexes. [At present there are many operational definitions of the status levels that define mobility. Therefore, the hypothesis must include a statement of the index that is to be used; see part 4 for available indexes.]

Such specific formulations have the advantage of assuring that research is practicable and significant, in advance of the expenditure of effort. It furthermore increases the validity of the results, since the broader the terms the easier it is to fall into the trap of using selective evidence. The fame of most prophets and fortune-tellers lies in their ability to state predictions so that almost any occurrence can be interpreted as a fulfillment. We can express this in almost statistical terms: the more specific the prediction, the smaller the chance that the prediction will actually be borne out as a result of mere accident. Scientific predictions or hypotheses must, then, avoid the trap of selective evidence by being as definite and specific as possible.

What to do: Never be satisfied with a general prediction, if it can be broken into more precise subhypotheses. The general prediction of war is not enough, for example: we must specify time, place, and participants. Predicting the general decline of a civilization is not a hypothesis for testing a theory. Again, we must be able to specify and measure the forces, specify the meaning and time of decline, the population segments involved, etc. Often this can be done by conceptual analysis and the formulation of related hypotheses: e.g., we may predict that urbanization is accompanied by a decline in ferility. However, we gain in precision if we attempt to define our indexes of urbanization; specify which segments will be affected, and how much (since in the United States the various ethnic and religious segments are affected differently); specify the amount of fertility decline, and the type (percentage childless, net reproduction rate, etc.). Forming subhypotheses (1) clarifies the relationship between the data sought and the conclusions; and (2) makes the specific research task more manageable.

4. *Hypotheses should be related to available techniques.* Earlier, the point was repeatedly made that theory and method are not opposites. The theorist who does not know what techniques are available to test his hypotheses is in a poor way to formulate usable questions.

This is not to be taken as an absolute injunction against the formulation of hypotheses that at present are too complex to be handled by contemporary technique. It is merely a sensible requirement to apply to any problem in its early stages in order to judge its researchability.

There are some aspects of the impossible hypothesis that may make its formulation worth while. If the problem is significant enough as a possible frame of reference, it may be useful whether or not it can be tested at the time. The socioeconomic hypotheses of Marx, for example, were not proved by his data. The necessary techniques were not available either then or now. Nevertheless, Marxian frameworks are an important source of more precise, smaller, verifiable propositions. This is true for much of Emile Durkheim's work on suicide. His related formulations concerning social cohesion have also been useful. The work of both men has been of paramount importance to sociology, even though at the time their larger ideas were not capable of being handled by available techniques.

Furthermore, posing the impossible question may stimulate the growth of technique. Certainly some of the impetus toward modern developments in technique has come from criticisms against significant studies that were considered inadequate because of technical limitations. In any serious sociological discussion, research frontiers are continuously challenged by the assertion that various problems "ought" to be investigated even though the investigations are presently impossible.

What to do: Look for research articles on the subject being investigated. Make a list of the various techniques that have been used to measure the factors of importance in the study. If you are unable to locate any discussion of technique, you may find it wiser to do a research on the necessary research techniques. You may, instead, decide that this lack of techniques means your problem is too large and general for your present resources.

Some items, such as stratification or race attitudes, have been studied by many techniques. Try to discover why one technique is used in one case and not in another. Note how refinements in technique have been made, and see whether one of these may be more useful for your purposes. Look for criticisms of previous research, so as to understand the weaknesses in the procedures followed.

Again, other problems may have been studied with few attempts at precise measurement. Study the literature to see why this is the case. Ascertain whether some subareas (for example, of religious behavior) may be attacked with techniques used in other areas (for example, attitude measurement, stratification measures, research on choice making, etc.).

5. *The hypothesis should be related to a body of theory.* This criterion is one which is often overlooked by the beginning student. He is more likely to select subject matter that is "interesting," without finding out whether the research will really help to refute, qualify, or support any existing theories of social relations. A science, however, can be cumulative only by building on an existing body of fact and theory. It cannot develop if each study is an isolated survey.

Although it is true that the clearest examples of crescive theoretical development are to be found in the physical and biological sciences, the process can also be seen in the social sciences. One such case is the development of a set of generalizations concerning the social character of intelligence. The anthropological investigations at the end of the nineteenth century uncovered the amazing variety of social customs in various societies, while demonstrating conclusively that there were a number of common elements in social life: family systems, religious patterns, an organization of the socialization process, etc.

The French school of sociology, including Lucien Lévy-Bruhl, Emile Durkheim, Marcel Mauss, Henri Hubert, and others, formulated a series of propositions, at the turn of the century, which suggested that the intellectual structure of the human mind is determined by the structure of the society. That is, perception and thought are determined by society, not alone by the anatomical structure of our eyes, ears, and other senses. Modes of thought vary from society to society. Some of these formulations were phrased in an extreme form that need not concern us now, and they were often vague. Nevertheless, the idea was growing that the intelligence of a Polynesian native could not be judged by European standards; his thinking was qualitatively, not merely quantitatively, different.

At the same time, however, better techniques were being evolved for measuring "intelligence," which came to be standardized in the form of scores on various IQ tests. When these were applied to different groups it became clear that the variation in IQ was great; children of Italian immigrants made lower grades on such tests, as did Negroes. Northern Negroes made higher grades than whites from many Southern states. American children of Chinese and Japanese parents made rather high scores. Since it was generally assumed that these tests measured "innate intelligence," these data were sometimes generalized to suggest that certain "racial" groups were by nature inferior and others superior.

However, such conclusions were opposed on rational grounds, and liberal sentiments suggested that they be put to the test. There were, then, two major sets of conclusions, one suggesting that intelligence is in the main determined by social experience, the other suggesting that the IQ is innately determined. To test such opposing generalizations, a research design was needed for testing logical expectations in more specific situations. If, for example, it is true that the intelligence of individuals who are members of "inferior" groups is really determined biologically, then changes in their environments should not change their IQ. If, on the other hand, the social experience is crucial, we should expect that such changes in social experience would result in definite patterns of IQ change.

Further deductions are possible. If identical twins are separated and are placed in radically different social experiences at an early age, we might expect significant differences in IQ. Or, if a group of rural Negro children moves from the poor school and social experience of the South to the somewhat more stimulating environment of the North, the group averages would be expected to change somewhat. Otto Klineberg, in a classic study, carried out the latter research. He traced Negro children of various ages after they had moved to the North and found that, in general, the earlier the move to the North occurred, the greater the average rise in the IQ. The later the move, the smaller the increase. Even if one assumes that the "better," more able, and more daring adult Negroes made this move, this does not explain the differences by time of movement. Besides, of course, the subjects were children at the time of the migration.[1]

In this research design a particular result was predicted by a series of deductions from a larger set of generalizations. Further, the prediction was actually validated. In justice to the great number of scholars who have been engaged in refining and developing IQ tests, it should be mentioned that other tests and investigations of a similar order have been carried out by many anthropologists, sociologists, and social psychologists. They do not invalidate the notion that IQ is based in part on "innate" abilities, but they do indicate that to a great extent these abilities must be stimulated by certain types of experience in order to achieve high scores on such tests.

From even so sketchy an outline of a theoretical development as the foregoing is, it can be seen that when research is systematically based upon a body of existing theory, a genuine contribution in knowledge is more likely to result. In other words, to be worth doing, a hypothesis must not only be carefully stated, but it should possess theoretical relevance.

What to do: First, of course, cover the literature relating to your subject. If it is impossible to do so, then your hypothesis probably covers too much ground. Second, try to abstract from the literature the way in which various propositions and sets of propositions relate to one another (for example, the literature relating to Sutherland's theory of differential association in criminology, the conditions for maximum morale in factories, or the studies of prediction of marital adjustment). Third, ascertain whether you can deduce any of the propositions, including your own hypothesis, from one another or from a small set of major statements. Fourth, test it by some theoretical model, such as Merton's "Paradigm for Functional Analysis in Sociology" (*Social Theory and Social Structure*, pp. 50–54), to see whether you have left out major propositions and determinants. Fifth, especially compare your own set of related propositions with those of some classic author, such as Weber on bureaucracy or Durkheim on suicide. If you find this task of abstraction difficult, compare instead with the propositions of these men as explained by a systematic interpreter such as Talcott Parsons in his *Structure of Social Action.* What is important is that, whatever the source of your hypothesis, it must be logically derivable from and based upon a set of related sociological propositions.

Note

1. Otto Klineberg, *Negro Intelligence and Selective Migration* (New York: Columbia University Press, 1935).

1.8 SCIENCE: OBSERVATIONAL, EXPERIMENTAL, HISTORICAL

Instructions for Use of Guides to Study Design: Guides 1.8, 1.9, 1.10

The study design involves such decisions as that of whether a historical analysis, statistical sampling survey, qualitative structured observation, or controlled experimentation is needed. In the following, Raymond Siever, a physical scientist, describes varieties and styles of science and stresses the importance of the problem and its relation to scientific method.

SCIENCE: OBSERVATIONAL, EXPERIMENTAL, HISTORICAL*

Raymond Siever

A question that has concerned many scientists for about as long as sciences started to differentiate from each other is, "Are there different sciences or is there just one science?" A related question can be put, "Is there *a* scientific method, or are there many scientific methods?" Discussion of these points is usually obfuscated by the speaker's background, in particular, what science he happens to be doing at the moment. It also, of course, is characteristically confused by mixing subject matter with the way in which an investigation is carried out. I will give my idea of how the different conventional groupings of sciences relate to each other and propose some answers to the question of whether there is just one science or many. It is not that these ideas are new. It is more that we need to remind ourselves of our philosophical underpinnings, especially now that branches of science have become more specialized and yet at the same time have joined together in attacks on complex systems.

Observational versus Experimental

The distinction between an observational science and an experimental science is often made. In this context in some people's language, the word "observa-

---

* Reprinted from *American Scientist* 56, no. 1 (1968): 70–77. Copyright by *Sigma Xi,* Princeton, N.J.

tional" is associated with the thought "solely descriptive" and the word "experimental" is usually associated with an analytical approach. There is an extension of these associations by which some scientists, thereby qualifying themselves as superior, imply that there is "good" or "bad" science by linking observational with bad and experimental with good. This choice of terms is dictated by diplomacy within the scientific community, for it is not good policy to refer to work that one's colleagues in another field are doing as bad; it is much better simply to call it "descriptive." We all know that there are appropriate uses for the words bad and good, but properly only as applied to an individual piece of work.

There are, of course, other terms that we are familiar with. There are the "hard" sciences and, by implication I suppose, the "soft" sciences. We also know that a good many other words have been juxtaposed to distinguish between "two cultures" within science (table 1). Without trying to wreck diplomacy, it is worthwhile to point out just how these words, observational, descriptive, experimental, analytical, are being used.

It must be taken as given, I think, that all sciences observe and describe. An example is one product of science that has been with us for a long time, the heat flow equation, an equation that is fundamentally based on simple observation. The laws that Newton first formulated for heat flow are simpler than the more elegant mathematical statements that we now use. But this elegant formulation with which we are able to do so much rests on rather elementary kinds of observations. So it is silly to speak of a nonobservational or a nondescriptive science.

There are said to be scientists who describe things and do not wish to make any analysis of them. They say description for its own sake is worthwhile science. It is true, of course, that many sciences in their early stages of development are characterized by an extraordinarily high ratio of data collecting to data analysis. This rarely implies that those who accumulate the data are not thinking about what they are describing or trying to integrate it into some pattern. It is obvious that those who describe are making a choice of what to describe and that analysis is involved in the selection of the object to be described. We ordinarily do not consider it science for somebody to observe everything that could be catalogued about a particular process, phe-

Table 1 *Words That Have Been Used in Characterizing Differences among the Sciences*

Analytical	Descriptive
Experimental	Observational
Soft	Hard
Non-mathematical	Mathematical
Good	Bad
Interesting	Dull
"Stamp Collecting"	Crucial experimentation
Classical	Modern
The general equation	The encyclopedic monograph
Rigorous	Inexact
Easy	Difficult
Exploding	Mined-out

nomenon, object, or other, though the point may be argued, and probably will be when the first man lands on the moon.

There is no denying that the scientific population includes some who do describe for its own sake, who admit that description is their only goal. As such they bear the same relationship to science as the inventory-taker does to business. But most who solely describe will say that they are only temporarily so engaged, that they are always working toward the goal of analysis (usually put off to some future time).

If it is true that description for its own sake, without any analysis of what to describe or how to integrate it after description, is not what we usually call science, then we really cannot speak of a descriptive or nondescriptive science. When some scientists say of another scientist's work or of another field within science, "It's descriptive," they really mean that it is not science.

The kind of statement made above may also be interpreted to mean, with good grace, that the proportion of description to analysis is high compared to those in some other field. The proportion varies, of course, with the stage of development of the field and it varies, obviously, with the person. Even within a field that is largely beyond the stage where description is in a high ratio to analysis, the invention of a new instrument can lead to new kinds of observations, temporarily producing a great abundance of data relative to analysis.

If one of the major objects of scientific endeavor is to make general laws from specific observations, then it must also be granted that the endeavor is more or less difficult. Physics has come to be, by and large, the domain of those who work where generalizations are relatively easy to make from limited data (though no one would claim physics as an easy field in terms of mental effort). Another way to put it is that the data have small variance and the generalizations are very good. It is also true that in certain fields, of which perhaps the social sciences are the most obvious example, the data have such high variance that the generalizations are either difficult or almost impossible to make. This inevitably leads to differences in the overall logical structure of disciplines. A great many parts of physics are tied together with a strong interconnecting network of fundamental physical theory from which all other parts can be derived, so-called first principles. On the other hand we have fields, such as some areas of engineering, where empiricism is the order of the day simply because there is no generally valid group of first principles from which to operate.

Experiment and Science

Experiments have always been associated with science, and have rightly been considered the most powerful tools of science. Our vision of experiment is largely based on those that have been done in physics and chemistry. But there are a number of ways in which one can look at experiments. They can be divided into controlled and uncontrolled experiments. Alternatively, we can formulate experimentation as either natural or artificial. The artificial experiment we all know about; one chooses the starting materials and conditions of the experiment, then one observes the process in action or the final results.

The natural experiment we are somewhat less familiar with, except for those of us whose primary interest lies in biology, the earth sciences, or astronomy. We may ask what would have happened had Newton one day seen the mythical apple on the ground, somewhat overripe, partly eaten, and decayed. From such an observation, could he have extracted a generalization on gravity? I think it not improbable that he might have, but perhaps at a much greater cost in time and effort and with much less assurance. Many geochemists, for example, have to go about analyzing chemical processes on the earth in a special way. It would be as if someone who wanted to find out what was going on in an elementary chemistry laboratory would go to the laboratory when no one was in it, analyze what he found in the sink, and analyze what he found in the sewer leading from the laboratory. Noting how the laboratory is equipped he could make some deductions as to the experiments that were performed and guess what the starting reagents might have been. So natural experimentation has built into it restricted control and limited information on the nature of the starting materials. Natural experimentation, of course, has the same restrictions as artificial experimentation; one must pick the right observational parameters.

The natural experiment can be refined by looking at separable parts of it or by choosing the chance event that has resulted in a specially controlled or restricted experiment. In a multivariate situation we look for the occasional place or time when the variables are fewer. Those who have spent a good deal of time looking for controlled natural experiments can speak with feeling about the rarity or impossibility of finding the perfectly controlled natural experiment. They all have defects. And so those who work with such data seem always to be trying to draw some generalizations from rather poor experiments.

Restrictions on artificial experimentation possibilities in science are many. The first restriction is the largeness of some systems. Scaling factors are not always available or adequate to reduce the system in size for examination in the laboratory. The two most notable sciences in this regard are astronomy and geology. Here again, restricted bits and pieces of these large systems can be removed and taken to the laboratory, but the interrelatedness of the system itself cannot be reproduced.

The complexity and interrelatedness of some systems restrict the experiment. Warren Weaver (1955) applied the words "strongly coupled" and "weakly coupled" to the sciences. Weaver applied these terms to differentiate the natural from the social sciences, but I think the point can equally be taken to differentiate among the natural sciences. Some aspects of the study of the oceans, for example, the general oceanic circulation, appear to be relatively weakly coupled, in that one considers a few interactions between the motion of the planet, its atmosphere, and the heat budget of the earth and the oceans. Another branch of oceanography, ecology, is a very strongly coupled science. Ecology in the ocean is so strongly coupled that it is difficult even to distinguish the variables from each other. It appears that most natural phenomena of large scale on the earth's surface are rather strongly coupled in the sense that the variables are not separable either for experimental or analytical purposes.

There are, of course, large-scale artificial experiments that have been done and have revealed a great deal of information. I would class the modern air and water pollution disaster as an obvious, though socially evil, experiment. I can offer more examples: Bomb-C^{14} spread through the atmosphere and exchanged with the ocean to give us a much better picture of the circulation of CO_2 and its equilibrium between the ocean and the atmosphere than we had had previously. Attempts to counter the current pollution of the Great Lakes may be an experiment in reversibility; we have the social hope but scientific uncertainty that the Lakes can be cleaned up. Whether reversible or not, the pollution and the counter measures are certainly giving us a good deal of scientific (or engineering?) information.

In the past, social taboos have prevented a whole class of experiments, but it now seems that even these have broken down at some times, most notably with Nazi so-called "experimentation" in some concentration camps. There have been suggestions that warfare in Viet Nam involves certain experimental tests of new equipment and ideas. But it is still largely true that, for scientists, areas considered important in biological experimentation are taboo for what we consider good and sufficient social reasons.

Simulated or "hypothetical" experiments and systems analysis have been used to circumvent social control or for large systems that cannot be taken to the laboratory. But such "experiments" are only as good as the first principles that allow them to be carried on in the mind alone. Theoretical physics is a clear choice for the field in which such experiments have great value. But in most of the world of scientific practice, scientists use hypothetical experiments as a prelude to actual experimentation or further observation. One does not perform hypothetical experiments for their own sake. We grant that as teachers we have frequent recourse to such devices. As research workers in science they are of little value of and for themselves.

It appears then, that experimental science is of many different kinds, that though the nature of experiment is the same no matter where one sees it, the controls may vary and the ability to observe different parts of the experiment may be limited, and finally that there are experiments that simply cannot be done for social reasons.

Historical versus Nonhistorical Science

This topic, a recurring theme in the dialogue on the nature of science (Nagel, 1952), has been explored recently by G. G. Simpson (1963) and R. A. Watson (1966). It appears to me that there is no fundamental difference between historical and nonhistorical science except as it may be economically profitable or culturally desirable to determine as exactly as possible what happened at a certain place and time. Thus we really do not care, as Watson puts it, exactly how the Grand Canyon of the Colorado River was formed. We only care how the generic class of Grand Canyons forms and has formed in the past, assuming that canyon-cutting was not a unique event. This is true in the same way that a chemist does not care what the particular numbers of an individual experiment are. His only concern is in repeating and generalizing that experiment so that the results from his or anybody else's operation of the same kind will fall into the same pattern. In fact, one rarely sees the particular numbers of any experiment. The raw data are of little interest except as an intermediate stage in the calculation of the quantities that are usually of true interest, quantities the significance of which has been established by earlier scientific studies. So, though we measure a particular mass and volume, we quote the important number as the density.

We may differentiate the historical sciences from the so-called nonhistorical sciences by the time scale of the processes involved. Though a chemical reaction has a "history," that history is usually faster than most processes we consider "historical." Even slow chemical reactions are extraordinarily fast compared to geological processes. In astronomy, too, a great many processes are very slow, although there are others that are fast. But even the history of a chemical reaction can be of major importance, for the study of chemical kinetics is just this. Again, though it is a historical event, the chemist studying the course of a reaction is rarely interested in any particular one performed at any particular time in his laboratory, but rather in the general repeatable experiment that anyone can do.

What is different about historical sciences is that many times only one natural experiment is observable, or so few that generalization is difficult if not impossible. We have on this earth, apparently, only one example of organic macroevolution. The general appearance of oxygen in the earth's primitive atmosphere probably happened only once. In modern times, the change in our lives caused by the development of the atomic bomb could happen only once. If the essence of experiment, whether artificial or natural, is that it be repeatable and that one needs at least one degree of freedom in order to make an average or to generalize, then we are destroyed by the uniqueness of some events. This is not to say, of course, that they are unique in the universe; they are only unique as far as our observational capabilities are concerned. It is for this reason that there is interest among biologists about the possibilities of some form of life on the moon or on Mars. They are simply seeking the additional experiment. Almost worse than the unique experiment is the availability of a very few experiments with a high variance. We have on the Earth only a few continents. In the development of the structure of the North American continent there have been only a few major evolutionary patterns of geosynclines and mountain chain evolution on the borders of the continent. There are only a few terrestrial planets. The social sciences to some extent are plagued by the same. There are as yet only a few nations that have atomic bombs.

Styles in Science

Each scientist selects the discipline he works in for variety of reasons, but many styles can be found in all. I use the word "style" because, as has already become apparent, I reject the notion that there are different kinds of science, or scientific disciplines. There are many different personalities that go into science, and each of these personality types has his own way of doing things, as pointed out by Kubie (1953) and Eiduson (1962). Though there may be some correlation between personality and the discipline selected, I do not wish to discuss that issue.

Style is a word that has many meanings, ranging from a particular historical "school" in any subject (for example, "classical style") to a designation of a particular approach to any intellectual effort that is the product of the interaction of a personality with his time and his subject. It is the latter meaning of the word that I will use exclusively. Styles are probably related to personality, but they are always modified by the field in which that person works. An obvious recent example of different styles is that given by the contrast in the addresses of two recent Nobel laureates in physics, Richard Feynman (1966) and Julian Schwinger (1966). Here two men working in the same field of physics reveal very different styles of tackling the same kind of problem and writing about it.

We can recognize and tag some of the more distinctive styles that are common to all fields. We recognize that some of these are cross-coupled and one may indulge in several styles at different periods or as the mood strikes:

The rigorous formalist
The brilliant phenomenologist
The painstaking laboratory methodologist and his equivalent, the careful, detailed
  field observer
The quick and dirty cream skimmer
The niche-lover or horizontal monopolist
The subgeneralist or vertical monopolist
The dilettante and his brother, the versatile virtuoso, separated by the difference
  between success and failure
The older, wiser generalist

This is a parlor game that anyone can play and apply to his friends and colleagues.

Value judgments are usually made about the relative worth of various stylists' contribution. But it is probably so that all of these styles are necessary for science to advance, for everyone leans on everyone else. There is some danger at the present time that there will be too much emphasis on certain styles in picking the leaders of science, and that style will be confused with discipline and with fundamental ability of the individual to make advances in science. Pluralism and diversity make for more interest in science as they do elsewhere in life. But let us have differences in style and subject and recognize that invidious distinctions between "kinds" of science serve only to build hierarchies of position and privilege.

References

EIDUSON, BERNICE T. *Scientists: Their Psychological World.* New York: Basic Books, 1962.

FEYNMAN, RICHARD P. "The Development of the Space-Time View of Quantum Electrodynamics." *Science* 153 (1966): 699–708.

KURIE, L. S. "Problems of the Scientific Career." *Scientific Monthly* 74 (1953). Reprinted in H. FEIGLE and M. BRODBECK, *Readings in the Philosophy of Science.* New York: Appleton-Century-Crofts, 1953. Pp. 688–700.

SCHWINGER, JULIAN. "Relativistic Quantum Field Theory." *Science* 153 (1966): 949–53.

SIMPSON, G. G. "Historical Science." In *The Fabric of Geology,* edited by C. C. Albritton, Jr. Reading, Mass.: Addison-Wesley, 1963. Pp. 24–27.

WATSON, R. A. "Is Geology Different: A Critical Discussion of 'The Fabric of Geology.'" *Philosophy of Science* 33 (1966): 172–85.
WEAVER, WARREN, "Science and People." *Science* 122 (1955): 1255–59.

Guides for Design, Model Building, and Large-Scale Research

At this point one must decide the nature of proof desired, taking into consideration the level of one's hypotheses, the size of one's budget, the amount of personnel and their skills, the time required, etc. It is now generally accepted that the model of the controlled experiment is always a valuable guide even if, in practice, deviation is necessary. "Some Observations on Study Design" (1.9) by Samuel A. Stouffer is regarded as the single most useful statement of design requirements for social investigation.

Hans L. Zetterberg explains the problems facing the researcher who wishes to use controlled observation and explains how alternative hypotheses can be tested with pseudo-experimental designs. See 1.10, an excerpt from *On Theory and Verification in Sociology.*

Model building has become an integral part of scientific work. "The Role of Models in Research Design" (1.11) describes various types of models in current use.

Edward Suchman in 1.12 has listed some "General Considerations of Research Design." These are realistic appraisals often needed when ideal plans must be compromised. The professional researcher keeps these guides before him.

Factors affecting the validity of the research design are described in 1.13. Large-scale group research has grown in volume and in scope. Delbert C. Miller has written "The Shaping of Research Design in Large-Scale Group Research" (1.14) to provide a case study for the team research proposal. The breaking down of the problem into manageable parts is illustrated. The importance of individual differences among researchers is highlighted. Note also the progression of research stages. This guide is for the guidance of design in large-scale research only.

SOME OBSERVATIONS ON STUDY DESIGN*   *1.9*

Samuel A. Stouffer

We must be clear in our own minds what proof consists of, and we must, if possible, provide dramatic examples of the advantages of relying on something more than plausibility. And the heart of our problem lies in study design *in advance,* such that the evidence is not capable of a dozen alternative interpretations.

Basically, I think it is essential that we always keep in mind the model of a controlled experiment, even if in practice we may have to deviate from an ideal model. Take the simple accompanying diagram.

* Reprinted from Samuel A. Stouffer, "Some Observations on Study Design," *American Journal of Sociology* 55 (January 1950): 356–59. Copyright 1950 by the University of Chicago.

	Before	After	After–Before
Experimental group	x_1	x_2	$d = x_2 - x_1$
Control group	x_1'	x_2'	$d' = x_2' - x_1'$

The test of whether a difference d is attributable to what we think it is attributable to is whether d is significantly larger than d'.

We used this model over and over again during the war to measure the effectiveness of orientation films in changing soldiers' attitudes. These experiences are described in Volume III of our *Studies in Social Psychology in World War II.*[1]

One of the troubles with using this careful design was that the effectiveness of a single film when thus measured turned out to be so slight. If, instead of using the complete experimental design, we simply took an unselected sample of men and compared the attitudes of those who said they had seen a film with those who said they had not, we got much more impressive differences. This was more rewarding to us, too, for the management wanted to believe the films were powerful medicine. The gimmick was the selective fallibility of memory. Men who correctly remembered seeing the films were likely to be those most sensitized to their message. Men who were bored or indifferent may have actually seen them but slept through them or just forgot.

Most of the time we are not able or not patient enough to design studies containing all four cells as in the diagram above. Sometimes we have only the top two cells, as in the accompanying diagram. In this situation we have two observations of the same individuals or groups taken at different

x_1	x_2

$d = x_1 - x_2$

times. This is often a very useful design. In the army, for example, we could take a group of recruits, ascertain their attitudes, and restudy the same men later. From this we could tell whose attitudes changed and in what direction. (It was almost always for the worse, which did not endear us to the army!) But exactly what factors in the early training period were most responsible for deterioration of attitudes could only be inferred indirectly.

The panel study is usually more informative than a more frequent design, which might be pictured thus:

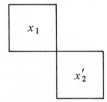

Here at one point in time we have one sample, and at a later point in time we have another sample. We observe that our measure, say, the mean, is greater for the recent sample than for the earlier one. But we are precluded from observing which men or what type of men shifted. Moreover, there is always the disturbing possibility that the populations in our two samples were initially different; hence the differences might not be attributable to conditions taking place in the time interval between the two observations. Thus we would study a group of soldiers in the United States and later ask the same questions of a group of soldiers overseas. Having matched the two groups of men carefully by branch of service, length of time in the army, rank, etc., we hoped that the results of the study would approximate what would be found if the same men could have been studied twice. But this could be no more than a hope. Some important factors could not be adequately controlled, for example, physical conditions. Men who went overseas were initially in better shape on the average than men who had been kept behind; but, if the follow-up study was in the tropics, there was a chance that unfavorable climate already had begun to take its toll. And so it went. How much men overseas changed called for a panel study as a minimum if we were to have much confidence in the findings.

A very common attempt to get the result of a controlled experiment without paying the price is with the design that might be as shown in the accompanying diagram. This is usually what we get with correlation analysis. We have two or more groups of men whom we study at the same point in time.

$$\begin{array}{|c|} \hline x_2 \\ \hline x_2' \\ \hline \end{array}$$

Thus we have men in the infantry and men in the air corps and compare their attitudes. How much of the difference between x_2' and x_2 we can attribute to experience in a given branch of service and how much is a function of attributes of the men selected for each branch we cannot know assuredly. True, we can try to rule out various possibilities by matching; we can compare men from the two branches with the same age and education, for example. But there is all too often a wide-open gate through which other uncontrolled variables can march.

Sometimes, believe it nor not, we have only one cell:

$$\begin{array}{|c|} \hline x_2 \\ \hline \end{array}$$

When this happens, we do not know much of anything. But we can still fill pages of social science journals with "brilliant analysis" if we use plausible conjecture in supplying missing cells from our imagination. Thus we may find that the adolescent today has wild ideas and conclude that society is going to the dogs. We fill in the dotted cell representing our own yesterdays with hypothetical data, where x_1 represents us and x_2 our offspring. The tragicomic part is that most of the public, including, I fear, many social scientists, are so acculturated that they ask for no better data.

I do not intend to disparage all research not conforming to the canons of the controlled experiment. I think that we will see more of full experimental design in sociology and social psychology in the future than in the past. But I am well aware of the practical difficulties of its execution, and I know that there are numberless important situations in which it is not feasible at all. What I am arguing for is awareness of the limitations of a design in which crucial cells are missing.

Sometimes by forethought and patchwork we can get approximations that are useful if we are careful to avoid overinterpretation. Let me cite an example:

In Europe during the war the army tested the idea of putting an entire platoon of Negro soldiers into a white infantry outfit. This was done in several companies. The Negroes fought beside white soldiers. After several months we were asked to find out what the white troops thought about the innovation. We found that only 7 percent of the white soldiers in companies with Negro platoons said that they disliked the idea very much, whereas 62 percent of the white soldiers in divisions without Negro troops said they would dislike the idea very much if it were tried in their outfits. We have:

	Before	After
Experimental		7%
Control		62%

Now, were these white soldiers who fought beside Negroes men who were naturally more favorable to Negroes than the cross section of white infantrymen? We did not think so, since, for example, they contained about the same proportion of southerners. The point was of some importance, however, if we were to make the inference that actual experience with Negroes reduced hostility from 62 to 7 percent. As a second-best substitute, we asked the white soldiers in companies with Negro platoons if they could recall how they felt when the innovation was first proposed. It happens that 67 percent said they were initially opposed to the idea. Thus we could tentatively fill in a missing cell and conclude that, under the conditions obtaining, there probably had been a marked change in attitude.

Even if this had been a perfectly controlled experiment, there was still plenty of chance to draw erroneous inferences. The conclusions apply only to situations closely approximating those of the study. It happens, for example, that the Negroes involved were men who volunteered to leave rear-area jobs for combat duty. If other Negroes had been involved, the situation might have been different. Moreover, they had white officers. One army colonel who saw this study and whom I expected to ridicule it because he usually opposed innovations, surprised me by offering congratulations. "This proves," he said, "what I have been arguing in all my thirty years in the army— that niggers will do all right if you give 'em white officers!" Moreover, the study applied only to combat experiences. Other studies would be needed to justify extending the findings to noncombat or garrison duty. In other words, one lone study, however well designed, can be a very dangerous thing if it is exploited beyond its immediate implications.

Now experiments take time and money, and there is no use denying that we in social science cannot be as prodigal with the replications as the biologist who can run a hundred experiments simultaneously by growing plants in all kinds of soils and conditions. The relative ease of experimentation in much—not all—of natural science goes far to account for the difference in quality of proof demanded by physical and biological sciences, on the one hand, and social scientists, on the other.

Though we cannot always design neat experiments when we want to, we can at least keep the experimental model in front of our eyes and behave cautiously when we fill in missing cells with dotted lines. But there is a further and even more important operation we can perform in the interest of economy. That lies in our choice of the initial problem.

Note

1. Carl I. Hovland, Arthur A. Lumsdaine, and Fred D. Sheffield, *Experiments on Mass Communication* (Princeton, N.J.: Princeton University Press, 1949).

ON THE DECISIONS IN VERIFICATIONAL STUDIES*   *1.10*

Hans L. Zetterberg

The advantages of the experimental design, however, rest with the possibility of a random assignment of cases to the experimental and control groups and on the possibility of producing what the working hypothesis terms the cause. Unfortunately, in sociology we rarely have these possibilities.

Certainly many factors are intentionally introduced into society by politicians, educators, welfare agencies, etc. But these phenomena are seldom or never produced, because they are termed causes in a scientific social theory. Furthermore, when compulsory education, socialized medicine, public housing projects, etc., are introduced into a society, the very complexity of the new phenomena does not make them suitable as indicators of concepts of a theory.

In the second place, we can rarely introduce randomization of the persons

* From H. L. Zetterberg, *On Theory and Verification in Sociology,* 2nd ed. rev. (Totowa, N.J.: Bedminster Press, 1963), pp. 61–66.

supposed to enjoy these intentionally produced phenomena without violating strong moral sentiments. As to the social programs of the welfare state Chapin makes the comment:

> The conventional method of equalizing factors that are known and also unknown (by R. A. Fisher's design of experiment) is to select at random both the experimental group that receives treatment and the control group that serves as a reference group for comparison. In social research the program of social treatment cannot be directed toward a randomly selected group because the prevailing mores require that this treatment be directed to a group of individuals who are eligible because of greater *need*. Thus precise control of unknown is impossible and the only factors that can be controlled are factors that are known to be in the particular social situation because of previous studies.[1]

It seems that this inability to satisfy the conditions for a profitable use of the experimental design would definitely curtail the sociologist's prospect to verify his theories. However, the situation is by no means disastrous: sciences like meteorology and astronomy have verified theories without the employment of the experimental method.

For control of alternative hypotheses, the sociologist is to a large extent dependent on what might be called *pseudoexperimental* designs. These designs control propositions known as alternative ones, but, unlike the experimental designs, these designs cannot control unknown alternatives.

The most commonly used method in sociology for control of known alternative propositions is multivariate analysis, which has been formalized by Paul Lazarsfeld.[2] Skill in its use has become essential for most sociological research; those who know how to use it deserve to be called "modern sociologists." The technique controls alternative propositions by testing the hypothesis in subsamples that are homogeneous with respect to the determinants specified by the alternative propositions. It can be used to control all known alternative determinants provided the sample used is large enough.

The simplest relation between two variates X and Y is a fourfold table:

	X	non-X
Y		
non-Y		

To discover whether a third variable, Z, accounts for any of the relations found in such a table, we break it into two parts:

	X	non-X			Z X	non-X			non-Z X	non-X
Y			$=$	Y			$+$	Y		
non-Y				non-Y				non-Y		

If the relation between X and Y still holds in all subclasses of Z, we may retain, for the time being, our trust in the proposition that X affects Y. To this kind of design many new alternative determinants can be added, and it works equally well for qualitative and quantitative varieties.

However, the advantages do not end here. We can tabulate:

							Y			non-Y	
	X	non-X			X	non-X			X	non-X	
Z				Z				Z			
			=				+				
non-Z				non-Z				non-Z			

and also:

							X			non-X	
	Y	non-Y			Y	non-X			Y	non-Y	
Z				Z				Z			
			=				+				
non-Z				non-Z				non-Z			

The purpose of these tabulations is to discover the actual linkage between the three variables. It would carry us far to review all the rules of interpretation involved here. However, if certain assumptions about the time lag between the variates can be made, it is possible to use such tabulations to disentangle a wide variety of causal chains, as shown in the diagram (below) adapted from Dahlström.[3]

(1) $X \longrightarrow Y \longrightarrow Z$ (2) $X \longrightarrow Z \longrightarrow Y$

(3) $Z \longrightarrow X \longrightarrow Y$ (4)

(5)   (6)   (7)

(8)   (9)   (10)

(11)   (12)   (13)

Another method of pseudoexperimental control is that of *matching,* advocated by F. S. Chapin.[4] An experimental group and a control group are made equal on some criteria by discarding cases in one group for which no "twin" can be found in the other group. One disadvantage of this procedure is that the matched groups so obtained are not representative of the original groups. When this way of matching is employed, we do not quite know to what population the results can be generalized.

Control in pseudoexperimental design can be obtained through the use of other statistical adjustments. Various applications of the *multiple regression* approach can be made, provided variables fitting the rather rigid assumptions are used. The most common methods are those of partial correlation and analysis of covariance. These methods become rather laborious if the number of factors to be controlled is more than three or four.

Experimental designs and pseudoexperimental designs may be cross-sectional or longitudinal. We have already pointed out that longitudinal designs are more effective than cross-sectional designs and that experimental designs are more effective than pseudoexperimental designs. We can now reach a typology of designs:

		The test of the null-hypothesis	
		Cross-sectional	Longitudinal
The control of alternative hypotheses	No control		
	Pseudoexperimental		
	Experimental		

The closer a design comes to the longitudinal experimental, the better it is. However, we know little or nothing about how to evaluate crosswise combinations of the two criteria. We have no way in which to tell whether a pseudoexperimental longitudinal design (such as a panel with multivariable anslysis) is as effective as the cross-sectional experimental design (the conventional laboratory experiment).

Notes

1. F. Stuart Chapin, "Experimental Designs in Social Research," *American Journal of Sociology* 55 (1950): 402.
2. Paul F. Lazarsfeld, "Interpretation of Statistical Relations as a Research Operation," in *The Language of Social Research,* ed. Paul F. Lazarsfeld and Morris Rosenberg (Glencoe, Ill.: Free Press, 1955), pp. 115–25.
3. Edmund Dahlström, "Analys av surveymaterial," in *Sociologiska metoder,* ed. Georg Karlsson et al. (Stockholm: Svenska Bokförlaget, 1961), p. 193.
4. F. Stuart Chapin, *Experimental Designs in Sociological Research* (New York: Harper, 1947).

For further reading the advanced student should see F. Stuart Chapin, *Experimental Designs in Sociological Research,* rev. ed. (New York: Harper, 1955); Ernest Greenwood, *Experimental Sociology: A Study in Method* (New York: King's Crown, 1945); Claire Selltiz, Marie Jahoda, Morton Deutsch, and Stuart W. Cook, *Research Methods in Social*

Relations, rev., 1 vol. (New York: Henry Holt, 1959), chap. 4; Russell L. Ackoff, *The Designs of Social Research* (Chicago: University of Chicago, 1953), chap. 3; Abraham Kaplan, *The Conduct of Inquiry* (San Francisco: Chandler, 1964).

THE ROLE OF MODELS IN RESEARCH DESIGN

1.11

Instructions for Use of Guide 1.11

Model building has been an integral part of social science for a long time. The work of Herbert Spenser and his followers based on a biological model of society would fill a small library. Physics has also served to encourage social scientists to seek social analogues. August Comte often used the term *social physics* to describe modern sociology.

Model building has been accentuated and accelerated by many forces in contemporary life. Models seem appropriate to the new world of computers, automation, and space technology; and they have conferred new status on the scientist in government, industry, and the military. Model building has become "modeling," and the language of social science now includes such terms as game models (gaming), simulation models, mathematical models, trend models, stochastic models, laboratory models, information and cybernetic models, causal and path models, and many more. Even theory itself is being fractionalized into "theoretical models." All these terms stand for a closed system from which are generated predictions (or hypotheses) that, when made, require some kind of empirical test.

In trying to bring some order out of the variety of models, it is soon discovered much overlapping and widely different usages exist. There is no common agreement on the classification of models. In the following description five categories of models and their variants are set out.[1] Don't hesitate to use models if they assist in identifying significant variables in such a way that tests of hypotheses can be defined more sharply.

I. Physical Models

A physical model is a concrete object fashioned to look like the represented phenomena. These objects incorporate static or structural properties. Examples include skeletons, organs, molecules, atoms, small-scale buildings, airplanes, and air tunnels. Perhaps the most famous model in contemporary science is the double-helix model showing the structuring of the DNA code gene that governs human reproduction. Pilot operating models introduce dynamic systems patterns to represent functioning mechanisms in many fields.

A cognitive function is performed by the physical model in almost every field of science and branch of technology from sewing to architecture and aeronautical engineering. Sociology has made limited use of physical models, but F. S. Chapin has experimented with models to demonstrate institutions and social space and D. C. Miller with models of group and power relations. Many possibilities present themselves.

Basic Reading

CHAPIN, F. S. "A Theory of Social Institutions." In *Contemporary American Institutions.* New York: Harper & Bros., 1935. Pp. 319–52.

MILLER, DELBERT C. "The Research, Administrative, and Teaching Uses of Sociological Models in Depicting Group Relations." *Proceedings of the Pacific Sociological Society* 19 (June 1951): 98–102.

II. Theoretical Models

The term model is often used loosely to refer to any scientific theory phrased in symbolic, postulational, or formal styles. If there is any value in using "theory" and "model" as synonymous, it probably exists when a theory is set forth as a set of postulations with the relations among the parts clearly specified or exhibited. Thus Talcott Parsons and Charles Ackerman argue that the "social system is a theoretical device which maximizes analytical attention to its connectedness and it does so in a disciplined manner."[2]

Basic Reading

DUBIN, ROBERT. *Theory Building, A Practical Guide to the Construction and Testing of Theoretical Models.* New York: Free Press, 1969.

LAND, KENNETH C. "Formal Theory." In *Sociological Methodology 1971,* edited by Herbert L. Costner. San Francisco: Jossey-Bass, 1971.

LAVE, CHARLES A., and MARCH, JAMES G. *An Introduction to Models in the Social Sciences.* New York: Harper & Row, 1975.

III. Mathematical Models

Applied in the social sciences, a mathematical model refers to the use of mathematical equations to depict the behavior of persons, groups, communities, states, or nations. Common use of mathematics can be observed in trend, causal, path, stochastic models.

Trend models refer to the fitting of time-series data to equations or curves postulated as change principles or laws.

Research Examples

BARTOS, OTOMAR. J. *Simple Models of Group Behavior.* New York: Columbia University Press, 1967.

COLEMAN, JAMES S. *The Mathematics of Collective Action.* Chicago: Aldine, 1973.

DODD, STUART CARTER. "Testing Message Diffusion in Controlled Experiments: Charting the Distance and Time Factors in the Interactance Hypothesis." *American Sociological Review* 18 (August 1952): 410–16.

HART, HORNELL. "Logistic Social Trends." *American Journal of Sociology* 50 (March 1945): 337–52.

HENRY, LOUIS. *Population Analysis and Models.* New York: Academic Press, 1977.

HERNES, GUDMUND. "The Process of Entry into First Marriage." *American Sociological Review* 37 (April 1972): 173–82.

KEMF, WILLIAM F., and REPP, BRUNO H. *Mathematical Models for Social Psychology.* New York: Wiley, 1977.

RESTLE, FRANK. *Mathematical Models in Psychology.* Baltimore: Penguin, 1971.

STOUFFER, SAMUEL A. "Intervening Opportunities: A Theory Relating Mobility and Distance." *American Sociological Review* 5 (December 1940): 845–67.

Causal and path models involve the construction of a simplified model of social reality in which variables are presumed to act in a causal or processual sequence. The most important variables affecting some dependent (outcome) variable or criterion are sought and arranged according to their influence or impact. All other variables entering into the causal system are regarded as residuals.

Research Examples

DUNCAN, O. D. "Path Analysis: Sociological Examples." *American Journal of Sociology* 72 (July 1966): 1–16.

————, and BLAU, PETER. "The Process of Stratification." In *The American Occupational Structure.* New York: Wiley, 1967. Pp. 163–77.

SEWELL, WILLIAM H.; HALLER, ARCHIBALD O.; and OHLENDORF, GEORGE W. "The Educational and Early Occupational Status Attainment Process: Replication and Revision." *American Sociological Review* 35 (December 1970): 1014–27.

A stochastic model refers to a probability construction in which a sequence of behavioral events occurs in time and to which are assigned probabilities for the joint occurrence of such events. Such models deal with "stochastic processes."

Research Examples

DODD, S. C. "Diffusion Is Predictable: Testing Probability Models for Laws of Interaction." *American Sociological Review* 20 (August 1955): 392–401.

GALASKIEWICZ, JOSEPH, and WASSERMAN, STANLEY. "A Dynamic Study of Change in a Regional Corporate Network." *American Sociological Review* 46 (August 1981): 475–84.

HUNTER, ALBERT. "Community Change: A Stochastic Analysis of Chicago's Local Communities, 1930–60." *American Journal of Sociology* 39 (January 1974): 923–47.

Basic Reading

BARTHOLOMEW, D. J. *Stochastic Models for Social Processes.* 2nd ed. New York: Wiley-Interscience, 1974.

COLEMAN, JAMES S. *Introduction to Mathematical Sociology.* New York: Free Press of Glencoe, 1964.

DOREIAN, PATRICK, and HUMMON, NORMAN. *Modeling Social Processes.* New York: Elsevier, 1976.

FARARO, THOMAS J. *Mathematical Sociology.* New York: Wiley-Interscience, 1973.

KEMENY, JOHN G., and SNELL, LAURIE. *Mathematical Models in the Social Sciences.* Cambridge, Mass.: MIT Press, 1962.

LAZARSFELD, PAUL F. *Mathematical Thinking in the Social Sciences.* Glencoe, Ill.: Free Press, 1954.

TUFTE, EDWARD R. *Data Analysis for Politics and Policy.* Englewood Cliffs, N.J.: Prentice-Hall, 1974.

IV. Mechanical Models

In social science mechanical models use concepts from physics to provide analogues for social behavior. Mathematics was to be the handmaiden for building the field and bringing new rigor and validity. Increasingly, interest has grown in machine models; these are an extension of the concern with mathematical models since they are based on mathematical language and symbolic logic. The computer is the focus of the machine model, and the term *computer simulated model* or *electronic simulated model* is current. The game model is clearly related.

The *computer simulated model* is focused on the use of a computer program to provide a test of a set of constructs that are internally consistent and have presumed explanatory power in order to derive generalizable propositions from the coded empirical data. Electronic computers are increasingly used to substitute for mathematical derivations in formal models. The postulates of the model can be programmed onto the computer (making the computer program the theory), and the computer will calculate the behavior that the program (i.e., theory) dictates.

Research Examples

BESHERS, JAMES M. *Computer Methods in the Analysis of Large Scale Social Systems.* Cambridge, Mass.: MIT Press, 1965.

COHEN, KALMAN J., and CYERT, RICHARD M. "Simulation of Organizational Behavior." In *Handbook of Organizations,* edited by James G. March. Chicago: Rand McNally, 1965. Pp. 305–34.

GUETZKOW, HAROLD; KOTLER, PHILIP; and SCHULTZ, RANDALL R. *Simulation in Social and Administrative Science.* Englewood Cliffs, N.J.: Prentice-Hall, 1972.

GULAHORN, JOHN T., and JEANNE E. "Some Computer Applications in Social Science." *American Sociological Review* 30 (June 1965): 363–65.

HARE, PAUL A.; RICHARDSON, R.; and SCHEIBLECHNER, HARTMAN. "Computer Simulation of Small Group Decisions." Vienna: Institute for Higher Studies, February 1968.

ROBY, THORNTON B. "Computer Simulation Models for Organization Theory." In *Methods of Organizational Research,* edited by Victor H. Vroom. Pittsburgh: University of Pittsburgh Press, 1967. Pp. 171–211.

Microanalytic simulation models are used to examine the effects of various kinds of policies on the demographic structure of the population, saving and tax behavior, income security during retirement, social-class differences in health and disease, and numerous other aspects of the population and its well-being. The microanalytic system (MASS) was originally developed by Guy Orcutt of Yale University. It is a computer approach to capture many of the complexities of a nation's social and economic structure. It is sophisticated enough to handle research problems as complex as the real-life events that affect the economic lives of whole populations of human beings: marrying and divorcing, giving birth, changing residence, becoming unemployed and finding new jobs, retiring, and dying. Research involving general simulation modeling to capture very large sets of human behaviors is still rare. A research leader in this work is Dr. James D. Smith at the

Institute of Social Research, University of Michigan, Ann Arbor, MI. For further information, contact him at that address. See his book cited below.

Research Examples

HAVEMAN, ROBERT H., and HOLLENBECK, KEVIN, eds. *Microeconomic Simulation Models for Public Policy Analysis.* 2 Vols. New York: Academic Press, 1980.

HOUSE, PETER W., and McLEOD, JOHN. *Large Scale Models for Policy Evaluation.* New York: Wiley, 1977.

SMITH, JAMES D. *Modeling the Distribution and Intergenerational Transmission of Wealth.* Chicago: University of Chicago Press, 1980.

Basic Reading

BRIER, ALAN, and ROBINSON, IAN. *Computers and the Social Sciences.* London: Hutchinson, 1974.

DYKE, BENNETT, and MacCLUER, JEAN WALTERS, eds. *Computer Simulation in Human Population Studies.* New York: Academic Press, 1973 [1974].

Game models rest on a mathematical theory that pertains to the determination of optimum strategies in a competitive situation (game of strategy) involving two or more individuals or parties. Games of strategy, in contrast to games where the outcomes depends only on chance, are games in which the outcome depends also, or entirely, on the moves chosen by the individual players.

Research Examples

FELDT, ALLAN G. *CLUG: Community Land Use Game.* New York: Free Press, 1972.

GAMSON, WILLIAM A. *SIMSOC: Simulated Society.* 2nd ed. New York: Free Press, 1972.

GUETZKOW, HAROLD and VALADEZ. *Simulated International Processes: Theories and Research in Global Modeling.* Beverly Hills, Calif.: Sage, 1981.

HORN, ROBERT E., and CLEAVES, ANNE, eds. *The Guide to Simulations (Games for Education and Training.* 4th ed. Beverly Hills, Calif.: Sage, 1980.

SHIRTS, R. GARY. *Star Power.* La Jolla, Calif.: Simile II, 1969.

SHUBICK, MARTIN. *The Uses and Methods of Gaming.* New York: Elsevier, 1975.

SINGLETON, ROBERT R., and TYNDALL, WILLIAM F. *Games and Programs: Mathematics for Modeling.* San Francisco: Freeman, 1974.

WINTERS, P. R. *The Carnegie Tech Management Game: An Experiment in Business Education.* Homewood, Ill.: Irwin, 1964.

YATES, DAVID JULES. *Community Interaction Game.* Cambridge, Mass.: Simulmatics, 1967.

Basic Reading

BARTON, RICHARD F. *A Primer on Simulation and Gaming.* Englewood Cliffs, N.J.: Prentice-Hall, 1970.

DUKE, RICHARD. *Gaming, The Future's Language.* New York: Halsted, 1974.

GIBBS, G. IAN. *Dictionary of Gaming, Modeling, and Simulation.* Beverly Hills: Calif: Sage, 1978.

GREENBLAT, C., and DUKE, R., eds. *Gaming-Simulation: Rationale, Designs, and Applications.* New York: Halsted, 1975. Rev. 1981.

INBAR, MICHAEL, and STOLL, CLARENCE S. *Simulation and Gaming in Social Science.* New York: Free Press, 1972.

SHUBICK, MARTIN. *Games for Society, Business, and War.* New York: Elsevier, 1975.

Simulation and Games. An interdisciplinary form for scholarly communication on all aspects of theory, design, and research bearing on the use of man, man-machine, and machine simulations of social processes. Editor: Cathy S. Greenblat, Rutgers University. Publisher: Sage, Beverly Hills, Calif.; published quarterly in March, June, September, and December.

V. Symbolic Interactionist Models

Symbolic interactionist models address themselves to the meanings that actors give to the symbols they use or encounter. In social interaction, cues to behavior are transmitted by word and gesture. Behavior is constantly changing as transactions occur. There are many nuances of meaning too subtle to be treated as mechanical phenomena. Some symbolic interactionist models are simple constructs involving few persons; others are more elaborate and use the computer to seek out patterns and generalizations. All models tend to be simulation models, i.e., they are based on contrived situations or structured concepts that are isomorphic to reality situations.

Laboratory models refer to contrived situations simulating groups or organizations in which actors play roles that are either structured or unstructured according to the design of the researcher. Generally such behavior is observed in a closed environment where observation and recording devices can be employed. Well-known examples can be cited from the small-group laboratory. Somewhat less attention has been given to the organization in the laboratory, but research is increasing rapidly.

Research Examples

BALES, ROBERT F. *Interaction Process Analysis: A Method for the Study of Small Groups.* Cambridge, Mass.: Addison-Wesley, 1950.

BURKE, PETER J. "The Development of Task and Social-emotional Role Differentiation." *Sociometry* 30 (December 1968): 379–92.

SLATER, PHILIP E. "Role Differentiation in Small Groups," *American Sociological Review* 20 (June 1955): 300–310.

WEICK, KARL E. "Laboratory Experimentation with Organizations." In *Handbook of Organizations,* edited by James G. March. Chicago: Rand McNally, 1965. Pp. 194–260.

———. "Organizations in the Laboratory." In *Methods of Organizational Research,* edited by Victor H. Vroom. Pittsburgh: University of Pittsburgh Press, 1967. Pp. 1–56.

Basic Reading

BALES, ROBERT F. "Interaction Process Analysis." In *International Encyclopedia of Social Sciences,* edited by D. L. Sills. New York: Macmillan, Free Press, & Colliers Encyclopedia, 1968.

———. *Personality and Interpersonal Behavior.* New York: Holt, Rinehart & Winston, 1970.

HARE, PAUL A. *Handbook of Small Group Research.* 2nd ed. New York: Free Press of Glencoe, 1975.

Information and cybernetic models depict information inputs, flows, and outputs within communication systems.[3] Models may range from mechanical to symbolic interactionist, where meaning becomes more significant. The computer may or may not be a useful adjunct. Models may treat with noise, redundancy, looping, and feedback. The most common analog is human intelligence and the functioning of the brain. The scientific base is the information-scientific principle as explained by Pieter J. van Heerden:[4]

The Information-Scientific Principle of Intelligence

We have a black box with an input signal $f(t)$ which is a function of the time t only, and an output signal $g(t)$; both are binary time series:

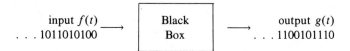

input $f(t)$ $\longrightarrow$ Black $\longrightarrow$ output $g(t)$
. . . 1011010100   Box   . . . 1100101110

Figure 1. Basic Model of Artificial Intelligence

The black box is the analogy of the brain of living intelligent beings. The input signal forms the analogy of the psychological drives, while the output is analogous to the command, from the brain, through the nerves, to the muscles of hands, feet, mouth, etc. In a machine, the input series would be any information with which we want to disturb the machine and cause it to react; the output would operate any physical means we may wish to make available to it. A simple example would be an intelligent machine which operates a number of elevators, and the input would be formed by the buttons people push, and the complaints they utter, translated in a binary code.

Research Examples

DeFleur, Melvin L., and Larsen, Otto N. *The Flow of Information: An Experiment in Mass Communication.* New York: Harper, 1958.

Dodd, S. C. "Diffusion Is Predictable: Testing Probability Models for Laws of Interaction." *American Sociological Review* 20 (August 1955): 392–401.

Singer, Benjamin D. *Feedback and Society.* Lexington, Mass.: D. C. Heath, 1973.

Basic Reading

Fuchs, Walter R. *Cybernetics for the Modern Mind.* New York: Macmillan, 1971.

Klír, Jiri, and Valach, Miroslav. *Cybernetic Modeling.* Princeton, N.J.: Van Nostrand, 1967.

McKay, Donald. *Information, Mechanism, and Meaning.* Cambridge, Mass.: MIT Press, 1969.

Weiner, Norbert. *Cybernetics.* New York: Wiley, 1948.

Notes

1. Cf. Charles A. Lave and James G. March, *An Introduction to Models in the Social Sciences* (New York: Harper & Row, 1975); see also Lyndhurst Collins, ed., *The Use of Models in the Social Sciences,* (Boulder, Colo.: Westview Press, 1976).

2. Gordon J. DiRenzo, ed., *Concepts, Theory and Explanation in the Behavior Sciences* (New York: Random House, 1967), pp. 6–27.

3. These concepts are often used interchangeably. Information theory is concerned with the making of representations (i.e., symbolism in its most general sense) and of measuring changes in knowledge. Norbert Wiener, often called the father of cybernetics, said the term *cybernetics* would be used to cover "the entire field of control and communication theory whether in the machine or in the animal." Norbert Weiner, *Cybernetics* (New York: Wiley, 1948), p. 8.

4. Pieter J. van Heerden, *The Foundation of Empirical Knowledge with a Theory of Artificial Intelligence* (Wassenar, The Netherlands: N. V. Uitoererij Wistik, 1968).

1.12 GENERAL CONSIDERATIONS OF RESEARCH DESIGN*

Edward A. Suchman

1. It seems to us futile to argue whether or not a certain design is "scientific." The design is *the plan of study* and, as such, is present in all studies, uncontrolled as well as controlled and subjective as well as objective. It is not a case of scientific or not scientific, but rather one of good or less good design. The degree of accuracy desired, the level of "proof" aimed at, the state of existing knowledge, etc., all combine to determine the amount of concern one can have with the degree of "science" in one's design.

2. The proof of hypotheses is never definitive. The best one can hope to do is to make more or less plausible a series of alternative hypotheses. In most cases multiple explanations will be operative. Demonstrating one's own hypotheses does not rule out alternative hypotheses and vice versa.

3. There is no such thing as a single "correct" design. Different workers will come up with different designs favoring their own methodological and theoretical predispositions. Hypotheses can be studied by different methods using different designs.

4. All research design represents a compromise dictated by the many practical considerations that go into social research. None of us operates except on limited time, money, and personnel budgets. Further limitations concern the availability of data and the extent to which one can impose upon one's subjects. A research design must be *practical*.

5. A research design is not a highly specific plan to be followed without deviation, but rather a series of guideposts to keep one headed in the right direction. One must be prepared to discard (although not too quickly) hypotheses that do not work out and to develop new hypotheses on the basis of increased knowledge. Furthermore, any research design developed in the office will inevitably have to be changed in the face of field considerations.

1.13 FACTORS JEOPARDIZING INTERNAL AND EXTERNAL VALIDITY OF RESEARCH DESIGNS

Campbell and Stanley list twelve factors jeopardizing the validity of various experimental designs.

---

* From *An Introduction to Social Research,* edited by John T. Doby with the assistance of Edward A. Suchman, John C. McKinney, Roy G. Francis, and John P. Dean, pp. 254–55. By permission of Edward A. Suchman and the Stackpole Company, 1954. The statements above are from chap. 10, "The Principles of Research Design."

FROM EXPERIMENTAL AND QUASI-EXPERIMENTAL DESIGNS FOR RESEARCH*

Donald T. Campbell and Julian C. Stanley

Fundamental to this listing is a distinction between *internal validity* and *external validity. Internal validity* is the basic minimum without which any experiment is uninterpretable: Did in fact the experimental treatments make a difference in this specific experimental instance? *External validity* asks the question of generalizability: To what populations, settings, treatment variables, and measurement variables can this effect be generalized? Both types of criteria are obviously important, even though they are frequently at odds in that features increasing one may jeopardize the other. While *internal validity* is the *sine qua non,* and while the question of *external validity,* like the question of inductive inference is never completely answerable, the selection of designs strong in both types of validity is obviously our ideal.

Relevant to *internal validity,* eight different classes of extraneous variables will be presented; these variables, if not controlled in the experimental design, might produce effects confounded with the effect of the experimental stimulus. They represent the effects of:

1. *History,* the specific events occurring between the first and second measurement in addition to the experimental variable.
2. *Maturation,* processes within the respondents operating as a function of the passage of time per se (not specific to the particular events), including growing older, growing hunger, growing more tired, and the like.
3. *Testing,* the effects of taking a test upon the scores of a second testing.
4. *Instrumentation,* in which changes in the calibration of a measuring instrument or changes in the observers or scores used may produce changes in the obtained measurements.
5. *Statistical regression,* operating where groups have been selected on the basis of their extreme scores.
6. Biases resulting in differential *selection* of respondents for the comparison groups.
7. *Experimental mortality,* or differential loss of respondents from the comparison groups.
8. *Selection-maturation interaction,* etc., which in certain of the multiple-group quasi-experimental designs is confounded with, i.e., might be mistaken for, the effect of the experimental variable.

The factors jeopardizing *external validity* or *representativeness* are:
9. The *reactive* or *interaction effect of testing,* in which a pretest might increase or decrease the respondent's sensitivity or responsiveness to the experimental variable and thus make the results obtained for a pretested population unrepresentative of the effects of the experimental variable for the unpretested universe from which the experimental respondents were selected.
10. The *interaction* effects of *selection* biases and the *experimental variable.*
11. *Reactive effects of experimental arrangements,* which would preclude generalization about the effect of the experimental variable upon persons being exposed to it in nonexperimental settings.

* Reprinted from Donald T. Campbell and Julian C. Stanley, *Experimental and Quasi-Experimental Designs for Research* (Chicago: Rand McNally, 1966), pp. 5–6. By permission of American Educational Research Association.

12. Multiple-treatment interference, likely to occur whenever multiple treatments are applied to the same respondents, because the effects of prior treatments are not usually erasable. This is a particular problem for one-group designs.

The value of such a list is that it gives the researcher some cautions before finalizing a design. To increase the degree of accuracy desired, these factors cannot be ignored. What is put into a research design directs what will come out after the data are collected and analyzed.

1.14 THE SHAPING OF RESEARCH DESIGN IN LARGE-SCALE GROUP RESEARCH*

Delbert C. Miller

This paper examines some of the problems and opportunities in the shaping of research design posed by a large-scale group research project undertaken by the University of Washington for the U.S. Air Force.

The project began in June 1951 under a contract with the Human Resources Research Institute calling for an exploration of human relations problems of air force personnel manning isolated Air Defense radar stations "with reference to job requirements, morale factors, and leadership under stressful noncombat conditions and to develop methods for improving effectiveness." The contract was concluded in December 1953. During the thirty-two months of active research, the project moved from exploration to descriptive and diagnostic study. Some cross-sectional experimental studies were undertaken in the final phase. The full research program included a national survey of the U.S. Air Defense Command Aircraft Control and Warning Stations, a study of the Japan Air Defense Command (A. C. and W.), and numerous investigations in the 25th Division of the Pacific Northwest. All these undertakings centered on personnel problems and squadron efficiency.

It is the theme of this paper that research design in a group project is a product of a social process. That process is influenced by a number of organizational demands as well as by the dynamic interplay of personalities and

* Reprinted from *Social Forces* 33 (May 1955): 383–90. This paper is based on the conclusions of the writer as director of the Air Site Project. Other members of the project have contributed in many different ways to the experiences described. Appreciation is acknowledged to Orvis F. Collins (Southern Illinois University), Edward Gross (University of Washington), F. James Davis (Illinois State University at Normal, Illinois), Glenn C. McCann (North Carolina State College), Nahum Z. Medalia (Oakland University at Rochester, Michigan), Charles D. McGlamery (University of Alabama at Birmingham), professional sociologists; David S. Bushnell, Donald L. Garrity, Robert Hagedorn, John Hudson, Harold Kant, Alvin S. Lackey, Robert Larson, Herman Loether, Duane Strinden, Wes Wager, Shirley Willis, and David Yaukey, research fellows; all are now professional sociologists in the United States.

The research was supported in part by the U.S. Air Force under contract number AF-33-038-26823, monitored by the Human Resources Research Institute, Air Research and Development Command, Maxwell Air Force Base, Alabama. Permission is granted for reproduction, translation, publication, and disposal in whole and in part by or for the U.S. government.

I am especially indebted to the continuous encouragement of Dr. Raymond V. Bowers, director of the Institute from 1949–52, and to Dr. Abbott L. Ferriss, chief of the Human Relations Division, whose administration efforts made possible our access to many research fields.

experiences that are encountered by the group as research penetration continues. It is believed that it is entirely fallacious to consider group research as
individual research simply grown big.

Research design for group research must be sensitive to needs of individual
researchers, to organizational demands, and to research growth through contact with the problem. Indeed, it should be clearly recognized that individual
researchers do not become group researchers merely by joining group research. The problem of research design becomes one of wedding the logic
of scientific method to the social pressures of many internal and external
considerations. Four major factors affected research design on the Air Site
Project. These were: (I) the characteristic imperatives of group research,
(II) the personal wants of researchers, (III) the demands of education, and
(IV) the accumulation of empirical and theoretical knowledge.

I. The Characteristic Imperatives of Group Research

A. *The Restrictions of Interdependent Research Relationships.* The individual
researcher confronting group research is asked to change many research habits
that he may value highly. The change in habits may be experienced as a
set of onerous restrictions. He may find that he cannot choose his problem,
and the problem assigned to him may require collaboration with others that
reduces still further his area of free movement. He discovers that he has
come to live in a web of interrelationships in which his work is intertwined.
His own methods of work undergo close scrutiny of the group. He is subordinate to the final approval of a research director. Status and craft comparisons
may clearly become causes of interpersonal conflict.[1] If the researcher does
not or cannot adjust to this new social environment, conflict processes are
intensified and spread to the group. In this atmosphere, even interpretation
of words can become a serious source of wrangling.[2] Learning to live together
in close interdependence does not come easy. And in group research for a
client, many additional pressures are added.

B. *The Demands of a Time Schedule.* Group research for a client usually
has a number of deadlines. Our military client required quarterly, interim,
and final reports on given dates. No longer could researchers regard as indefi-
nite the date for concluding a study. The demand for a report often meant
intensified work, and this brought to some workers a sense of frustration
that quality had been sacrificed for lack of time to do one's best.

C. *Conciliation of Other Pressures.* The client—or, as in our project, the
monitoring agent—may offer suggestions and instructions as the research
proceeds. These are usually accepted as persuasions to modify or intensify
work in a given direction. These come to the project director and are transmitted through his actions or instructions to the group researchers. Sometimes
the reason is not understood, or it may be understood but resented as an
outside idea, foreign to the group process, and emotionally rejected.

Scientific canons of rigor may be opposed by demands for exploratory or
applied research on problems for which hypotheses and measurement tools
cannot be readied. A researcher whose pride system has incorporated strict
and rigid standards of craftsmanship may quail before problems whose solu-

tion requires simple exploration or vulgar practicality (expecially if he does not see how he can get a published paper from it).

The requirements of expense accounts, security clearances, permission for entry to the research field, "logistic support," and numerous matters of red tape are often further irritations—a headache to researchers and director alike.

The airmen and officers in the research field also exert subtle pressure on the researchers. The questions, "What's this all about? What are you trying to find out?" are continuous and require some kind of answer. The challenge, "You won't be able to do any good" is even more difficult to meet. It can undermine the feeling of acceptance and make fieldwork a resented rather than a welcome experience.

All these new elements call for personal adjustments. It is apparent that a number of strains must be borne by group researchers who have not confronted these factors before. Who are these researchers that come into the group and what do they want?

II. The Personal Wants of Researchers

A. *Motivations of Researchers.* Young researchers are attracted to group research. If they are graduate students, the prospect of funds and a thesis presents an opportunity both to do research and to eat. Young Ph.D.s see opportunity for publication, promotion, and freedom from teaching. Both of these groups are seeking to build research reputations through publication. This motive serves to make the burdens of fieldwork sufficiently acceptable to get the necessary data collecting done, but marriage, parenthood, and sedentary proclivities all contrive to make absence from the home an increasing burden.

B. *Security Needs of Researchers.* Research staffs are often recruited from among those persons who are seeking permanent employment. When contracts are on a year-to-year basis with no fixed guarantee as to their duration, a job insecurity is added to the social influences that bear upon the researchers' morale and productivity. As individual contracts begin to approach termination, personal insecurities mount and are intensified by group interaction. The feelings of insecurity are expressed in many different ways, which may include demands for more say in both policy and administrative decisions, safeguards for individual publication rights, and almost single-minded preoccupation with the acquisition of the *next* research contract.

A research design is under the stress of individual wants, for group thinking is colored every step of the way by these personal concerns. Each person wants to know what part of the design he can claim for his research publications. Each person wants to have an opportunity to guide his fieldwork in such a way as to minimize its burdens. Each wants the maximum opportunity to determine his working conditions.

C. *Role of the Research Director.* The research director takes his place in the center of all the forces that have been described. His role is to direct group processes, ascertain group sentiment, and make decisions so that research can be designed and executed with harmony and efficiency. He must see that role definitions for each member are clearly outlined. He must interpret the external demands on the project and relate them to his research personnel so that appropriate action is taken. He must come to recognize that he will get little opportunity to do field research himself. And he must accept the fact that some interpersonal friction will accompany his most valiant efforts to make group research palatable, especially during the early period when a number of individual researchers are learning to live together as group researchers. He will come to understand that each member of the group is concerned with his reputation as the result of his membership. He wants to have his say as to what others do when he feels his own standards are being violated. This is at once a source of group power and of group conflict. The director will often be challenged as to how these group motivations can be channeled.

A research director who wishes to manage by the use of democratic methods must know the dilemmas of leadership in the democratic process and find his own way to cope with them.[3] Softhearted, inexperienced democratic leadership rivals autocratic blindness in creating poor conditions for efficiency and morale.

III. The Demands of Education

The major problem facing organization of group research within a university is to secure opportunity for each researcher to have maximum freedom to apply his talents to a project whose major problems have been outlined in a contract for him. This is no little task. A professional researcher, we have said, wants to choose his problem, be given the proprietary right of publication for his work, and have control over his working conditions. The university is concerned that graduate students receive broad research training and not be employed at mere clerical tasks. The research design must be constructed in recognition of these concerns and the staff organized in optimum-size working groups so that the best combination of professional staff and graduate students may be obtained.

The basic research unit of the Air Site Project was made up of a professional sociologist and two graduate students; in 1952–53, there were four such units in the Project. Graduate students alternated fieldwork and classwork so that both types of training were secured. In the close association of professional sociologist and graduate student, both educational and research functions were served.

IV. The Accumulation of Empirical and Theoretical Knowledge

Research progress on a central problem usually proceeds through stages— first, exploration of the social setting of the problem, the factors involved, and the criteria that may be used to measure or appraise the problem; then descriptive and diagnostic study may be possible. Hypotheses are set up, factors are isolated, measured, and relationships ascertained. Still later, experimental studies may be undertaken. Research design keeps changing as hypotheses are modified, eliminated, and substituted. Each stage of research requires the use of new skills, the recasting of theory, the introduction of new revised factors, and perhaps reinterpretation of results.[4]

A. *Exploratory Study.* The Air Site Project began as a military requirement to investigate the morale and personnel problems of air force personnel in radar squadrons. We agreed to go to the research field and discover the personnel problems and personnel needs. At the same time we were to find the most significant problems for basic research into morale and motivation. Three professional sociologists developed a plan of sampling and interviewing and devoted three months between July and October 1951 to field visits and analysis of seven squadrons in one Air Defense division.[5] Detailed interviews were held with a representative sample of air force personnel in each squadron. We lived with and observed the operations and leisure activities of each squadron for a number of days. From our interviews and notes a common record was prepared by the research team for each squadron. This record ranked the major personnel problems as reported to us in each squadron, the needs as expressed by air force personnel, and research clues that we determined through our experiences in the field. Table 1 gives a record of major personnel needs and research clues for one air force squadron.

Interviews were coded and an analysis of major personnel problems was made to determine possible associations with age, martial status, education, length of service, and isolation of site. Various tables were constructed to show analyses of interview data—Analysis of Management Problems, Impact of Isolation on Operating Problems, and Personnel Needs as Defined by Site Personnel. All these tables were prepared especially for top military leaders and were presented in briefing sessions to them for their guidance. On the basis of these facts and others, new facilities were subsequently made available to the squadrons.

Meanwhile, research clues were combed to find the most significant research problems. General clusters of factors that we called research sectors were set forth as the ones we believed to be most directly related to the adjustment of air force personnel.[6] We selected (1) The Job and the Career, (2) Organization and Communication, (3) Leadership, and (4) Morale and Motivation. We pressed forward without an overall theory;[7] rather, research teams were formed and these teams selected a research sector, set up hypotheses, and began field research in the fall of 1951.

B. *Descriptive and Diagnostic Study.* In January 1952, six months after the initiation of the project, the research design was composed of the parts shown on page 58. The central problem had become the adjustment of the person to a military organization. Morale, motivation, and management or personnel problems had been chosen as the principal objects of study. Guttman scaling techniques were being applied to the study of various attitude areas. Nonverbal indices, such as rate of promotion, were being developed. Later, as a squadron efficiency rating system was developed by the officers of one air division (assisted by the Air Site Project), this criterion was introduced. Against these criteria we sought to determine the relationship of many social and social-psychological variables.

The illustration on page 58, Basic Generalities of Social Organization, became our overall design. It was based essentially on the importance of studying certain difficult sociological problems *intensively* while ascertaining the full scope of other problems *extensively*. The six research sectors that received intensive study were those of Personal History, Job Adjustment,

Table 1 *Major Personnel Needs and Research Clues for One Air Force Squadron*

Problems encountered

1. Recreational outlets on the base.
2. Access to city or large town.
3. Degree of supervision.
4. Housing for the married man and his family.
5. Living on Indian Reservation and adjustment to Indian people.
6. Restrictions imposed on minors.
7. Career misassignment.
8. Pressures from division and group commands.
9. Irritations from GI regulations.
10. Inequities in promotions and advancements.
11. Supply problems.
12. Access to weapon and monotony of tracking.
13. Organizational change to larger unit.
14. Relative deprivation.
15. Organizational cleavages.

Basic research clues for possible future study

1. Study relationship between humor and tension. Compare a tense and relaxed site, watching for differences.
2. Study of emotional outbursts as manifested in attitude and in behavior such as AWOL, chewing out, or fighting.
3. Time sampling study of a group of highly motivated and poorly motivated personnel.
4. A study of newcomers over an extended time period to watch acculturation.
5. A study of the effect of increasing size on organizational and morale changes.
6. Relations of age, marital status, military experience, and residence and education to adjustment of highly and poorly adjusted persons.
7. A validation of relative deprivation.
8. A study of language functions, especially jargon and argot.
9. Socialization of the civilian to military culture.
10. Description of military culture.
11. The relation of job satisfaction to civilian training, experience, and goals.
12. Extent to which realization alone of choice of job is related to job satisfaction.

Observation clues for possible future measurement

1. Evaluate condition of uniform and military bearing at spot point.
2. Number of persons found in various places—barracks, dayroom, mess hall (goldbricking).
3. Count number who leave camp every day—check those who leave on 2-day-off periods.
4. Turnover as a generalized aspect of military organizations.
   —among officers (upward mobility involves spatial mobility).
   —among airmen (stay only 18 months in a site).
5. What is relation of high turnover to problem of morale, organization, and leadership, to identification with the site, fellows, CO?

Group Integration, Leadership, Organization, and Family and Community. In these sectors researchers attempted to find relationships in areas where it was difficult to secure the relevant data and in which understanding could come only through patient, skillful, and persistent study. Such study was usually confined to one or two sites.[8] As crucial variables were identified and quantitative measures were developed, these variables were considered ready for extensive intersite test. The intersite design called for a testing of variables on a selected sample of air force men in all (or representative sample of all) sites in the population studied. Here, the criteria of morale, personnel problems, and efficiency were measured by the most refined measures that

BASIC GENERALITIES OF SOCIAL ORGANIZATION
Relationships Validated in the
Air Defense Command

Management
Information
Manuals

Basic
Science
Contributions

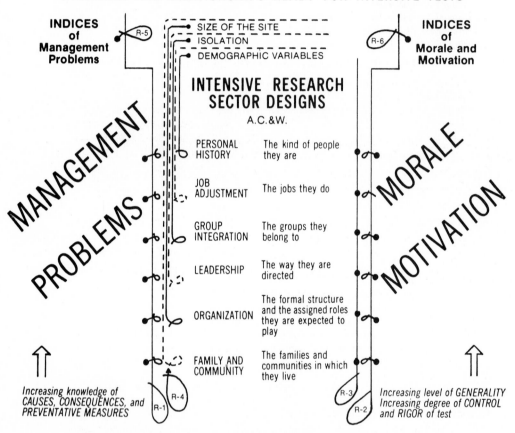

EXTENSIVE INTERSITE RESEARCH DESIGNS
Relationships Validated in the 25th Air Division A.D.C.

Site 1	Site 2	Site 3	Site 4	Site 5	Site 6	Site 7	Site 8	Site 9	Site 10
A.C.&W.	E.W.	A.C.&W.	A.C.&W.	A.C.&W.	E.W.	E.W.	A.C.&W.	A.C.&W.	E.W.

VARIABLES AND RELATIONSHIPS READY FOR INTERSITE TESTS

INDICES
of
Management
Problems

R-5

SIZE OF THE SITE
ISOLATION
DEMOGRAPHIC VARIABLES

R-6

INDICES
of
Morale and
Motivation

INTENSIVE RESEARCH
SECTOR DESIGNS
A.C.&W.

MANAGEMENT
PROBLEMS

PERSONAL
HISTORY — The kind of people they are

JOB
ADJUSTMENT — The jobs they do

GROUP
INTEGRATION — The groups they belong to

LEADERSHIP — The way they are directed

ORGANIZATION — The formal structure and the assigned roles they are expected to play

FAMILY AND
COMMUNITY — The families and communities in which they live

MORALE
MOTIVATION

Increasing knowledge of CAUSES, CONSEQUENCES, and PREVENTATIVE MEASURES

R-4
R-1

R-3
R-2

*Increasing level of GENERALITY
Increasing degree of CONTROL
and RIGOR of test*

The general research design of large-scale investigation into the human factors affecting morale, motivation, and efficiency of radar sites.

could be constructed or utilized. Selected social, demographic, and ecological variables were employed as independent variables to determine significant relationships to criteria measures. Intersite questionnaires were administered in twelve sites of one division[9] (May 1952), and in the Japan Air Defense Command[10] (August–September 1952); and a national survey of the Air Defense Command was executed in April and May 1953.

The design reflects the twofold objectives: (1) to carry on basic research in morale (or personal adjustment) at the descriptive level, and (2) to work on personnel problems at the diagnostic level. The design thus reflects both the canons of basic research and the requirements of the client for operational results. The balance between these two foci was often beset by subtle pressures deriving from professional standards, on the one hand, and the practical concerns of the military officials, on the other. The research director who seeks to advance knowledge must see that the research work is so designed that the long-run concerns of basic science are carried along and, at the same time, good diagnostic studies of operational problems are produced that convince his client that research can be of service to him on the problems he faces *now*. He must persuade his staff of the importance of these twin demands, and he must protect them so that there is ample opportunity to achieve both basic and operational research. The basic research design of the Air Site Project grew out of these pressures, and it sought to satisfy them.

But more than this, the design must be understood as an expression of the researcher's desire for freedom to attack his problem in his own way. Some researchers took to the field at once to explore their problem. Others began to devise measuring instruments and to work out sampling plans. Some planned much observational work in the field; others planned fieldwork only to make pretests of questionnaires and scales. These differences seemed to be explained sometimes by differences in research approach (interactionists versus statistical testers) and sometimes by different adjustments to fieldwork. The deprivations of fieldwork and the new role relationships of a fieldworker (in contrast to those of the classroom teacher and library researcher) presented adjustment problems to all staff members. Some found field contact exciting and satisfying; others found absence from home and from customary routines of office a deprivation and sought to center their research in the university. It has already been suggested that the home plays an influential role in shaping the attitudes of the field researcher and thus indirectly the research work itself.

C. *Experimental Study*. Samuel Stouffer has written that "the necessary condition for dealing with a collection of variables is to isolate and identify them and, in addition, it is useful if they can also be measured. Until the relevant variables can be identified, empirical tests of a conceptual scheme involving these variables hardly can be expected."[11]

In the Air Site Project we identified the objects of study and were able to measure some of them. We ascertained many relationships between our criteria and social, demographic, and ecological factors. Many hypotheses were tested by field teams. Experimental work of a cross-sectional type was carried out.[12] Perhaps one of the most important relationships tested was that between morale in a squadron and the efficiency of the squadron. It is widely believed that good human relations are related positively to high efficiency. However, only a few tests have been made under experimental conditions involving a control group.[13]

The assignment of air force men is made according to the training specialty of available personnel and according to organizational needs. The assignment of men who are drawn out to fill quotas results in near stratified-random selection. As a result it is possible to find squadrons that have almost identical characteristics as to mean age, length of service, marital status, education, rank structure, degree of isolation, work conditions, and living conditions. In one division we studied twelve squadrons. Efficiency ratings of these squadrons were made each quarter by the responsible division officials. We constructed Guttman-type scales or items measuring such areas of morale as satisfaction with air site, satisfaction with air force, job satisfaction, and acceptance of mission goals. The relationship of morale to efficiency under controlled conditions was ascertained in our population. Because of the randomization in the squadron populations, control by frequency distribution could be employed. Squadrons were selected from the total universe (one division) and matched on variables believed to affect efficiency. The significance of differences between means were determined. Replication of this design was made on our larger universe of squadrons from all divisions.[14]

D. *Projected Experimentation.* Plans had been made for moving to the stage of true experimental study by taking before and after measures of experimental and control groups under controlled conditions. This would have consummated the direction of research movement. Unfortunately, the sharp curtailment of funds for human relations research in 1953 made it impossible to proceed into this type of experimentation. Projected experiments were not undertaken earlier because needed measures of morale, leadership, and efficiency had to be constructed first. Moreover, a high degree of confidence and cooperation from line military officers had to be earned before such work would have been possible. This is a hard social fact that cannot be ignored.

Four major factors influenced the shaping of research design on one large-scale group research project. These were: the characteristic imperative of group research, the personal wants of researchers, the demands of education, and the accumulation of empirical and theoretical knowledge.

These factors created both problems and opportunities. Problems have been considered in much of this paper, but opportunities were also abundant. Adequate financing of research brings professional, clerical, and technical assistance, permitting a rapid increase in the quantity and quality of research. Access to the research field and cooperation within it opens a new wealth of social data. A long-standing weakness of social science research has been the inability to get enough individual cases or organizational units so that relationships could be validated through replication. This is possible in large-scale group research. These opportunities can be capitalized, but only as the social processes of group research are marshaled. Social processes ever blend with scientific thinking to mold research design. As an end product of group research, it is a precipitate of personal feelings, thoughts, habits, and hopes.

Notes

1. Joseph W. Eaton, "Social Process of Professional Teamwork," *American Sociological Review* 16 (October 1951): 707–13; Alfred M. Lee, "Individual and Organizational Research in Sociology," *American Sociological Review* 16 (October 1951): 707–7.

2. Urie Bronfenbrenner and Edward C. Devereux, "Interdisciplinary Planning for Team Research on Constructive Community Behavior," *Human Relations* 5 (1952): 187–203;

William Caudill and Bertram H. Roberts, "Pitfalls in the Organization of Interdisciplinary Research," *Human Organization* 10 (Winter 1951): 12–15.

3. Chester I. Barnard, "Dilemmas of Leadership in the Democratic Process," *Organization and Management* (Cambridge, Mass.: Harvard University, 1949), pp. 24–50.

4. Robert K. Merton, "The Bearing of Empirical Research upon the Development of Social Theory," *American Sociological Review* 13 (October 1948): 505–15.

5. Squadrons varied in size from approximately 100 to 300 men, depending on type and function of the station.

6. For a full report of this exploratory survey see F. James Davis, Edward Gross, and Delbert C. Miller, *Survey Report on Military Management Problems in Aircraft Control and Warning Stations in the Air Defense Command* (Human Resources Research Institute, Air University, Maxwell Air Force Base, Ala., 1951).

7. This was a source of much concern to some of our researchers, and we held many staff meetings groping for such a theory. Some members of the staff believed we should not set out at all until a fully-developed theory was in hand. Others believed theory should wait until the research and field experience were more advanced.

8. For published reports of this work see: F. James Davis, "Conceptions of Official Leader Roles in the Air Force," *Social Forces* 32 (March 1954): 253–58; F. James Davis and Robert Hagedorn, "Testing the Reliability of Systematic Field Observations," *American Sociological Review* 19 (June 1954): 345–48; F. James Davis, Robert Hagedorn, and J. Robert Larson, "Scaling Problems in the Study of Conceptions of Air Force Leader Roles," *Public Opinion Quarterly* 18 (Fall 1954): 279–86; Edward Gross, "Some Functional Consequences of Primary Controls in Formal Work Organizations," *American Sociological Review* 18 (August 1953): 368–73; Edward Gross, "Primary Functions of the Small Group," *American Journal of Sociology* 60 (July 1954): 24–29; Herman J. Loether, "Propinquity and Homogeneity as Factors in the Choice of Best Buddies in the Air Force," *Pacific Sociological Review* 3 (Spring 1960): 18–22; C. D. McGlamery, "Developing an Index of Work Group Communications," *Research Studies, State College of Washington* 21 (1953): 225–30; Nahum Z. Medalia, "Unit Size and Leadership Perception," *Sociometry* 17 (February 1945): 64–67; Nahum Z. Medalia, "Authoritarianism, Leader Acceptance, and Group Cohesion," *Journal of Abnormal and Social Psychology* 51 (September 1955): 207–13.

9. The Human Resources Research Institute published interim reports in 1952.

10. A final report has been prepared for Human Resources Research Institute by Edward Gross and Orvis Collins, *American Air Sites in Japan: An Analysis of Human Relations in A. C. & W. Detachment Within the Japan Air Defense Force* (12 January 1953).

11. Samuel A. Stouffer et al., *The American Soldier* (Princeton, N.J.: Princeton University Press, 1949), 1:34.

12. Stouffer writes, "I would trade a half dozen army-wide surveys on attitudes toward officers for one good controlled experiment. Keeping the model of the controlled experiment as an ideal, it is sometimes possible for one to approximate it. . . . Ingenuity in locating ready-made situations is much needed. In any program of future research, I would put far more emphasis on this than ever has been done in the past." Robert K. Merton and Paul F. Lazarsfeld, eds., *Studies in the Scope and Method of "The American Soldier"* (Glencoe, Ill.: Free Press, 1950), p. 211.

13. See Daniel Katz, Nathan Maccoby, and Nancy C. Morse, *Productivity, Supervision and Morale in an Office Situation*, pt. 1 (Ann Arbor: Institute for Social Research, University of Michigan, 1950); Daniel Katz, Nathan Maccoby, Gerald Gurin, and Lucretia G. Floor, *Productivity, Supervision, and Morale Among Railroad Workers* (Ann Arbor: Survey Research Center, University of Michigan, 1951); Irving R. Weschler, Murray Kahane, and Robert Tannenbaum, "Job Satisfaction, Productivity and Morale: A Case Study," *Occupational Psychology* 1 (January 1952): 1–14; Gunner Westerlund, *Group Leadership, A Field Experiment* (Stockholm: Nordisk Rotogravyr, 1952).

14. This research is described by Nahum Z. Medalia and Delbert C. Miller in "Human Relations Leadership and the Association of Morale and Efficiency in Workgroups: A Controlled Study with Small Military Units," *Social Forces* 33 (May 1955): 348–52. See also D. C. Miller and N. Z. Medalia, "Efficiency, Leadership, and Morale in Small Military Organizations," *Sociological Review* 3 (July 1955): 93–107; Edward Gross and D. C. Miller, "The Impact of Isolation on Worker Adjustment in Military Installations of the United States and Japan," *Estudios de Sociologia,* Buenos Aires, 1 (Fall 1961): 70–86; Glenn C. McCann, Nahum Z. Medalia, and Delbert C. Miller, "Morale and Human Relations Leadership as Factors in Organizational Effectiveness," in *Studies of Organizational Effectiveness,* ed. R. V. Bowers (Washington, D.C.: Air Force Office of Scientific Research, 1962), pp. 85–114.

1.15   THE SAMPLING CHART

Instructions for Use of Guide 1.15

A sample is a smaller representation of a larger whole. The use of sampling allows for more adequate scientific work by making the time of the scientific worker count. Instead of spending much of his time analyzing a large mass of material from one point of view, he can use that time to make a more intensive analysis from many points of view. The researcher can also save much time and money by sampling, thus making possible investigations that could not otherwise be carried out.

The sampling problems may be divided into those that affect (1) the definition of the population, (2) the size of the sample, and (3) the representativeness of the sample. In regard to the definition of the population, the important problem is to decide the group about which the researcher wishes to generalize his findings. In regard to size of sample, consideration must be given to the persistent disappearance of cases in a breakdown analysis. This disappearance should be foreseen as clearly as possible. Dummy tables help provide for such planning. The third and perhaps most intricate sampling problem arises in connection with the method of securing a representative sample. The essential requirement of any sample is that it is as representative as possible of the population or universe from which it is taken.

Three methods of sampling are commonly used. These are *random sampling, stratified sampling,* and *judgmental* or *"purposive" sampling.*

Random Sampling. A random sample is one that is drawn in such a way that every member of the population has an equal chance of being included. The most rigorous method of random sampling employs a table of random numbers. In this method, a number is assigned to each member of the population. Those members are included in the sample whose numbers are taken from the table of random numbers in succession until a sample of predetermined size is drawn. A more common method is to write the names or numbers of the members of a population on cards or discs, shuffling these, and then drawing. A convenient method, known as systematic sampling, which is not exactly equivalent to random sampling, but is often close enough for practical purposes, is to take every n^{th} item in the population, beginning at some random member in the population.

Stratified sampling. The aforementioned methods assume that the composition of the total group is not known, and that a representative sample will be best approximated by a strictly random selection or a selection by regular intervals. In some cases the more or less exact composition of the total group with respect to some significant characteristics is known before we select our sample. For example, we may know the exact ratio of men to women in the population and that sex differences are related to the variables we wish to test. In such cases we can increase the chances of selecting a representative sample by selecting subsamples proportionate in size to the significant characteristics of the total population. Thus, we can select a sample that is mathematically absolutely representative with regard to some significant characteristics. There are numerous forms of stratified random sampling techniques as shown in the Ackoff Sampling Chart, which follows on pages 64–65.

Judgment or "purposive" sampling. When practical considerations preclude the use of probability sampling, the researcher may seek a representative sample by other means. He looks for a subgroup that is typical of the population as a whole. Observations are then restricted to this subgroup, and conclusions from the data obtained are generalized to the total population. An example would be the choice of a particular state or county as a barometer of an election outcome, relying upon the results of past elections as evidence of the representativeness of the sample for the nation or state. Sampling errors and biases cannot be computed for such samples. For this reason judgmental sampling should be restricted to the following situations: (1) when the possible errors are not serious and (2) when probability sampling is practically impossible. Data from judgmental samples at best suggest or indicate conclusions, but in general they cannot be used as the basis of statistical testing procedures.

These three forms of sampling do not exhaust the range of sampling procedures. The Ackoff Sampling Chart lists such types as multistage random sampling, cluster, stratified cluster, and repetitive sampling. A description of these forms may be found in Russell Ackoff, *The Design of Social Research,* pp. 123–26. He writes:

> From practical as well as purely scientific purposes it is necessary to use selection procedures whose errors are measurable. A procedure should be capable of characterization relative to bias and variability. The fundamental procedure satisfying these conditions is simple random sampling, a method in which each individual has an equal chance of being selected. Simple random sampling is performed with the aid of random numbers, while systematic sampling is a variation which proceeds from a random start to select elements at a preset interval.
>
> By breaking the population into subgroups, we may select a sample in stages. If a random sample is selected at each stage, we have a multistage random sample. If a complete count of sampling units is taken at one stage other than the last, we have a stratified sample. If a complete count is made at the last stage, we have a cluster sample. The probability of selecting any subgroup may be made proportionate to some function of the size of the subgroup, and the number of units selected from any subgroup may also be made proportionate to some such function. Proportionate sampling tends to reduce sampling errors. Stratification and clustering can be combined to yield efficient samples, particularly where stratification and/or clustering is based on geographic properties (i.e., in area sampling). Area sampling reduces the complexity of preparing sampling lists and permits the clustering of subjects so that they come in bunches.

Sampling Chart *

Type of sampling	Brief description	Advantages	Disadvantages
A. Simple random	Assign to each population member a unique number; select sample items by use of random numbers	1. Requires minimum knowledge of population in advance 2. Free of possible classification errors 3. Easy to analyze data and compute errors	1. Does not make use of knowledge of population which researcher may have 2. Larger errors for same sample size than in stratified sampling
B. Systematic	Use natural ordering or order population; select random starting point between 1 and the nearest integer to the sampling ratio (N/n); select items at interval of nearest integer to sampling ratio	1. If population is ordered with respect to pertinent property, gives stratification effect, and hence reduces variability compared to A 2. Simplicity of drawing sample; easy to check	1. If sampling interval is related to a periodic ordering of the population, increased variability may be introduced 2. Estimates of error likely to be high where there is stratification effect
C. Multistage random	Use a form of random sampling in each of the sampling stages where there are at least two stages	1. Sampling lists, identification, and numbering required only for members of sampling units selected in sample 2. If sampling units are geographically defined, cuts down field costs (i.e., travel)	1. Errors likely to be larger than in A or B for same sample size 2. Errors increase as number of sampling units selected decreases
1. With probability proportionate to size	Select sampling units with probability proportionate to their size	1. Reduces variability	1. Lack of knowledge of size of each sampling unit before selection increases variability
D. Stratified 1. Proportionate	Select from every sampling unit at other than last stage a random sample proportionate to size of sampling unit	1. Assures representativeness with respect to property which forms basis of classifying units; therefore yields less variability than A or C 2. Decreases chance of failing to include members of population because of classification process 3. Characteristics of each stratum can be estimated, and hence comparisons can be made	1. Requires accurate information on proportion of population in each stratum, otherwise increases error 2. If stratified lists are not available, may be costly to prepare them; possibility of faulty classification and hence increase in variability
2. Optimum allocation	Same as 1 except sample is proportionate to variability within strata as well as their size	1. Less variability for same sample size than 1	1. Requires knowledge of variability of pertinent characteristic within strata
3. Disproportionate	Same as 1 except that size of sample is not proportionate to size of sampling unit but is dictated by analytical considerations or convenience	1. More efficient than 1 for comparison of strata or where different errors are optimum for different strata	1. Less efficient than 1 for determining population characteristics; i.e., more variability for same sample size

Sampling Chart—Continued

Type of sampling	Brief description	Advantages	Disadvantages
E. Cluster	Select sampling units by some form of random sampling; ultimate units are groups; select these at random and take a complete count of each	1. If clusters are geographically defined, yields lowest field costs 2. Requires listing only individuals in selected clusters 3. Characteristics of clusters as well as those of population can be estimated 4. Can be used for subsequent samples, since clusters, not individuals, are selected, and substitution of individuals may be permissible	1. Larger errors for comparable size than other probability samples 2. Requires ability to assign each member of population uniquely to a cluster; inability to do so may result in duplication or omission of individuals
F. Stratified cluster	Select clusters at random from every sampling unit	1. Reduces variability of plain cluster sampling	1. Disadvantages of stratified sampling added to those of cluster sampling 2. Since cluster properties may change, advantage of stratification may be reduced and make sample unusable for later research
G. Repetitive: multiple or sequential	Two or more samples of any of the above types are taken, using results from earlier samples to design later ones, or determine if they are necessary	1. Provides estimates of population characteristics which facilitate efficient planning of succeeding sample, therefore reduces error of final estimate 2. In the long run reduces number of observations required	1. Complicates administration of fieldwork 2. More computation and analysis required than in nonrepetitive sampling 3. Sequential sampling can only be used where a very small sample can approximate representativeness and where the number of observations can be increased conveniently at any stage of the research
H. Judgment	Select a subgroup of the population which, in the basis of available information, can be judged to be representative of the total population; take a complete count or subsample of this group	1. Reduces cost of preparing sample and fieldwork, since ultimate units can be selected so that they are close together	1. Variability and bias of estimates cannot be measured or controlled 2. Requires strong assumptions or considerable knowledge of population and subgroup selected
I. Quota	Classify population by pertinent properties; determine desired proportion of sample from each class; fix quotas for each observer	1. Same as above 2. Introduces some stratification effect	1. Introduces bias of observers' classification of subjects and nonrandom selection within classes

*Reprinted from Russell L. Ackoff, *The Design of Social Research* (Chicago: University of Chicago, 1953), p. 124. By permission of The University of Chicago Press. Copyright 1953 by The University of Chicago.

In double sampling a first sample can be used to provide information which can in turn be used to design an efficient second sample. Such sampling can also be used to reduce the number of observations required, on the average, for coming to a conclusion. When double sampling is generalized, it yields sequential sampling, a method of drawing one item or set of items at a time and using the data obtained to decide whether to continue sampling or not.

—The ultimate basis for selecting a sampling procedure should be minimization of the cost of getting the sample and the expected cost of errors which may result from using the method. Expert assistance should be employed in making such evaluations.

The sampling chart summarizes in a very brief way the description, advantages, and disadvantages of the various sampling procedures discussed.

1.16   A SELECTED BIBLIOGRAPHY ON RESEARCH DESIGN

ACKOFF, RUSSELL L. *The Design of Social Research.* Chicago: University of Chicago Press, 1953.

ACKOFF, RUSSELL L., and EMERY, FRED E. *On Purposeful Systems.* Chicago: Aldine, 1972.

ALWIN, DUANE F., ed. *Survey Design and Analysis.* Beverly Hills: Sage, 1978.

ARMER, MICHAEL, and GRIMSHAW, ALLEN, eds. *Comparative Social Research: Methodological Problems and Strategies.* New York: Wiley, 1973.

BLALOCK, HUBERT M., JR. *Theory Construction.* Englewood Cliff, N.J.: Prentice-Hall, 1969.

———. *An Introduction to Social Research.* Englewood Cliffs, N.J.: Prentice-Hall, 1970.

———. *Conceptualization and Measurement in the Social Sciences.* Beverly Hills, Calif.: Sage, 1982.

BLALOCK, HUBERT M., JR., ed. *Causal Models in the Social Sciences.* Chicago: Aldine, 1971.

———. *Quantitative Sociology: International Perspectives on Mathematical and Statistical Modeling.* New York: Academic Press, 1975.

———. *Sociological Theory and Research.* New York: Free Press, 1980.

BOGUE, GRANT. *Basic Sociological Research Design.* Glenview, Ill.: Scott, Foresman, 1981.

BOUDON, RAYMOND. *The Logic of Sociological Explanation.* Harmondsworth: Penguin Education, 1974.

BREWER, MARILYNN B., and COLLINS, BARRY E. *Scientific Inquiry and the Social Sciences.* San Francisco: Jossey-Bass, 1981.

BROSS, IRWIN D. J. *Design for Decision.* New York: Macmillan, 1953.

CANNON, WALTER BRADFORD. *The Way of an Investigator.* New York: Hafner, 1961.

CHURCHMAN, C. W. *Theory of Experimental Inference.* New York: Macmillan, 1948.

COCHRAN, W. G., and COX, G. N. *Experimental Designs.* 2nd ed. New York: Wiley, 1957.

COHEN, MORRIS, and NAGEL, E. *An Introduction to Logic and Scientific Methods.* Rev. ed. New York: Harcourt, Brace & World, 1960.

COOK, THOMAS D., and CAMPBELL, DONALD T. *Quasi-Experimentation.* Chicago: Rand McNally, 1979.

DENZIN, NORMAN. *The Research Act.* Chicago: Aldine, 1973.

DIENER, EDWARD, and CRANDALL, RICK. *Ethics in Social and Behavioral Research.* Chicago: University of Chicago Press, 1978.

DiRENZO, GORDON J., ed. *Concepts, Theory, and Explanation in the Behavioral Sciences.* New York: Random House, 1967. See especially Paul F. Lazarsfeld, "Concept Formation and Measurement," pp. 144–202.

DUBIN, ROBERT. *Theory Building, a Practical Guide to the Construction and Testing of Theoretical Models.* New York: Free Press, 1969.

EDWARDS, ALLEN L. *Experimental Design in Psychological Research.* New York: Holt, Rinehart and Winston, 1960.

FICHTER, JOSEPH H. *One-Man Research, Reminiscences of a Catholic Sociologist.* New York: Wiley-Interscience, 1973.

FISHER, R. A. *The Design of Experiments.* 7th rev. ed. New York: Hafner, 1960.

FORCESE, DENNIS P., and RICHER, STEPHEN, eds. *Stages of Social Research: Contemporary Perspectives.* Englewood Cliffs, N.J.: Prentice-Hall, 1970. Forty-one authors describe such stages as the Scientific Approach, Conceptualization, Measurement, Research Format, Sampling, Data Collection, Data Analysis and Interpretation.

GIBBS, JACK. *Sociological Theory Construction.* Hinsdale, Ill.: Dryden, 1972.

GINSBURG, G. P., ed. *Emerging Strategies in Social Psychological Research.* New York: Wiley, 1979.

GLASER, BARNEY G., and STRAUSS, ANSELM L. *The Discovery of Grounded Theory.* Chicago: Aldine, 1967.

GLOCK, CHARLES Y. *Survey Research in the Social Sciences.* New York: Russell Sage Foundation, 1967.

GOLDSTEIN, HARVEY. *The Design and Analysis of Longitudinal Studies.* New York: Academic Press, 1979.

GOODE, WILLIAM J., and HATT, PAUL K. *Methods in Social Research.* New York: McGraw-Hill, 1952.

GREER, SCOTT. *The Logic of Social Inquiry.* Chicago: Aldine, 1969.

HAMMOND, P. E., ed. *Sociologists at Work: Essays on the Craft of Social Research.* New York: Basic Books, 1964.

HARGENS, LOWELL L. *Patterns of Scientific Research: A Comparative Analysis of Research in Three Scientific Fields.* ASA Rose Monograph Series. New York: Cambridge University Press, 1975.

HERBST, P. G. *Socio-Technical Design: Strategies in Multidisciplinary Research.* London: Tavistock, 1974.

HOOVER, KENNETH R. *The Elements of Social Scientific Thinking.* 2nd ed., New York: St. Martins Press, 1980.

HYMAN, HERBERT. *Survey Design and Analysis: Principles, Cases and Procedures.* Glencoe, Ill.: Free Press, 1955.

KAPLAN, ABRAHAM. *The Conduct of Inquiry.* San Francisco: Chandler, 1964.

KERLINGER, FRED N. *Foundations of Behavioral Research.* New York: Holt Rinehart and Winston, 1964.

KISH, LESLIE. *Survey Sampling.* New York: Wiley, 1965.

KRATOCHWILL, THOMAS R., ed. *Single Subject Research: Strategies for Evaluating Change.* New York: Academic Press, 1978.

LAVE, CHARLES A., and MARCH, JAMES G. *An Introduction to Models in the Social Sciences.* New York: Harper & Row, 1975.

LAZARSFELD, PAUL F., and REITZ, JEFFREY G. *An Introduction to Applied Sociology.* New York: Elsevier, 1975. See especially chap. 4, "Translating a Practical Problem into Research," pp. 66–97.

LIN, NAN. *Foundations of Social Research.* New York: McGraw-Hill, 1976.

MITROFF, IAN, I., and KILMANN, RALPH H. *Methodological Approaches to Social Science.* San Francisco: Jossey-Bass, 1978.

NAGI, SAAD Z., and CORWIN, RONALD G. *The Social Contexts of Research.* New York: Wiley Interscience, 1972.

NORTHROP, F. S. C. *The Logic of the Sciences and the Humanities.* New York: Macmillan, 1947.

ORENSTEIN, ALAN, and PHILLIPS, WILLIAM R. F. *Understanding Social Research.* Boston: Allyn and Bacon, 1978.

PHILLIPS, BERNARD S. *Social Research: Strategy and Tactics.* New York: Macmillan, 1966.

POPPER, KARL R. *The Logic of Scientific Discovery.* New York: Basic Books, 1959.

RILEY, MATILDA WHITE. *Sociological Research: A Case Approach.* New York: Harcourt, Brace & World, 1963.

ROSENBERG, MORRIS. *The Logic of Survey Analysis.* New York: Basic Books, 1968.

SANDERS, WILLIAM B. *The Sociologist as Detective: An Introduction to Research Methods.* New York: Praeger, 1974.

SAXE, LEONARD, and FINE, MICHELLE. *Social Experiments: Methods for Design and Evaluation.* Beverly Hills, Calif.: Sage, 1981.

SJOBERG, GIDEON, and NETT, ROGER. *A Methodology for the Social Sciences.* New York: Harper & Row, 1968.

SKIDMORE, WILLIAM. *Theoretical Thinking in Sociology.* Cambridge, England: Cambridge University Press, 1975.

SMITH, H. W. *Strategies of Social Research: The Methodological Imagination.* Englewood Cliffs, N.J.: Prentice-Hall, 1975.

STINCHCOMBE, ARTHUR, L. *Constructing Social Theories.* New York: Harcourt, Brace, & World, 1968.

STOUFFER, SAMUEL. *Social Research to Test Ideas.* New York: Free Press, 1962.

SUCHMAN, EDWARD A. *Evaluative Research, Principles, and Practice in Public Service and Social Action Programs.* New York: Russell Sage Foundation, 1968.

SUDMAN, SEYMOUR. *Applied Sampling.* New York: Academic Press, 1972.

WALLACE, WALTER R. *The Logic of Science in Sociology.* Chicago: Aldine, 1971.

WATSON, JAMES D. *The Double Helix.* New York: North American Library, 1968.

WHITEHEAD, ALFRED N. *A Philosopher Looks at Science.* New York: Philosophical Library, 1965.

WILLIAMS, BILL. *A Sampler on Sampling.* New York: Wiley, 1978.

ZELLER, RICHARD A., and CARMINES, EDWARD G. *Measurement in the Social Sciences: The Link Between Theory and Data.* New York: Cambridge University Press, 1980.

ZETTERBERG, HANS L. *On Theory and Verification in Sociology.* 3rd rev. ed. Totowa, N.J.: Bedminister Press, 1965.

Guides to Methods and Techniques of Collecting Data in Library, Field, and Laboratory; Social Science Data Libraries and Research Centers

THE collection of data is the crucial operation in the execution of a good research design. The quality of the research rests upon the quality of the data. In this section the methods and techniques of social research are presented according to their common situs of research: library, field, and laboratory. Advantages and disadvantages of principal methods are pointed out. Guides to the construction of questionnaires, interviews, and scales are described.

A listing of social science data libraries is given. These social science archives are available to research scholars and offer many excellent opportunities for research. The collection of data is expensive, and the ability to use data previously collected offers the possibility of superior research at a greatly lowered cost. The guide to the U.S. Census and Bureau of Labor Statistics is especially thorough, to make known and usable the rich mine of data available to social researchers.

Finally, directories of social science research centers in the United States, England, and throughout the world are provided to aid the researcher. A list of important research associations and institutes affiliated with the International Sociological Association may be valuable contact points to determine the status of current research and comparative research advances in various fields.

The collection of data occurs in a designed inquiry only after a long series of steps including:

1. The definition of the problem
2. The construction of the theoretical framework
3. The stating of hypotheses
4. The establishment of the design of inquiry
5. The determination of sampling procedures

This section introduces the most common methods of social science research and presents a brief set of instructions for the construction of questionnaires, interviews, and scales. These instructions will assist the researcher in evaluating the appropriate method for his problem. He should consult methods books for a thorough explanation of each method or technique.

Methods are handmaidens of designed inquiry. It is important to distinguish carefully between four terms: methodology, situs, methods, and techniques.

Methodology is a body of knowledge that describes and analyzes methods, indicating their limitations and resources, clarifying their presuppositions and consequences, and relating their potentialities to research advances. In this part the methods of social science are first examined in order to set forth the advantages and disadvantages of each method. The aim is to help the researcher to understand the process of gathering data and what his choice of method entails.

Situs refers to the place in which the data is gathered. For most sciences, the most used situses are the library, the field, and the laboratory.

Method refers to the means of gathering data that are common to all sciences or to a significant part of them. Thus methods include such procedures as the making of observations and measurements, performing experiments, building models and theories, or providing explanations and making predictions. The social sciences use documentary analysis, the mailed questionnaire, and the personal interview most frequently.

Techniques refer to specific procedures that are used in a given method. For example, the field method worker may employ such techniques as use of sociometric scales to measure social variables and personality inventories to identify personal traits. The research worker such as a demographer may draw heavily on statistical documents and use various statistical techniques to describe relationships or gain statistical control over the data.

The following aids first present an outline of methods and techniques as employed in the three situses: library, field, and laboratory. Then aids are presented for the most common methods and techniques. A list of reference books is given that describes various methods and techniques in detail.

Situs	Methods	Techniques
Library	1. Analysis of historical records: primary records—letters, diaries, etc.; secondary interpretations of events 2. Analysis of documents: statistical and nonstatistical records of formal agencies 3. Literature search for theory and previous research in books, journals, and monographs	Recording of notes Content analysis Tape and film listening and analysis Statistical compilations and manipulations Reference and abstract guides Microfilm, microfiche searches Computer information probes
Field	1. Mail questionnaire	Identification of social and economic background of respondents Use of sociometric scales to ascertain such variables as social status, group structure, community and social participation, leadership activity, and family adjustment Use of attitude scales to measure morale, job satisfaction, marital adjustment, etc.
	2. Personal interview Structured interview schedule	Interviewer uses a detailed schedule with open and closed questions Sociometric scales may be used
	3. Focused interview	Interviewer focuses attention upon a given experience and its effects; he knows in advance what topics or questions he wishes to cover
	4. Free story interview	Respondent is urged to talk freely about the subjects treated in the study
	5. Group interview	Small groups of respondents are interviewed simultaneously; any of the above techniques may be used
	6. Telephone survey	Used as a survey technique for information and for discerning opinion May be used for follow-up of a questionnaire mailing to increase return
	7. Case study and life history	For case study, cross-sectional collection of data for intensive analysis of a person emphasizing personal and social factors in socialization For life history, longitudinal collection of data of intensive character also emphasizing socialization over an extended period of time
	8. Nonparticipant direct observation	Use of standard score cards and observational behavior scales
	9. Participant observation	Interactional recording; possible use of tape recorders and photographic techniques
	10. Mass observation	Recording mass or collective behavior by observation and interview using independent observers in public places
Laboratory	Small group study of random behavior, play, problem solving, or stress behavior of individuals and/or groups; organizational and role analysis	Use of contrived and nonconstructed situations, use of confederates; use of audiovisual recording devices; use of observers behind one-way mirror.

The research question that motivates research generally comes first in the history of any research project. Then a search of the scientific literature becomes paramount. Social scientists often minimize this step. Sometimes they mistakenly believe that their problem is so "novel" that past literature will not apply. But all too often they simply do not give enough importance to the way in which their work will help build on past research to validate a test hypothesis or theory and thus make a growing accumulation of findings. They underestimate past work and sell short the future requirements of their science.

Physical and biological scientists dare not take such risks because they know that fellow scientists will quickly detect these faults in scientific work. Social scientists have to learn that they cannot do so with impunity.

The resources for making the literature research are great and marvelous. They fall into four categories: (1) indexes to periodical literature, (2) computer assisted reference services, (3) microfilm-microfiche-microprint media, and (4) specialized source books.

Indexes to Periodical Literature

The following indexes are of most value to the social scientist and are described in the order in which they are usually consulted:

1. *Social Sciences Index* is a cumulative index to English-language periodicals. The main body of the index consists of author and subject entries to periodicals in the fields of anthropology, area studies, economics, environmental sciences, geography, law and criminology, medical sciences, political sciences, psychology, public administration, sociology, and related subjects. In addition there is an author listing of citations to book reviews following the main body of the index. This index, which is published quarterly with bound cumulation each year, has a fairly long history. It began in 1907 as the *International Index;* in 1955 its name was changed and it continued as the *Social Science and Humanities Index.* The growing body of knowledge necessitated a division of the index into a separate *Social Sciences Index* and a *Humanities Index* (1974). This division continues today. The periodicals shown below are indexed; all data reflect the latest information available.*

Periodicals Indexed

Academy of Political Science. Proceedings. $22. q 619 W 114th St, Suite 500, New York, N.Y. 10025

Acta Sociologica. $38. q Universitetsforlaget, P.O. Box 7508, Skillebekk, Oslo 2, Norway

Adolescence. $25. q Libra Publishers Inc, P.O. Box 165, 391 Willets Rd, Roslyn Heights, L.I. N.Y. 11577

Advances in Thanatology. $60. 4 times a yr Arno Press, 3 Park Ave, New York, N.Y. 10016

* Reprinted with permission of H. W. Wilson Co., publishers of the Social Sciences Index.

Africa Today. $15. q Africa Today Associates, c/o Graduate School of International Studies, University of Denver, Denver, Colo. 80208

African Studies. R20. bi-ann Witwatersrand University Press, Jan Smuts Ave, Johannesburg 2001, South Africa

African Studies Review. $45. 3 times a yr Subscription Department, African Studies Assn, 255 Kinsey Hall, University of California, Los Angeles, Calif. 90024

American Academy of Political and Social Science. Annals. $18. bi-m 3937 Chestnut St, Philadelphia, Pa. 19104

American Anthropologist. $50. q American Anthropological Assn, 1703 New Hampshire Ave, NW, Washington, D.C. 20009

The American Behavioral Scientist. $45. bi-m Sage Publications, Inc, 275 S Beverly Drive, Beverly Hills, Calif. 90212

The American Economic Review. $43. 5 times a yr Rendings Fels, 1313 21st Ave. South, Nashville, Tenn. 37212
    May number has added title: Papers and Proceedings of the Annual Meeting of the American Economic Association

The American Economic Review; Papers and Proceedings. See American Economic Review

The American Economist. $6. 2 times a yr University of Alabama, Department of Economics, PO Drawer AS, Ala. 35486

American Journal of Correction. See Corrections Today

The American Journal of Economics and Sociology. $10. q 50 E 69th St, New York, N.Y. 10021

The American Journal of International Law. $47. 4 times a yr American Society of International Law, 2223 Massachusetts Ave, NW, Washington, D.C. 20008

American Journal of Nursing. $15. m Subscription Department, 555 W 57th St, New York, N.Y. 10019

American Journal of Orthopsychiatry. $22. q AOA Publications Sales Office, 49 Sheridan Ave, Albany, N.Y. 12210

American Journal of Physical Anthropology. $214. 8 times a yr Alan R. Liss, Inc, 150 5th Ave, New York, N.Y. 10011

American Journal of Political Science. $30. q University of Texas Press, Box 7819, Austin, Tex. 78712

The American Journal of Psychiatry. $27. m American Psychiatric Association, Circulation Dept, 1700 18th St, NW, Washington, D.C. 20009

The American Journal of Psychology. $30. q University of Illinois Press, 54 E. Gregory Drive, Box 5081, Station A, Champaign, Ill. 61820

American Journal of Public Health. $40. m American Public Health Assn, 1015 18th St, NW, Washington, D.C. 20036

The American Journal of Sociology. $40. bi-m University of Chicago Press, 5801 Ellis Ave, Chicago, Ill. 60637

American Opinion. $18. m(Ag-Je) R. Welch, Inc, 395 Concord Ave, Belmont, Mass. 02178

American Planning Association. Journal. $22. q American Planning Assn, 1776 Massachusetts Ave, NW, Washington, D.C. 20036

The American Political Science Review. $50. q American Political Science Association, 1527 New Hampshire Ave, NW, Washington, D.C. 20036

American Psychologist. $25. m Subscription Section, American Psychological Association, Inc, 1200 17th St, NW, Washington, D.C. 20036

American Society for Psychical Research. Journal. $20. q American Society for Psychical Research Inc, 5 W 73d St, New York, N.Y. 10023

American Sociological Review. $30. bi-m American Sociological Association, 1722 N St, NW, Washington, D.C. 20036

Anthropological Quarterly. $18. q Catholic University of America Press, Washington, D.C. 20064

Anthrops. International Review of Ethnology and Linguistics. Swiss Fr 140. 3 times a yr Editions Saint-Paul, 1700 Fribourg, Switzerland

Archaeology and Physical Anthropology in Oceania. $15. 3 times a yr Mackie Building, University of Sydney, New South Wales, Australia 2006

Asia. $10. bi-m Asia Society, P.O. Box 379, Fort Lee, N.J. 07024

Asian Affairs; Journal of the Royal Society for Asian Affairs. $20. 3 times a yr The Royal Society for Asian Affairs,

42 Devonshire St, London, W1N 1LN, England

Asian Survey. $37.50 m University of California Press, Berkeley, Calif. 94720

Association of American Geographers. Annals. $30. q Association of American Geographers, 1710 16th St, NW, Washington, D.C. 20009

The Atlantic Community Quarterly. $15. q The Atlantic Council of the United States, 1616 H St, NW, Washington, D.C. 20006

Aztlan; International Journal of Chicano Studies Research. $20. 3 times a yr Chicano Studies Center, 405 Hilgard Ave, Los Angeles, Calif. 90024

The Bell Journal of Economics. free. semi-ann American Telephone & Telegraph Co, 195 Broadway, New York, N.Y. 10007

The Black Scholar; Journal of Black Studies and Research. $16. bi-m P.O. Box 908, Sausalito, Calif. 94965

Boston College Environmental Affairs Law Review. $20. q Boston College Law School, 885 Centre St, Newton Centre, Mass. 02159

The British Journal of Criminology; Delinquency and Deviant Social Behaviour. $37.50 q Fred B. Rothman & Co, 57 Leuning St, S Hackensack, N.J. 07606

British Journal of Political Science. $99. q Cambridge University Press, 32 E 57th St, New York, N.Y. 10022

The British Journal of Psychology. $100. q Distribution Center, Blackhorse Road, Letchworth, Herts SG6 1HN, United Kingdom

The British Journal of Sociology. $50. q Routledge Journals, 9 Park St, Boston, Mass. 02108

Brookings Papers on Economic Activity. $15. 3 times a yr 1775 Massachusetts Ave, NW, Washington, D.C. 20036

Bulletin on Narcotics. $10. q United Nations Sales Section, New York, N.Y. 10017

Business and Society Review. $38. q Warren, Gorham & Lamont, Inc, 870 7th Ave, New York, N.Y. 10019

Business History Review. $20. q Harvard Graduate School of Business Administration, 215 Baker Library, Soldiers Field, Boston, Mass. 02163

The Canadian Forum; an Independent Journal of Opinion and the Arts. $15. m 70 The Esplanade, 3d floor, Toronto, Ont. M5E 1A6

The Canadian Geographer. $25. q Canadian Assn. of Geographers, Burnside Hall, McGill University, 805 Sherbrooke St, W, Montreal, H3A 2KG, Canada

Canadian Geographic. $17. bi-m Royal Canadian Geographical Society, 488 Wilbrod St, Ottawa, K1N 6M8, Ont.

Canadian Journal of Economics. $36. q University of Toronto Press, 5201 Dufferin St, Downsview, M3H 5T8, Ont.

Canadian Journal of Political Science. $35. q Wilfrid Laurier University Press, Waterloo, Ont. N2L 3C5

Canadian Journal of Psychology/Revue Canadienne de Psychologie. $35. q Canadian Psychological Assn, King Edward Ave, Ottawa, Ont. K1N 7N6

Caribbean Studies. $8. q University of Puerto Rico, Institute of Caribbean Studies, Box BM, University Station, Rio Piedras, Puerto Rico, 00931

The Center Magazine. $5. bi-m Fund for the Republic, Inc, 2056 Eucalyptus Hill Rd, Santa Barbara, Calif. 93108

Child Development. $50. q University of Chicago Press, 5801 Ellis Ave, Chicago, Ill. 60637

China Quarterly; an International Journal for the Study of China. $30. q. Contemporary China Institute, School of Oriental and African Studies, Malet St, London, WC1E 7HP, England

Civil Rights Digest. See Perspectives; the Civil Rights Quarterly

Civil Service Journal. $5.75. q Supt. of Documents, Government Printing Office, Washington D.C. 20402
Ceased publication with v 19 no 4

Community Development Journal; an International Forum. $17.50. 3 times a yr Journals Manager, Oxford University Press, Press Rd, Neasden, London, N.W. 10, England

Community Mental Health Journal. $50. q Human Science Press, 72 5th Ave, New York, N.Y. 10011

Comparative Political Studies. $32. q Sage Publications, Inc, 275 S Beverly Drive, Beverly Hills, Calif. 90212

Comparative Politics. $25. q Subscription Fulfillment, Transaction Periodicals Consortium, Rutgers University, New Brunswick, N.J. 08903

Contemporary Drug Problems. $24. q Federal Legal Publications Inc, 157 Chambers St, New York, N.Y. 10007

Crime and Delinquency. $20. q National Council on Crime and Delinquency, Continental Plaza, 411 Hackensack Ave, Hackensack, N.J. 07601

Corrections Today. $18. bi-m American Correction Assn, Inc, 4321 Hartwick Rd, Suite L-208, College Park, Md. 20740
Formerly American Journal of Correction; name changed with v41 no 1 January 1980

Criminology; an Interdisciplinary Journal. $32. q Sage Publications, 275 S Beverly Drive, Beverly Hills, Calif. 90212

The Crisis; a Record of the Darker Races. $6. 10 times a yr 1790 Broadway, New York, N.Y.10019

Current Anthropology; a World Journal of the Sciences of Man. $44. 6 times a yr University of Chicago Press, 5801 Ellis Ave, Chicago, Ill. 60637

Demography. $35. q Business Manager, Population Association of America, P.O. Box 14182, Benjamin Franklin Station, Washington, D.C. 20044

Development/The International Development Review. $15. q Society for International Development, 1346 Connecticut Ave, NW, Washington, D.C. 20036

Developmental Psychology. $36. bi-m Subscription Section, American Psychological Association, Inc, 1200 17th St, NW, Washington, D.C. 20036

Dissent. $17. q Foundation for the Study of Independent Social Ideas, 505 5th Ave, New York, N.Y. 10017

East European Quarterly. $12. q 1200 University Ave, Boulder, Colo. 80302

Econometrica. $63. bi-m Tieto Ltd, 4 Bellevue Mansions, Bellevue Rd, Clevedon, Avon, BS21 7NU, England

Economic Development and Cultural Change. $40. q University of Chicago Press, 5801 Ellis Ave, Chicago, Ill. 60637

Economic Geography. $18.50 q Business Manager, Clark University, Worcester, Mass. 01610

The Economic History Review. $30. q Titus Wilson & Son Ltd, 28 Highgate, Kendal Cumbria LA9 4TB, England

Economic Inquiry. $65. q Western Economic Assn, Executive Office, Department of Economics, California State University, Long Beach, Calif. 90840

The Economic Journal. $72. q Cambridge University Press, American Branch, 32 E 57th St, New York, N.Y. 10022

Economica. $32. q Tieto Ltd, 5 Elton Rd, Clevedon, Avon, BS21 7RA, England

The Economist. $85. w Subscription Department, P.O. Box 190, 23a St James St, London, SW1A 1HF, England
Note magazine printing error on masthead of March 15 1980; should read vol 274 not vol 275

Education and Urban Society. $32. q Sage Publications Inc, 275 S Beverly Drive, Beverly Hills, Calif. 90912

Ekistics: the Problems and Science of Human Settlements. $36. 10 times a yr Athens Center of Ekistics, PO Box 471, Athens, Greece

Environment. $22. 10 times a yr Scientists' Institute for Public Information, 4000 Albemarle St, N.W. Washington, D.C. 20016

Environment and Behavior. $32. q Sage Publications, Inc, 275 S Beverly Drive, Beverly Hills, Calif. 90212

Environmental Research. $61. bi-m Academic Press, Inc, 111 5th Ave, New York, N.Y. 10003

Ethics: an International Journal of Social, Political, and Legal Philosophy. $30. q University of Chicago Press, 5801 Ellis Ave, Chicago, Ill. 60637

Ethnic Groups; an International Periodical of Ethnic Studies. $67.50. q Gordon and Breach Science Publishers Inc, 42 William IV St, London, WC2, England

Ethnohistory. $10. q American Society for Ethnohistory, c/o Arizona State Museum, University of Arizona, Tucson, Ariz. 85721

Ethnology; an International Journal of Cultural and Social Anthropology. $17. q Department of Anthropology, University of Pittsburgh, Pa. 15260

European Economic Review. $172.50. for 2 volumes. 3 times a yr North Holland Publishing Co, Box 211, Amsterdam, The Netherlands

European Journal of Sociology/Archichives Européennes de Sociologie. $53.50. 2 times a yr Cambridge University Press, 32 E 57th St, New York, N.Y. 10022

Far Eastern Economic Review. $62. w Datamovers, Inc, 38 W 36th St, New York, N.Y. 10018

Federal Probation. free. q Administrative Office of the U.S. Courts, Supreme Court Building, Washington, D.C. 20544

Foreign Affairs. $18. 5 times a yr Subscription Dept. P.O. 2615, Boulder, Colo. 80322

Foreign Policy. $12. q P.O. Box 984, Farmingdale, N.Y. 11735

Freedomways. $4.50. q Freedomways Associates, 799 Broadway, New York, N.Y. 11737

Futures; the Journal of Forecasting and Planning. $67. bi-m IPC Business Press, Ltd, 205 E 42d St, New York, N.Y. 10017

The Futurist; a Journal of Forecasts, Trends and Ideas about the Future. $21. bi-m World Future Society, P.O. Box 30369, Bethesda Branch, Washington, D.C. 20014

The Geographical Journal. $55. 3 times a yr Royal Geographical Society, 1 Kensington Gore, London, SW7 2AR, England

The Geographical Magazine. $35.20. m IPC Business Press Ltd, Oakfield House Perrymount Rd, Haywards Heath, West Sussex RH16 3DH, England

Geographical Review. $40. q American Geographical Society, Broadway & 156th St, New York, N.Y. 10032

Geography. $15. q George Philip & Son Ltd, 12–14 Long Acre, London, WC2E 9LP, England

The Gerontologist. $25. bi-m Gerontological Society, 1835 K St, NW, Washington, D.C. 20006

Government and Opposition. $60. q London School of Economics and Political Science, Houghton St, London, WC2A 2AE, England

History of Political Economy. $28. q Duke University Press, 6697 College Station, Durham, N.C. 27708

Human Ecology. $65. q Plenum Press, 227 W 17th St, New York, N.Y. 10011

Human Organization. $25. q Society for Applied Anthropology, 1703 New Hampshire Ave, NW, Washington D.C. 20009

Human Relations; a Journal of Studies towards the Integration of the Social Sciences. $115. m Plenum Publishing Co, 227 W 17th St, New York, N.Y. 10011

Impact of Science on Society. French Fr 40. q UNIPUB, Box 433, Murray Hill Station, New York, N.Y. 10016

The Indian Historian. $7. q 1451 Masonic Ave, San Francisco, Calif. 94117

Inter-American Economic Affairs. $20. q Box 181, Benjamin Franklin Station, Washington, D.C. 20044

International Affairs. $25. q Oxford University Press, Press Rd, London, NW10 0DD, England

International Economic Review. $46. 3 times a yr Department of Economics, McNeil Building CR, University of Pennsylvania, Philadelphia, Pa. 19104

International Journal of Comparative Sociology. $42.77. q E. J. Brill, Leiden, The Netherlands

International Journal of Middle East Studies. $95. 8 times a yr Cambridge University Press, 32 E 57th St, New York, N.Y. 10022

International Journal of Offender Therapy and Comparative Criminology. $28. 3 times a yr 199 Gloucester Place, London, NW1 6BU, England

International Journal of Social Psychiatry. $50. q Avenue Publishing Co, 18 Park Ave, London, NW11 7SJ, England

International Organization; a Journal of Political and Economic Affairs. $30. q Journals Department, University of Wisconsin Press, 114 N. Murray St, Madison, Wis. 52701

International Review of Social History. $26.15. 3 times a yr Royal VanGorcum, Assen, Netherlands

International Social Science Journal. French Fr 70. q UNIPUB, Inc, P.O. Box 433, New York, N.Y. 10016

International Studies Quarterly. $40. q Sage Publications Inc, 275 S Beverly Drive, Beverly Hills, Calif. 90212

JEI/Journal of Economic Issues. $20. q Association for Evolutionary Economics, Fiscal Office, Dept. of Economics,

University of Nebraska, Lincoln, Neb. 68588

Jewish Social Studies; a Quarterly Journal Devoted to Contemporary and Historical Aspects of Jewish Life. $25. q Conference on Jewish Social Studies, 250 W 57th St, New York, N.Y. 10019

Journal of Abnormal Psychology. $34. bi-m American Psychological Association Inc, 1200 17th St, NW, Washington, D.C. 20036

Journal of Anthropological Research. $16. q Subscription Manager, University of New Mexico, Albuquerque, N.Mex. 87131

Journal of Applied Behavior Analysis. $22. q University of Kansas, Department of Human Development, Lawrence, Kan. 66045

The Journal of Applied Behavioral Science. $23. q NTL Institute for Applied Behavioral Science, P.O. Box 9155, Rosslyn Station, Arlington, Va. 22209

Journal of Applied Psychology. $38. bi-m American Psychological Association, Inc, 1200 17th St, NW, Washington, D.C. 20036

Journal of Asian and African Studies. $26.52. q E. J. Brill, Leiden, Netherlands

Journal of Black Studies. $36. q Sage Publications, Inc, 275 S Beverly Drive, Beverly Hills, Calif. 90212

Journal of Common Market Studies $57. q Basil Blackwell, 108 Cowley Rd, Oxford, OX4 1JF, England

The Journal of Conflict Resolution: Research on War and Peace Between and Within Nations. $45. q Sage Publications, 275 S Beverly Drive, Beverly Hills, Calif. 90212

Journal of Consulting and Clinical Psychology. $50. bi-m American Psychological Association Inc, 1200 17th St, NW, Washington, D.C. 20036

Journal of Contemporary Asia. $26. q P.O. Box 49010, Stockholm 49, Sweden

Journal of Counseling Psychology. $30. bi-m Subscription Section, American Psychological Assn, Inc, 1200 17th St, NW, Washington, D.C. 20036

The Journal of Creative Behavior. $9. q Managing Editor, State University College at Buffalo, 1300 Elmwood Ave, Buffalo, N.Y. 14222

The Journal of Criminal Law & Criminology. $25. q Northwestern University School of Law, 357 E Chicago Ave, Chicago, Ill. 60611

The Journal of Development Studies. $49.50. q Frank Cass & Co. Ltd, 11 Gainsborough Rd, London, E11 1RS, England

The Journal of Economic History. $25. q Eleutherian Mills Historical Library, Wilmington, Del. 19807

Journal of Economic Theory. $138. bi-m Academic Press, 111 5th Ave, New York, N.Y. 10003

Journal of Experimental Psychology: Animal Behavior Processes. $14. q American Psychological Association, Inc, Subscription Section, 1200 17th St, NW, Washington, D.C. 20036

Journal of Experimental Psychology: General. $16. q American Psychological Association, Inc, Subscription Section, 1200 17th St, NW, Washington, D.C. 20036

Journal of Experimental Psychology: Human Learning and Memory. $30. bi-m American Psychological Association, Inc, Subscription Section, 1200 17th St, NW, Washington, D.C. 20036

Journal of Experimental Psychology: Human Perception and Performance. $20. q American Psychological Association, Inc, Subscription Section, 1200 17th St, NW, Washington, D.C. 20036

Journal of Experimental Social Psychology. $53. bi-m Academic Press, Inc, 111 5th Ave, New York, N.Y. 10003

The Journal of General Psychology. $54. q 2 Commercial St, Provincetown, Mass. 02657

Journal of Gerontology. $35. bi-m Gerontological Society, 1835 K St, NW, Washington, D.C. 20006

Journal of Health and Social Behavior. $16. q American Sociological Assn, 1722 N St, NW, Washington, D.C. 20036

Journal of Housing. $33. 11 times a yr National Association of Housing and Redevelopment Officials. The Watergate Building, 2600 Virginia Ave, NW, Washington, D.C. 20037

The Journal of Human Resources; Education, Manpower, and Welfare Policies. $28. q 4 times a yr Journals Department, University of Wisconsin Press, 114 N Murray St, Madison, Wis. 53715

Journal of Humanistic Psychology. $18. q Association of Humanistic Psychology, 325 9th St, San Francisco, Calif. 94103

Journal of Interamerican Studies and World Affairs. $36. q Sage Publications, 275 S Beverly Drive, Beverly Hills, Calif. 90212

Journal of International Affairs. $12. semi-ann Columbia University, 420 W 118th St, New York, N.Y. 10027

Journal of International Economics. $117. q North-Holland Publishing Co, P.O. Box 211, Amsterdam-C, Netherlands

Journal of Latin American Studies. $33. 2 times a yr Cambridge University Press, 32 E 57th St, New York, N.Y. 10022

Journal of Law and Economics. $20. 2 times a yr University of Chicago Law School, 1111 E 60th St, Chicago, Ill. 60637

Journal of Leisure Research. $15. q National Recreation & Park Assn. 1601 North Kent St, Arlington, Va. 22209

Journal of Marriage and the Family. $30. q National Council on Family Relations, 1219 University Ave, SE, Minneapolis, Minn. 55414

The Journal of Modern African Studies; a Quarterly Survey of Politics, Economics and Related Topics in Contemporary Africa. $46.50. q Cambridge University Press, American Branch, 32 E 57th St, New York, N.Y. 10022

Journal of Money, Credit and Banking. $17.50. q Ohio State University Press, 2070 Neil Ave, Columbus, Ohio 43210

The Journal of Parapsychology. $15. q Box 6847, College Station, Durham, N.C. 27708

Journal of Peace Research. $28. q P.O. Box 258, Irvington-on-Hudson, New York, N.Y. 10533

Journal of Personality and Social Psychology. $80. m Subscription Section, American Psychological Association, Inc, 1200 17th St, NW, Washington, D.C. 20036

Journal of Police Science and Administration. $25. q International Association of Chiefs of Police, 11 Firstfield Road, Gaithersburg, Md. 20760

Journal of Political Economy. $30. bi-m University of Chicago Press, 5801 Ellis Ave, Chicago, Ill. 60637

Journal of Politics. $19. q Manning J. Dauer, Managing Editor, University of Florida, Gainesville, Fla. 32611

Journal of Psychedelic Drugs. $30. q Student Association for the Study of Hallucinogens, 118 S Bedford St, Madison, Wis. 53703

The Journal of Psychology; the General Field of Psychology. $54. 6 times a yr 2 Commercial St, Provincetown, Mass. 02657

Journal of Research in Crime and Delinquency. $12. 2 times a yr National Council on Crime and Delinquency, 411 Hackensack Ave, Hackensack, N.J. 07601

Journal of Social History. $25. q Carnegie-Mellon University, Pittsburgh, Pa. 15213

The Journal of Social Issues. $32. q Society for the Psychological Study of Social Issues, P.O. Box 1248, Ann Arbor, Mich. 48106

Journal of Social Psychology. $54. bi-m Box 543, 2 Commercial St, Provincetown, Mass. 02657

Journal of Studies on Alcohol. $50. m Publications Division, Center of Alcohol Studies, P.O. Box 969 Piscataway, N.J. 08854

Journal of Verbal Learning and Verbal Behavior. $72. bi-m Academic Press Inc, 111 5th Ave, New York, N.Y. 10003

Kyklos; International Review for Social Sciences. Swiss Fr 70. q Kyklos-Verlag, Postfach 524, CH-4000, Basel 2, Switzerland

Latin American Research Review. $30. 3 times a yr LARR Subscription, 316 Hamilton Hall, University of North Carolina, Chapel Hill, N.C. 27514

Law and Contemporary Problems. $20. q Duke University Press, Box 6697, College Station, Durham, N.C. 27708

Law and Society Review. $35. q Executive Office, Law and Society Assn, University of Denver College of Law, 200 W 14th Ave, Denver, Colo. 80204

Man; the Journal of the Royal Anthropological Institute. $52. q Royal Anthropological Institute, 56 Queen Anne St, London, W1M 9LA, England

The Manchester School of Economic and Social Studies. $37.50. q Manchester University, Department of Economics, Dover St, Manchester, M13 9PL, England

Mankind. $18. 2 times a yr Anthropological Society of NSW, c/o Department of Anthropology, University of Sydney, Sydney, Australia

The Middle East Journal. $15. q 1761 N St, NW, Washington, D.C. 20036

Middle Eastern Studies. $71.85. q Frank Cass & Co, Ltd, Gainsborough House, Gainsborough Rd, London, E11 1RS, England

Modern Age. $10. q Intercollegiate Studies Institute, Inc, 14 S Bryn Mawr Ave, Bryn Mawr, Pa. 19010

Modern Asian Studies. $95. q Cambridge University Press, American Branch, 32 E 57th St, New York, N.Y. 10022

Monthly Review; an Independent Socialist Magazine. $24. 11 times a yr 62 W 14th St, New York, N.Y. 10011

National Wildlife. $7.50. bi-m National Wildlife Federation, Inc, 1412 16th St, NW, Washington, D.C. 20036

New Left Review. $35. bi-m 7 Carlisle St, London, W1V 6NL, England

New Statesman. $44. w 10 Great Turnstile, London, WC1V 7HJ, England

Nursing Outlook. $17. m 555 W 57th St, New York, N.Y. 10019

Oceania; a Journal Devoted to the Study of the Native Peoples of Australia, New Guinea and the Islands of the Pacific Ocean. $17.50. q University of Sydney, New South Wales, Australia 2006

Oceans. $15. bi-m Oceanic Society, Fort Mason, San Francisco, Calif. 94123

Orbis: a Journal of World Affairs. $25. q 3508 Market St, Suite 350, Philadelphia, Pa. 19104

Oxford Economic Papers. $30. 3 times a yr Oxford University Press, Walton St, Oxford, OX2 6DP, England

Parliamentary Affairs. $34. q Oxford Journals, Press Rd, Neasden, London, NW10 0DD, England

Perspectives; the Civil Rights Quarterly. $15. q Commission on Civil Rights, 1121 Vermont Ave, NW, Washington, D.C. 20425

Formerly Civil Rights Digest; name changed with v 12 no 1 Spring 1980

Phylon; the Atlanta University Review of Race and Culture. $12. q Atlanta University, Atlanta, Ga. 30314

The Political Quarterly. $41.60 q 4 Bloomsbury Sq, London, WC1, England

Political Science Quarterly. $24. q Academy of Political Science, 619 W 114th St, Suite 500, New York, N.Y. 10025

Political Studies. $44. q Political Studies Assocation of the United Kingdom, Oxford University Press, Press Rd, Neasden, London, NW10 0DD, England

Politics and Society. $28. q Geron-X Inc, Publishers, Box 1108, Los Altos, Calif. 94022

Population Bulletin. $25. bi-m Circulation Department, Population Reference Bureau, Inc, 1337 Connecticut Ave, Washington, D.C. 20036

Problems of Communism. $10. bi-m Superintendent of Documents, US Government Printing Office, Washington, D.C. 20402

The Professional Geographer. $19. q Association of American Geographers, 1710 16th St, NW, Washington, D.C. 20009

Psychiatry. Journal for the Study of Interpersonal Processes. $24. q 1610 New Hampshire Ave, NW, Washington, D.C. 20009

The Psychological Record. $21.50. q Kenyon College, Gambier, Ohio 43022

Psychological Reports. $112. bi-m Box 9229, Missoula, Mont. 59807

Psychological Review. $26. bi-m American Psychological Association, 1200 17th St, NW, Washington, D.C. 20036

Public Administration Review. $35. bi-m American Society for Public Administration, 1225 Connecticut Ave, NW, Washington, D.C. 20036

The Public Interest. $12. q Box 542, Old Chelsea Post Office, New York, N.Y. 10011

Public Management. $15. m International City Management Assn, 1140 Connecticut Ave, NW, Washington, D.C. 20036

The Public Opinion Quarterly. $28. q Elsevier North-Holland, Inc, 52 Vanderbilt Ave, New York, N.Y. 10017

Public Policy. $25. q John Wiley & Sons, Inc, 605 3d Ave, New York, N.Y. 10158

The Quarterly Journal of Economics. $30. q John Wiley and Sons, Inc, 605 3d Ave, New York, N.Y. 10016

The Quarterly Review of Economics and Business. $17. q 428 Commerce West, Urbana, Ill. 61801

The Review of Black Political Economy. $15. q Rutgers University, New Brunswick, N.J. 08903

The Review of Economic Studies. $67. 5 times a yr Longman Group Ltd, Journals Division, 43–45 Annandale St, Edinburgh, EH7 4AT, Scotland

The Review of Economics and Statistics. $56. q North-Holland Publishing Co, P.O. Box 211, Amsterdam, Netherlands

The Review of Politics. $10. q University of Notre Dame, Ind. 46556

Review of Social Economy. $18. 3 times a yr Association for Social Economics, DePaul University, 25 E. Jackson Blvd, Chicago, Ill. 60604

The Round Table; the Commonwealth Journal of International Affairs. $30. q Professional & Scientific Publications, Tavistock House East, Tavistock Sq, London, WC1H 9JR, England

Rural Sociology. $28. q Rural Sociological Society, 325 Morgan Hall, University of Tennessee, Knoxville, Tenn. 37916

Scandinavian Review. $15. q American-Scandinavian Foundation, 127 E 73d St, New York, N.Y. 10021

Science & Society; an Independent Journal of Marxism. $20. q John Jay College, CUNY, 445 W 59th St, New York, N.Y. 10019

Simulation and Games; an International Journal of Theory, Design, and Research. $32. q Sage Publications, 275 S Beverly Drive, Beverly Hills, Calif. 90212

Social and Economic Studies. $15. q University of the West Indies, Institute of Social and Economic Research, Mona, Jamaica

Social Biology. $35. q University of Wisconsin, 1180 Observatory Drive, Madison, Wis. 53706

Social Casework; the Journal of Contemporary Social Work. $25. m(S-Je) Family Service Association of America, 44 E 23d St, New York, N.Y. 10010

Social Forces; an International Journal of Social Research. $15.60. q University of North Carolina Press, Box 2288, Chapel Hill, N.C. 27514

Social Policy. $15. bi-m Room 1212, 33 W 42d St, New York, N.Y. 10036

Social Problems; Official Journal of the Society for the Study of Social Problems. $35. 5 times a yr 208 Rockwell Hall, State University College, 1300 Elmwood Ave, Buffalo, N.Y. 14222

Social Psychology Quarterly. $16. q American Sociological Assn, 1722 N St, NW, Washington, D.C. 20036

Social Research; an International Quarterly of the Social Sciences. $20. q New School for Social Research, 66 W 12th St, New York, N.Y. 10011

Social Science Quarterly. $30. q University of Texas Press, Box 7819, Austin, Tex. 78712

The Social Service Review. $22. q University of Chicago Press, 5801 Ellis Ave, Chicago, Ill. 60637

Social Theory and Practice. $21. 3 times a yr Florida State University, Department of Philosophy, Tallahassee, Fla. 32306

Social Work; Journal of the National Association of Social Workers. $30. bi-m 49 Sheridan Ave, Albany, N.Y. 12210

Sociological Quarterly. $15. q Southern Illinois University, Department of Sociology, Carbondale, Ill. 62901

The Sociological Review. New series. $30. q University of Keele, Staffordshire, ST5 5BG, England

Sociology and Social Research; an International Journal. $30. q University of Southern California Press, University Park, Los Angeles, Calif. 90007

Sociology of Education; a Journal of Research in Socialization and Social Structure. $16. 4 times a yr American Sociological Assn, 1722 N St, NW, Washington, D.C. 20036

Sociology; The Journal of the British Sociological Association. $50.26. 3 times a yr 10 Portugal St, London, WC2A 2HD, England

Southern Economic Journal. $30. q Hanes Hall 019-A, Chapel Hill, N.C. 27514

The Soviet Review; a Journal of Translations. $25. q M. E. Sharpe, Inc, 901 N Broadway, White Plains, New York, N.Y. 10603

State Government. $12. q P.O. Box 11910 Lexington, Ky. 40578

Studies in Comparative Communism; an International Interdisciplinary Journal. $22. q Editorial and Business Offices, VKC 330, School of International Relations, University of Southern California, University Park, Los Angeles, Calif. 90007

Survey: a Journal of East and West Studies. $27. q Oxford University Press, Subscription Department, Press Rd, Neasden, London, NW10 0DD, England

Technology and Culture. $27. q University of Chicago Press, 5801 Ellis Ave, Chicago, Ill. 60637

Town and Country Planning. $20. 11 times a yr Town and Country Planning Assn, 17 Carlton House Terrace, London, SW1Y 5AS, England

Town Planning Review. $36. q Liverpool University Press, 123 Grove St, Liverpool, 17 7AF, England

Trial; the National Legal Newsmagazine. $18. m Assn. of Trial Lawyers of America, P.O. Box 3717, 1050 31st St. NW, Washington, D.C. 20007

Urban Affairs Quarterly. $40. q Sage Publications, Inc, 275 S Beverly Drive, Beverly Hills, Calif. 90212

Urban Life; a Journal of Ethnographic Research. $32. q Sage Publications, Inc, 275 S Beverly Drive, Beverly Hills, Calif. 90212

Urban Studies. $38. 3 time a yr Longman Group Ltd, Journals Division, 43–45 Annandale St, Edinburgh, EH7 4AT, Scotland

The Washington Monthly. $20. 11 times a yr 1611 Connecticut Ave, NW, Washington, D.C. 20009

The Western Political Quarterly. $20. q D. W. Hanson, Editor, University of Utah, Salt Lake City, Utah 84112

World Marxist Review; Problems of Peace and Socialism. $7.50. m. Progress Subscription Service, 71 Bathurst St, Toronto, Ont. M5V 2P6

World Politics: a Quarterly Journal of International Relations. $22.50. q Princeton University Press, Princeton, N.J. 08540

The World Today. $27. m Oxford University Press, Press Rd, Neasden, London, NW10 0DD, England

2. *Sociological Abstracts* is an index that describes briefly every research article within twenty-four major information areas: methodology and research technology; sociology-history and theory; social psychology; group interactions; culture and social structure; complex organizations (management); social change and economic development; mass phenomena; political interactions; social differentiation; rural sociology and agricultural economics; urban structures and ecology; sociology of the arts; sociology of education; sociology of religion; social control; sociology of science; demography and human biology; the family and socialization; sociology of health and medicine; social problems and social welfare; sociology of knowledge; community development; planning, forecasting, and speculation.

It is indexed by subject and by author. A cumulative index for each volume is published as the last (eighth) issue of the year and includes a table of contents, a subject index, a periodical index, a monograph index, an author index, and a list of abbreviations. Abstracts of the papers of the annual meetings of the American Sociological Association are published annually as a supplement and includes a table of contents, abstracts, and an author index.

Sociological Abstracts has been published since 1952 and is especially valuable after an article has been identified as of interest to the researcher. The abstract conveys the findings and enables the researcher to decide whether the original article has significance for the work pursued. Eight issues are published each year.

3. *Social Sciences Citation Index* (SSCI) is a calendar-year index begun in 1966 that continues currently. The items covered in SSCI are taken from over a thousand of the world's most important social science journals in the following disciplines: anthropology, archaeology, area studies, business and finance, communication, community health, criminology and penology, demography, economics, educational research, ethnic group studies, geography, history, information and library sciences, international relations, law, linguistics, management, marketing, philosophy, political science, psychiatry, psychology, sociology, statistics, and urban planning and development.

Undertaking a Search in the SSCI. Using the *Social Sciences Citation Index* is a relatively simple affair. In a citation index the subject of a search is symbolized by the starting reference rather than by a word or subject heading. Consequently, searching is independent of special nomenclatures or artificial languages. The searcher starts with a reference or an author he has identified through a footnote, book, encyclopedia, or conventional word or subject index. He then enters the "Citation Index" section of the *Social Sciences Citation Index* and searches for that particular author's name. When he locates the author's name, he checks to see which of several possible references best fits his particular interest. Under the year, journal, volume, and page number of the selected reference, he then looks to see who has currently cited this work. After noting the bibliographic citations of authors who are citing the work, the searcher then turns to the "Source Index" section and obtains complege bibliographic data for the works he has found.

The fundamental question one can answer quickly through the SSCI is, Where and by whom has this paper been cited in the literature? The SSCI is also used by scientists to determine whether their work has been applied or criticized by others. It can facilitate feedback in the communication cycle. Any author may choose to ignore citations to his own work and still use the index to retrieve publications that cite works by other social scientists. The SSCI can be used to identify researchers currently working on special problems or to determine whether a paper has been cited, whether there has been a review of a subject, or whether a concept has been applied, a theory confirmed, or a method improved. Because indications of corrections are published in the SSCI, it is also useful as an aid in following particular articles. Only the user's imagination limits the extent to which the SSCI can be a useful tool for the scientist and librarian. Among the many questions that the SSCI can answer are these:

Has this paper been cited?
Has there been a review on this subject?
Has this theory been confirmed?
Has this work been extended?
Has this method been improved?
Has this suggestion been tried?
Is this idea really original?
Was this "to be published" paper published, and where?
Where is the full paper for this preliminary communication?
Has this technical report been published in a journal?
Have subsequent errata and correction notes been published?
Where are the data for an introduction to this paper?

Where are the raw data for a review article on this subject?
Is there sufficient new information to warrant updating a chapter in a book?
What are the raw data for an analytical historical network diagram?
Who else is working in this field?
Are there data to delineate this field of study?
What are some potential new markets for this product?
Has this theory or concept been applied to a new field?
What published work originated from this organization?
Has this article been abstracted in primary journals?
What are all the current works in which this person is primary author?
What are all the current works in which this person is secondary author?
What other works has this person written?
Has this person's work been compiled?

Current Information about Published Work

4. *Current Contents in the Social Behavioral Sciences* is a weekly listing of the contents of journals and some books in the social and behavioral sciences. It also includes an index by first author and principal words in the titles of articles.

Related Indexed Areas of Interest to the Social Science Researcher.

5. *Psychological Abstracts* does for psychology what *Sociological Abstracts* does for the wider field of social science. Social scientists often work in similar areas. In *Psychological Abstracts* there are sixteen major content classifications including general psychology, psychometrics, experimental psychology (human and animal), physiological psychology, physiological intervention, communication systems, developmental psychology, social processes and social issues, experimental social psychology, personality, physical and psychological disorders, treatment and prevention, professional personnel and professional issues, educational psychology, and applied psychology. There is a subject index and an author index. This index service goes back to 1927.

6. *Resources in Education* is a monthly abstract journal published by the Educational Resources Information Center (ERIC) of the National Institute of Education (NIE). *Resources in Education* announces research reports and other nonjournal literature of interest to the educational community. These documents are cataloged, abstracted, and indexed by subject, author or investigator, and responsible institution.

Resources in Education started publication in November 1966 and can be purchased in single copies or on subscription from the Superintendent of Documents, U.S. Government Printing Office, Washington, D.C. 20402. Annual cumulative sets have been reprinted and can be obtained from Macmillan Information, 216R Brown Street, Riverside, N.J. 08075.

Macmillan Information also publishes *Current Index to Journals in Education* (CIJE), which indexes articles in over seven hundred journals. These journals represent the core of the periodical/serial literature in the field of education.

Individual monthly volumes and yearly cumulations of *Resources in Education* and *Current Index to Journals in Education* are available in many college and university libraries, as well as in some special libraries. Most of these libraries are open to the public for on-site reference, and many also have complete ERIC microfiche collections. *Resources in Education* is also available in the offices of many school systems at the state and local level. All routine searches for documentary material should begin with *Resources in Education.*

All of the indexes—the *Social Science Index, Sociological Abstracts, Social Sciences Citation Index, Psychological Abstracts,* and *Resources in Education*—are housed in almost all college libraries and in many larger public libraries. The same information is available in Computer Assisted Reference Services in major university libraries. These same reference data are also commonly on microfilm or microfiche in major libraries. Interlibrary loan from major universities makes everything available to the smallest college anywhere in the United States and to many parts of the world.

Computer Assisted Reference Service (CARS)

Many major libraries provide searches by computer of bibliographic citations. More than 400 university libraries in the United States are currently on-line. Topics best suited for CARS searches include the following:

1. Searches on topics so new or specialized that they may not appear as subject headings in printed indexes. *Examples:* cognitive mapping; splinter skills in children.
2. Searches that require the coordination of two or more separate concepts. *Example:* effect of parental divorce on children's self-concept.
3. Searches on topics for which there are so many synonyms that a manual search of a key-word-in-context index would take an extremely long time. *Example:* adolescents; teenagers; juveniles; youth; young adults; students.
4. Searches that are relatively narrow in scope and are likely to result in a fairly small number of citations. *Example:* PCBs in Indiana.

The advantages of such computer assisted search are many:

1. It is quick. CARS can often locate appropriate citations in minutes while you might have to spend several days going through printed indexes.
2. It is comprehensive. CARS can search several sets of sources, which is probably more than your time would allow you to do manually.
3. It is precisely focused. Printed indexes restrict the number of index terms more than a machine readable data base does. CARS gives you many additional access points to a given article.
4. It provides good copy. Your citations may be printed on-line during the search for immediate delivery or you can have them printed off-line (usually a cheaper option) to be mailed for delivery within 3 to 4 days. An average search will usually cost between $15 and $30 depending on the data base(s) used and the extent of the search, as well as the number of citations ordered.

Data bases are numerous. For a full list of them, see Martha E. Williams et al., eds., *Computer-Readable Data Bases: A Directory and Data Source Book* (Washington D.C.: American Society for Information Science, 1980). The most important for the social scientist include:

Sociological Abstracts
Social Scisearch

Psychological Abstracts
Population Bibliography
U.S. Political Science Documents
American Statistics Index (CIS, Inc.)
SSIE Current Research (Smithsonian Science Information)
CIS/Index (Congressional Information Services)
GPO Monthly Catalog (U.S. Government Printing Office)
ERIC*

Specialized Indexes of Interest to Social Science

Population Index attempts to cover the bibliography of demographic research for demographers. To this end, the editors scan as much as possible of the world literature and select some 2500 titles a year. These are presented in a scheme of topics, with titles translated into English and with annotations or indicative abstracts of varying length provided for the majority. The material indexed consists of publications in 20 Western and Slavic languages, as well as the maximum feasible coverage in Oriental languages. The index includes government documents, periodical articles, books, monographs, and pamphlets. Excluded are unpublished materials, maps and other graphics, and newspaper articles. Selection favors the citation of primary source material and substantive studies of primary data by analytical methods. *Population Index* is based in the offices of Population Research at Princeton University.

Population Bibliography (1966–present, 47,500 records, bimonthly updates; University of North Carolina Population Center, Chapel Hill) is the world's largest single computer data base covering monographs, journals, technical reports, government documents, conference proceedings, dissertations, and many unpublished reports on population. The bibliography is a principal source for information on abortion, demography, migration, family planning, fertility studies, and general areas of population research such as population policy and law, population education, and population research methodology.

The *International Population Census Bibliography: Revision and Update, 1945–1977,* compiled by Doreen S. Goyer (University of Texas, Austin), 1980, has over 13,000 citations of reports from population censuses taken from 1945 through 1977, almost as many publications in the past thirty-two years as there were in the over 200-year period preceding. No other reference work in the field duplicates exactly the scope of these publications. The *Revision and Update* is a reference tool to aid the researcher and guide the librarian through the maze of census publications. For the researcher it presents the results of a country's census production in a logical manner using familiar bibliographic descriptions. It tells where a copy of almost every item listed may be found in the United States for consultation in person or via interlibrary loan. On the surface it may seem to have many more

---

* ERIC was originally conceived in the U.S. Office of Education in the mid-1960s as a system of providing ready access to recent educational research and other education related literature. The ERIC Processing and Reference Facility is a centralized information processing facility serving Central ERIC and sixteen decentralized clearinghouses, each specializing in a branch of knowledge. For further information, write ERIC Processing and Reference Facility, 4833 Rugby Avenue, Suite 303, Bethesda, MD 20014. Telephone (301) 656–9723.

conveniences for the librarian; but if the librarian has control of the literature, the researcher reaps the benefits.

American Statistics Index is a comprehensive index of the statistical publications from more than 400 central or regional issuing agencies of the U.S. government. Statistical data include population and economic censuses, foreign trade data, Consumer Price Index reports, unemployment statistics, agricultural data, vital statistics, educational data, and much more. A computer data base covering the same material is available.

Statistical Reference Index is a new index offering information on state government publications, statistical studies by universities, independent research organizations, and business organizations and associations.

Microfilm—Microfiche—Microprint Services*

These services provide reproductions of books, newspapers, magazines, scientific journals, and doctoral dissertations. Because it is relatively cheap to acquire and reproduce, use of microfiche especially is growing rapidly. It "packs a lot of information" in an incredibly small space. Most librarians call it the media of the future—at least until the computer takes over all reference work. Today many journals are acquired in microfiche to save money and space.

Major newspapers are available generally on microfilm. Such newspapers include the *New York Times, Washington Post, Christian Science Monitor, Los Angeles Times, Manchester Guardian, London Times, Observer,* and *Chicago Tribune.*

Microprint was developed earlier than the other two services. It is a positive print, in contrast to the negative prints of microfilm and microfiche. It holds less data, is more expensive, and is more difficult to store.

What is significant for the research scholar is that major indexes like *Sociological Abstracts* are available on microfiche. This means a missing page or volume of the printed book need not delay the researcher; it is available with high reliability on microfiche. Interlibrary loan can fill your needs anywhere in the United States.

University Microfilms International makes available journal articles and issue reprints of nearly 10,000 magazines and journals, by article or issue and in single or multiple copies. All of the major journals in sociology and the social sciences generally can be obtained for a fee. Every periodical cited in the UMI catalog is available either in paper or microform (microfilm or microfiche). For further information contact the UMI Article Reprint Department, 300 North Zeeb Road, Ann Arbor, MI 48106. In England the address is 18 Bedford Row, London WCIR4EJ.

---

* For a full list of available microforms, see *Microforms in Print, Incorporating International Microforms in Print.* This is an annual publication listing author, subject, prices, type of microform, and publisher. Available from Microform Review Inc., 520 Riverside Avenue, Westport, CT 06880. Johnson Associates has complete sets of 80 sociological journals available in microfiche; if not in your library, they may be purchased by set or volume. For further information write for the catalog *A Selection of Journals in Sociology Available in Microfiche* to: JAI Press, Inc., 165 W. Putnam Avenue, Greenwich, CT 06830.

Online Computer Library Center (OCLC) operates a computer network used by more than 2400 libraries in the United States and Canada, of which over 300 are U.S. federal libraries. Founded in 1967 as the Ohio College Library Center, it has grown rapidly into an international center for library automation. To reflect its broadened geographic scope, the name was changed in 1977 to OCLC, Inc., the acronym by which it had already become known throughout the world. More than 3800 remote computer terminals in the network are linked to OCLC's computer center in Dublin, Ohio. Libraries use the OCLC system to catalog books, order custom-printed catalog cards, maintain location information on library materials, and arrange for interlibrary lending of materials. The files contain more than 6 million records of books and other library materials such as U.S. government documents.

You can use a terminal to check bibliographic information (author, title, etc); find out whether your library owns the item; locate items in other libraries. Most college and university libraries make no charge for these services. This is the Super Card Catalog of the future, operating now.

2.3 DESCRIPTION OF IMPORTANT DOCUMENTARY RESOURCES AVAILABLE IN THE LIBRARY*

Statistical Sourcebooks

The social science researcher commonly uses reference books to assist him. Among the most useful are:

U.S. Bureau of the Census. *Statistical Abstract of the United States, 1981.* 102d ed. Washington, D.C.: U.S. Government Printing Office, 1981.

> Arranged in 33 sections: population; vital statistics, health, and nutrition; immigration and naturalization; education; law enforcement, federal courts, and prisons; area, geography, and climate; public lands, parks, recreation, and travel; labor force, employment, and earnings; national defense and veterans affairs; social insurance and welfare services; income, expenditures, and wealth; prices; elections; federal government finances and employment; state and local government finances and employment; banking, finance, and insurance; business enterprise; communications; power; science; transportation—land; transportation—air and water; agriculture—farms, land, and finances; agriculture—production, marketing, and trade; forests and forest products; fisheries, mining and mineral products; construction and housing; manufactures; distribution and services; foreign commerce and aid; outlying areas under the jurisdiction of the United States; comparative international statistics. Three appendixes. Index of names and subjects. Clothbound.

U.S. Census of Population by States. Washington, D.C.: U.S. Government Printing Office, 1981.

> Contains the following information for most urban places of 2500 or more: size of population by sex; major occupational groups by sex; income for stated year of total families and unrelated individuals; major industry groups by sex; color of population by sex; age of population by sex; years of school completed; marital status of males and females, fourteen years and above; country of birth of foreign born white (a decennial publication).

* This guide was originally assembled by John Pease, University of Maryland; additions have been made in revised editions by the author with much assistance by Herman Loether.

U.S. Bureau of the Census. *Historical Statistics of the United States: Colonial Times to 1970.* Washington, D.C.: U.S. Government Printing Office, 1975.

Historical data on population; vital statistics and health and medical care; migration; labor; prices and price indexes; national income and wealth; consumer income and expenditures; social statistics; land, water, and climate; agriculture; forestry and fisheries; minerals; construction and housing; manufactures; transportation; communication; power; distribution and services; foreign trade and other international transactions; business enterprise; productivity and technological development; banking and finance; government; colonial statistics. Index of names and subjects. Clothbound.

City Directories

Often useful in giving a wide range of information about industries and social organizations of the community. Contains alphabetical lists of persons and typically lists occupation and address of each adult.

The County and City Data Book. Washington, D.C.: U.S. Government Printing Office.

Lists numerous tables for each county and cities of 25,000 or more. Contains such tables as labor force, income, elections, banking and finance, business enterprises, and education.

A Comparative Atlas of America's Great Cities by John S. Adams and Ronald Abler. Minneapolis: University of Minnesota Press, 1977.

A comparative analysis of the nation's twenty largest cities.

The Municipal Year Book. Chicago: International City Managers' Association. Issued yearly.

Authoritative reference book on municipal governments. Facts available about the role of city governments including education, housing, welfare, and health make it possible to compare any city with other cities on hundreds of items.
    For specialized purposes consult:
U.S. Census of Manufacturers, Area Statistics
U.S. Census of Population, Census Tract Bulletin
Poor's Register of Directors and Executives
Rand McNally's International Bankers' Directory
Moody's Industrial Manual
Editor and Publisher Market Guide
Sales Management, Survey of Buying Power
Fortune Magazine Directory of 500 Largest Corporations
The Economic Almanac
Labor Fact Book
Directory of National and International Labor Unions in the United States
*Who's Who in America, Who's Who in the East, Who's Who in the Midwest, Who's
    Who in the South and Southwest, Who's Who on the Pacific Coast*
Directory of Scholars, Social and Behavioral Sciences
Who's Who in Commerce and Industry
Who's Who in Labor

America's Governments: A Fact Book on Census Data on the Organization, Finances, and Employment of Federal, State, and Local Governments. Compiled by Richard P. Nathan and Mary M. Nathan. New York: Wiley, 1979.

Contains data compiled from U.S. Bureau of Census Documents that describe the form, functions, and finances of the more than 80,000 governments of the United States. Text, tables, and charts enable the researcher to find out how a particular large government is organized and financed and how its major characteristics compare to other governments in the nation.

World Handbook of Political and Social Indicators by Bruce M. Russett, Haywood R. Alker, Jr., Karl W. Deutsch, and Harold D. Lasswell. New Haven: Yale University Press, 1964. Revised 2nd ed. by Charles Lewis Taylor and Michael C. Hudson, Yale University Press, 1972.

An extensive compilation of 75 variables for 133 states and colonies based on indices covering human resources, government and politics, communication, wealth, health, education, family and social relations, distributions of wealth and income, and religion. A matrix of intercorrelation is presented for the 75 variables and an analysis of trends and patterns is presented showing how the data can be used to investigate a wide variety of political and social questions.

UNESCO STATISTICAL Yearbook, 1981 UNIPUB, Box 433, Murray Hill Station, New York, NY 10016.

Topics covered world-wide include:

Population: Tables outline population by area and density from 1960 through 1976, and estimate major areas from 1970–2000.

Education: Summary tables for all levels of education are cited. Public expenditure on education is given at the current market prices and by level of education.

Science and technology: Manpower is inventoried by research and experimental development. Expenditures in the field are totaled.

Libraries: Summarizes libraries and their holdings by category of library, collections, borrowers, works loaned-out, current expenditures, personnel.

Publishing: Book production is delineated by number of titles published, language, number of copies, subject groups, translations, and authors. Totals of newspapers and other periodicals, paper production, and consumption are aggregated.

Media: Seating capacity and annual attendance at cinema is given. Radio/TV tables provide statistical information on transmitters, receivers, and programs.

Basic Statistical References for Education: Elementary, Secondary, and Adult Education; American and World Universities

Standard Education Almanac. 1980–81. Chicago: Marquis Academic Media.

Compiled from latest government and private statistics, this unique almanac provides the most complete coverage of elementary, secondary, and adult education in the United States today. Completely updated, this edition includes statistical information ranging from historical to current, plus projection, in some cases, through the year 2000. A substantial body of information on current trends is presented through articles, reports, and evaluative studies.

For coverage of Special Education and Adult Education, see Marquis *Yearbook of Special Education and Yearbook of Adult and Continuing Education.*

Yearbook of Higher Education, 1980. Chicago: Marquis Academic Media.

This directory provides both statistical and descriptive data about higher education. Part 1 provides essential information about more than 3400 two- and four-year colleges and universities in the United States and Canada. Part 2 provides updated statistics relating to such areas as enrollment, faculty/staff, income, expenditures, degrees, and the role of the federal government in higher education. Part 3 provides information on higher education association and accrediting bodies, statewide agencies for postsecondary education, ERIC clearinghouses, and more.

Other Marquis Books follow. *See* Reference Books Published by Marquis Academic Media.

International Handbook of Universities and other Institutions of Higher Education. 7th ed. Edited by H. M. R. Keyes and D. J. Aitkew. Paris, France: International Association of Universities, 1977.

Commonwealth Universities Yearbook, 1980. 4 vols. London, England: Association of Commonwealth Universities.

Directory of Educational Research Institutions (U1074). New York: UNESCO, 1980. 208 pp.

This first edition of the Directory has been compiled by UNESCO on the basis of feedback from a preliminary version circulated in late 1979 to the institutions concerned. It is intended to familiarize the educational researchers with such institutions and to serve as a link between institutions and researchers, helping to breach the isolation that too often prevents cross-fertilization between them. It contains over 550 entries and covers 117 regions and countries.

Reference books published by Marquis Academic Media: Chicago, Ill.

Annual Register of Grant Support
Consumer Protection Directory
Current Audiovisuals for Mental Health Education
Directory of Certified Psychiatrists and Neurologists
Directory of Publishing Opportunities
Directory of Registered Lobbyists and Lobbyist Legislation
Environmental Protection Directory
Family Factbook
Grantsmanship: Money and How to Get It
Mental Health in America: The Years of Crisis
NASA Factbook
NIH Factbook
NSF Factbook
The Selective Guide to Audiovisuals for Mental Health and Family Life Education
The Selective Guide to Publications for Mental Health and Family Life Education
Sourcebook of Equal Educational Opportunity
Sourcebook on Aging
Sourcebook on Food and Nutrition
Sourcebook on Mental Health
Standard Education Almanac
Standard Medical Almanac
Yearbook of Adult and Continuing Education
Yearbook of Higher Education
Yearbook of Special Education
Worldwide Directory of Computer Companies
Worldwide Directory of Federal Libraries

Abstracts

Abstracts of the Papers of the Annual Meetings of the American Sociological Association. Sociological Abstracts, Inc., 2315 Broadway, New York, NY 10024.

1961. Annually. Table of contents. Abstracts. Author index. Published as a supplement to *Sociological Abstracts.*

Catholic University of America Studies in Sociology Abstract Series. Catholic University of America Press, 620 Michigan Avenue, N.W., Washington, D.C. 20017.

1950. Irregularly. Abstracts of dissertations in sociology from the Catholic University of America.

Sociological Abstracts. Sociological Abstracts, Inc., 2315 Broadway, New York, NY 10024.

For full description refer back to Guide 2.2.

Communication Abstracts. Sage Publications, Inc., P.O. Box 776, Beverly Hills, CA 90213

1978. Quarterly. Each issue provides 250 in-depth abstracts of recent communication-related literature from publishers, research institutions, universities, and information services. Sixty professional journals are searched regularly.

Sociology of Education Abstracts. School of Education, University of Liverpool, 19 Abercromby Square, Liverpool 7, England.

1965. Quarterly. Education study areas index. Sociological study areas index. List of abstractors.

Almanacs

GENDELL, MURRAY, and ZETTERBERG, HANS L., eds. *A Sociological Almanac for the United States.* 2nd ed. New York: Scribner's, 1964. 109 pp.

Three essays—"The United States Summed Up by Browsing in a Sociological Almanac," "The Organization of a Sociological Almanac," and "How to Read a Table"— and 96 tables about American society organized in terms of 9 major topics: human resources; nonhuman resources; polity and order; economy and prosperity; science and knowledge; religion and sacredness; art and beauty; ethics and virtue; community—local and national. Paperbound.

BRITTAIN, J. MICHAEL, and ROBERTS, STEPHEN A. *Inventory of Information Resources and the Social Sciences.* Lexington, Mass.: Heath, 1975.

This book provides a detailed list of specialized information resources and services in the social sciences and related fields in Western Europe, Scandinavia, Canada, and Japan. The inventory covers query answering and referral centers, bibliography sources, and ongoing research into information systems. For each resource listed, details are given of the full name and address, range of subjects covered and information handled, availability of services, and relevant changes. Comprehensive title, subject, and geographical indexes are provided; these, together with headings in the text and the editorial introduction, are given in French and English.

Bibliographies

International Bibliography of the Social Sciences—Sociology. Aldine Publishing Co., Saw Mill River Road, Hawthorne, N.Y. 10532

1952–54, vols. 1–4 published in Current Sociology; 1955–59, vols. 5–9 published as *International Bibliography of Sociology, 1960.* Annually. List of periodicals consulted. Classification scheme. Bibliography. Author index. Subject index.

Dictionaries and Glossaries

BOGARDUS, EMORY S. "Selected Sociological Concepts for Beginning Students in Sociology." *Sociology and Social Research* 44 (January–February 1960): 200–208.

A brief definition of and discussion about 52 sociological concepts recommended to beginning sociology students.

FAIRCHILD, HENRY PRATT, ed. *Dictionary of Sociology.* New Students Outline Series. Paterson, N.J.: Littlefield, Adams, 1961. 350 pp.

This is a reprint, unchanged, of the original edition that appeared in 1944. Paperbound.

GOULD, JULIUS, and KOLB, WILLIAM L., eds. *A Dictionary of Social Science.* New York: Free Press, 1964. 777 pp.

Each entry outlines a brief history of usage and discusses the variations in current usage. Foreword by the Secretariat of UNESCO. Clothbound.

MIHANOVICH, CLEMENT S.; MCNAMARA, ROBERT J.; and TOME, WILLIAM N., eds. *Glossary of Sociological Terms.* Milwaukee, Wisc.: Bruce, 1957. 40 pp.
MITCHELL, G. DUNCAN, ed. *A Dictionary of Sociology.* Hawthorne, N.Y.: Aldine, 1968. 232 pp.

Especially prepared to introduce students to the language of the discipline.

MITCHELL, G. DUNCAN, ed. *A New Dictionary of the Social Sciences.* Hawthorne, N.Y.: Aldine, 1979.

Updated and expanded edition of above to cover all social sciences.

READING, HUGH F., *A Dictionary of the Social Sciences.* Boston: Routledge and Kegan Paul, 1977.

Designed for students of the social sciences, public administration, social administration, and social work, this dictionary will also be useful to those who work in specialized agencies and international organizations. The dictionary defines over 7500 terms.

THEODORSON, GEORGE A., ed. *Modern Dictionary of Sociology.* New York: Crowell, 1969.

Encyclopedias

SELIGMAN, EDWIN R. A., and JOHNSON, ALVIN, eds. *Encyclopedia of the Social Sciences.* New York: Macmillan, 1930–35. 15 vols. (now issued in an 8-vol. set).

Volume 1, in addition to regular articles, includes 23 essays in two introductory sections: "The Development of Social Thought and Institutions" and "The Social Sciences as Disciplines." Volume 15, in addition to regular articles, includes a complete index.

SILLS, DAVID L., ed. Foreword by Alvin Johnson. *International Encyclopedia of the Social Sciences.* New York: Macmillan and Free Press, 1968. 17 vols.

Volume 17 is a complete index. Comprehensive, thorough, authoritative. Succinct information on all important subjects in one source.

Guides to the Literature

BLAU, PETER M., and MOORE, JOAN W. "Sociology." In *A Reader's Guide to the Social Sciences,* edited by Bert F. Hoselitz. Glencoe, Ill.: Free Press, 1959; rev., 1975. Pp. 158–87.

Arranged in two major sections. The first section, "The Development of Sociology," includes early social philosophy, the separation of state and society, inevitable evolutionary forces, concern with social reform, history and sociology, the scientific study of social facts, implications, and reactions. The second section, "Contemporary Sociological Literature in Selected Areas," includes social theory, interviewing surveys, social psychology, demography and human ecology, social differentiation in community and nation, formal and informal organization.

BOTTOMORE, T. B. *Sociology: A Guide to Problems and Literature.* 2nd ed. New York: Pantheon, 1971.

LEWIS, PETER R. "Sociology." In *The Literature of the Social Sciences: An Introductory Survey and Guide.* London: Library Association, 1960. Chap. 10.

Arranged in five parts; bibliographies, guides, and reference books; sociological theory; sources on social conditions; social services; libraries and library problems.

LU, JOSEPH K. *U.S. Government Publications in the Social Sciences: An Annotated Guide.* Beverly Hills, Calif.: Sage, 1975.

LIBRARY OF CONGRESS, *A Dictionary of Information Resources in the United States: Social Sciences.* Washington, D.C.: U.S. Government Printing Office, 1973.

MUKHERJEE, A. K. "Sociology, Social Psychology, and Allied Topics." In *Annotated Guide to Reference Materials in the Human Sciences.* London: Asia Publishing House, 1962. Pp. 177–256.

Chapter 4 is arranged in 8 parts: dictionary, encyclopedia, yearbook, directory, handbook, bibliography, abstract and index, historical material. Chapter 5 covers Specialized Journals. Chapter 6 is arranged in 16 parts: basic source material and standard treatise—sociology, rural and urban sociology, social change, social problems, family and kinship, social survey and methodology, social case work, race problems, social psychology, culture and personality, personality study, ethno-psychology, somat-psychology, author index, subject index.

UNESCO study. *Main Trends of Research in the Social and Human Sciences.* Pt. 1. *The Social Sciences.* New York: Mouton, 1980.

An examination of the present state as well as the perspectives for development of various social science disciplines and inter- and multidisciplinary dimensions of research in these fields.

WHITE, CARL M., and Associates. *Sources of Information in the Social Sciences, A Guide to the Literature.* 2nd ed. Chicago: American Library Association, 1973.

ZETTERBERG, HANS L. "Sociology." In *Sources of Information in the Social Sciences: A Guide to the Literature,* edited by Carl M. White with an annotated bibliography by Thompson M. Little and Carl M. White. Totowa, N.J.: Bedminster Press, 1964. Pp. 183–228.

Zetterberg's essay is arranged in 20 parts, organized under 4 major headings: general orientation, sociological theory, topics of sociology, methods of sociology. Little and White's bibliography is organized under the following 14 headings: guides to the literature; reviews of the literature; abstracts and digests; bibliographies—current; bibliographies—retrospective; dictionaries; encyclopedias and encyclopedic sets; directories and biographical information; atlases and pictorial works; handbooks, manuals, compendia; yearbooks; statistical sources; sources of scholarly contributions; sources of unpublished information.

Handbooks, Sourcebooks, and Reviews

BART, PAULINE, and FRANKEL, LINDA. *The Student Sociologist's Handbook.* Morristown, N.J.: General Learning Press, 1971; 2nd ed. 1975.

BLUMER, HERBERT, ed. "Special Semicentennial Issue." *American Journal of Sociology* 50 (May 1945): 421–548.

An editorial foreword and 14 articles especially prepared for this issue and arranged in 4 parts: developments in the last fifty years of sociology in the United States, the proximate future of American sociology, trends in sociology.

CHRISTENSEN, HAROLD T., ed. *Handbook of Marriage and the Family.* Chicago: Rand McNally, 1964.

DUIGNAN, PETER, and RABUSHKA, ALVIN, eds. *The United States in the 1980s.* Stanford, Calif.: Hoover Institution Press, 1980.

An exhaustive compilation of hard facts and tough opinions, this definitive sourcebook for the 1980s covers the widest possible range of domestic and foreign issues.

FARIS, ROBERT E. L., ed. *Handbook of Modern Sociology.* Chicago: Rand McNally, 1964. 1096 pp.

A collection of 27 articles written especially for this volume and aimed at summarizing "all major growing research areas of modern sociology." Each article includes an extensive bibliography. Index of names. Index of subjects. Clothbound.

GOSLIN, DAVID A., ed. *Handbook of Socialization Theory and Research.* Chicago: Rand McNally, 1969.

GOULDNER, ALVIN, and MILLER, S. M., eds. *Applied Sociology: Opportunities and Prospects.* Glencoe. Ill.: Free Press, 1964.

Experts describe application of sociology to numerous fields of activity.

HANDY, ROLLO, and KURTZ, PAUL. "Sociology." In *A Current Appraisal of the Behavioral Sciences.* Great Barrington, Mass.: Behavioral Research Council, 1964. Pp. 25–34.

Arranged under 9 headings: working specification of the field; other specifications of the field; schools, methods, techniques; results achieved; contemporary controversy; problems of terminology; comment and evaluation; selected bibliographies; germane journals.

HARE, A. PAUL. *Handbook of Small Group Research.* 2nd ed. New York: Free Press, 1976.

HAUSER, PHILIP M., ed. *Handbook for Social Research in Urban Areas.* Paris: UNESCO, 1964.

HOSELITZ, BERT F., ed. *A Readers Guide to the Social Sciences.* Rev. ed. New York: Free Press, 1975.

General introduction and guide to the literature of the social sciences. Covers historical development of sociology, psychology, anthropology, geography, and economics with appraisals of the classics in the field, systematic review of current output, and critical comments on present trends and directions. Bibliography.

JANOWITZ, MORRIS. *The Last Half-Century: Societal Change and Politics in America.* Chicago: University of Chicago Press, 1978.

Comprehensive systematic analysis of the major trends in American society during the past fifty years.

LAZARSFELD, PAUL F.; SEWELL, WILLIAM H.; and WILENSKY, HAROLD L., eds. *The Uses of Sociology.* New York: Basic Books, 1967. 913 pp.

Introduction and 31 articles written especially for this volume and arranged in 6 parts: sociological perspectives, the uses of sociology in the professions, the uses of sociology in establishments, social problems and formal planning, rapid social change, institutional problems in applied sociology. Index of names. Index of subjects. Clothbound.

LINDZEY, GARDNER, and ARONSON, ELLIOT, eds. *Handbook of Social Psychology.*
5 vols. Reading, Mass.: Addison-Wesley, 1968–70.
LIPSET, SEYMOUR MARTIN, and SMELSER, NEIL J., eds. *Sociology, the Progress of
a Decade: A Collection of Articles.* Englewood Cliffs, N.J.: Prentice-Hall, 1961. 646
pp.

Introduction and 64 articles arranged in 4 parts: the discipline of sociology; the major
boundaries of social systems; the production and allocation of wealth, power, and
prestige; the balance between stability and change in society. Clothbound.

MARCH, JAMES G., ed. *Handbook of Organizations.* Chicago: Rand McNally, 1965.
MCINNIS, RAYMOND G., and SCOTT, JAMES W. *Social Science Research Handbook.*
New York: Barnes and Noble, 1974.
MADGE, JOHN. *The Origins of Scientific Sociology.* New York: Free Press of Glencoe,
1962.

A review of selected work by outstanding sociologists who have contributed to the
building of a scientific sociology.

MERTON, ROBERT K.; BROOM, LEONARD; COTTRELL, LEONARD S., JR., eds. *Sociology Today: Problems and Prospects.* New York: Basic Books, 1959. 658 pp.

Introduction and 25 articles written especially for this volume and arranged in 5
parts: problems in sociological theory and methodology, problems in the sociology
of institutions, the group and the person, problems in demographic and social structure,
selected applications of sociology. Index of names and subjects. Clothbound. Also
available in a two-volume paperbound set from Harper & Row of New York.

————, RILEY, MATILDA WHITE, eds. *Sociological Tradition from Generation to
Generation: Glimpses into the American Experience.* Norwood, N.J.: Ablex, 1980.
MITCHELL, G. DUNCAN. *A Hundred Years of Sociology.* Chicago: Aldine, 1968.

A concise history of the major ideas, figures, and schools of sociological thought.

MOHAN, RAJ P., and MARTINALE, DOW. *Handbook of Contemporary Developments
in World Sociology.* Westport, Conn.: Greenwood Press, 1975.

This collection brings together a number of notable sociologists, all of whom were
asked to examine how sociology, a transnational discipline, has been and continues
to be shaped by the individual nation-states of the world. Differences in methodology,
viewpoint, and emphasis are apparent throughout the work. The split in French sociology between a global, humanistic sociology and a historical microsociology is explored,
as is the impact of an outmoded university system, religion, and regional divisions
on the development of sociology in Italy. The complex and often contradictory effects
of American sociological thought on the Western Hemisphere and Russian thought
on Eastern Europe are detailed. The receptivity of Japan and Australia to Western
empirical methods is analyzed.

OLSON, DAVID H., ed. *Inventory of Marriage and Family Literature.* 7 vols. Beverly
Hills, Calif.: Sage, 1977–81.

Systematic, comprehensive listing of current literature.

PARSONS, TALCOTT, ed. *American Sociology: Perspective, Problems, Methods.* New
York: Basic Books, 1968. 368 pp.

Introduction and 24 essays especially prepared for this volume and arranged in 6
parts and a conclusion: components of social systems; methods of investigation; functional subsystems; sociology of culture; strain, deviance, and social control; total societies and their change; conclusion. Index of names of subjects. Clothbound.

SHILS, EDWARD A. *The Calling of Sociology and Other Essays on the Pursuit of Learning.* Chicago: University of Chicago Press, 1980.
SHORT, JAMES F., JR., ed. *The State of Sociology: Problems and Prospects.* Beverly Hills: Sage, 1981.

Assessments of accomplishments in methodology, theory, empirical knowledge, and application of sociology over the past twenty-five years.

STOGDILL, RALPH M. *Handbook of Leadership, Theory, and Research.* New York: Free Press, 1974.
WAKEFIELD WASHINGTON ASSOCIATES. *Family Research: A Source Book, Analysis, and Guide to Federal Funding.* Westport, Conn.: Greenwood Press, 1980.

GUIDES FOR SELECTION AND CONSTRUCTION OF QUESTIONNAIRES AS UTILIZED IN FIELD RESEARCH

2.4

The mail questionnaire is a list of questions for information or opinion that is mailed to potential respondents who have been chosen in some designated manner. The respondents are asked to complete the questionnaire and return it by mail.

This means of gathering information is very popular because it promises to secure data at a minimum of time and expense. The popularity of the method is often defeating because many respondents are overburdened by the number of questionnaires that reach them. In the competition for their time, respondents increasingly examine the purpose of the study, the sponsorship, the utility of findings to them, the time required to fill out the questionnaire, the clarity and readability of the type, and perhaps the quality of the paper.

Decision-making criteria: Every researcher who chooses the mail questionnaire should consider its value in a highly competitive environment in which the majority of respondents will probably not complete and return the questionnaire. The researcher should examine carefully the advantages and disadvantages described below. The disadvantages are shown first to emphasize their importance. If the advantages override these disadvantages, and if the method fits the study, then the questionnaire is appropriate. A guide to questionnaire construction follows that should prove useful. Also note the guide to techniques for increasing percentage of returns.

Disadvantages of the Mail Questionnaire*

MAJOR WEAKNESSES:

1. Problem of nonreturns.
   a. Response rates to mail questionnaires usually do not exceed 50 percent when conducted by private and relatively unskilled persons.
   b. Intensive follow-up efforts are required to increase returns.
2. Those who answer the questionnaire may differ significantly from the nonrespondents, thereby biasing the sample.

---

* Cf. David Wallace, "A Case For—and Against—Mail Questionnaires," *Public Opinion Quarterly* 18 (1954): 40–52.

    a. Nonrespondents become a collection about whom virtually nothing is known.

    b. Special efforts must be made (registered letter, telephone calls, personal interviews, etc.), to assess how nonrespondents compare with respondents.

    c. The most thorough of follow-up efforts bring the researcher up against persons who cannot be located, who may be inaccessible, or unreachable. The residual group of "no response" or "refuse to answer" can be considerable.

Advantages of Mail Questionnaire

1. Permits wide coverage for minimum expense both in money and effort.

2. Affords wider geographic contact.

3. Reaches people who are difficult to locate and interview.

4. Greater coverage may yield greater validity through larger and more representative samples.

5. Permits more considered answers.

6. More adequate in situations in which the respondent has to check information.

7. More adequate in situations in which group consultations would give more valid information.

8. Greater uniformity in the manner in which questions are posed.

9. Gives respondent a sense of privacy.

10. Affords a simple means of continual reporting over time.

11. Lessens interviewer effect.

Guide to Questionnaire Construction*

A. Reclarify the relation of the method to problem and hypotheses. Obtain a thorough grasp of the area to be studied and a clear understanding of the objectives of the study and the nature of the data needed.

    In a *descriptive* inquiry the investigator is seeking to estimate as precisely and comprehensively as possible a problem area; in an *explanatory* inquiry of a theoretical type the investigator is seeking to test some particular hypothesis about the determinants of a dependent variable or factor. In either type, economy and efficiency are important criteria. The rule is: Gather the data you need but not more than is needed. Know how you will use and analyze your data. Make your dummy tables now if possible and challenge their adequacy for describing the possible distributions or relationships that are related to your problem or hypotheses.

B. Formulate questions.

    1. Keep the language pitched to the level of the respondent.

        Interviews given only to specialized respondents can use the terminology with which they are familiar. But interviews given to the general public must use language with more common usage.

    2. Try to pick words that have the same meaning for everyone.

        A questionnaire involving American and British respondents might ask, "How often do you have tea?" To the American, tea would refer to a drink. To the British, tea would refer to a light meal.

---

* Cf. Paul F. Lazarsfeld, *Qualitative Analysis: Historical and Critical Essays* (Boston: Allyn & Bacon, 1972), chap. 8.; See also Don A. Dillman, "Writing Questions," chap. 3 in *Mail and Telephone Surveys* (New York: Wiley Interscience, 1978).

3. Avoid long questions.

    When questions become long they often become ambiguous and confusing.

4. Do not a priori assume that your respondent possesses *factual* information or firsthand opinions.

    A mother may be able to report what books her child reads, but a child himself must be questioned to know how he feels about reading those books.

5. Establish the frame of reference you have in mind.

    Don't ask: How many magazines do you read?

    Ask: Which magazines do you read?

6. In forming a question, either suggest all possible alternatives to the respondent or don't suggest any.

    Don't ask: Do you think the husband should help with dressing and feeding the small children when he's home?

    Ask: Do you think the husband should help with dressing and feeding the small children when he's home, or do you think it's the wife's job in any case?

    Or: Who should dress and feed the children when the husband is home?

7. Protect your respondent's ego.

    Don't ask: Do you know the name of the chief justice of the Supreme Court?

    Ask: Do you happen to know the name of the chief justice of the Supreme Court?

8. If you're after unpleasant orientations, give your respondent a chance to express positive feelings first so that he or she is not put in an unfavorable light.

    Ask: What do you like about X?

    Then: What don't you like about X?

9. Decide whether you need a direct question, an indirect question, or an indirect followed by a direct question.

    Direct: Do you ever steal on the job?

    Indirect: Do you know of anyone ever stealing on the job?

    Combination: Do you know of anyone ever stealing on the job? Have you ever taken anything from the job?

10. Decide whether the question should be open or closed.

    Open: It is believed that some people in this community have too much power. Do you think this is true? Who are they?

    Closed: It is believed that some people in this community have too much power. Is this statement ☐ True. ☐ False. ☐ Don't know. If true, who are they? ☐ Negroes. ☐ Jews. ☐ Poles. ☐ Italians. ☐ _____ .

11. Decide whether general or specific questions are needed.

    It may be enough to ask: How well did you like the book?

    It may be preferable to also ask: Have you recommended the book to anyone else?

12. Avoid ambiguous wording.

    Don't ask: Do you usually work alone?

    Ask: ☐ No, I never work alone. ☐ Yes, I work alone less than half the time. ☐ Yes, I work alone most of the time.

13. Avoid biased or leading questions.

    Don't ask: Did you exercise your right as an American citizen to vote in the last election?

    Ask: Did you vote in the last election?

14. Phrase questions so that they are not unnecessarily objectionable.

Instead of: Did you graduate from high school?

Ask: What is the highest grade in school you completed?

15. Decide whether a personal or impersonal question will obtain the better response.

Impersonal: Are working conditions satisfactory or not satisfactory where you work?

Personal: Are you satisfied or dissatisfied with working conditions in the plant where you work?

16. Questions should be limited to a single idea or a single reference.

Don't ask: Do you favor or oppose increased job security and the guaranteed annual wage?

Ask: Do you favor or oppose increased job security?

And: Do you favor or oppose the guaranteed annual wage?

C. Organize the questionnaire.

1. Start with easy questions that the respondent will enjoy answering.

Don't start with age, occupation, or marital status.

Ask questions to arouse interest.

2. Don't condition answers to subsequent questions by preceding ones.

a. Go from the general to the specific.

How do you think this country is getting along in its relations with other countries?

How do you think we are doing in our relations with Russia?

b. Go from the easy to the difficult.

3. Use the sequence of questions to protect the respondent's ego. Save the personal questions such as income for later.

4. Decide whether one or several questions will best obtain the information for a given objective.

5. With free-answer questions, it is sometimes helpful to have the questions in pairs, asking for the pros and cons of a particular issue.

6. Open-ended questions which require most thought and writing should be kept to a minimum. Generally, these should be placed at the end to assure that the closed questions will be answered.

7. The topics and questions should be arranged so that they make the most sense to the respondent. The aim is to secure a sequence that is natural and easy for the respondent.

D. Pretest the questionnaire.

1. Select a number of respondents representative of those you expect to survey and interview them. Encourage them to ask any questions that they have as they respond to your items. Watch for misunderstanding, ambiguity, and defensiveness. Ask them how they would restate a question that is difficult to understand or to answer.

2. Never omit pretesting!

E. Select paper and type carefully. The use of type-print can produce a mimeographed questionnaire on good paper that looks like a printed copy.

F. Consider how you can present the strongest possible sponsorship. The person, persons, or group that will support your efforts through a covering letter is important. Note the increase of 17 percent return reported in the technique guide for increasing percentage of returns.

G. Examine each of the techniques for increasing return of the questionnaire and decide which will maximize returns for you. See Guide 2.9.

Techniques for Increasing Percentage of Returns

Method	Possible increase of total % of returns	Optimal conditions
Follow-up*	50%	More than one follow-up may be needed. If possible, returns may be increased by using double postcards with the most important questions on follow-ups. The telephone can often be used effectively for follow-up. Researcher should find out if respondent needs another copy of the questionnaire (it may have been destroyed or misplaced). Sewell and Shaw report a 87.2% return on 9007 from parents of Wisconsin high school students using 3 waves of mailed questionnaires and final telephone interview. *American Sociological Review* 33 (April 1968): 193.
Sponsor	17%	John K. Norton found that people the respondent knew produced the best results. A state headquarters received the second best rate. Others following in order were: a lower-status person in a similar field, a publishing firm, a college professor or student, and a private association or foundation.
Length	22%	If a questionnaire is short, then the shorter the better. A double postcard should produce the best results. However, if the questionnaire is over 10 pages at the minimum, length may cease to be a factor. Sewell and Shaw used a double postcard in the study reported.
Introductory letter	7%	An altruistic appeal seems to have better results than the idea that the respondent may receive something good from it.
Type of questions	13%	Questionnaires asking for objective information receive the best rate, and questionnaires asking for subjective information receive the worst.

H. Observe the brief excerpt from a questionnaire. Note how open and closed questions are phrased.

Experiences of Researchers with the Mail Questionnaire: Guides 2.5, 2.6, 2.7, and 2.8

The records that follow were selected from a large universe of mail questionnaires. Guide 2.5 is a compilation of return rates from many different populations with different content in the questionnaire. This record shows the wide range of returns that may be expected. Guide 2.6 is a model of outcomes from a long questionnaire mailed to more than 18,000 college graduates from different colleges across the United States. This record shows how the problems of eligibility, location, accessibility, and acceptability diminish returns. Guide 2.7 is an analysis of returns from a study of top leaders on the East Coast of the United States. This compilation displays the importance of occupational type and indicates how the geocultural character of a city can diminish returns. Guide 2.8 is a summary of response rates based on 183 published studies that used a mail questionnaire. This guide displays the wide variation in response rate and highlights the successful use of follow-up mailings.

2.5   A RECORD OF RETURN RATES FROM MANY DIFFERENT MAIL QUESTIONNAIRES

Instructions for Use of Guide 2.5

This compilation is based on a selection of questionnaires to show the range of returns that follow a mailing of questionnaires. Note that there are populations representing the general public, adult women, and powerful eastern urban leaders from business, labor, government, religious, and civic and civil rights groups. These populations yield returns varying from 3 to 71 percent.

The populations following these are those of college and high school graduates; note that these yield a range of from 24 to 90 percent return. The succeeding populations are as various as (1) members of the American Sociological Association, (2) deans of professional schools in the United States (3) women cafeteria employees, and (4) women faculty members. Returns range from 24.5 to 65 percent.

2.6   A MODEL OF OUTCOMES FROM A LONG MAIL QUESTIONNAIRE

Instructions for Use of Guide 2.6

This guide reports on a study made in 1963 by Robert Calvert, Jr., of male liberal arts graduates from a wide selection of colleges and universities across the United States.* The years sampled are for graduates in 1948, 1953, and 1958. This means that fifteen, ten, and five years had elapsed since graduation for the respective classes. The questionnaire was long: twenty pages. The population consisted of highly educated persons. Two follow-up mailings were made.

This guide will alert the researcher to the difficulties of follow-up studies under the conditions of this model.

The questionnaire was prepared by the Survey Research Center of the University of California, whose director is Charles Y. Glock. The study was financed by the U.S. Office of Education and the Carnegie Foundation.

* Reprinted by permission of the Carroll Press, Cranston, R.I., from Robert Calvert, Jr., *Career Patterns of Liberal Arts Graduates,* rev. ed. Copyright © 1973. From tables 114 and 115, p. 214.

A Record of Return Rates from Many Different Mail Questionnaires

Population	Aim and date of questionnaire	Length	Number sent	Number returned	Percent returned	Number of follow-ups	Research agent
Statewide samples of general public in Arizona, Indiana, North Carolina, and Washington (see section 2.10 for details including published source)	To find views about living in communities of various sizes 1970-71-73	12 pages (8 pages in Indiana)	Wash. 4137; N. Car. 4470; Ariz. 2021; Ind. 7558	Wash. 3103; N. Car. 3116; Ariz. 1441; Ind. 5360	Wash. 75; N. Car. 69.7; Ariz. 71.3; Ind. 70.9	3 in all states	Independent researchers Don A. Dillman, Edwin H. Carpenter, James A. Christensen, and Ralph M. Brooks
Adult women who were given or wrote in for questionnaire; reached through N.Y. Chapter of NOW and ads in newspapers, magazines, and church bulletins	To study the sexual conduct of females 1972-73	5 pages (60 items)	100,000	3000	3	None	Independent researcher Shere Hite (published in *The Hite Report*)
Key and top leaders in urban affairs in Boston-Washington, D.C. region (see section 2.7 for details)	To find out how leaders functioned in solving urban problems and in working with other business, labor, government, religious, and civic leaders (1968-69) as well as with organizations	12 pages	200 key leaders and 200 top leaders	100 key leaders and 78 top leaders	50 for key leaders and 39 for top leaders	3 plus new appeal and another questionnaire	Delbert C. Miller *Power and Leadership in Bos-Wash Megalopolis*
High school students from 10 Illinois high schools 15 years after graduation	To discover achievements and problems in the transition to adulthood, especially sex differences in educational attainment and age at marriage: (1972)	Not known	Original (1957) sample of 8617	6498	75 (44 by mail, 31 by shorter telephone interview)	1 (telephone)	Margaret Mooney Marini, "The Transition to Adulthood: Sex Differentials in Educational Attainment and Age at Marriage," *American Sociological Review* 43 (August 1978).

Population	Aim and date of questionnaire	Length	Number sent	Number returned	Percent returned	Number of follow-ups	Research agent
June graduates from 135 colleges and universities; sample designed to be representative of June 1961 graduates receiving degrees from accredited colleges and universities	To discover intended career field and plans for graduate study; reactions to various aspects of college life (1961)	19 pages	42,209, of which 2231 subsequently declared ineligible	33,982 eligible returns	85	Not known	National Opinion Research Center; James A. Davis, study director (published as *Undergraduate Career Decisions*)
Liberal arts graduates of a national sample (see section 2.6 for details)	To survey activities of graduates. November 1963–June 1964	20 pages	17,449	10,877	62.3	2 mailings with copy of questionnaire	Survey Research Center, University of California at Berkeley; Charles Y. Glock, director
Graduates, arts and sciences, Miami University	To survey activity of the class of 1976 one year after graduation (1977); to survey activity of class of 1978 one year after graduation (1979)	1 page each	792 in 1977; 700 in 1978	572 in 1977; 532 in 1978	72 in 1977; 76 in 1978	None	Office of Dr. C. K. Williamson, dean of college of A & S, Miami University published in *Miami: Alumnus.* January 1980
Graduates, Miami University, Oxford, Ohio, 1893–1971	To secure information about employment and activities (1971)	3 pages	6158 (one to every sixth alumni in pool of 45,000)	2958	48	None	Douglas M. Wilson, director of Alumni Affairs, Miami University (published in *Miami University Alumni News.* September 1971)

Population	Purpose	Questionnaire	Number sent	Number returned	Percentage returned	Special notes	Source
Graduates, all campuses. Indiana University	Survey of present background and activities of class of 1970, ten years later	3 pages with covering letter from president	9200	2676	29.2 (no return postage)	None	Indiana University Alumni Association (published in university alumni association magazine, January 1980)
Short supplementary study of graduates of Indiana University	Survey of present background and activities of class of 1970, ten years later	1½ pages with letter from alumni secretary	9200	2172	23.6 (no return postage)	None	I. U. Alumni Association
Doctoral graduates, Indiana University	Survey of background and activities of class of 1970, ten years later	3 pages with letter from president	570	228	40 (no return postage)	None	I. U. Alumni Association
Graduates of DePauw University, 1975 and 1976	To secure information about employment, 1976 and 1977	1 page	407 (1975 class); 465 (1976 class)	367 (1975 class); 421 (1976 class)	90 (1975 class); 90 (1976 class)	None	President's Office, DePauw University, Greencastle, Indiana
Members of the American Sociological Association	To find out if respondents thought ASA should publish a non-technical journal; 1979	1 page	2000	489	24.5	None	ASA Committee on Publication (See *Footnotes* of ASA. October 1979)
Deans of professional schools in the United States	To secure a ranking of outstanding schools; 1977	3 pages	1180	621	53	Shortened questionnaire increased return to 76%	Peter M. Blau, Professor of Sociology, Columbia University; financed by NSE

Population	Aim and date of questionnaire	Length	Number sent	Number returned	Percent returned	Number of follow-ups	Research agent
Women employees of cafeterias in Indiana University dormitories	To secure information about satisfaction with work, personal life, and husband's attitudes; June 1977	2 pages	80 (handed a questionnaire to fill out during coffee break)	52	65	None	Susie Holly, independent journalist (published in *Indiana Daily Student*, June 17, 1977)
Women faculty and staff members in telephone directory of Indiana University	as above; June 1977	2 pages	145 (randomly chosen from populations of 921; mailed questionnaires through campus mailing system)	72	50	None	Holly, as above

In November 1963 the 20-page booklet was mailed to 18,004 liberal arts male graduates with a covering letter and a prepaid envelope. A second mailing was made in January 1964 and a third in March 1964 with a cutoff date of June 1964. Each mailing included a copy of the questionnaire and a prepaid envelope. The response to the mail questionnaire is shown in Table 1.

Table 1 *Response to Mail Questionnaire*

Outcome	Number	Percent
Returned, complete, and eligible	10,877	60.4
Returned, ineligible[a]	277	1.4
Unlocatable[b]	1,312	7.2
Inaccessible[c]	5	negligible
No response or refused to answer[d]	5,583	31.0
Total mailed	18,004	100.0

[a] *Ineligible:* A subject was considered ineligible if his returned questionnaire or letter from him or a relative indicated that he was not a male U.S. citizen or foreign citizen residing in the United States who graduated from one of the sample schools with a liberal arts major in 1948, 1953, or 1958.

[b] *Unlocatable:* A graduate was counted as unlocatable if questionnaires mailed to him were returned as undeliverable by the post office and no new address could be obtained from the post office or from his college or university.

[c] *Inaccessible:* A graduate was classified as inaccessible if he was locatable but unable to answer because of illness or a similar legitimate reason.

[d] *No response:* Residual group not meeting the criteria for classification in the above categories of the 5583 included here. Of the group, 161 wrote letters stating that they refused to answer or returned blank questionnaires.

All questionnaires were sent with a return request. When questionnaires were returned without a forwarding address, the college was contacted to ask for a more current address of the graduate or his parents. More than 3000 address corrections were obtained and an additional 1250 mailings were made.

A follow-up study was undertaken to gain additional information about the 5583 who did not respond and to ascertain how they differed from the respondents. A systematic random sample of 555 was drawn and various approaches taken to reach them. A registered letter was first mailed to each member of the sample asking for his completion of a brief questionnaire. Those not responding were next contacted by telephone if a telephone number could be obtained for them. At least three calls were made to each subject at his home or office before he was considered unreachable for the follow-up study. Subjects without known telephone numbers were mailed a second registered letter asking for their cooperation. The outcomes of these activities are presented in table 2.

The author concludes: "There is a group of non-respondents about whom virtually nothing is known. These are the graduates who proved totally unlocatable, either because their college had no address for them or because they were unreachable through their last known address. Such graduates comprised approximately 14 percent of all graduate of the cooperating institutions who might have been included in the survey. They must remain a potential and essentially unassessable bias in the results presented."

This study should alert the researcher to the persistent problems of (1)

Table 2. *Response to Follow-Up Study*

Outcome		N	%
Unlocatable (registered letter undeliverable)		47	8.5
Contacted by phone or mail		420	75.7
Eligible and completed follow-up questionnaire	360		64.9
Found ineligible	24		4.3
Refused to cooperate	36		6.5
Inaccessible (hospitalized, abroad for extended period or classified assignment, etc., as reported by person at last address)		17	3.0
Unreachable (registered letter unanswered, no telephone number available)		71	12.8
Total follow-up sample		555	100.0

getting the questionnaire to its desired destination (7.2 percent not locatable or accessible in this study); (2) no-response (31.0 percent); (3) ineligible respondents (1.4 percent); (4) the importance of conducting a special effort (registered letter, telephone calls, etc.) to assess how nonrespondents compare with respondents (note that 64.9 percent of the follow-up sample finally completed a questionnaire); (5) the almost impossible task of removing all bias of findings because of the difficulty of securing all respondents in the sample (14 percent in this study).

2.7 VARIABILITY OF RESPONSE RATE BY OCCUPATION AND CITY OF RESIDENCE FOR POWERFUL LEADERS AS SHOWN BY THE BOS-WASH MEGALOPOLIS LEADERSHIP STUDY

This study shows how wide variations in questionnaire returns are correlated with occupational group and city of residence. The returns in this study were secured by three mailings of a 12-page questionnaire. The first mailing was sent to all 200 key and 200 top leaders (April 11, 1969). A follow-up mailing 18 days later (April 29) went to those leaders who had not answered. A third mailing was made 15 days later (May 14). In each follow-up a short appeal for a return was attached to another copy of the questionnaire. The final record of returned questionnaires shows 100 returned by key leaders (50 percent) and 78 returned by top leaders (39 percent).

Key leaders were those judged by panels of experts as the most influential leaders in urban affairs in the Boston to Washington, D.C. region; top leaders were those judged as influential but not as much so as the key leaders.

The final returns are drawn from a population of leaders judged most important in Megalopolis and probably the busiest. The questionnaires reached persons who could not have been interviewed easily. All had offices at some central point, but many were likely to be away for various periods of time. Busy people can "sandwich" mail questionnaires into their schedules (probably when they answer their mail) when they cannot (or will not) yield valuable interview time. This was our experience after many attempts to conduct interviews with key leaders.

Table 1 shows a widely varying response based on occupational types of

Table 1. *Variability of Response Rate by Occupation and City of Residence*

	Questionnaire returns by occupational type and influence rating of leader			Questionnaire returns by northeastern city and influence type of leader	
	N = 200 Key	N = 200 Top		N = 200 Key	N = 200 Top
Religion	67%	47%	Baltimore	67%	73%
Business	51	27	Boston	67	27
Labor	51	51	Philadelphia	60	54
Civic	43	45	Washington, D.C.	37	43
Political-government	43	23	New York	37	20

Source: From Delbert C. Miller, *Leadership and Power in the BOS-WASH Megalopolis* (New York: Wiley, 1975, p. 380).

leaders, influence rating of leaders, and residence of respondent leaders. Note that highest returns come from *religious, business,* and *labor* leaders of key influence living in *Baltimore, Boston,* and *Philadelphia.* Lowest returns come from civic and political leaders of key and top influence living in Washington, D.C., and New York.

These findings should alert researchers to the disparity that may be expected based on occupation, influence, and place of residence. Of special significance is the impact of the names of all respondents appearing on the questionnaire. Key leaders responded to sociometric questions pertaining to 200 other key leaders named on the questionnaire. Top leaders saw the names of key leaders but not their own names. A reduction in response seems to have followed as a result of this difference. (It will be recalled that 50 percent of the key leaders returned the questionnaire, whereas only 39 percent of the top leaders did so.) A researcher should list *all* respondents on his questionnaire if this is feasible. This gives the respondent a feeling of identity with a given population.

SUMMARY OF RESPONSE RATES BASED ON A LARGE NUMBER OF MAIL QUESTIONNAIRES WITH A WIDE VARIETY OF STUDIES   *2.8*

Table 1. *Summary of Response Rates Based on Mail Questionnaires*

Percent response from	N	Mean	SD	Percentiles				
				5	25	Median	75	95
Initial mailing	183	48.1	19.9	18.6	30.1	47.4	62.1	82.4
Follow-up 1	58	19.9	7.7	7.5	14.0	19.5	25.6	31.6
Follow-up 2	40	11.9	6.2	3.0	7.8	10.7	15.5	24.5
Follow-up 3	25	10.0	5.1	2.8	6.8	8.1	14.3	19.3

Source: Based on the report of Thomas A. Heberlein and Robert Baumgartner, "Factors Affecting Response Rate to Mailed Questionnaires" *American Sociological Review* 43 (August 1978): 451. Permission to reprint granted by the American Sociological Association and the authors.

Note in order in table 1:

1. Response rates from 183 studies where *on the average* 48 percent of those who received one mailing of the questionnaire returned it. Examine the wide deviation in response from these 183 studies.

2. A follow-up mailing nets, *on the average,* nearly 20 percent of the initial sample as reported in 58 studies. Again observe the wide deviation reported.

3. Second ($N = 40$ studies) and third ($N = 25$ studies) follow-ups, *on the average,* yield about 12 and 10 percent returns respectively. There is again substantial variation in effectiveness, which makes simple generalizations difficult.

4. Not shown in the table are 31 studies that had four follow-up contacts, but the response rate for these studies was not significantly better than for three contacts (83.9 percent compared to 80.6 percent).

5. Finally, the following chart reports on 214 studies that utilized one or more follow-ups:

				Percentiles				
	N	Mean	*SD*	5	25	Median	75	95
Final response rate percent based on studies utilizing one or more follow-ups	214	60.6	24.3	21.2	40.9	60.8	82.9	96.6

2.9 TECHNIQUES FOR INCREASING PERCENTAGE OF QUESTIONNAIRE RETURNS

Method	Possible increase of total % of returns	Optimal conditions
Follow-up contacts 1. By mail	40% to 50%. Based on a large number of studies, *one follow-up* nets, on the average, 20% more responses. A *second* and *third follow-up*, on the average, yield about 12% and 10% higher return respectively.[a]	See sections 2.8 and 2.10, which show conclusively that follow-up mailings pay off. In the Calvert study, after a registered letter was mailed with the first questionnaire, the telephone was used if the questionnaire was not returned. Three calls were made to each subject at his home or office before he was considered unreachable for follow-up study (75.7% final return).
2. By telephone	Increase in returns depends on whether the telephone is used solely or as a supplement to mail follow-ups. As a supplement another 15% to 30% may be obtained.	Sewell and Shaw report a 87.2% return from a population of 9007 parents of Wisconsin high school students using 3 waves of mailed questionnaires and a final telephone interview (*American Sociological Review* 33 [April 1968]: 193). A 15-year follow-up of high school students gave a 44% return to a mailed questionnaire; there was a 31% increase with a telephone follow-up. (See M. M. Marini in section 2.5.)

Method	Possible increase of total % of returns	Optimal conditions
Type of population surveyed	Response varies with education, income, occupation, and geographic location of respondent populations. (See section 2.7, which reports variations ranging from 23% to 67% for different occupational groups and from 20% to 73% for city of residence.)	1. The better educated are more likely to return questionnaires; among them, professionals are more likely to return questionnaires. One of the highest returns reported in the research literature is that by Rensis Likert. In a study of the League of Women Voters (commissioned by the League) a cross-sectional sample of 2905 League members and officers showed the following percent of return: 79% of members; 95% of board members; 100% of chapter presidents. 2. Remember: Nonreaders and nonwriters are excluded from participation automatically.
Salience of content	30% to 40%.	Questionnaires are more likely to be returned if they are judged as salient to the respondent. Heberlein and Baumgartner report that 43 surveys with nonsalient questionnaires averaged a 42% return while 26 questionnaires judged to be salient for the respondent obtained a 77% return.[b]
Nature of sponsor and covering letter	Not well known, but range could be considerable.	The sponsor and letter describing importance of questionnaire are seldom self-evident. Sponsor and appeal are very important. The most prestigious and respected person to make the appeal is one who can most influence returns, all other factors held constant. An altruistic appeal seems to get better results than the idea that the respondent may receive something of personal value. The Bureau of Social Science Research, Inc., 1200 Seventeenth Street N.W., Washington, DC 20036, has compiled completion rates in mail surveys undertaken by BSSR. Data compiled by Lenore Reid. They report a 65% to 90% return with as many as four follow-ups. *Covering letter from institutional sponsor believed very important.*
Sensitive areas of inquiry	Not well known, but range can be very wide. More sophisticated approaches are now being utilized to increase returns.	Substantial drop in response if questions probe areas regarded by the respondent as private and/or a threat to him or his immediage group (fam-

Method	Possible increase of total % of returns	Optimal conditions
	Among these are the Randomized Response Technique and the Multiplicity Technique.[c]	ily, company, neighborhood, church, political party, etc.). A promise of complete confidentiality may help. If respondent does not need to place his name on the questionnaire, some fear may be dispelled.
		Personal sexual behavior is often one of the most sensitive areas. Note that Shere Hite received only 3% return on her questionnaire to 100,000 adult women seeking information about their sexuality.
		Often questions about income or education dampen the return. Important variations can occur between respondents of different nations because of varying cultural "sensitivities."
Inducements	Not clearly established.	*Response Analysis,* a private research organization, reports that a monetary incentive raises response by 40%. *Response Analysis* mailed questionnaires to a random sample of 700 Delaware residents in March 1980. The sample was divided into four groups of 175 each: monetary incentive, sponsor letterhead; monetary incentive, *Response Analysis* letterhead; no monetary incentive, sponsor letterhead; no monetary incentive, *Response Analysis* letterhead. Completion rates varied from 76% for the first group to 35% for the fourth group.[d]
		Research reviews of the literature show that relatively few studies have used monetary incentives. Two studies paid $1.00 and had 80% returns; 9 paid $.50 and had 66% returns; 7 paid $.25 and had 45% returns (all using only one contact). Most studies (*N* = 187) used no incentives and averaged a 62% response. There is a suggestion that incentives have a linear trend effect, but there is no significant zero-order effect.[e]
		University sponsorship, type of population, and type of questionnaire could make such inducements unnecessary. Consider promise of report to respondent as inducement; appeal to advancement of knowledge.

Method	Possible increase of total % of returns	Optimal conditions
Method of return	Not known.	Special techniques include use of registered letter, double postcards, sending respondent another copy of the questionnaire, and inclusion of stamped addressed envelope. A regular stamped envelope produces better results than business reply envelope.
Time of arrival	Not known.	The questionnaire, if sent to the home, should arrive near the end of the week.
Format	Not known.	Sletto found a need for an aesthetically pleasing cover, a title that would arouse interest, an atractive page format, a size and style of type easily readable under poor illumination and for people with poor vision, and photographs to illustrate the questionnaire. (See section 2.10 for further instructions.)
Length of questionnaire	Not significant.	In their study of 214 mailed questionnaires Heberlein and Baumgartner found no significant correlation between any of the length measures and overall responses. Length varied from a single page to 22 pages.[f]

[a] Thomas A. Heberlein and Robert Baumbartner, "Factors Affecting Response Rates to Mailed Questionnaires," *American Sociological Review* 43 (August 1978): 460.

[b] Ibid., p. 451.

[c] The Randomized Response Technique places a random device such as a coin in the hands of the respondent and asks that he select by chance one of two questions: a sensitive question related to the topic under study or a nonsensitive question. For example, in a study of abortion, two questions might be: (1) I had an abortion during the past year; (2) I was born in the month of April. The respondent would be instructed to merely reply Yes or No to the selected statement without telling the interviewer which question was being answered. The interviewer can point out that the interviewer will *never know* which question was asked and answered. And the respondent can now answer without fear of embarrassment or reprisal. The researcher knowing the percentage of women born in April can deduce the desired finding.

The Multiplicity Technique allows respondents to avoid a self-report by asking them to report anonymously on the behavior of specified individuals such as close friends or relatives. This approach has its highest utility when the behavior being studied is likely to be denied by a considerable portion of respondents (e.g., in the case of illegal or stigmatized behavior, as in drug use). For further information write: Dr. Patricia Fishburne, Research Director, *Response Analysis*, Research Park, Route 206, Princeton, NJ 08540.

[d] Results from the 1980 study almost duplicate those from a 1977 research project conducted with the same design. Completion rates in the 1977 study ranged from 78% for the first group to 39% for the fourth group (no monetary incentive group). There was a consistent favorable bias when the sponsor's letterhead was used. This verifies the importance of the sponsor, as indicated earlier. The results favoring a monetary incentive may be due to an identification with a private research organization. University sponsorship may explain the conflicting evidence reported in previous research studies. See *The Sampler from Response Analysis* (Research Park, Princeton, N.J.), no. 19 (Winter 1981): 1–2.

[e] Heberlein and Baumgartner, Factors Affecting Response Rates," p. 453.

[f] Ibid., p. 452.

Response rates to mail questionnaires are typically low, usually not exceeding 50 percent. Recent research indicates that much better return rates can be achieved by skilled use of questionnaire construction and follow-up procedures. Four researchers are so sure of their methods that they assert "with a mail methodology available which will consistently provide a high response, poor return rates can no more be excused than can inadequate theory or inappropriate statistics."[1]

The effectiveness of a particular method for eliciting response to lengthy questionnaires (85–165 items) was tested on large statewide samples of the general public in Arizona, Indiana, North Carolina, and Washington. The methods utilized produced response rates of from 69.7 percent to 75.2 percent. They were equally effective in rural and urban regions. The quality of the data was uniformly high throughout the items.

Increasing Returns of Mail Questionnaires

The method of achieving such results can be detailed in successive steps:

1. Prepare questionnaire as a booklet by photo reduction and multilithing. (This makes it seem less formidable.)
2. Make the cover page attractive and eye-catching.
3. Use straightforward, unambiguous questions carefully ordered and presented in a visually attractive manner. (See 2.4 for sample page of a questionnaire.) Questions in the first pages should be designed largely to attract respondents' interest in order to increase the likelihood that important questions of limited interest and appeal will be answered.
4. Prepare a cover letter and emphasize the social usefulness of the study and the individual importance of each respondent to the success of the study.
5. Make full use of personalization procedures.[2] Address salutation by name of respondent, not *Dear Sir* or *Madam;* sign your name; etc.
6. Mail questionnaire as first-class mail.
7. Use postcard follow-up one week later.
8. Prepare letter with replacement questionnaire and send at the end of the third week.
9. Send final letter with replacement questionnaire by certified mail after seven weeks.[3]

Table 1 shows the cumulative response rates to the four mailings used in each study.[4]

Expected Results

Note that the final response rates for the four states vary just over five percentage points from highest to lowest. Since there was high similarity in content, there is evidence that the topic per se made no difference.

Table 1 *Cumulative Response Rates to Four Mailings Used in Each Study* *

Mailing	Time	Washing-ton 1970 $N = 4137^1$	Washing-ton 1971 $N = 4175^1$	North Carolina 1973 $N = 4470^1$	Arizona 1973 $N = 2021^1$	Indiana 1973 $N = 7558^1$	Overall Mean
1. First mailing	Week 1	27.0%	26.3%	20.6%	26.5%	18.6%	23.8%
2. Postcard follow-up	Week 2	45.7	51.1	35.1	41.6	36.5	42.0
3. First replacement questionnaire	Week 4	59.2^2	67.6	53.0	60.1	55.3	59.0
4. Second replacement questionnaire sent by certified mail	Week 7	75.0	75.2	69.7	71.3	70.9	72.4

^1N = number of *potential* respondents. This is slightly less than the original mailing. Those dropped included persons (1) who had moved from the state so were no longer eligible, (2) to whom a questionnaire could not be delivered (usually because of moving and either leaving no forwarding address or leaving one that expired), (3) who had died, or (4) who were physically incapable of responding (usually due to infirmities of old age). The first two categories accounted for approximately three-fourths of the drops. The numbers (and percent of the original mailing) dropped in each state are as follows: Washington 1970, 363 (8.1%); Washington 1971, 325 (7.2%); North Carolina, 612 (12.0%); Arizona, 229 (10.2%); Indiana, 479 (5.9%).

In this study the third mailing did not include a replacement questionnaire.

*Used with permission of the author and the American Sociological Association.

The table reveals the importance of intensive follow-ups. Without the final two mailings, the probable final response rates would have been less than 50 percent for four of the five studies. The third mailing increased returns by an average of 17.0 percent. The fourth mailing (the final mailing) was only slightly less productive with a 13.4 percent return.

Cost of Data Collection Process

Low cost is one of the major advantages of the mail survey compared with personal interviews. Costs are incurred in such categories as labor, postage, printing, and supplies. What researchers have at their disposal can make a big difference in unit costs. Needless to say, costs do not stabilize; they continue to rise. For further information on costing, see the section on Costing, in part 5.

Notes

1. Don A. Dillman, James A. Christensen, Edwin H. Carpenter, and Ralph M. Brooks, "Increasing Mail Questionnaire Response: A Four State Comparison," *American Sociological Review* 39 (October 1974): 755.
2. Don A. Dillman and James H. Frey, "The Contribution of Personalization to Mail Questionnaire Response as an Element of a Previously Tested Method," *Journal of Applied Psychology* 59, no. 3 (1974): 297–301. Cf. E H. Carpenter as cited in bibliography.
3. Dillman et al., "Increasing Questionnaire Response." Adapted from p. 746.
4. Ibid., p. 748.
5. Ibid., p. 754.

A RESEARCH FOLLOW-UP ON THE TOTAL DESIGN METHOD FOR MAIL SURVEYS*

Don A. Dillman

Forty-eight mail surveys have been reported by Dillman since the first mail survey was described by him and his co-workers. Each of these were conducted by what Dillman calls the Total Design Method (pp. 160–98) and as spelled out in the previous article. The surveys were done by a large number of investigators under 37 different projects most of which were of populations in Washington State. Surveys have been conducted in nine different states, and six were national in scope. Most have been conducted from college and university settings. No nationwide survey has been undertaken by the TDM method, nor have any surveys been conducted in the largest metropolitan centers.

With this note of caution, the results of the 48 surveys show an average response rate of 74 percent. No survey obtained less than a 50 percent response rate. Results from some of the studies exhibit response rates near 90 percent.

References to Factors Affecting Response Rates to Questionnaires

ALWIN, DUANE F. ed., "Survey Design and Analysis," Special Issue. *Sociological Methods and Research* 6 (November 1977).

> Articles included are: Duane F. Alwin, "Making Errors in Surveys: An Overview"; Howard Schuman and Stanley Presser, "Question Wording as an Independent Variable in Survey Analysis"; Seymour Sudman, Norman Bradburn, Ed Blair, and Carol Stocking, "Modest Expectations: The Effects of Interviewers' Prior Expectations on Responses"; Lloyd Lueptow, Samuel A. Mueller, Richard R. Hammes, and Lawrence S. Master, "Response Rate and Response Bias Among High School Students Under the Informed Consent Regulations"; Gideon Vigderhous, "Analysis of Patterns of Response to Mailed Questionnaires"; Jae-on Kim and James Curry, "The Treatment of Missing Data in Multivariate Analysis"; William T. Bielby and Robert M. Hauser, "Response Error in Earnings Functions for Nonblack Males."

American Statistical Association Conference on Surveys of Human Population. "Report on the ASA Conference on Surveys of Human Populations." *American Statistician* 28 (February 1974): 30–34.

ARMSTRONG, J. SCOTT. "Monetary Incentives in Mail Surveys." *Public Opinion Quarterly* 39 (Spring, 1975): 111–16.

BACHRACK, STANLEY D., and SCOBLE, HARRY M. "Mail Questionnaire Efficiency: Controlled Reduction of Non-Response." *Public Opinion Quarterly* 31(Summer 1967): 264–71.

BERDIE, DOUGLAS R. "Questionnaire Length and Response Rate." *Journal of Applied Psychology* 58 (October 1973): 278–80.

BOEK, WALTER E., and LADE, JAMES H. "A Test of the Usefulness of the Postcard Technique in a Mail Questionnaire Study." *Public Opinion* Quarterly 27 (Summer 1963): 303–6.

CARPENTER, EDWIN H. "Personalizing Mail Surveys: A Replication and Reassessment." *Public Opinion Quarterly* 38 (Winter 1974–75): 614.

---

* From Don A. Dillman, *Mail and Telephone Surveys* (New York: Wiley Interscience, 1978). For a list of the 48 mail surveys and the response rates, see pp. 22–24.

CHAMPION, DEAN J., and SEAR, ALAN M. "Questionnaire Response Rates: A Methodological Analysis." *Social Forces* 47 (March 1969): 335–39.

DILLMAN, DON A. "Increasing Mail Questionnaire Response in Large Samples of the General Public." *Public Opinion Quarterly* 36 (Summer 1972): 254–57.

_____. *Mail and Telephone Surveys: The Total Design Method.* New York: Wiley Interscience, 1978.

> An 18-page bibliography on mail and telephone surveys may be found in pages 299–318.

_____; CARPENTER, EDWIN; CHRISTENSON, JAMES; and BROOKS, RALPH. "Increasing Mail Questionnaire Response: A Four State Comparison." *American Sociological Review* 39 (October 1974): 744–56.

_____, and FREY, JAMES H. "The Contribution of Personalization to Mail Questionnaire Response as an Element of a Previously Tested Method." *Journal of Applied Psychology* 59 (1974): 297–301.

DUNNING, BRUCE, and CAHALAN, DON. "By Mail vs. Self-Administered Questionnaires." *Public Opinion Quarterly* 37 (Winter 1973–74): 618–24.

FERRISS, ABBOTT L. "A Note on Stimulating Response to Questionnaires." *American Sociological Review* 16 (April 1951): 247–49.

KERLINGER, FRED. *Foundations of Behavioral Research.* New York: Holt, 1973.

LEIK, ROBERT K. *Methods, Logic and Research of Sociology.* Indianapolis: Bobbs-Merrill, 1972.

LEUTHOLD, DAVID A., and SCHEELE, RAYMOND J. "Patterns of Bias in Samples Based on Telephone Directories." *Public Opinion Quarterly* 35 (Summer 1961): 296–99.

MACLEAN, MAVIS. *Methodological Issues in Social Surveys.* Atlantic Highlands, N.J.: Humanities Press, 1979.

National Research Council Panel on Privacy and Confidentiality. *Privacy and Confidentiality as Factors in Survey Response.* Washington, D.C.: National Academy of Sciences, 1979.

PERRY, JOSEPH, JR. "A Note on the Use of Telephone Directories as a Sample Source." *Public Opinion Quarterly* 32 (Fall 1968): 691–95.

POTTER, DALE R.; SHARPE, KATHRYN; HENDEE, JOHN C.; and CLARK, ROGER N. *Questionnaires for Research: An Annotated Bibliography on Design, Construction and Use.* USDA Forest Service Research Paper, PNW-140. Portland: Pacific Northwest Forest and Range Experiment Station, 1972.

ROSENBERG, MILTON J. "The Conditions and Consequences of Evaluation Apprehension." In *Artifact in Behavioral Research,* edited by R. Rosenthal and R. Rosnow. New York: Academic Press, 1969. Pp. 279–341.

ROSENTHAL, ROBERT, and ROSNOW, RALPH L. "The Volunteer Subject." In *Artifact in Behavioral Research,* edited by R. Rosenthal and R. Rosnow. New York: Academic Press, 1969. Pp. 61–118.

SCHUMAN, HOWARD, and JOHNSON, MICHAEL P. "Attitudes and Behavior." In *Annual Review of Sociology,* vol. 2, edited by Alex Inkeles. Palo Alto: Annual Reviews, 1976. Pp. 161–207.

SCHWARTZ, SHALOM H. "Normative Influences on Altruism." In *Advances in Experimental Social Psychology,* vol. 10, edited by L. Berkowitz. New York: Academic Press, 1977. Pp. 222–79.

SLETTO, RAYMOND F. "Pretesting of Questionnaires." *American Sociological Review* 5 (April 1940): 193–200.

SLOCUM, W. L.; EMPEY, L. T.; and SWANSON, H. S. "Increasing Response to Questionnaires and Structured Interviews." *American Sociological Review* 21 (April 1956): 221–25.

SUDMAN, SEYMOUR, and BRADBURN, NORMAN. *Response Effects in Surveys.* Chicago: Aldine, 1974.

VINCENT, CLARK E. "Socioeconomic Status and Familiar Variables in Mail Questionnaire Responses." *American Journal of Sociology* 69 (May 1964): 647–53.

2.11   ## GUIDES FOR SELECTION AND USE OF PERSONAL INTERVIEWS AS UTILIZED IN FIELD RESEARCH

The interview represents a personal contact between an interviewer and a respondent usually in the home or office of the respondent. The interview can range from a highly structured situation with a planned series of questions to a very informal talk with no structure except for some areas of discussion desired by the interviewer. The degrees of freedom represent opportunity and danger: opportunity to explore many subjects with intensity but with the danger that the interview may not yield the appropriate data. It is often not susceptible to codification and comparability.

The researcher may not appreciate that every open-ended question will take considerable interview time. The analysis of open-ended questions requires a code guide and careful independent observers to establish the validity and reliability of the coding for each question. In general the rule is: Present closed rather than open-ended questions. If you must employ open-ended questions, choose a few with care and with the precise aims of the study in mind. If hypotheses are to be tested, make sure that the questions bear directly upon them. Open-ended questions are appropriate and powerful under conditions that require probing of attitude and reaction formations and ascertaining information that is interlocked in a social system or personality structure.

In general, keep the interview within a 45-minute time span. Public-opinion interviewers have reported that most respondents begin to weary and show less interest in the interview at this point. It is true that some respondents will "warm up" as the interview proceeds, and there are examples of six- and eight-hour interviews in the literature. (Robert Dahl with community leaders in New Haven, Connecticut, and Neal Gross in planned interviews with Massachusetts School Superintendents in Cambridge, Massachusetts).[1] These long interviews are exceptional and can occur only under specially prepared conditions.

The interview may be identified in three forms: (1) The Structured Interview Schedule, (2) The Focused Interview, and (3) The Free Story. These forms and their characteristics are shown in the Outline Guide to Situses, Principal Methods, and Techniques of the Social Science Researcher (p. 72). Common techniques that may be employed include inclusion of scales to measure social factors, attitudes, and personality traits. Secret ballots and panel techniques are often employed.

The guide that follows lists advantages and disadvantages of the interview. Use it as a check list noting with a plus mark those advantages that are important or essential; mark a minus for the disadvantages that will affect your use of the interview. You now have an adequate base for your choice or rejection of the personal interview.

Other field methods are available including the group interview, telephone interview, case study and life history, direct observation, participant observation, and mass observation. Guides have not been prepared for these methods, but a list of reference books is appended to this part describing in detail all the methods and techniques.

Guide for Appraisal of Personal Interview for Data Collection

The researcher should check the advantages important for his study. Then check the disadvantages that cannot be overcome. Appraise the choice. Reconsider documentary analysis, mail questionnaire, telephone interview, observation, or other methods suggested in the Outline Guide to Situses, Principal Methods, and Techniques of the Social Science Researcher.

Advantages of Personal Interview

1. The personal interview usually yields a high percentage of returns, for most people are willing to cooperate.
2. It can be made to yield an almost perfect sample of the general population because practically everyone can be reached by and can respond to this approach.
3. The information secured is likely to be more correct than that secured by other techniques since the interviewer can clear up seemingly inaccurate answers by explaining the questions to the informant. If the latter deliberately falsifies replies, the interviewer may be trained to spot such cases and use special devices to get the truth.
4. The interviewer can collect supplementary information about the informant's personal characteristics and environment that is valuable in interpreting results and evaluating the representatives of the persons surveyed.
5. Scoring and test devices can be used, the interviewer acting as experimenter to establish accurate records of the subject.
6. Visual material to which the informant is to react can be presented.
7. Return visits to complete items on the schedule or to correct mistakes can usually be made without annoying the informant. Thus greater numbers of usable returns are assumed than when other methods are employed.
8. The interviewer may catch the informant off guard and thus secure more spontaneous reactions than would be the case if a written form were mailed out for the informant to mull over.
9. The interviewer can usually control which person or persons answer the questions, whereas in mail surveys several members of the household may confer before the questions are answered. Group discussions can be held with the personal interview method if desired.
10. The personal interview may take long enough to allow the informant to become oriented to the topic under investigation. Thus recall of relevant material is facilitated.
11. Questions about which the informant is likely to be sensitive can be carefully sandwiched in by the interviewer. By observing the informant's reactions, the investigator can change the subject if necessary or explain the survey problem further if it appears that the interviewee is about to rebel. In other words, a delicate situation can usually be handled more effectively by a personal interview than by other survey techniques.
12. More of the informant's time can be taken for the survey than would be the case if the interviewer were not present to elicit and record the information.
13. In cases where a printed schedule is not used (cf. disadvantage *2*, below), the

language of the survey can be adapted to the ability or educational level of the person interviewed. Therefore, it is comparatively easy to avoid misinterpretations or misleading questions.

14. The length of the interview does not affect refusal rates.[2]

Disadvantages of Personal Interview

Especially in large metropolitan areas, two factors have had an impact on personal interviewing: higher costs and lower response rates than were encountered previously.

1. Higher costs have been encountered in all phases of the interview operation. Salaries both in the field and in the central office of survey agencies have followed the inflationary spiral. Travel costs for visiting sample households have spiraled along with the price of gasoline, which has more than doubled in recent years.[3]

2. Lower response rates are being reported in all quarters, especially in large metropolitan areas where increases in personal and property crimes have altered the life styles of residents. Locked, central entrances to apartment buildings and a greater concern among residents about opening their doors to strangers prevent interviewing in many multiunit dwellings. There is also an increasing reticence to admit strangers in single-family dwellings in areas with high crime rates. Some interviewers refuse to enter areas perceived to be dangerous. In large metropolitan areas the final proportion of respondents who are located and consent to an interview is declining to a rate close to 50 percent.[4]

3. The above disadvantages have focused more attention on the telephone survey (to be described in the following section). Consideration is also being given to a combination of data collection methods utilizing the mail questionnaire, a telephone survey, and a personal interview where indicated. For example, if the largest possible return is sought, a personal interview may be required as the follow-up to round out the sample after telephone and mail inquiries have exhausted their usefulness.

4. Unless personal interviewers are properly trained and supervised, data may be inaccurate and incomplete. A few poor enumerators may make a much higher percentage of returns unusable than if informants filled out and mailed the interview form to survey headquarters.

5. The personal interview usually takes more time than the telephone interview, providing the persons who can be reached by telephone are a representative sample of the population to be covered by the survey. For a sample of the general public, however, a telephone inquiry is no substitute for a personal interview. The lowest-income groups often do not have telephones.[5]

6. If the interview is to be conducted in the home during the day, the majority of informants will be housewives. If a response is to be obtained from a male member of the household, most of the fieldwork has to be done in the evenings or on weekends. Since only an hour or two can be used for evening interviewing, the personal interview method requires a large staff if studies need contacts with the working population.

7. The human equation may distort the returns. Interviewers with a certain economic bias, for example, may unconsciously ask questions so as to secure confirmation of their views. In opinion studies especially, such biases may operate. To prevent such coloring of questions, most opinion surveyors instruct their interviewers to ask the question exactly as it is printed in the schedule.

8. Researchers should be aware that funding agencies may be reluctant to make grants to projects relying heavily on the personal interview. Given all the disadvantages, especially those associated with higher costs and lower response rates, the applicant for a grant may be placed on the defensive.

Notes

1. Robert A. Dahl, *Who Governs* (New Haven: Yale University Press, 1961), p. 334. Neal Gross, Ward S. Mason, and Alexander W. McEachern, *Explorations of Role Analysis: The Superintendency Role* (New York: Wiley, 1958), p. 85.

2. In a study of 500 adults testing 25-minute and 75-minute interviews, no relationship was found between interview length and overall item response. BSSR, *Newsletter of the Bureau of Social Science Research* 14, no. 3 (Fall 1980), 1–2.

3. See the Section on Costing in part 5 for a more detailed description of costs for the personal interview, mailed questionnaire, and telephone survey.

4. Robert M. Groves and Robert L. Kahn, *Surveys by Telephone: A National Comparison with Personal Interviews* (New York: Academic Press, 1979), p. 3.

5. True, but telephone availability has grown with more than 90 percent of all residences in the United States now possessing telephones. Many persons can be reached on business telephones.

DESCRIPTION AND INSTRUCTIONS FOR PREPARATION OF A TELEPHONE INTERVIEW SURVEY   *2.12*

Description

With increasing frequency, social science researchers are utilizing the telephone for social investigation. There are a number of reasons for this use including the following:

1. Almost all residences in the United States now have a telephone. It is estimated that at least 90 percent of all persons in a cross-sectional sample can be reached by telephone. The probability of social-class bias stemming from telephone availability has greatly diminished.[1]

2. Personal interview costs have risen greatly, and telephone surveys can be made for only 45 to 65 percent of personal interview costs.[2] (For further information on costing, see section 5.)

3. Personal interviews are incurring falling response rates in large cities, and telephone interviewing is competitive in response rate achieved on national populations. They are running only 5 to 10 percent lower than those of comparable in-person surveys.[3]

4. A comparison of response rates for mail surveys with telephone surveys favors the telephone. Dillman reports an average response of 91 percent for 31 surveys, a full 17 percentage points higher than the average for 48 mail surveys. The difference persists for both specialized and general populations. These results were obtained in the State of Washington.[4]

5. The rapid emergence of the telephone as a survey research tool means that the social science community has little information about telephone surveys. Among the unknowns may be listed:

   a. What response rates to expect for various populations.
   b. How long different people will stay on the telephone.
   c. The unique requirements of telephone interviews in contrast with the familiar mail and personal interview survey.

It is believed that most surveyors have adapted their normal interviewing procedures to the telephone and are simply employing "face-to-face interviews" by telephone. This procedure is not recommended.[5] Groves and Kahn contend that "the transition from personal interview methods to telephone methods requires a total reorganization for collecting data."[6]

Groves believes surveys in the future may combine telephone and personal interviews so that the two modes can complement each other and possibly provide greater precision than is possible with either one alone. It is known that proportionately more telephone respondents feel uneasy about discussing some topics, especially financial status and political attitudes. Yet in large metropolitan areas respondents feel more comfortable about answering questions on the telephone than about inviting strangers into their homes. A combination of telephone and personal interviewing would take advantage of the lower costs of telephone interviews and maintain representation of households without telephones.[7]

Instructions for the Telephone Interview*

The telephone interview contrasts sharply with the mail questionnaire. Telephone interviews depend entirely on verbal communication, and the interviewer must build rapport with the respondent in an interchange during which neither sees the other. And unlike face-to-face interviews, the telephone interviewer cannot use visual aids to help explain questions, and cannot observe respondents' facial expressions for hints that something is misunderstood.

The design of the telephone questionnaire must be shaped to meet the needs of three audiences: respondents, interviewers, and coders.

Respondents. Responding to a telephone interview is difficult. Respondents may be called to the telephone unexpectedly and asked to do something they do not fully understand. They may be in the midst of another activity, such as preparing dinner, playing a game, reading the newspaper, or listening to the radio of TV. Their feelings may range from frustration, suspicion, anxiety, and downright hostility. Subtle ways must be found to discourage respondents from beginning or continuing with other activities that may distract their attention from the interview. "Getting through" may mean that the respondent needs time to get used to the interviewer's way of speaking, understanding different words and the meaning of questions, etc. Being interviewed by telephone is a new experience, and the respondent may need time to think through answers. Most respondents need support and encouragement.

Interviewers. The interviewer must secure completion of a telephone questionnaire with information that is accurate and can be accurately recorded. The interviewer must determine who of the household is eligible to respond and get this person on the phone. The first few seconds are all-important in determining whether a successful interview will take place. The interviewer may be faced with such questions as: How do I know who you say you are? What are you trying to sell? I don't know anything about you or your product—why don't you call someone else? I have a call that I am expecting—you will have to hang up now. Can you call later?

---

* Based on Dillman, *Mail and Telephone Surveys,* pp. 200–281. Users of the telephone survey should consult this thorough treatment, which includes constructing telephone questionnaires and administering the survey.

The interviewer must "prove" *his* legitimacy and the *worth* of his project, and must stimulate the respondent to begin. As the interview proceeds the interviewer must move the conversation from question to question, write answers while mentally preparing to ask the next question, listen intently for any changes of mood, record unsolicited comments, hold the telephone receiver, and turn the pages of the questionnaire.

Coders. Methods of facilitating rapid data compilation are important. Precoding identifies the computer card columns and punches for each response category on the questionnaire. Precoding marks and additional instructions for coders usually do not interfere with the requirements of the interviewer.

Some important steps:

1. Prepare the telephone questionnaire so that all questions are straightforward, unambiguous, and carefully ordered. Begin the questionnaire with items central to the topic that seem easy to answer, interesting, and socially important. All topical questions are asked before questions relating to personal characteristics.

2. A well-constructed questionnaire will maximize the probability that interviewers will administer it in exactly the same fashion to each respondent: Each response category is assigned an identifying number that is used to represent it on a computer punch. The final version should be carefully pretested, and interviewers might role-play the interviewer-respondent interchange.

3. The most difficult part of conducting telephone surveys is combining all elements in the research design for administration. Each act of preparation is oriented to the single critical act of the initial interviewing. A countdown list of activities that must be completed prior to the start of interviewing has been prepared by Dillman. Use of it will help prevent oversights and organizational failures.

Countdown List of Activities That Must Be Done Prior to the Start of Interviews*

Draw Sample
___Names, street addresses, and telephone numbers drawn from directories typed onto gummed labels and attached to cover page of questionnaire
[*or*]
___Random numbers generated by computer (or manually from table) and printed on lists for distribution to interviewers

Facilities and Equipment
___Access to telephones arranged
___Telephones checked to be sure they are in working order
___Access to leased lines arranged (if needed)
___Chairs and tables assembled (if needed)
___Labeled boxes for sorting questionnaires into appropriate categories (e.g., refusals, completions, and call-backs)

Computer Related Needs (If immediate data processing is planned)
___Arrange access to computer
___Arrange access to computer equipment (e.g., keypunch, and sorter reproducer)
___Decide analysis programs to be used and set up format statements for their use.

* Reprinted with permission from the publisher and Don A. Dillman, *Mail and Telephone Surveys: The Total Design Method* (New York: Wiley, 1978) p. 274. Copyright © 1978 by John Wiley and Sons, Inc.

___Do preliminary computer runs with "Dummy" data to check for errors in analysis
   programs

Materials
___Questionaires
   ___Duplicated
   ___Assembled
   ___Cover page and selection procedures (if any) added
   ___Directory listing attached to cover page (if applicable)
   ___Randomized for distribution to interviewers
___"What the Respondent Might Like to Know" duplicated
___"Rules Book" duplicated
___Special dialing instructions duplicated (if needed)
___Pencils and notepads, thumbtacks, rubber bands, and other miscellaneous supplies
___All of the above placed at each interviewing station

Advance Letter
___Printed, personalized, and stuffed into envelopes
___Each letter is mailed three to five days before call is likely to be made

Personnel
___Interviewers
   ___Hired
   ___Trained
   ___Scheduled
___Supervisory personnel schedule
___Persons to check questionnaires for completeness scheduled
___Coders and/or keypunchers
   ___Hired
   ___Trained
   ___Schedule
___Person to "trouble-shoot" disconnected numbers and other problem calls scheduled

Other Resources
___Telephone directories that cover study area (to aid in checking possible errors)
___Notify relevant officials that survey is in process

Dillman has an 18-page reference bibliography on mail and telephone surveys, which is coded as follows: M = an explicit treatment of mail surveys; T = an explicit treatment of telephone surveys; G = not an explicit treatment of either mail or telephone surveys, but has implications for conducting them. See Dillman, *Mail and Telephone Surveys,* pp. 299–318.

Notes

1. Don A. Dillman, *Mail and Telephone Surveys* (New York: Wiley Interscience, 1978), p. 10).
2. Robert M. Groves, "Telephone Helps Solve Survey Problems," *Newsletter of the Institute of Social Research* (University of Michigan) 6, no. 1 (1980): 3.
3. Ibid.
4. Dillman, *Mail and Telephone Surveys,* p. 28.
5. Ibid., p. 11.
6. Robert M. Groves and Robert L. Kahn, *Surveys by Telephone* (New York: Academic Press, 1979, p. 4.
7. Groves, "Telephone Helps Solve Survey Problems," p. 3.

The development of telephone interviews and procedures for sampling households by means of random-digit dialing may be the most important innovations in survey research since the introduction of multistage probability sampling. But comparisons of telephone surveys with personal interviews raise many questions:

1. *Are Telephone Responses as Reliable and as Valid as Those Given in Personal Interviews?*

There is no simple answer to this question even when all conditions of sample and survey content are held constant—and that is almost impossible. However, hard data are available in regard to such important matters as sample coverage, selection of respondents in households, overall rates of response and nonresponse, and validity of response.

On sample coverage. With more than 90 percent of all households in the United States reachable by telephone, the overall coverage of telephone samples begins to approach the levels typically obtained by personal interviews of an area probability sample of households. For some subpopulations, however, households not covered by telephone are crucial. These include poor households where there are more nonsubscribers; rural households, which tend to have lower incomes than urban households; elderly people, who tend to have lower incomes and experience more hearing difficulties; households of young adults, who are more transient and possess lower incomes than middle-aged adults.

One cannot assume that nonsubscribers are like subscribers, but the proportion of nonsubscribers continues to shrink. The bias in statistics linked to the absence of nonphone households depends on the nature of measurements taken.

On selection of respondents in households. The selections of respondents within sample households must be done at the time of the interview. In personal interview surveys, household selection is done by using a full listing of household members. In telephone surveys, the procedure can be simplified by using a grid corresponding to different numbers of male and female adults. The telephone interviewer determines the total number of adults in the household and the number of them who are women. Use of the grid then indicates the individual selected as respondent. Use of this procedure showed it yielded an error in selection in about 10 percent of the sample households![1]

On different rates of response. The response rate of national telephone surveys remains at least five percentage points lower than that expected in personal surveys. This has been a rather stable comparison despite numberous changes in training interviewers, monitoring and feedback procedures, and techniques of introducing the survey to the respondent.[2]

On validity of response. Later studies using validity checks find small, generally negligible differences between telephone and personal interviews on reports of embarrassing events such as personal bankruptcy and arrests for drunken driving.[3]

2. *Are There Systematic Differences in the Content or Depth of the Answers People Give by Telephone and Those They Give in Person?*

Consistent differences in interviewing speed between telephone and personal modes have been noted by researchers. The faster pace of telephone interviews is associated with differences both in the number and type of responses to open-ended items. Some people begin telephone interviews but do not complete them. A lower response rate (5 percent lower) has already been noted for the telephone interview. In spite of these differences, very few response discrepancies have been found between the two sets of data that were large enough to be considered statistically significant.[4]

Many studies have concentrated on reports of embarrassing or sensitive data. These studies have generally found no or only slight difference between telephone and personal interviews. Most results vary because of differences in research design, populations studied, or kinds of data collected. A general statement is inappropriate.[5]

There is a real concern about rapport between respondent and interviewer in the telephone survey. Nonresponse rates suggest that respondents find the telephone interview to be a less rewarding experience and more of a chore than the personal interview. A first priority for future research must be given to telephone techniques to establish motivation and trust equal to the face-to-face survey.[6]

3. *Are There Large Gains in Efficiency When Sample Households Are Interviewed by Telephone?*

Personnel needs for a national telephone survey are smaller than those for an equivalent personal interview survey. Take the case of a personal interview survey requiring 200 interviewers, each conducting 7 or 8 interviews. National telephone surveys are often conducted in the same amount of time using 30–40 interviewers, each doing 40–50 interviews. Supervisory and coordinating staff are similarly reduced.[7] Clearly, cost advantages exist for telephone interviewing. (For a comparative analysis of costs for mail questionnaire, personal interview, and telephone surveys, see section on Costing, part 5 of this Handbook.)

Efficiency results by having questionnaires of the telephone survey coded soon after they are taken. Interviewer errors discovered during coding are quickly detected and corrected. Feedback to interviewers can be quickly reported on interview behavior and results obtained.

Increasingly, sampling is done by random-digit dialing (RRD). Random-digit dialing refers to direct selection of numbers listed in telephone books. Generally, a set of randomly chosen digits corresponds to a working telephone number. This means a random sample can be quickly and easily located. A detailed description of the RRD procedure is clearly stated by Klecka and Tuchfarber.[8] Stratified random design and cluster designs are often employed. For a discussion of these, see Groves and Kahn.[9]

Notes

1. Robert M. Groves and Robert L. Kahn, *Surveys by Telephone* (New York: Academic Press, 1979), p. 217.
2. Ibid., p. 219.

3. Ibid., pp. 8–9.

4. Ibid., p. 231.

5. Ibid., p. 9.

6. Ibid., pp. 222–23.

7. Ibid., p. 8.

8. W. Klecka and A. Tuchfarber, "Random-Digit Dialing: A Comparison to Personal Surveys," *Public Opinion Quarterly* 42 (1978): 105–14. For further information about a study design for a statewide survey program, see Alan Booth, Lynn White, David R. Johnson, and Joan Litze, "Combining Contract and Sociological Research: The Nebraska Annual, Social-Indications Survey," *American Sociologist* 15 (November 1980): 226–32.

9. Groves and Kahn, *Surveys by Telephone,* pp. 215–16.

CHOOSING AMONG THE MAIL QUESTIONNAIRE, PERSONAL INTERVIEW, AND TELEPHONE SURVEY

2.14

The choice of a mode of collecting data involves many factors. The projection of results expected is speculative because in one sense every sample and the conditions surrounding it are unique. Even changes in world events during administration can make a difference. If the researcher is prepared to utilize many follow-ups or a combination of methods, then a prediction of higher response can be projected.

Table 1 is an evaluation of the modes of field operation covering eight

Table 1. *Choosing among the Mail Questionnaire, Personal Interview, and Telephone Survey**

Code: 1 = most favorable ranking
2 = intermediate ranking
3 = least favorable ranking

Factors influencing coverage and information secured	Mailed questionnaire	Personal interview	Telephone survey
Lowest relative cost	1	3	2
Highest percentage of return	3	1	2
Highest accuracy of information	2	1	3
Largest sample coverage	3	1	2
Completeness including sensitive material	3	1	2
Overall reliability and validity	2	1	3
Time required to secure information	3	2	1
Ease of securing information	1	3	2
Total Number of rankings 1, 2, 3	2, 2, 4	5, 1, 2	1, 5, 1

* Based on author's evaluation of findings for cross-sectional samples of student and adult populations. All evaluations are based on "average" determinations.

important factors. The researcher must determine what is most important among these factors for the design selected and choose accordingly.

Cost is of high priority. It can be seen that the mailed questionnaire is the cheapest, the telephone survey is of intermediate cost, and the personal survey is the most expensive. If the telephone survey involves substantial long-distance calling, however, the cost figures change quickly to give telephoning a less favorable position in comparison with the personal survey. (For a full description on comparative costs see the section on Costing, part 5 of this Handbook.)

Note that cost is in inverse relation to almost all the other factors when comparing the mailed questionnaire with the personal interview. The personal interview, unless placed among the most vulnerable conditions of dangerous sections in large, urban environments, easily leads in desirable factors. The telephone survey yields a very consistent set of rankings in the intermediate range; this accounts for its growing popularity.

2.15 THE PANEL TECHNIQUE AS A RESEARCH INSTRUMENT

Social scientists are giving even greater attention to methods for analyzing time data. It has been noted that all the social science disciplines have moved from static to dynamic models. The panel technique is an important research instrument. So much attention is being given to it currently, it seems almost to have been rediscovered.

Definition. The panel technique involves interviewing the *same* group of people on *two* or *more occasions*. It is mainly used for studying changes in behavior or attitudes with repeated interviews or "waves." Most panel studies contain a set of core questions or observations that are repeated on all or nearly all the waves. Considerable supplementary material may be obtained at each or different waves to be used in interpreting changes found in the core questions.

Uses. The panel is used in many areas of investigation, such as political polls, occupational and income movements, consumer habits, and mass communications. We can distinguish two major kinds of panels: those which focus mainly on attitudes and opinions; and those which deal mainly with factual material regarding economic, consumption, and communications behavior.

Panel studies focusing on opinion and attitude changes generally have a limited number of waves, usually ranging from two to four, and rarely exceeding seven. Since they seek specifically to pin down a particular fact or a reason that accounts for the changes noted, they are ordinarily restricted to the study of short-range changes of specific attitudes.

Advantages of the Panel Technique

The researcher has two options in searching for short-range changes of specific attitudes: (1) Information can be obtained involving facts or experiences during the course of time from a *single* contact with the respondent. Such questions as, "For whom did you intend to vote one month ago?" or, "Have you recently made a change in your job?" may be asked. Such information may not be accurate, for the memory of the respondent may be inadequate for the question; it may be deceptive or both. (2) Based as it is on repeated contact, the panel technique can be trusted to be more reliable and valid with a number of distinct advantages. Ziesel has listed these as follows:

*Repeated Cross-Sections Versus Panel Technique**

Cross-Sections	Panel
1. Recording changes In comparing, for example, the "Proportion of users of XX-brand soap" at two different periods, one obtains the difference in the total proportion of users at each interview: the net change.	In addition to the net change, one obtains an accurate picture of the number and direction of individual shifts, which, when added together, account for the net change.
2. Reasons for observed changes For instance, whether or not a certain type of propaganda has influenced a person's political attitude. This is difficult to ask and to answer.	By analyzing separately those who were exposed to a certain piece of propaganda and those who were not, the panel can ascertain whether the number and direction of attitude changes are different for the two groups.
3. Amount of collected information Since the respondents differ from survey to survey, one does not know more about each one respondent than can be gathered in any one interview.	Repeated interviews with the same respondents yield an ever increasing amount of information. In a three interview panel study we can get two or three hours worth of information about each member of our panel.
4. Data referring to time periods One-interview surveys will yield accurate results if the question refers to the time instant at which the interview takes place. If the respondent is to recall events that extend over a time period, one must rely on memory. Such data are most always required if certain research concepts are to be defined: If we want to find out a person's "reading habits" or whether he is a "regular listener" to a certain radio program, we must rely entirely on the respondent's memory and judgment.	Only through the panel can one avoid reliance on the respondent's memory if one aims at data that refer to an extended period of time. Repeated interviews yield objective data on the consistency and fluctuations of habits and attitudes. Such distinctions as that of "regular" vs. "nonregular" listener can be made with accuracy and reliability.
5. Reliability of results The statistical significance of observed changes from survey to survey depends upon the size and structure of the particular sample.	In most cases an observed change in a panel will be of higher statistical significance than a change of equal size observed in repeated cross-sections that equal the panel in size and structure.

* Hans Zeisel, *Say It with Figures*, 4th ed. (New York: Harper & Row, 1957, pp. 217–18. Copyright © 1957 by Harper & Row. Reprinted with permission of Harper & Row.

Difficulties Inherent in the Panel Technique

There are two basic difficulties in the use of the panel technique:

1. Mortality is the loss of panel members as a percent of the difficulty of reaching the same person for two or more contacts, or because of the refusal of their continuous cooperation. Since different sections of the panel may show a different mortality rate, some danger of a biased sample arises.
2. Reinterviewing bias is the effect of repeated discussions on certain topics on the respondent's behavior or attitude toward these very topics. Thus, the fact of being repeatedly interviewed may in itself induce changes of opinion.

Panel Mortality

There is bound to be a loss of panel members over time—and the longer the time, the greater the loss. The main reason for failure in reinterviewing is the temporary absence from the original place of interview or a complete change of address. This problem can be partly overcome by recording both home and business addresses at the time of the first interview and by persistent efforts to reach the respondent at the time of repeat interviews. If telephone interviewing has been the manner of contact, then the mailed questionnaire or a personal interview may be tried. A certified letter may increase response.

Mortality bias is a concern that increases with the loss of panel members. This is particularly true because mortality does not occur at random. It is well known that younger people and people in large cities, as well as people in the lower-income brackets, have a higher mobility than the old, small-town, and upper-class respondents (see Zeisel, *Say It with Figures,* p. 246). We must find out in each case whether such a bias exists. Most efforts to do this center on the nonrespondents. A vigorous effort is made to secure as many of these by different approaches and very persistent efforts. When returns are secured from the previously nonrespondent group, the researcher carefully analyzes to see if mortality bias has been introduced and how serious it may be for interpreting the findings.

Reinterviewing Bias

Bias may be introduced by reinterviewing simply because the first interview may have heighted the respondent's attention. There is possibly more thought given to the topic, and the ultimate effect may be a bias. The increasing familiarity gained by reinterviewing may add to the biasing of respondents' opinions.

To detect the presence of such bias a control group parallel to the panel may be interviewed. At the time of the first panel interview a field sample, matching the structure of the panel, is interviewed on the same topic. Again, at the time of second panel interview, a different field sample is interviewed. Now, any resulting bias can be discovered by comparing the change within the panel with the change between the two field samples.

These two principal sources of error in panel studies, mortality and reinterviewing bias, must receive attention. Nevertheless, studies have shown that neither of these two factors seriously endangers the use of the panel; it is a highly promising and powerful tool in the field of social research. See Lee

Wiggins, Panel Analysis: Latent Probability Models for Attitude and Behavior Processes (San Francisco: Jossey-Bass, 1973).

There are a number of important decisions to be made in designing a panel study. Each of these is briefly described below.

Problems of Administration and Suggestions for Dealing With Them

Administration problem	Suggestion
1. Number of waves The number of waves must consider the extent of cooperativeness on the part of respondents. They may become bored, annoyed, or irritated by repeated interviews. Repeated interviewing is also expensive. Like energy, cheap interviewing is gone.	The number of waves should usually be reduced to the minimum.
2. Interval Between waves Deciding on the interval between waves is governed by the factors of freshness of memory, type of information desired, and the speed with which a situation changes. If too long an interval elapses the panel member may suffer a loss of memory of previous events and may distort the answer.	The type of information desired is the most important factor in determining the appropriate interval. Consumer panels: ordinarily run waves at intervals of one or two weeks. Political panels: ordinarily, waves of one to two months apart are about right. In an exciting political campaign or a political crisis, short intervals are preferable.
3. Sample size Sampling error can be reduced with larger samples but this increases cost. A larger sample size can compensate for dropout mortality anticipated prior to first wave (1200 set up in the original sample so that a desired 1000 is available for interview). The problem here is that the original mortality may differ from the group that is interviewed.	Check sampling error associated with different sample sizes. Within the limitations imposed by cost, the researcher can either try to reduce the original mortality by repeated call-backs or try to obtain a sample of the original mortality.
4. Sample type—quota vs. area Quota samples have the advantage of being easier and cheaper to use than area samples. If respondents could be selected on the streets according to specific quota requirements, the speed and cost would be very desirable. After obtaining respondents' names and addresses, they could conduct interviews next time in their homes. This has not proved feasible as much of the original sample is lost for various reasons. The area sample is subject to considerably less mortality.	Whenever possible, personal interview panels should be conducted on an area basis in the home.

5. Incentives An incentive of some sort is needed to obtain the respondent's cooperation and participation. This is especially true in a panel study involving respondent's cooperation over fairly long periods and many waves of reinterviewing. The researcher faces the problem of first securing and then sustaining cooperation.	Two major incentives are usually effective depending on type of sponsor and the panel respondents. These are tangible (money, premiums, etc.) or prestigious (sponsorship, ego enhancement) incentives. Consumer panels: Use some sort of tangible reward such as points redeemable for premiums. Consider a small monetary payment. Government and educationally sponsored panels: Stress prestige and duty as citizen in advancing knowledge or improving society.
6. Type of interview: personal, telephone, mail Personal interviews have been most common in panel studies but this is the most expensive form of interview and is becoming more expensive. Telephone interviewing is becoming more common since the telephone is almost universally available at the home or work address. It is more difficult to get many kinds of sensitive information and attitudinal data by telephone. The mail interview involves two problems not present in personal or telephone interviews. a. Mail interviews become impractical when the interval between waves is important since there is no control over the time factor. b. Mail interviews are open to the very real possibility of a bias introduced by a discussion of answers with family members or neighbors.	The telephone interview is gaining in popularity as expenses of personal interviewing rise. New techniques and interview skills are making telephone interviewing more reliable and valid. Avoid the mail interview unless the telephone or personal interview is not feasible. The mail interview has some merit where it is not safe to enter areas of the city or where sensitive data is difficult to secure.

General References

HYMAN, MARTIN D. "Panel Analysis." In *Handbook of Social Sciences,* vol 2, *Quantitative Social Research,* edited by Robert B. Smith. New York: Irvington, 1980.

JAHODA, MARIE; DEUTSCH, MORTON; and COOK, STUART W., eds. *Research Methods in Social Relations.* New York: Dryden Press, 1951. Pp. 587–610.

KESSLER, RONALD C., and GREENBERG, DAVID E. *Linear Panel Analysis: Models of Quantitative Change.* New York: Academic Press, 1981.

LAZARSFELD, PAUL F.; PASANELLA, ANN K.; and ROSENBERG, MORRIS, eds. *Continuities in the Language of Social Research.* Rev. ed. of *Language of Social Research.* New York: Free Press of Macmillan, 1975. See section on Panel Analysis.

WIGGINS, LEE M. *Panel Analysis: Latent Probability Models for Attitude and Behavior Processes.* San Francisco: Jossey-Bass, 1973.

ZEISEL, HANS. *Say It with Figures,* 5th ed. New York: Harper & Row, 1965. Pp. 215–54.

Methodological References for Advanced Students

CLARRIDGE, BRIAN R.; SHEEHY, LINDA L.; HAUSER, TARISSA S. "Tracing Members of a Panel: A 17-Year Follow-Up." In *Sociological Methodology 1978,* edited by Karl F. Schuessler. San Francisco: Jossey-Bass, 1978.

DUNCAN, OTIS DUDLEY. "Unmeasured Variables in Linear Models for Panel Analysis." In *Sociological Methodology 1972,* edited by Herbert L. Costner. San Francisco: Jossey-Bass, 1972.

————. "Testing Key Hypotheses in Panel Analysis." *Sociological Methodology 1980,* edited by Karl F. Schuessler. San Francisco: Jossey-Bass, 1980.

GOODMAN, LEO A. "Causal Analysis of Data from Panel Studies and Other Kinds of Survey." *American Journal of Sociology* 78 (March 1973): 1135–91.

————. "A Brief Guide to the Causal Analysis of Data from Surveys," *American Journal of Sociology* 84 (March 1979): 1078–95.

HANMAN, MICHAEL T., and YOUNG, ALICE A. "Estimation in Panel Models: Results on Pooling Cross-Sections and Time Series." In *Sociological Methodology 1977,* edited by David R. Heise. San Francisco: Jossey-Bass, 1977.

MORGAN, JAMES N.; DUNCAN, GREG; and the Staff of the Economic Behavior Program. *Five Thousand American Families—Patterns of Economic Progress: Analyses of the Panel Study of Income Dynamics.* Vols. 1–7. Ann Arbor: Mich: Institute of Social Research, University of Michigan, 1974–79.

vol. 1, *Analyses of the First Five Years* (1974, 436 pp.);
vol. 2, *Special Studies of the First Five Years* (1974, 376 pp.);
vol. 3, *Analyses of the First Six Years* (1975, 490 pp.);
vol. 4, *Analyses of the First Seven Years* (1976, 520 pp.);
vol. 5, *Analyses of the First Eight Years* (1977, 534 pp.);
vol. 6, *Analyses of the First Nine Years* (1978, 528 pp.);
vol. 7, *Analyses of the First Ten Years* (1979, 392 pp.).

The analyses in these seven volumes constitute an intensive investigation into the factors that affect changes in the economic well-being of families over time. For ten years this massive, pioneering study has documented the lives of a large and representative sample of the entire U.S. population. Over 15,000 families were studied in 1968 and more than 2000 new families have been added to the panel as members of the original households split off to form new households.

A Panel Study of Income Dynamics: Documentation for Interviewing Years 1968 to 1977. Vol. 1, *Study Design, Procedures, Available Data* (1968–72, 400 pp.); vol. 2, *Tape Codes and Indexes* (1968–72 1100 pp.); Supplements 1973–78.

Complete documentation for this ongoing study of factors affecting family economic well-being over time are presented in these volumes. Data tape available (#7439).

PELZ, DONALD C., and ANDREWS, FRANK M. "Detecting Causal Priorities in Panel Study Data." *American Sociological Review* 29 (December 1964): 836–54.

WHEATON, BLAIR; MUTHÉN, BERGT; ALWIN, DUANE F.; and SUMMERS, GENE F. "Assessing Reliability and Stability in Panel Models." In *Sociological Methodology 1979* edited by David R. Heise. San Francisco: Jossey-Bass, 1977.

2.16 GUIDES FOR THE SELECTION AND CONSTRUCTION OF SOCIAL SCALES AND INDICES

Scaling techniques play a major role in the construction of instruments for collecting standardized, measurable data. Scales and indices are significant because they provide quantitative measures that are amenable to greater precision, statistical manipulation, and explicit interpretation. However, before constructing a new scale, it is exceedingly important that a very careful survey of the literature be made to ascertain if an appropriate scale is already available to measure the dependent or independent variables in a given study. The general rule is: Use the available scale if it has qualities of validity, reliability, and utility (and in that order of priority). With such a scale comparative and accumulative research is possible. The need to develop a new scale can almost be considered a disciplinary failure unless the variable represents a factor never before considered as open to measurement. We shall begin, therefore, at the point at which the literature has not revealed an appropriate scale and the researcher decides to construct an index or scale.

How does one "think up" a number of indicators to be used in empirical research?

This question is answered by Paul F. Lazarsfeld and Morris Rosenberg as follows:

> The first step seems to be the creation of a rather vague image or construct that results from the author's immersion in all the detail of a theoretical problem. The creative act may begin with the perception of many disparate phenomena as having some underlying characteristic in common. Or the author may have observed certain regularities and is trying to account for them. In any case, the concept, when first created, is some vaguely conceived entity that makes the observed relations meaningful. Next comes a stage in which the concept is specified by elaborate discussion of the phenomena out of which it emerged. We develop "aspects," "components," "dimensions," or similar specifications. They are sometimes derived logically from the overall concept, or one aspect is deduced from another, or empirically observed correlations between them are reported. The concept is shown to consist of a complex combination of phenomena, rather than a simple and directly observable item. In order to incorporate the concept into a research design, observable indicators of it must be selected.[1]

Indices and scales are often used interchangeably to refer to all sorts of measures, absolute or relative, single or composite, the product of simple or elaborate techniques of measurement.

Indices may be very simple. For example, one way to measure morale is to ask the direct question, "How would you rate your morale? Very good, good, fair, poor, very poor." This might be refined slightly so that the responses are placed on a numerical scale. Note that there are nine points on the following scale.

How Would You Rate Your Morale?								
Very good		Good		Fair		Poor		Very poor
1	2	3	4	5	6	7	8	9

The basis for construction is logical inference and the use of a numerical scale requires the assumption of a psychological continuity which the respondent can realistically act upon in self-rating. Face validity is usually asserted for such a scale although it would be possible to make tests of relations with criteria such as work performance, absenteeism, lateness, amount of drinking, hours of sleep, etc.

A composite index is one or a set of measures, each of which is formed by combining simple indexes. For example, morale may be considered as a composite of many dimensions.

Four measures can be combined by such questions as

How satisfied are you with your job?
How satisfied are you with your company or organization?
How satisfied are you in your personal life?
How satisfied are you with your community?

Response choices of very good, good, fair, poor, and very poor may be offered for each question with weights of 5, 4, 3, 2, and 1. A range from 4 to 20 points is possible. Such a composite index may improve precision, reliability, and validity.

Rigor is introduced as greater attention is paid to tests of validity and reliability. At a certain point a given means of measurement reaches its limit of improvement and a more refined technique becomes necessary for greater precision. Many scaling techniques concern themselves with linearity and equal intervals or equal-appearing intervals. This means that the scale follows a straight line model and that a scoring system is devised, preferably based on interchangeable units and subject to statistical manipulation. This is a major attribute of the Thurstone attitude scaling technique.

Unidimensionality or homogeneity is another desired attribute assuring that only one dimension is measured and not some mixture of factors. This is a prime concern of the Guttman scaling technique. Reproducibility is a characteristic that enables the researcher to predict the pattern of a respondent's answers by knowing only the total scale score. This attribute is built into Guttman scaling techniques.

The intensity of feeling is introduced in the Likert technique. The respondent is usually asked to indicate his feelings on a five-point scale ranging from strongly agree to strongly disagree. Tests of item discrimination are applied.

There is no single method that combines the advantages of all of them.[2] It is, therefore, important that we understand their respective purposes and the differences between them.

Notes

1. Paul F. Lazarsfeld and Morris Rosenberg, eds., *The Language of Social Research: A Reader in the Methodology of Social Research* (Glencoe, Ill.: Free Press 1962), p. 15.
2. The Scale Discrimination Technique developed by Allen Edwards makes an excellent attempt to secure a combination of the Thurstone, Likert, and Guttman features. See the following pages. Cf. Allen L. Edwards and Kathryn Claire Kenney, "A Comparison

of the Thurstone and Likert Techniques of Attitude Scale Construction," *Journal of Applied Psychology* 30 (1946): 72–83.

2.16.a. THURSTONE EQUAL-APPEARING INTERVAL SCALE

NATURE: This scale consists of a number of items whose position on the scale has been determined previously by a ranking operation performed by judges. The subject selects the responses that best describe how he feels.

UTILITY: This scale approximates an interval level of measurement. This means that the distance between any two numbers on the scale is of known size. Parametric and nonparametric statistics may be applied. See part 3, guide 5 of this handbook.

CONSTRUCTION:

1. The investigator gathers several hundred statements conceived to be related to the attitude being investigated.
2. A large number of judges (50–300) independently classify the statements in eleven groups ranging from most favorable to neutral to least favorable.
3. The scale value of a statement is computed as the median position to which it is assigned by the group of judges.
4. Statements that have too broad a spread are discarded as ambiguous or irrelevant.
5. The scale is formed by selecting items that are evenly spread along the scale from one extreme to the other.

Example: Brayfield and Roethe's Index of Job Satisfaction. This index is reproduced in part 4, section 1. The Thurstone technique is used in the initial development of the scale to provide equal-appearing intervals. The full scale contains eighteen items with Thurstone scale values ranging from 1.2 to 10.0 with approximately .5 step intervals. Some items from the scale representing the job satisfaction continuum are:

My job is like a hobby to me.

I am satisfied with my job for the time being.
I am often bored with my job.
Most of the time I have to force myself to go to work.

RESEARCH APPLICATIONS: Scales have been constructed to measure attitudes toward war, the church, capital punishment, the Chinese, blacks, whites, and institutions.

2.16b. LIKERT-TYPE SCALE

NATURE: This is a summated scale consisting of a series of items to which the subject responds. The respondent indicates agreement or disagreement with each item on an intensity scale. The Likert technique produces an ordinal scale that generally requires nonparametric statistics. See part 3, guide 5 of this handbook.

UTILITY: This scale is highly reliable when it comes to a rough ordering of people with regard to a particular attitude or attitude complex. The score includes a measure of intensity as expressed on each statement.

CONSTRUCTION:

1. The investigator assembles a large number of items considered relevant to the attitude being investigated and either clearly favorable or unfavorable.
2. These items are administered to a group of subjects representative of those with whom the questionnaire is to be used.
3. The responses to the various items are scored in such a way that a response indicative of the most favorable attitude is given the highest score.
4. Each individual's total score is computed by adding his or her item scores.
5. The responses are analyzed to determine which items differentiate most clearly between the highest and lowest quartiles of total scores.
6. The items that differentiate best (at least six) are used to form a scale.

Example: Rundquist and Sletto Scales of Morale and General Adjustment. See the Minnesota Survey of Opinions (long and short form) as reproduced in part 4, section 1. The scales to measure morale and general adjustment, and also inferiority, family, law, and economic conservatism, are examples of the Likert attitude scale technique. A significant characteristic is that each selected statement has been carefully researched to determine its discrimination through a criterion of interval consistency. A second feature is the addition of the intensity dimension to each statement as follows:

The Future Looks Very Black
Strongly agree^5 Agree^4 Undecided^3 Disagree^2 Strongly disagree^1
Most People Can Be Trusted
Strongly agree^1 Agree^2 Undecided^3 Disagree^4 Strongly disagree^5

2.16.c. GUTTMAN SCALE-ANALYSIS

NATURE: The Guttman technique attempts to determine the unidimensionality of a scale. Only items meeting the criterion of reproducibility are acceptable as scalable. If a scale is unidimensional, then a person who has a more favorable attitude than another should respond to each statement with equal or greater favorableness than the other.*

UTILITY: Each score corresponds to a highly similar response pattern or scale type. It is one of the few scales where the score can be used to predict the response pattern to all statements. Only a few statements (five to ten) are needed to provide a range of scalable responses. Note the analysis below showing how fourteen subjects responded (yes) to several statements and how scores reflect a given pattern of response.

---

* An excellent manual on how to construct and apply a unidimensional scale in social research is now available for novice researchers. See Raymond L. Gordon, *Unidimensional Scaling of Social Variables* (Riverside, N.J.: Free Press, 1977). For a critical analysis, see Nan Lin, *Foundations of Social Research* (New York: McGraw-Hill, 1976), p. 189.

Respondent	Item 7	Item 5	Item 1	Item 8	Item 2	Item 4	Item 6	Item 3	Score
7	yes	yes	yes	yes	yes	yes	yes	—	7
9	yes	yes	yes	yes	yes	yes	yes	—	7
10	yes	yes	yes	yes	yes	yes	—	—	6
1	yes	yes	yes	—	yes	yes	—	yes	6
13	yes	yes	yes	yes	yes	yes	—	—	6
3	yes	yes	yes	yes	yes	—	—	—	5
2	yes	yes	yes	yes	—	—	—	—	4
6	yes	yes	yes	yes	—	—	—	—	4
8	yes	yes	yes	—	—	yes	—	—	4
14	yes	yes	yes	yes	—	—	—	—	4
5	yes	yes	yes	—	—	—	—	—	3
4	yes	yes	—	—	—	—	—	—	2
11	—	—	—	—	yes	—	—	—	1
12	yes	—	—	—	—	—	—	—	1

CONSTRUCTION:

1. Select statements that are felt to apply to the measurable objective.
2. Test statements on a sample population (about 100).
3. Discard statements with more than 80 percent agreement or disagreement.
4. Order respondents from most favorable responses to fewest favorable responses. Order from top to bottom.
5. Order statements from most favorable responses to fewest favorable responses. Order from left to right.
6. Discard statements that fail to discriminate between favorable respondents and unfavorable respondents.
7. Calculate coefficient of reproducibility.
   a. Calculate the number of errors (favorable responses that do not fit pattern)

   b. $\text{Reproducibility} = 1 - \dfrac{\text{Number of errors}}{\text{Number of responses}}$

   c. If reproducibility equals .90, a unidimensional scale is said to exist.
8. Score each respondent by the number of favorable responses or response patterns.

EXAMPLE:

This Handbook reproduces one scale constructed by the Guttman Scaling Technique. This is Wallin's scale for measuring women's neighborhood practices, as shown on pages 411–12.

When attitudes are measured, the statements must permit a range of opinions and evoke a definite feeling. Note the statements scaled on air force personnel reflecting their satisfaction with the air force.

I have a poor opinion of the air force most of the time.
Most of the time the air force is not run very well.
I am usually dissatisfied with the air force.
The air force is better than any of the other services.
If I remain in military service I would prefer to remain in the air force.[*]

[*] From Delbert C. Miller and Nahum C. Medalia, "Efficiency, Leadership and Morale in Small Military Organizations," *Sociological Review* 3 (July 1955): 93–107.

2.16.d. SCALE-DISCRIMINATION TECHNIQUE

NATURE: This technique seeks to develop a set of items that meet the requirements of a unidimensional scale, possess equal-appearing intervals, and measure intensity. Aspects of the construction of Thurstone's equal-appearing intervals, Likert's summated scales, and Guttman's scale analysis are combined in this technique of Edwards and Kilpatrick.

UTILITY: Three distinct advantages of separate scaling techniques are combined. The interval scale quality of the Thurstone technique can be achieved. The discriminability between respondents and the addition of an intensity measure are derived from the Likert technique, and unidimensionality from the Guttman technique. Caution: Item analysis will eliminate items in the middle of the scale.

CONSTRUCTION:

1. Select a large number of statements that are thought to apply to the attitude being measured.
2. Discard items that are ambiguous or too extreme.
3. Give the statements to judges and have them judge the favorableness of each statement and place it in one of eleven categories.
4. Discard half the items with the greatest scatter or variance.
5. Assign scores to the remaining items as the median of the judges' scores.
6. Formulate the statements in the form of a summated scale and give to a new set of judges.
7. Perform an item analysis to determine which questions discriminate best between the lowest and highest quartiles.
8. Select twice the number of items that are wanted in the final scale. Select from each scale interval the statements that discriminate best.
9. Divide these statements in half.
10. Submit halves to separate test groups.
11. Determine coefficients of reproducibility for each test group and use if .90 or above.

2.16.e. RATING SCALES

NATURE: This technique seeks to obtain an evaluation or a quantitative judgment of personality, group, or institutional characteristics based upon personal judgments. The rater places the person or object being rated at some point along a continuum or in one of an ordered series of categories; a numerical value is attached to the point or the category.

UTILITY: Rating scales can be used to assess attitudes, values, norms, social activities, and social structural features.

CONSTRUCTION:

1. Divide the continuum to be measured into an optimal number of scale divisions (approximately 5–7).
2. The continuum should have no breaks or divisions.
3. The positive and negative poles should be alternated.
4. Introduce each trait with a question to which the rater can give an answer.
5. Use descriptive adjectives or phrases to define different points on the continuum.
6. Decide beforehand upon the probable extremes of the trait to be found in the group in which the scale is to be used.
7. Only universally understood descriptive terms should be used.
8. The end phrases should not be so extreme in meaning as to be avoided by the raters.

9. Descriptive phrases need not be evenly spaced.

10. Pretest. Ask respondents to raise any questions about the rating and the different points on the continuum if they are unclear.

11. To score, use numerical values as assigned.

Example: Miller's Scale Battery of International Patterns and Norms, reproduced in part 4, section J, contains twenty rating scales to ascertain important norms and patterns within national cultures. The significant feature is the meaningful continuum that can be developed with approximately worded statements or adjectives for each point on the continuum. The scale can be designed so that the researcher or the respondent may make the rating. An example of a rating scale is item 7, Moral Code and Role Definitions of Men and Women, taken from the Miller Scale Battery of International Patterns and Norms.

7. Moral Code and Role Definitions of Men and Women

1	2	3	4	5	6

Single code of morality prevails for men and women. Separate occupational and social roles are not defined for men and women. Similar amounts and standards of education prevail.	Variations between moral definitions for men and women exist for certain specified behaviors. Occupational and social role definitions vary in degree. Varying educational provisions for the sexes.	Double code of morality prevails. Separate occupational and social roles for men and women exist and are sharply defined. Amount and standards of education vary widely between the sexes.

2.16.f. LATENT DISTANCE SCALES

NATURE: A technique for scalogram analysis based on a probability model, that attempts to apply to qualitative data the principles of factor analysis providing ordinal information. The basic postulate is that there exists a set of latent classes such that the manifest relationship between any two or more items on a questionnaire can be accounted for by the existence of these latent classes and by these alone.

UTILITY: Unlike scalogram analysis, this technique includes imperfect scale types in the analysis without considering them as mistakes.

CONSTRUCTION:

1. List questions believed to be related to the latent attitude.

2. Dichotomize answers to questions in terms of positive-negative, favorable-unfavorable, etc.

3. Calculate proportion of respondents who demonstrate latent attitude in each response.

4. Arrange items in terms of their manifest marginals.

5. Compute the latent class frequencies through inverse-probability procedures.

6. Rank response patterns in terms of average latent position or use an index to characterize each response pattern.

Example: Latent Distance Scale on Neurotic Inventory

1. Have you ever been bothered by pressure or pains in the head?
    Positive answer: Yes, Often or Yes, Sometimes or No
                    Answer   13.8%
2. Have you ever been bothered by shortness of breath when you were not exercising
    or working hard?
    Positive answer: Yes, Often or Yes, Sometimes or No
                    Answer   30.7%
3. Do your hands ever tremble enough to bother you?
    Positive answer: Yes, Often or Yes, Sometimes or No
                    Answer   43.1%
4. Do you often have trouble in getting to sleep or staying asleep?
    Positive answer: Very Often or No Answer   57.1%

Complete Analysis of Latent Distance Scale on Neurotic Inventory

Response pattern 1 2 3 4	Percent of each pattern in latent class n_I	n_{II}	n_{III}	n_{IV}	n_V		Fitted total	Actual total
+ + + +	94.9%	4.2%	0.8%	0.1%	0.0%	100%	76.8	75
+ + − +	90.0	3.9	0.7	4.6	0.8	100%	14.6	10
+ + + −	90.4	4.0	0.7	0.1	4.8	100%	5.8	8
+ − + +	66.8	2.9	24.5	5.0	0.8	100%	16.3	14
− + + +	2.5	79.3	14.7	3.0	0.5	100%	108.3	110
− − + +	0.3	8.8	73.5	14.9	2.5	100%	145.4	141
− + − +	1.3	38.9	7.2	45.1	7.5	100%	39.7	49
+ − − +	24.5	1.1	9.0	56.1	9.3	100%	8.0	11
− − − +	0.0	1.4	11.9	74.3	12.4	100%	161.9	161
+ + − −	36.7	1.6	0.3	1.9	59.5	100%	2.6	3
− + + −	1.3	40.7	7.6	1.5	48.9	100%	15.2	11
+ − + −	25.9	1.2	9.5	1.9	61.5	100%	3.0	8
− − + −	0.1	1.5	12.8	2.6	83.0	100%	60.2	64
− + − −	0.1	2.5	0.5	2.9	94.0	100%	44.0	41
+ − − −	1.3	0.0	0.5	3.0	95.2	100%	10.9	9
− − − −	0.0	0.1	0.5	3.0	96.4	100%	287.3	285
Total in each class	109.9	129.5	161.3	181.4	417.9		1,000.0	1,000

The above items were taken from a neurotic inventory presented by Samuel A. Stouffer, *The American Soldier: Measurement and Prediction* (Princeton, N.J.: Princeton University Press, 1949), 4: 445. Consult the book for instruction in this technique or see section 2.9 of this handbook. The bibliography on Index and Scale Construction will prove useful. Paul F. Lazarsfeld developed latent structure analysis. See Lazarsfeld, "Recent Developments in Latent Structure Analysis," *Sociometry* 18 (December 1955): 647–59.

2.16.g. PAIRED COMPARISONS

NATURE: This technique seeks to determine psychological values of qualitative stimuli without knowledge of any corresponding respondent values. By asking respondents to select the more favorable of a pair of statements or objects over a set of several pairs, an attempt is made to order the statements or objects along a continuum. It is sometimes called the forced-choices technique.

Note how it is applied in the Neal and Seeman Powerlessness Scale reproduced in part 4, section J.

UTILITY: The ordering by paired comparisons is a relatively rapid process for securing a precise and relative positioning along a continuum. Comparative ordering generally increases reliability and validity over arbitrary rating methods.

CONSTRUCTION:

1. Select statements that relate to the attribute being measured.
2. Combine statements in all possible combination of pairs. $\dfrac{N(N-1)}{2}$
3. Ask judges to select which statement of each pair is the more favorable.
4. Calculate the proportion of judgments each statement received over every other statement.
5. Total the proportions for each statement.
6. Translate the proportions into standardized scale values.
7. Apply an internal consistency check by computing the absolute average discrepancy.
8. Present statements to respondents and ask them to indicate favorableness or unfavorableness to each statement.
9. Respondent's score is the median of his favorable responses.

Example: Hill's Scale of Attitudes Toward Involvement in the Korean War*

Item set favorable to U.S. involvement in Korea	Paired comparison scale score
1. I suppose the United States has no choice but to continue the Korean war.	0.00
2. We should be willing to give our allies in Korea more money if they need it.	0.74
3. Withdrawing our troops from Korea at this time would only make matters worse.	0.98
4. The Korean war might not be the best way to stop communism, but it was the only thing we could do.	1.07
5. Winning the Korean war is absolutely necessary whatever the cost.	1.25
6. We are protecting the United States by fighting in Korea.	1.46
7. The reason we are in Korea is to defend freedom.	1.71

2.16.h. SEMANTIC DIFFERENTIAL

NATURE: The semantic differential seeks to measure the meaning of an object to an individual. The subject is asked to rate a given concept (e.g., "Negro," "Republican," "wife," "me as I would like to be," "me as I am") on a series of seven-point, bipolar rating scales. Any concept, whether it is a politi-

* From Richard J. Hill, "A Note on Inconsistency in Paired Comparison Judgments," *American Sociological Review* 18 (October 1953): 564–66. Richard Ofshe and Ronald E. Anderson have translated Hill's Korea items to Vietnam and the Vietnam scale is described in "Testing a Measurement Model," in *Sociological Methodology,* ed. Edgar F. Borgatta (San Francisco: Jossey-Bass, 1969).

cal issue, a person, an institution, or a work of art, can be rated. The seven-point scales include such bipolar scales as the following: (*A*) fair–unfair, clean–dirty, good–bad, valuable–worthless; (*B*) large–small, strong–weak, heavy–light; (*C*) active–passive, fast–slow, hot–cold. The rating is made according to the respondent's perception of the relatedness or association of the adjective to the word concept. Osgood and his colleagues have inferred that the three subgroups (*A*), (*B*), and (*C*) measure the following three dimensions of attitude:

A—the individual's *evaluation* of the object or concept being rated, corresponding to the favorable–unfavorable dimension of more traditional attitude scales.
B—the individual's perception of the *potency* or power of the object or concept.
C—his perception of the *activity* of the object or concept.

The authors suggest that the measuring instrument is not grossly affected by the nature of the object being measured or by the type of persons using the scale. For further information see the developers of the semantic differential: Charles E. Osgood, George J. Suci, and Percy H. Tannenbaum, *The Measurement of Meaning* (Urbana: University of Illinois Press, 1957).

UTILITY: A 100-item test can be administered in about ten to fifteen minutes. A 400-item test takes about one hour. The semantic differential may be adapted through choice of concepts and scales to the study of numerous phenomena. It may be useful in constructing and analyzing sociometric scales.

CONSTRUCTION:

1. Prepare a list of concepts appropriate to the theory guiding the variable to be measured.
2. Pairs of polar adjectives are selected on a priori grounds.
3. Selection of adjectives is determined empirically by asking different groups (comparative or experimental-control design) to take prescribed orientations in responding to an adjective-rating task. For example, one group of respondents is asked to rate as it believes a person would rate the concept if he held a positive attitude; another group of respondents is asked to rate as it believes a person would rate the concept if he held a strong negative attitude.

   Respondents are given the standard instructions for using the semantic differential form (Osgood, Suci, and Tannenbaum, *Measurement of Meaning*). Analyze data and select adjective pairs that distinguish clearly between the groups.
4. Select new groups of respondents who take prescribed orientations in rating the concepts. Analyze data. For guidance, again see Osgood, Suci, and Tannenbaum.

2.16.i. MULTIDIMENSIONAL SCALING

The majority of scaling techniques that have been described produce one-dimensional scales, i.e., the scales consist of a single continuum along which are located a succession of the opinion items. Multidimensional scaling is a technique that is increasingly of interest to the social sciences. In psychophysics multidimensional scaling has been utilized for some time.[1] In the study of attitudes, however, there is a dearth of satisfactory methods, but there is nothing to prevent the adoption of the multidimensional method to the attitude domain. The key concept involved is that of social or psychological

A Sample of a Semantic Differential Scale*

Fifteen concepts:

Love, Child, My Doctor, Me, My Job, Mental Sickness, My Mother, Peace of Mind, Fraud, My Spouse, Self-control, Hatred, My Father, Confusion, Sex
Each concept was rated on the following ten scales:

valuable	____:____:____:____:____:____:____	worthless
clean	____:____:____:____:____:____:____	dirty
tasty	____:____:____:____:____:____:____	distasteful
large	____:____:____:____:____:____:____	small
strong	____:____:____:____:____:____:____	weak
deep	____:____:____:____:____:____:____	shallow
fast	____:____:____:____:____:____:____	slow
active	____:____:____:____:____:____:____	passive
hot	____:____:____:____:____:____:____	cold
tense	____:____:____:____:____:____:____	relaxed

* This sample Semantic Differential was used in a study reported by Charles E. Osgood and Zella Luria, "A Blind Analysis of a Case of Multiple Personality Using the Semantic Differential," *Journal of Abnormal and Social Psychology* 49 (1954): 579–91. For detailed information see James G. Snider and Charles E. Osgood, eds. *Semantic Differential Technique, A Sourcebook.* Hawthorne, N.Y. Aldine, 1969.

distance. Social distance is well known; see, for example, the Bogardus scale and the research cited in part 4. Psychological distance is a concept employed in approach and avoidance gradient theory[2] and in Lewin's field theory.[3]

If social or psychological distance can be analyzed as though it were physical distance, it would be possible to draw a "map" of the way in which an individual structures the similarities and differences among attitudes (or behavioral or organizational characteristics) in a given domain. On such a map, short distances would represent similarity or agreement, and long distances would represent dissimilarity or disagreement. Multidimensional scales based upon the interpretation of dissimilarities or disagreements as distances have already been constructed with nonpsychological stimuli.[4]

For students interested in multidimensional scaling, a good model is that of Robert P. Abelson, "A Technique and a Model for Multi-Dimensional Attitude Scaling," *Public Opinion Quarterly* (Winter 1954–55): 405–18. Also reprinted in Martin Fishbein, ed., *Readings in Attitude Theory and Measurement* (New York: Wiley, 1967), pp. 147–56.

Students interested in applying multidimensional scaling to social characteristics should see Joel H. Levine, "The Sphere of Influence," *American Sociological Review* 37 (February 1972): 14–27. Levine describes an analysis of a network of interlocking directorates, specifically the network in which the boards of major banks interact with the boards of major industrials in the United States. He constructs maps showing "spheres of influence." The sectors of the sphere represent similarly linked corporations, and the relations among the sectors represent the relations among bank industrial communities. Smallest-space analysis is utilized.

Another very interesting application of multidimensional scaling can be found in Edward O. Laumann, "The Social Structure of Religious and Ethnoreligious Groups in a Metropolitan Community," *American Sociological Review* 3, 4 (April 1969): 182–97. The relatively new technique of smallest-space analysis is used to analyze the formation of friendship relations among 15 religious and 27 ethnoreligious groups. Indexes of Dissimilarity of friendship choices are computed, and three dimensional solutions are mapped.

Good treatments of multidimensional scaling for advanced students are Clyde H. Coombs, *A Theory of Data* (New York: Wiley, 1967), pp. 444–95; Warren S. Torgerson, *Theory and Methods of Scaling* (New York: Wiley, 1960), pp. 247–97; Susan S. Schiffman, M. Lance Reynolds, and Forrest W. Young, *Introduction to Multidimensional Scaling* (New York: Academic Press, 1981).

Notes

1. M. W. Richardson, "Multidimensional Psychophysics," *Psychological Bulletin* 35 (1938): 659–60.
2. N. Miner, "Comment on Theoretical Models," *Journal of Personality* 20 (1951): 82–100.
3. Kurt Lewin, *Principles of Topological Psychology* (New York: McGraw-Hill, 1936).
4. F. L. Klingberg, "Studies in Measurement of the Relations Among Sovereign States," *Psychometrika* 6 (1941): 335–52; C. E. Osgood and G. J. Suci, "A Measure of Relations Determined by Both Mean Difference and Profile Information," *Psychological Bulletin* 49 (1952): 251–62. For other applications see Roger N. Shepard, A. Kimball Romney, and Sarah Beth Nerlove, eds., *Multidimensional Scaling: Theory and Applications in the Behavioral Sciences, vols. I, II* (New York: Academic Press, 1972).

GUIDE TO BODIES OF COLLECTED DATA FOR THE SOCIAL SCIENCE RESEARCHER: DATA REFERENCES AND DATA ARCHIVES   *2.17*

Instructions for the Use of Guide 2.17

Two major kinds of information resources are important to the researcher. The first contains bibliographic *references* to documents that contain data; the second consists of *collected data* such as population characteristics, public opinion, or voting records. The modern researcher explores both sources before embarking on the expensive task of collecting new data. Today great stores of data are available, often at no cost or limited cost. Data seldom are exhaustively analyzed by the original research effort, although the initial collection may have cost hundreds of thousands of dollars. It may be an unexplored gold mine of data for the problem a researcher wishes to investigate. A review of data sources is now as important as a review of the research literature.

Data References

Directory of Data Bases in the Social and Behavioral Sciences, edited by Vivian Sessions. Science Associates/International, Inc., 23 East 26 Street, New York, N.Y. 10010. 1974. 300 pp.

Contains references for some 1500 groups of data files from over 650 organizations throughout the world, representing the data holdings of governmental, academic, and commercial organizations. Information on data files includes major subject field, title, time frame of data, geographic coverage, data sources, and data collection agency. Also contains profiles of reporting organizations. Completely indexed.

The National Archives and Statistical Research, edited by Meyer H. Fishbein. Ohio University Press, Athens, Ohio 45701. 1973. 255 pp.

Proceedings of a conference held May 27 and 28, 1968, cosponsored by the National Archives and Records Service and the National Academy of Science. Examines statistical data available in the records of the National Archives; discusses uses by economists, historians, geographers, political scientists, sociologists, and statisticians; and discusses current production of conventional and electronic statistical source records as well as criteria for preserving records for future research.

The Review of Public Data Use. Data Use and Access Laboratories (DUALabs), Suite 900, 1601 North Kent Street, Arlington, Va. 22209.

This is an interdisciplinary journal published by a nonprofit corporation and devoted to the spectrum of intellectual activity associated with public data access and use. It publishes primary articles and current awareness information on social science research and methodology using publicly available data bases as well as planning and research in state and local government fields. In addition, it covers computer software for accessing statistical data files, information technology, technical problems of data file use, legislation and administrative actions affecting public access, and foreign developments.

S S Data. Newsletter of Social Science Archival Acquisitions, 321A Schaffer Hall, University of Iowa, Iowa City, Iowa 52242. Published quarterly in September, December, March, and June by the Laboratory for Political Research of the University of Iowa.

Its purpose is to communicate information on the current acquisitions of social science data archives to social science researchers. More than 40 archives are now cooperating in providing information about the original data collection agency and principal investigator, the time period of the data, the population covered, and a paragraph describing the substance of the study.* The information received is classified under Sociology, Political Science, History, Public Opinion Surveys, and Miscellaneous. The newsletter also publishes descriptions of the archives participating in the project and information on new technical developments that enhance the use of machine-readable data for research and instruction.

1975 Directory of Computerized Data Files and Related Software Available from Federal Agencies. National Technical Information Service, Springfield, Va. 1975. This directory is a product of the National Technical Information Service (NTIS) of the U.S. Department of Commerce.

This is essentially a bibliographic project. A few of the 72 subject fields are consumer affairs, elections, immigration, price statistics and price indexes, state and local government finance, and international relations. Although originally weak in the "soft sciences," the system is now more heavily committed to the social sciences, and to the urban area in particular. NTIS, for those who are unfamiliar with it, offers numerous bibliographic information services: a weekly index to documents wholly or partially funded by federal money in just about every aspect of human endeavor, a weekly

* See List of Cooperating Archives as shown in this Handbook, pp. 150–52.

abstract service for the most significant documents in specialty areas, information retrieval services either in batch mode through direct query to NTIS or on-line through both the Lockheed and the Systems Development dial-up systems, and physical access to the documents themselves in either microform or hard copy. Each NTIS reference to a data file has an identifying title, a date, name of the generating agency, the distributing agency (if different), notes about the number of tapes in each file, the density of the tapes, the number of tracks, and the coding structure. There is also an abstract of about 100 words describing the contents of the file as to subject, kinds of variables, and the number of records in the file. The subject index, in addition to providing subject access to the contents of the 530 computerized data files listed in this edition of the *Directory*, is also a good source of terminology for others who are faced with the problem of analyzing the contents of data files. (This description is drawn from Vivian S. Sessions, *Public Data Use* 3 [January 1975]: 3.) Of special interest to the social scientist is the weekly *Behavior and Society*, containing government abstracts of social research projects.

University On-Line Computer Searches for Social Scientists

An increasing number of universities are providing their own on-line bibliographic search. For example, Indiana University has a contract with the Lockheed Retrieval Service which furnishes the following data references:

Sociological Abstracts On-Line.

Over 60,000 citations from the world's sociological literature. Coverage is from 1963 to present. File is updated quarterly.

Social Scisearch On-Line.

Equivalent to printed *Social Sciences Citation Index*. Journal literature and books in the social and behavioral sciences. Covers from 1972 to present. Updated monthly. Growth is 80,000 items per year.

Social Science Data Archives in the United States*

The Inter-university Consortium for Political and Social Research is essentially a vast archive of machine-readable data. The results of numerous studies and a huge number of facts are available to potentially every researcher in the world. The ICPSR is a federation of 240 colleges and universities worldwide. Each make available data that are often not fully explored by the researchers who collect them and through the Consortium they are made available for continuing study by others. Many of the major studies of the Institute of Social Research, University of Michigan, are in the ICPSR archive. Major studies of the National Opinion Research Center's General Social Survey are also available. Frequently requested data sets in the huge archive are those from the decennial Census of the United States from the beginning of its history until 1980. ICPRS has both the National Archive for Computerized Data on Aging and the Criminal Justice Archive and Information Network.

*Assembled and described by David Nasatir, asst. research sociologist, Survey Research Center, University of California, Berkeley, Calif. *The American Sociologist* 2 (November 1967): 207–12.

Inquiries about ICPSR and its data holdings and services should be addressed to: Executive Director, Inter-university Consortium for Political and Social Research, P.O. Box 1248, Ann Arbor, MI 48106.

Because the list of the 240 ICPSR archives is too large to publish, two smaller but very significant archive confederations are shown. The first contains members of the original Council of Social Science Data Archives. The type of data and subject matter are shown. The second list contains those archives currently cooperating with the Laboratory for Political Research, University of Iowa. There is overlap but together the two lists represent a fairly exhaustive bibliography of social data. For employment of data banks those researchers described by Hymans demonstrate how productive use can be made of such archival data.* Deutsch's statement about comparisons across time, space, concepts, and methods illustrate that the surface of prospects for data bank use is barely scratched.†

Table 1. *Members of the Council of Social Science Data Archives*[1]

Name of data library	Address	Type of data	Subject matter
Archive on Political Elites in Eastern Europe	Dept. of Political Science 1028 H Cathedral of Learning University of Pittsburgh Pittsburgh, PA 15123	Biographical information	Political elites in Eastern Europe
Archive on Comparative Political Elites	Dept. of Political Science University of Oregon Eugene, OR 97403		
Bureau of Applied Social Research	Columbia University 605 West 115 Street New York, NY 10025	Sample surveys	Health and welfare occupations and professions, mass communications, politics, education, organizations
Bureau of Labor Statistics[2]	United States Department of Lab.		
Carleton University, Social Science Data Archive	Dept. of Political Science Carleton University Colonel By Drive Ottawa 1, Canada	Sample surveys, Biographies, Election statistics, Census data	Politics and public opinion
Center for International Studies Data Bank	Mass. Inst. of Technology E53-365, Herman Building Cambridge, MA 02139	Sample surveys	Politics, social behavior, public opinion

* Herbert Hyman, *Secondary Analysis of Sample Surveys* (New York: Wiley, 1972).

† Karl W. Deutsch, "The Impact of Complex Data Bases on the Social Sciences," in *Data Bases, Computers and the Social Sciences,* ed. Ralph Bisco (New York: Wiley, 1970), pp. 19–41.

Table 1. (*Continued*)

Name of data library	Address	Type of data	Subject matter
Columbia University School of Public Health and Administrative Medicine Research Archives	630 West 168 Street New York, NY 10032	Sample surveys, Operational data	Administrative medicine, public health
Council for Inter-Societal Studies	Northwestern University 1818 Sheridan Road Evanston, IL 60201		
National Opinion Research Center	University of Chicago 6030 South Ellis Avenue Chicago, IL 60637	Sample surveys	Health and welfare, mass communication, community problems
Political Science Research Library and Political Data Program	Yale University 89 Trumbell Street New Haven, CT 06520	Sample surveys	Studies from Roper ICPR in political science
Public Opinion Survey Unit	Research Center, School of Business & Public Administ. University of Missouri Columbia, MO 65201	Sample surveys	Politics and public opinion in Missouri,
Project Talent Data Bank	132 North Bellefield Avenue Pittsburgh, PA 15213	Sample surveys	High school student attitudes surveys, career plans, aptitude tests
Roper Public Opinion Research Center[2]	Williams College Williamstown, MA 01267	Sample surveys	Politics, economics, business, education, public opinion
Social Science Data and Program Library Service[2]	Social Systems Research Inst. Rm. 4451, Social Science Bldg. University of Wisconsin Madison WI 53703	Sample surveys	Economics, demography
Survey Research Laboratory	437 David Kinley Hall University of Illinois Urbana, IL 61801	Sample surveys, Statistics	Politics, economics, public opinion
UCLA Political Behavior Archive	Dept. of Political Science University of California Los Angeles, CA 90024		
Yale Growth Center	Yale University 52 Hillhouse Avenue New Haven, CT 06520	National accounts	Country analysis of underdeveloped nations
Graduate School of Industrial Administration	Carnegie Inst. of Technology Pittsburgh, PA 15213	Ecological statistics, Sample surveys	French cantons: election and demographic statistics
Human Relations Area Files	Yale University P.O. Box 2054 Yale Station New Haven, CT 06520	Some machine-readable data, reports, bibliographies, texts	Social structure, organization: diet practices, kinship

Table 1. (*Continued*)

Name of data library	Address	Type of data	Subject matter
International Data Library and Reference Service[2]	Survey Research Center 2220 Piedmont Avenue University of California Berkeley, CA 94720	Sample surveys	Politics, communication, social behavior. Emphasis on Asia, Latin America
International Development Data Bank	Michigan State University 322 Union Building East Lansing, MI 48823		List of Archive holdings is available
Inter-University Consortium for Political Research[2]	University of Michigan P.O. Box 1248 Ann Arbor MI 48106	Sample surveys	Political behavior, Public opinion
Laboratory for Political Research	Dept. of Political Science University of Iowa Iowa City, IA 52240	Sample surveys, Voting studies	Politics; biography data on American and Argentine legislators
Louis Harris Political Data Center[2]	Dept. of Political Science University of North Carolina Cardwell Hall Chapel Hill, NC 27514	Public-opinion surveys	Politics in individual states in U.S.

[1] This is not an exhaustive list of data archives as it contains only those who had affiliated with the Council of Social Science Data Archives. The Council itself is not currently active. The List of Archives Cooperating with the Laboratory for Political Research, University of Iowa (below) provides a list of archives cooperating in political research.

[2] General purpose, service-oriented libraries. Materials in these libraries are routinely available to the entire community of social scientists.

Table 2. *List of Archives Cooperating with the Laboratory for Political Research, University of Iowa.* *

Project TALENT Data Bank
American Institute for Research
P.O. Box 1113
Palo Alto, CA 94302

Alfred J. Tuchfarber, Jr., Director
Behavioral Sciences Laboratory
University of Cincinnati
Cincinnati, OH 45221

Phillippe Laurent
Belgian Archives for the Social Sciences
Place Montesquieu, 1 Boite 18
B-1348 Louvain-la-Neuve, Belgium

Celade Latin American Population Data Bank
United Nations Latin American Demographic Center (CELADE)
Casilla 91
Santiago, Chile

Social Science Data Librarian
Center for Social Analysis
State University of New York
Binghamton, NY 13901

Center for Quantitative Studies in Social Sciences
117 Savery Hall
DK-45
University of Washington
Seattle, WA 98195

Per Nielsen
Danish Data Archives
Odense University
Niels Bohrs Alle 25
DK-5230 Odense M
Denmark

Table 2. (*Continued*)

Alice Robbin
Data and Program Library Service
4451 Social Science Building
University of Wisconsin
Madison, WI 53706

Laine Ruus
Data Library
6356 Agricultural Road
Room 206
University Campus
Vancouver, British Columbia
Canada V6T 1W5

Data Librarian
Data Library
Survey Research Center
University of California
Berkeley, CA 94720

Drug Abuse Epidemiology Data Center
Institute of Behavioral Research
Texas Christian University
Fort Worth, TX 76129

Librarian
Information Documentation Center
Dualabs, Inc.
1601 N. Kent Street, Suite 900
Arlington, VA 22209

**European Consortium for Political Re-
search**
Data Information Service
Fantoftvegen 38
N-5036 Fantoft-Bergen
Norway

Thomas Atkinson, Director
Data Bank
Institute for Behavioral Research
York University
4700 Keele Street
Downsview, Ontario
Canada

Assistant Director for Member Services
**Inter-University Consortium for Political
and Social Research**
P.O. Box 1248
Ann Arbor, MI 48106

E. M. Avedon
Leisure Studies Data Bank
University of Waterloo
Waterloo, Ontario
Canada N2L 3G1

Reference Service
Machine-Readable Archives Division
(NNR)

National Archives and Records Service
Washington, DC 20408

Patrick Bova
National Opinion Research Center
University of Chicago
6030 South Ellis Avenue
Chicago, IL 60637

Lorraine Borman
**Northwestern University Information
Center**
Vogelback Computing Center
Northwestern University
Evanston, IL 60201

**Norwegian Social Science Data Ser-
vices**
Universiteet i Bergen
Hans Holmboesgt. 22
N-5014 Bergen-Univ.
Norway

Robert Darcy
Oklahoma Data Archive
Center for the Application of the Social
Sciences
Oklahoma State University
Stillwater, OK 74074

Stuart J. Thorson
Polimetrics Laboratory
Department of Political Science
Ohio State University
Columbus, OH 43210

Political Science Data Archive
Department of Political Science
Michigan State University
East Lansing, MI 48823

Gerald Wright, Director
**Political Science Laboratory and Data
Archive**
Department of Political Science
248 Woodburn Hall
Indiana University
Bloomington, IN 47401

David K. Miller, Director
Project Impress
Dartmouth College
Hanover, NH 03755

Machine-Readable Archives
Public Archives Canada
395 Wellington Street
Ottawa, Ontario
Canada K1A ON3

Table 2. (*Continued*)

Roper Center, Inc. Box U-164R University of Connecticut Storrs, CT 06268	Sue A. Dodd **Social Science Data Library** University of North Carolina Room 10 Manning Hall Chapel Hill, NC 27514
Social Data Exchange Association 229 Waterman Street Providence, RI 02906	Judith S. Rowe **Social Science User Service** Princeton University Computer Center
Social Science Computer Research In- **stitute** 621 Mervis Hall University of Pittsburgh Pittsburgh, PA 15260	87 Prospect Avenue Princeton, NJ 08540 Patricia Meece **SRL Data Archive** Survey Research Laboratory
James Grifhorst **Social Science Data Archive** Laboratory for Political Research 321A Schaeffer Hall University of Iowa Iowa City, IA 52242	1005 W. Nevada Street University of Illinois Urbana, IL 61801 Director **SSRC Survey Archive** University of Essex
JoAnn Dionne **Social Science Data Archive** Social Science Library Yale University Box 1958 Yale Station New Haven, CT 06520	Wivenhoe Park, Colchester Essex, England Jack Citrin, Director **State Data Program, Survey Research** **Center**
Social Science Data Archives Department of Sociology and Anthropol- ogy Carleton University Colonel By Drive Ottawa, Ontario Canada K1S 5B6	2538 Channing Way University of California Berkeley, CA 94720 Robert M. deVoursney **State Government Data Base** Council of State Governments Iron Works Pike Lexington, KY 40578
Everett C. Ladd, Jr. **Social Science Data Center** University of Connecticut Storrs, CT 06268	**Steinmetzarchief** Herengracht 410–412 1017 BX Amsterdam Netherlands
James Pierson **Social Science Data Center** University of Pennsylvania 353 McNeil Bldg. CR 3718 Locust Walk Philadelphia, PA 19104	**Zentral Archive fur Empirische Sozial** **Forschung** Universitat zu Koln Bachemer str. 40 D-5000 Koln 41 West Germany

* List from *S.S. Data, Newsletter of Social Science Archival Acquisitions* 10 (Spring 1981): 7–8.

Base for Archives of Institutional Change

An organization has been formed in Washington, D.C., to survey the social responses of institutions devoted to the advancement and application of knowledge. The Archives of Institutional Change is a nonprofit documentation center that collects reports and published findings of studies of educational and research institutions, libraries, learned and professional societies, museums, experimental social services, and comparable establishments, primarily in North America. In cooperation with Acropolis Books of Washington, D.C., the Archives has published a number of institutional studies in a series with the overall title of *Prometheus*. The titles of the first four books were as follows: *The Bankruptcy of Academic Policy; Scientific Institutions of the Future; Talent Waste—How Institutions of Learning Misdirect Human Resources;* and *Documenting Change in the Institutions of Knowledge—A Prometheus Bibliography.*

Inquiries are invited and may be addressed to the Archives of Institutional Change, Georgetown Office Service Center, 3160 O Street, N.W., Washington, DC 20007.

Major Data Sources of Political Statistics for the United States*

The Almanac of American Politics, 1976. By Michael Barone, Grant Ujifusa, and Douglas Matthews. (New York: Dutton, 1975. Pp. xviii, 1054. $7.95.)

Congressional District Data Book, 93d Congress. Bureau of the Census, Social and Economic Statistics Administration, U.S. Department of Commerce. (Washington, D.C.: U.S. Government Printing Office, 1973. Pp. xvii, 550. $8.30.)

Congressional Directory, 1976, 94th Congress, 2nd Session. Joint Committee on Printing. (Washington, D.C.: U.S. Government Printing Office, 1976. Pp. xxxii, 1146. $8.50 in cloth, $6.50 in paper.)

County and City Data Book, 1972. Bureau of the Census, Social and Economic Statistics Administration, U.S. Department of Commerce. (Washington, D.C.: U.S. Government Printing Office, 1973. Pp. lvi, 1020. $18.65.)

The Gallup Poll: Public Opinion 1935–1971. By George H. Gallup. (New York: Random House, 1972. Pp. xliv, 2388, in 3 volumes. $95.00.)

Guide to U.S. Elections. Edited by Robert A. Diamond. (Washington, D.C.: Congressional Quarterly, 1975. Pp. xvi, 1103. $48.50.)

Party Strength in the United States, 1872–1970. By Paul T. David. (Charlottesville, Va.: University of Virginia Press, 1972. Pp. xiii, 310. $9.75.)

The Political Marketplace. Edited by David L. Rosenbloom. (New York: Quadrangle Books and Campaign Communications Institute for Politics, Inc., 1972. Pp. xix, 949. $25.00.)

1973 Republican Almanac. Produced by the Political/Research Division, Republican National Committee, 310 First Street, S.E., Washington, DC 20003. (Washington, D.C.: 1973. Pp. 422. No price.)

1970, 1972, and *1974 Congressional Vote Statistics.* National Republican Congressional Committee, Pierre M. Purves, Director, Statistics. (Washington, D.C.: National Republican Congressional Committee, 1971, 1973, and 1975. No pagination, each volume approximately 500 pages. No price.)

State and National Voting in Federal Elections, 1910–1970. By Edward Franklin Cox. (Hamden, Conn.: Archon Books, Shoe String Press, 1972. Pp. xv, 280. $15.00.)

Statistical Abstract of the United States, 1975. Bureau of the Census, U.S. Department of Commerce. (Washington, D.C.: U.S. Government Printing Office, 1975. Pp. xx, 1050. $8.00 in paper, $10.50 in cloth.)

Voting and Registration in the Election of November 1972. U.S. Bureau of the Census, *Current Population Reports,* Series P-20, No. 253. (Washington, D.C.: U.S. Government Printing Office, 1973, Pp. iii, 214. $3.30.)

* Compiled by Edward R. Tufte. See his "Political Statistics for the United States: Observations on Some Major Data Sources," *American Political Science Review* 71 (March 1977): 305–314.

The Human Relations Area Files

Any student or research scholar interested in a question involving cross-cultural and comparative material will find the Human Relations Area Files useful. These files have been called a vast ethnographic encyclopedia. There is information on more than 300 cultural groups around the world, and for them there are 888 different categories of cultural and natural information. The material may be found on 5 x 8 paper slips or 3 x 5 microfilm cards depending on the institution. These have accumulated by the tens of thousands with more than a thousand items added yearly.

Most major universities house these files. For more than a quarter of a century, the Human Relations Area Files Inc. (HRAF), a nonprofit research organization sponsored by 25 major universities, has served the educational community by making available primary research materials and by encouraging systematic cross-cultural research. Useful publications of HRAF include:

LAGACE, ROBERT O. *Nature and Use of the HRAF Files.* New Haven, Conn.: Human Relations Area Files, 1974. 49 pp. $1.00 Paper.

———, ed. *Sixty Cultures: A Guide to the HRAF Probability Sample Files.* New Haven, Conn: *Human Relations Area Files,* 1977. 507 pp. $10.00 Cloth.

NAROLL, RAOUL; MICHIK, GARY L.; and NAROLL, FRADA. *Worldwide Theory Testing,* New Haven, Conn.: Human Relations Area Files, 1976. 138 pp. $5.00 Paper.

For further information write: Human Relations Area Files, 755 Prospect Street, New Haven, CT, Box 2054, Yale Station 06520. Representative examples of published research drawing on HRAF files, listed in order of publication, are:

MURDOCK, GEORGE PETER. *Social Structure.* New York, 1949.

FREEDMAN, LAWRENCE Z., and FERGUSON, VERA M. "The Question of 'Painless Childbirth' in Primitive Cultures." *American Journal of Orthopsychiatry* 20 (1950).

FORD, CLELLAN S., and BEACH, FRANK A. *Patterns of Sexual Behavior.* New York, 1951.

WHITING, JOHN W. M., and CHILD, IRVING L. *Child Training and Personality: A Cross-Cultural Study.* New Haven, 1953.

SPRIO, M. E., and D'ANDRADE, ROY. "A Cross-Cultural Study of Some Supernatural Beliefs," *American Anthropologist* 60 (1958).

UDY, STANLEY. *Organization of Work.* New Haven, 1959.

ROBERTS, J. M.; ARTH, M. J.; BUSH, R. R. "Games in Culture." *American Anthropologist* 61 (1959).

NAROLL, RAOUL. "A Tentative Index of Culture Stress." *International Journal of Social Psychiatry* 5 (1959).

NAG, MONI. *Factors Affecting Human Fertility in Nonindustrial Societies: A Cross-Cultural Study.* YUPA No. 66, 1962.

STEPHENS, WILLIAM N. *The Family in Cross-Cultural Perspective.* New York, 1963.

TEXTOR, ROBERT B. *A Cross-Cultural Summary.* New Haven, 1967.

2.18   **GUIDE TO THE U.S. CENSUS AND BUREAU OF LABOR STATISTICS: DATA REFERENCES AND DATA ARCHIVES**

Instructions for the Use of Guide 2.18

The U.S. Census is one of the richest sources of primary data for the social scientist. The data are collected at ten-year intervals as a national enumeration of the U.S. population. Various survey samples of many different kinds are taken at intervals between the decennial censuses. Because of its magnitude and importance, a special section has been prepared. Data references are first shown and then the character of the data bank is described. Almost every field of sociology can draw upon this magnificent collection, and the U.S. Census staff are anxious to help the researcher.

The Bureau of Labor Statistics in the Department of Labor is an excellent complement to the U.S. Census. It gathers a large amount of information on occupations and the changes affecting them. It is a major source of data about cost of living, wages, strikes, and industrial relations generally. The Bureau will cooperate with researchers seeking data relevant to the responsibilities of the office.

Data References: A Primer on 1980 Census References and Guides

1980 Census Users' Guide

The primary guide for serious users of 1980 census data. This is the reference source to turn to for more information on all aspects of the 1980 census, from collection and processing methodology, to products and services. The new Guide is issued on a subscription basis so that users will automatically receive occasional updates and supplementary material.

Data User News

The Bureau's monthly newsletter for data users. It reports on new publications and computer tapes, developments in Bureau services to users, upcoming conferences and training courses, and related matters. It includes the quarterly supplement, *1980 Census Update.*

Bureau of the Census Catalog

Issued quarterly with monthly supplements, the *Catalog* provides a comprehensive listing of all new publications, computer tape files, and special tabulations.

1980 Census Indexes

Comprehensive subject matter and geographic indexes to data tables from both published reports and computer tape files from the 1980 Census.

There are a number of specialized guides which are fully listed in *Census '80: Continuing the Factfinder Tradition,* U.S. Department of Commerce, Bureau of the Census (a text prepared by Charles P. Kaplan and Thomas L. Van Valey), U.S. Government Printing Office, Washington, D.C., 1980, pp. 351–59.

U.S. Census Data Files and Special Tabulations

The Bureau of the Census publishes only essential and widely useful data in its printed reports of censuses and surveys, but much more information is available to the public. The Bureau maintains data files that can be processed to provide almost unlimited subject cross-classifications and area tabulations. Some of these tape and punchcard files, which do not contain confidential individual records, may be purchased and used by the purchaser for making tabulations. All files, under appropriate circumstances, can be used by the

Bureau to prepare tabulations specified by customers. Special tabulations can also be prepared directly from files of filled-in questionnaires. Tabulations made from individual records are subject to review to make certain that the results are in such summary form that no individual information is disclosed. Some unpublished nonstatistical information is also available, including maps, computer programs, and address directories of public officials.

The materials are arranged according to major subject field. Within each field, the items generally are separated into two groups, Data Files and Selected Special Tabulations, with the occasional use of a third category, Other Materials. Under Data Files are listed the large machine-readable files that have become available during the period covered by this issue of the *Catalog;* the contents of each are described, and the description indicates whether the files are for sale or may be used only by the Census Bureau to prepare tabulations for individual customers. Under Selected Special Tabulations are listed examples of tabulations prepared during the current period for individual users. Under Other Materials are maps and computer programs as well as materials that have become available during the period covered by this issue of the *Catalog.*

A section describing available machine-readable materials first appeared in the 1964 *Catalog.* It provided information on many data files of the 1960 Censuses of Population and Housing, the 1959 Census of Agriculture, the 1958 Census of Business and Manufactures, the 1962 Census of Governments, the *County and City Data Book,* and other series which have not been repeated in later issues of the *Catalog.* The 1969 edition of *Guide to Census Bureau Data Files and Special Tabulations* provides a cumulative inventory of items still available for the period 1958 through 1968.

For detailed information about any item listed, write to the Chief of the Division named at the beginning of each section. When inquiring about a file or special tabulation, please specify the catalog item number.

The Bureau's data files are of two basic types: (1) those containing the basic records on the individual respondents (i.e., the returns for each person, establishment, and the like), and (2) those containing statistical totals (i.e., summarizations for small areas or for detailed subject classifications). The description of each file indicates whether it is for sale or may be used only by the Census Bureau for preparation of special tabulations for the buyer.

Basic record tapes. The tapes containing basic individual records are in nearly all cases confidential; therefore the Bureau cannot sell them but can prepare special tabulations from them. However, certain sets of nonconfidential individual records on tapes and punchcards (as described in the *Guide to Census Bureau Data Files and Special Tabulations* mentioned above) can be purchased from the Bureau. The Bureau has prepared for sale tape files containing 1/100, 1/1000, and 1/10,000 samples of individual records from the 1960 and 1970 Censuses of Population and Housing by removing all information that might make possible identification of any person, household, or housing unit. The Bureau also makes available the nonconfidential returns from some of the public agencies that report on their activities for the Bureau's surveys; for example, information from each building permit-issuing jurisdiction is available on computer tapes.

Summary tapes. Many summary tapes are available; these contain small-area totals that were subsequently added together by the computer to obtain the results required for the published tables. Summary tapes are generally useful for further machine processing to obtain totals for areas not shown separately in the published reports or for preparing derived measures (averages, ratios, etc.) for specific geographic areas. The data on these tapes can also be obtained as printouts of the tape content. Such displays are accompanied by technical memoranda explaining the content and organization of the display and supplying identification for the totals.

In addition to the data described above, some files contain the same statistics found in published reports; these files are made available for users who wish to summarize further or to rearrange the published data. Examples of such data files are the computer tape "copies" of all editions of the *County and City Data Book,* which are also available on punchcards on a special-order basis.

Documentation furnished with tapes. Furnished with all purchases of computer tapes are descriptions of the data, a layout of the record format, the code structure used, and other needed technical documentation.

Maps. Maps are generally published as part of the corresponding reports. Some of the computer tape products are available on *microfiche.*

Data Archive: The U.S. Census as a Data Bank

The U.S. Census is a gold mine of data for the social science researcher.* The 1980 census content and coverage shown below indicates the scope of information compared with the 1970 census gathered in the decennial census on population and housing.

Table 1. *Population and Housing Items: 1980 Census Items Compared to 1970*

The sample percentages population and housing items included in the 1980 census in comparison with the items in the 1970 census are shown below. Please note that as new items have been added to the census questionnaire, others have had to be dropped. The 1980 Census has added more products and services that were formulated in response to needs for more racial, ethnic group, and small area data. For information about these changes, see David E. Silver and Lucille D. Catherton, "1980 Census Data Products and Coverage Improvements," *Statistical Reporter* (August 1979), pp. 279–288.

Population Items	1980	1970	Housing Items	1980	1970
Household relationship	100	100	Coverage questions	100	100
Sex	100	100	Access to unit	100	100
"Race"	100	100	Complete plumbing facilities	100	100
Age	100	100	Number of rooms	100	100
Marital status	100	100	Tenure (whether unit is owned		
Spanish/Hispanic origin			or rented)	100	100
or descent	100	5	Condominium	100	—
School enrollment	21	15	Acreage and presence of		
Educational attainment	21	20	commercial establishment	100	100
Place of birth	21	20	Value of home	100	100
Citizenship and year of			Monthly rent	100	100
immigration	21	5	Occupancy and vacancy status	100	100
Current language	21	—	Description of building	21	20
Ancestry	21	—	Stories, elevator in structure	21	5
			Acreage and crop sales	21	20

* For excellent descriptions of census applications in urban and regional planning in business, use of population and housing by geographers and by social demographers, see chapters 11, 12, 13, and 14 in *Census '80: Continuing the Factfinder Tradition, op. cit.,* pp. 363–432.

Population Items	1980	1970	Housing Items	1980	1970
Place of residence 5 years ago	21	15	Source of water	21	15
Activity 5 years ago	21	20	Sewage disposal	21	15
Veteran status	21	15	Year built	21	20
Disability	21	5	Year present occupant		
Children ever born	21	20	moved into house	21	15
Marital history	21	5	Heating equipment	21	20
Employment status	21	20	Fuels	21	5
Hours worked last week	21	20	Cost of utilities and fuels	21	20
Place of work	21	15	Complete kitchen facilities	21	100
Travel time to work	21	—	Number of bedrooms	21	5
Mode of transportation to			Number of bathrooms	21	15
work	21	15	Telephone	21	100
Carpooling	21	—	Air conditioning	21	15
Year last worked	21	20	Number of automobiles	21	—
Industry, occupation, class			Number of light trucks and		
of worker	21	20	vans	21	—
Work and weeks looking			Basement	—	100
for work previous year	21	20	Clothes washing machine	—	5
Income last year	21	20	Clothes dryer	—	5
Birthplace of parents	—	15	Dishwasher	—	5
Mother tongue	—	15	Home food freezer	—	5
Vocational training	—	5	Television	—	5
Industry, occupation, and			Radio	—	5
class of worker 5 years			Second home	—	5
ago	—	5			

Table 2. *Published Census Tract Report—Population Data*

Table P-1. General characteristics of persons	Table P-2. Social Characteristics of Persons: 1980*
Census Tracts	**Census Tracts**
AGE	**NATIVITY AND PLACE OF BIRTH**
Total persons	Total persons
Under 5 years	Native
5 to 9 years	Born in State of residence
10 to 14 years	Born in different State
15 to 19 years	Born abroad, at sea, etc.
20 to 24 years	Foreign born
25 to 34 years	
35 to 44 years	**LANGUAGE SPOKEN AT HOME AND ABILITY TO SPEAK ENGLISH**
45 to 54 years	Persons 5 to 17 years
55 to 64 years	Speak a language other than English at home
65 to 74 years	Percent who speak English not well or not at all
75 years and over	
3 and 4 years	Persons 18 years and over
16 years and over	Speak a language other than English at home
18 years and over	Percent who speak English not well or not at all
21 years and over	
60 years and over	
62 years and over	

Table P-1. General characterics of persons	Table P-2. Social Characteristics of Persons: 1980*

Median

Female
Under 5 years
5 to 9 years
10 to 14 years
15 to 19 years
20 to 24 years
25 to 34 years
35 to 44 years
45 to 54 years
55 to 64 years
65 to 74 years
75 years and over

3 and 4 years
16 years and over
18 years and over
21 years and over
60 years and over
62 years and over

Median

HOUSEHOLD TYPE AND RELATIONSHIP
Total persons
In households
  Householder
    Family householder
    Nonfamily householder
     Living alone
  Spouse
  Other relatives
  Nonrelatives
Inmate of institution
Other, in group quarters

Persons per household
Persons per family

Persons 65 years and over
In households
  Householder
    Nonfamily householder
     Living alone
  Spouse
  Other relatives
  Nonrelatives
Inmate of institution
Other, in group quarters

FAMILY TYPE BY PRESENCE OF OWN CHILDREN
Families
With own children under 18 years
  Number of own children under 18 years

SCHOOL ENROLLMENT AND TYPE OF SCHOOL
Persons 3 years old and over enrolled in school
Nursery school
  Private
Kindergarten
  Private
Elementary (1 to 8 years)
  Private
High school (1 to 4 years)
  Private
College

YEARS OF SCHOOL COMPLETED
Persons 25 years old and over
Elementary: 0 to 4 years
           5 to 7 years
           8 years
High School: 1 to 3 years
           4 years
College: 1 to 3 years
       4 or more years
Percent high school graduates

FERTILITY
Women 35 to 44 years
  Children ever born
    Per 1,000 women

RESIDENCE IN 1975
Persons 5 years and over
Same house
Different house in United States
  Same county
  Different county
    Same State
    Different State
      Northeast
      North Central
      South
      West
Abroad

JOURNEY TO WORK
Workers 16 years and over
Private vehicle: Drive alone
               Carpool
Public transportation
  Bus or streetcar
  Subway, elevated train, or railroad
Walked only
Other means
Worked at home

Table P-1.   General characteristics of persons

Married-couple families
With own children under 18 years
  Number of own children under 18 years

Female householder, no husband present
With own children under 18 years
  Number of own children under 18 years

MARITAL STATUS

Male, 15 years and over
Single
Now married, except separated
Separated
Widowed
Divorced

Female, 15 years and over
Single
Now married, except separated
Separated
Widowed
Divorced

Table P-2.   Social Characteristics of Persons: 1980*

Persons per private vehicle
Mean travel time to work   Minutes

Worked in county of residence
Worked outside county of residence
Place of work not reported

Table P-3.   Labor Force and Disability Characteristics of Persons: 1980

Census Tracts

LABOR FORCE STATUS

Persons 16 years and over
Labor force
    Percent of persons 16 years and over
  Civilian labor force
  Employed
  Unemployed
    Percent of civilian labor force

Female, 16 years and over
Labor force
    Percent of female, 16 years and over
  Civilian labor force
  Employed
  Unemployed
    Percent of civilian labor force
With own children under 6 years
  In labor force
Married, husband present
  In labor force

Civilian persons 16 to 19 years
Not enrolled in school
  Not high school graduate
    Employed

Table P-4.   Income and Poverty Status in 1979: 1980

Census Tracts

INCOME IN 1979

Households
Less than $5,000
$5,000 to $7,499
$7,500 to $9,999
$10,000 to $14,999
$15,000 to $19,999
$20,000 to $24,999
$25,000 to $34,999
$35,000 to $49,999
$50,000 or more
Median
Mean
Owner-occupied households
  Median income
  Mean income
Renter-occupied households
  Median income
  Mean income
Families
  Median income
  Mean income
Unrelated individuals 15 years and over
  Median income
  Mean income
Per capita income

Table P-3.   Labor Force and Disability Characteristics of Persons: 1980

Unemployed
Not in labor force

OCCUPATION AND SELECTED INDUSTRIES

Employed persons 16 years and over

Managerial and professional specialty occupations
  Executive, administrative, and managerial occupations
  Professional specialty occupations
Technical, sales, and administrative support occupations
  Technicians and related support occupations
  Sales occupations
  Administrative support occupations, including clerical
Service occupations
  Private household occupations
  Protective service occupations
  Service occupations, except protective and household
Farming, forestry, and fishing occupations
Precision production, craft, and repair occupations
Operators, fabricators, and laborers
  Machine operators, assemblers, and inspectors
  Transportation and material moving occupations
  Handlers, equipment cleaners, helpers, and laborers

Manufacturing
Wholesale and retail trade
Professional and related services

Class of worker

Private wage and salary workers
Government workers
  Local government workers
Self-employed workers

LABOR FORCE STATUS IN 1979

Persons 16 years and over, in labor force in 1979
Percent of persons 16 years and over
  Worked in 1979
    40 or more weeks
      Usually worked 35 or more hours per week
    50 to 52 weeks

Table P-4.   Income and Poverty Status in 1979: 1980

INCOME TYPE IN 1979

Households
With earnings
  Mean earnings
With Social Security income
  Mean Social Security income
With public assistance income
  Mean public assistance income

MEAN FAMILY INCOME IN 1979 BY FAMILY TYPE

Families
  With own children under 18 years
  Without own children under 18 years
Married-couple families
  With own children under 18 years
  Without own children under 18 years
Female householder, no husband present
  With own children under 18 years
  Without own children under 18 years

ALL INCOME LEVELS IN 1979

Families
Householder worked in 1979
With related children under 18 years
Female householder, no husband present
  Householder worked in 1979
  With related children under 18 years
    With related children under 6 years
Householder 65 years and over

Unrelated individuals for whom poverty status is determined
65 years and over

Persons for whom poverty status is determined
Under 18 years
  Related children under 18 years
    Related children 5 to 17 years
18 to 59 years
60 years and over
  65 years and over

INCOME IN 1979 BELOW POVERTY LEVEL

Families
Percent below poverty level
Householder worked in 1979
With related children under 18 years
Female householder, no husband present
  Householder worked in 1979
  With related children under 18 years
    With related children under 6 years
Householder 65 years and over

Table P-3.   Labor Force and Disability
Characteristics of Persons: 1980

Usually worked 35 or more hours
per week
With unemployment in 1979
Percent of those in labor force in
1979
Unemployed 15 or more weeks
Mean weeks of unemployment

DISABILITY STATUS OF NONINSTITUTIONAL PERSONS

Male, 16 to 64 years
With a work disability
Not in labor force
Prevented from working

Female, 16 to 64 years
(Repeat as Male, 16 to 64)

Persons 16 to 64 years
With a public transportation disability
With a work disability

Persons 65 years and over
With a public transportation disability

WORKERS IN FAMILY IN 1979

No workers
  Mean family income
1 worker
  Mean family income
2 workers
  Mean family income
3 or more workers
  Mean family income

Table P-4.   Income and Poverty Status
in 1979: 1980

Unrelated individuals for whom
poverty status is determined
Percent below poverty level
65 years and over
**Persons for whom poverty status
is determined**
Percent below poverty level
Under 18 years
  Related children under 18 years
    Related children 5 to 17 years
18 to 59 years
60 years and over
  65 years and over

INCOME IN 1979 BELOW SPECIFIED POVERTY LEVEL

Percent of persons for whom poverty status is determined:
  Below 75 percent
  Below 125 percent
  Below 150 percent
  Below 200 percent

* Source: Peter A. Bounpane, Acting Chief, Decennial Census Division Memorandum, PHC80–2 Census Tracts, U.S. Bureau of Census, Jan. 21, 1982

Geographic Areas

The 1980 census provides data for more geographic areas than any other census. These areas are classified as either governmental or statistical areas. Figure 1 lists all Census Bureau geographic units and the hierarchical relationships for which census data are available. Figure 2 shows the subdivisions of a standard metropolitan statistical area as they appeared in the 1970 census. These divisions are all continued in the 1980 census including census regions and divisions of the United States and ZIP code areas.

The Bureau initiated a Neighborhood Statistics Program in 1980. Certain summary statistics are tabulated for officially designated neighborhoods in municipalities of 10,000 or more population that chose to take part in the voluntary program. The neighborhoods were defined by local officials in terms of census tracts and blocks.

New data were tabulated for 269 federal and state Indian reservations. This is the first decennial census for which the Bureau has systematically identified the boundaries of Indian reservations.

Figure 1. Census Bureau Geographic Units—Their Hierarchical Relationships. These figures illustrate hierarchical or "nesting" relationships among census geographic areas. Note that the hierarchies overlap, e.g., counties are subdivided into minor civil divisions or census county divisions (Figure A), into urban and rural components (Figure C), and, inside SMSA's, into census tracts (Figure B). Note also the relationship among governmental and statistical units as data summary areas.

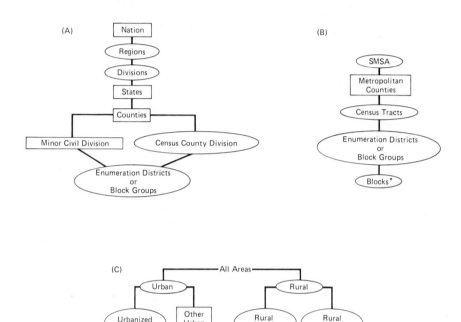

KEY:

▭ Governmental Units

⬭ Statistical Units

* Blocks do not cover the entire SMSA, only the urbanized part.

Potential users of the 1980 census now have tabulated data available for 43,000 census tracts, 300,000 block groups and enumeration districts, and over 2.5 million blocks. In addition, government geography data have been tabulated for 3136 counties; 20,000 legally incorporated villages, towns, and cities; and 35,000 minor civil divisions or census county divisions.*

These geographical areas show how data are summarized in many different ways. For example, summary tape file STF 1 (1982) provides 321 cells of complete-count population and housing data. Data are summarized for the United States, regions, divisions, states, SCSA's, SMSA's, urbanized areas, congressional districts, counties, county subdivisions, places, census tracts,

* Charles P. Kaplan and Thomas L. Van Valey, *Census 80: Continuing the Factfinding Tradition* (Washington, D.C.: U.S. Government Printing Office, 1980), pp. 128–57.

Figure 2.   Geographic Areas in 1980 Census Reports

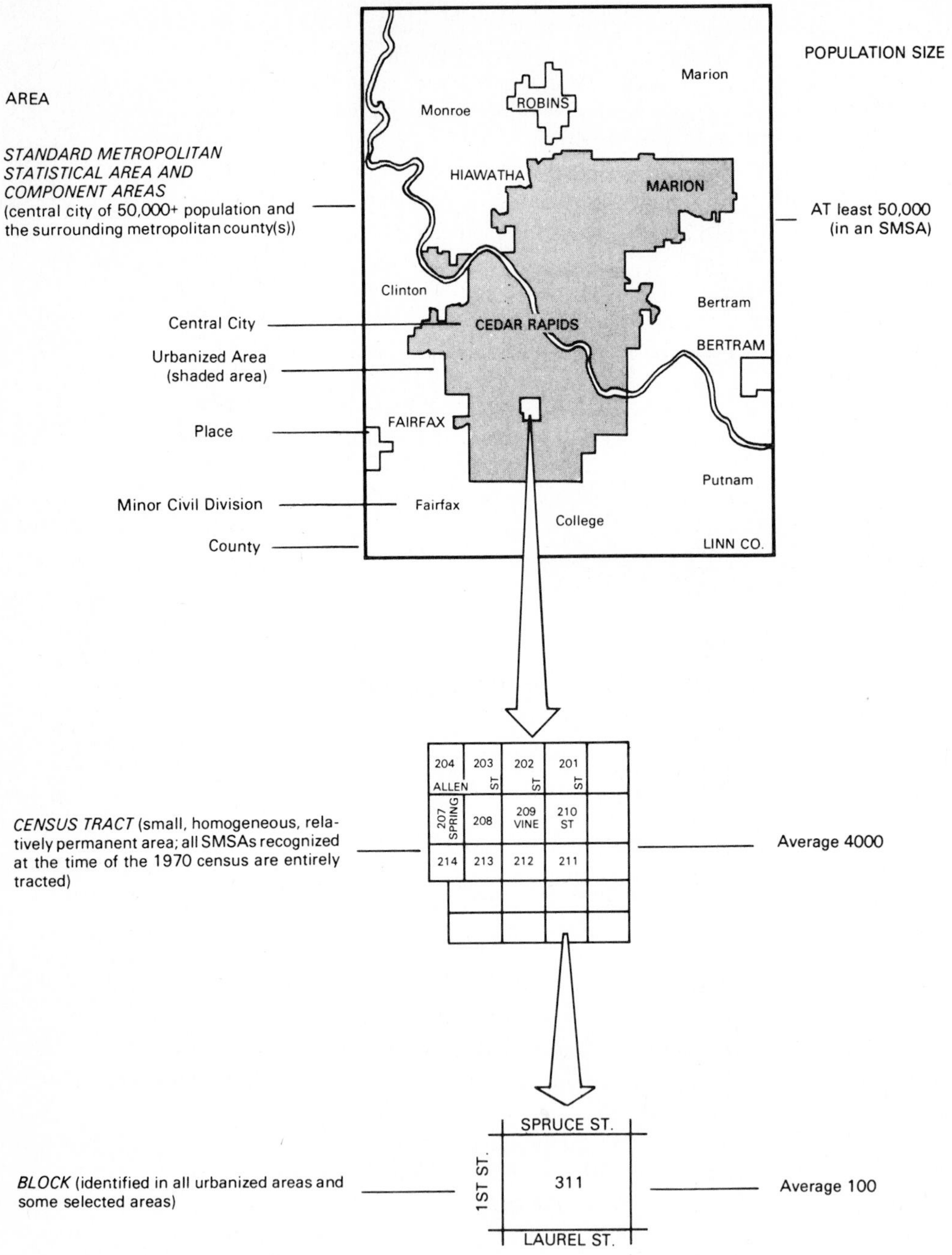

enumeration districts in unblocked areas, and blocks and block groups in blocked areas. These tape data are in a file set that will appear in printed reports PHC80–1, PHC80–3, and PC80–1–A.

Of all these geographical units, the census tract is often the most valuable. As shown in figure 2, it is a small, homogeneous, relatively permanent area.

Because it has many common social and economic characteristics it offers many comparative study opportunities in community study.

The information on population items is generally of most interest to the social scientist. The tables that follow have been selected from the census tract data to show items of some social and labor force characteristics of the United States population. Statistics for most of the population and housing subjects included in the 1980 census are presented for census tracts in SMSA's and in other tracted areas in the final printed report series PHC80–2 (1983).

Also available are other census tract tables which include breakdowns of General Characteristics, Social and Labor Force Characteristics for White Persons, 1980 and Black Persons, 1980; Occupation, Income in 1979, and Poverty Status in 1979 of White Persons and Black Persons. The same data sets can be secured for American Indian, Eskimo, and Aleut Persons, 1980; Asian and Pacific Islander Persons, 1980; Spanish Origin Persons, 1980. Other tables include Structural, Equipment, and Household Characteristics of Housing Units: Total Population, 1980. All of these items are then broken down for the White Householder, the Black Householder, the American Indian, Eskimo, and Aleut Householder, Asian and Pacific Householder, and Householders of Spanish origin. Additional information by census tract is available on Financial Characteristics of Housing Units, each in turn broken down by the same racial and geographic units specified above.

General and Specialized Summaries of U.S. Census Data

Congressional District Data Book

Population and housing data with maps for each district; votes cast for President and Congress.

County and City Data Book

Demographic, social, and economic data for states, counties, cities, and unincorporated places of 25,000 or more, and for metropolitan and urbanized areas.

Historical Statistics of the United States, Colonial Times to 1970—Bicentennial Edition, 1975.

Demographic, social, and economic trends. Analytical text and detailed source notes. Comprehensive index.

Pocket Data Book, U.S.A.

A condensation of the Statistical Abstract, simplified for ready reference, with charts on current trends. Index and glossary of terms.

Statistical Abstract of the United States

The standard annual summary of statistics on the social, political, and economic characteristics of the nation. Extensive guide to public and private sources. Comprehensive index.

Subject and U.S. Area Reports

U.S. summaries for specific censuses.

Public Use Samples of the U.S. Census* could prove especially valuable to social scientists who want to perform detailed analyses that would exhaust samples of the usual size of 1500 to 3000. For example, detailed cross-tabulation of race, sex, and occupation become quite feasible with the public use sample (PUS). The U.S. Bureau of the Census has released a collection of samples of the U.S. population as of April 1, 1970, which contains data on individuals and their households. The *Public Use Samples of Basic Records* from the 1970 census come from the sample questionnaires administered to the population as part of the decennial census. No names, addresses, or other identifying information are included in the data, but all other data collected through the sample questionnaire are coded onto computer-readable magnetic tapes. These individual and household data are a major resource for social science research, for they provide flexibility in analysis that the aggregate (tabulated) data released by the Bureau cannot provide. PUS is a collection of six statistically independent samples, each reporting data from a 1 percent sample of households permitting a pooling of approximately 12 million observations (or 6 percent of households). An interesting application of the PUS is described by Richard C. Rockwell, "Applications of the 1970 Census Public Use Samples in Affirmative Action Programs," *American Sociologist* 19 (February 1975): 41–46.

For users of small-area statistics, *Data User News* is valuable. This publication is issued monthly by the Social and Economic Statistics Administration of the Department of Commerce, Washington, DC. For information, write Editor, Data User Services Division, Bureau of the Census, Washington, DC 20233.

Community leaders will find *Census Data for Community Action* suitable for their use. Several examples are provided of the types of community problems the solution of which begin with analysis of census statistics. In one, the census results are used to evaluate the impact of alternate routes for an expressway on various neighborhoods in a community. Another shows how census data on age, education, and other population characteristics can establish the need for adult education programs. A third indicates how census data can help in assessing a community's need for day-care centers. Income figures, households headed by a woman, and the number of children under five years of age are all utilized in this analysis.

Copies of the booklet may be obtained from the Publications Distribution Section, Social and Economic Statistics Administration, Washington, DC 20233.

For more detailed research activity in the local area, the *Census Use Study* is the required resource.

The *Census Use Study* was established by the U.S. Bureau of the Census to explore the current uses and future needs for small-area data, and data handling and display techniques in local, state, and federal agencies. There

---

* U.S. Bureau of the Census, *Public Use Samples of Basic Records from the 1970 Census: Description and Technical Documentation* (Washington, D.C.: U.S. Government Printing Office, 1972).

is a growing need to improve the system for relating census data with local agency data. Linking of data from census and local sources is essential for enhancing the analysis of various urban problems and trends of change. For example, in the study of crime and delinquency statistics, agencies are interested in linking incident reports prepared by law enforcement agencies with neighborhood socioeconomic data available from the Census Bureau. Similarly, in transportation planning, local data on land use and travel patterns must be related to specific demographic and social characteristics for small areas such as traffic zones. Trip generation rates as related to the socioeconomic characteristics of study areas can then be computed and used to estimate future transportation facility requirements. Other areas of interest include educational planning, health planning, housing and redevelopment planning, public safety planning, and various subjects of concern to commerce and industry such as studies of telephone and bank service users in relation to the socioeconomic characteristics of small groups of the population.

Data Access Descriptions are intended as a means of access to unpublished data of the Bureau of the Census for persons with data requirements not fully met by the published reports. These are published as occasional reports when various kinds of data become available. *Data Access Description,* U.S. Bureau of the Census, Washington, DC 20233.

Data Access News is published by the Clearinghouse and Laboratory for Census Data (CLCD) six to eight times a year. The CLCD also publishes a quarterly *Review of Public Data Use.* The CLCD is operated by Data Use and Access Laboratories with a grant from the National Science Foundation. CLCD offices: Suite 900, 1601 North Kent Street, Arlington, VA 22209. These are significant references for current information about research and data for behavioral sciences.

Current Population Reports represents a data resource of great value to demographers and social scientists generally. In addition to the findings of the Census of Population, conducted every few years, the Bureau of the Census publishes continuing and up-to-date statistics on population counts, characteristics, and other special studies on the American people. Data are issued under eight subject areas and released under the general title *Current Population Reports.* The eight categories are:

P-20 Population Characteristics
P-23 Special Studies
P-25 Population Estimates and Projections
P-26 Federal-State Cooperative Program for Population Estimates
P-27 Farm Population
P-28 Special Census
P-60 Consumer Income
P-65 Consumer Buying Indicators

Of these, P-20 Population Characteristics and P-23 Special Studies have most general utility to the social scientist.

The P-20 series began in September 1947. Since then, approximately ten reports a year have been issued covering current national and, in some cases, regional data on geographic residence and mobility, fertility, education, school enrollment, martial status, numbers and characteristics of household and families, and so on. Almost three hundred reports have appeared.

Census Bureau Methodological Research is available to researchers interested in methodological problems centered on census surveying and data processing. This annual publication is an annotated list of papers and reports on the status of methodological research within the Bureau of the Census. The first list covered the years 1963–66; the list has been issued annually since then. Sections include Statistical Theory and Sampling Methods; General Planning and Procedures for Censuses and Surveys; Measurement of Coverage and Response Error; Census of Population and Housing Evaluation Projects; Data Processing; Concepts and Techniques of Analysis; Data Access and Use; Other Documents of Methodological Interest; Selected Methodological Reports Conducted in Past Years.

Where to Find Census Reports

Most college and university libraries contain census reports. Many public libraries obtain the principal census reports for their communities; if your branch library does not, try the main library. The city planning office, city government library, mayor's office, chamber of commerce, or similar public and private agencies also often have census reports on hand.

A community-action group may discover that it has frequent need to refer to census reports. If so, copies are available at a reasonable cost. Department of Commerce field offices in forty-three cities stock many of the reports for their cities and surrounding areas, or orders may be sent directly to the U.S. Superintendent of Documents. Order forms may be obtained by writing to the Publications Services Division, Social and Economic Statistics Administration, Washington, DC 20233.

Bureau of Labor Statistics

The Bureau of Labor Statistics is a fact-finding agency engaged in the collection, interpretation, and dissemination of economic information. It conducts research on employment, manpower, prices, wages and industrial relations, productivity, safety and health, and economic growth. In many of these areas the Bureau has experience dating back to 1884. A description of the Bureau's current activity may be found in *Major Programs* (published annually), U.S. Department of Labor, Bureau of Labor Statistics, Washington, DC 20212.

Publications include the *Monthly Labor Review, Occupational Outlook Quarterly, Handbook of Labor Statistics* (annually), *B.L.S. Handbook of Methods, and Publications of the Bureau of Labor Statistics,* a semiannual annotated catalog listing all current Bureau publications.

Of particular interest to social scientists are the *Special Labor Force Reports.* Copies may be obtained from the Bureau of Labor Statistics in Washington, DC, or at any of its regional offices. In your library the reports will be filed under U.S. Bureau of Labor Statistics, Special Labor Force Reports, Government Classification No. L. 2.98.

Long Hours and Premium Pay, May 1976 (No. 196)
New Labor Force Projections to 1990 (No. 197)

Where to Find Research Assistance

A Primer on Data User Services

Specialists at the Bureau's Washington headquarters and 12 regional offices can provide answers to questions concerning Census data products and services:

Is the information I need available?

In what media is it available—on computer tape, in a printed report, on microfiche?

If it is on computer tape, who can I get to print-out tabulations for me?

For what geographical areas can I get the data?

How do I order the maps, tapes, or reports I need?

Workshops, conferences, training courses, and seminars are conducted at locations throughout the country. These educational and training activities introduce users in businesses, academic institutions, and government to Bureau programs, products, and services.

Washington contact: Data User Services Division, Bureau of the Census, Washington, DC 20233 (301) 763–2400.

Regional office contacts: Data User Services Officer, Bureau of the Census.

Atlanta, GA 1365 Peachtree St., NE, Room 638, 30309 (404) 881–2274.

Boston, MA 441 Stuart St., 8th Floor, 02116 (617) 223–0668.

Charlotte, NC 230 South Tryon St., Suite 800, 28202 (704) 371–6144.

Chicago, IL 55 E. Jackson Blvd., Suite 1304, 60604 (312) 353–0980.

Dallas, TX 1100 Commerce St., Room 3C54, 75242 (214) 767–0625.

Denver, CO 575 Union Blvd., 80225 (303) 234–5825.

Detroit, MI Federal Bldg. & U.S. Courthouse, Room 565, 231 West Lafayette, 48226 (313) 226–4675.

Kansas City, KS One Gateway Center, 4th & State Sts., 66101 (816) 374–4601.

Los Angeles, CA 11777 San Vincente Blvd., 8th Floor, 90049 (213) 824–7291.

New York, NY 26 Federal Plaza, Federal Office Bldg., Room 37–130, 10007 (212) 264–4730.

Philadelphia, PA 600 Arch St., Room 9226, 19106 (215) 597–8314.

Seattle, WA 915 2nd Ave., Rm. 312, 98174 (206) 442–7080.

The Labor Force Patterns of Divorced and Separated Women, March 1975 (No. 198)

Employment and Unemployment in 1976 (No. 199)

Students, Graduates, and Dropouts in the Labor Market, October 1976 (No. 200)

Work Experience of the Population, 1976 (No. 201)

The Extent of Job Search by Employed Workers, May 1976 (No. 202)

Year-Round Full-Time Earnings in 1975 (No. 203)

Going Back to School at 35 and Over, October 1976 (No. 202)

Children of Working Mothers, March 1976 (No. 205)

Martial and Family Characteristics of the Labor Force in March 1976 (No. 206)

Absence from Work—Measuring the Hours Lost, May 1973–76 (No. 207)

Labor Force Trends: A Synthesis and Analysis; and a Bibliography, October 1977 (No. 208)

Educational Attainment of Workers, March 1977 (No. 209)

Job Search of the Unemployed, May 1976 (No. 210)

Multiple Jobholders in May 1977 (No. 211)

Employment and Unemployment Trends During 1977 (No. 212)

Women Who Head Families: A socioeconomic Analysis, March 1977 (No. 213)

Long Hours and Premium Pay, May 1977 (No. 214)

Students, Graduates, and Dropouts in the Labor Market, October 1977 (No. 215)

Martial and Family Characteristics of Workers, March 1977 (No. 216)

Children of Working Mothers, March 1977 (No. 217)

Employment and Unemployment During 1978: An Analysis (No. 218)

Martial and Family Characteristics of Workers, 1970–78 (No. 219)

Divorced and Separated Women in the Labor Force—An Update, October 1978 (No. 220)

Multiple Jobholders in May 1978 (No. 221)

Job Search of Recipients of Unemployment Insurance, February 1979 (No. 222)

Students, Graduates, and Dropouts in the Labor Market, October 1978 (No. 223)

Work Experience of the Population in 1977 (No. 224)

Educational Attainment of Workers—Some Trends from 1973 to 1978 (No. 225)

Long Hours and Premium Pay, May 1978 (No. 226)

Back to School at 35 and Over, October 1978 (No. 227)

Labor Force Patterns of Single Women, August 1979 (No. 228)

Absent Workers and Lost Hours, May 1978 (No. 229)

Median Earnings in 1977 Reported for Year-round Full-time Workers, June 1979 (No. 230)

Occupational Mobility During 1977 (No. 231)

Workers on Late Shift in a Changing Economy (No. 232)

Young Workers and Families: A Special Section (No. 233)

Employment and Unemployment During 1979: An Analysis (No. 234)

Job Tenure Declines as Work Force Changes (No. 235)

Work of Experience of the Population in 1978 (No. 236)

Martial and Family Characteristics of the Labor Force, March 1979 (No. 237)

Percent Working Long Hours Show First Post-Recession Decline (No. 238)

Women Share of Moonlighting Nearly Doubles During 1969–79 (No. 239)

Educational Attainment of Workers, March 1979 (No. 240)

School and Work Among Youth During the 1970's (No. 241)

Women in Domestic Work: Yesterday and Today (No. 242)

The Employment Situation for Military Wives (No. 243)

Employment and Unemployment: A Report on 1980 (No. 244)

The Department of Labor has a unique set of longitudinal data on labor-force behavior and work attitudes, which is available to interested users for a fee. The opportunities are described in Herbert S. Parnes, "The National Longitudinal Surveys: New Vistas for Labor Market Research," *American Economic Review* 65, no. 2 (May 1975): 244–49. The Department of Labor may support research using data from the tapes either by (1) small grants for dissertion research by doctoral candidates on manpower-related subjects or (2) contracts or grants for research that is likely to have significant implications for manpower policies or programs. Write Howard Rosen, Director, Office of Manpower Research and Development, Patrick Henry Building, 601 D. Street N.W., Washington, DC 20213. Challenging problems in this area may be found in Willard Wirtz, *The Boundless Resource: A Prospectus for an Educational/Work Policy,* The New Republic Book Co. Inc., 1220 19 Street N.W., Washington, DC 20036.

GUIDE TO PRIVATE PROFESSIONAL SERVICES FOR THE SOCIAL RESEARCHER

2.19

This guide is not a complete directory, but rather a selected compilation of certain services that are available at various prices. They are services rendered by universities, government, and private companies. Perhaps the NORC General Social Survey of the National Opinion Research Center is the most valuable commercial social data service, bringing to fruition an idea long nurtured by researchers, that is, to provide a nationwide sample of data available on an annual basis such that time-series analysis might be possible. Such a sample was also needed by sociologists to make selected data available that, for various reasons, could not be delivered by the U.S. Census.

Other services provide research in progress within specified fields, such as designing a sample, developing questionnaires or interview schedules, collecting data by mail or personal interview, and completing analysis. The researcher can even get help on budgeting and funding.

NORC also provides a variety of services for the social survey researcher. These include sample design, questionnaire construction, pretesting of questionnaires, coding, data processing, and analyses. NORC has had twenty-five years' experience in data collection maintaining a national probability sample and a staff of trained and experienced interviewers.

For information, write: National Opinion Research Center, University of Chicago, 6030 South Ellis Avenue, Chicago, IL 60637.

The NORC General Social Survey

This is a program of social indicators research and a data diffusion system. The data come from annual personal interviews administered to national cross sections of about 1500 adults, using a standard questionnaire repeated each year. The questionnaire content covers a broad spectrum of sociological interests.

With the completion of the 1980 General Social Survey the combined surveys, 1972–80, include nearly 500 variables and cover 12,120 respondents. It is now possible to study social trends and consistencies. A social indicator series is in place. The survey covers a full range of demographics: behavioral items on such topics as organizational membership, voting, gun ownership, smoking, and drinking; attitudinal items in such areas as abortions, crime and punishment, governmental spending preferences, race relations, violence, and women's rights; and personal evaluations of happiness, satisfaction, and anomia.

The data may be purchased from the Roper Center, U-164R, University of Connecticut, Storrs, CT 06268.

The basic idea of GSS is to provide a nationwide sample of data so that time-series data of high quality is available on an annual basis. The rationale for the enterprise stems from NORC's opinion that the field of sociology shows a number of research weaknesses when compared to other social science disciplines. An unhealthy division exists between a handful of investigators associated with major research institutes and the great majority of sociologists who can obtain national data only on a hand-me-down basis after the original investigation or when Uncle Sam is tired of the materials. It is hoped this resource will stimulate research and make available high-quality national data.

Given the scope of the questionnaire, a variety of analyses can be performed. For example:

1. Replicating findings from previous studies, perhaps introducing variables that were not available to the original author.
2. Testing one's own hypotheses.
3. Studying small population groups by merging studies across years. (This is possible because of the repetition of questions.)
4. Studying trends over time by comparing current results with those in the various baseline studies. The codebooks give references to the original study for each item drawn from a previous national sampling.
5. Since respondent age is reported to the year, one can use the cohort method in studying age trends for variables reported by age in the original study.

The data can also be used in classwork in a number of ways:

6. Students can use the data to test hypotheses derived from readings and lectures.
7. Methods classes can use the data for practice in analyses. Many content areas have enough items for exercises on scale and index construction.
8. Teachers can run data to bring their lectures up to date.

Reference

CITRO, CONSTANCE F., with the assistance of JAMES A. DAVIS. "The NORC General Social Survey." *Public Data Use* 2 (October 1974): 28–31.

National Opinion Research Center. "The NORC General Social Survey: Questions and Answers." All questionnaire items classified by broad content type and causal stage. Revised and updated, March 1974.

Broadly speaking, the measures of the GSS survey fall into the following content scheme:

1. Ecology
2. Family and life cycle
   a. Age
   b. Marriage and family structure
   c. Sex (gender, behavior, and roles, especially employment)
   d. Children and fertility
   e. Miscellaneous
3. Socioeconomic status
   a. Occupational level
   b. Education
   c. Income
   d. Class consciousness

4. Primordial groups
  a. Ethnicity
  b. Religion
  c. Race
  d. Politics
5. Social psychology
  a. Interaction
  b. Social integration
  c. Other
6. Miscellaneous
  a. Deviance
  b. Health
  c. Other

An *Annotated Bibliography of Papers Using the General Social Surveys,* 1981 edition, has just been completed by the National Data Program for the Social Sciences. This 200-page bibliography cites over 650 scholarly papers, articles, government reports, and books that use the General Social Surveys as a data source. Each citation includes a list of the variables and surveys used and an abstract. In addition, there is a mnemonic index that allows the user to quickly locate literature using variables of interest. The bibliography can be ordered for $5 from: Patrick Bova, Library, National Opinion Research Center, 6030 South Ellis Avenue, Chicago, IL 60637.

Response Analysis

This organization, like NORC, offers a full range of research services. It will collect data, design a sample, consult on questionnaire development, or do analysis. Response Analysis advertises the advantages of its services as follows:

> We can undertake any kind of study, anywhere. We have developed our own national probability sample and also possess expertise in the design and implementation of local and regional studies. We have a national resident staff of over 500 personally trained interviewers, including specially trained elite interviewers.
> We are cost-efficient. We insist on quality work, but we do it efficiently for reasonable budgets.
> We get the job done when you need it, and have developed a special field control system toward that end.

For further information, write: Response Analysis, Research Park, Route 206, Princeton, NJ 08540.

Smithsonian Science Information Exchange (SSIE) (Research Retrieval)

The SSIE is a nonprofit corporation of the Smithsonian Institution. It calls itself the national source for information on research in progress.

By maintaining a data base of information about ongoing or recently completed research projects, the SSIE has been serving research investigators and managers in the social sciences since 1963. The SSIE receives project information from over 1300 federal and other organizations that support research, indexes it, and stores it in a computerized file. Exchange scientists conduct searches of this file upon requests from users in government agencies and research laboratories in universities and private industry. Information is collected at the time a project is funded and is usually available for retrieval well before reports are made at professional meetings or articles appear in the published literature.

The current data base, which covers ongoing research and research initiated and completed between July 1973 and the present, contains information on more than 8000 projects in all areas of the social sciences. This research is sponsored by organizations such as the National Science Foundation; the U.S. Department of Health, Education, and Welfare; the Social Science Research Council; and many other public and private groups.

For further information, write Ann Riordan, Chief, Social Sciences Branch, Smithsonian Science Information Exchange, Room 300, 1730 M Street N.W., Washington, DC 20036.

NEXUS, a Baker and Taylor Information Service (Literature Retrieval)

NEXUS is a data storage and retrieval firm specializing in research tools to serve the academic community throughout the English-speaking world. The word *nexus* means "a link," a link between modern computer technology and traditional research methods to furnish speedy, efficient access to large bodies of published scholarly source materials.

NEXUS promises an individually tailored resource list and describes its services as follows:

> *Preliminary Bibliographies with Englightening Speed.* We have on computer the authors and abstracted titles of all articles ever printed in any of 534 history, political science and sociology journals (see list inside) published the world over, obscure and well-known both, since these journals began—more than 350,000 articles in all, going back to 1834. We'll search the file by computer on any topic you select, furnishing a bibliography individually tailored to your needs. The computer will dig out citations either by a specific author *or* about a specific subject (your choice).
>
> *Periodical Guide.* In effect, we're a computerized periodical literature guide covering pertinent (sometimes esoteric) journals of most interest to the serious researcher. Based on your own "key word" choices, our bibliography homes in directly on your specific research target. With one search, it can cover the entire 140-year archive. In the handy form of computer printouts, our source lists are easily tucked into a notebook or pocket and carried along with you.

For further information, write: NEXUS, P.O. Box 1517, Costa Mesa, CA 92705.

Institute for Scientific Information (Literature Retrieval)

The Institute offers an individualized weekly service of reporting on any of 68 topics in the social and behavioral sciences as they appear in the world's leading professional journals. ASCATOPICS is a computer system to locate articles relevant to the topics the researcher selects.

For further information, write: Institute for Scientific Information, 325 Chestnut Street, Philadelphia, PA 19106.

Academic Media (*Literature Search*)

This organization searches for directories, fact books, almanacs, and other sources for information desired by the researcher. For further information, write: Academic Media, 14852 Ventura Blvd., Sherman Oaks, CA 91403.

Inventory Services Available in Public Institutions

For examples of inventories and of their great variety in format and content, the following are illustrations: *A Guide to Resources and Services of the Inter-University Consortium for Political Research, 1972–73* (Ann Arbor: Institute for Social Research, University of Michigan); *Canadian Social Science Data Catalog* (Institute for Behavioral Research, York University, April 1974); and Latin American Data Bank, *File Inventory* (Gainesville: Center for Latin American Studies, University of Florida, August 1974).

Clearinghouses Offer Sociologists Variety of Services

Several clearinghouses that are operating in this country can be usefully employed by sociologists to keep posted on research projects, to conduct literature searches, to maintain currency with the existing information, and to circulate their products.

Content of the clearinghouses ranges from broad, general topics such as mental health to narrow, limited topics such as commuting students.

Among the services provided by clearinghouses are computer-generated bibliographies tailored to specific requests; notification of new literature in the field through the mailing of concise summaries of abstracts; specialized bibliographies on selected subjects of wide interest, a variety of publications including books, monographs, newsletters, digests, and directories; and referrals to other sources that have more complete information. Many services are provided free of charge. For more information write to the clearinghouses whose addresses are presented below.

National Clearinghouse for Mental Health Information, 5600 Fishers Lane, Rockville, MD 20852.

National Clearinghouse for Alcohol Information, P.O. Box 2345, Rockville, MD 20852.

National Clearinghouse for Drug Abuse Information, P.O. Box 1908, Rockville, MD 20850.

National Criminal Justice Reference Service, Law Enforcement Assistance Administration, U.S. Dept. of Justice, Washington, DC 20530.

Child Abuse and Neglect Clearinghouse Project, Herner and Company, 2100 M Street, N.W., Suite 316, Washington, DC 20037.

National Female Offender Resource Center, 1705 DeSales Street, N.W., Washington, DC 20036.

Clearinghouse, Bureau of Research and Training (MH), Eastern Pennsylvania Psychiatric Institute, Henry Avenue and Abbottford Road, Philadelphia, PA 19129.

National Clearinghouse on Revenue Sharing, 1785 Massachusetts Ave., N.W., Washington, DC 20036.

National Clearinghouse for Commuter Programs, 1211 Student Union, University of Maryland, College Park, MD 20742.

Association for the Development of Religious Information Systems, Dept. of Sociology and Anthropology, Marquette University, Milwaukee, WI 53233.
The National Agricultural Library, 10301 Baltimore Blvd., Beltsville, MD 20705.
National Library of Medicine, 8600 Rockville Pike, Bethesda, MD 20014.

2.20 DIRECTORIES OF SOCIAL RESEARCH CENTERS IN THE UNITED STATES, ENGLAND, AND THE WORLD

Research Centers in the United States

Research Centers Directory. Gale Research Co., Detroit, MI 48226, 1979. 6th edition. Updated supplements.
Lists 3200 research centers in the following:

1. Agriculture, Home Economics, and Nutrition
2. Astronomy
3. Business, Economics, and Transportation
4. Conservation
5. Education
6. Engineering and Technology
7. Government and Public Affairs
8. Labor and Industrial Relations
9. Law
10. Life sciences
11. Mathematics
12. Physical and Earth Sciences
13. Regional and Area Studies
14. Social Sciences, Humanities, and Religion
    A total of 376 centers are listed including Anthropology, Communications, Human Development, Population, Religion, Sociology, History, Ethnic Folklore, Linguistics, Journalism, Creativity, Family Study, Behavior, Race Relations.
15. Multidisciplinary Programs
16. Research Coordinating Offices

A typical entry shows the information given:

2750 Columbia University
CENTER FOR THE SOCIAL SCIENCES (1976)
(formerly Bureau of Applied Social Science)
Founded 1937
8th Level, 420 West 118th St.
New York, New York 10027
Dr. Jonathon R. Cole, Director   Phone (212) 280–3093

Integral unit of graduate faculties of Columbia University. Supported by parent institution, U.S. Government, state and local agencies, foundations, non-profit social organizations, and industry. Staff: 41 research professionals, 7 supporting professionals, 20 graduate research assistants, 15 others, plus research fellows, interns, and part-time student interviewers, coders, and statistical clerks.

Principal Fields of research: Public and elite opinion formation; political behavior; international comparative studies; manpower and populations; sociology of professions; formal organizations; community studies and evaluation of social programs. Also collects cases of application of social research to practical problems, codifies social research methods, develops new methods for study of aggregate aspects of mass social behavior, and provides empirical social science research training for graduate students and visiting foreign scholars. Maintains its own IBM data processing equipment.

Research results published in books, monographs, professional journals, project reports, and graduate student doctoral dissertations. Publication: *CSS Newsletter* (tri-annually) Also a Preprint Series, a Reprint Series, and Impact on Policy Monograph Series. Holds periodic seminars on social and political problems and applications of social science research methodology.

World Directory of Research Institutes

The World of Learning. Europe Publications, Ltd., 18 Bedford Square, London, England 1980–81. 31st edition.

A compilation, for all countries of the world, of academies, learned societies, research institutes, libraries, museums, art galleries, and universities (including lists of faculty) in all fields of knowledge. This coverage is excellent for most purposes but often fails to include research organizations within academic departments and the university generally.

In the United States the Gale *Research Centers Directory* is superior. For additional information, consult the Social Science Research Council, 230 Park Avenue New York, NY 10017.

World Directory of Social Science Institutions, UNESCO, 1977. UNIPUB, Box 433, Murray Hill Station, New York, NY 10016.

This comprehensive reference tool is based on collections of the UNESCO Social Science Documentation Centre. The Centre systematically acquires social science data relating to social science research, social scientists, research projects, research publications, and social science periodicals.

LIST OF IMPORTANT RESEARCH ASSOCIATIONS AND INSTITUTES AFFILIATED WITH THE INTERNATIONAL SOCIOLOGICAL ASSOCIATION   *2.21*

This guide should assist research scholars who wish to communicate with other sociological researchers across the world. The list is not definitive. Not all research organizations are affiliated with the International Sociological Association. Many members belong to the older International Institute of Sociology, and a scholar should try to contact their members to have a more complete channel of communication. *The World of Learning* cited in the previous guide will be helpful.

Collective Members Directory of the International Sociological Association

Members in Category A: National Sociological Associations:

Africa

EGYPT	Egyptian Sociological Association
	National Center for Sociological & Criminological
	Research
	Gezira P.O., Cairo
GHANA	Ghana Sociological Association
	Department of Sociology
	University of Ghana
	Legon, Accra
MOROCCO	Centre Universitaire de la Recherche Scientifique
	Université du Marco
	Avenue Ibn Batota
	B.P. 447
	Rabat
NIGERIA	Nigerian Anthropological and Sociological
	Association
	Department of Sociology
	University of Ibadan
	Ibadan
TUNISIA	Institut de Planification Statistique et d'Etudes
	Juridiques, Economiques et Sociales
	23, rue d'Espagne
	Tunis

Asia

CYPRUS	Cyprus Sociological Association
	P.O. Box 4688
	Nicosia
INDIA	Indian Sociological Society
	Centre for the Study of Social Systems
	Jawaharlal Nehru University
	New Delhi 110057
IRAN	Institute for Social Studies and Research
	Faculty of Social Sciences and Cooperative Studies
	University of Tehran
	P.O. Box 13
	1155 Tehran
ISRAEL	Israel Sociological Society
	Department of Sociology
	Hebrew University
	Jerusalem
KOREA	Korean Sociological Association
	Department of Sociology
	Korea University
	Seoul
JAPAN	Japan Sociological Society
	Department of Sociology
	Faculty of Letters
	University of Tokyo
	Bunkyo-ku, Tokyo

MONGOLIA	Academy of Sciences of the Mongolian People's Republic Institute of Philosophy, Sociology and Law Str. Peace, Building "B" 54 Ulan-Bator
TAIWAN	Chinese Sociological Association Department of Agricultural Extension National Taiwan University Taipei
Australia and New Zealand	Sociological Association of Australia and New Zealand Department of Sociology La Trobe University Bundoora, Victoria 3083

Eastern Europe

BULGARIA	Bulgarian Sociological Association 27B Moskowska Street Sofia
CZECHOSLOVAKIA	Czechoslovak Sociological Society Ul. 1, Listopadu Nouzove stavby cp. 804 Praha 4—Nusle
DDR	Nationalkomitee für Soziologische Forschung bei der Akademie der Wissenschaften der Deutschen Demokratischen Republik Otto-Nuschke-strasse 22/23 108 Berlin
HUNGARY	Institute of Sociology Hungarian Academy of Sciences Uri Utca 49 Budapest 1
POLAND	Polish Sociological Association Warsaw University Department of Sociology 72 Nowy Swiat Warsaw 00 330
RUMANIA	Comitetul National de Sociologie Academy of Social and Political Sciences Str. Onesti Nr. 11, Sectorul 1 Bucharest
USSR	Soviet Sociological Association Novocheremushkinskaya 46 Moscow 117418

Western Europe

AUSTRIA	Österreichische Gesellschaft für Soziologie Fleischmarkt 3–5 A-1010 Wien
BELGIUM	Belgian Sociological Society Van Evenstraat 2C B-3000 Louvain
DENMARK	Danish National Institute of Social Research Borgergade 28 DK-1300 Copenhagen K

FRG	Deutsche Gesellschaft für Soziologie Universität Mannheim Lehrstuhl für Soziologie Schloss, 68 Mannheim 1
FINLAND	The Westermarck Society PL 85 00511 Helsinki 51
FRANCE	Société Française de Sociologie 82 rue Cardinet 75017 Paris
GREAT BRITAIN	British Sociological Association 13, Endsleigh Street Skepper House London W.C. 1
GREECE	Hellenic Sociological Association "Alexander Papanastassiou" 1, Pesmajoglou Str. Athens 121
IRELAND	The Economic and Social Research Institute 4 Burlington Road Dublin 4
ITALY	Asociazione Italiana di Scienze Sociali Istituto di Sociologia Facolta di Magistero Universita di Torino 10100 Torino
NETHERLANDS	Nederlandse Sociologische en Antropologische Vereniging Mauritsweg 26A Rotterdam 3002
NORWAY	Norsk Sosiologforening P.O. Box 41 Blindern Oslo 3
SWEDEN	Sveriges Sociologforbund Sociologiska Institutionen Drottninggatan 1A S-752 20 Uppsala
SWITZERLAND	Société Suisse de Sociologie Case 152 1000 Lausanne 24
YUGOSLAVIA	Yugoslav Sociological Association Studentski trg. 1 11000 Belgrad

Latin America*

CUBA	Universidad de la Habana Relaciones Internacionales La Habana
MEXICO	Asociacion Mexicana de Sociologia Providencia 330 Col. del Valle Mexico 12, D.F.

* For further information see Gunther Remmling, *South American Sociologists: A Directory* (Austin: Institute of Latin American Studies, University of Texas, 1966).

VENEZUELA	Asociacion Venezolana de Sociologia Apdo. 80044 Caracas 108

North America

CANADA	Canadian Sociology and Anthropology Association P.O. Box 878 Montreal, P.Q.
	Association Canadienne des Sociologues et Anthropologues de Langue Française Dépt. de Sociologie Université de Montréal C.P. 6128 Montréal, P.Q.
US	American Sociological Association 1722 N. Street, N.W. Washington, DC 20036
	The Society for the Study of Social Problems Executive Office: Social Problems P.O. Box 533 Notre Dame, IN 46556

Members in Category B: International and Multinational Regional Associations of Sociologists

Western Europe

FRANCE	International Council for Research in Cooperative Development 7, avenue Franco-Russe Paris 7
	Association Internationale des Sociologues de Langue Française 17, rue de la Sorbonne Paris 5
	European Association of Experimental Social Psychology Université de Provence 13100 Aix-en-Provence
FRG	Arbeitsgemeinschaft Sozialwissenschaftliches Institut Plittersdorfer Str. 21 53 Bonn-Bad Godesberg
	European Society for Rural Sociology Nussallee 21 Bonn
SWITZERLAND	Institut International de Sociologie Palais Wilson C.P. 7 1211 Genève 14

Africa

SOUTH AFRICA	Association for Sociology in Southern Africa Centre for Intergroup Studies University of Cape Town Rondebosch 7700

Members in Category C: Research Institutes and University Departments

Africa

MOZAMBIQUE	Course of Economics University of Lourenço Marques Lourenço Marques
DAHOMEY	Département de Sociologie Centre de Recherches Appliquées du Dahomey B.P. 6 Porto-Novo
REPUBLIQUE DU NIGER	Institut de Recherche en Sciences Humaines Université de Niamey B.P. 318 Niamey
SUDAN	Department of Social Anthropology and Sociology Faculty of Economic and Social Studies University of Khartoum Khartoum
	Economic and Social Research Council P.O. Box 1166 Khartoum
SOUTH AFRICA	Centre for Intergroup Studies c/o University of Cape Town Rondebosch 7700
	Department of Sociology and Criminology University of Fort Hare Private Bag 314 Alice 5700
	The School of Social Sciences University of Cape Town Department of Sociology Private Bag, Rondebosch, C.P.
New Zealand	Department of Sociology University of Auckland Private Bag Auckland

Asia

CYPRUS	Social Research Centre Charalambides Building Grivas Dighenis Avenue Nicosia
HONG KONG	Social Research Centre Chinese University of Hong Kong 545 Nathan Rd. On Lee Building, 10/F Kowloon
INDIA	Indian Statistical Institute 203, Barrackpore Trunk Rd. 35 Calcutta

Western Europe

AUSTRIA	Institut für Musiksoziologie und Musikpädagogische Forschung Lothringerstrasse 18 A-1030 Wien

BELGIUM	Sociologische Onderzoeksinstituut Katholieke Universiteit Leuven Van Evenstraat 2B 3000 Louvain
	Centre de Recherches Sociologiques Université Catholique de Louvain Van Evenstraat 2B 3000 Louvain
FRANCE	Centre d'Etudes Sociologiques Centre National de la Recherche Scientifique 82, rue Cardinet 75017 Paris
	Centre de Recherches Sociologiques de Toulouse Faculté des Lettres et des Sciences Humaines 56, chemin du Mirail 31 Toulouse
FRG	Forschungsinstitut für Soziologie der Universität Köln Zulpicher strasse 182 5 Köln–Sulz
	Institut für Marxistische Studien und Forschungen Liebigstrasse 6 6 Frankfurt/Main
	Zentralarchiv für Empirische Sozialforschung der Universität zu Köln D-5000 Koln 41 (Lindenthal) Bachemer Strasse 40
	Institut für Soziologie der Rheinisch-Westfälischen Technischen Hochschule Kopernikusstrasse 16 51 Aachen
GREECE	Centre National de Recherches Sociales 1, rue Sophocleous Athens 122
ITALY	Istituto di Sociologia Facolta di Magistero Via S. Ottavio 20 10124 Torino
	Istituto di Studi Sociali Facolta di Scienze Politiche Universita degli Studi di Perugia 06100 Perugia
	Centro Nazionale di Prevenzione e Difesa Sociale Piazza Castello 3 20121 Milano
	Istituto per gli studi di servizio sociale Via Arno 2 Roma 00198
	Istituto di Socialogia Facolta di Scienze Politiche Universita degli Studi di Milano Via Conservatorio 7 20122 Milano
	Dipartimento di Sociologia e de Scienze Politica Universita della Calabria Arcavacata 87100 Cosenza

Servizio Richerche Sociologiche e Studi sull' Org.
della Ing. C. Olivetti & Co.
Via Jervis 24
10015 Ivrea

SPAIN

Instituto "Balmes" de Sociologia
4 Duque de Medinaceli
Madrid 14

Instituto de Estudios Politicos
Plaza de la Marina Espanola 8
Madrid 13

SWITZERLAND

Département de Sociologie
Université de Genève, C.P. 141
1211 Genève 24

Latin America

ARGENTINA

Centro de Investigaciones
Sociales del Instituto Torcuato
di Tella
Superi 1502
Buenos Aires

Asociacion de Graduados en Sociologie de la
Facultad de Ciencias Sociales
Universidad del Salvador
Callao 542
Buenos Aires

BRAZIL

Departmento de Ciencias Sociales e Filosofia
Universidade Federal do Ceara
C.P. 1257
Fortaleza 60000
Ceara

CHILE

Instituto de Sociologia
Universidad Catolica de Chile
Casilla 1114-D
Santiago

DOMINICAN REPUBLIC

Escuela de Sociologia
Universidad Nacional Pedro Henriquez Urena
Santo Domingo

HAITI

Centre Haïtien d'Investigation en Sciences Sociales
rue Bonne Foi, 23
B.P. 1294
Port-au-Prince

PARAGUAY

Centro Paraguayo de Estudios Sociologicos
Eligio Ayala 973
Asuncion

VENEZUELA

Centro de Investigaciones en Ciencias Sociales
Apartado 12863
Caracas 101

WEST INDIES

Department of Sociology
Faculty of Social Sciences
University of the West Indies
St. Augustine
Trinidad

Department of Economics
University of the West Indies
Cave Hill Campus
G.P.O. Box 64
Barbados

North America

CANADA   Queen's University
                            Department of Sociology
                            Kingston, Ontario

U.S.   Rural Sociological Society
                            306A Comer Hall
                            Auburn University
                            Auburn, AL 36830

                            Sociological Abstracts Inc.
                            P.O. Box 22206
                            San Diego, CA 92122

Members in Category E: Supporting Organizations and Institutions

FRG   Forschungsgruppe für Gerontologie
                            Am Bergwerkswald 16
                            63 Giessen

                            Lehrstuhl für Betriebswirtschaftslehre
                            Universität München
                            Amalienstrasse 73
                            8 München 73

GREAT BRITAIN   National Documentation Centre for Sport,
                              Physical Education and Recreation
                            University of Birmingham
                            P.O. Box 363
                            Birmingham B15 2TT

A BIBLIOGRAPHY OF METHODS GUIDES   *2.22*

Documents

ALLPORT, GORDON. *The Use of Personal Documents in Psychological Science.* New York: Social Science Research Council, 1942.

GOTTSCHALK, L.; KLUCKHOHN, C.; and ANGELL, R. *The Use of Personal Documents in History, Anthropology, and Sociology.* New York: Social Science Research Council, 1945.

THOMAS, W. I., and ZNANIECKI, F. *The Polish Peasant in Europe and America.* New York: Dover Publications, 1958.

WEBB, EUGENE J.; CAMPBELL, DONALD T.; SCHWARTZ, RICHARD D.; and SECHREST, LEE. *Unobtrusive Measures: Nonreactive Research in the Social Sciences.* Chicago: Rand McNally, 1966. See chaps. 3 and 4.

Content Analysis

BERELSON, BERNARD. *Content Analysis in Communication Research.* New York: Free Press, 1952.

HOLSTI, OLE R. *Content Analysis for the Social Sciences and Humanities.* Reading, Mass.: Addison-Wesley, 1969.

KRIPPENDORFF, KLAUS. *Content Analysis: An Introduction to Its Methodology.* Beverly Hills, Calif: Sage, 1980.

ROSENGREN, KARL ERIK, ed. *Advances in Content Analysis.* Beverly Hills, Calif.: Sage, 1981.

STONE, PHILLIP J., et al., *The General Inquirer: A Computer Approach to Content Analysis.* Cambridge, Mass: MIT Press, 1966.

Direct Observation

BALES, ROBERT F. *Interaction Process Analysis.* Reading, Mass.: Addison-Wesley, 1949. Cf. his revised work, *Personality and Interpersonal Behavior.* New York: Holt, Rinehart & Winston, 1970.

DUNPHY, DEXTER C. *The Primary Group. A Handbook for Analysis and Field Research.* New York: Appleton-Century-Crofts, 1972.

RILEY, MATILDA, and NELSON, EDWARD E., eds. *Sociological Observation: A Comparative Strategy for New Social Knowledge.* New York: Basic Books, 1974.

WEBB, EUGENE J.; CAMPBELL, DONALD T.; SCHWARTZ, RICHARD D.; and SECHREST, LEE. *Unobtrusive Measures: Nonreactive Research in the Social Sciences.* Chicago: Rand McNally, 1966. See chaps. 5 and 6.

Historical and Theoretical Methods in Research

ERICKSON, KAI I.; TILLY, CHARLES; and WALLACE, ANTHONY F. C. "Essays on Social Historical Research" *Contemporary Sociology* 9 (March 1980): 185–94.

FREESE, LEE, ed. *Theoretical Methods in Sociology: Seven Essays.* Pittsburgh: University of Pittsburgh Press, 1981.

OUTHWAITE, WILLIAM. *Understanding Social Life: The Method Called Verstehen.* New York: Holmes and Meier, 1976.

TILLY, CHARLES. *As Sociology Meets History.* New York: Academic Press, 1981.

Participation Observation

BRUYN, SEVERYN T. *The Human Perspective in Sociology: The Methodology of Participant Observation.* Englewood Cliffs, N.J.: Prentice-Hall, 1966.

FRIEDRICKS, J., and LUDTKE, H. *Participant Observation Theory and Practice.* Lexington, Mass.: Heath, 1975.

JACOBS, GLENN, ed. *The Participant Observer.* New York: Braziller, 1970.

POWDERMAKER, HORTENSE. *Stranger and Friend, The Way of an Anthropologist.* New York: Norton, 1966.

SPRADLEY, JAMES P. *Participant Observation.* New York: Holt, Rinehart & Winston, 1980.

Questionnaire Construction

LABAW, PATRICIA. *Advanced Questionnaire Design.* Cambridge, Mass.: Abt Books, 1981.

LAZARSFELD, PAUL F., and BARTON, ALLEN. "Some General Principles of Questionnaire Classification." In *The Language of Social Research,* edited by Paul F. Lazarsfeld and Morris Rosenberg. Glencoe, Ill.: Free Press, 1962. Pp. 83–92.

OPPENHEIM, A. N. *Questionnaire Design and Attitude Measurement.* New York: Basic Books, 1966. See chaps. 2 and 3.

SCHUMAN, HOWARD, and PRESSER, STANLEY. *Questions and Answers in Attitude Surveys.* New York: Academic Press, 1981.

Interview

BRADBURN, NORMAN M.; SUDMAN, SEYMOUR; and ASSOCIATES. *Improving Interview Method and Questionnaire Design.* San Francisco: Jossey-Bass, 1979.

CANNELL, CHARLES F.; LAWSON, SALLY A.; and HAUSSER, DORIS L. *A Technique for Evaluating Interviewer Performance: A Manual for Coding and Analyzing Inter-*

CANNELL, CHARLES F.; OSKENBERG, LOIS; and CONVERSE, JEAN M. *Experiments in Interviewing Techniques: Field Experiments in Health Reporting. 1971–1977.* Ann Arbor: Mich: Institute of Social Research, University of Michigan, 1979.

GORDON, RAYMOND L. *Interviewing: Strategy, Techniques, and Tactics.* Rev. ed. Homewood, Ill.: Dorsey Press, 1975.

HYMAN, HERBERT H., et al. *Interviewing in Social Research.* Chicago: University of Chicago Press, 1954; reissued 1975.

KAHN, ROBERT L., and CANNELL, CHARLES F. *The Dynamics of Interviewing.* New York: Wiley, 1957.

MERTON, ROBERT K., et al. *The Focused Interview: A Manual of Problems and Procedures.* Glencoe, Ill.: Free Press, 1956.

Staff of the Survey Research Center. *Interviewer's Manual.* Rev. ed. Ann Arbor, Mich.: Institute for Social Research, University of Michigan, 1976.

Index and Scale Construction

BAUER, RAYMOND A., ed. *Social Indicators.* Cambridge, Mass.: MIT Press, 1966.

CARLEY, MICHAEL. *Social Measurement and Social Indicators.* London: Allen and Unwin, 1981.

COMBS, CLYDE H.; DAWES, ROBIN M.; and IVERSKY, AMOS. "Scaling and Data Theory." In *Mathematical Psychology: An Elementary Introduction.* Englewood Cliffs, N.J.: Prentice-Hall, 1970.

EDWARDS, ALLEN. *Technique of Attitude Scale Construction.* New York: Appleton-Century-Crofts, 1957.

LAND, KENNETH C., and SPILERMAN, SEYMOUR, eds. *Social Indicator Models.* New York: Russell Sage Foundation, 1975.

MARANELL, GARY M., ed. *Scaling: A Sourcebook for Behavioral Scientists.* Chicago: Aldine, 1974.

OPPENHEIM, A. N. *Questionnaire Design and Attitude Measurement.* New York: Basic Books, 1966. See chap. 5.

RILEY, MATILDA W.; RILEY, JOHN W.; and TOBY, JACKSON. *Sociological Studies in Scale Analysis.* New Brunswick, N.J.; Rutgers University Press, 1954.

SHAW, MARVIN E., and WRIGHT, JACK M. *Scales for the Measurement of Attitudes.* New York: McGraw-Hill, 1967.

SHELDON, ELEANOR B., and MOORE, WILBERT E. *Indicators of Social Change: A Symposium of Concepts and Measures.* New York: Russell Sage Foundation, 1968.

STOUFFER, SAMUEL, et al. *The American Soldier: Measurement and Prediction,* vol. 4. Princeton, N.J.: Princeton University Press, 1949. See chaps. on Scaling and on Latent Structure Analysis.

TORGERSON, W. *Theory and Methods of Scaling.* New York: Wiley, 1958.

The Sample Survey (Vehicle for Data Collection)

ALWIN, DUANE F., ed. *Survey Design and Analysis: Current Issues:* Beverly Hills, Calif.: Sage, 1978.

HOINVILLE, ROGER J., and Associates. *Survey Research Practice.* Exeter, N.H.: Heinemann 1978.

HYMAN, HERBERT. *Survey Design and Analysis: Principles, Cases, and Procedures.* Glencoe, Ill.: Free Press, 1955.

HYMAN, HERBERT. *Secondary Analysis of Sample Surveys: Principles, Procedures and Potentialities.* New York: Wiley, 1972.

JENSEN, RAYMOND. *Statistical Survey Techniques.* New York: Wiley, 1978.
NAMBOODIRI, N. KRISHNAN, ed. *Survey Sampling and Measurement.* New York: Academic Press. 1978.
ROSENBERG, MORRIS. *The Logic of Survey Analysis.* New York: Basic Books, 1968.
SUDMAN, SEYMOUR, and BRADBURN, NORMAN M. *Response Effect in Surveys: A Review and Synthesis.* Chicago: Aldine, 1974.
WARWICK, DONALD P. *The Sample Survey.* New York: McGraw-Hill, 1975.

Use of Panels

For references and instructions in the use of panels see section on The Panel Technique as a Research Instrument.

Use of Informants

SEIDLER, JOHN. "On Using Informants: A Technique for Collecting Quantitative Data and Controlling Measurement Error in Organizational Analysis." *American Sociological Review* 39 (December 1974): 816–31.

Field Methods for Studying Social Organizations

FELDMAN, ELLIOT J. *A Practical Guide to the Conduct of Field Research in the Social Sciences.* Boulder, Colo.: Westview Press, 1981.
GLAZER, MYRON. *The Research Adventure: Promise and Problems of Field Work.* New York: Random House, 1972.
HABENSTEIN, ROBERT W., ed. *Pathways to Data: Field Methods for Studying Ongoing Social Organizations.* Chicago: Aldine, 1970.
HAMMOND, PHILLIP E., ed. *Sociologists at Work.* New York: Basic Books, 1964; reprinted in 1970 as Doubleday Anchor Book.
SHAFFIR, WILLIAM B., ed., *Fieldwork Experience: Qualitative Approaches to Social Research.* New York: St. Martin's Press, 1980.

General Bibliography on the Understanding of Research Processes and Methods

BELL, COLIN, and NEWBY, HOWARD, eds. *Doing Sociological Research.* New York: Free Press, 1977.
BUNKER, BARBARA B.; PEARLSON, HOWARD B.; and SCHULZ, JUSTIN W. *Students' Guide to Conducting Social Science Research.* New York: Human Sciences Press, 1975.
ECKHARDT, KENNETH W., and ERMAN, M. DAVID. *Social Research Methods: Perspective, Theory, and Analysis.* New York: Random House, 1977.
GOLDEN, M. PATRICIA. *The Research Experience.* Itasca, Ill.: Peacock, 1976.
HARTMAN, JOHN J., and HEDBLOM, JACK H. *Methods for the Social Sciences.* Westport, Conn.: Greenwood Press, 1980.
ISAAC, STEPHEN, with MICHAEL, WILLIAM B. *Handbook in Research and Evaluation.* San Diego, Calif.: EDITS, 1980.
ORENSTEIN, ALAN, and PHILLIPS, WILLIAM R. F. *Understanding Social Research: An Introduction.* Boston: Allyn & Bacon, 1978.
RUNCIE, JOHN F. *Experiencing Social Research.* Rev. ed. Homewood, Ill: Dorsey Press, 1980.

STERN, PAUL C. *Evaluating Social Science Research.* New York: Oxford University Press, 1979.

Social Research Methodology Abstracts 1. Annual review, Summer 1979. Edited by C. Van De Merwe, G. W. Kantebeen, M. Bosch. Rotterdam, The Netherlands: Erasmus University Rotterdam SRM-Documentation Centre, 1979. 149 pp. NPL, paper.

Social Research Methodology Bibliography 1, no. 3. Autumn 1979. Edited by C. Van De Merwe, G. W. Kantebeen, M. Van Logchem, and G. M. Van Den Bosch. Rotterdam, The Netherlands: Erasmus University Rotterdam, SRM-Documentation Centre, 1979. 87 pp. NPL, paper.

Social Research Methodology Bibliography 1, no. 4. Winter 1979. Edited by C. Van De Merwe, G. W. Kantebeen, M. Van Logchem, and G. M. Van Den Bosch. Rotterdam, The Netherlands: Erasmus University Rotterdam, SRM-Documentation Centre, 1979. 83 pp. NPL, paper.

Each volume of the *Abstracts* consists of a subject index and an index of descriptors; the former provides enumerations of reference numbers by subject, and the latter consists of a referenced alphabetical index of research and methdological terms. Review of pertinent literature is presented in two separate sections: Primary Abstracts and Secondary Abstracts. Primary Abstracts contains original reviews by SRM indexers presented alphabetically by author. Secondary Abstracts contains not reviews but references and descriptors. The purpose is to inform the reader of current literature and to indicate the subject(s) covered. These annual publications are comparable in style to other abstracts and easy to use. The contents cover research methods and related interests in a thorough manner nowhere else duplicated. Researchers and students will find these to be an invaluable resource.

The *Bibliographies* provide a cross-listing of references arranged in 318 categories (e.g., levels of theories, research design, types of interviews, multidimensional scales). *Sample:*

(Reviewed by Nancy K. Johnson, University of Connecticut, in *Contemporary Sociology,* 10 (November 1981) 819–820.)

HUMAN RELATIONS SKILLS IN SOCIAL RESEARCH   *2.23*

Interviewing and field research require social skills of rapport, participation, involvement, and communication. The researcher who seeks to be effective in personal contact might be well advised to read some of the references below, which grew out of the efforts of researchers who learned through the hard lessons of experience.

BAIN, ROBERT K. "The Researcher's Role: A Case Study." *Human Organization* 9 (Spring 1950): 23–28.

BELLACK, ALAN S., and HERSEN, MICHAEL, eds. *Research and Practice in Social Skills Training.* New York: Plenum, 1979.

BEAUCHAMP, TOM L. et al., eds., *Ethical Issues in Social Science Research,* Baltimore, Md.: Johns Hopkins Press, 1982.

Covers major areas of controversy over experimentation in the social sciences: harm and benefit; informed consent and deception; privacy and confidentiality; and government regulation.

FORM, WILLIAM H. "The Sociology of Social Research." In *The Organization, Management, and Tactics of Social Research,* edited by Richard O'Toole. New York: Schenkman, 1971. Pp. 3–42.

Describes human relations and social dimensions that surround research activity.

GEORGES, ROBERT A., and JONES, MICHAELO. *People Studying People: The Human Element in Field Work.* Berkeley: University of California Press, 1980.

Reports of field workers' experiences.

GOULDNER, ALVIN W. *Patterns of Industrial Bureaucracy.* New York: Free Press, 1954.

See especially the appendix: Field Work Procedures: The Social Organization of a Student Research Team.

HAMMOND, PHILLIP E., ed. *Sociologists at Work: The Craft of Social Research.* New York: Doubleday, 1967.

Relates research experiences of skilled social investigators including Peter M. Blau, James C. Coleman, Melville Dalton, James A. Davis, Renee C. Fox, Herbert Hyman, Seymour Lipset, David Reisman, Jeanne Watson, and Robert N. Bellah. Especially useful for the beginning researcher is Blanche Greer's "First Days in the Field," pp. 372–98.

HOLLINGSHEAD, A. B. *Elmtown's Youth.* New York: Wiley, 1949.

See especially field procedures as utilized in this community-based research.

JOHNSON, JOHN M. *Doing Field Research.* New York: Free Press, 1975.

Excellent chapters on Developing Trust, Gaining and Managing Entree in Field Research, Personal Relations, and Data Collection.

MADAN, T. N., ed. *Encounter and Experience: Personal Accounts of Fieldwork.* Honolulu: University Press of Hawaii, 1975.

Good statement stressing importance of personal relations in the field.

MANN, FLOYD C. "Human Relations Skills in Social Research." *Human Relations* 4, no. 4 (1951): 341–54.

An outstanding description. Outlines a *field* of study.

REINHARZ, SHULAMIT. *On Becoming a Social Scientist: From Survey Research and Participant Observation to Experiential Analysis.* San Francisco: Jossey-Bass, 1979.

This book seeks to prepare the student for the human relations problems encountered in research. Contents: Encountering the World of Sociology; The Ritual of Survey Empiricism; Dilemmas of Participant Observation; The Stress of Detached Fieldwork; Reclaiming Self-Awareness as a Source of Insight; Analysis of the Team Fieldwork Experience; Dimension of an Experiential Sociological Method; The Integration of Person, Problem, and Method.

REYNOLDS, PAUL DAVIDSON. *Ethical Dilemmas and Social Science Research: Moral Issues Confronting Investigators in Research Using Human Participants.* San Francisco: Jossey-Bass, 1979.

Individual investigators are now being held accountable for deception of research participants, failure to secure informed consent, physical discomfort and psychic stress experienced by volunteers, invasions of privacy, and other effects of their studies.

part 3

Guides to Statistical Analysis and Computer Resources

THIS part includes guides that should prove useful to researchers as they seek statistical tools and computer resources to test hypotheses. Researchers may find it necessary to reformulate initial hypotheses in order to use the most powerful statistical test. There is a reciprocal relationship between research design and statistical analysis. Superior designs are developed when the researcher has a command of both the required research knowledge and the full scope of statistical treatments available. Imaginative research questions require the fullest possible weighing of research implementation. When the twin conditions are realized, research options of maximum effectiveness open to stir the creative imagination.

Qualitative and quantitative variables require appropriate statistics to provide tests of association or of significant differences between groups. In this part statistical tests are organized to deal with both kinds of variables. In addition, the question of the probability of normal distribution of the data forces the researcher to make a distinction between parametric and nonparametric statistics in drawing inferences from samples. These distinctions are presented with the description of the statistics.

Computations being done in the social sciences today increasingly use high-speed computers through user terminals that resemble typewriters or television screens. User terminal clusters are located in universities or in organizations such as banks and insurance offices. The hardware will be found in some central location. Since the 1970s the explosion of mini- and micro-computer technology has generated mini- and micro-computers in almost every department of the university. Home computers are also increasingly available.

For smaller sets of data and more limited analysis, there are punchcard sorters, counter sorters, and various types of scanners. Desk calculators are becoming more sophisticated and less expensive. Electronic calculators are noiseless and more reliable than the earlier models and often contain storage and program keys that greatly increase their usefulness.

All this hardware makes possible complex and sophisticated statistical analyses, and important scientific questions can be searched as never before. The computer can swallow masses of data and organize their relationships at split-second speed.

With these tools available, the student is challenged to develop statistical knowledge and a creative imagination. Computers can be used for generating formal models of social systems; for simulating the behavior of persons, groups, or nations; and for retrieving large amounts of documentary material such as abstracts of journal articles (as explained in part 2). The cost of computer time requires more attention than ever before to research design, especially statistical planning.

Statistical planning is an integral part of designed research. The sooner attention can be given to this part of research, the better. After the problem, theory, study design, and hypotheses are chosen, the time for statistical planning has arrived. Researchers should not wait until they are in the process of gathering or analyzing data. This caveat applies especially to young researchers wishing to avoid mistakes, but all researchers will have better research designs if their statistical planning is done before fieldwork begins.

Causal analysis refers to the depicting of the causal relationships of the variables. Zetterberg listed thirteen possible causal chains for three variables.[1] The selection of an appropriate chain is an important first step in designing statistical analysis.

Example: Two major determinants influencing the productivity or effectiveness of a work group are leadership behavior and the morale of workers. The causal relationship is often assigned to the chain that identifies Leadership Behavior as the independent variable (x), Morale as an intervening variable (y), and Productivity as the outcome (or dependent) variable (z). The causal chain can be diagrammed as $x \rightarrow y \rightarrow z$. The statistical tests of hypotheses now are given form, and appropriate techniques are applied. Alternate assumptions about the causal relationships of these three variables would call for different treatments.

A multivariate problem with many interacting variables poses more elaborate constructions. A *path model* is important if many independent and intervening variables are involved in measuring relationships with a dependent variable.

Example: Path analysis is discussed in 3.9 where a path diagram is shown. This model diagrams the interrelationships of variables believed to influence the son's current occupation. Father's occupation and father's education are shown as independent variables, son's education and son's first job as intervening variables. The algebraic representation of the causal scheme now rests on a system of equations rather than the single equation often employed in multiple regression analysis.

Dummy statistical tables become the statistical plan for qualitative data. These tables represent the actual tables to be used for analysis when data are collected and frequencies or values are inserted within them. By setting up dummy tables in advance, a careful appraisal of the appropriate statistics can be made and a selection of the best technique chosen. If the researcher wants help from a statistician, these tables are a necessity. With them decisions can be made as to the statistic, techniques, and confidence that may be entertained. Perhaps a recasting of the data collection process may be called for. Or different types of data are needed. This is the stage at which the researcher needs this kind of information. Later it may not be possible, and valuable time and money may be lost.

Example: Note how Allen Barton in 3.2, "The Idea of Property Space in Social Research," has prepared dummy tables for dichotomous and trichotomous attributes in two-, three-, and four-dimensional space. The variables involve relationships of father's occupation, father's political party with son's occupation, and political party. The dummy tables are particularly useful in permitting the effects of the various background variables to be compared, holding the others constant in each case.

Skeleton primary tables are tables proposed for future display of published data. The scientific worth of the tables depends upon the soundness of the reasoning underlying the classifications and associations of the data. The originator of a set of tables should ask:

What important fact or facts should this table emphasize?
How can these facts be made most evident?
Is the form adapted for the vehicle of publication?[2]

Example of a Skeletal Primary Table:

Product-Moment Correlations between Socioeconomic Status and Sentence Length for Crime Categories in Three States[3]

	New York r r^2 N	Colorado r r^2 N	Mississippi r r^2 N
2nd Degree murder	— — —	— — —	— — —
Forcible rape	— — —	— — —	— — —
Burglary	— — —	— — —	— — —
Embezzlement	— — —	— — —	— — —
Drug offenses	— — —	— — —	— — —

This table will show the product-moment correlation (Pearsonian r) between the socioeconomic status level of defendants and the sentences received for specific crimes within three states. Also to be shown is the proportion of variance(r^2) in one variable that is explained by the other, as well as the sample size (N) for each crime category. Levels of statistical significance for computed correlation coefficients will be shown where relevant.[4]

Reluctance to take these steps in statistical design means that the research is placed under greater risk. The execution of these steps means the heart of the completed product is projected in advance for appraisal and evaluation. Improvements can be made and risks of failure minimized.

No limited set of guides can replace a good text in statistics. However, the researcher can find an array of concepts so organized here that he may be able to survey the dimensions of his problem. Computation guides have been included for the use of the most commonly used statistical measures.

A section on causation and multivariate analysis includes an introduction to the computer, path analysis, and factor analysis.

The bibliography at the end of this part has been selected to provide additional information on statistics, tables, and graphic presentation. Each reference enables the reader to follow step-by-step explanations. A brief dictionary of some newer statistical tools and methodological techniques has been prepared in order to acquaint the uninformed reader with the general meaning of the terms.

Notes

1. See Hans L. Zetterberg, "On the Decisions in Verificational Studies," p. 39 of this book.
2. For further information about construction of such tables, see Mary Louise Mark, *Statistics in the Making,* Bureau of Business Research Publication 92 (Columbus, Ohio: College of Commerce and Administration, Ohio State University, 1958), pp. 156–79.
3. The suggestion for this table is drawn from Theodore G. Chiricos and Gordon P. Waldo, "Socioeconomic Status and Criminal Sentencing: An Empirical Assessment of a Conflict Proposition," *American Sociological Review* 40 (December 1975): 760.
4. For presentation of the data in graphic form, see Calvin F. Schmid, *Handbook of Graphic Presentation* (New York: Ronald, 1954). For a brief description of graphic presentation, see Pauline V. Young, *Scientific Social Surveys and Research,* 3rd ed. (Englewood Cliffs, N.J.: Prentice-Hall, 1956), pp. 360–405.

William Lurie

Instructions for Use of Guide 3.1

This article should sharpen researchers' awareness of the dimensions of their hypotheses as they prepare to test them. As Lurie puts it: "It is the scientist's responsibility to decide exactly what his hypotheses are, what these hypotheses are about, and how sure he wants to be of their correctness. . . . And the more the scientist becomes aware of his responsibilities, and takes them into account in his work, so much more accurate and valid will his conclusions be, and so much more properly related to the reality with which he deals."

Prologue

It has become fashionable to ornament science with statistical embellishments. No equation is complete without at least a double summation sign somewhere in it, sub-ij's attach themselves to familiar Xs, Ys and Zs; and phrases like "polymodal distribution," "inverse reciprocal correlation," and "multivariate deviations" now can be seen on practically every other page of "The Journal of the Society for Thus-and-So," "The Transactions of the Association for Such-and-Such," and "The Proceedings of the Symposium on Etc., Etc."

But in addition to providing mathematical and linguistic ornamentation for these publications, the statistician, if he is really to assist the scientist, must perform a necessary, but irritatingly annoying task: he must ask the scientist impertinent questions. Indeed, the questions, if bluntly asked, may appear to be not only impertinent but almost indecently prying—because they deal with the foundations of the scientist's thinking. By these questions, unsuspected weaknesses in the foundations may be brought to light, and the exposure of weaknesses in one's thinking is a rather unpleasant occurrence.

The statistician will, then, if he is wise in the ways of human beings as well as learned in statistics, ask these questions diplomatically, or even not ask them as questions at all. He may well guide the discussion with the scientist in such a way that the answers to the questions will be forthcoming without the questions having been even explicitly asked.

And if happily the scientific and statistical disciplines reside within one mind, and it is the scientist's statistical conscience that asks him these questions, instead of impertinent questioning there is valid scientific soul-searching.

Regardless, then, of whether these questions arise inside or outside the scientist's own mind, what are they? These:

1. With respect to the experiment you are performing, just what are your ideas?
2. With respect to the scientific area to which these ideas refer, just what are they about?
3. How sure do you want to be of the correctness of these ideas?

* Reprinted by permission of author and *American Scientist* 46 (March 1958): 57–61.

In order to understand the statistician's reasons for asking these questions, let us first see how the scientist's activities look to the statistician.

From the statistician's point of view, what the scientist does, is: performs experiments and/or makes observations to obtain data relating to *an idea he has* about the organization of *that portion of the world he is interested in,* so that he can decide *whether his idea was correct or not.*

For each of these italicized aspects of the scientist's activity, there is a corresponding question.

Let us, then, examine each of these aspects of the scientist's activities, and the purpose for and consequences of the question concerning it.

An Idea He Has

The impertinent questioner must take the risk of appearing to imply that the scientist is not thinking clearly. And, of course, even an implication to this effect is not calculated to endear the implier to the heart of the implyee. But it is exactly this implication that, perhaps innocently, is associated with the question, "Just what are your ideas?"

Why does the statistician ask this impertinent question? Because it is a precondition for the statistician's being able to help the scientist accomplish his objective. A hazily formulated idea not only can be discussed, at best, with difficulty, but further, it is practically impossible to test its correctness. Therefore, the statistician has a rule, his name for which is: EXPLICIT HYPOTH-ESIZATION. This rule expresses the requirement that the idea, whose correctness is to be determined by the experiment, should be stated in as clear, detailed, and explicit form as possible, preferably before the experiment is conducted. This idea can relate either to the influence of one factor or to the influence of several factors, or to the numerical characterization of a property (or properties) of whatever is being experimented on. In the early stages of an investigation, where what are being sought are the influential factors (i.e., those which, when they are at varying levels, give rise to suffi-ciently varied results), the idea (or hypothesis) need not be specific, but it must be explicit. The hypothesis can be broad, but it must be explicitly broad:—that is, even though it is not a hypothesis about details, its boundary must be sharply delineated.

For example, "Factors, *A, B, C,* and *D* individually influence the results," "Factors *A* and *B*, acting in conjunction, influence the results differently than would be expected from the effects of *A* alone and *B* alone," "Factors *A, B,* and *C*, acting in conjunction, etc., etc." Or later in the investigation, and more specifically, "The measurement of the effect of factor *A* at level a_1, will result in the numerical value $N \pm n$."

To emphasize unmistakably the requirement for explicit hypothesization, let us use an obviously exaggerated example dealing with a particular subject: the task of an industrial psychologist who has been given the job of finding out why the accounting clerks are making too many errors in addition. (The problem of deciding how many errors are "too many" is another statistical problem, which will not be considered here.)

The psychologist, for the purposes of this example, may say to himself: "My training as a psychologist tells me that the situation in which a person operates affects his behavior. So let me find out what the situation is that is causing the clerks to make these errors." If the formulation of the psychologist's idea goes no further than this, he can obviously continue to attempt to find out what the situation is, from now on forever, since "The Situation" has no boundaries.

It might, for example, not only include the working circumstances of the clerks, but their home circumstances, their childhood histories, their dream life; and it is seen that the possibilities are unlimited. As then is obvious, the hypothesis has not been sufficiently explicitly formulated, nor the situation covered by it clearly enough delineated, for a decision to be able to be arrived at as to the correctness of the hypothesis.

But now, let the psychologist's statistical conscience awaken, and his ideas begin to crystalize out of their original diffuseness. "The Situation?—Well, to be more specific, let's just consider the office situation. And within the office situation, I'll pick three factors that I believe affect the performance of the clerks. The factors I'm selecting to study for their effects are: Temperature, Humidity, and Noise. And now, my explicit hypothesis: It makes a difference what the levels of temperature, humidity, and noise are with respect to the number of errors in addition made by the accounting clerks." The hypothesis could (and probably should) have been even more explicitly formulated (e.g., including as factors Illumination Level, Desk Space per employee, etc.) but the direction of the path to statistical virtue has been pointed out, and further travel along that path is left to the reader.

Now, assuming that the hypothesis has been sufficiently explicitly formulated, the scientist and statistician can together review the plan (or design) of the experiment, and assure themselves that such data will be obtained as will be sufficient to determine the correctness (or noncorrectness) of the scientist's idea.

That Portion of the World He Is Interested In

Again, the impertinent questioner must be careful in asking: "Just what are your ideas about?" Even though one may admit that his ideas are not as clearly and explicitly formulated as he would like, the question "Just what are your ideas about?" carries with it, to the person being asked, the implication that he isn't clear about the subject-matter of his ideas, surely not a flattering implication. The statistician has a reason for his implied aspersion on the basis of the scientist's self-esteem. The statistician's reason can be stated to the scientist thus: "It's for your own good. If I am to help you decide, on the basis of the experimental facts, whether your ideas are correct or not, I have to know, as explicitly as possible, not only what your ideas are, but *what they are about.* My name for this requirement is: MODEL FORMULATION." Technically, model formulation establishes the requirement that a clear differentiation be made as to whether the scientist's ideas are intended to be applicable only to the conditions of the experiment (the narrower range of application) or to conditions (i.e., levels of the factors) other than those specific ones under which the experiment is being conducted (the broader range of application). Why the necessity for this differentiation? Because, when the experimental data have been obtained, the analysis of the data is carried on in different ways, depending on whether the hypotheses are intended to have the broader or narrower range of application.

Let us again, for exemplification, return to our industrial psychologist. And, let us say, his experimental conditions are, for temperature, 40°, 55°, and 70°F.; for humidity, 40, 55, and 70 percent; and for noise level, 40, 55, and 70 decibels.

It may well make a difference in the way the experimental data are analyzed to arrive at conclusions (i.e., decisions as to correctness of ideas), and whether any conclusions can be arrived at, and, if so, what they are, depending on whether the scientist wants his conclusions to apply only to the three levels of temperature, humidity, and noise level that have been used in the experiment, or also to other (unspecified) temperature, humidity, and noise levels. Data that support narrow conclusions may not be sufficient to support broader conclusions. Therefore, the scientist must have clearly in mind what his hypotheses are about, and whether, consequently, his conclusions will be broad or narrow; and the statistician's effort to assure that the scientist does have this clearly in mind, may well, to the scientist, appear to be impertinent.

Whether His Idea Was Correct or Not

The statistician's third question—"How sure do you want to be of the correctness of your ideas?"—is the least impertinent of the three. This question, unlike the other two, does not probe the foundations of the scientist's thinking, but rather requests him to quantify a previously unquantified aspect of it. (In fact, the request is in accordance with the scientist's own predilection for quantitative data.) This aspect is that dealing with levels of assurance, for which ordinary language supplies us with qualitatively descriptive terms (somewhat sure, rather sure, quite sure, extremely sure). But these terms are not sufficiently explicit for scientific use. Therefore, the statistician asks the scientist to decide upon and express his desired level of assurance in quantitative terms, so that it can be determined, by analysis of the quantitative data, whether the desired level of assurance of the conclusions has been achieved. The statistician's name for the choice and quantitative expression of the desired level of assurance is: SIGNIFICANCE LEVEL SELECTION. And how does the statistician help the scientist choose the desired level of assurance? By bringing to the forefront of the scientist's consciousness his already unconscious awareness of the inherent variability of events (i.e., that, because of chance alone, no repetition of an experiment will give exactly the same results); by helping the scientist decide what assurance is desired that the hypothesis has not been "confirmed" just by the operation of chance alone; and by furnishing the mathematical tools to decide, on the basis of the experimental data, whether the desired level of assurance has been attained. Say, for example, in the temperature-humidity-noise level experiment, when all the data have been accumulated, and the scientist is preparing them for analysis so that he may decide whether his hypotheses were correct or not, the statistician will then say to him: "You know, of course, that if you did the experiment over, under as near the same conditions as possible, you'd get slightly, or even somewhat different results. The results might even, just by chance, be different enough to lead you to believe that temperature does affect accuracy, even though it really doesn't. Or even if you didn't do the experiment over again, the particular experiment you've just done might be the one in which the data are such that you'd believe temperature has an effect though it really doesn't. *But I can test these data of yours.* I can assure you that when you state the conclusion, say, that temperature does affect accuracy, you'll have only a 5 percent, or 1 percent, or 1/10th of 1 percent chance of being wrong, as a result of that off chance I told you about. Now—what chance do you want to take? If you select a very small chance of being wrong in saying there is a temperature effect when there really isn't you're taking a bigger chance of saying there isn't a temperature effect when there really might be. I can figure this out for you also. So again, what chance do you want to take?"

When the scientist has selected the chance he is willing to take of being wrong (or what is equivalent, how sure he wants to be that he is correct) in his conclusions, the statistician can analyze the data and tell the scientist what conclusions he can validly draw (i.e., what decisions he can make about the correctness of his ideas).

Epilogue

One final word. *It is the statistician's responsibility to ask these questions, not to anwer them.* It is the scientist's responsibility to decide exactly what his hypotheses are, what these hypotheses are about, and how sure he wants to be of their correctness.

The statistician, in asking his impertinent questions, is just explicitly bringing to the scientist's attention responsibilities that the scientist may not have been aware that he had. And the more the scientist becomes aware of his responsibilities, and takes them into account in his work, so much more accurate and valid will his conclusions be, and so much more properly related to the reality with which he deals.

THE IDEA OF PROPERTY-SPACE IN SOCIAL RESEARCH*   *3.2*

Allen H. Barton

Instructions for Use of Guide 3.2

This guide presents a technique of classifying qualitative data so that associations may be discovered. Arranging data in "property-space" is particularly useful in permitting the effects of various background variables to be compared, while other variables are held constant in each case. The concept of property-space is valuable because it becomes a way of thinking about qualitative data and the way in which relations may be ascertained. Hans Zeisel, *Say It With Figures,* 5th ed. rev. (New York: Harper, 1968), presents a more elaborate description of causal analysis and the role of cross-tabulation for the reader who wishes additional knowledge. The more advanced student

---

* Reprinted by permission from Paul F. Lazarsfeld and Morris Rosenberg, eds., *The Language of Social Research* (Glencoe, Ill.: Free Press, 1955), pp. 40–44. Copyright 1955 by The Free Press, A Corporation.

should consult Herbert Hyman, *Survey Design and Analysis: Principles, Cases, and Procedures* (Glencoe, Ill.: Free Press, 1966). See also the selected readings on causal models and multivariate analysis in the bibliography at the end of part 3.

Everyone is familiar with the idea of indicating location in space by means of coordinates. Every point on this page can be described by two numbers: its distance from the left-hand side and its distance from the bottom (or from any other pair of axes we choose). The location of any point on the earth's surface can be indicated by giving its latitude and longitude, using as base lines the equator and the Greenwich meridian.

Other properties besides location in physical space can likewise be indicated by coordinates. A man can be characterized by his scores on tests of mathematical and linguistic ability, just as by his latitude and longitude. These two scores locate him in a "property-space" with the two dimensions of mathematical ability and linguistic ability. We can chart this property-space on paper by using mathematics score as one axis and linguistic score for the other, just as we can chart the earth's surface. Of course in the latter case we are making a spatial representation of actual spatial dimensions, only on a smaller scale. In the former our distances on paper represent the numbers of correct answers to questions given by people taking tests, or in a larger sense, the ability of their minds to perform certain tasks.

The dimensions on which we "locate" people in property-space can be of different kinds. Most psychological test scores are for all practical purposes *continuous variables,* but they usually do not have equal intervals or a meaningful zero point. They provide only a relative ordering of people. Once we have located a representative sample of the United States population in our mathematical-linguistic property-space, we can say that a man is in the fifth percentile of the population in mathematical ability and in the fortieth in linguistic ability. Sometimes social scientists do work with continuous variables that do have a zero-point and equal intervals, at least formally: age, income, size of community, number of hours spent watching television.

More often, probably, the dimensions will be qualitative properties, which locate cases in one of a number of classes, like "state of birth," "military rank," or "occupation." State of birth locates everyone born in the continental U.S. in one of 51 *unordered classes* (counting District of Columbia). Military rank locates members of the armed forces in what is by definition a set of *rank-ordered classes,* ranging from buck private up to five-star general. Occupations in themselves do not necessarily form a set of ranked classes, although some of them are specifically defined in terms of degree of "skill." We might simply list them arbitrarily, as in alphabetical order. Or we might draw upon outside information about them—for example average income, as known from census data, or prestige status, as discovered through surveys—to arrange them in one or another rank-order.

The simplest type of property by which an object can be characterized is a *dichotomous attribute,* such as voter/nonvoter, white/nonwhite, male/female, or Democrat/Republican. It is always possible to simplify a more complex property by reducing the number of classes that are distinguished. A continuous variable can be cut up to form a set of ranked classes, like income brackets or age levels. A set of ranked classes, in turn, can be simplified by combining all those above a certain point into one class and all those below into a second class, forming a dichotomy. This is done when we reduce the military hierarchy to the distinction between officers and enlisted men, or the income brackets to above or below a certain amount. By picking out one aspect of a set of unordered classes we can sometimes order them into a dichotomy, as when we classify states as east or west of the Mississippi, or occupations as manual or nonmanual.

When we chart the property-space formed by two qualitative characteristics the result is not, of course, a continuous plane, but an array of cells each representing one combination of values on two properties. For example, a study of the 1952 election described people's "political position" in October 1952 in terms of the two dimensions of "usual party affiliations" and "degree of political interest." If one asks Americans what their usual party affiliation is almost everyone falls into three categories: Republicans, Democrats, and independents. These are natural divisions. Degree of interest on the other hand can be divided into any number of ranked categories we please, depending on the alternatives we offer the respondent. In the present case they could rate themselves as having high, medium, or low interest. These two trichotomous dimensions then define a ninefold property-space as shown in table 1.

We can locate a person within this property-space by giving as coordinates his usual party affiliation and his degree of political interest.

There is no reason why we cannot characterize objects by as many properties as we want. We can add a test in historical knowledge to tests in mathematics and language, and characterize our subjects by three coordinates. These can still be presented in the form of a physical model, by using a box in which everyone is located by distance from the left-hand side, from the front, and from the bottom. If we add a fourth test, for instance, of reading speed, we can give our subjects four coordinates and locate them in a four-dimensional property-space. Thus we can say that someone is in the fifth percentile of the U.S. population in mathematics, the fortieth in language skill, the sixtieth in historical knowledge, and the twenty-ninth in reading speed. We can no longer represent this by a physical model, but we can perform mathematical operations on the four coordinates just as well as on two or three.

In dealing with qualitative property-spaces which have limited numbers of categories on each dimension, we can still chart the property-space on

Table 1. *A Qualitative Property-Space of Political Position*

USUAL PARTY AFFILIATION

		Republican	Democratic	Independent
Degree of Political Interest	High			
	Medium			
	Low			

paper even though it is three-dimensional or even higher-dimensional. Let us take the two dimensions of occupation, dichotomized as manual/nonmanual, and political preference, dichotomized as Democratic/Republican. These give us a fourfold table. If we add the dimension of father's occupation, again dichotomized as manual/nonmanual, we now have a "two-story" fourfold table: occupation and party of sons of manual workers and occupation and party of sons of nonmanually employed people. This can be physically represented by a cube with eight cells, with the original fourfold table repeated on both the "first floor" and the "second floor." If we want to represent this cube on a flat piece of paper, all we have to do is to lay the two "stories" side by side, as an architect would two floor plans. (See table 2.)

Now suppose that we ask a fourth question, for example, the father's usual party, again dichotomized as Democratic/Republican. Our property-space then becomes a four-dimensional "cube." But we can still lay out each level on this fourth dimension on paper as we did those on the third. (See table 3.)

The combination of dichotomous attributes produces a type of property-space that may be labeled "dichotomous attribute-space."[1] Position in a dichotomous attribute-space can be indicated as a response-pattern of plus and minus signs, where we have assigned these values (arbitrarily or otherwise) to the two sides of each dichotomy and arranged the dimensions in some order. Thus a Democratic manual worker, whose father was a Democratic manual worker, might be indicated by the coordinates ($++++$). A Republican nonmanually employed person, whose father was a Democratic manual

Table 2. *A Three-Dimensional Attribute-Space Laid Out in Two Dimensions*

Father Manual Occupation

Son's Occupation

Son's Party		Manual	Nonmanual
	Democrat		
	Republican		

Father Nonmanual Occupation

Son's Occupation

Son's Party		Manual	Nonmanual
	Democrat		
	Republican		

Table 3. *A Four-Dimensional Attribute-Space Laid Out in Two Dimensions*

<table>
<tr>
<td></td>
<td colspan="3" align="center">Father Manual
Occupation</td>
<td></td>
<td colspan="3" align="center">Father Nonmanual
Occupation</td>
</tr>
<tr>
<td></td>
<td colspan="3" align="center">Son's Occupation</td>
<td></td>
<td colspan="3" align="center">Son's Occupation</td>
</tr>
<tr>
<td>Father
Democrat</td>
<td></td>
<td align="center">Manual</td>
<td align="center">Nonmanual</td>
<td></td>
<td></td>
<td align="center">Manual</td>
<td align="center">Nonmanual</td>
</tr>
<tr>
<td></td>
<td>Son
Democrat</td>
<td></td>
<td></td>
<td></td>
<td>Son
Democrat</td>
<td></td>
<td></td>
</tr>
<tr>
<td></td>
<td>Republican</td>
<td></td>
<td></td>
<td></td>
<td>Republican</td>
<td></td>
<td></td>
</tr>
</table>

<table>
<tr>
<td></td>
<td colspan="3" align="center">Son's Occupation</td>
<td></td>
<td colspan="3" align="center">Son's Occupation</td>
</tr>
<tr>
<td>Father
Republican</td>
<td></td>
<td align="center">Manual</td>
<td align="center">Nonmanual</td>
<td></td>
<td></td>
<td align="center">Manual</td>
<td align="center">Nonmanual</td>
</tr>
<tr>
<td></td>
<td>Son
Democrat</td>
<td></td>
<td></td>
<td></td>
<td>Son
Democrat</td>
<td></td>
<td></td>
</tr>
<tr>
<td></td>
<td>Republican</td>
<td></td>
<td></td>
<td></td>
<td>Republican</td>
<td></td>
<td></td>
</tr>
</table>

worker, would have the coordinates ($--++$), and so on. (This system of notation is often used in "political score-sheets" that show how congressmen voted on a series of bills, a plus sign showing a "correct" vote and a minus sign a "wrong" vote, in terms of a given political viewpoint or economic interest.)

If we are particularly interested in one of the dimensions as a criterion or dependent variable, we may present a dichotomous attribute-space in abbreviated form by showing only the "background" factors as dimensions in the chart, and filling in each cell with a figure showing the percent who are "positive" on the criterion behavior. No information is lost since the attribute is a dichotomy, and all those not positive are classified as "negative" on the attribute. It is as if we had raised three-dimensional bars from the two-dimensional chart of background characteristics with a height proportional to the positive answers on the criterion behavior, and then replaced them with figures indicating their height just as altitudes are shown on a flat map. Thus table 3 could be presented as an eightfold table showing the dimensions of father's occupation, father's party, and son's occupation; the cells would be filled in with figures showing "percent Democrat" (or vice versa). (See table 4.)

Such tables are particularly useful in permitting the effects of the various background variables to be compared, holding the others constant in each case.[2]

To suggest how far the use of very high-dimension property-spaces has actually developed in social research, we need only note that the results of each interview in a survey are normally punched on an IBM card containing 80 columns, each with twelve rows. Such a card provides for an 80-dimensional

Table 4. *Abbreviated Presentation of a Four-Dimensional Attribute-Space*

	Father's Occupation			
	Manual		Nonmanual	
	Son's Occupation		Son's Occupation	
	Manual	Nonmanual	Manual	Nonmanual
Democratic	_____% Dem.	_____% Dem.	_____% Dem.	_____% Dem.
Father's Party				
Republican	_____% Dem.	_____% Dem.	_____% Dem.	_____% Dem.

property-space, with each property having twelve classes. In practice one never uses all eighty dimensions simultaneously to characterize a respondent; however, they are all available to use in whatever smaller combinations we select. If we consider each position in the 80 by 12 matrix as representing a dichotomous attribute (each can either be punched or not punched), we have the possibility of locating each respondent in a dichotomous attribute-space of 960 dimensions.

Notes

1. This has special characteristics that are used in latent-structure analysis, but this will not be discussed here. A dichotomous system is also equivalent to a binary number system, or an "off/on" system of information, as used in computing machines and in communication theory.
2. Many concrete examples can be found in chap. 10 in Hans Zeisel, *Say It With Figures* (New York: Harper, 1968).

3.3 SUMMARY OF COMMON MEASURES OF ASSOCIATION

Instructions for Use of Guide 3.3

Statistical methods enable us to study and to describe precisely averages, differences, and relationships. The number of statistical tests has risen considerably in the last thirty years and has become so large that not even a professional statistician can keep all of them at his fingertips. As these tests have become more numerous so have the kinds of hypotheses that can be tested by statistical procedures.

Common questions that the researcher often asks are:

Is there a significant difference between these two (or more) groups on this variable? What confidence can I have that observed differences did not occur by chance? Is there an association between these two (or more) variables? If so, how close is the association?

To ascertain the significance of differences between two or more groups on a given variable the most common statistics used include the t-test, χ^2, and F. A summary of the more common measures of association would include Pearson's product-moment r with its increasing display in correlation matrices, the correlation ratio eta, Gamma G, Spearman's rank difference coefficient rho, Lambda λ and the multiple correlation R.* Consult the bibliography Guide 3.11 for a statistical text describing these measures. Note that computation guides have been included in this handbook for the very useful statistics t, r, x^2, and r_s.

Guide 3.3, which follows, summarizes common measures of association. Since a major object of scientific inquiry is to discover relationships, these measures become standard equipment in the training of the scientist who uses statistical tests to ascertain relationships.**

a. Pearson product-moment r: For measuring relationships between two variables when both are continuous and the relationship is rectilinear. The coefficient of correlation is most reliable when based upon a large number of pairs of observations.

b. The correlation ratio eta: For measuring relationships between two continuous variables that are related in a curvilinear fashion.

c. Spearman's rank difference coefficient rho r_s: For measuring the association between two rankings. The measure is based on the difference between ranks. It is primarily used where rankings of individual cases on two variables are available so that rankings range from 1 to N for each variable. Rho will have a value of $+1.0$ for a perfect match of ranks, to a value of -1.0 if the ranks are exactly opposite.

d. Gamma G: For measuring the association between two ordinal variables, each of which is arranged in rank order. Gamma can always achieve the limiting values of -1.0 or $+1.0$ regardless of the number of ties between the pairs in the data.

e. Lambda λ: For measuring the association between two bivariate distributions where both variables are interpreted to be nominal variables. Lambda simply reverses the role of two variables predicting x from information about y.

f. Multiple correlation coefficient R: For measuring the maximum relationship that may be obtained between a combination of several continuous (independent) variables and some other continuous (dependent) variable.

g. Partial correlation coefficient $r_{12.3}$: For measuring the relationship between two continuous variables with the effects of a third continuous variable (or several others) held constant.

h. Biserial r: For measuring relationships when one variable is recorded in terms of a dichotomy and the other is continuous. Biserial r assumes that the individuals in each of the two categories represent a complete distribution (i.e., not just the two extremes), that the dichotomized variable is really

---

* Based on: Tests of Association Used in Journal Articles in ASR, AJS, and SF, as compiled by Kenneth J. Pollinger.

** See Herman J. Loether and Donald G. McTavish, *Descriptive Statistics for Sociologists* (Boston: Allyn and Bacon, 1974). Note especially pp. 256–57 for table listing current measures with formulas and guides to the selection of the measure appropriate to the dimensions of different problems.

continuous and normally distributed, and that the relationship between the two variables is rectilinear.

i. Point biserial r: For measuring the relationship between a truly dichotomous variable and a continuous variable.

j. Contingency coefficient c: For measuring the association between two variables that can be classified in two or more categories, but when the categories themselves are not quantitative.

k. Phi coefficient φ: For measuring the association between two variables that are truly dichotomous. Cf. with Yule's *Q* for appropriate use.

l. Kendall coefficient of concordance N: For measuring the degree of agreement among *m* sets of *n* ranks. If we have a group of *n* objects ranked by each of *m* judges, the coefficient of concordance tells us the degree of agreement among the *m* sets of ranks.*

3.4 FOUR LEVELS OF MEASUREMENT AND THE STATISTICS APPROPRIATE TO EACH LEVEL

Instructions for Use of Guide 3.4

In part 4 many sociometric scales have been included to measure social variables. These scales may be *nominal, ordinal, interval,* and *ratio* types.

A Nominal or Classificatory Scale refers to a level of measurement when numbers or other symbols are used simply to classify an object, person, or characteristic. *Example:* Folkways, Mores, Laws.

The Ordinal or Ranking Scale refers to a level of measurement when objects in various categories of a scale stand in some kind of *relation* to the categories.

Given a group of equivalence classes, if the relation *greater than* holds between some but not all pairs of classes, we have a partially ordered scale. If the relation *greater than* holds for all pairs of classes so that a complete rank ordering of classes arises, we have an ordinal scale. *Example:* Socioeconomic status as conceived by Warner in his ranking from Lower Lower to Upper Upper.

The Interval Scale refers to a level of measurement when a scale has all the characteristics of an ordinal scale, and when in addition the distances between any two numbers on the scale are of known size. Then, measurement considerably stronger than ordinality has been achieved. *Example:* Thurstone's Equal-Appearing Interval Scale.

The Ratio Scale refers to a level of measurement when a scale has all the characteristics of an interval scale and in addition has a true zero point as its origin. The ratio of any two scale points is independent of the unit of measurement. *Example:* Centigrade temperature scale.

Each of these scales has defining relations that make particular statistical tests appropriate. Nominal and ordinal scales require nonparametric tests; only interval and ratio scales may permit use of parametric tests. Since most indexes and scales are ordinal, the nonparametric test is of especial importance. It is necessary to match the appropriate statistic with the defining characteristics of the scale. The guide summarizes these relations between type of scale and appropriate statistic.

* For a good treatment of this coefficient see Sidney Siegel, *Nonparametric Statistics for the Behavioral Sciences* (New York: McGraw-Hill, 1956), pp. 229–38.

Four Levels of Measurement and the Statistics Appropriate to Each Level*

Scale	Defining relations	Examples of appropriate statistics	Appropriate statistical tests
Nominal	1. Equivalence	Mode Frequency Contingency coefficient	Nonparametric test
Ordinal	1. Equivalence 2. Greater than	Median Percentile Spearman r_S Kendall T Kendall W	Nonparametric test

Interval	1. Equivalence
	2. Greater than
	3. Known ratio of any two intervals
		Mean
		Standard deviation
		Pearson product-
		   moment correlation
		Multiple product-
		   moment correlation
			Nonparametric and
			  parametric tests

Ratio	1. Equivalence 2. Greater than 3. Known ratio of any two intervals 4. Known ratio of any two scale values	Geometric mean Coefficient of variation	Nonparametric and parametric tests

*By permission from Sidney Siegel, *Nonparametric Statistics for the Behavioral Sciences* (New York: McGraw-Hill, 1956). Copyright 1956 by McGraw-Hill Book Co., Inc.

NONPARAMETRIC STATISTICAL TESTS APPROPRIATE TO VARIOUS TYPES OF SCALES   *3.5*

Instructions for Use of Guide 3.5

In the development of modern statistical methods, the first techniques of inference that appeared were those that made many assumptions about the nature of the population from which the scores were drawn. Since population values are "parameters" these statistical techniques are called *parametric*. For example, a technique of inference may be based on the assumption that the scores were drawn from a normally distributed population. Or the technique of inference may be based on the assumption that both sets of scores were drawn from populations having the same variance (σ^2) or spread of scores. Such techniques produce conclusions that contain qualifications, i.e., "If the assumptions regarding the shape of the population(s) are valid, then we may conclude that. . . ."

More recently a large number of techniques of inference have been developed that do not make stringent assumptions about parameters. These newer nonparametric techniques are "distribution free," so that "Regardless of the shape of the population(s), we may conclude that. . . ."

In the computation of parametric tests, we add, divide, and multiply the scores from samples. When these arithmetic processes are used on scores that are not truly numerical, they naturally introduce distortions in those data and thus throw doubt on conclusions from the test. Thus it is permissible to use the parametric techniques only with scores that are truly numerical. The mean and standard deviation are the central concepts of position and dispersion. Many nonparametric tests, on the other hand, focus on the order or ranking of the scores, not on their "numerical" values. The advantages of order statistics for data in the behavioral sciences are especially pronounced since so many "numerical" scores are numerical in appearance only.

Guide 3.5 presents a wide range of various nonparametric statistical tests. Note that each row divides the tests into those appropriate for nominal, ordinal, and interval scales. The first column contains those tests that may be used when one wishes to determine whether a single sample is from a specified sort of population. Columns 2 and 3 contain tests that may be used when one wishes to compare the scores obtained from two samples— one set considers tests for two related samples, while the other considers tests for two independent samples. Columns 4 and 5 are devoted to significance tests for k (3 or more) samples; one of these presents tests for k related samples and the other presents tests for k independent samples. Column 6 gives nonparametric measures of association and the tests of significance that are useful with some of these.

The field of statistics has developed to the extent that we now have, for almost all research designs, alternative statistical tests that might be used in order to come to a decision about a hypothesis. Having alternative tests, the researcher has two choices—read carefully about criteria to follow in choosing among various tests applicable to a given research design or get advice from a professional statistician. Preferably, he should do both. In order to use Guide 3.5 intelligently, the researcher should note where his problem falls within the table and then consult Sidney Siegel, *Nonparametric Statistics for the Behavioral Sciences* (New York: McGraw-Hill, 1956).

Researchers at the Institute of Social Research, University of Michigan, have prepared a guide for selecting statistical techniques for both parametric and nonparametric statistics. The core of the guide—a "decision tree"—consists of sixteen pages of sequential questions and answers that lead the user to the appropriate technique. It presents a systematic but highly condensed overview of over one hundred currently used statistics and statistical techniques and their uses. These are indexed for the decision tree, which is built around two major questions:

How Many Variables Does the Problem Involve?

ONE VARIABLE_____   TWO VARIABLES_____
MORE THAN TWO VARIABLES_____

How Do You Want to Treat the Variables with Respect to Scale of Measurement?

NOMINAL_____   ORDINAL_____   INTERVAL_____
(Including all possible combinations for two and three variable measurements)

Appendices cite major references to each statistic, programs of the OSIRIS III computer software system that compute given statistics, and new or rarely

Guide 3.5 *Nonparametric Statistical Test*[a][b]

LEVEL OF MEASURE-MENT	One-sample case	Two-sample case		k-sample case		NONPARAMETRIC MEASURE OF CORRELATION
	Col. 1 (Chap. 4)	Col. 2 Related samples (Chap. 5)	Col. 3 Independent samples (Chap. 6)	Col. 4 Related samples (Chap. 7)	Col. 5 Independent samples (Chap. 8)	Col. 6 (Chap. 9)
Nominal	Binomial test, pp. 36–42; χ^2 one-sample test, pp. 42–47	McNemar test for the significance of changes, pp. 63–67	Fisher exact probability test, pp. 96–104; χ^2 test for two independent samples, pp. 104–11	Cochran Q test, pp. 161–66	χ^2 test for k independent samples, pp. 175–79	Contingency coefficient: C, pp. 196–202
Ordinal	Kolmogorov-Smirnov one-sample test, pp. 47–52; One-sample runs test, pp. 52–58	Sign test, pp. 68–75; Wilcoxon matched-pairs signed-ranks test, pp. 75–83[c]	Median test, pp. 111–16; Mann-Whitney U test, pp. 116–27; Kolmogorov-Smirnov two-sample test, pp. 127–36; Wald-Wolfowitz runs test, pp. 136–45; Moses test of extreme reactions, pp. 145–52	Friedman two-way analysis of variance by ranks, pp. 166–72	Extension of the median test, pp. 179–84; Kruskal-Wallis one-way analysis of variance by ranks, pp. 184–93	Spearman rank correlation coefficient: r_s, pp. 202–13; Kendall rank correlation coefficient: r, pp. 213–23; Kendall partial rank correlation coefficient: $r_{xy.z}$, pp. 223–29; Kendall coefficient of concordance: W, pp. 229–38
Interval		Walsh test, pp. 83–87; Randomization test for matched pairs, pp. 88–92	Randomization test for two independent samples, pp. 152–56			

[a] Each column lists, cumulatively downward, the tests applicable to the given level of measurement. For example, in the case of k related samples, when ordinal measurement has been achieved both the Friedman two-way analysis of variance and the Cochran Q test are applicable.

[b] For use of this table, consult Sidney Siegel, *Nonparametric Statistics for the Behavioral Sciences* (New York: McGraw-Hill, 1956).

[c] The Wilcoxon test requires ordinal measurement not only within pairs, as is required for the sign test, but also of the differences between pairs. See the discussion on pp. 75–76 of Siegel.

used statistical techniques.[1] The new edition contains an expanded coverage of multivariate analysis.

Note

1. Frank M. Andrews, Laura Klem, Terrence N. Davidson, Patrick M. O'Malley, and Willard L. Rodgers, *A Guide for Selecting Statistical Techniques for Analyzing Social Science Data,* 2nd ed. (Ann Arbor, Mich.: Institute of Social Research, University of Michigan, 1981).

3.6   COMPUTATION GUIDES*

Instructions for Use of Guide 3.6

The computation guides that follow describe procedures for computing four statistics commonly needed by research workers in the behavioral sciences. Statistics t and r are parametric statistics, assuming randomness and normality of the populations; χ^2 and r_s are nonparametric or "distribution free," only randomness is generally assumed.

The computation design for the t test of the significance of the difference between two means is for the case of two independent samples. This is the test commonly used to test the difference between two means because we are often dealing with small samples, and we cannot assume that our data and values of t derived from them are normally distributed as are the parameters of large samples of 500 or more observations. However, it is assumed that the observations are drawn from normally distributed populations. The computation design for r, Pearson's product-moment coefficient of correlation, is useful when the number of cases is relatively large and the correlation chart is desired as a substitute for machine calculation. Pearson's r is for measuring relationships between two variables when both are continuous and the relationship is rectilinear. Both t and r may be used when the scores under analysis result from measurement in the strength of at least an *interval scale.*

The computation design for χ^2 is for testing significance of association between two attributes; for the general $r \times s$ case and for the special 2×2 table. This is the most widely used statistic for use with qualitative variables. The Spearman rank order coefficient r_s is the nonparametric statistic corresponding to the parametric Pearsonian r. This statistic is based on two sets of rankings of the same set of items. The Spearman rank order coefficient is not limited by the restrictions of normality and linearity imposed upon the Pearsonian product-moment r. While χ^2 is a test of the *existence* of a possible association, r_s provides a measure of the *degree of relationship* between two sets of rankings. Both χ^2 and r_s may be used when the scores under analysis result from measurements of *ordinal* or *nominal scales.*

---

* It should be understood that computer programs exist for all common statistical measures. These guides are used by researchers working with small samples or when a computer is not available.

3.6.a. *t* TEST OF SIGNIFICANCE BETWEEN TWO MEANS OF INDEPENDENT SAMPLES

Computation Design for t Test of the Difference Between Two Means, for Two Independent Samples*

$$\text{from } S_1: \ \overline{X}_1 = \Sigma X_{1i}/N_1$$

$$\Sigma x_1{}^2 = \Sigma X_{1i}{}^2 - (\Sigma X_{1i})^2/N_1$$

$$\text{from } S_2: \ \overline{X}_2 = \Sigma X_{2i}/N_2$$

$$\Sigma x_2{}^2 = \Sigma X_{2i}{}^2 - (\Sigma X_{2i})^2/N_2$$

1. H_0 : (See below for instructions.)

2. $s_{\overline{x}1-\overline{x}2} = \sqrt{\left(\dfrac{\Sigma x_1{}^2 + \Sigma x_2{}^2}{N_1 + N_2 - 2}\right)\left(\dfrac{1}{N_1} + \dfrac{1}{N_2}\right)}$

    $=$

3. $t = \dfrac{\overline{X}_1 - \overline{X}_2}{s_{\overline{x}1-\overline{x}2}} =$

4. d.f. $= N_1 + N_2 - 2 =$

5. $P =$

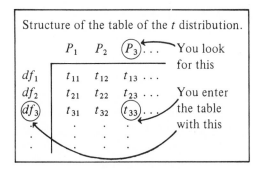

Structure of the table of the *t* distribution.

1. Formulate the null hypothesis you wish to test. This will determine whether you are to make a two-sided or one-sided test. The chief null hypotheses are $\mu_1 = \mu_2$ (two-sided), $\mu_1 \leqslant \mu_2$, or $\mu_1 \geqslant \mu_2$ (both one-sided). Write the hypothesis on line 1.

2. Compute the standard error of the difference by pooling estimates of the sums of squares. Enter on line 2.

3. Assume that both samples are normally and independently distributed; assume also that they have equal variances; then the distribution of *t*, which is the difference between the means divided by the estimated standard error of the difference, follows the *t* distribution with $N_1 + N_2 - 2$ degrees of freedom. Enter *t* on line 3 and d.f. on line 4.

---

* From Morris Zelditch, Jr., *A Basic Course in Sociological Statistics* (New York: Holt, 1959), p. 245. See Theodore R. Anderson and Morris Zelditch, Jr., *A Basic Course in Statistics: With Sociological Applications,* 3rd ed. (New York: Holt, 1975), pp. 272–77, for further discussion.

4. With the value of t and d.f. you enter the table of t. You are looking for P, the probability that a value of t this large or larger would have been obtained by chance if the null hypothesis were true. P will be shown along the head of the table, d.f. down the side, and the values of t will be shown in the body of the table. The probability shown will be two-tailed (i.e., the *sum* of the probability to the right of t and to the left of $-t$); if the hypothesis is one-sided, use one-half the tabled probability.

5. If P is equal to, or less than, 0.05, reject the null hypothesis. (Set the level of significance at 0.01 if you prefer greater certainty.) If P is greater than 0.05, accept the null hypothesis.

3.6b. PEARSONIAN r TO MEASURE LINEAR CORRELATION BETWEEN TWO VARIABLES

A scatter diagram should be prepared and carefully observed. If the distribution is judged to be rectilinear, proceed to analyze for the strength of the correlation.

Product Moment Correlation for Ungrouped Data

$$r = \frac{\Sigma XY - \dfrac{(\Sigma X)(\Sigma Y)}{N}}{\sqrt{\Sigma X^2 - \dfrac{(\Sigma X)^2}{N}} \sqrt{\Sigma Y^2 - \dfrac{(\Sigma Y)^2}{N}}}$$

X	Y	X^2	Y^2	XY
—	—	—	—	—
—	—	—	—	—
—	—	—	—	—
—	—	—	—	—
ΣX	ΣY	ΣX^2	ΣY^2	ΣXY

1. List X and Y scores in adjacent columns.
2. Compute each X^2, Y^2, and XY.
3. Obtain ΣX, ΣY, ΣX^2, ΣY^2, ΣXY, and N
4. Substitute in formula. Compute Standard Error of r.

$$\sigma r = \frac{1 - r^2}{\sqrt{N}} \cdot \text{Evaluate. See Interpretation of } r.$$

Interpretation of r:

1. .00–.20 little or no relationship.
   .20–.40 some slight relationship
   .40–.60 substantial relationship
   .60–.80 strong useful relationship
   .80–1.00 high relationship
2. The usefulness of a correlation is determined by its size. The sign has no bearing on the strength of the relationship. It only determines the direction of the relationship: direct or inverse.

3. A significant correlation means: Population from which the data were drawn probably does not have a zero correlation.

3.6.c χ^2 TEST OF ASSOCIATION

Computation Design for χ^2 for Testing Significance of Association Between Two Attributes for the General $r_1 \times s$ Case and for the Special 2×2*

n_{11}	n_{12}	n_{13} $\cdots$ n_{1s}	$n_1.$
n_{21}	n_{22}	n_{23} $\cdots$ n_{2s}	$n_2.$
n_{31}	n_{32}	n_{33} $\cdots$ n_{3s}	$n_3.$
$\cdot$	$\cdot$	$\cdot$ $\quad$ $\cdot$	$\cdot$
n_{r1}	n_{r2}	n_{r3} $\cdots$ n_{rs}	$n_r.$
$n._1$	$n._2$	$n._3$ $\cdots$ $n._s$	N

1	2	3	4	5
O	E	$O - E$	$(O - E)^2$	$(O - E)^2/E$
n_{11}	$n_1.n._1/N$			
n_{12}	$n_1.n._2/N$			
n_{13}	$n_1.n._3/N$			
$\cdot$	$\cdot$			
n_{rs}	$n_r.n._s/N$			

$$\chi^2 = \Sigma \left[(O - E)^2/E \right]$$
$$\text{d.f.} = (r - 1)(s - 1)$$

1. Enter the observed frequencies in column 1.

2. Calculate the expected values, E, as follows: find the marginal in the rows containing the cell ij and the marginal in the column containing the cell, and multiply them together, giving $n_i.n._j$; then divide by N, the total number of observations in the table, giving $n_i.n._j/N$, and enter in column 2.

3. Subtract the expected values from the observed, column 2 from 1, and enter the result in column 3.

4. Square the differences obtained and enter in column 4.

5. Divide each entry in column 4 by the expected values in column 2 and enter in column 5.

6. Add up column 5. This gives you χ^2.

---

* From Zelditch, *Basic Course in Sociological Statistics,* p. 290. See also Theodore R. Anderson and Morris Zelditch, Jr., *A Basic Course in Statistics: With Sociological Applications,* 3rd ed. (New York: Holt, Rinehart & Winston, 1975), pp. 256–64.

7. To find the number of degrees of freedom with which you enter the table, take one less than the number of rows times one less than the number of columns $(r - 1)(s - 1)$.

Interpretation of χ^2 as a Test of Relationship Between Variables

As reported by David Gold in "A Note on Statistical Analysis in the American Sociological Review," "qualitative data are by far the most common data with which the sociologist concerns himself.—It is evident that, on the most elementary descriptive level, there is markedly inadequate statistical analysis of qualitative data."

These statements should alert the social science researcher to the importance of the correct use and interpretation of χ^2. It is this coefficient which appears most frequently in social science research as a test of association and significance. The following article by Thomas J. Duggan and Charles W. Dean should be "must" reading for all social scientists.

3.6.d. COMMON MISINTERPRETATIONS OF SIGNIFICANCE LEVELS IN SOCIOLOGICAL JOURNALS*

Thomas J. Duggan and Charles W. Dean

Periodically, the uses and misuses of probability statistics in social and behavioral science research have been reviewed. For instance, in 1949 Lewis and Burke pointed to several misuses of the chi-square test[1] and in 1959 an article by Selvin stimulated discussion on the general question of using statistics in social surveys.[2] Most recently, Skipper, Guenther, and Nass reviewed the discussion of substantive interpretation associated with significant levels.[3] While such discussions have served to clarify some of the technical requirements and have corrected some of the misunderstandings often associated with the use of statistical tests, one crucial matter has received relatively little attention. This concerns the substantive interpretation of significance tests and the consequences of such interpretations.

The frequently used chi-square test, and the interpretations given to data analyzed by this statistic, will serve to illustrate the problem. This statistic can be used to test goodness of fit or independence although it is the latter which is more frequently used in reporting research. Since this is a test of the independence of variables, significant values of chi-square are often taken to indicate a dependence or relationship between variables. In interpreting such relationships, there are two serious problems which are often overlooked. The first concerns the strength of relationship and the second the form of relationship.

Strength of Relationship

As to the first problem, if the chi-square is significant at the chosen level, then the investigator routinely rejects the null hypothesis of independence

---

* Reprinted from *American Sociologist* 3 (February 1968): 45–46.

Table 1

Variable Y	Variable X			
	Very high	High	Low	Very low
High	5	24	17	9
Moderate	12	18	9	3
Low	19	22	16	2

$\chi^2 = 14.0, P < .05, G = -.30.$

Table 2

Variable Y	Variable X		
	High	Moderate	Low
High	24	18	10
Moderate	19	12	7
Low	19	18	21

$\chi^2 = 6.2, P < .20, G = .22.$

and tentatively accepts the alternate hypothesis that the variables are dependent or are related. Regardless of how low the probability associated with
the obtained value of chi-square, nothing can be inferred about the strength
or degree of that relationship. However, in practice, this point is often overlooked.

Consider table 1, which was reported in a major sociological journal within
the last year.[4] According to the author's interpretation, the significance level
of the chi-square test was so high that if variables X and Y were not clearly
separate measures, "We would suspect the relationship to be tautological."
Since the authors failed to report the degree of association, Goodman and
Kruskels' gamma was computed. In this instance, gamma equalled $-.30$,
which suggests a relationship which is far from tautological. The difference
in the interpretation based on chi-square and gamma should be noted and
emphasized. In contrast to the above data, consider table 2, which was presented in the same article.

In this case, the probability is such that the sociologist normally would
accept the null hypothesis of independence. However, gamma was computed
for these data and G equalled .22. Here, data non-significant according to
chi-square has a relationship only slightly lower than that of the preceding
example, where it was concluded that the variables were highly related. To
further demonstrate the need for sensitivity to the difference between significance level and strength of association, table 3 was constructed.[5]

Table 3 clearly demonstrates that while chi-square, properly used, may
be sensitive to the dependence of variables, after dependence is shown the
usefulness of this statistic is exhausted. As the data of table 3 show, significance
at the .001 level could mean that the relationship between the variables could
be less than .09 or more than .80. At the .001 level, the distribution of the
strength of association appears to approach randomness. While these data

Table 3 *A Comparison of Level of Significance and Strength of Relationship*
(n = 45 articles)

Level of significance	Strength of Relationship								
	.00 to .09	.10 to .19	.20 to .29	.30 to .39	.40 to .49	.50 to .59	.60 to .69	.70 to .79	.80 to .89
.001	3	2	2	8	· ·	1	· ·	2	3
.01	1	· ·	6	· ·	2	· ·	· ·	· ·	· ·
.05	4	3	· ·	· ·	· ·	· ·	· ·	· ·	· ·
.10	1	· ·	1	· ·	· ·	· ·	· ·	· ·	· ·
.20	1	1	1	· ·	· ·	· ·	· ·	· ·	· ·
.30+	· ·	3	· ·	· ·	· ·	· ·	· ·	· ·	· ·

do show that non-significance, or significance at or about the arbitrary .05 level, will usually result in a relationship which is consistently weaker, the relationship is as likely to be above .10 at the .30 level as at the .05 level. Still, all three tables reporting significance above the .30 level had gammas ranging between .10 and .19. In contrast, of the seven tables reporting significance at .05, only three had gammas in the .10 to .19 range, while four tables had gammas below .10. If more non-significant tables were reported in the journals, the distribution of measures of association would probably be even broader. Generally, the lower the significance level, the greater the probability of a low relationship, but this cannot be assumed. These data emphatically demonstrate that a measure of strength of association is necessary before statements about strength of relationship can be made.

These data illustrate the serious problem in interpreting significance levels of the chi-square test of independence and indicate the need for a reminder that statistical significance is not equatable with practical significance. A significant chi-square value, at best, permits one to say that *probably* there is some dependence between variables in the population, but the extent of dependence may be virtually zero *regardless of the significance level.* The consequences for understanding the phenomena under investigation and for the construction of theories require constant awareness of the limited interpretations which can be given to statistical significance.

Form of Relationship

The second problem refers to the form of relationship between variables. In using tables three by three or larger, users of the chi-square are often prone to think and interpret results in terms of linear relationships, but the contingency table and the chi-square statistic are not sensitive to and provide no basis for assuming the existence of this form of relationship.

The data of table 4, also presented in a major sociological journal within the last year, illustrate the error in interpreting the direction of the relationship in linear terms. The author stated that the data of this table confirmed the hypothesis that the greater the degree of variable X, the greater the degree of variable Y. An inspection of the table reveals that this is not the case. As table 4 indicates, the largest number of subjects ranking in the "frequent" category of variable X rank in the low category of variable Y. However,

Table 4

	Variable X		
Variable Y	Frequent	Occasional	Infrequent
High	3	9	6
Moderate	14	30	12
Low	17	12	6

χ^2 (4df) = 8.51; $P < .05$.

the largest number of subjects in the "occasional" and "infrequent" categories of variable X rank in the "moderate" category of variable Y. Only those ranking "low" on variable Y are distributed in the expected pattern.

Another team of authors in a recent edition of another sociological journal presented data similar to that of table 4 to test the hypothesis that the greater the degree of variable A, the higher the degree of variable B. They computed chi-square values for their data table and stated, "The relationship shown is significant beyond the .001 level; therefore, the hypothesis is accepted." Throughout the article, the authors made similar statements from similar data about linear relationships.

While the above authors did not attempt to disguise their acceptance of linearity, frequently, other researchers state a linear hypothesis, present the data, table, accept the hypothesis on the basis of the chi-square probability and then discuss only those proportions of the table which fit the linear model. This more subtle but equally erroneous procedure appears frequently in the sociological literature.

A linear relationship exists only if the pattern of concentration of subjects lies along a diagonal of the table. If this is not the case, the relationship cannot be interpreted as a linear one. If the phenomenon of possible nonlinearity is not taken into account or if the implication of linearity is made in interpreting chi-square, serious consequences again arise in interpreting data and in developing explanatory theories. This problem can be averted by inspecting the data table, outlining the pattern of concentration and describing the pattern.

Conclusion

To avoid these errors of confusing significance with strength of association and of misinterpreting form of relationship, two elementary safeguards can be exercised in reporting results. One is routinely to compute and report a measure of degree of association in addition to the statistical test whenever this is possible. The second safeguard is the introduction of care and caution in the verbal interpretation of data tables and the inferred association of variables.[6]

In this day when computer technology is so drastically improving the analytical tools of the sociologist, it seems paradoxical that there is a need to remind researchers of such basic rules of interpretation.

Notes

1. Don Lewis and C. J. Burke, "The Use and Misuse of The Chi-square Test," *Pscyhological Bulletin* 46 (1949): 433–89.
2. Hanan Selvin, "A Critique of Tests of Significance in Survey Research," *American Sociological Review* 22 (October 1957): 519–27.
3. James K. Skipper, Anthony L. Guenther, and Gilbert Nass, "The Sacredness of .05: A Note Concerning the Uses of Statistical Levels of Significance in Social Science," *American Sociologist* 2 (February 1967): 16–18.
4. Since the purpose of these tables is to illustrate peculiarities in the use of chi-square rather than to criticize individual research, no tables will identify either author, journal or original variables actually treated. However, all tables were reported in refereed sociological journals within a year prior to the writing of this piece.
5. These data were derived from major sociological journals published between 1955 and 1965 in a systematic search for three by three tables, both variables ordinal.
6. For detailed information see Denton E. Morrison and Ramon E. Henkel, *The Significance Test Controversy, A Reader* (Hawthorne, N.Y.: Aldine, 1970).

3.6.e. SPEARMAN'S RANK ORDER CORRELATION

Computation Design for Spearman Rank Order Coefficient, r_s*

K_i designates an ordered position. K_{xi} designates the position of the *i*th observation in an array of the X variable; K_{yi} designates the position of the *same* observation in the Y array. If, for example, the first observation, O_1, is first in the X array and fourth in the Y array, the first row of the layout form below should read

$$K_{x1} = 1, K_{y1} = 4, K_{x1} - K_{y1} = -3, (K_{x1} - K_{y1})^2 = 9$$

(1) O_i	(2) K_{xi}	(3) K_{yi}	(4) d	(5) d^2
O_1	K_{x1}	K_{y1}	$K_{x1} - K_{y1}$	$(K_{x1} - K_{y1})^2$
O_2	K_{x2}	K_{y2}	$K_{x2} - K_{y2}$	$(K_{x2} - K_{y2})^2$
.	.	.	.	.
.	.	.	.	.
O_N	K_{xN}	K_{yN}	$K_{xN} - K_{yN}$	$(K_{xN} - K_{yN})$

$$\Sigma(K_{xi} - K_{yi})^2 = \Sigma d^2 =$$

$$r_s = 1 - \frac{6\Sigma d^2}{N(N^2 - 1)} =$$

$$t = r_s \sqrt{\frac{N - 2}{1 - r_s^2}} = \qquad\qquad, \text{d.f.} = N - 2.$$

* From Zelditch, *Basic Course in Sociological Statistics*, p. 326. See also Anderson and Zelditch, *Basic Course in Statistics: With Sociological Applications*, pp. 126–32.

1. Form an array of the observations on the X variable. (Start with the "best," "smallest," "highest." You may choose the starting point at will, but you must be consistent on both X and Y, or the sign of r_s will be meaningless.) Order the observations on the variable Y in the same manner.

2. Replace the X value of each observation by its rank in the X array and the Y value of each observation by its rank in the Y array. In column 2 at the right enter ranks of the observations on the X variable and in column 3 enter ranks of the observations on the Y variable. Ranks in the same row must be for the *same* observation.

3. Take the difference between ranks and enter in column 4.

4. Square these differences, enter in column 5, and sum column 5.

5. Compute r_s from the formula shown above.

6. For $N > 10$, to test $H_0 : \rho_s = o$, use t, computed from the formula shown above with $(N - 2)$ d.f. (ρ_s [read "rho sub-s"] is the population parameter corresponding to r_s.)

CAUSATION AND MULTIVARIATE ANALYSIS　　　　　*3.7*

From Univariate and Bivariate Problems to Multivariate Analysis of Social Behavior

It was once generally thought that for every effect there existed only one cause; if several causes were discovered, it was assumed the effect must really be more than one. The history of social theory is largely a series of statements asserting that one factor is the sole cause of social change. These notions have been called determinisms and include geographic, physical, racial, psychological, religious, political, economic, technological, and familial determinism. And there are many more.

It is characteristic of all these notions of determinism to assert that the sole factor operates according to its own inherent laws independently of all factors including human will and desires. These single-factor theories were relatively simple to understand and appealed to scholars and lay persons alike. They seemed to draw truth from the complex phenomena presented by social problems. But in their oversimplification the single-factor theories distorted reality and foisted a great amount of mischief and misery on people. For example, racial determinism bred prejudice and discrimination in every country of the world. In Hitler's Germany, it brought humankind's most cruel inhumanity.

Modern humans know better, although single-factor theories still abound. The contemporary approach involves allowing for and expecting a number of different causes for a single effect.

Four Manifestations of Causes

Causes may manifest themselves in a *sequence,* as a *convergence* or cluster, as producing *dispersion* effects, or as a *complex network.*

1. Causes may occur in a sequence, like the links on a chain. Some of these causes are direct and immediate, others are indirect and remote. Thus, a decline in worker motivation and sense of personal responsibility may be due to the direct fact that much labor is performed in the large corporation on highly repetitive jobs; the remote causes are the factory system and mass market, which in turn were brought about by the steam engine, the electric motor, and machine tools.

2. Several causes may converge to produce a change. Thus electric power and several transportation and communication inventions have converged to augment the decentralization of industry. These converging causes are often called a cluster.

3. The effects of a single cause may be dispersed outward into many different sectors of a society. Thus the average increase of formal education that is being acquired by Americans has many different effects on family, church, community, military organization, and labor relations.

4. The phenomena of convergence and of dispersion may be tied in with the phenomena of sequence to produce a complex network of causes. This is a very common manifestation, but the complexity can be simplified by recognizing that causes vary in importance, and important causes may be identified that account for a large part of the effects observed.

Future Developments

New technology is ready to deal with these more complex notions of causation. Loether and McTavish have written about future developments in theory, research methods, and statistics stressing the importance of multivariage analysis.

Herman J. Loether and Donald G. McTavish *

The increasing availability of computers has shifted the emphasis in sociology from the study of univariate and bivariate problems to the study of multivariate problems. To be efficient predictors, sociological theories generally need to be stated in multivariate terms. Before computers, multivariate statistical techniques were so tedious that they were not commonly used. The computer has now made these techniques accessible and practical. In response to this breakthrough, sociological theories are increasingly becoming multivariate in form. It is becoming increasingly important for the sociologist to be a knowledgeable computer user. Computer technology is racing forward at a breathtaking pace, and the potential uses of computers for sociological analysis stagger the imagination.

Another very promising development in sociology is the gradual but dramatic disappearance of the chasm separating theory and research. Sociology appears to be moving forward by returning to the model which Durkheim set for us in the nineteenth century. The effect of this long overdue marriage of theory and research is the development of theory that is researchable and the appearance of more theory-oriented research. The advent of the computer in sociology and the increasing emphasis upon multivariate analysis have done much to facilitate this development.

There is a third important development that promises to have a significant impact on sociology and on the academic preparation of future sociologists.

* Herman J. Loether and Donald G. McTavish, *Inferential Statistics for Sociologists* (Boston: Allyn & Bacon, 1974), pp. 283–84.

Traditionally, sociologists have used a structure rather than a process to theorizing and researching. Social behavior has been viewed in static terms, and much research has focused on single points in time, much like stopping a movie and studying a single frame. Sociologists are now beginning to realize that what is orderly about social behavior may be the way in which it changes rather than the way in which it resists change. This perspective focuses attention on time series and longitudinal analysis. The shift in statistics is toward the increasing use of stochastic processes and techniques of time series analysis. This emphasis will make the understanding of calculus an important requirement in the academic training of future sociologists. It seems inevitable that process models involving the use of calculus will appear with increasing frequency in the sociological literature.

Obviously sociology is coming of age. The public and our public leaders are beginning to realize that the pressing problems of today and the forseeable future are those for which solutions are encouched in a knowledge of social behavior. Sociology is in a position to contribute that knowledge. This is an exciting time in which to be a part of it. We believe that those students of sociology who will make important contributions to that knowledge will be those who are well versed in theory, research methods, and statistics.

3.7.a. THE STATISTICAL WORLD OF MULTIVARIATE ANALYSIS

Multivariate analysis has now developed techniques for dealing with more than three variables or attributes at a time. The type of analysis to use in attempting to unravel a complex of variates in a real-life situation depends on what will best bring out the essential relationships under scrutiny. Multivariate analysis may give increased precision to prediction problems (the relation of a number of predictor variables to a criterion), offer greater control of interfering or confounding variables (holding more variables constant), and furnish guiding principles in the development of attitude scales, rating scales, psychological tests, and criterion measures (finding dimensions of behavior). Some of the most important multivariate techniques include:

Multiple Correlation and Classification Analysis
Path Analysis
Factor Analysis
Partial Correlation Analysis
Analysis of Variance and Covariance
Multiple Discriminant Analysis

The full description of these techniques is beyond the scope and purpose of the Handbook. Nevertheless, computer technology is advancing at a rapid rate and is an indispensable adjunct to multivariate analysis. An Introduction to the Computer is presented in 3.8 for those who are seeking guidance in utilizing computer programs. Descriptions of Multiple Correlation and Classification Analysis (3.7.b), Path Analysis (3.9), and Factor Analysis (3.10) are also set out to provide an introduction to these forms of multivariate analysis now so common to sociological research.

3.7.b.   MULTIPLE CORRELATION AND CLASSIFICATION ANALYSIS

R as a Coefficient

The multiple correlation ($R_{1.234}$) is simply the correlation between the actual scores on a single dependent variable and the scores derived from any linear combination of independent variables. The multiple correlation, like the simple product-moment correlation (r), varies on a scale from 0 to +1. The smaller the coefficient, the poorer the correlation; and the larger the coefficient, the stronger the correlation. The multiple correlation can be interpreted by squaring it. R^2 is called the coefficient of multiple determination and expresses the proportion of the variation in the dependent variable that is explained by the regression equation.

Scope of Application

The utility of R has been known for some time. But it was originally cumbersome to calculate when more than four or five independent variables (predictors) were introduced. The computer has erased that limitation, but a second limitation intervened. The coefficient was adaptable only when the variables were continuous. Modern methods of *multiple classification analysis* have removed this limitation. There are computer techniques that can handle predictors with no better than nominal measurement and interrelationships of any form among predictors or between predictors or between a predictor and the dependent variable. Many of the most interesting analysis problems involve the simultaneous consideration of several predictor variables (i.e., "independent" variables) and their relationships to a dependent variable. Sometimes one wants to know *how well* all the variables together explain variation in the dependent variable. Other times it is necessary to look at each predictor separately to see how it relates to the dependent variable, either considering or neglecting the effects of other predictors. A criterion generally used is its contribution to reduction in unexplained variance or "error." Another is the extent to which its class means differ from the grand mean.

A different but related concern is the matter of predicted relations. Instead of asking *how well* one can predict, one sometimes asks *what level* (i.e., what particular value or score) would one predict for a person or other unit having a certain combination of characteristics. This is the classic problem to which multiple regression has frequently been applied.

Finally, one sometimes wants to know whether one's ability to predict is significantly better than chance.

The Multiple Classification Analysis devised by Frank M. Andrews, James N. Morgan, John A. Sonquist, and Laura Klem (reported in section 3.8.b) implements a multivariate technique that is relevant for all the above problems and that may be applied to many kinds of data for which the simpler forms of the traditional techniques would be inappropriate. Its chief advantage over conventional dummy variable regression is a more convenient input arrangement and understandable output that focuses on sets of predictors, such as occupation groups, and on the extent and direction of adjustments made for intercorrelations among the sets of predictors.

Research Examples of Multivariate Analysis

DUNCAN, OTIS DUDLEY. "A Socioeconomic Index for All Occupations." In Albert J. Reiss, *Occupations and Social Status*. New York: Free Press of Glencoe, 1961. Pp. 109–38.

HODGE, ROBERT W.; SIEGEL, PAUL M.; and ROSSI, PETER H. "Occupational Prestige in the United States, 1925–1963." *American Journal of Sociology* 70 (November 1964): 286–302.

HOUSE, JAMES S., and MASON, WILLIAM M. "Political Alienation in America, 1952–68." *American Sociological Review* 40 (April 1975): 123–47.

LADINSKY, JACK L. "Occupational Determinants of Geographic Mobility Among Professional Workers." *American Sociological Review* 32 (April 1967): 253–64.

SCOTT, JOSEPH W., and EL-ASSAL, MOHAMED. "Multiversity, University Size, University Quality, and Student Protest: An Empirical Study." *American Sociological Review* 34 (October 1969): 702–9.

Brief Treatments of Multiple Correlation and Regression

LOETHER, HERMAN J., and McTAVISH, DONALD G. *Descriptive Statistics for Sociologists: An Introduction*. Boston: Allyn & Bacon, 1974. Pp. 306–40.

SCHUESSLER, KARL. *Analyzing Social Data*. Boston: Houghton Mifflin, 1971. Pp. 10–30.

General References

ANDERSON, T. W. *An Introduction to Multivariate Statistical Analysis*. New York: Wiley, 1958.

BENNETT, S., and BOWERS, DONALD W. *An Introduction to Multi-Variate Techniques for the Social and Behavioral Sciences*. New York: Halsted, 1976.

BLALOCK, HUBERT M., JR. *Social Statistics*. 2nd ed. New York: McGraw-Hill, 1972.

COLEMAN, JAMES S. "Multivariate Analysis." In *Introduction to Mathematical Sociology*. New York: Free Press of Glencoe, 1964. Pp. 189–240.

COOLEY, WILLIAM W., and LOHNES, PAUL R. *Multivariate Procedures for the Behavioral Sciences*. New York: Wiley, 1962. See chap. 3, "Multiple and Canonical Correlation."

COSTNER, HERBERT L., ed. *Sociological Methodology*. San Francisco: Jossey-Bass, 1971. See especially chap. 5 by George Bohrnstedt and T. Michael Carter, "Robustness in Regression Analysis"; also chap. 6 by Morgan Lyons, "Techniques for Using Ordinal Measures in Regression and Path Analysis."

DRAPER, NORMAN R., and SMITH, HARRY. *Applied Regression Analysis*. New York: Wiley, 1966.

DUBOIS, PHILIP H. *Multivariate Correlation Analysis*. New York: Harper & Row, 1957.

EZEKIAL, MORDECAI, and FOX, KARL A. *Methods of Correlation Analysis*. 3rd ed. New York: Wiley, 1959.

GORDON, ROBERT A. "Issues in Multiple Regression." *American Journal of Sociology* 73 (March 1968): 592–616.

KENDALL, M. G. *A Course in Multivariate Analysis*. London: Griffin, 1961.

JORESKOG, KARL G., and VAN THILLO, MARIELLE. *LISREL: A General Computer Program for Estimating a Linear Structural Equation System Involving Multiple Indicators of Unmeasured Variables*. Princeton, N.J.: Educational Testing Service, 1972.

LAZARSFELD, PAUL F.; PASANELLA, ANN K.; and ROSENBERG, MORRIS, eds. *Continuities in the Language of Social Research.* Rev. ed. of *Language of Social Research.* New York: Free Press of Macmillan, 1975. See section on Multivariate Analysis for articles and selected examples.

For additional references see section 3.12, Selected Readings on Causal Models and Multivariate Analysis for the Advanced Student.

3.8 AN INTRODUCTION TO THE COMPUTER

Purpose

The purpose of any process of data analysis is to condense information contained in a body of data into a form that can be easily comprehended and interpreted. Sometimes this process is used simply to describe a body of empirical data, but it is far more common for social science data analysis to involve a search for meaningful patterns of relationships among sets of variables, that is, a means to test empirical social theory. Computers are extremely useful for the routine processing of large quantities of data. Indeed, the need for large-scale processing led directly to the development of the computer. Such processing includes the classification, sorting, storing, and retrieval of data that have been presented to the computer in a suitable coded form. These routine tasks, termed *data processing,* constitute the most important use of computers at present.

Steps in the Use of the Computer

Generally, (1) data is gathered in the form of responses to items on a survey schedule or coded specifically in experimental situations. These responses are then usually (2) transferred to *80-column IBM computer cards.* These cards contain punches that are indicative of the original response code. There is always at least one card per case, but frequently more cards are necessary to complete the listing of all the information pertinent to that case. These cards are (3) punched upon a machine called a *keypunch.* This machine closely resembles a typewriter; however, it punches IBM cards instead of typing letters. Once the data has been recorded, it is often (4) reproduced on a machine called a *reproducer.* This permits the researcher to make a spare deck of data with a minimum amount of work in the event that his original deck is lost or damaged.

Once a deck of data cards has been made, other pieces of equipment can be utilized. For example, after the original deck has been reproduced on the reproducer, the new deck can be placed in a device called (5a) a *lister.* The lister prints in standard numerals and alphabetic letters the content of the punches on each particular card. This print appears at the top of every individual card. If a more easily read listing of the content of the cards is desired, the deck may be placed into a different machine, (5b) a *printer,* which will list the content on a computer sheet printout. This method of listing allows for the rapid scanning of the information by the researcher in order to check for typographical errors and punctuation that might lead to computer rejection of the data, or for the simple search for a particular case or variable.

The *card sorter,* another piece of unit record equipment, allows the researcher to separate his data deck into several categories. That is, the researcher may wish to (5c) separate several types of traits or subject responses from the others, and this is made possible through the employment of the card sorter. For example, it may be desirable to place all the subjects into categories based upon occupation. The card sorter can be adjusted to cause all cards with a specific number in a specific column—the code for a particular occupation—to fall into one bin, all cards with a different number in that same column to fall into another bin, and so forth.

Finally, once the data have been prepared accurately, they can either be (6) submitted to the computer in card form or transferred to a magnetic tape and then submitted. In addition, the data, however their initial form, cards or tape, can be (6a) retained by the computer for a specified period of time in the form of a storage file. This file is usually stored on a disc within the computer system. Once the data have been appropriately prepared and submitted and the computer has been programmed to handle the data, which is almost always done by computer specialists, (7) various data analytic procedures can be employed to obtain the desired statistics. These procedures are only restricted by the particular computer language used, the programming of the computer, and the scale level (nominal, ordinal, interval, ratio) of the data.

Computer languages vary widely in terms of their capabilities and structure. The appropriate language for data analysis depends to a great extent upon the kind of analysis to be done and the form of the data. For most social science data analysis, the fairly recent development and refinement of the SPSS (Statistical Package of the Social Sciences) packaged programs have been of great assistance. However, other computer languages may frequently prove to be more appropriate. Computer consultants and operators, who are present at all computer facilities, are normally capable not only of assisting the researcher with the selection of the best language, but also of aiding him in any usage problems that may appear.

When trouble in running a program is incurred, however, the computer consultant is an invaluable aid to research. It must always be borne in mind that computer time is extremely valuable and, consequently, extremely expensive; thus errors must be eliminated before using the computer facility if possible. Careful preparation and intelligent use of consultants is essential to rapid and economical data analysis.[1]

There is a sound warning to be observed in using a computer consultant. A widespread and erroneous belief has it that when a researcher has a data problem for the computer, he goes to a computer consultant, who solves the problem and turns over a finished computer answer to the researcher. This belief is based on the assumption that the computer expert understands behavioral science problems, data, and methods. Another belief is that computer methods are uniform and applicable to all substantive problems. It is not realistic to expect computer consultants to know the range of research problems represented by psychology, sociology, economics, and political science. It is the responsibility of the researcher to learn at least enough programming to be able to talk knowledgeably to programmers. The Indiana University Computing Network reports the following experiences by their "consultants":

> The term "consultant has come to mean different things to different people. The first consultants that users should encounter are our front-line, part-time student consultants. Currently we have ten hourly undergraduate and graduate students and seven graduate assistants stationed at HPER, Memorial, Ballantine, and the Lindley terminal cluster for a total of 187 hours per week. We try to double up during the extra busy periods of time, which adds another 22 consultant hours. These front-line consultants serve hundreds of users every week and are confronted with a wide variety of problems ranging from very simple to highly sophisticated. Just a few of the things that consultants encounter are questions on the CDC 6600/172, DEC-10, PRIME, and IBM computers; PASCAL, BASIC, FORTRAN, LISP, PL/1, SNOBOL, and other programming languages; information storage and retrieval on magnetic tape and disk using programs such as SIR, INFOL, ARCHIVE and RETRIEV; text processing using programs such as TFORM, RUNOFF, UCEDIT, and VW; statistical programming using such packages as SPSS and BMDP; and a myriad of other computing areas.
>
> As the Indiana University Computing Network has grown, more systems have been added. This in turn has required more expertise in greater areas. We cannot reasonably expect any one person to be an expert in all these areas. We can and do, however, try to cover all the areas by selective recruiting. Thus a consultant might be a whiz at PASCAL but may have an insufficient statistical background to consult on SPSS problems. The job of this particular consultant, then, when faced with an SPSS problem is to steer you, the user, to the appropriate WCC individual who may be another part-time or one of the full-time User Services staff who serve as backup and are sometimes also referred to as consultants.[2]

The first user, or even the experienced user, can have frustrating experiences, waste a good deal of time, and perhaps be prepared to give up all future computer use. Nevertheless, the work involved and the frustrations encountered are more than balanced by the power acquired over research analysis. The student who writes his first program for real data and makes it work will never look back. The student of social science who does not acquire this facility is not ready to march confidently into modern research. Computer literacy is a must.

Computer science specialists are making predictions like this:

> The 1980s will be a decade of revolution in academic computing. By the end of the decade, we can expect students to own microcomputers just as they own calculators today. Floppy disks will be sold in university bookstores and university computing will be focused on supporting the massive communications requirements posed by hundreds of mini and micro computers, providing technical support to faculty and students with their own systems, and running supercomputers which will dwarf the capacity of our big systems today but which will be smaller physically and which will be running in supercooled environments.[3]

Notes

1. For an excellent set of computer instructions for the beginning student, see Gerald S. Ferman and Jack Levin, *Social Science Researcher: A Handbook for Students* (Cambridge, Mass.: Schenkman, 1975), pp. 91–136.

2. *Random Bits* 16 (May 1981): 3, 8. Marshal H. Wrubel Computing Center, Indiana University, Bloomington.

3. Edward E. Pollack, director, Computing Services, Indiana-Purdue University, at the Eighth Annual Indiana University Network Conference, as quoted in *Random Bits* 16 (May 1981): 1.

3.8.a. PREPARING DATA FOR THE COMPUTER: PUNCHCARD PROCESSING

Two major steps must be taken before raw data is ready for the computer. You must organize the data in a systematic fashion for storage and retrieval. Punching raw data into the "hollerith" or IBM card is step 1. After that, a software program must be selected. *Software* refers to a set of computer programs that can be "set up" or activated on a data file by recording characteristics of the file in specified positions on IBM cards (or other media, such as magnetic tapes). These programs are designed to automatically perform a variety of operations on the data. Each program has particular specifications. Many students believe they must take a course in computer language before they can competently use software programs. This is totally incorrect; software program write-ups can be easily understood by the average student. No technical or specialized language is needed to utilize the tremendous capabilities of computers.

The section that follows lists a number of software programs. But the first step is punchcard processing.

PUNCHCARD PROCESSING*

Herman J. Loether and Donald G. McTavish

Once data have been carefully collected (by observation, interview, mail questionnaire, copying documents or records), it is important to take steps to keep them under control in order to assure that added biases and errors do not creep in. Nearly any organized and workmanlike procedure will suffice, although there are some checks and procedures that experience has shown to be worthwhile considering.

Much contemporary sociological analysis is done with the aid of computers or other mechanical aids so that the procedures described below are nearly always relevant.

1. *Assign Identification Numbers.* Immediately upon receipt of the completed questionnaires, schedules, or other data documents, each case or subject is assigned a unique case number in order from 1 to the sample size (*N*).

This serves several purposes: (*a*) it permits detection of missing cases simply by checking the sequence and consecutiveness of ID numbers; (*b*) it permits cases to be ordered for easy cross-referencing between punched hollerith cards and the original source documents; and (*c*) it permits one to double-

---

* From Herman J. Loether and Donald G. McTavish, *Statistical Analysis for Sociologists: A Student Manual* (Boston: Allyn & Bacon, 1974), pp. RS43–47. Reprinted by permission.

EXAMPLE OF A HOLERITH CARD WITH SOME DATA ENTERED

check new decks which may be created or new information which is added to old decks of hollerith cards to be sure that information about a subject appears only on his card.

2. *Edit the Returns.* Returned questionnaires or schedules should be checked for accuracy and completeness. If this is done early it may be possible to detect missing information or errors in interviewing or responding which can be corrected by additional training of interviewers or additional instructions. Schedules might be returned to interviewers to collect any missing information.

3. *Create a Codebook.* Specify which of the 80 columns on a hollerith card will be used for punching coded responses to each question. If more than 80 columns are needed, additional cards can be used but each card should contain the subject identification number assigned in No. 1 above, in addition to some type of number to indicate which card is card 1, 2, etc.

Special column assignments frequently included in a punched deck are:

a. Case numbers are frequently assigned the first three or four columns of a card so that they can be more easily located and read later on.

b. Project and deck numbers are sometimes punched in the last three or four columns of a card (i.e., columns 77, 78, 79, 80) to differentiate several projects and/or cards per subject used in the course of an investigation. In the event that decks are accidentally mixed, this number permits separating the cards. (See the codebook, example following.)

c. Interviewers or coders may be assigned code numbers so that one can check on an interviewer or coder bias.

d. Source-of-data codes. An investigator may wish to include codes for the date of return of mailed questionnaires; the state, block, or area from which the case was sampled; or the volume, date, and page number of documents from which data were taken.

4. *Code the Data.* If the questionnaires or interview schedules have been pre-coded (hollerith card columns and category codes pre-assigned and printed in the form), the editing step may be sufficient to remove any ambiguity in the data so that keypunches can punch the data directly from the questionnaires.

If there are open-ended items they must be read and assigned to relevant categories. This code may be written in the proper place on a precoded questionnaire form. If the questionnaire is complex or if it is not pre-coded, codes may be written by a coder on a separate form such as that reproduced below. The keypuncher then punches from this form.

Numbers corresponding to the response of individual subjects are entered in the boxes corresponding to card columns assigned to items in the codebook. The codebook is used at this point to determine which number goes where. Separate coding forms would be used for separate subjects. If more than one card is needed for the responses of a single subject, more than one such form would be needed per subject.

EXAMPLE OF A CODING FORM WITH SOME DATA ENTERED

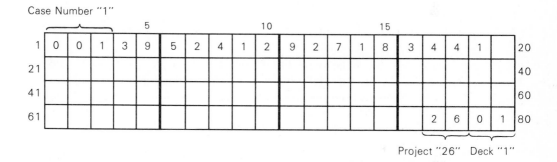

Case Number "1"

Project "26" Deck "1"

5. *Keypunching.* Once the data have been carefully coded and the coding double-checked as much as possible (often a sample is drawn and independently re-coded to serve as a check on the nature and extent of errors—all cases are re-coded if sufficient errors are discovered in some column), the data are ready to be keypunched.

From the keypuncher's point of view a long series of numbers is to be punched into a card. It is important to organize this part of the work to eliminate number-reading/punching errors. The coding form is one such aid. Neatly drawn block numbers using a number 2, sharpened pencil is another aid to the keypuncher.

Checking the keypunching. It is especially worthwhile to have data verified (checked) by: (*a*) punching two decks independently and then comparing them by machine (the reproducing punch will compare two decks). If there are any mismatches these cases can be resolved by referring to the original codesheets or questionnaires. (*b*) Another way to check the keypunching is to have the keypuncher re-punch the deck on a Card Verifying Machine. This permits a comparison of the second punching with the first without actually punching a separate deck of cards.

6. *Vertical Deck Cleaning.* Several final checks are generally required before punched information can be reasonably assumed to reflect the original data. One of these checks consists of tabulating the number of each different punch (0, 1, 2, etc.) in each column of the entire deck. This can be done easily on a computer, using standard programs.

These "marginals" for each item are checked against the codebook to see whether punches were made for which no code was assigned. For example, if a "3" was punched in some card in the deck in the column for sex where only "1" and "2" punches were assigned, one would know that this constituted an error either in coding or in keypunching (probably in the coder's writing). These cards can be quickly sorted (by a sorter) out of the deck, the identification number checked, the original questionnaire examined again, and the correction made.

7. *Horizontal Deck Cleaning.* Another type of machine check on the accuracy of data consists of checking for logical inconsistencies in punched responses to sets of two or more questions. For example, cases coded as male should not answer questions asked only of females. Again, error cards can be sorted out, checked, and corrected.

8. *Insurance.* Accurately punched cards are rather valuable in terms of the time and expense required to create them. It is prudent to take steps to protect the investment. Often intermediate protection of a kind similar to that described below is "taken out" as early as step 5.

Insurance is generally of two kinds: (*a*) creating a printed listing of the data cards which can be filed and used to punch a new card when necessary without necessitating reference to the original questionnaires (which may have been destroyed to help preserve anonymity, for example), and (*b*) a copy of the cleaned decks is generally filed in some safe place. Copies can be made by machine.

A note on card storage. PUNCH-CARD machines are constructed to close tolerances and damaged or worn cards frequently will not be accepted. Damage can come about in several ways: physical bending, ripping, stapling, etc., and by swelling caused by storing the cards in high humidity areas. It is best to store decks in a reasonably low humidity area where the cards can be kept flat and square and preferably under some pressure (weighted or squeezed). Heat is also damaging to cards.

9. *Periodic Double-checking.* If cards are used extensively—especially if they are used by several different people—it is a good idea to compare a work deck against an original master deck. This can be done in a number of mechanical ways. In addition, as the deck is used, the number of cards can be double-checked to see that no data cards have been lost.

10. *Work Decks.* Sometimes part of the analysis calls for creating indices, scale scores, etc., or combining on one card variables originally punched in several different cards. Such special work decks may be created by machine. When new work decks are created it is important to compare case numbers to be sure that information pertaining to one subject is kept together. It is also important that the card layout for the work deck be recorded in the codebook. New deck numbers are assigned for each new deck that is created so that cards from different decks are not mixed.

It is generally the case (except for special programs on computers) that all variables to be simultaneously compared must appear on the same, single hollerith card for each subject.

11. *Grouping Variables.* It is not uncommon that insufficient cases appear in some category of a variable for proper statistical analysis. This can often be detected by examining the "marginals" created in step 6. In this event, the more elaborate code originally used may be condensed into fewer categories.

For example, if marital status is punched, too few "widowed" individuals may be included in the sample to provide a basis for analysis as a separate category. A new "grouped" code may then be assigned where, for example, divorced, separated, and widowed may be grouped into an "other" category. The new code should be noted in the codebook for decks in which this new grouping appears. Punch-card machines can be used to create new grouped codes from single variables as well as new indices and scale scores from combinations of variables. Many computer programs permit one to group categories for analysis without actually punching the new grouped code in the source cards.

12. *Analysis.* Quite naturally, the cards are used in various ways to create frequency distributions, tables, etc. There is virtually no restriction on the type of analysis that can be carried out by using data in punched-card form. See write-ups of existing computer programs or machine manuals for help in machine data analysis.

In addition, each category of response to the questions should be assigned a specific code number which corresponds to a punch in a hollerith card (a hollerith card has 12 possible single punches in a single column: 0, 1, 2, 3, 4, 5, 6, 7, 8, 9, −, and +.[1] Generally, each item is punched in a separate column and only one punch is punched in that column to indicate the subject's response to one item.

For example, the investigator may decide to assign the question about the sex of the respondent to column 10 of a hollerith card. If the subject is male he may be assigned a "1" punch in column 10; if female the subject may be assigned a "2" punch in column 10. Thus, in the completed deck of cards, if a card has a "1" punch in column 10, the codebook will tell one that this means the subject was a male.

Some codes are so extensive that they require a "field" of two or more adjacent columns on a hollerith card. Age might be punched in a two-column field (in columns 23 and 24, for example). The age "75" would be indicated by punching the 7 in column 23 and the 5 in column 24. Again, only one numeric code is punched in any single column.

Items are assigned to columns of a hollerith card in the simplest way, which is generally in the order they appear in the questionnaire or source document. At this point the easiest possible way to organize the task will result in fewer coder errors, less confusion, and some coder efficiency which will be reflected in costs. Once the cards have been keypunched, a new deck of cards can be created with items (from many decks) appearing in the desired order and this can be done simply by machine.

It is good practice to record in the codebook exactly how codes are to be assigned and how ambiguities are (were) resolved so that later in the research one will know exactly what is included in a certain category. The codebook might also indicate the question number in the questionnaire (or source document) used in coding in order to facilitate later cross-checking in interpreting the findings. (An example of a codebook follows.)

EXAMPLE OF A COMPUTER DATA CODE BOOK

Selected Characteristics of Juveniles in Minnesota Department of Corrections Group Homes, 1969

This data set concerns Minnesota juveniles who were adjudicated delinquent and placed in group foster homes operated by the Minnesota Department of Corrections. Group homes are private family homes which have four or more delinquent youths placed under their supervision.

Variable* number	Variable label*	Variable description	Card column	Frequency**	Percent**
		Identification Number	1–5		
1	Homeage	Age when entered home	6–7		
		01 12			
		02 13			
		04 14			
		05 15			
		06 16			
		07 17			
		08 19			
		09 20			
		10 21			
2	Sex	Sex	8		
		1 Male			
		2 Female			
3	Changes	No. of changes in household of residence prior to last offense	9		
		1 2			
		2 1–2			
		3 3–5			
		4 6 or more			
4	Ethnic	Bioethnic background	(10)		
		1 American Indian			
		2 Black			
		3 White			
		5 Mexican			
		6 Other			
5	Guardian	Legal guardianship	(11)		
		1 Parents			
		2 Relatives			
		3 Private Agency			
		4 Public			
		5 Self			

* Often computer programs permit the labeling, with numbers and/or short names, of the variables, and it is important to keep a record of these in a codebook.

** Frequency and percent are often added to a codebook.

Any punch may be assigned to any category of response to an item, but there is usually some efficiency (given current programs and machines) in assigning codes in a sequence starting with 0, 1, 2 . . . to 9, −, and +, depending upon the number of response categories there are. Some investigators reserve a zero or + punch to stand for "no response" for each item. This is often good practice rather than merely leaving a column blank if the subject does not respond to an item. While consistency may aid the memory, the more important point is to assign one of the codes at the end of the sequence of codes to this category since it will likely be dropped in the final analysis.

Note

1. A hollerith card has 80 columns and 12 rows. (See the illustration on page 228 which shows standard alphabetic and numeric punch codes.) The 80 columns are numbered from left to right. The twelve rows start with "9" at the bottom of the card (the "9-edge") and proceed up the card, 8, 7, 6, 5, 4, 3, 2, 1, 9. Above the 0-punch there are two more rows of punches. The next row above the zero-row is called a "−" (minus) punch (also called an X, eleven, or zone punch). The row along the top of the card is called + (also called Y, R, zone or 12-punch). Some standard computer programs cannot treat the 11 and 12 punches as separate categories so they are generally assigned only if there are as many as 11 or 12 categories of response to an item and where programs will be available to handle these "zone" punches. If there are more than 10 (or 12) categories of response, two columns of the hollerith card are used.

3.8.b. COMPUTER PROGRAMS (SOFTWARE)

The Institute of Social Research at Indiana University in Bloomington has the following programs currently running on the Indiana University Computer Network System. All programs except SAS run on the CDC6600/Cyber-172 computer system (WCC system)

SPSS: Statistical Package for the Social Sciences
BMD: Biomedical Computer Programs
SAS: Statistical Analysis System, currently running on the IBM4341 at IUPUI in Indianapolis, Indiana
LISREL: Analysis of Linear Structural Relationships by the Method of Maximum Likelihood, version 4*
EFAP: Exploratory Factor Analysis version 2*
COFAMM: Confirmatory Factor Analysis with Model Modification*
ECTA: Everyman's Contingency Table Analyzer (log-linear analysis)*
RATE: continous time, discrete state, Markov models for events data*
KYST-2: Multidimensional Scaling and Unfolding*
STRUCTURE: a computer program providing basic data for the analysis of empirical positions in a system of actors*

SPSS Program

The institute relies mainly on the SPSS computer program write-ups maintained in the University Computer Center. These include:

---

* The Institute of Social Research maintains the write-ups of these programs.

One-Way Frequency Distributions
Descriptive Statics for Aggregated Data Files
Contingency Tables and Related Measures of Association
Description of Subpopulations and Mean Difference Testing: Subprograms, Break-
    downs and t-Test
Bivariate Correlation Analysis: Pearson Correlation, Rank-Order Correlation, and
    Scatter Diagrams
Partial Correlation
Multiple Regression Analysis
Path Analysis and Causal Interpretation
Analysis of Variance and Covariance
Discriminant Analysis
Factor Analysis
Canonical Correlation Analysis
Guttman Scalogram Analysis

For an initial understanding of SPSS, consult *SPSS Primer* by William R. Klecka, Norman H. Nie, and C. Hadlai Hull (New York: McGraw-Hill, 1975). The presentation begins with background material on computers and progresses to information on how to describe numerical data to SPSS, how to create and save a "system file," recode data values, and identify missing data; and how to use several basic statistical procedures. After studying this text, you should be able to prepare a simple SPSS computer run for the analysis of your data.

For more extensive use of SPSS, you should read the manual on which the primer is based: Norman H. Nie et al., *SPSS: Statistical Package for the Social Sciences,* 2nd ed. (New York: McGraw-Hill, 1975). This larger book provides a complete description of the SPSS system. In particular it describes alternative means of supplying data to SPSS, the full use of alphabetic variables, the complete set of transformation instructions, the full range of statistical procedures, and numerous other details. In addition, *SPSS* includes detailed descriptions of the statistics available in each statistical procedure, information not provided in the *Primer*. Numerous update releases of *SPSS* have been published and are available from the book's publisher.

SCSS Program

Norman H. Nie et al., *SCSS: A User's Guide to the SCSS Conversational System* (New York: McGraw-Hill, 1980), refers to a sister program to *SPSS*. Nevertheless, *SCSS* is not just an extension or modified version of *SPSS* but a new package with a somewhat different language. The major parallel to *SPSS* is that both packages encompass approximately the same statistical procedures.

Conversational, or interactive, computing allows users to obtain immediate feedback while retaining step-by-step control over the computational process. For researchers, *SCSS* would be most useful for purposeful and theoretically guided model building and testing. Promising avenues of investigation can be quickly distinguished from dead ends. For teachers, *SCSS* might provide a means for students to explore empirically a substantive area using basic cross-tabulation techniques on a carefully limited data set.

OSIRIS

OSIRIS is another widely used package of computer programs designed for the analysis of social science data. The statistical analysis capabilities include a variety of multivariate and nonparametric analysis programs. Potential users should read *Data Processing in the Social Sciences with OSIRIS* by Judith Rattenburg and Paula Pelletier (Ann Arbor: Institute of Social Research, University of Michigan, 1974).

OSIRIS is intended to guide researchers and their assistants in the field of social science through all the stages necessary for processing data with a computer. No previous knowledge of computers is assumed, although at least theoretical knowledge of data collection and analysis is expected.

The monograph describes procedures and strategies geared to studies involving relatively large bodies of data. Discussed are the basic components of computers and the different kinds of software necessary for using a computer, different types of data and analysis, the various steps of the processing stages, and the kinds of errors commonly made when using a computer for data processing and how they can be avoided.

Users of OSIRIS who need assistance in writing or modifying a computer program should consult Judith Rattenburg and Neal Van Eck, *OSIRIS: Architecture and Design* (Ann Arbor: Institute of Social Research, University of Michigan, 1974). This monograph provides technical documentation.

OSIRIS IV: Statistical Analysis and Data Management Software System by the Computer Support Group, Survey Research Center (Ann Arbor: Institute of Social Research, University of Michigan, 1979), is the latest update of the OSIRIS IV software system. The volume describes the major features basic to the system and it includes a general description of the program, special terminology, command features, printed output, data input and output, restrictions, examples, and keywords as appropriate.

Other Computer Languages

COBOL: The COBOL language is well suited for handling large amounts of data and is the most frequently chosen language for business applications. Topics include basic program structure, file manipulation (soft/merge), the report writer, and features unique to the CDC COBOL compiler.

FORTRAN: Topics covered are an introduction to computer organization, algorithms and flowcharts, FORTRAN language statements and syntax, and program debugging.

Advanced FORTRAN: Designed for researchers and students who are experienced FORTRAN programmers. Topics include learning how to interpret an exchange package, speedy input/output procedures, representation of data on CDC machines, bufferin overlays, the segment loader, basic data structures, and advanced FORTRAN Syntax.

PASCAL: Intended for persons with little or no programming experience. Topics include the advantages of programming in Pascal, how to prepare a Pascal program, and solving problems via computer programs. The most basic statements of Pascal: assignment, conditionals, iteratives, declarations, types, case statements, procedures, functions, and using arrays.

Advanced PASCAL: Intended for persons with programming experience in at least one other higher-level language: data structures (e.g., linked lists, binary trees, AVL trees). Other topics include disk input/output using the RIOLIB library, interactive Pascal in information systems, and terminal screen cursor addressing.

Introduction to Telex and Kronos Control Language: Intended for all persons planning to use computers for research or academic work. A must for computer science majors. Good background for TFORM users. Topics include using a computer terminal, logging into Telex, permanent and local files, status commands, using the UCEDIT text editor, manipulating files, the configuration of computers, optimizing turnaround, adjusting time and memory requirements, using magnetic tapes, direct access permanent files, common files, and dealing with large data bases.

Telex for Programming: For individuals who already know at least one high-level language such as FORTRAN or Pascal. Learn how to run such programs interactively from Telex commands frequently needed by programmers (e.g., creating files, using the editor, tape handling procedures, and more).

Telex for Text Processing: If you plan to use the computer only for text processing, then this language is tailored to your needs. The essential commands and procedures are discussed: how to log on, create files, use the editor, use text formatting programs, and use tapes. No prior computing experience is required.

SPSS Manova: For a variety of multivariate analytic techniques such as multivariate analysis of variance, multiple discriminant function analysis, and canonical correlation.

SPSS REPORT Generator: Version 8.0 of SPSS contains a procedure, named REPORT, that enables the user to generate complex, hierarchial reports from an SPSS data set or system file. The REPORT procedure contains many options for labeling and data placement.

Specialized Computer Programs

The Institute for Social Research at the University of Michigan is currently offering the following Computer Techniques in Social Science Research:

ANDREWS, FRANK M., and MESSENGER, ROBERT C. *Multivariate Nominal Scale Analysis: A Report on a New Analysis Technique and a Computer Program.* 1975.

This monograph describes a powerful new technique for conducting multivariate analysis of categorical dependent variables. It applies the most common analytic model—the additive one—to categorical dependent variables and arrives at answers to the usual questions addressed by multivariate analysis. It is uniquely useful in exploring the interrelationships of theoretical concepts involving categorical dependent variables and substantial numbers of independent variables at various levels of measurement.

ANDREWS, FRANK M.; MORGAN, JAMES N.; SONQUIST, JOHN A., and KLEM, LAURA. *Multiple Classification Analysis: A Report on a Computer Program for Multiple Regression Using Categorical Predictors.* 1967; rev. ed., 1974.

Multiple Classification Analysis is a technique for examining the interrelationship between several predictor variables and a dependent variable within the context of an additive model. The program will handle missing data on both the dependent and predictor variables.

MORGAN, JAMES N., and MESSENGER, ROBERT C. *THAID: A Sequential Analysis Program for the Analysis of Nominal Scale Dependent Variables.* 1973.

Like its companion volume, *Multivariate Nominal Scale Analysis,* this monograph describes a recently developed technique for conducting multivariate analyses of categorical dependent variables. Although common in social research, such variables have, until now, been difficult to handle with available statistical techniques. THAID describes a searching process that provides an efficient and effective means for sorting through a variety of analytic models to find the most able to produce useful predictions. The program searches for subgroups that differ maximally as to their distribution; it assumes neither additivity nor linearity, so requires substantial samples of 1000 or more cases.

RATTENBURY, JUDITH. *Introduction to the IBM 360 Computer and OS/JCL (Job Control Language).* 1971; rev. 1974.

This monograph will be of value to both the complete novice and to those who have used other computers. It not only gives details of the most used subset of the IBM 360 job control language but also attempts to make it meaningful by describing the physical characteristics of tapes and disks and by explaining how the operating system works.

SONQUIST, JOHN A. *Multivariate Model Building: The Validation of a Search Strategy.* 1970; reprinted, 1971.

This book undertakes the validation of the Automatic Interaction Detection (AID) technique. It uses computer techniques for data-generation to produce models in which the actual structure of the relationship between variables is completely known. Then, applying both AID and Multiple Classification Analysis (MCA) techniques to the data, it explores the ability of each algorithm to lead the analyst to a correct assessment of the structure of the predictive model implicit in the data. The conclusion leads to further developments in a strategy for the back-to-back use of AID and MCA in the task of multivariate building.

SONQUIST, JOHN A.; LAUH BAKER, ELIZABETH; and MORGAN, JAMES N. *Searching for Structure.* 1971; rev. ed., 1974.

This report presents an approach to analysis of substantial bodies of micro-data and documentation for a computer program. The new computer program—AID 111—is a descendant of the original Automatic Interaction Detector program that started the application of search strategy; several new features have been added to the new program.

The Community and Family Study Center of the University of Chicago has the following computer techniques available:

Techniques for Making Population Projections: How To Make Age-Sex and Functional Projections by Electronic Computer, by DONALD J. BOGUE. Manual No. 12.

This manual presents the basic methodology of population forecasting and the techniques necessary for forecasting the future size of functional subgroupings of the population.

Mini-Regression: A Small Computer Program for Performing Multiple Regression Analysis, by MAURICE J. MOORE. Manual No. 14.

Basic principles of multiple regression analysis are presented. A computer program for calculating regression coefficients and related statistics is included.

Techniques of Pregnancy History Analysis, by DONALD J. BOGUE and ELIZABETH J. BOGUE.

> This manual systematizes data collection, computerizes data processing, and codifies the steps involved in adjusting and interpreting the data of pregnancy histories. Computer programs for use on small computers are included.

The Fertility Components and Contraceptive History Techniques for Measuring Contraceptive Use-Effectiveness, by DONALD J. BOGUE and JAMES NELSON.

> A contribution to the methodology for measuring and interpreting the implications of contraceptive use-effectiveness for fertility rates. The manual includes techniques for a new system of measurement, practicable procedures for data collection, and a "packaged" computer program for small computers.

An Empirical Model for Demographic Evaluation of the Impact of Contraception and Marital Status on Birth Rates with Computerized Applications to the Setting of Targets and Quotas for Family Planning Programs, by DONALD J. BOGUE, SCOTT EDMONDS, and ELIZABETH J. BOGUE.

> This manual attempts to solve the practical problem of the valid projection of family-planning targets. It develops an empirical model which links birth rates to contraceptive behavior in a new form able to yield realistic results. A "packaged" computer program for small computers is included.

Mini-Tab Edit, Mini-Tab Frequencies and Mini-Tab Tables: A Set of Three Interrelated Statistical Programs for Small Computers, by HENRY G. ELKINS.

> A set of simplified and versatile programs written in basic FORTRAN to tabulate social data where large computers and more elaborate programs are not readily available.

ADDLIB: A Computer Program for Addressing Mail and Indexing Libraries, by THOMAS MOSSBERG. Family Planning Research and Evaluation Manual No. 13.

> ADDLIB is a computer program which performs two important functions: (1) It addresses labels for all mailings. Names and addresses written on ordinary punched cards can be selected, sorted, and printed on labels with respect to any desired combinations of up to five criteria of selection. (2) ADDLIB prints out bibliographies of items contained in a library, permitting selection by subject for any desired combinations of up to five subject matter classifications. Written for small (32K) computers, it eliminates costly addressing equipment and permits rapid information retrieval at many additional sites throughout the world.

Introductory References to the Role of the Computer

HARMON, MARGARET. *Stretching Man's Mind: A History of Data Processing.* New York: Mason/Charter, 1975.

HOFEDITZ, CALVIN A. *Computers and Data Processing Made Simple.* Garden City, N.Y.: Doubleday, 1979.

KENNEDY, JOHN G. *Man and the Computer.* New York: Scribner's, 1972.

KLEINBERG, HARRY. *How You Can Learn to Live with Computers.* New York: Penguin, 1977.

LATEL, PIERRE DE. *Thinking by Machine.* Boston: Houghton Mifflin, 1957.

MICALLEF, BENJAMIN A. *An Introduction to Data Processing.* Menlo Park, Calif.: Cummings, 1971.

PYLYSHYN, Z. W., ed. *Perspectives on the Computer Revolution.* Englewood Cliffs, N.J.: Prentice-Hall, 1970.

TAVISS, I., ed. *The Computer Impact.* Englewood Cliffs, N.J.: Prentice-Hall, 1970.

Technical Treatments of the Computer

DESMONDE, WILLIAM H. *Computers and Their Uses.* 2nd ed. Englewood Cliffs, N.J.: Prentice-Hall, 1971.

FAVRET, ANDREW G. *Digital Computer, Principles and Applications.* New York: Van Nostrand Reinhold, 1972.

LAVER, MURRAY. *Computers, Communications, and Society.* New York: Oxford University Press, 1975.

MARTIN, JAMES. *The Wired Society.* Englewood Cliffs, N.J.: Prentice-Hall, 1978.

Applications of the Computer to the Social Sciences

BRIAR, ALAN, and ROBINSON, IAN. *Computers and the Social Sciences.* London: Hutchinson, 1974.

DUTTON, JOHN M., and STARBUCK, WILLIAM H. *Computer Simulation of Human Behavior.* New York: Wiley, 1971.

GREENBERGER, MARTIN; CRENSON, MATTHEW A.; and CRISSEY, BRIAN L. *Models in the Policy Process.* New York: Russell Sage Foundation, 1976.

PATH ANALYSIS   *3.9*

Path Analysis as Causal Analysis

Path analysis has become a popular form of data analysis because it provides possibilities for causal determinations among sets of measured variables. A principal objective of science is to build theoretical explanations of social phenomena. Kaplan has said,

> Science is a search for constancies, for invariants. It is the enterprise of making those identifications in experience which prove to be most significant for the control or appreciation of the experience to come. The basic scientific question is "what the devil is going on around here?"[1]

When the underlying assumptions of path analysis are met, theory and data may be related in situations where many variables are to be handled simultaneously. Path analysis is essentially a data analytic technique using standardized multiple regression equations in examining theoretical models.

Extravagant hopes for causal explanations should not be entertained—at least not yet. The inability to deal with all variables in a social system, to measure and plot their exact interactions, makes the results in most problems only first approximations to causality. But the power of the technique continues to challenge researchers, and its use is proliferating.

A researcher commonly wishes to discover the relationship of independent factors to a dependent variable. Simple and multiple correlations are utilized and often yield important relationships, yet they never demonstrate causality. For example, if we wish to relate father's occupational status to son's occupational status, then, using correlational techniques, their correlational relationship can be determined, but causality can only be inferred. Using path analysis it is possible to postulate that such independent factors as father's educational attainment and occupational status are causal factors in the son's subsequent educational attainment, the status of the first job achieved, and the status of the current job.

Six Steps in the Application of Path Analysis

1. Develop a causal scheme or model.
2. Establish a pattern of associations between the variables in the sequence.
3. Depict a path diagram.
4. Calculate path coefficients for the basic model.
5. Test for "goodness of fit" with the basic model.
6. Interpret the result.

Step 1: Develop a Causal Scheme. Path analysis allows the social theorist to state a theory in the form of a linear causal model. The crucial question has to do with the order of priority for the variables in the system in a causal or processual sequence. Causal models involve the construction of an oversimplified model of social reality in the sense that the model takes into account only a very limited number of variables that are of interest in the specific research area. The most important variables are sought; all others are regarded as "residual." The social scientist represents the process assumed to be in operation among the variables based upon the results of past research and current theory.

Let us suppose that we utilize stratification theory and research. We postulate that status changes in the life cycle of a cohort of males indicate that father's educational attainment (A) and father's occupational attainment (B) will determine the subsequent educational attainment of the son (X), his first job (Y), and his current job (Z). This is the linear statement or temporal order and may be written as follows:

$$(A \longrightarrow B) \longrightarrow X \longrightarrow Y \longrightarrow Z$$

The earlier variables may affect a later one not only through intervening variables but also directly.

Step 2: Establish a Pattern of Associations Between the Variables in the Sequence. The conceptual framework must be translated into quantitative estimates. This is done by establishing the pattern of association of the variables in the sequence. A correlation matrix is developed utilizing the simple correlations for the five status variables in the model. An adaptation of Blau and Duncan shows the matrix of their occupational mobility study (see table 1).[2] Simple correlation measures the gross magnitude of the effect of an antecedent variable upon the consequent variable. The current job status is the expected outcome of all the other four antecedent variables. Reading across the first row it is observed that all four antecedent variables show significant correlation to current job status, the highest being for the son's

Table 1. *Simple Correlations for Five Status Variables*

Variable	Z	Y	X	B	A
Z Son's current occupational status	—	.541	.596	.405	.322
Y Son's first-job status		—	.538	.417	.332
X Son's education			—	.438	.453
B Father's occupational status				—	.516
A Father's education					—

education ($r = .596$), and the next being his first job status ($4 = .541$). As expected, father's occupational status and father's education are related in somewhat diminished magnitude ($r = .405$ and $r = .322$ respectively). The second row reports correlations with first-job status and again the same pattern of relationship with father's occupation and education appears. The third row repeats expected relationships of son's education to father's occupation and education. The fourth row demonstrates the high correlation of father's occupation and education ($r = .516$).[3]

Step 3: Depict a Path Diagram. Path diagrams are generally illustrated, as in figure 1, by means of one-headed arrows connecting some or all of the variables included in the basic model. Variables are distributed from left to right, depending upon their theoretical ordering. The first independent variables are placed at the extreme left. In this case, these are father's education and father's occupation, and the link is shown as an arrowhead at both ends to distinguish it from other paths of influence. Intercorrelations (zero-order) between variables not influenced by other variables in the model are called *exogenous* variables, which refer to all variables prior to and outside the model.

The remaining subset of variables (which may consist of only one variable) is taken as dependent, and these variables are called *endogenous* (*X, Y,* and *Z*). As contrasted with the exogenous variables, this subset is considered totally determined by some combination of the variables in the system. The straight lines above running from one measured variable to another represent

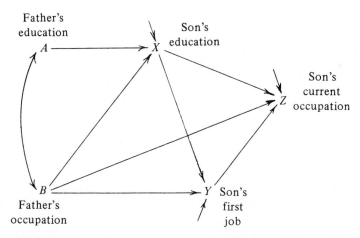

Figure 1. Basic Model of the Process of Stratification. Reprinted by permission and adapted from Blau and Duncan, *American Occupational Structure* (New York: Wiley, 1967). The algebraic representation of the causal scheme now shown in the path model rests on a system of equations rather than the single equation more often employed in multiple regression analysis. This feature permits a flexible ordering of the inferred influences. Each line represents a search and a determination of direct (or net) influences. Note how much emphasis Blau and Duncan have given to the father's occupation as a causative factor as path coefficients are traced to son's education, first job, and current job. Father's education, on the other hand, is traced only through the son's education.

the direct influences of one variable upon another. There are also indirect influences, as illustrated in the diagram under analysis. Variables recognized as effects of certain antecedent factors may, in turn, serve as causes for subsequent variables. For example, X is caused by A and B, which in turn influences Y and Z, thus Y and Z are affected indirectly by both A and B, in addition to any direct effects.

Finally, residual paths must be drawn. These are the lines with no source indicated carrying arrows to each of the endogenous or effect variables. Residuals are represented as the arrows coming from outside the system to X, Y, and Z, and are due to causes not recognized or measured, errors of measurement, and departures of the true relationships from additivity and linearity, properties that are assumed throughout the analysis.

Step 4: Calculate Path Coefficients. Path coefficients reflect the amount of direct contribution of a given variable on another variable when effects of other related variables are taken into account. Path coefficients are identical to partial regression coefficients (the betas) when the variables are measured in standard form. Two ways of computing path coefficients are frequently employed. The first uses regression programs that take raw data and compute partial coefficients from standardized input data. Both path coefficients and multiple correlation coefficients are generally provided by standard computer regression programs.[4] The second method uses only zero-order correlations among variables, a researcher can employ the "basic theorem" to compute the path coefficients.[5]

In figure 2 the path coefficients have been entered on the path diagram with the exception of antecedent variables A and B. The path basic model is now complete and awaits evaluation.

Step 5: Test for "Goodness of Fit" with Basic Model. The crux of the analysis is the test for "goodness of fit" between the observed data and the basic model. Three general approaches may be made:

1. Examining the amount of *variation* in dependent variables that is *explained* by variables linked as specified in the model
2. Examining the *size of path coefficients* to see whether they are large enough to warrant the inclusion of a variable or path in the model
3. Evaluating the ability of the model to *predict correlation coefficients* that were not used in computation of the path coefficients themselves[6]

An investigator usually contrasts the usefulness of the model in these three respects with alternative models. This is the heart of explanatory progress in any science.

The partial regression coefficients in standard form and the coefficients of determination for specified combinations of variables are essential for applying the first "goodness of fit" criterion. Table 2 is an adaption of the Blau and Duncan data. This table shows that the coefficient of determination for father's occupation, father's education, and son's education is .26, which is to say that 26 percent of the variation in son's education may be accounted for by the father's occupation and education.

Similarly, 33 percent of the variation in son's first job may be accounted for by father's occupation, father's education, and son's education. Finally, 43 percent of the variation in son's current occupation is due to father's

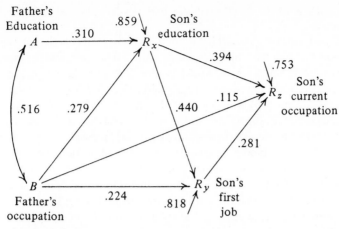

Figure 2. The Path Model for the Causal Scheme. Reprinted by permission and adapted from Blau and Duncan, *American Occupational Structure* (New York: Wiley, 1967), p. 170.

occupation, father's education, son's education, and son's first job. Note that father's education is not helpful in explaining this variance. The unexplained variation $1 - R^2_{4.123} = .57$. The model leaves unexplained 57 percent of the variance in son's current job. This is not as satisfactory as might be hoped. The "unexplained" variation is due to variables or measurement error not included in the model and, for sake of completeness, the square root of these $1 - R^2$ values are ascribed to the residual variables, R_x, R_y and R_z as shown in figure 2. These "residual" paths are large and the investigator must reexamine his causal scheme. However, it must not be assumed that the size of the residual is necessarily a measure of success in explaining the phenomenon under study. "The relevant question about the residual is not really its size at all, but whether the unobserved factors it stands for are properly represented *as being uncorrelated* with the measured antecedent factors."[7]

In terms of the second criterion of goodness of fit, the model fares well. Most of the path coefficients are significant. It turned out that the net regressions of both father's occupation and son's first job on father's education were so small as to be negligible. Hence, father's education could be disregarded without loss of information.[8] One might consider eliminating father's

Table 2 *Partial Regression Coefficients in Standard Form (Beta Coefficients) and Coefficients of Determination, for Specified Combinations of Variables*

Dependent variable	First job	Son's education	Father's occupation	Father's education	Coefficient of determination (R^2)
Son's education			.279	.310	.26
First job		.433	.214	.026	.33
Current occupation	.282	.397	.120	−.014	.43

education as a factor because of its low coefficients and recompute path coefficients.

Third, one could examine the "fit" between observed correlations not previously used in formulas for calculating path coefficients and predictions of correlation coefficients which would be derived from the model. In this instance the correlation between father's education and son's first job (as well as between current job) was not used to estimate path coefficients.

The question of testing an alternative model involves a thorough reexamination of the basic mode. Two possibilities present themselves: (*a*) substituting factors in the basic model believed to be more important, (*b*) adding new factors to the basic model. Whether a path diagram or the causal scheme it represents is adequate depends on both theoretical and empirical considerations. The causal scheme must be complete in the sense that all causes are accounted for. Unmeasured causes presumed to be uncorrelated with the dependent variable must be represented.

Step 6: Interpret the Result. The variables in the causal scheme may be studied for their direct and indirect effects. The direct effect of father's occupation on son's education, first job, and current occupation is shown by path coefficients of .279, .224, and .115, none of which are particularly large. Nevertheless, the cumulative indirect effects are significant. Father's occupation and education do influence son's education, and this in turn influences the son's first job, which in turn influences the son's current occupation. At the same time, many other factors of even greater influence are clearly operating to determine this last dependent variable of interest.

The technique of path analysis is not a method of discovering causal laws but a procedure for giving a quantitative interpretation of an assumed causal system as it operates within a given population.

Nygreen has reported a program called the Interactive Path Analyzer to increase the practical power of path analysis. He describes on-line path analysis for those who have access to computer facilities. He writes:

> In many locations, social science researchers are beginning to gain access to computer facilities via remote typewriter-like "time-sharing" terminals. The increasing ubiquity of such "on-line" computer resources has given many social scientists access to the computational power of digital computers in a much more convenient form than has been the case in the past. Time-sharing computers are becoming increasingly commonplace on college campuses either in addition to or in lieu of the more conventional "batch" processing techniques.
>
> In a time-sharing environment, the analyst can "talk" with the computer by specifying different input criteria to his problem and observing the results immediately. These characteristics of the "conversational" environment provide an advantageous setting in which path analyses can be performed. Specifically, the researcher can think through and then specify his causal model, but the computer can do the numerical calculations, displaying the coefficients for inspection almost immediately. The sociologist is able to postulate alternative theoretical causal formulations, modify his current model[9] and again have the lengthy computations performed in milliseconds, with the results arrayed on the typewriter before him. Properly utilized, the time-sharing computer environment increases the practical power of path analyses, reducing turn-around time literally to seconds.

A program called the Interactive Path Analyzer (IPA) has been written and tested in this on-line environment with very favorable results.[10] The availability of the time-shared computer and the Interactive Path Analyzer lend flexibility and convenience to an otherwise tedious procedure in calculating path coefficients.

Notes

1. Abraham Kaplan, *The Conduct of Inquiry* (San Francisco: Chandler, 1964), p. 85.
2. Peter M. Blau and Otis Dudley Duncan, *The American Occupational Structure* (New York: Wiley, 1967), p. 169.
3. Ibid.
4. For explanations of this procedure in the most understandable terms, see one of the following: Blau and Duncan, *American Occupational Structure,* pp. 171–77; Herman J. Loether and Donald C. McTavish, *Descriptive Statistics for Sociologists* (Boston: Allyn & Bacon, 1974), pp. 321–28. Other references are appended.
5. G. T. Nygreen, "Interactive Path Analysis," *American Sociologist* 6 (February 1971): 37–43.
6. Kenneth C. Land, "Principles of Path Analysis," in *Sociological Methodology, 1969,* ed. Edgar F. Borgatta (San Francisco: Jossey-Bass, 1969).
7. Blau and Duncan, *American Occupational Structure,* p. 175.
8. Ibid., p. 173.
9. Evaluation procedures that require reformulation of the causal model and recomputation of the path coefficients will not be dealt with in this paper.
10. Nygreen, "Interactive Path Analysis," p. 41; requests for copies of this program should be directed to Ms. Judith Rowe, Office for Survey Research and Statistical Studies, O-S-17 Green Hall, Princeton University, Princeton, NJ. Source decks and listings with documentation are available for $10.

Brief Treatment of Path Analysis

BOYLE, RICHARD P. "Path Analysis and Ordinal Data." *American Journal of Sociology* 75 (January 1970): 461–80.

DUNCAN, OTIS D. "Path Analysis: Sociological Examples." *American Journal of Sociology* 72 (July 1966): 1–16. Traces history of path analysis and provides many examples.

LOETHER, HERMAN J., and McTAVISH, DONALD G. *Descriptive Statistics for Sociologists.* Boston: Allyn & Bacon, 1974, Pp. 321–28.

Research Examples of Path Analysis

BLAU, PETER M., and DUNCAN, OTIS DUDLEY. *The American Occupational Structure.* New York: Wiley, 1967. Pp. 163–205.

FEATHERMAN, DAVID L. "Achievement Orientations and Socioeconomic Career Attainments." *American Sociological Review* 37 (April 1972): 131–43.

KELLEY, JONATHAN. "Causal Chain Models for the Socioeconomic Career." *American Sociological Review* 38 (August 1973): 481–93.

LAND, KENNETH C. "Path Models of Functional Theories of Social Stratification as Representations of Cultural Beliefs on Stratification." *Sociological Quarterly* 11 (Fall 1970): 474–84.

ROBINSON, ROBERT V., and KELLEY, JONATHAN. "Class as Conceived by Marx and Dahrendorf: Effects on Income Inequality and Politics in the United States and Great Britain." *American Sociological Review* 44 (February 1979): 38–58.

SEWELL, WILLIAM H.; HALLER, ACHIBALD O.; and OHLENDORF, GEORGE W. "The Educational and Early Occupational Status Attainment Process: Replication and Revision." *American Sociological Review* 35 (December 1970): 1014–27.

General References for Path Analysis

BLALOCK, HUBERT M., JR. *Causal Inferences in Nonexperimental Research.* Chapel Hill, N.C.: University of North Carolina Press, 1964.

BOUDON, RAYMOND. "A Method of Linear Causal Analysis: Dependence Analysis." *American Sociological Review* 30 (June 1965): 365–74.

COSTNER, HERBERT L., and LEIK, ROBERT K. "Deductions from 'Axiomatic Theory.'" *American Sociological Review* 29 (December 1964): 819–35.

FORBES, H. D., and TUFTE, E. R. "A Note of Caution in Causal Modelling." *American Political Science Review* 62 (December 1968): 1258–64.

HEISE, D. R. "Problems in Path Analysis and Causal Inference." In *Sociological Methodology,* edited by Edgar Borgatta. San Francisco: Jossey-Bass, 1969. Pp. 38–71.

LI, C. C. *Population Genetics.* Chicago: University of Chicago Press, 1955.

SIMON, HERBERT A. *Models of Man.* New York: Wiley, 1957.

STINCHCOMBE, ARTHUR. *Construction of Social Theories.* New York: Harcourt, Brace & World, 1968. See chap. 3 and Appendix for application of path analysis to tests of sociological theories.

WRIGHT, SEWELL. "The Method of Path Coefficients." *Annals of Mathematical Statistics* 5 (1934): 161–215.

———. "Path Coefficients and Path Regressions: Alternative or Complementary Concepts?" *Biometrics* 16 (June 1960): 189–202.

———. "The Treatment of Reciprocal Interaction, with or without Lag in Path Analysis." *Biometrics* 16 (September 1960): 423–45.

For additional references see section 3.12, Selected Readings on Causal Models and Multivariate Analysis.

3.10   FACTOR ANALYSIS

Explaining Relations among Numerous Variables in Simpler Terms

The purpose of this introduction is to provide the sociological researcher with a working knowledge of the basic concepts of factor analysis without burdening him with statistical details. It will be assumed in the following discussion, however, that the user has some grasp of the meaning of correlation and regression coefficients. Factor analysis is a procedure for investigating the possibility that a large number of variables have a small number of factors in common which account for their intercorrelations. As Schuessler explains, "We observe that pupils who score high in reading tend to score high in spelling and arithmetic. We ascribe this consistency, or correlation, in pupils' marks to the general factor of intelligence."[1] Thus, it can be seen in brief that this principle holds that a circumstance common to a succession of categorically identical events, which otherwise have nothing in common, may be regarded as a cause of that event. Therefore, to discover the cause of an event, we search for the lone circumstance that is always present when the event occurs. In a similar manner, by means of factor analysis, we seek to isolate those common elements that are present in two or more variables and to which the intercorrelations among these variables may be attributed. It can be seen then that factor analysis is an arithmetical procedure for determining whether the intercorrelations among many variables could be due to a few common factors.

C may be considered as either a cause of both X and Y or simply an element present in both variables. Factor analysis considers the possibility that X and Y are indicators of the same thing. From the observed correlation between X and Y, the inference can be drawn that they were produced by the same cause or that they are, in varying degrees, different aspects of the same thing.

Finding Underlying Factors

To distinguish the observed variables, which are manipulated, from the common variables, which are hidden components in them, it is customary to speak of the latter as factors rather than variables. Thus, for the simplest case of two variables, Z_1 and Z_2, where each is the sum of the two parts, one part common (A) and one part distinct to each variable (B_i), where

$$Z_1 = A + B_1$$
$$Z_2 = A + B_2$$

Z is conventionally spoken of as a variable and A and B_i as factors. Before proceeding any further, it should be emphasized that factors are statistical variables in the usual sense in all respects: factors possess both a mean and a variance, they may be symmetrically distributed, and they may also be correlated with other factors. The special term "factor" serves to maintain the distinction between the composite variable, which is observed, and its component parts, which are hypothetical.

Data Reduction Capability of Factor Analysis

The single most distinctive characteristic of factor analysis is its data-reduction capability. This means that given an array of correlation coefficients for a set of variables, factor-analytic techniques enable the researcher to see whether some underlying pattern of relationships exist such that the data may be "rearranged" or reduced to a smaller set of factors that may be considered source variables accounting for the observed interrelations in the data. There are multiple uses for this statistical capability, but the most frequent applications of the method fall into one of the following three categories: (1) exploratory uses, the exploration and detection of patterning of variables with a view to the discovery of new concepts and a possible reduction of data; (2) confirmatory uses, the testing of hypotheses about the structuring of variables in terms of the expected number of significant factors and factor loadings;

and (3) uses as a measuring device, the construction of indices to be used as new variables in later analysis.[2]

Factor Analysis as Research Design

Factor analysis presents one of the few methods capable of teasing out what *would* happen through manipulation where manipulation is impossible. It seeks conclusions by statistical techniques rather than the more traditional experimental route of manipulative control.

Three Major Steps in Factor Analysis Procedure

Factor analysis includes a fairly large variety of statistical techniques, but there are basically three steps in a factor analysis procedure. The three usual steps are: (1) the preparation of a correlation matrix; (2) the extraction of the initial factors—the exploration of possible data reduction; and (3) the rotation to a terminal solution—the search for simple and interpretable factors. Major options at each of these three stages may be summed up by three dichotomies: R-type versus Q-type factor analysis in step 1, defined versus inferred factors in step 2, and orthogonal versus oblique in step 3. These are defined in detail in the treatments of factor analysis listed in the following bibliography.

Notes

1. Karl Schuessler, *Analyzing Social Data* (Boston: Houghton Mifflin, 1971), p. 44.
2. N. H. Nie et al., *Statistical Package for the Social Sciences* (New York: McGraw-Hill, 1970).

Research Examples of Factor Analysis

BALES, ROBERT F., and COUCH, ARTHUR S. "The Value Profile: A Factor Analytic Study of Value Statements." *Sociological Inquiry* 39 (Winter 1969): 3–17.
CREW, ROBERT E. "Dimensions of Public Policy: A Factor Analysis of State Expenditures." *Social Science Quarterly* 50 (September 1969): 381–88.
MCRAE, DUNCAN, JR. *Issues and Parties in Legislative Voting.* New York: Harper & Row, 1970.
NEAL, ARTHUR, and RETTIG, SOLOMON. "On the Multidimensionality of Alienation." *American Sociological Review* 32 (February 1967): 54–63.

Brief Treatment of Factor Analysis

COMREY, ANDREW L. *A First Course in Factor Analysis.* New York: Academic Press, 1973.
COTTRELL, RAYMOND F. Factor Analysis. An Introduction to Essentials. I. The Purpose and Underlying Models." *Biometrics* 21 (March 1965): 190–215. II. "The Role of Factor Analysis in Research." *Biometrics* 21 (June 1965): 405–35.
KIM, JAE-ON, and MUELLER, CHARLES. *Introduction to Factor Analysis: What It Is and How to Do It.* Beverly Hills, Calif.: Sage, 1978.
RUMMEL, RUDOLPH J. "Understanding Factor Analysis." *Journal of Conflict Resolution* 11 (December 1967): 444–80.

SCHUESSLER, KARL. *Analyzing Social Data.* Boston: Houghton Mifflin, 1971. Pp. 44–84.

General References for Factor Analysis

FRUCHTER, BENJAMIN. *Introduction to Factor Analysis.* Princeton, N.J.: Van Nostrand, 1954.

CATTELL, RAYMOND B. *Factor Analysis: An Introduction and Manual for the Psychologist and Social Scientist.* New York: Harper & Row, 1952.

HARMAN, HARRY H. *Modern Factor Analysis.* 2nd ed. Chicago: University of Chicago Press, 1967.

HORST, PAUL. *Factor Analysis of Data Matrices.* New York: Holt, Rinehart & Winston, 1965.

JORESKOG, K. G. *Advances in Factor Analysis and Structural Equation Models.* Cambridge, Mass.: Abt Books, 1979.

KIM, JAE-ON, and MUELLER, CHARLES. *Factor Analysis: Statistical Methods and Practical Issues.* Beverly Hills, Calif.: Sage, 1978.

NIE, N. H.; BENT, D. H.; and HULL, C. H. *Statistical Package for the Social Sciences.* New York: McGraw-Hill, 1970.

RUMMEL, RUDOLPH J. *Applied Factor Analysis.* Evanston, Ill.: Northwestern University Press, 1970. Recent applications of factor analysis in political and social research are listed in a special chapter.

THURSTONE, LOUIS L. *Multiple Factor Analysis.* Chicago: University of Chicago Press, 1947.

A BIBLIOGRAPHY OF STATISTICAL METHODS   *3.11*

The writing of introductory statistics is as prolific as the writing of introductory sociology texts—perhaps more so since many departments of a university teach introductory courses. It is difficult to find the "best" text for a given class. Royce Singleton, Jr., of Holy Cross College was asked to review the following introductory texts:

DANIEL, WAYNE W. *Introductory Statistics with Applications.* Boston: Houghton Mifflin, 1977. 475 pp.

LEVIN, JACK. *Elementary Statistics in Social Research.* 2nd ed., New York: Harper & Row, 1977. 293 pp.

MALEC, MICHAEL A. *Essential Statistics for Social Research.* Philadelphia: Lippincott, 1977. 235 pp.

PINE, VAN-DERLYN R. *Introduction to Social Statistics.* Englewood Cliffs, N.J.: Prentice Hall, 1977. 415 pp.

RUNYON, RICHARD P. *Winning with Statistics: A Painless First Look at Numbers, Ratios, Percentages, Means, and Inference.* Reading, Mass.: Addison-Wesley, 1977. 210 pp.

SCHUTTE, JERALD G. *Everything You Always Wanted to Know about Elementary Statistics (But Were Afraid to Ask).* Englewood Cliffs, N.J.: Prentice Hall, 1977. 230 pp.

Singleton's approach to this problem of assessment is instructive to all who must make a choice among introductory statistics books. To begin with, he identified the first four listed books as "texts." The latter two he regarded as textbook supplements. He describes his method of judging as follows:

For a summary comparison of the textbooks, I rated each in six areas: adequacy and effectiveness of presentation of (1) Univariate Description (frequency distributions and their graphs; central tendency; variability), (2) Bivariate Description (contingency table analysis, including nominal and ordinal measures of association; correlation and regression), (3) Probability (fundamental laws, definitions, and calculus; sampling distributions), and (4) Inferential Statistics (logic of; hypothesis testing; estimation; ANOVA), (5) Communication Effectiveness (readability; use and explanation of symbols; use of illustrations, drawings, tables, graphs, etc.) and (6) Use of Examples, and Exercises (number and pedagogical value). A 1 to 4 scale with pluses and minuses was used, in which 1 is inadequate, 2 is adequate, 3 is good, and 4 is superior. These ratings are found in table 1. It is apparent that I judged none of these texts to be superior. Indeed, in my judgment, all four are much inferior to Blalock's *Social Statistics* and Mueller, Schuessler, and Costner's *Statistical Reasoning in Sociology.**

Table 1. *Summary Ratings of Four Introductory Statistics Textbooks*

	Daniel	Levin	Malec	Pine
Univariate description	1	3	3	3−
Bivariate description	1+	2	3+	2+
Probability	3+	2	2	2
Inferential statistics	3+	2+	2	2−
Communication effectiveness	2	3	3+	3−
Use of examples & exercises	3	4−	2	3

The following books are especially valuable when the researcher is seeking a readable step-by-step explanation or procedure. The selections are based on the simplicity of the description and the inclusion of illustrative examples.

ANDERSON, THEODORE R., and ZELDITCH, MORRIS, JR. *A Basic Course in Statistics: With Sociological Applications.* 3rd ed. New York: Holt, Rinehart & Winston, 1975.

Step-by-step computation guides for all basic statistics; well illustrated.

BERNSTEIN, ALLEN L. *A Handbook of Statistical Solutions for the Behavioral Sciences.* New York: Holt, Rinehart & Winston, 1964.

Presents solutions to typical problems.

BOHRNSTEDT, GEORGE W., and KNOKE, DAVID. *Statistics for Data Analysis in the Social Sciences,* Itasca, Ill.: Peacock, 1981.

Current applications of statistics to data analysis. See Chapter 12 for "path analysis."

BLALOCK, HUBERT M., JR. *Social Statistics.* 2nd ed. New York: McGraw-Hill, 1972.

Well-written book introducing the student to modern developments.

CHILD, DENNIS. *The Essentials of Factor Analysis.* New York: Holt, Rinehart & Winston, 1973.

Elementary treatment with examples and application to psychology, sociology, and the medical sciences.

CONWAY, FREDA. *Sampling: An Introduction for Social Scientists.* New York: Humanities Press, 1967.

Lucid, neatly organized book on statistics using large-sample theory.

* Royce Singleton, Jr., *Contemporary Sociology* 8 (January 1979): 114–16.

COOMBS, CLYDE H.; DAWES, ROBYN M.; and TVERSKY, AMOS. *Mathematical Psychology: An Elementary Introduction.* Englewood Cliffs, N.J.: Prentice-Hall, 1970.

An elementary treatment with applications to psychology.

CROWLEY, FRANCIS J., and COHEN, MARTIN. *Basic Facts of Statistics.* New York: Collier Books, 1963.

Digests elementary statistics in a very brief and comprehensive manner within 62 pages.

EDWARDS, ALLEN. *Statistical Methods.* 2nd ed. New York: Holt, Rinehart & Winston, 1967.

Statistical techniques and methods presented for the student with a minimum amount of mathematical knowledge. Parametric and nonparametric methods are integrated into the text.

FREUND, JOHN E.; LIVERMORE, PAUL E.; and MILLER, IRVIN. *Manual of Experimental Statistics.* Englewood Cliffs, N.J.: Prentice-Hall, 1960.

Presents in outline form the most frequently used statistical techniques, including appropriate computing formulas and completely worked out examples of each method.

HANUSHEK, ERIC A., and JACKSON, JOHN E. *Statistical Methods for Social Scientists.* New York: Academic Press, 1977.

Contemporary methods of quantitative analysis as used in sociology, economics, and political science. Good coverages of telephone surveys.

HAUSER, PHILIP M. *Social Statistics in Use.* New York: Russell Sage Foundation, 1975.

Stresses importance of and shows how social statistics are put to public use.

HOLLANDER, MYLES, and WOLFE, DOUGLAS A. *Nonparametric Statistical Methods.* New York: Wiley, 1973.

An updated description of nonparametric statistics.

LEVIN, JACK. *Elementary Statistics in Social Research.* 2nd. ed. New York: Harper & Row, 1977.

This edition had descriptions of twelve research situations with data and instructions to the student to select the appropriate statistical measure.

LOETHER, HERMAN J., and MCTAVISH, DONALD G. *Descriptive Statistics for Sociologists.* Boston: Allyn & Bacon, 1974.

Careful treatment of statistical techniques that sociologists commonly use and illustrations showing how sociologists make use of them. A companion volume, *Inferential Statistics for Sociologists,* is available by these same writers and focuses attention on statistical techniques that make inferences possible from samples.

MAXWELL, ALBERT E. *Analyzing Qualitative Data.* New York: Wiley, 1961.

The book, which might have been given the title x^2 tests, aims at providing the research worker with a simple but up-to-date account of statistical techniques available for the analysis of qualitative data.

MORONEY, M. J. *Facts from Figures.* Baltimore: Penguin, 1956.

Lucid explanation of the background of statistics; well illustrated.

MUELLER, JOHN H.; SCHUESSLER, KARL F.; and COSTNER, HERBERT. *Statistical Reasoning in Sociology.* 3rd ed. Boston: Houghton Mifflin, 1977.

Emphasizes reasons for each statistical procedure.

SCHMID, CALVIN F. *Handbook of Graphic Presentation.* New York: Ronald Press, 1954.

Methods for presenting social statistics in a visual manner.

SMITH, G. MILTON. *A Simplified Guide to Statistics for Psychology and Education.* 3rd ed. New York: Holt, Rinehart & Winston, 1962.

Integrates most commonly used tools.

TANUR, JUDITH M. *Statistics: A Guide to Political and Social Issues.* San Francisco: Holden-Day, 1977.

Statistics applied to current political and social issues.

TANUR, JUDITH M.; MOSTELLER, FREDERICK; KRUSKUL, WILLIAM H.; LINK, RICHARD F.; PIETERS, RICHARD S.; and RISING, GERALD R. *Statistics: A Guide to the Unknown.* San Francisco: Holden-Day, 1972.

Everyday use of statistics.

WALKER, HELEN M. *Mathematics Essential for Elementary Statistics: A Self-Teaching Manual.* Rev. ed. New York: Henry Holt, 1951.

Material permits student to proceed with mathematical training by self-instruction.

WEISS, ROBERT S. *Statistics in Social Research.* New York: Wiley, 1968.

The traditional topics are treated from the point of view of someone guiding a student through the research process.

WIKE, EDWARD L. *Data Analysis: A Statistical Primer for Psychology Students.* Chicago: Aldine-Atherton, 1971.

A "how to do it" text that illustrates the use of statistics in data obtained from small samples. Intended for students who are conducting experiments for the first time. Organized around types of experimental designs.

ZEISEL, HANS. *Say It with Figures.* 5th ed. New York: Harper & Row, 1968.

A guide to the assembly and interpretation of social statistics.

ZELLER, RICHARD A., and CARMINES, EDWARD G. *Statistical Analysis of Social Data.* Chicago: Rand McNally, 1978.

Good applications for the political science student.

3.12 A SPECIALIZED BIBLIOGRAPHIC SECTION FOR THE ADVANCED STUDENT

Selected Readings on Causal Models and Multivariate Analysis

BISHOP, Y. M. M.; FINEBERG, S. E.; and HOLLAND, P. W. *Discrete Multivariate Analysis.* Cambridge, Mass.: MIT Press, 1975.

BLALOCK, HUBERT M., JR., ed. *Measurement in the Social Sciences: Theories, and Strategies.* Chicago: Aldine, 1974.

_____. *Causal Inferences in Non-Experimental Research.* Chapel Hill: University of North Carolina Press, 1964.

_____, and BLALOCK, ANN B., eds. *Methodology in Social Research.* New York: McGraw-Hill, 1968.

_____; AGANBEGIAN, A.; BORODKIN, F. M.; BOUDON, RAYMOND; and CAPECCHI, VITTORIO, eds. *Quantitative Sociology, International Perspectives on Mathematical and Statistical Modelling.* New York: Academic Press, 1975.

BOHRNSTEDT, GEORGE W., and BORGATTA, EDGAR F., eds. *Social Measurement: Current Issues.* Beverly Hills, Calif.: Sage, 1981.

COOLEY, WILLIAM W., and LOHNES, PAUL R. *Multivariate Data Analysis.* New York: Wiley, 1971.

COOMBS, CLYDE H. *A Theory of Data.* New York: Wiley, 1964.

COSTNER, HERBERT L., ed. *Sociological Methodology.* San Francisco: Jossey-Bass, 1974.

DUNCAN, OTIS D. *Introduction to Structural Equation Models.* New York: Academic Press, 1975.

GOLDSTEIN, MATHEW, and DILLON, WILLIAM R. *Discrete Discriminant Analysis.* New York: Wiley, 1978.

GRAWOIG, DENNIS E. *Decision Mathematics.* New York: McGraw-Hill, 1967.

HABERMAN, SHELBY J. *Analysis of Qualitative Data.* Vol. 2. *New Developments.* New York: Academic Press, 1979.

HEISE, DAVID R. *Causal Analysis.* New York: Wiley, 1975.

KERLINGER, FRED N., and PEDHAZUR, ELAZAR J. *Multiple Regression in Behavioral Research.* New York: Holt, Rinehart & Winston, 1973.

LEIK, ROBERT K., and MEEKER, BARBARA F. *Mathematical Sociology.* Englewood Cliffs, N.J.: Prentice-Hall, 1975.

LIEBERMAN, BERNHARDT. *Contemporary Problems in Statistics: A Book of Readings for the Behavioral Sciences.* New York: Oxford University Press, 1971.

MCCLEARY, RICHARD; HAY, RICHARD A., JR.; and Associates. *Applied Time Series Analysis for the Social Sciences.* Beverly Hills, Calif.: Sage, 1980.

MORRISON, DONALD F. *Multivariate Statistical Methods.* New York: McGraw-Hill, 1967.

NOWAK, S. "Some Problems of Causal Interpretation of Statistical Relationships." *Philosophy of Science* 27 (January 1960): 23–38.

POLK, KENNETH. "A Note on Asymmetric Causal Models." *American Sociological Review* 27 (August 1962): 539–42.

ROBINSON, W. S. "Asymmetric Causal Models: Comments on Polk and Blalock," *American Sociological Review* 27 (August 1962): 545–48.

SCHUESSLER, KARL. *Analyzing Social Data.* Boston: Houghton Mifflin, 1971.

SIMON, HERBERT A. "Causal Ordering and Identifiability." In *Studies in Econometric Methods,* edited by W. C. Hood and T. C. Koopmans. New York: Wiley, 1953. Pp. 49–74.

_____. "Spurious Correlation: A Causal Interpretation." *Journal of the American Statistical Association* 49 (September 1954): 467–79.

_____. *Models of Man: Social and Rational.* New York: Wiley, 1957. Pp. 37–49.

TUFTE, EDWARD R. *Data Analysis for Politics and Policy.* Englewood Cliffs, N.J.: Prentice-Hall, 1974.

WOLD, HERMAN. "Causal Inference from Observational Data." *Journal of the Royal Statistical Society* 119, ser. A, pt. 1 (1956): 28–60.

_____, and JUREEN, L. *Demand Analysis: A Study in Econometrics.* New York: Wiley, 1953.

3.12.a. SELECTED BIBLIOGRAPHY FOR THE APPLICATION OF MATHEMATICS TO SOCIAL ANALYSIS AND SPECIAL PROBLEMS

AIGNER, D. J., and GOLDBERGER, A. S., eds. *Latent Variables in Socioeconomic Models.* Amsterdam: North-Holland, 1977.

BIJNEN, E. *Cluster Analysis.* Netherlands: Tilburg University Press, 1973.

A sociologist describes cluster analysis and its social applications.

BOUDON, RAYMOND. *Mathematical Structures of Social Mobility.* San Francisco: Jossey-Bass, 1973.

BOX, G. E. P., and JENKINS, G. M. *Time Series Analysis: Forecasting and Contract.* San Francisco: Holden-Day. 1976.

COLEMAN, JAMES S. *Introduction to Mathematical Sociology.* Glencoe, Ill.: Free Press, 1964.

The emphasis in this book is on mathematics as a tool for the elaboration of sociological theory.

————. *The Mathematics of Collective Action.* Chicago: Aldine, 1973.

A theory relating the decisions and actions of social groups with instrumental powers to the specific interests and resources of group members.

DODD, STUART C., and CHRISTOPHER, STEFAN C. "The Reactants Models." In *Essays in Honor of George Lundberg.* Great Barrington, Mass.: Behavioral Research Council, 1968. Pp. 143–79.

A search for laws of communicative behavior by fitting curves to diffusion data as item moves through a population.

DOREIAN, PATRICK. *Mathematics and the Study of Social Relations.* New York: Schocken, 1971.

GOLDBERG, SAMUEL. *Introduction to Difference Equations.* New York: Wiley, 1958.

Revised edition of monograph on difference equations written in 1954 at the invitation of SSRC Committee on the Mathematical Training of Social Scientists.

HAMLIN, ROBERT L.; JACOBSEN, R. BROOKE; and MILLER, JERRY L. *A Mathematical Theory of Social Change.* New York: Wiley, 1973.

HAYES, PATRICK. *Mathematical Methods in Social and Managerial Sciences.* New York: Wiley Interscience, 1975.

HARMAN, HARRY H. *Modern Factor Analysis.* 2nd ed. Chicago: University of Chicago Press, 1967.

HORST, PAUL. *Factor Analysis of Data Matrices.* New York: Holt, Rinehart, & Winston, 1967.

JACKSON, DAVID J., and BORGATTA, EDGAR F., eds. *Factor Analysis and Measurement: A Multi-Dimensional Perspective.* Beverly Hills, Calif.: Sage, 1981.

KEMENY, JOHN G., and SNELL, LAURIE J. *Mathematical Models in the Social Sciences.* Boston: Blaisdell, 1962.

This book is for a mathematics course, not a social science course; the problems in the social sciences are introduced only as an incentive to learn mathematics.

LAZARSFELD, PAUL F. "Notes on the History of Quantification in Sociology—Trends, Sources, and Problems." In *Quantification,* edited by Harry Woolf. Indianapolis: Bobbs-Merrill, 1961.

————, ed. *Mathematical Thinking in the Social Sciences.* Glencoe, Ill.: Free Press, 1954.

LUNDBERG, GEORGE A. "Statistics in Modern Social Thought." In *Contemporary Social Theory,* edited by Harry Elmer Barnes, Howard Becker, and Francis Bennett Becker. New York: Appleton Century, 1940. Pp. 110–40.

Historical account of the rise of social statistics.

MARTINDALE, DON. "Limits to the Uses of Mathematics in the Study of Sociology." In *Mathematics and the Social Sciences,* edited by James C. Charlesworth. Philadelphia: American Academy of Political and Social Science, June 1963. Pp. 95–121.

MCGINNIS, ROBERT. *Mathematical Foundations for Social Analysis.* Indianapolis: Bobbs-Merrill, 1965.

Provides an introduction to mathematical procedures which are being increasingly employed in sociology: sets, relations, real numbers, matrices, and limits.

MERTON, ROBERT K.; COLEMAN, JAMES C.; and ROSSI, PETER H., eds. *Qualitative and Quantitative Social Research: Papers in honor of Paul F. Lazarsfeld.* New York: Free Press, 1979.

MOKKEN, R. J. *A Theory and Procedure of Scale Analysis.* The Hague, Paris: Mouton, 1971.

Theoretical and practical issues of Guttman Scale techniques.

MORRISON, DENTON E., and HENCKEL, RAMON E., eds. *The Significance Test Controversy: A Reader.* Chicago: Aldine, 1970.

RASHEVSKY, NICHOLAS. *Mathematical Biology of Social Behavior.* Chicago: University of Chicago Press, 1950.

Application of mathematical methods to study of social stratification.

SOLOMON, HERBERT, ed. *Mathematical Thinking in the Measurement of Behavior.* Glencoe, Ill.: Free Press, 1960.

Includes contributions by James S. Coleman on mathematics and small-group research; Ernest W. Adams on utility theory; and Herbert Solomon on factor analysis.

STONE, RICHARD. "Mathematics in the Social Sciences." *Scientific American* 211, no. 3 (September 1964): 168–86.

STOUFFER, SAMUEL A.; GUTTMAN, LOUIS; SUCHMAN, EDWARD A.; LAZARSFELD, PAUL F.; STAR, SHIRLEY A.; and CLAUSEN, JOHN A. *Measurement and Prediction.* Princeton, N.J.: Princeton University Press, 1950.

Theoretical and empirical analysis of scales and problems of prediction.

WHITE, HARRISON. "Uses of Mathematics in Sociology." In *Mathematics and the Social Sciences,* edited by James C. Charlesworth. Philadelphia: American Academy of Political and Social Science, June 1963. Pp. 77–94.

———. *An Anatomy of Kinship.* Englewood Cliffs, N.J.: Prentice-Hall, 1963.

Attempt to analyze logic underlying kinship systems by mathematical methods.

ZIPF, GEORGE KINGSLEY. *Human Behavior and the Principle of Least Effort.* Cambridge, Mass.: Addison-Wesley, 1949.

Quantitative Applications in the Social Sciences

Brief, clearly articulated explanations of advanced methodological concepts have been developed by research specialists and published as a series by Sage Publications, 275 S. Beverly Drive, Beverly Hills, CA 90212. Titles include:

Analysis of Variance by Gudmund Iversen and Helmut Norroth
Operations Research Methods by Stuart Nagel with Marian Neef
Causal Modeling by Herbert B. Asher
Tests of Significance by Ramon E. Henkel

Cohort Analysis by Norval D. Glenn
Canonical Analysis and Factor Comparison by Mark S. Levine
Analysis of Nominal Data by H. T. Reynolds
Analysis of Ordinal Data by David K. Hildebrand, James D. Laing, and Howard Rosenthal
Time Series Analysis: Regression Techniques by Charles W. Ostrom, Jr.
Ecological Inference by Laura Irwin Langbein and Allan J. Lichtman
Multidimensional Scaling by Joseph B. Kruskal and Myron Wish
Multiple Indicators: An Introduction by John L. Sullivan and Stanley Feldman
Exploratory Data Analysis by Frederick Hartwig with Brian E. Dearing
Reliability and Validity Assessment by Edward G. Carmines and Richard A. Zeller
Analyzing Panel Data by Gregory B. Markus
Analysis of Covariance by Albert R. Wildt and Olli T. Ahtola
Introduction to Factor Analysis: What It Is and How To Do It by Jae-on Kim and Charles Mueller
Factor Analysis: Statistical Methods and Practical Issues by Jae-on Kim and Charles Mueller
Discriminant Analysis by William R. Klecka
Log-Linear Models by David Knoke and Peter J. Burke
Interrupted Time Series Analysis by David McDowall, Richard McCleary, Errol E. Meidinger and Richard A. Hay, Jr.
Applied Regression: An Introduction by Michael S. Lewis-Beck
Research Designs by Paul Spector
Unidimensional Scaling by John P. McIver and Edward G. Carmines
Magnitude Scaling: Quantitative Measurement of Opinions by Milton Lodge

Contents of Sociological Methodology 1969–80

Sociological Methodology is an official publication of the American Sociological Association. It is an annual series that began in 1969 and was designed to keep social scientists abreast of methodological changes and innovations in all areas of sociological inquiry. Because of its importance in defining the cutting edge of the discipline, the contents are reproduced to provide a ready reference for the researcher. All volumes are published by Jossey-Bass, Inc., 615 Montgomery Street, San Francisco, CA 94111.

1969: Edgar F. Borgatta and George W. Bohrnstedt, eds.
  Part One: Path Analysis, Causal Inferences, and the Measurements of Change
   1. "Principles of Path Analysis," Kenneth C. Land
   2. "Problems in Path Analysis and Causal Inference," David R. Heise
   3. "Contingencies in Constructing Causal Models," Otis Dudley Duncan
   4. "Observations on the Measurement of Change," George W. Bohrnstedt

  Part Two: General Papers
   5. "Logic and Levels of Scientific Explanation," John T. Dody
   6. "Ecological Variables," Desmond S. Cartwright
   7. "Convariance Analysis in Sociological Research," Karl Schuessler
   8. "Stochastic Processes," Thomas J. Fararo

  Part Three: Shorter Papers and Notes
   9. "Testing a Measurement Model," Richard Ofshe and Ronald E. Anderson
   10. "Use of Ad Hoc Definitions," Jeffrey K. Hadden
   11. "Probabilities from Longitudinal Records," Peter A. Morrison

1970: Edgar F. Borgatta and George W. Bohrnstedt, eds.

Part One: Theory Building and Causal Models
  1. "Causal Inference from Panel Data," David R. Heise
  2. "Heise's Causal Model Applied," Donald C. Pelz and Robert A. Lew
  3. "Partials, Partitions, and Paths," Otis Dudley Duncan
  4. "Evaluating Axiomatic Theories," Kenneth D. Bailey

Part Two: Measurement, Reliability, and Validity
  5. "Statistical Estimation with Random Measurement Error," H. M. Blalock, Caryll S. Wells, and Lewis F. Carter
  6. "Validity, Invalidity, and Reliability," David R. Heise and George Bohrnstedt
  7. "Effect of Reliability and Validity on Power of Statistical Tests," T. Anne Cleary, Robert L. Linn, and G. William Walster
  8. "Bivariate Agreement Coefficients for Reliability of Data," Klaus Krippendorff
  9. "Validity and the Multitrait-Multimethod Matrix," Robert P. Althauser and Thomas A. Heberlein
  10. "Validation of Reputational Leadership by the Multitrait-Multimethod Matrix," Gene F. Summers, Lauren H. Seiler, and Glenn Wiley

Part Three: Statistical Techniques
  11. "Statistics According to Bayes," Gudmund R. Iversen
  12. "Uncertainty Analysis Applied to Sociological Data," Doris R. Entwisle and Dennis Knepp
  13. "Multivariate Analysis for Attribute Data," James S. Coleman
  14. "Statistical Significance as a Decision Rule," G. William Walster and T. Anne Cleary

Part Four: Mathematical Sociology
  15. "Mathematical Formalization of Durkheim's Theory of Division of Labor," Kenneth C. Land
  16. "Status Dynamics," Thomas J. Fararo
  17. "Structure of Semantic Space," Andy B. Anderson

1971: Herbert L. Costner, ed.

Part One: Strategies of Data Production
  1. "Systematic Observation of Natural Social Phenomena," Albert J. Reiss, Jr.
  2. "Detection Theory and Problems of Psychosocial Discrimination," Darrell K. Adams and Z. Joseph Ulehla
  3. "Coding Responses to Open-Ended Questions," Kenneth C. W. Kammeyer and Julius Roth

Part Two: Measurement Error in Regression and Path Analysis
  4. "The Treatment of Unobservable Variables in Path Analysis," Robert M. Hauser and Arthur S. Goldberger
  5. "Robustness in Regression Analysis," George W. Bohrnstedt and T. Michael Carter
  6. "Techniques for Using Ordinal Measures in Regression and Path Analysis," Morgan Lyons

Part Three: Path and Process Models
  7. "Formal Theory," Kenneth C. Land
  8. "Key Variables," Phillip Bonacich and Kenneth D. Bailey
  9. "Coleman's Process Approach," Martin Jaeckel

Part Four: Association and Prediction of Variables
  10. "Integrated Approach to Measuring Association," Robert K. Leik and Walter R. Grove

11. "Continuities in Social Prediction," Karl Schuessler

1972: Herbert L. Costner, ed.
1. "Strategies for Meaningful Comparison," Ronald Schoenberg
2. "Unmeasured Variables in Linear Models for Panel Analysis," Otis Dudley Duncan
3. "Polythetic Reduction of Monothetic Property Space," Kenneth Bailey
4. "The Generation of Confidence: Evaluating Research Findings by Random Subsample Replication," Bernard M. Finifter
5. "Technique for Analyzing Overlapping Memberships," Phillip Bonacich
6. "Retest of a Measurement Model," Cynthia J. Flynn and Lewis F. Carter
7. "Using Monotone Regression to Estimate a Correlation Coefficient," Lawrence S. Mayer

1973–74: Herbert L. Costner, ed.
Prologue, Herbert L. Costner
1. "Some Issues in Sociological Measurement," David R. Heise
2. "Theta Reliability and Factor Scaling," David J. Armor
3. "Construction of Composite Measures by the Canonical-Factor-Regression Method," Michael Patrick Allen
4. "Approaches to the Interpretation of Relationships in the Multitrait-Multimethod Matrix," Duane F. Alwin
5. "Inferring Validity from the Multitrait-Multimethod Matrix: Another Assessment," Robert P. Althauser
6. "Correlation of Ratios or Difference Scores Having Common Terms," Glenn V. Fuguitt and Stanley Lieberson
7. "Alternative Approaches to Analysis-of-Variance Tables," Peter J. Burke and Karl Schuessler
8. "Hierarchical Models for Significance Tests in Multivariate Contingency Tables: An Exegesis of Goodman's Recent Papers," James A. Davis
9. "Questions About Attitude Survey Questions," Howard Schuman and Otis Dudley Duncan
10. "Problems of Statistical Estimation and Causal Inference in Time-Series Regression Models," Douglas A. Hibbs, Jr.
11. "Spectral Analysis and the Study of Social Change," Thomas F. Mayer and William Ray Arney
12. "Social Mobility Models for Heterogeneous Populations," Burton Singer and Seymour Spilerman

1975: David R. Heise, ed.
1. "Toward the Integration of Content Analysis and General Methodology," John Markoff, Gilbert Shapiro, and Sasha R. Weitman
2. "Cluster Analysis," Kenneth D. Bailey
3. "Scaling Replicated Conditional Rank-Order Data," Forrest W. Young
4. "Method for Classifying Interval-Scale and Ordinal-Scale Data," Kenneth R. Bryson and David P. Phillips
5. "Multiple Indicators and the Relationship Between Abstract Variables," Lawrence S. Mayer and Mary Sue Younger

1976: David R. Heise, ed.
1. "Local Structure in Social Networks," Paul W. Holland and Samuel Leinhardt
2. "Comparing Causal Models," David A. Specht and Richard D. Warren
3. "The Relationship Between Modified and Usual Multiple-Regression Approaches to the Analysis of Dichotomous Variables," Leo A. Goodman

4. "Analyzing Contingency Tables with Linear Flow Graphs," D. Systems and James A. Davis
5. "Predictive-Logic Approach to Causal Models of Qualitative Variates," David K. Hildebrand, James D. Laing, and Howard Rosenthal
6. "Effects of Grouping on Measures of Ordinal Association," Roland K. Hawkes
7. "Can We Find a Genuine Ordinal Slope Analogue?," H. M. Blalock, Jr.
8. "Using Assumptions of Linearity to Establish a Metric," Phillip Bonacich and Douglas Kirby
9. "Monotonic Regression Analysis for Ordinal Variables," Richard K. Leik
10. "Causal Models with Nominal and Ordinal Data," Richard K. Leik
11. "Rank-Sum Comparisons Between Groups," Stanley Lieberson

1977: David R. Heise, ed.
1. "The Epistemological Bases of Social Order: Toward Ethnoparadigm Analysis," Allen W. Imershein
2. "Estimation in Panel Models: Results on Pooling Cross-Sections and Time Series," Michael T. Hannan and Alice A. Young
3. "Assessing Reliability and Stability in Panel Models," Blair Wheaton, Bengt Muthén, Duane F. Alwin, and Gene F. Summers
4. "On Analyzing the Effects of Policy Interventions: Box-Jenkins and Box-Tiao Versus Structural Equation Models," Douglas A. Hibbs, Jr.
5. "Estimates for Differential Equation Models of Social Phenomena," Patrick Doreian and Norman P. Hummon
6. "Estimating Rates From Retrospective Questions," Aage B. Sørensen
7. "Network Time Series from Archival Records," Ronald S. Burt and Nan Lin
8. "An Examination of CONCOR and Related Methods for Blocking Sociometric Data," Joseph E. Schwartz
9. "Statistical Inference and Statistical Power in Applications of the General Linear Model," William T. Bielby and James R. Kluegel

1978: Karl F. Schuessler, ed.
1. "Understanding World Models," Nathan Keyfitz
2. "Forecasting Sociological Phenomena: Application of Box-Jenkins Methodology to Suicide Rates," Gideon Vigderhous
3. "Analyzing Political Participation Data with a MIMIC Model," David C. Stapleton
4. "The Allocation of Time Among Individuals," Christopher Winship
5. "Using Boolean Algebra to Analyze Overlapping Memberships," Phillip Bonacich
6. "Parametrizing Age, Period, and Cohort Effects: An Application to U.S. Delinquency Rates, 1964–1973," Thomas W. Pullum
7. "Measures of Association for Multiple Regression Models with Ordinal Predictor Variables," Lawrence S. Mayer and Jeffrey A. Robinson
8. "Multiple Regression with a Categorical, Interval-Level Control Variable: The Between-Groups Component," Robert H. Somers
9. "Tracing Members of a Panel: A 17-Year Follow-Up," Brian R. Clarridge, Linda L. Sheehy, and Taissa S. Hauser
10. "Statistical Analysis of Qualitative Variation," Alan Agresti and Barbara F. Agresti
11. "The Reliability of Variables Measured as the Number of Events in an Interval of Time," Paul D. Allison
12. "The Reliability of Products of Two Random Variables," George W. Bohrnstedt and Gerald Marwell

1979: Karl F. Schuessler, ed.

1. "Identification and Estimation of Age-Period-Cohort Models in the Analysis of Discrete Archival Data," Stephen E. Fienberg and William M. Mason
2. "Multiway Contingency Analysis with a Scaled Response or Factor," Otis Dudley Duncan and James A. McRae, Jr.
3. "On the Design Matrix Strategy in the Analysis of Categorical Data," Mark Evers and N. Krishnan Namboodiri
4. "A Note on Fitting and Interpreting Parameters in Models for Categorical Data," Stephen E. Fienberg
5. "The Utility of Systems of Simultaneous Logistic Response Equations," Stephen S. Brier
6. "Simultaneous Equation Models and Two-Stage Least Squares," John Fox
7. "Detection of Specification Errors in Linear Structural Equation Models," W. E. Saris, W. M. de Pijper, and P. Zegwaart
8. "Clustering on the Main Diagonal in Mobility Matrices," Burton Singer and Seymour Spilerman
9. "Approaches to the Censoring Problem in Analysis of Event Histories," Nancy Brandon Tuma and Michael T. Hannan
10. "The Assessment of 'No Opinion' in Attitude Surveys," Howard Schuman and Stanley Presser
11. "Some Problems of Inference from Chain Data," Bonnie H. Erickson
12. "A Note on Classifying Ordinal-Scale Data," Nan M. Laird
13. "Exploratory Data Analysis: An Introduction to Selected Methods," Samuel Leinhardt and Stanley S. Wasserman

1980: Karl F. Schuessler, ed.

1. "The Welfare Approach to Measuring Inequality," Joseph Schwartz and Christopher Winship
2. "The Continuing Debate over the Use of Ratio Variables: Facts and Fiction," Susan B. Long
3. "Measurement Models for Response Errors in Surveys: Issues and Applications," Duane F. Alwin and David J. Jackson
4. "Binary Variables and Index Construction," Jae-On Kim and James Rabjohn
5. "Assessing the Reliability of Linear Composites," Vernon L. Greene and Edward G. Carmines
6. "The Interpretation of Net Migration Rates," Stanley Lieberson
7. "Multidimensionality in Population Analysis," Nathan Keyfitz
8. "Modeling Macro Social Change," Kenneth C. Land
9. "Testing Key Hypotheses in Panel Analysis," Otis Dudley Duncan
10. "A Reexamination of Selection and Growth Processes in the Nonequivalent Control Group Design," David A. Kenny and Steven H. Cohen
11. "Maximum-Likelihood Estimation in Panel Studies with Missing Data," Margaret Mooney Marini, Anthony R. Olsen, and Donald B. Rubin
12. "When Can Interdependence in a Dynamic System of Qualitative Variables Be Ignored?" Nancy Brandon Tuma
13. "A Stochastic Model for Directed Graphs with Transition Rates Determined by Reciprocity," Stanley S. Wasserman
14. "Some Exploratory Methods for Modeling Mobility Tables and Other Cross-Classified Data," Robert M. Hauser
15. "The Measurement and Decomposition of Causal Effects in Nonlinear and Nonadditive Models," Ross M. Stolzenberg
16. "The Algebra of Blockmodeling," Phillip Bonacich and Maureen J. McConaghy
17. "The Application of Bayseian Techniques in Randomized Response," John D. Spurrier and W. J. Padgett

18. "Quantitative Coefficients for Selecting a Measure of Central Location," Jean D. Gibbons and Gordon R. Stavig

Selected References to Multiple Discriminant Analysis

HOEL, P. G. *Introduction to Mathematical Statistics.* 3rd ed. New York: Wiley, 1962.

KLECKA, WILLIAM R. *Discriminant Analysis.* Beverly Hills: Sage, 1980.

LOY, JOHN, W., JR. "Social Psychological Characteristics of Innovators." *American Sociological Review* (February 1969): 73–82.

RAO, C. R. *Advanced Statistical Methods in Biometric Research.* New York: Wiley, 1952.

RETTIG, SOLOMON. "Multiple Discriminant Analysis: An Illustration." *American Sociological Review* 29 (June 1964): 398–402.

RULON, PHILLIP J. "Distinctions Between Discriminant and Regression Analysis and a Geometric Interpretation of the Discriminant Function." *Harvard Educational Review* 21 (Spring 1951): 80–90.

TIEDEMAN, DAVID V. "The Utility of the Discriminant Function in Psychological and Guidance Investigations." *Harvard Educational Review* 21 (Spring 1951): 71–80.

Recent Trends

Recent trends in sociological methodology reported by Schuessler include:

1. Increasing use of the language of causal modeling.

2. Development of methods for analyzing categorical or qualitative data.

3. Increased application of statistical mathematics to theory building and theory testing.

4. Growing interest in methods for analyzing time data.

5. Building and testing structural equation theory.

6. Increasing dependence of theory building and theory testing on the high speed computer.*

Bohrnstedt has reviewed methodology employed by the social sciences generally over the past twenty-five years and concludes that five common themes can be distinguished:

1. All social science disciplines have moved from rather crude description to the development of a set of more or less precise mathematical models.

2. The social sciences have rather freely borrowed methods from one another.

3. All social science disciplines have moved from static to dynamic models.

4. As the disciplines have matured, the models have become increasingly complex.

5. The final commonality is the apparent failure of most models to do much more than account for the observed data in the sample on which the models were developed. Most models are rather precise mathematical descriptions of a set of observations bound by time and culture rather than powerful predictive instruments.**

---

* For a detailed looked at these trends see Karl F. Schuessler, "Quantitative Methodology in Sociology: The Last 25 Years," *American Behavioral Scientist* 23, no. 6 (July/August 1980): 835–60.

** George Bohrnstedt, "Social Science Methodology: The Past 25 Years," *American Behavioral Scientist* 23, no. 6 (July/August 1980): 781–87.

The concepts in this section are among those that commonly appear in the
sociological research writing found in major journals. The explanations given
are attempts to state as simply as possible what these concepts mean. References are given at the end of each concept to indicate research applications.
The aim is to provide the reader with understanding but not to formulate
operational procedures. This latter kind of information can be found in the
various statistical bibliographies cited previously.

Bayesian Methods: Bayesian Inference, Bayesian Statistics

Bayesians believe that scientists should qualify their opinions as probabilities
before performing their experiments, do the experiment so as to collect data
bearing on these opinions, and then use a Bayesian theorem formally to
revise prior probabilities to yield new posterior probabilities. Posterior probabilities are scientists' revised opinions in the light of information provided
by the data. That is the key idea behind all Bayesian methods.

Statistically, a Bayesian inference is simply a conditional probability. It
gives the probability of a cause (hypothesis) on condition that the effect
(evidence) has occurred. The usual ordering of reasoning is reversed: from
effect to cause rather than the other way around. In its emphasis on subjective
beliefs, a Bayesian inference has the distinctive characteristic of refining one's
probability.

Bayesian methods are seldom used in sociology, although they have been
used advantageously in economics and psychology. A Bayesian approach
would seem to have value to sociology whenever the social analyst works
backward from effect to causes, as indicated in the method of analytical
induction. In this method the cause must be present whenever the effect is
present; it must be absent whenever the effect is absent. The body of statistics
dealing with Bayesian inferences are called Bayesian statistics. Such statistical
methods utilize prior information (objective or subjective) about parameters.
The term has also been applied to statistical methods based on the concept
of subjective or personal probability.

References

FOSCHI, MARTHA, and FOSCHI, RICARDO, "Bayesian Model for Performance Expecta-
tions." *Social Psychology Quarterly* 42 (1979): 232–42.
LINDLEY, D. V. *Introduction to Probability and Statistics from a Bayesian Viewpoint*,
parts 1 and 2. Cambridge: Cambridge University Press, 1965.
PHILLIPS, LAWRENCE D. *Bayesian Statistics for Social Scientists.* London: Thomas
Nelson and Sons, 1973.
SCHMITT, SAMUEL A. *Measuring Uncertainty: an Elementary Introduction to Bayesian
Statistics.* Reading, Mass.: Addison-Wesley, 1969.
SCHUESSLER, KARL F. "Prologue." *In Sociological Methodology 1980.* San Francisco:
Jossey-Bass, 1981.

Canonical Correlation

The canonical correlation is the maximum correlation between two sets of independent and dependent variables. It can be compared to the simpler coefficient of multiple correlation, which provides the maximum correlation between a number of independent variables with a single dependent variable.

The basic idea of canonical correlation is that, through least squares analysis, two linear composites are formed, one for the independent variables, X_J, and one for the dependent variables, Y_N. The correlation between these two composites is the canonical correlation R_c. The square of the canonical correlation, R_c^2, is an estimate of the variance shared by the two composites.

References

KERLINGER, FRED N., and PEDHAZUR, ELAZAR J. *Multiple Regression in Behavior Research.* New York: Holt, Rinehart, & Winston, 1973. Pp. 341–49.

LEVINE, MARK S. *Canonical Analysis and Factor Comparison.* Beverly Hills, Calif.: Sage, 1977.

REEVE, VANNEMAR, and PAMPEL, FRED C. "The American Perception of Class and Status," *American Sociological Review* 42 (June 1977): 432–37.

Cluster Analysis

A method of analysis in which the researcher identifies items that "cluster" together, as shown by item intercorrelation, is called *cluster analysis.* For example, we know that people choose jobs because of such factors as the ability to exercise originality and creativity and to work with people and the desire to earn a substantial sum of money and accumulate property. If various questions about job characteristics were posed to respondents, the researcher might find that items would fall into three general clusters. Each cluster would include items that are more highly intercorrelated with others in their cluster than with items outside that cluster.

A correlation matrix can be developed and rows and columns of the matrix rearranged so that the more highly intercorrelated items form triangular "bunches" at different points along the diagonal. In this way, the nature of interacting forces can be revealed with precision.

References

ANDERBERG, MICHAEL R. *Cluster Analysis for Applications.* New York: Academic Press, 1973.

EVERITT, BRIAN. *Cluster Analysis.* London: Heinemann Educational Books, 1974.

LOETHER, HERMAN J., and McTAVISH, DONALD G. *Descriptive Statistics for Sociologists: An Introduction.* Boston: Allyn & Bacon, 1974. Pp. 343–48.

Cohort Analysis

A cohort refers to persons of similar age or other selected characteristics matched so that the defining characteristic can be held constant. A cohort analysis refers to the study of one or more cohorts in which designated variables are assessed.

Such analysis is very valuable for occupational and industrial sociology because cohorts in the labor force are studied both in cross-sectional and longitudinal designs. Population, health sciences, criminology, gerontology, and many other fields frequently use cohort analysis.

References

GLENN, NORVAL D. *Cohort Analysis.* Beverly Hills, Calif.: Sage, 1977.

LANE, ANGELA. "The Occupational Achievement Process, 1940–1949: A Cohort Analysis." *American Sociological Review* 40 (August 1975): 472–82.

RILEY, MATILDA W. "Aging and Cohort Succession: Interpretations and Misinterpretations." *Public Opinion Quarterly* 37 (1973): 35–49.

Decomposition of a Dependent Variable

Many social variables are composites. For example, population growth is the sum of natural increase and net migration; each of the latter may be further decomposed. Natural increase can be calculated as births minus deaths; net migration is the difference between in- and out-migration. When such decomposition is possible, it is of interest (1) to compute the relative contributions of the components to variation in the composite variable and (2) to ascertain how causes affecting the composite variables are transmitted through the respective components.

Reference

DUNCAN, OTIS DUDLEY. "Path Analysis: Sociological Examples." *American Journal of Sociology* 72 (July 1966).

Decomposition of Effects in Causal Modeling

It is important to interpret patterns of direct and indirect causation in path models and other structural equation models. Such interpretation helps answer questions of the form: "How does variable X affect variable Y?" "How much does mechanism Z contribute to the effect of X or Y?" "Does mechanism Z contribute as much to explaining the effect of X on Y in population A as in population B?"

Causal modeling usually entails decomposing the total effect of the antecedent variable into direct and indirect components. The direct effect of one variable on another is simply that part of the total effect not transmitted via intervening variables. Indirect effects are those parts of a variable's total effect transmitted or mediated by variables intervening between the cause and effect interest in a model. Decomposition here means calculating total, direct, and indirect effects in multiequation models.

References

ALWIN, DUANE F., and HAUSER, ROBERT M. "The Decomposition of Effects in Pattern Analysis." *American Sociological Review* 40 (February 1975): 37–47.

PARCEL, TOBY L. "Race, Regional Labor Markets, and Earnings." *American Sociological Review* 44 (April 1979): 262–79.

SCHLAIFER, ROBERT. "The Relay Assembly Test Room: An Alternative Statistical Interpretation." *American Sociological Review* 45 (December, 1980): 995–1005. See esp. p. 997, "Importance of Explanatory Variables and Decomposition of R^2.

Discriminant (Function) Analysis

The discriminant function was originally proposed by R. A. Fisher in "The Use of Multiple Measurements in Taxonomic Problems," *Annals of Eugenics* 7 (1936): 179–88. It was designed to aid in the classification of an individual observation into one of two groups. The discriminant function has been defined as a linear combination of a set of n variables that will classify into two different classes (or groups) the events or items for which the measurements of the n variables are available, and will do so with the smallest possible proportion of misclassifications. It is useful, for example, in the problem of classifying persons into two social groups, such as culturally assimilated or culturally alienated.

References

KLECKA, WILLIAM R. *Discriminant Analysis.* Beverly Hills, Calif., Sage, 1978.

VAN DE GEER, JOHN P. *Introduction to Multivariate Analysis for the Social Sciences.* San Francisco: Freeman, 1971. Pp. 243–72.

VANNEMAN, REEVE, and PAMPEL, FRED C. "The American Perception of Class and Status." *American Sociological Review* 42 (June 1977): 422–37.

Multiple Discriminant (Function) Analysis

The discriminant function technique has been extended by Fisher to include more than two groups. See R. A. Fisher, "The Statistical Utilization of Multiple Measurements," *Annals of Eugenics* 13 (1938): 376–86. With the computer it is now possible to study a large number of groups simultaneously across many variables.

Multiple discriminant function analysis provides three kinds of information:

1. It determines whether in fact certain groups are really distinct with respect to selected characteristics.
2. It tells on what factors the groups may be best discriminated.
3. It indicates whether an individual is like other individuals in the group to which he has been assigned. That is, it indicates the extent to which individuals have been theoretically misclassified.

References

VAN DE GEER, JOHN P. *Introduction to Multivariate Analysis for the Social Sciences.* San Francisco: Freeman, 1971. Pp. 267–70.

See also Selected References to Multiple Discriminant Analysis on page 261 of this book.

Dummy Variable: Dummy Variable Regression Analysis

Dummy variables are dichotomous variables employed when the researcher is working with categorical or nominal variables. The binary nature of the computer is most happy with dummy variables that indicate the presence (scored 1) or absence (scored 0) of a certain characteristic for each individual respondent. For qualitative variables it is especially useful. For example, marital status can be coded using four dummy variables.

Marital Status	Dummy Variables
Currently married	1 = yes; 0 = no.
Never married	1 = yes; 0 = no.
Widowed	1 = yes; 0 = no.
Separated	1 = yes; 0 = no.
Divorced	(A pattern of 0, 0, 0, 0 would indicate that a person is divorced. No dummy variable needed.)

If a person were widowed, rather than having a score of 3, he would have four scores, one on each of the four dummy variables: 0010.

These dummy variables are all included in the usual multiple regression analysis. When a zero score appears for an individual on one of the dummy variables, that is the regression weight placed in the regression equation. Otherwise, the regression weight becomes the value assigned by the researcher to a particular status.

Dummy variables can be used as independent variables in standard score or raw-score form, and they can be used in path analysis. Dummy variables are useful if a researcher wishes to "score" specific combinations of values of variables to search for expected statistical interaction in a multiple regression equation when otherwise the model would assume an additive relationship among variables. These efforts are called *dummy variable regression analysis*.

References

Koo, Hagen, and Houg, Doo-Seung. "Class and Income Inequality in Korea." *American Sociological Review* 45 (August 1980): 610–26.

Loether, Herman J., and McTavish, Donald G. *Descriptive Statistics for Sociologists*. Boston: Allyn & Bacon, 1974. Pp. 333–34.

Rindfuss, Ronald R.; Bumpass, Larry; and St. John, Craig. "Education and Fertility: Implications for the Roles Women Occupy." *American Sociological Review* 45 (June 1980): 431–47.

Log-Linear Modeling and Analysis

A recent development in contingency table analysis, log-linear modeling refers to new techniques for analyzing multidimensional tables. In the past, purely categorical data have been difficult to analyze, especially in the construction of multivariate models. Leo A. Goodman has said log-linear models not only help one find bivariate relationships and higher-order interactions in complex tables but can be viewed as analogous to the analysis of simultaneous equations. The promise is that the exploration of polls and surveys may have caught up with causal and path analysis. Some researchers caution that the same concepts they employ in studying interval-level data may not apply unambiguously in interpreting cross-classifications of categorical data.

Essential to log-linear modeling is building a model for the expected frequences in a multidimensional population cross-classification by introducing so-called main and interaction effects. It is sometimes more convenient to work with the natural logarithms of the expected frequencies. A model is to be described by the set of "fitted marginals" tables used in estimating the expected frequencies under the model.

References

GOODMAN, LEO A. "Causal Analysis of Data from Panel Studies and Other Kinds of Surveys." *American Journal of Sociology* 79 (March 1973): 1135–1191.
———. *Analyzing Qualitative Categorical Data: Log-Linear Models and Latent Structure Analysis.* Cambridge, Mass. Abt Books, 1978.
KNOKE, DAVID, and BURKE, PETER J. *Log-Linear Models.* Beverly Hills, Calif.: Sage, 1980.
REYNOLDS, H. T. "Some Comments on the Causal Analysis of Surveys with Log-Linear Models." *American Journal of Sociology* 83 (July 1977): 127–43. See excellent bibliography.
SWAFFORD, MICHAEL. "Three Parametric Techniques for Contingency Table Analysis." *American Sociological Review* 45 (August 1980): 664–90.

Markov Chains

Markov chains are models predicting changes taking place over time. Imagine a problem predicting the outcomes over time as some persons move from job to job while others stay on the same job. When the data consist of a chain of M-1 turnover tables (*see* Turnover Tables), it is natural to wonder whether the observed frequencies might be accounted for by a simple probability law. Markov's law (simple) would account for a stationary, but not necessarily equal, division of movers and stayers toward the end of the time sequence. A Markov chain might be found for all kinds of change behavior stated in dichotomous terms: those who change their minds before election day, those who never change their minds; those whose morale changes daily, those whose morale remains fixed; and so on.

References

BLUMEN, I.; KOGAN, M.; and MCCARTHY, P. J. *The Industrial Mobility of Labor as a Probability Process.* Ithaca, N.Y.: Cornell University Press, 1955.
SURESH, L., KONDA, and STEWMAN, SHELBY. "An Opportunity Labor Demand Model and Markovian Labor Supply Models Comparative Tests in an Organization." *American Sociological Review* 45 (April 1980): 276–301. See excellent bibliography.

Matrix Algebra

This branch of mathematics provides one of the most powerful tools for conceptualizing and analyzing psychological, sociological, and educational research data. Matrix algebra is a system of notations that relates to vectors and matrices using sums, sums of squares, and cross products. The need for such calculations occurs repeatedly in multivariate analysis. Matrix algebra notation and thinking fit in nicely with the conceptualization of computer programming and use.

References

KERLINGER, FRED N., and PEDHAZUR, ELAZAR J. *Multiple Regression in Behavioral Research.* New York: Holt, Rinehart, & Winston, 1973. Pp. 454–66.
VAN DE GREER, JOHN P., *Introduction to Multivariate Analysis for the Social Sciences.* San Francisco: W. H. Freeman, 1971. See Part I, Introduction to Matrix Algebra, 3–82.

Multicollinearity Problem

Multicollinearity is a term used to describe a common situation in multiple regression analysis where there is such a high degree of correlation between two or more explanatory (independent) variables that it is impossible to measure their individual effects on the explained (dependent) variable. In a matrix many important theoretical variables are highly intercorrelated, and the empirical associations among them may be underestimated due to random measurement errors. It is suggested that a correction of this multicollinearity problem will require a combination of large samples and good measurement.

Reference

BLALOCK, JR., HUBERT M. "Measurement and Conceptualization Problems: The Major Obstacle to Integrating Theory and Research." *American Sociological Review* 44 (December 1979): 881–94.

Smallest Space Analysis

A mapping technique developed by James C. Lingoes and Louis F. Guttman that depicts social phenomena in graphic terms is called smallest space analysis. The social objects are graphed according to their proximity on selected social characteristics. One-, two-, and three-dimensional space solutions may be applied.

References

LAUMANN, EDWARD O. "The Social Structure of Religious and Ethno-Religious Groups in a Metropolitan Community." *American Sociological Review* 34 (April 1969): 182–97.
———, and MARSDEN, PETER V. "The Analysis of Oppositional Structures in Political Elites: Identifying Collective Actors." *American Sociological Review* 44 (October 1979): 713–32.
———, and GUTTMAN, LOUIS. "The Relative Associational Contiguity of Occupations in an Urban Setting." *American Sociological Review* 31 (April 1966): 169–78.
LINGOES, JAMES C. *The Guttman-Lingoes Non-metric Program Series.* New York: Academic Press, 1973. Or see "An IBM-7070 Program for Guttman-Lingoes Smallest Space Analysis." *Behavioral Science* 10 (April 1965): 183–84.
MORTIMER, JOHN T. "Patterns of Intergenerational Occupational Movements: A Smallest-Space Analysis." *American Journal of Sociology* 79 (March 1974): 1278–99.

Stochastic Processes

In the study of random processes one is generally concerned with sequences of random variables with special reference to their interdependence and limiting behavior. Random processes are governed at least in part by some random mechanism and may be expressed by a corresponding mathematical model.

Examples of random processes in physical nature are provided by the growth of populations such as bacterial colonies. Similarly, stochastic probability processes may be considered as models of human mobility, population growth, and migration.

References

FARARO, THOMAS J. "Stochastic Processes." In *Sociological Methodology, 1969,* edited by Edgar F. Borgatta and George W. Bohrnstedt. San Francisco: Jossey-Bass, 1970.

McGINNIS, ROBERT. "A Stochastic Model of Social Mobility." *American Sociological Review* 33 (October 1968): 712–22.

PARZEN, EMANUEL. *Stochastic Processes.* San Francisco: Holden-Day, 1962.

Structural Equations and Structural Equation Models

Structural equations are equations that relate a dependent variable to various structural components believed to have causal influence on the dependent variable. Various *structural equation models* may be developed. Each "dependent" variable must be regarded explicitly as completely determined by some combination of variables in the system. In problems in which complete determination by measured variables does not hold, a residual variable uncorrelated with other determining variables must be introduced.

For example, let us posit a stratification system in which rewards assure the placement and motivation of persons in various occupational positions within a social structure. Rewards may include prestige, income, leisure, and other amenities. Prestige may be designated dependent variable X_3 and other rewards such as income, leisure, and amenities may be designated as a second dependent variable X_4. Now suppose we postulate the theorem that the rated functional importance of an Occupation X_1 and Required Skill X_2 will deliver appropriate rewards of prestige, income, and leisure, and will draw the aspiring incumbent into an achieved status position.

Using X to stand for the standard score of a given variable, one could express the relationship as a path of influence in which:

$$\text{Prestige } X_3 = p_{31}X_1 + p_{32}X_2 + p_{3a}X_a$$

$$\text{Other}$$
$$\text{Rewards } X_4 = p_{41}X_1 + p_{42}X_2 + p_{4b}X_b$$

These structural equations correspond to multiple regression equations. In these equations, p is a path coefficient* and the subscripts indicate the variable it connects. X_a and X_b are included to reflect variables external to Prestige (X_3) and Income (X_4) and measurement errors that may influence

---

* Path coefficients are identical to beta coefficients in the standard multiple regression equation.

the dependent variables. These are sometimes called *residual variables*. This is a "fully" recursive model because all the possible one-way arrows are drawn between four explicit variables: X_1, X_2, X_3, and X_4.

A recursive system refers to a system of equations (as above) in which correlations between any pair of variables can be written in terms of paths leading from common antecedent variables. In path diagrams this is represented by using one-way arrows leading from each determining variable to each variable dependent upon it.

Nonrecursive systems involve instantaneous reciprocal action of variables; thus, no path of influence can be plotted for such systems.

References

BERK, RICHARD A.; LENIHAW, KENNETH J.; and ROSSI, PETER H. "Crime and Poverty: Some Experimental Evidence from Ex-Offenders." *American Sociological Review* 45 (October 1980): 766–86.

An example of a nonrecursive model.

DUNCAN, OTIS DUDLEY. "Path Analysis: Sociological Examples." *American Journal of Sociology* 72 (July 1966): 1–12.
———. *Introduction to Structural Equation Models.* New York: Academic Press, 1975.
GOLDBERGER, ARTHUR S., and DUNCAN, OTIS DUDLEY, eds. *Structural Equation Models in the Social Sciences.* New York: Academic Press, 1973.

Many different applications.

HODGE, ROBERT W., and TREIMAN, DONALD J. "Social Participation and Social Status." *American Sociological Review* 33 (October 1968): 722–40.
JUDD, CHARLES M., and MILBURN, MICHAEL M. "The Structure of Attitude Systems in the General Public: Comparisons of a Structural Equations Model." *American Sociological Review* 45 (August 1980): 627–43.

An example of a fully recursive model.

LOETHER, HERMAN J., and McTAVISH, DONALD G. *Descriptive Statistics for Sociologists.* Boston: Allyn & Bacon, 1974. Pp. 306–40.

Turnover Tables (Panel Analysis)

When the same persons (panel) are cross-classified on the same dichotomy, y, at two points in time, the result is a 2×2 turnover table; when the same persons are cross-classified on two dichotomies, y and x, at two points in time, the result is a 4×4 turnover table; when the same persons are cross-classified on the same dichotomy at three or more (m) points in time, the result is a chain of m-1 turnover tables.

Reference

SCHUESSLER, KARL. "Quantitative Methodology in Sociology." *American Behavioral Scientist* 23 (July/August 1980): 850–52.

part 4

Selected Sociometric Scales and Indexes

THERE are literally thousands of scales and indexes to measure social variables. Social scientists have often elected to construct new measures even when scales of high reliability and validity have been available. This practice is wasteful of time, energy, and money. In addition, it makes replication and accumulation of research findings difficult if not impossible. The selection of scales to be found in this handbook was based on such criteria as validity, reliability, and utility. The variables most commonly used in social measurement were studied and measures for them were sought. Those with the highest reliability and validity were selected. It is hoped that this handbook will encourage greater use of these scales or stimulate the search for better ones.

In general, three groups of variable factors need to be observed and measured in any research design that seeks to test a basic hypothesis or social relationship.

First, there is the dependent variable, the effect we wish to observe and describe.

Second, there is the independent variable (or variables) that has been designated as the causal factor. Sometimes this factor must be broken down into the component parts that operate more or less as a unit pattern.

Third, there are intervening or other independent variables that must be controlled lest they obscure the relationship we wish to measure by use of experimental design.

Sociometric scales have been constructed in substantial numbers to permit quantitative description of these factors in human relations.

Three areas of social measurement can be identified. These are:

1. Psychometric and social psychological scales: psychological measurements including intelligence scales, personality tests and scales, attitude tests and scales.

    Examples of these scales that are included in this part are the Minnesota Multiphasic Personality Inventory, the Authoritarian Personality (F) Scale, Morale and Job Satisfaction Scales, as well as attitude scales to measure leisure satisfactions; community attitudes, achievement orientation, and alienation.

2. Demographic Scales: measurements of the forms or results of social behavior in large units such as the community, state, or nation.

    Examples in this part include community rating scales, community services activity, citizen political activity, and a community solidarity index.

3. Sociometric Scales: measurements of the social structure and process.

    Examples in this part include sociometric tests to measure informal friendship constellations, measurements of social participation, of social distance, and of group cohesiveness. Other scales are provided to assess marital adjustment and group dimensions. The measurement of social status is of such crucial importance that a number of scales are included, such as *Duncan's Socioeconomic Index, Siegel's Prestige Scores, Nam-Powers Socioeconomic Status Scores, Hollingshead's Two Factor Index of Social Position, Alba Edwards' Socioeconomic Scale, Warner's Revised Occupational Scale for Social Class.*

If you do not find a scale that fits your particular research interest, consult the inventory of measures used by researchers represented in the *American Sociological Review* during 1965–80. This inventory has been placed in section M of part 4. Introducing this inventory is a listing of major sources for scale information and appraisal. One very important source are the occupational, political, and social psychological scales carefully selected and appraised by John P. Robinson and his co-workers at the Institute of Social Research of the University of Michigan. A complete listing is shown on pages 550–60.

Also presented in part 4 (m.6) is the list of attitude scales from Marvin E. Shaw and Jack M. Wright, *Scales for the Measurement of Attitudes* (New York: McGraw-Hill, 1967). The complete scale can be found in their book.

Scale construction yields four types of scales: the *nominal* scale, consisting simply of distinguishable categories with no implication of "more" or "less"; the *ordinal* scale, on which positions can be identified in a rank order with no implication as to the distance between positions; the *interval* scale, which has equal distance between any two adjacent positions on the continuum; and the *ratio* scale, which has not only equal intervals but an absolute zero.

The ideal scale is a ratio scale, but with the possible exception of the procedures for measuring certain psychophysical phenomena, none of the measurement techniques currently used fits the requirements for a ratio scale. The nominal scale permits neither rank ordering nor a metric scale. It is so elemental as a classification scheme that such scales are generally regarded as first approximations toward the quantification of a social variable. The result is that ordinal and interval scales are the most frequent types in use. There is considerable disagreement over whether an ordinal or interval scale provides the most appropriate model for social data. Some writers have taken the view that few, if any, of the techniques now in use provide data that can be considered appropriate to more than ordinal scales. Others believe that various types of scales may properly be treated as conforming to interval scales. Still others have taken the position that, although most of the measurements used do not go beyond ordinal scales, little harm is done in applying statistics to them that are appropriate to interval scales.

The result is that statistics appropriate to interval scales continue to be widely used in the analysis of social data whether the assumptions are met or not. However, there is also an increasing use of statistics that are specifically appropriate to ordinal scales. The statistical tools included in part 3 of the handbook are for the use of the ordinal and interval scales included in this section.

The selection of a good scale involves weighing a number of criteria. Frequency of use is one useful criterion for choice of a scale because of the possibility of maximizing accumulated research in the test of hypotheses. In the selection of scales for the revised edition this frequency criterion has been utilized. However, it is not the only determinant. Frequency can be misleading. New and better scales are constantly appearing. Moreover, use of a scale by others does not guarantee that they have chosen the "best" scale as described by rigorous criteria. For this reason some of the scales selected for this section may not be high on frequency count, but it is believed that they are the scales the researcher should use *now*. The most important single consideration is validity. Does the scale measure what it purports to measure? How much and what kind of evidence is available? Does the scale fit the problem selected for study?

Other considerations include its reliability, its precision, its simplicity and ease of administration. In recent years there has been considerable emphasis on unidimensionality. The Guttman technique enables the researcher to identify and construct scales of a single dimension. This may be very important in increasing the precision and predictability of a given variable. However, two qualifications must be kept in mind. Such a scale may not be the most effective either for measuring attitudes toward complex objects or for making predictions about behavior in relation to such objects. It must also be remembered that a given scale may be unidimensional for one group of individuals but not for another.

The scales assembled in this part include those constructed by arbitrary or judgmental ranking, by item analysis techniques, by Thurstone's equal-appearing interval method, by Guttman's technique of scale analysis, and by factor analysis. Regardless of the method used in construction, what the researcher seeks is the scale that best fits his problem, has the highest reliability and validity, is precise, and is relatively easy to apply.[1] When he has made his selection he must be aware of the statistical techniques he may subsequently apply. Generally, he will be using nonparametric statistics for ordinal scales and parametric statistics for interval scales and for those ordinal scales that do not deviate too far from the assumptions of randomness and normal distribution.

Note

1. For an excellent discussion of these criteria, see Paul F. Lazarsfeld and Morris Rosenberg, *The Language of Social Research* (Glencoe, Ill.: Free Press, 1955): Hans Zeisel, *Say It with Figures,* 5th ed., rev. (New York: Harper, 1968), pp. 76–102. Cf. George W. Bohrnstedt, "A Quick Method for Determining the Reliability and Validity of Multiple-Item Scales," *American Sociological Review* 34 (August 1969): 542–48. For a critique of Likert, Thurstone, and Guttman scales see Nan Lin, *Foundations of Social Research* (New York: McGraw-Hill, 1976), pp. 182–192.

Social Status

Social class or status is one of the most important variables in social research. The socioeconomic position of a person affects his or her chances for education, income, occupation, marriage, health, friends, and even life expectancy. The variable has proved difficult to measure in a pluralistic, equalitarian, and fluid society such as exists in the United States. Nevertheless, many researchers have tried to identify the social strata and measure variables associated with them. Nearly 30 percent of all research articles in major sociological journals are devoted to social stratification. Occupation has been shown to be the best single predictor of social status, and overall occupational prestige ratings have been found to be highly stable. A number of factors act in close relationship between occupation and social status. Both individual income and educational attainment are known to be correlated with occupational ranks. Education is a basis for entry into many occupations, and for most persons, income is derived from occupation. House type and dwelling area constitute other highly correlated factors.

Seven scales are presented here for the researcher's choice. They vary in length and in the number of factors included in the scale.

1. O. D. Duncan's Socioeconomic Index
2. Siegel's (NORC) Prestige Scores
3. Treiman's Standard International Prestige Scale
4. Nam-Powers Socioeconomic Status Scores
5. August B. Hollingshead's Two Factor Index of Social Position
6. The Revised Occupational Rating Scale from Warner, Meeker, and Eell's Index of Status Characteristics.
7. Alba M. Edwards' Social-Economic Grouping of Occupations

Of the seven, the standard Duncan Socioeconomic Index is most widely used and is generally considered to be superior for most survey and large-sample situations. It takes into account income, education, and occupational prestige. Siegel's (NORC) Prestige Scores are based on respondents' subjective rankings to establish the standing of a large number of occupations. It represents an effort to secure a "pure" prestige rating. Treiman has a prestige scale that is superior for studying international comparisons of occupational status.

Nam-Powers, which is based on the 1970 U.S. census, has used socioeconomic status scores for occupations listed in that census. Scores are based on average levels of education and income for U.S. males and females in 1970. Researchers have the option of choosing the Nam-Powers Socioeconomic Scores if they wish to employ a measurement without prestige weights. A correlation of .97 is reported between the Duncan Socioeconomic Index and Nam-Powers Socioeconomic Status scores.

Hollingshead's Two Factor Index of Social Position is based on occupation and education. The occupation scale differentiates among kinds of professionals and the size and economic strength of business. The seven-point educational scale is premised upon the assumption that men and women who possess similar educations will tend to have similar tastes and similar attitudes and will exhibit similar behavior patterns. The Hollingshead and Duncan indices have been shown to be moderately correlated. When they differ it is usually because Duncan has had to use one of the grosser census categories. Researchers concerned especially about the professional and business personnel in their sample may elect Hollingshead's index.

Choose the Warner, Meeker, and Eell's Occupational Rating Scale if a short scale is desired. This seven-point occupation scale is probably the most sophisticated short classification available. Occupation is one measure in the Index of Status Characteristics. Other measures include source of income, house type, and dwelling area. If these data are available, somewhat greater precision can be obtained. The scale provides scores ranging from 12 to 84, but occupations are grouped into 7 classifications. The scale is comparable to Edwards' socioeconomic groupings, but the Warner scale obtained greater rigor by increased homogeneity of its classifications.

Choose Edwards' socioeconomic grouping if a relatively broad classification is satisfactory for your problem. This grouping makes it possible to use the U.S. census for many kinds of comparative purposes. This nominal scale has been used widely in research on occupational mobility and occupational trends generally. The most often cited criticisms of the Edwards' classifications concern the lack of homogeneity of the categories and the weak scale properties of hierarchical grouping.

Two questions concern the researcher: What is the relative validity of the available social status scales? Can social status be regarded as unidimensional and measurable by a single socioeconomic index? Some tentative answers are possible.

THE RELATIVE VALIDITY OF SOCIAL STATUS SCALES

The researcher will probably find that the problem under study indicates a choice among Duncan's SEI, Siegel's (NORC) Prestige Scores, and Nam-Powers Socioeconomic Status Scores. A summary of the relative measures is shown.

The small range of possible score values marks the Hollingshead Two Factor Index of Social Position, Warner's Index of Status Characteristics,

Duncan's SEI	Siegel's prestige scores	Nam-Powers socioeconomic status scores
Combines education, income, and prestige in a multi-item index.	Prestige index only.	Combines education, income, and occupation in a multi-item index.
Provides a composite socio-economic and prestige measure.	Provides a direct subjective measure of prestige.	Provides a direct, objective measurement of SES.
Underrates clergymen, farmers, and certain blue-collar workers (e.g., machinists, carpenters); overrates entertainers, newspaper personnel, and sanitation workers.	Respondents who judged occupations biased some scores because of respondents' own status and familiarity with various occupations in the middle of the status scale.	Will underrate some occupations and overrate others where income and education are not principal factors in social status.
Provides scores for men only.	Provides scores for men only.	Provides scores for men and women.

and Edwards' Social-Economic Grouping of Occupations. As the range of possible score values decreases, the scales seem to approach what should be called ordinal scales—in contrast to the interval scales of Duncan, Siegel, and Nam-Powers. This reduction of range blunts the precision of coding and the validity of any given score, but there is no denying that limited-range scales are easier to code and manipulate statistically.

Specific problems beset all current measures. Haug has said that all of the major occupational stratification schemes indicated in the scales presented have a common parent in government census classification: "Given that occupations provide the best or at least the most feasible single indicator of relative standing in a societal system, the problem still remains of defining them, deciding on the most valid way to order them, and determining the most theoretically sound way to group and utilize them."[1]

Haug elaborates on this issue by pointing out that in the framework of the Weberian dimensions of class, status, and power, researchers developing methods of ordering occupations hierarchically have selected the first two dimensions as guidelines, but have not always kept them conceptually distinct. There is, moreover, a neglect of the power dimension. Updating is constantly needed because changes are constantly jeopardizing validity of the measures. Haug pleads that "overcoming measurement shortcomings in the fundamental sociological concept of stratification calls for top scientific priority for the whole discipline."[2] Haug and Sussman mention the need for a valid index based on the theoretical distinction between class (economic position) and social status (prestige) and adapted to current structural realities.[3] They express concern over the changes in income and education in various age cohorts since the construction of the scales. Nevertheless, remarkable stability in occupational stratification has been reported by Robert W. Hodge, Paul M.

Siegel, and Peter H. Rossi, who found only small changes in prestige ratings and conclude that "there have been no substantial changes in occupational prestige in the United States since 1925."[4]

These reassuring facts about stability do not resolve some difficulties that are inherent in the differing social repute assigned to education and income. Because status variables are only loosely intertwined, the vast majority of individuals in modern societies are able to advance some legitimate claims to recognition and the other rewards of society. Those with little education may still achieve ample incomes, and those with modest incomes may land a prestigious job. At the moment the only way to weigh the merits of a scale is for the researcher to examine the data on occupations among his or her respondents and compare the categories incorporated in the scales.

The researcher is urged to consider the second question: Can socioeconomic status be considered unidimensional? Caplow and Hatt say no;[5] Hodge goes still further and urges a multidimensional approach, claiming that different indicators of social participation and psychological well-being are in fact associated with different indicators of socioeconomic status. "Any attempt to combine these indicators—educational attainment, occupational pursuit, family income or occupational origins—into a single index of socioeconomic status will prove unsatisfactory because its component parts have different consequences for the same variable."[6]

Researchers have options. Regression, factor analysis, and path analysis all offer an opportunity to use socioeconomic characteristics as independent variables when seeking correlations with a dependent variable. When appropriate, the "best" indexes of social status should be utilized. With all their shortcomings, there is good evidence that the socioeconomic indexes described in this section are among the most valid and useful scales used as sociological instruments. If your problem so indicates, employ them; they will permit your research findings to be cumulative and therefore valuable to the advancement of social knowledge.

Notes

1. Marie R. Haug, "Measurement in Social Stratification," *Annual Review of Sociology* 3 (1977): 73.

2. Ibid., p. 75. See the brief statement of this article under the Bibliography of Assessments.

3. Marie R. Haug and Marvin B. Sussman, "The Indiscriminate State of Social Class Measurement," *Social Forces* 49 (June 1971): 549–63. See the commentary by Hollingshead, defending his index, on pp. 563–67.

4. Robert W. Hodge, Paul M. Siegel, and Peter H. Rossi, "Occupational Prestige in the United States, 1925–1963," *American Journal of Sociology* 70 (November 1964): 296.

5. Theodore Caplow, *Sociology of Work* (Minneapolis: University of Minnesota Press, 1954), pp. 33–57; Paul K. Hatt, "Occupation and Social Stratification," *American Journal of Sociology* 55 (May 1950): 538–43.

6. Robert W. Hodge, "Social Integration, Psychological Well-Being, and their SES Correlates," in *Social Stratification: Research and Theory for the 1970's,* ed. E. O. Laumann (Indianapolis: Bobbs-Merrill, 1970), pp. 182–206.

ASSESSMENTS OF STATUS SCALES

HALLER, ARCHIBALD O., and BILLS, DAVID B. "Occupational Prestige Hierarchies: Theory and Evidence." *Contemporary Sociology* 8 (September 1979): 721–34.

Excellent review of Treiman's Standard International Occupational Prestige Scale; brief history of prestige measurement; discussion of prestige hierarchies; good bibliography.

HAUG, MARIE R. "Measurement in Social Stratification." *Annual Review of Sociology* 3 (1977): 51–77.

Reviews Hollingshead, Duncan, Siegel, Canadian and British measures, Treiman, and Edwards. Critical judgment is excellent.

HAUSER, ROBERT M., and FEATHERMAN, DAVID L. *The Process of Stratification: Trends and Analysis.* New York: Academic Press, 1977.

Excellent analysis of Duncan, Siegel, and Treiman scales. Uses research demonstrations to show differences among the three scales.

RAINWATER, LEE, and COLEMAN, RICHARD. *Social Standing in America: New Dimensions of Class.* New York: Basic Books, 1978.

Assessment of measures of class; presents original status scales with sophisticated interview techniques to capture the many complexities of our social-class system.

ROBINSON, JOHN B.; ATHANASIOU, ROBERT; and HEAD, KENDRA B. *Measures of Occupational Attitudes and Occupational Characteristics.* Ann Arbor: Institute of Social Research, University of Michigan, 1969. Pp. 335–76.

Evaluations of Socio-Economic Status Scale (Duncan 1961); Socio-Economic Status Scores (Bureau of Census 1963); Occupational Ratings (North and Hatt 1947, 1965); Index of Status Characteristics (Warner et al. 1949); Index of Social Position (Hollingshead and Redlich 1958); Class Identification (Centers and others 1949–66); Facets of Job Evaluation (Guttman 1965); Occupation Scale (Warner et al. 1949).

STANDARD WORKS AND BIBLIOGRAPHIES OF STRATIFICATION RESEARCH

BLAU, PETER, and DUNCAN, OTIS DUDLEY. *The American Occupational Structure.* New York: Wiley, 1967.

FEATHERMAN, DAVID L., and HAUSER, ROBERT M. *Opportunity and Change.* New York: Academic Press, 1978. (Replication in 1973 of Blau and Duncan Study of 1962.)

GLENN, NORVAL D.; ALSTON, JON P.; and WEINER, DAVID. *Social Stratification: A Research Bibliography.* Berkeley: Glendessary Press, 1970.

LAUMANN, E. O. ed., *Social Stratification: Research and Theory for the 1970's.* Indianapolis: Bobbs-Merrill, 1970.

———; SIEGEL, P. M.; and HODGE, ROBERT W. *The Logic of Social Hierarchies.* New York: Markham, 1970.

Stratification and Inequality Essays. *Contemporary Sociology* 9 (January 1980): 1–63.

TUMIN, M. M. *Social Stratification,* Englewood Cliffs, N.J.: Prentice-Hall, 1967.

VARIABLE MEASURED: A socioeconomic index relating such basic characteristics as occupational prestige, education, and income.

DESCRIPTION: This measure was developed to secure two objectives: (1) to extend the North-Hatt (NORC) occupational prestige scores from 90 to 446 occupations in the detailed classification of the 1950 Census of Population; and (2) to obtain a socioeconomic index in terms of the relationship between the NORC prestige ratings and socioeconomic characteristics of the population. This index has been developed and has face validity, in terms of its constituent variables, and sufficient predictive efficiency with respect to the NORC occupational prestige ratings.

The Duncan index differs from NORC prestige scores in that NORC scores rely solely on subjective occupational ratings of representative samples of respondents. Duncan constructed the occupational socioeconomic index in terms of the relationship between the NORC prestige ratings X_1 and socioeconomic characteristics of the occupations, such as education X_2 and income X_3 with a multiple correlation of $R_{123} = 0.91$. Each occupation was given an education weight (X_2) based on the percentage of those in the occupation who were high school graduates. Income weights (X_3) were determined by those in each occupation reporting $3500 or more in 1949. Occupational scores on each of these indicators were compared with NORC prestige scores (X_1) for the 45 occupations on the NORC list that were reasonably equivalent to U.S. Census titles. In addition to specific socioeconomic scores, a population decile scale was constructed permitting the researcher the option of arranging his data in a ten-point ranking order. For more information on the construction of the index, the researcher is referred to citations under *Where Published* below.

WHERE PUBLISHED: Initial Scale, 1961: Albert J. Reiss, with O. D. Duncan, Paul K. Hatt, and C. C. North, *Occupations and Social Status* (Glencoe, Ill.: Free Press, 1961).

Revised Scale, 1975: Robert M. Hauser and David L. Featherman, *The Process of Stratification: Trends and Analysis* (New York: Academic Press, 1977). Appendix A contains new socioeconomic indices based on the 1970 Census Classification of Occupations.

Revised Scale, 1982: David L. Featherman and Gillian Stevens made another updating of the Duncan Socioeconomic Index using more recent measures of income and educational attainments of the labor force, providing a better approximation of the prestige measure, and considering attributes of both the male and total labor force. Researchers should examine this revision, titled "A Revised Socioeconomic Index of Occupational Status: Application in Analysis of Sex Differences in Attainment," Chapter 7 in *Social Structure and Behavior: Essays in Honor of William Hamilton Sewell* (New York: Academic Press, 1982).

RELIABILITY: Reliability problems emerge as respondent's description of his occupation is translated into an occupational code number using the U.S. Census *Index of Occupations and Industries* or the *Dictionary of Occupa-*

tional Titles published by the U.S. Department of Labor. For increasing reliability or expediting of clerical labor, see Donald G. McTavish, "A Method for More Reliable Coding Detailed Occupations into Duncan's Socio-Economic Categories," *American Sociological Review* 29 (June 1964): 402–6; Robert F. Winch, Samuel A. Mueller, and Lois Godiksen, "The Reliability of Respondent-Coded Occupational Prestige," *American Sociological Review* 34 (April 1969): 245–51.

VALIDITY: The prestige variable is rather highly related to each predictor: with education, $r = 0.84$; with income, 0.85. The multiple correlation between the three variables, $R_{1(23)} = 0.91$. Overall occupational ratings have been found to be highly stable over time ($r = .99$ from 1947 to 1963) and across social systems. See Hodge, Siegel, and Rossi, "Occupational Prestige in the United States."

Hauser and Featherman present many validating coefficients between Duncan SEI scores with father's education, father's occupation, son's education, son's first job, and son's current occupation. Interscale correlations over major occupation groups, Duncan (1961) SEI scores, and Siegel prestige scores (1971) show correlations as follows for Australian men aged 20 and over in 1965 and U.S. men aged 20–64 in 1962:

	Father's occupation		Current occupation	
	Australia	U.S.	Australia	U.S.
Duncan-Siegel	.7904	.7224	.8585	.9013

See Robert M. Hauser and David L. Featherman, *The Process of Stratification: Trends and Analysis* (New York: Academic Press, 1977), pp. 18–19.

A moderate correlation ($r = .74$) has been found between the Hollingshead and Duncan indices. However, these scales are constructed differently, and the correlation can be explained. See August B. Hollingshead, "Commentary on 'The Indiscriminate State of Social Class Measurement,'" *Social Forces* 49 (June 1971): 567. It is of consequence, however, that the two "leading" measures of social status express such a variance.

Certain anomalies appear. For example, since clergymen typically earn small salaries, their Duncan score is considerably below that found by more subjective procedures. In the blue-collar world, large differences are found among semiskilled workers in various industries. Important regional differences are not expressed. For these reasons Duncan does not recommend that the scale be used for comparisons within certain regions of the country or within certain segments of the status hierarchy, such as skilled workers. The researcher concerned with these discrepancies should consult Haug and Sussman, "The Indiscriminate State of Social Class Measurement," *Social Forces* 49 (June 1971): 549–63.

UTILITY: The basic data required are the subject's description of his or her occupation. This description must then be translated into an occupational code by the researcher, and the occupational title is then converted into a preexisting Duncan SEI score (or NORC transformed prestige score if desired). There are many subtleties in the art of occupation coding, especially for blue-collar occupations. One should reserve adequate time for training and cross-checking. Anyone planning detailed occupation coding should heed the sound recommendations of McTavish, "Method for More Reliable Coding," and Winch, Mueller, and Godiksen, "Reliability of Respondent-Coded Occupational Prestige." For codes and decile scores, see John B. Robinson et al., *Measures of Occupational Attitudes and Occupational Characteristics* (Ann Arbor: Survey Research Center, University of Michigan, 1969), pp. 342–58.

RESEARCH APPLICATIONS:

BLAU, PETER M. "The Flow of Occupational Supply and Recruitment." *American Sociological Review* 30 (August 1965): 475–90. See p. 476.

CLARK, JOHN P., and WENNINGER, EUGENE P. "Socioeconomic Class and Areas as Correlates of Illegal Behavior among Juveniles." *American Sociological Review* 27 (December 1962): 826–34. See p. 828.

———. "Goal Orientations and Illegal Behavior among Juveniles." *Social Forces* 42 (October 1963): 49–59. See p. 51.

ECKLAND, BRUCE K. "Academic Ability, Higher Education, and Occupational Mobility." *American Sociological Review* 30 (October 1965): 735–46. See p. 739.

———. "Social Class and College Graduation: Some Misconceptions Corrected." *American Journal of Sociology* 70 (July 1964): 36–50. See p. 43.

ERBE, WILLIAM. "Social Involvement and Political Activity: A Replication and Elaboration." *American Sociological Review* 29 (April 1964): 198–215. See p. 203.

REISS, IRA L. "Social Class and Premarital Sexual Permissiveness: A Reexamination." *American Sociological Review* 30 (October 1965): 747–56. See p. 749.

For more recent research use, see all references in the period 1965–80 in the *American Sociological Review Inventory* under Duncan's Socioeconomic Index Section 4.M.1, p. 497, pp. 504–505, and p. 519.

4.A.2   SIEGEL'S (NORC) PRESTIGE SCORES

Social Prestige as a Social Variable

Occupations can be differentiated with respect to the knowledge or skill required to perform them. So, too, they can be differentiated with respect to the economic power their incumbents will wield. All of the attributes attached to occupational roles give rise to corresponding differences in privilege. Privilege begets *prestige*. Prestige is seen as a symbolic definition of an occupational role based on deference entitlements. It is on the basis of knowledge, skill, power, and privilege that persons grant deference to themselves and claim it from others. It is on the basis of simultaneous assessments of their own and others' deference that they regulate their conduct toward others and anticipate the deferential responses of others.

Power and privilege are universally valued. Treiman contends that the prestige ordering of occupations is fundamentally invariant in all complex societies, past or present.[1] He bases this generalization on a comparative analysis of some 85 studies of occupational prestige conducted in nearly 60 countries throughout the world ranging from highly industrialized countries such as the United States to traditional peasant societies in India, Thailand, Nigeria, and New Guinea.[2]

What is the difference between social status and prestige? When should the researcher use a social status scale and when a prestige scale? Can the researcher use Duncan's Socioeconomic Index of Occupations to measure either social status or prestige?

Researchers working closely with prestige insist that social status and prestige are not identical dimensions, although the correlations between the underlying factors are high.[3] (Prestige with education, $r = 0.84$, and with income, $r = 0.85$. The multiple correlation between the three variables 0.91 indicates that about 83 percent of the variance in the prestige of individual occupations can be attributed to a combination of the education and income of the incumbents.) It is asserted that "a socioeconomic index is a better indicator than a prestige index of the way occupations serve as *resources* that facilitate the transmission of advantage from one generation to the next or the conversion of one form of advantage into another. On the other hand, prestige as a major occupational reward may be a better indicator of occupational attainment."[4]

Duncan's SEI and the NORC Prestige Scores reflect approximately equivalent prestige and socioeconomic status for most occupations, but for a substantial number they do not. This can be seen in the category "farmers" (owners and tenants); they have average prestige but very low socioeconomic status (because of limited education and low reported monetary returns). Because of numerous disparities like this, the Duncan scale cannot be adequate for prestige scores. Socioeconomic factors are the main determinants of prestige; but prestige is determined by other factors as well.[5]

What, then, are appropriate criteria for choosing between a prestige and a socioeconomic scale of occupational status? One answer is: Use a prestige measure if the dependent variable is "status attainment"; use a socioeconomic index if the dependent variable is "occupational mobility."[6] Another answer is to code occupations in alternative ways and investigate the results obtained. Duncan's Socioeconomic Index of Occupations has become the most widely used occupational status scale in research carried out on American data. Siegel's (NORC) prestige scores are most commonly used in prestige measurement in the United States. It is useful to compare the two scales for occupations included in a research sample. For cross-national comparability, the Standard International Occupational Prestige Scale (Treiman) should be used.

Notes

1. Donald J. Treiman, *Occupational Prestige in Comparative Perspective* (New York: Academic Press, 1977), p. 5.
2. Ibid., p. 25
3. Frank D. Bean and Gray Swicegood, "Intergenerational Occupational Mobility and Fertility: A Reassessment," *American Sociological Review* 44 (August 1974): 608–19. See also Aage B. Sørensen, "A Model and a Metric for the Analysis of the Intergenerational Status Attainment Process," *American Journal of Sociology* 85 (September 1979): 361–84.

4. Treiman, *Occupational Prestige in Comparative Perspective,* p. 212.

5. Treiman, *Occupational Prestige in Comparative Perspective,* p. 208.

6. Robert M. Hauser and David L. Featherman, *The Process of Stratification: Trends and Analyses* (New York: Academic Press, 1977). Hauser and Featherman have made the most careful investigation of the relative efficacy of the Duncan socioeconomic index and the Siegel (NORC) and Treiman prestige scales. They conclude: "Occupational socioeconomic status captures the major axis of occupational preference, aspiration, and inter and intragenerational mobility. A socio-economic index for occupations is substantively, and statistically, preferable to prestige indexes in stratification research" (p. xxiii).

Similarly, they warn: "A socioeconomic status is a more valid status index *only* with reference to occupational *mobility;* other occupational processes may be less responsive to the purely socioeconomic hierarchy of these roles than is mobility and may be more responsive to other desirable 'prestigious' but non-socioeconomic occupational dimensions. Therefore 'prestige' is indeed a multi dimensional concept and one needs to be quite specific about the occupational process one is discussing in identifying the most salient or valid dimension of status" (p. 50).

SIEGEL'S (NORC) PRESTIGE SCORES

VARIABLE MEASURED: An index measuring the prestige of a stratification system.

DESCRIPTION: The North-Hatt-NOTC study of occupational prestige appeared in 1947 and thereafter was widely used in research on prestige. Prestige scores were obtained for 90 occupations by a national sample of the American adult population. See Albert J. Reiss, Jr., and Others, *Occupations and Social Status* (New York: Free Press of Glencoe, 1961). In 1963, under a National Science Foundation Grant to the National Opinion Research Center, a replication was undertaken to provide definitive prestige scores for a more representative sample of occupations and in order to uncover some of the characteristics of occupations that generate their prestige scores. As in the 1947 study, occupational ratings were elicited by asking respondents to judge an occupation as having excellent, good, average, somewhat below average, or poor standing (along with a "don't know" option) in response to the item: "For each job mentioned, please pick out the statement that best gives your own personal opinion of the general standing that such a job has."

One indicator of prestige position is the proportion of respondents (among those rating an occupation) giving either an "excellent" or a "good" response. Another measure can be derived from a matrix of ratings by occupation by weighting the various responses with arbitrary numerical values. Assigning to an "excellent" rating a numerical average of these arbitrarily assigned values over all respondents rating the occupation yields the NORC prestige score. This latter measure has received rather widespread use, despite arbitrariness in the numerical weights assigned to the five possible ratings.

The NORC Occupational Prestige Ratings of 1963 were limited to 90 occupations (compared with the more than 500 occupation scores available in the Duncan SEI). By 1970 this limitation was removed as Robert W. Hodge, P. M. Siegel, and P. H. Rossi established prestige scores on more than 400 occupations. More recently, Wisconsin researchers have transformed the 1964–65 NORC prestige scores (reported in Siegel for the 1960 census detailed occupational titles) into the 1970 Classification System. These scores are shown in table 4.A.5.

WHERE PUBLISHED: P. M. Siegel, "Prestige in the American Occupational Structure" (Ph.D. dissertation, Department of Sociology, University of Chicago, 1971); David L. Featherman, Michael Sobel, and David Dickens, *A Manual for Coding Occupations and Industries into Detailed 1970 Categories and a Listing of 1970-Basis Duncan Socioeconomic and NORC Prestige Scores,* Working Paper #75–1 (Madison: Center for Demography and Ecology, University of Wisconsin, 1975); Robert M. Hauser and David L. Featherman, *The Process of Stratification: Trends and Analyses* (New York: Academic Press, 1977), Appendix B, pp. 319–29.

RELIABILITY: The respondent's own social status and familiarity with various occupations have been found to affect scores. Lowered reliability has also been found for occupations in the middle of the status scale. Guttman scale analysis of Hatt's data (1950) failed to find a single underlying prestige dimension. However, Hatt did find internally homogeneous scales with eight occupational groups: political, professional, business, recreation, agriculture, manual, military, and service.

VALIDITY: A correlation of 0.87 is reported by Siegel (1971) between Duncan's SEI scores (1960) and NORC Prestige Scores. The correlation between NORC prestige scores and Treiman's Standard International Prestige Scores is 0.95. The Duncan SEI seems to underrate clergyman, farmers, and certain blue-collar workers (e.g., machinist, carpenter) while overrating entertainers, newspaper personnel, and sanitation workers. NORC scores show discrepant ratings of these occupations when compared with Duncan ratings, and one may prefer to substitute NORC ratings for these occupations. See John P. Robinson, Robert Athanasiou, and Kendra B. Head, *Measures of Occupational Attitudes and Occupational Characteristics* (Ann Arbor: Institute for Social Research, University of Michigan, 1969), p. 337.

Because of the way they were created (weights used in combining income and education were those that maximized scale scores with prestige) Duncan's scores have often been treated as estimates of the relative prestige of occupations, but in fact the correlations between Duncan scores and actual prestige scores are far from perfect. Some significant discrepancies have been pointed out. But the best demonstrated finding is that prestige scores in toto are less valid indicators of the dimension of status that underlies occupational mobility than are Duncan SEI scores. Prestige measures may be more responsive to nonsocioeconomic occupational dimensions. See Hauser and Featherman, *The Process of Stratification,* pp. 37, 50.

UTILITY: The best strategy is to code occupations in alternative ways and investigate differences in the results obtained. If the researcher wishes to settle on a single occupational status index for American data, there are two advantages to the Duncan index: (1) it is the most widely used and offers opportunities for comparative analysis; (2) it will capture more joint variance with education and income than would a prestige scale. When other information on socioeconomic status is available for individuals, the NORC prestige ratings will avoid artificially inflated correlations with income and education. See Donald J. Treiman, *Occupational Prestige in Comparative Perspective* (New York: Academic Press, 1977), pp. 311–12. Cf. Edward O. Laumann, P. M. Siegel, and Robert W. Hodge, *The Logic of Social Hierarchies* (New York: Markham, 1970).

RESEARCH APPLICATIONS:

ALEXANDER, C. NORMAN. "Status Perceptions." *American Sociological Review* 37 (December 1972): 767–73.

HODGE, ROBERT W.; SIEGEL, P. M.; and ROSSI, PETER H. "Occupational Prestige in the United States, 1925–63." *American Journal of Sociology* 70 (November 1964): 286–302.

LABOVITZ, SANFORD. "The Assignment of Numbers to Rank Order Categories." *American Sociological Review* 35 (June 1970): 515–24.

LANE, ANGELA. "The Occupational Achievement Process, 1940–1949: A Cohort Analysis." *American Sociological Review* 40 (August 1975): 472–82.

PARCEL, TOBY L. "Race, Regional Labor Markets and Earnings." *American Sociological Review* 44 (April 1979): 262–79.

SIMMONS, ROBERTA G., and ROSENBERG, MORRIS. "Functions of Children's Perceptions of the Stratification System." *American Sociological Review* 30 (April 1971): 235–49.

SNYDER, DAVID, and HUDIS, PAULA M. "Occupational Income and the Effects of Minority Competition and Segregation: A Re-Analysis and Some New Evidence." *American Sociological Review* 41 (April 1976): 209–34.

VANNEMAN, REEVE, and PAMPEL, FRED C. "The American Perception of Class and Status." *American Sociological Review* 42 (June 1977): 422–37.

4.A.3.   TREIMAN'S STANDARD INTERNATIONAL OCCUPATIONAL PRESTIGE SCALE

VARIABLE MEASURED: A standardized prestige measure that can be used to code occupations in any country and to make cross-national comparisons.

DESCRIPTION: The scale consists of prestige scores for 509 occupations, 288 unit groups, 84 minor groups, and 11 major categories. The scale has a range of 92 points from "chief of state" with a score of 90 to "gatherer" with a score of −2. The mean scale score computed over the 509 occupations is 43.3.

WHERE PUBLISHED: Donald J. Treiman, *Occupational Prestige in Comparative Perspective* (New York: Academic Press, 1977).

RELIABILITY: The scale has been shown to be highly reliable. The average intercountry correlation based on seven countries is .97.

VALIDITY: The Standard Scale is extremely highly correlated with prestige hierarchies of 55 countries. The mean correlation of intercountry correlations with the Standard Scale is .91 computed over the 55 countries with pure prestige data. Of the 55 countries only 7 exhibit correlations with the Standard Scale smaller than .87. For the United States and Great Britain the correlations exceed .96.

UTILITY: Because of the basic similarity of prestige evaluations in all societies, Donald Treiman has been able to produce the first prestige scale that can be validly used to assign prestige scores to occupations in any country.

RESEARCH APPLICATIONS:

TREIMAN, DONALD J. "Correlations of (60) Individual Country Prestige Scores with the Standard Scale and with Version of Standard Scale Excluding Scores for the Country in Correlation. In *Occupational Prestige in Comparative Perspective.* New York: Academic Press, 1977. Pp. 175–77. Determination of Prestige Scores for each country in the analysis, pp. 318–493.

————, and TERRELL, KERMIT. "Sex and the Process of Status and Attainment. A Comparison of Working Women and Men." *American Sociological Review* 40 (April 1975): 174–200.

————. "The Process of Status Attainment in the United States and Great Britain." *American Journal of Sociology* 81 (November 1975): 563–83.

Because of its length, the Standard International Occupational Prestige Scale is not reproduced. For the complete scale, see Appendix A in *Occupational Prestige in Comparative Perspective,* pp. 235–60. Standard Scale scores for the 1960 U.S. Census, Detailed Occupational Classification, are on pp. 299–315.

NAM-POWERS SOCIOECONOMIC STATUS SCORES

4.A.4

VARIABLE MEASURED: The socioeconomic status score is a multiple-item measure derived by averaging scores for the component items of occupation, education, and family income. A companion measure of status consistency is also available.

DESCRIPTION: In the 1960s Charles B. Nam, Mary G. Powers, and their associates worked at the U.S. Bureau of the Census where they devised socioeconomic status scores for occupations (without use of prestige ratings) based on 1960 census data for income and education. There was interest at that time in constructing an occupational status index that was more detailed and homogeneous than the Alba Edwards classification scheme, which, since about 1930, had permitted arrangement of occupations into major groupings that formed a crude social scale. The Census Bureau's group decided that homogeneity could best be achieved not only by stratifying occupations per se but by developing a multiple-item index of socioeconomic status that combined independent ratings of education and income with ratings of occupations.

The procedure employed to compute the scores is similar to that used by Duncan, but with these differences: (1) median education and income, rather than percentages of specified education and income levels, were used; (2) Duncan indirectly standardized scores by age; (3) Duncan used the 1947

NORC prestige ratings in deriving weights for census characteristics. The similarity between the census and Duncan's index is attested to, however, by the Pearsonian coefficient of .97, as previously reported.

In planning for the 1970 census, the Census Bureau decided to drop the practice of generating socioeconomic scores using any procedure.

Nam and Powers take cognizance of the controversy between the pure prestige approach (Siegel's [NORC] Prestige Scores) and those of SES determination of prestige of occupations. They believe a third option, the direct measurement of SES without reference to prestige, deserves a more careful assessment. This approach was used in the work of August B. Hollingshead and Frederick C. Redlich, *Social Class and Mental Illness: A Community Study* (New York: Wiley, 1958) and by Peter M. Blau and Otis Dudley Duncan, *The American Occupational Structure* (New York: Wiley, 1967). This orientation begins with the notion that often one wants a measure of class or life chances or objective status conditions; any of these criteria for valuing occupations leads one to pure socioeconomic indicators of occupational rankings. This third, purely socioeconomic approach has been evident in work produced by the U.S. Bureau of the Census for the past century.

Nam and Powers have continued to generate new occupational status scores based on 1970 census data. For the first time, SEI scores have been made available for both men and women, and these are shown in table 4.A.5. A rationale for their "pure" socioeconomic multiple-item measure is presented in "The Measurement of Socioeconomic Status: Current Issues," in *Socioeconomic Status: Concepts and Measurement Issues,* ed. Mary G. Powers (Boulder, Colo.: Westview Press, 1982).

WHERE PUBLISHED: Initial work on 1960 census data appears in U.S. Bureau of the Census, *Methodology and Scores of Socioeconomic Status,* Working Paper No. 15 (Washington, D.C.: U.S. Government Printing Office, 1963); U.S. Bureau of the Census, U.S. Census of Population, 1960, *Socioeconomic Status,* Final Report PC(2)–5C (Washington, D.C.; U.S. Government Printing Office, 1967). More recent work on 1970 census data, incorporating SES scores for males, females, full-time year-round female workers, and both sexes, appears in Charles B. Nam, John LaRocque, Mary G. Powers, and Joan Holmberg, "Occupational Status Scores: Stability and Change," *Proceedings of the American Statistical Association, Social Statistics Section* (1975), pp. 570–75.

RELIABILITY: When Nam and Powers compared the full list of detailed occupations for men for 1950 and 1960, they calculated a correlation coefficient between the two sets of scores of .96. The 1950–60 correlation coefficient using the 126 occupations is .95. The calculation for men in the 126 occupations in 1960 and 1970 provides a correlation coefficient of .97, indicating that an extremely high degree of stability in status scores has been maintained. Even the correlation coefficient between scores for men in 1950 and 1970 is .91. For all women, the coefficient for 1960–70 was .85, reasonably high but much lower than for men. Apparently, the changing roles of women in recent years have modified status levels of some occupations in a significant way. An examination of scores for specific occupations shows that, while for the vast majority of occupations status scores changed very little between censuses, for a minority of occupations changes were notable and most often in a downward direction.

VALIDITY: Measured against prestige measures (Duncan or Siegel), very high correlations are reported. While these two dimensions, socioeconomic status and prestige, are highly associated, there is a tendency for occupational status to vary more over time than occupational prestige. See Ronald M. Pavalko, *Sociology of Occupations and Professions* (Itasca, Ill.: Peacock, 1971), pp. 132, 140.

UTILITY: Women have become increasingly involved in the labor force, and labeling occupations as exclusively men's or women's is disappearing. Scores for both men and women are shown in table 4.A.5.

RESEARCH APPLICATIONS:

BROMAN, SARAH H.; NICHOLS, PAUL L.; and KENNEDY, WALLACE A. *Preschool IQ: Prenatal and Early Developmental Correlates.* New York: Wiley, 1975.

CHIRICOS, THEODORE G., and WALDO, GORDON P. "Socioeconomic Status and Criminal Sentencing: An Empirical Assessment of a Conflict Proposition." *American Sociological Review* 40 (December 1975): 753–72.

MYRIANTHOPOULOS, N. C., and FRENCH, K. S. "An Application of the U.S. Bureau of the Census Socioeconomic Index to a Large, Diversified Patient Population." *Social Science and Medicine* 2 (1968).

NAM, CHARLES B. "Changes in the Relative Status Level of Workers in the United States, 1950–1960." *Social Forces* 47 (December 1968): 167–70.

———, and POWERS, MARY G. "Variations in Socioeconomic Structure by Race, Residence, and the Life Cycle." *American Sociological Review* 30 (February 1965): 97–103.

———; POWERS, MARY G.; and GLICK, PAUL C. "Socioeconomic Characteristics of the Population: 1960." *Current Population Reports,* Series P-23, no. 12 (1964).

POWERS, MARY G., and HOLMBERG, JOAN J. "Occupational Status Scores: Changes Introduced by the Inclusion of Women." *Demography* 15: (May 1978): 183–204.

In table 1, the Duncan, Siegel, and Nam-Powers scores are shown for the occupational group codes developed for the 1970 census. The Duncan and Nam-Powers SEI scores can take values approximately between 0 and 100 on both indexes, but since they are constructed somewhat differently, it is not appropriate to make direct comparisons. The Siegel prestige scores have a much smaller range, with bootblacks at 09.3 and various college and university teachers at 78.3. When wide variations appear on any of the indexes, caution should be used in interpreting the status of individual occupations. This is especially true in comparisons of men and women workers.

Table 1 shows Socioeconomic Index Scores for Major Occupation Groups by Duncan's SEI (weighted prestige, education, income), Siegel's and Treiman's Prestige Scores (subjective weighting of judges), and by Nam-Powers "pure" multiple-item Socioeconomic Scores (based on simple average of scores for occupation, education, and income for males of all ages in civilian labor force in 1970.)

Table 1.   *Group Occupational Status Scores for Men*

	Scales			
Occupation group	Duncan (1970)	Siegel (1970)	Treiman (1960)	Nam-Powers (1970)
Professional, technical and kindred	75	60	57	85
Managers, officials, proprietors	57	50	64	79
Clerical and kindred	45	39	44	56
Sales and kindred	49	34	40	66
Craft and kindred	31	39	41	49
Operatives	18	29	33	33
Service	17	25	31	25
Nonfarm labor	7	18	19	15
Farmers and farm managers	14	41	47	20
Farm laborers	9	19	27	4

Sources: Duncan, Siegel, and Treiman scale scores are drawn from Robert Hauser and David Featherman, *The Process of Stratification* (New York: Academic Press, 1977), p. 17. Nam-Powers scores appear in Mary G. Powers and Joan J. Holmberg, "Occupational Status Scores: Changes Introduced by the Inclusion of Women." *Demography* 15 (May 1978): 188. Nam and Powers report that major occupational groupings of the 1960 census are not at all homogeneous and constitute too crude a status scale to be useful in socioeconomic analysis. Among males, half of the detailed occupations under the category "Professional, technical and kindred workers" have status scores between 90 and 100 and two-thirds have status scores between 80 and 100; but one-third have scores less than 80, with several scores ranging between 40 and 59. The status scores for clerical occupations are widely distributed with over one-fourth below 45 and one-third 65 or above. Some service occupations have status scores of near zero, while others have scores near 70 or above. These variations are common for women as well as for men.

4.A.5   OCCUPATIONAL CLASSIFICATION SYSTEM OF THE U.S. BUREAU OF THE CENSUS WITH PARALLEL LISTINGS OF DUNCAN'S 1970 SEI SCORES, SIEGEL'S (1970 NORC) PRESTIGE SCORES, AND NAM-POWERS' (1970 CENSUS) SEI SCORES*

Occupation code[a]		1970 Duncan SEI Score (males)	1970 Siegel Prestige Score (males)	Nam-Powers (1970 U.S. Census) Score	
				(men, full-time)	(women, full-time)[b]
	Professional, technical, and kindred workers				
001	Accountants	76.3	55.9	88	87
002	Architects	85.2	66.7	95	100
	Computer specialists				
003	Computer programmers	65.0	50.6	84	97
004	Computer systems analysts	65.0	50.6	91	97

* I am indebted to Robert M. Hauser and David L. Featherman for the assembly of Duncan's SEI and Siegel's Prestige Scores in *The Process of Stratification* (New York, Academic Press, 1977), Appendices A, B, reprinted with permission of the authors and Academic Press; to Charles B. Nam, John La Rocque, Marty G. Powers, and Joan Holmberg for their (1970 census) SEI scores in "Occupational Status Scores: Stability and Change," *Proceedings of the American Statistical Association, Social Statistics Section,* 1975, pp. 570–75. Reprinted with permission of the American Statistical Association. Scores also available for female part-time workers and for both sexes combined.

Occupation code[a]		1970 Duncan SEI Score (males)	1970 Siegel Prestige Score (males)	Nam-Powers (1970 U.S. Census) Score	
				(men, full-time)	(women, full-time)[b]
005	Computer specialists, n.e.c.[c]	65.0	50.6	91	95
	Engineers				
006	Aeronautical and astronautical engineers	87.0	71.1	96	98
010	Chemical engineers	89.9	67.2	96	97
011	Civil engineers	84.0	67.8	93	98
012	Electrical and electronic engineers	84.0	69.4	94	97
013	Industrial engineers	85.5	55.6	91	94
014	Mechanical engineers	80.2	62.1	94	98
015	Metallurgical and materials engineers	83.1	58.4	95	97
020	Mining engineers	85.0	61.6	92	97
021	Petroleum engineers	81.0	57.1	95	97
022	Sales engineers	87.0	50.6	93	97
023	Engineers, n.e.c.	86.9	67.0	93	98
024	Farm management advisors	83.0	53.9	90	97
025	Foresters and conservationists	48.0	53.9	70	49
026	Home management advisors	83.0	53.9	58	98
	Lawyers and judges				
030	Judges	93.0	75.7	98	100
031	Lawyers	92.3	75.1	98	100
	Librarians, archivists, and curators				
032	Librarians	60.0	54.6	72	98
033	Archivists and curators	74.6	59.6	72	97
	Mathematical specialists				
034	Actuaries	81.0	55.4	97	92
035	Mathematicians	80.0	65.0	97	98
036	Statisticians	81.0	55.4	91	95
	Life and physical scientists				
042	Agricultural scientists	80.0	55.8	87	93
043	Atmospheric and space scientists	62.0	47.0	95	98
044	Biological scientists	80.0	67.7	91	98
045	Chemists	79.4	67.1	92	93
051	Geologists	80.0	67.2	97	98
052	Marine scientists			95	98
053	Physicists and astronomers	80.0	73.8	98	99
054	Life and physical scientists, n.e.c.	77.2	64.8	97	94
055	Operations and systems researchers and analysts	65.7	50.8	88	95
056	Personnel and labor relations workers	83.6	55.8	89	92
	Physicians, dentists, and related practitioners				
061	Chiropractors	75.0	60.0	93	97
062	Dentists	96.0	73.6	98	99
063	Optometrists	79.0	62.0	98	96
064	Pharmacists	81.3	60.3	93	97
065	Physicians, medical and osteopathic	92.1	81.2	99	100
071	Podiatrists	58.0	36.7	98	100
072	Veterinarians	78.0	59.7	98	100
073	Health practitioners, n.e.c.			87	100
	Nurses, dietitians, and therapists				
074	Dietitians	39.0	52.1	51	83
075	Registered nurses	44.3	60.1	62	91
076	Therapists	59.9	40.5	72	92
	Health technologists and technicians				
080	Clinical laboratory technologists and technicians	48.0	61.0	68	90

Occupation code[a]		1970 Duncan SEI Score (males)	1970 Siegel Prestige score (males)	Nam-Powers (1970 U.S. Census) Score	
				(men, full-time)	(women, full-time)[b]
081	Dental hygienists	48.0	61.0	85	95
082	Health record technologists and technicians	60.0	54.6	55	89
083	Radiologic technologists and technicians	48.0	61.0	70	85
084	Therapy assistants	48.0	61.0	61	59
085	Health technologists and technicians, n.e.c.	52.2	49.8	64	61
	Religious workers				
086	Clergymen	52.0	69.0	68	59
090	Religious workers, n.e.c.	56.7	55.0	61	70
	Social scientists				
091	Economists	74.4	53.6	95	97
092	Political scientists			97	99
093	Psychologists	81.0	71.4	96	100
094	Sociologists			91	99
095	Urban and regional planners	65.0	50.6	91	99
096	Social scientists, n.e.c.	81.0	65.6	91	90
	Social and recreation workers				
100	Social workers	64.0	52.4	80	96
101	Recreation workers	67.0	48.6	57	90
	Teachers, college and university				
102	Agriculture teachers	84.0	78.3	95	99
103	Atmospheric, earth, marine, and space teachers	84.0	78.3	94	99
104	Biology teachers	84.0	78.3	95	100
105	Chemistry teachers	84.0	78.3	95	100
110	Physics teachers	84.0	78.3	94	99
111	Engineering teachers	84.0	78.3	97	99
112	Mathematics teachers	84.0	78.3	92	99
113	Health specialties teachers	84.0	78.3	98	100
114	Psychology teachers	84.0	78.3	97	100
115	Business and commerce teachers	84.0	78.3	95	98
116	Economics teachers	84.0	78.3	97	99
120	History teachers	84.0	78.3	91	100
121	Sociology teachers	84.0	78.3	93	100
122	Social science teachers, n.e.c.	84.0	78.3	95	100
123	Art, drama, and music teachers	53.2	46.8	91	99
124	Coaches and physical education teachers	64.0	53.2	91	99
125	Education teachers	84.0	78.3	98	100
126	English teachers	84.0	78.3	91	99
130	Foreign language teachers	84.0	78.3	91	99
131	Home economics teachers	84.0	78.3	96	100
132	Law teachers	84.0	78.3	98	99
133	Theology teachers	84.0	78.3	89	99
134	Trade, industrial, and technical teachers	84.0	78.3	89	99
135	Miscellaneous teachers, college and university	84.0	78.3	92	100
140	Teachers, college and university, subject not specified	84.0	78.3	89	99
	Teachers, except college and university				
141	Adult education teachers	61.3	44.3	84	91
142(N)	Elementary school teachers (public)	71.2	58.9	79	96
143	Pre-kindergarten and kindergarten teachers (public)	72.0	56.1	52	91
144	Secondary school teachers (public)	70.2	59.8	85	98
145	Teachers, except college and university, n.e.c.	62.3	44.2	64	91

Occupation code[a]		1970 Duncan SEI Score (males)	1970 Siegel Prestige Score (males)	Nam-Powers (1970 U.S. Census) Score	
				(men, full-time)	(women, full-time)[b]
	Engineering and science technicians				
150	Agriculture and biological technicians, except health	62.0	47.2	60	70
151	Chemical technicians	62.0	47.0	72	82
152	Draftsmen	67.0	56.1	73	86
153	Electrical and electronic engineering technicians	62.0	51.6	76	73
154	Industrial engineering technicians	64.1	49.5	74	82
155	Mechanical engineering technicians	62.0	47.0	80	82
156	Mathematical technicians			81	82
161	Surveyors	48.4	53.1	61	79
162	Engineering and science technicians, n.e.c.	62.0	47.0	67	77
	Technicians, except health, and engineering and science				
163	Airplane pilots	79.0	70.1	93	76
164	Air traffic controllers	69.0	42.8	84	82
165	Embalmers	60.8	51.7	65	76
170	Flight engineers	48.0	48.2	89	76
171	Radio operators	69.0	42.8	57	49
172	Tool programmers, numerical control	62.0	47.0	83	76
173	Technicians, n.e.c.	62.0	47.2	67	83
174	Vocational and educational counselors	65.0	50.6	91	99
	Writers, artists, and entertainers				
175	Actors	60.0	55.0	64	92
180	Athletes and kindred workers	59.4	51.8	54	68
181	Authors	76.0	59.8	89	97
182	Dancers	45.0	37.6	47	50
183	Designers	70.5	56.5	87	95
184	Editors and reporters	82.0	51.2	89	95
185	Musicians and composers	52.0	46.0	45	85
190	Painters and sculptors	67.0	56.2	81	89
191	Photographers	50.0	40.5	69	56
192	Public relations men and publicity writers	82.0	56.7	90	96
193	Radio and television announcers	65.0	50.6	59	89
194	Writers, artists, and entertainers, n.e.c.	40.2	38.6	80	94
195	Research workers, not specified	65.0	50.6	88	97
	Managers and administrators, except farm				
201	Assessors, controllers, and treasurers; local public administration	61.2	50.9	71	61
202	Bank officers and financial	79.5	66.1	89	83
203	Buyers and shippers, farm products	50.5	43.0	60	77
205	Buyers, wholesale and retail trade	72.1	50.0	79	77
210	Credit men	74.0	48.8	81	74
211	Funeral directors	59.0	52.2	75	90
212	Health administrators	74.1	63.8	91	95
213	Construction inspectors, public administration	57.6	39.6	72	77
215	Inspectors, except construction, public administration	66.7	42.3	79	78
216	Managers and superintendents, building	32.0	38.3	61	31
220	Office managers, n.e.c.	75.1	57.6	83	84
221	Officers, pilots, and pursers; ship	49.9	56.7	62	77

Occupation code[a]		1970 Duncan SEI Score (males)	1970 Siegel Prestige Score (males)	Nam-Powers (1970 U.S. Census) Score	
				(men, full-time)	(women, full-time)[b]
222	Officials and administrators; public administration, n.e.c.	67.3	60.7	92	94
223	Officials of lodges, societies, and unions	59.8	48.4	82	95
224	Postmasters and mail superintendents	61.3	58.4	78	76
225	Purchasing agents and buyers, n.e.c.	74.7	46.4	82	86
226	Railroad conductors	58.2	40.9	68	77
230	Restaurant, cafeteria, and bar managers	37.6	38.7	63	34
231	Sales managers and department heads, retail trade	70.6	48.5	76	53
233	Sales managers, except retail trade	74.7	54.2	92	93
235	School administrators, college	77.9	70.6	97	99
240	School administrators, elementary and secondary	71.7	61.7	97	99
245	Managers and administrators, n.e.c.	62.0	50.8	67	51
	Sales workers				
260	Advertising agents and salesmen	66.1	42.3	86	88
261	Auctioneers	40.0	31.9	68	30
262	Demonstrators	35.0	28.3	64	48
264	Hucksters and peddlers	08.8	12.9	41	21
265	Insurance agents, brokers, and underwriters	66.0	46.8	82	76
266	Newsboys	27.0	15.4	11	16
270	Real estate agents and brokers	62.0	44.0	84	84
271	Stock and bond salesmen	72.3	51.2	95	89
280	Salesmen and sales clerks, n.e.c.[d]				
281	Sales representatives, manufacturing (Ind. 107–399)	65.0	49.1	86	70
282	Sales representatives, wholesale trade (Ind. 017–058, 507–599)	60.9	39.9	76	54
283	Sales clerks, retail trade (Ind. 608–699 except 618, 639, 649, 667, 668, 688)	39.0	28.7	44	23
284	Salesmen, retail trade (Ind. 607, 618, 639, 649, 667, 668, 688)	39.0	28.6	61	38
285	Salesmen of services and construction (Ind. 067–078, 407–499, 707–947)	52.7	35.8	77	51
	Clerical and kindred workers				
301	Bank tellers	52.0	49.5	50	47
303	Billing clerks	44.0	36.2	56	51
305(P)	Bookkeepers	50.8	47.3	64	57
310	Cashiers	44.0	31.4	32	31
311	Clerical assistants, social welfare			51	51
312	Clerical supervisors, n.e.c.	43.6	35.8	83	81
313	Collectors, bill and account	43.3	28.4	55	54
314	Counter clerks, except food	44.0	36.2	45	35
315	Dispatchers and starters, vehicle	39.9	33.3	62	48
320	Enumerators and interviewers	44.0	36.2	48	79
321	Estimators and investigators, n.e.c.	59.2	42.9	81	67
323	Expediters and production controllers	43.7	36.0	70	69
325	File clerks	44.0	31.4	41	42
326	Insurance adjusters, examiners, and investigators	62.1	47.6	80	79
330	Library attendants and assistants	44.0	40.4	42	76
331	Mail carriers, post office	53.0	42.3	64	73
332	Mail handlers, except post office	43.0	35.1	39	37

Occupation code[a]		1970 Duncan SEI Score (males)	1970 Siegel Prestige Score (males)	Nam-Powers (1970 U.S. Census) Score	
				(men, full-time)	(women, full-time)[b]
333	Messengers and office boys	28.2	19.4	23	31
334	Meter readers, utilities	44.0	36.2	46	50
	Office machine operators				
341	Bookkeeping and billing machine operators	44.9	43.7	51	50
342	Calculating machine operators	45.0	44.9	54	55
343	Computer and peripheral equipment operators	45.0	44.9	63	76
344	Duplicating machine operators	45.0	44.9	42	46
345	Key punch operators	45.0	44.9	60	60
350	Tabulating machine operators	45.0	44.9	51	69
355	Office machine operators, n.e.c.	45.0	44.9	42	42
360	Payroll and timekeeping clerks	44.0	41.2	64	69
361	Postal clerks	44.7	42.3	66	74
362	Proofreaders	44.0	36.2	70	61
363	Real estate appraisers	67.8	43.0	88	87
364	Receptionists	44.0	37.1	44	46
	Secretaries			66	76
370	Secretaries, legal	61.0	45.8		
371	Secretaries, medical	61.0	45.8		
372(Q)	Secretaries, n.e.c.	61.9	46.5	64	76
374	Shipping and receiving clerks	24.2	29.9	41	34
375	Statistical clerks	43.7	35.8	66	61
376	Stenographers	61.0	43.3	81	75
381	Stock clerks and storekeepers	44.0	25.0	42	50
382	Teacher aides, exc. school monitors	63.2	49.3	42	38
383	Telegraph messengers	22.0	29.8		
384	Telegraph operators	47.0	43.5	64	71
385	Telephone operators	45.0	40.4	49	52
390	Ticket, station, and express agents	59.8	35.4	70	87
391	Typists	61.0	41.3	48	54
392	Weighers	41.9	35.5	40	41
394	Miscellaneous clerical workers	43.7	36.2	54	45
395	Not specified clerical workers	44.0	36.2		
	Craftsmen and kindred workers				
401	Automobile accessories installers	21.6	32.5	35	48
402	Bakers	21.9	34.0	24	20
403	Blacksmiths	16.0	35.5	26	56
404	Boilermakers	32.6	30.6	51	56
405	Bookbinders	39.0	31.3	52	29
410	Brickmasons and stonemasons	27.0	35.7	35	42
411	Brickmasons and stonemasons, apprentices	32.0	40.8		
412	Bulldozer operators	19.7	32.3	23	49
413	Cabinetmakers	22.3	38.1	30	25
415(R)	Carpenters	18.9	39.7	33	56
416	Carpenter apprentices	31.0	40.8		
420	Carpet installers	12.0	32.8		
421	Cement and concrete finishers	19.0	31.6	21	57
422	Compositors and typesetters	52.0	38.0	61	45
423	Printing trades apprentices, exc. pressmen	40.0	40.8		
424	Cranemen, derrickmen, and hoistmen	21.0	38.7	39	55
425	Decorators and window dressers	40.0	37.4	53	36
426	Dental laboratory technicians	48.0	61.0	60	47

Occupation code[a]		1970 Duncan SEI Score (males)	1970 Siegel Prestige Score (males)	Nam-Powers 1970 U.S. Census) Score	
				(men, full-time)	(women, full-time)[b]
430	Electricians	44.0	49.2	66	64
431	Electrician apprentices	37.0	40.8		
433	Electric power linemen and cablemen	49.0	39.2	66	64
434	Electrotypers and stereotypers	55.0	38.0	65	42
435	Engravers, exc. photoengravers	47.0	41.2	46	57
436	Excavating, grading, and road machine operators; exc. bulldozer	22.8	31.5	30	45
440	Floor layers, exc. tile setters	17.3	31.4	41	57
441	Foremen, n.e.c.	49.7	45.3	70	61
442	Forgemen and hammermen	23.0	35.5	42	39
443	Furniture and wood finishers	17.8	29.1	22	14
444	Furriers	39.5	35.2	44	48
445	Glaziers	25.2	26.7	50	48
446	Heat treaters, annealers, and temperers	21.7	35.3	47	56
450	Inspectors, scalers, and graders; log and lumber	22.4	31.0	26	19
452	Inspectors, n.e.c.	41.2	31.3	61	36
453	Jewelers and watchmakers	36.4	37.5	49	29
454	Job and die setters, metal	33.5	46.4	50	51
455	Locomotive engineers	57.8	50.8	69	48
456	Locomotive firemen	45.0	36.2	69	48
461	Machinists	32.9	47.7	57	55
462	Machinist apprentices	41.0	40.8		
	Mechanics and repairmen				
470	Air conditioning, heating, and refrigeration	27.0	36.7	54	64
471	Aircraft	48.0	48.2	68	64
472	Automobile body repairmen	19.0	36.7	37	51
473(S)	Automobile mechanics	19.0	36.7	36	54
474	Automobile mechanic apprentices	25.0	40.8		
475	Data processing machine repairmen			78	73
480	Farm implement	27.0	32.6	33	58
481	Heavy equipment mechanics, incl. diesel	26.6	32.8	50	57
482	Household appliance and accessory installers and mechanics	27.0	32.6	50	56
483	Loom fixers	10.0	30.4	18	58
484	Office machine	35.9	33.8	61	65
485	Radio and television	36.0	35.0	56	59
486	Railroad and car shop	20.5	35.6	43	58
491	Mechanic, exc. auto, apprentices	34.0	40.8	52	58
492	Miscellaneous mechanics and repairmen	26.5	32.8	53	58
495	Not specified mechanics and repairmen	27.0	32.6	51	44
501	Millers; grain, flour, and feed	19.0	25.2	14	48
502	Millwrights	31.0	40.3	60	64
503	Molders, metal	12.0	39.1	30	28
504	Molder apprentices	33.0	40.8		
505	Motion picture projectionists	43.0	33.9	39	48
506	Opticians, and lens grinders and polishers	39.0	51.4	62	37
510	Painters, construction and maintenance	16.4	29.9	18	46
511	Painter apprentices	29.0	40.8		
512	Paperhangers	13.7	27.7	28	57
514	Pattern and model makers, exc. paper	43.0	38.7	70	61
515	Photoengravers and lithographers	63.0	40.1	73	52
516	Piano and organ tuners and repairmen	38.0	32.0	44	48

Occupation code[a]		1970 Duncan SEI Score (males)	1970 Siegel Prestige Score (males)	Nam-Powers (1970 U.S. Census) Score	
				(men, full-time)	(women, full-time)[b]
520	Plasterers	25.0	33.2	33	57
521	Plasterer apprentices	29.0	40.8		
522	Plumbers and pipe fitters	34.0	40.6	57	64
523	Plumber and pipe fitter apprentices	33.0	40.8		
525	Power station operators	50.0	38.8	71	75
530	Pressmen and plate printers, printing	46.3	39.3	60	46
531	Pressman apprentices	40.0	40.8		
533	Rollers and finishers, metal	22.0	36.0	47	41
534	Roofers and slaters	15.1	31.5	18	57
535	Sheetmetal workers and tinsmiths	33.0	36.8	59	62
536	Sheetmetal apprentices	33.0	40.8		
540	Shipfitters	34.0	35.5	52	56
542	Shoe repairmen	12.0	32.6	11	12
543	Sign painters and letterers	16.9	30.7	39	36
545	Stationary engineers	45.2	34.9	60	61
546	Stone cutters and stone carvers	24.0	31.7	20	48
550	Structural metal craftsmen	33.7	35.6	58	53
551	Tailors	22.0	34.0	22	19
552	Telephone installers and repairmen	48.8	39.1	68	65
554	Telephone linemen and splicers	49.0	39.2	60	40
560	Tile setters	28.2	38.4	42	57
561	Tool and die makers	49.2	42.3	70	64
562	Tool and die maker apprentices	41.0	40.8		
563	Upholsterers	21.1	29.9	22	19
571	Specified craft apprentices, n.e.c.	34.5	40.8		
572	Not specified apprentices	39.0	40.8		
575	Craftsmen and kindred workers, n.e.c.	25.7	42.1	45	29
580	Former members of the Armed Forces			38	48
	Operatives, except transport				
601	Asbestos and insulation workers	32.0	28.4	58	22
602(T)	Assemblers	17.2	27.5	41	33
603	Blasters and powdermen	11.0	32.1	26	22
604	Bottling and canning operatives	18.4	23.3	26	23
605	Chainmen, rodmen, and axmen; surveying	25.0	39.4	35	22
610	Checkers, examiners, and inspectors; manufacturing	19.2	36.1	42	32
611	Clothing ironers and pressers	17.8	21.9	12	08
612	Cutting operatives, n.e.c.	18.8	28.8	28	17
613	Dressmakers and seamstresses, except factory	23.0	31.7	12	18
614	Drillers, earth	21.6	26.2	36	35
615	Dry wall installers and lathers	24.5	36.4	45	22
620	Dyers	12.0	25.0	16	26
621	Filers, polishers, sanders, and buffers	18.7	23.1	19	23
622	Furnacemen, smeltermen, and pourers	18.1	32.9	35	49
623	Garage workers and gas station attendants	17.9	21.2	19	12
624	Graders and sorters, manufacturing	17.0	32.9	20	16
625	Produce graders and packers, except factory and farm	12.2	23.6	04	05
626	Heaters, metal	29.0	32.9		
630	Laundry and dry cleaning operatives, n.e.c.	15.0	18.2	15	07
631	Meat cutters and butchers, exc. manufacturing	28.8	32.0	47	25

Occupation code[a]		1970 Duncan SEI Score (males)	1970 Siegel Prestige Score (males)	Nam-Powers (1970 U.S. Census) Score	
				(men, full-time)	(women, full-time)[b]
633	Meat cutters and butchers, manufacturing	16.4	23.6	31	14
634	Meat wrappers, retail trade	18.0	19.4	20	43
635	Metal platers	19.8	30.3	37	34
636	Milliners	46.0	33.4	27	20
640	Mine operatives, n.e.c.	16.5	26.4	25	39
641	Mixing operatives	17.6	27.5	33	35
642	Oilers and greasers, exc. auto	15.0	24.2	31	44
643	Packers and wrappers, except meat and produce	18.0	19.5	25	23
644	Painters, manufactured articles	18.1	29.0	25	22
645	Photographic process workers	42.1	35.9	53	42
	Precision machine operatives				
650	Drill press operatives	21.8	31.7	39	38
651	Grinding machine operatives	21.9	19.0	47	49
652	Lathe and milling machine operatives	21.5	31.9	53	50
653	Precision machine operatives, n.e.c.	21.0	31.1	53	34
656	Punch and stamping press operatives	19.4	30.4	37	30
660	Riveters and fasteners	20.1	31.6	26	23
661	Sailors and deckhands	16.0	33.7	23	22
662	Sawyers	04.9	27.6	08	19
663	Sewers and stitchers	18.2	25.2	11	13
664	Shoemaking machine operatives	09.2	31.6	08	16
665	Solderers	23.8	35.4	26	31
666	Stationary firemen	16.6	31.7	38	20
	Textile operatives				
670	Carding, lapping, and combing operatives	03.1	28.9	07	18
671	Knitters, loopers, and toppers	21.0	29.4	17	18
672	Spinners, twisters, and winders	03.8	28.2	09	18
673	Weavers	05.9	25.0	12	26
674	Textile operatives, n.e.c.	06.1	28.8	11	17
680	Welders and flame cutters	24.0	40.1	41	40
681	Winding operatives, n.e.c.	19.6	32.0	50	28
690	Machine operatives, miscellaneous specified	19.0	28.4	21	29
692	Machine operatives, not specified	19.3	29.3	24	28
694	Miscellaneous operatives	19.2	29.1	16	15
695	Not specified operatives	19.2	29.1	24	28
701	Boatmen and canalmen	24.0	36.8	27	42
703	Bus drivers	24.0	32.4	36	28
704	Conductors and motormen, urban rail transit	32.5	28.0	60	42
705	Deliverymen and routemen	31.0	28.2	38	37
706	Fork lift and tow motor operatives	16.8	28.4	27	50
710	Motormen; mine, factory, logging camp, etc.	03.0	27.2	28	42
711	Parking attendants	18.8	22.0	18	42
712	Railroad brakemen	42.0	34.7	61	42
713	Railroad switchmen	44.0	32.8	60	64
714	Taxicab drivers and chauffeurs	10.0	21.5	26	21
715(U)	Truck drivers	15.1	32.1	31	51
	Laborers, except farm				
740	Animal caretakers, exc. farm	16.9	17.5	20	23
750	Carpenters' helpers	07.2	23.0	06	20
751(V)	Construction laborers, exc. carpenters' helpers	07.1	17.4	13	42
752	Fishermen and oystermen	10.6	30.3	07	20

Occupation code[a]		1970 Duncan SEI Score (males)	1970 Siegel Prestige Score (males)	Nam-Powers (1970 U.S. Census) Score	
				(men, full-time)	(women, full-time)[b]
753	Freight and material handlers	08.7	18.8	25	26
754	Garbage collectors	06.0	17.3	08	34
755	Gardeners and groundskeepers, exc. farm	10.9	22.1	06	17
760	Longshoremen and stevedores	11.0	24.4	29	20
761	Lumbermen, raftsmen, and woodchoppers	04.1	25.9	04	11
762	Stock handlers	16.7	20.6	19	22
763	Teamsters	08.0	12.2	08	20
764	Vehicle washers and equipment cleaners	08.6	18.5	10	16
770	Warehousemen, n.e.c.	08.3	20.3	40	47
780	Miscellaneous laborers	08.2	19.1	12	21
785	Not specified laborers	08.3	17.5	07	11
	Farmers and farm managers				
801(W)	Farmers (owners and tenants)	14.0	40.7	19	13
802	Farm managers	36.0	43.7	43	29
	Farm laborers and farm foremen				
821	Farm foremen	20.0	35.0	22	64
822	Farm laborers, wage workers	06.3	18.9	02	03
823	Farm laborers, unpaid family workers	17.0	18.4	13	15
824	Farm service laborers, self-employed	22.0	26.8	30	08
	Service workers, except private household				
	Cleaning service workers				
901	Chambermaids and maids, exc. private household	13.4	16.6	14	03
902	Cleaners and charwomen	07.8	18.4	07	06
903(X)	Janitors and sextons	12.7	19.5	10	14
	Food service workers				
910	Bartenders	19.0	19.9	36	22
911	Busboys	11.0	14.4	13	09
912	Cooks, except private household	15.0	26.4	18	08
913	Dishwashers	11.0	21.8	09	02
914	Food counter and fountain workers	17.0	15.4	17	12
915(Y)	Waiters	16.0	20.3	24	13
916	Food service workers, n.e.c. exc. private household	11.0	20.9	16	12
	Health service workers				
921	Dental assistants	38.0	47.8	40	49
922	Health aides, exc. nursing	25.0	26.3	34	34
923	Health trainees	51.0	45.1	35	45
924	Lay midwives	37.0	23.3	20	28
926	Practical nurses	13.7	36.8	43	46
	Personal service workers				
931	Airline stewardesses	31.0	36.4	68	89
932	Attendants, recreation and amusement	19.1	15.6	25	37
933	Attendants, personal service, n.e.c.	26.3	21.7	27	31
934	Baggage porters and bellhops	07.8	17.5	24	31
935	Barbers	17.0	37.9	31	34
940	Boarding and lodging house keepers	30.0	22.1	33	20
941	Bootblacks	08.0	09.3	00	31
942	Child care workers, exc. private household	28.2	24.0	32	18
943	Elevator operators	10.0	20.9	12	14

Occupation code[a]		1970 Duncan SEI Score (males)	1970 Siegel Prestige Score (males)	Nam-Powers (1970 U.S. Census) Score	
				(men, full-time)	(women, full-time)[b]
944	Hairdressers and cosmetologists	17.0	33.2	46	34
945	Personal service apprentices	31.0	40.8		
950	Housekeepers, exc. private household	31.0	36.4	48	28
952	School monitors	26.0	14.1	40	44
953	Ushers, recreation and amusement	25.0	14.9	16	31
954	Welfare service aides	11.0	14.4	47	32
	Protective service workers				
960	Crossing guards and bridge tenders	17.9	25.3	07	15
961	Firemen, fire protection	37.0	43.8	69	72
962	Guards and watchmen	18.2	22.2	32	47
963	Marshals and constables	21.0	45.8	52	64
964	Policemen and detectives	40.5	47.7	71	84
965	Sheriffs and baliffs	34.0	55.0	58	77
	Private household workers				
980	Child care workers, private household	07.0	22.6	10	03
981	Cooks, private household	07.0	18.0	06	01
982	Housekeepers, private household	10.7	20.1	06	02
983	Laundresses, private household	12.0	17.6	06	00
984(Z)	Maids and servants, private household	07.0	18.0	02	01

[a] Equivalent alphabetic codes follow some codes. Either code may be utilized, depending on the processing method.
[b] Readers with a special interest in the impact of women's labor force participation on occupational status scores should read Mary G. Powers and Joan J. Holmberg, "Occupational Status Scores: Changes Introduced by the Inclusion of Women," *Demography* 15 (May 1978): 183–204. The above scores for male incumbents are drawn from this article. Scores based on all incumbents, male and female, are also available for all of the above occupations.
[c] "N.e.c." means "not elsewhere classified."
[d] Category 280, "Salesmen and sales clerks, n.e.c." was subdivided in the census into 5 occupation groups dependent on industry. The industry codes are shown in parentheses.

4.A.6   HOLLINGSHEAD'S TWO FACTOR INDEX OF SOCIAL POSITION

VARIABLE MEASURED: Positions individuals occupy in the status structure.

DESCRIPTION: There are two- and three-factor forms of the index that have been used extensively. The two-factor index is composed of an occupational scale and an educational scale. The three-factor index includes a residential scale. Since the residential scale was based on sociological analysis previously made by Davis and Myers in New Haven, many communities would not be amenable until residential areas were mapped into a six-position scale. The two-factor index requires only knowledge of occupation and education.

The occupational scale is a seven-point scale representing a modification of the Edwards' system of classifying occupations into socioeconomic groups. The Edwards' system does not differentiate among kinds of professionals or the size and economic strength of businesses. The Hollingshead index of social position ranks professions into different groups and business by their size and value.

The educational scale is also divided into seven positions. In the two-factor index, occupation is given a weight of 7 and education is given a weight of 4. If one were to compute a score for the manager of a Kroger store who had completed high school and one year of business college, the procedure would be as follows:

Factor	*Scale Score* $\times$	*Factor Weight* $=$	*Partial Score*
Occupation	3	7	21
Education	3	4	12
Index of Social Position Score			33

The range of scores in each of five social classes (of New Haven, Connecticut) are:

Class	*Range of Scores*
I	11–17
II	18–31
III	32–47
IV	48–63
V	64–77

WHERE PUBLISHED: August B. Hollingshead, *Two Factor Index of Social Position* (copyright 1957), privately printed 1965, Yale Station, New Haven, Connecticut. August B. Hollingshead and Frederick C. Redlich, *Social Class and Mental Illness* (New York: Wiley, 1958), pp. 387–97.

RELIABILITY AND VALIDITY OF INDEX OF SOCIAL POSITIONS: High correlation is reported between the Hollingshead and Redlich measure and the index of class position devised by R. Ellis, W. Lane, and V. Olesen, "The Index of Class Position: An Improved Intercommunity Measure of Stratification," *American Sociological Review* 28 (April 1963): 271–77.

Various combinations of the scale score for occupation and education are reproducible in the Guttman sense, for there is no overlap between education-occupation combinations. If an individual's education and occupation are known, one can calculate his or her score; if one knows an individual's score, one can calculate both occupational and educational level.

Hollingshead and Redlich report a correlation between judged class with education and occupation as $R_{1(23)} = .906$. Judged class with residence, education, and occupation, $R_{.(234)} = .942$.

Hollingshead and others have made extensive studies of the reliability of scoring, and validity of the index on over one hundred variables. *See* Research Applications.

The researcher will find Hollingshead's account of the background and rationale for the two-factor scale in August B. Hollingshead, "Commentary on 'The Indiscriminate State of Social Class Measurement,' " *Social Forces* 49 (June 1971): 563–67.

UTILITY: Because of the difficulty in obtaining residential information where adequate ecological maps do not exist, the two-factor variation of the Index of Social Position has been used widely. Only occupation and education is needed and these data are relatively easy to obtain. The scale score can be quickly computed and individual social position established.

RESEARCH APPLICATIONS:

BELL, GERALD D. "Processes in the Formation of Adolescents' Aspirations." *Social Forces* 42 (December 1963): 179–86. See p. 182.

ELLIS, ROBERT A. "Social Stratification and Social Relations: An Empirical Test of the Disjunctiveness of Social Classes." *American Sociological Review* 22 (October 1957): 570–78. See p. 571.

HOLLINGSHEAD, AUGUST B., and REDLICH, FREDERICK C. "Social Stratification and Psychiatric Disorders." *American Sociological Review* 18 (April 1953): 163–69. See p. 165.

———. "Social Stratification and Schizophrenia." *American Sociological Review* 19 (June 1954): 302–6. See p. 302.

———. "Social Mobility and Mental Illness." *American Journal of Psychiatry* 112 (September 1955): 179–85. See pp. 180–82.

———. *Social Class and Mental Illness: A Community Study.* New York: Wiley, 1958. Pp. 390–91.

———; ELLIS, ROBERT; and KIRBY, E. "Social Mobility and Mental Illness." *American Sociological Review* 19 (October 1954): 577–84. See p. 579.

———, and FREEMAN, L. Z. "Social Class and the Treatment of Neurotics." In *The Social Welfare Forum.* New York: Columbia University Press, 1955. Pp. 194–205. See pp. 195.

HUNT, RAYMOND G.; GURSSLIN, ORVILLE; and ROACH, JACK L. "Social Status and Psychiatric Science in a Child Guidance Clinic." *American Sociological Review* 23 (February 1958): 81–83. See p. 81.

KOHN, MELVIN L. "Social Class and Parental Values." *American Journal of Sociology* 64 (January 1959): 337–51. See p. 338.

———, and CARROLL, ELEANOR E. "Social Class and the Allocation of Parental Responsibilities." *Sociometry* 23 (December 1960): 372–92. See p. 374.

LAWSON, EDWIN D., and BOCK, WALTER E. "Correlations of Indexes of Families' Socio-Economic Status." *Social Forces* 39 (December 1960): 149–52. See p. 150.

LEFTON, MARK; ANGRIST, SHIRLEY; DINITZ, SIMON; and PASAMANICK, BENJAMIN. "Social Class, Expectations, and Performance of Mental Patients." *American Journal of Sociology* 68 (July 1962): 79–87. See p. 82.

LESLIE, GERALD R., and JOHNSEN, KATHRYN P. "Changed Perceptions of the Maternal Role." *American Sociological Review* 28 (December 1963): 919–28. See p. 923.

LEVINGER, GEORGE. "Task and Social Behavior in Marriage." *Sociometry* 27 (December 1964): 433–48. See pp. 442 and 446.

LEWIS, LIONEL S. "Knowledge, Danger, Certainty, and the Theory of Magic." *American Journal of Sociology* 69 (July 1963): 7–12. See p. 9.

———, and LOPREATO, JOSEPH. "Arationality, Ignorance, and Perceived Danger in Medical Practices." *American Sociological Review* 27 (August 1962): 508–14. See p. 508.

MIZRUCHI, EPHRAIM H. "Social Structure and Anomia in a Small City." *American Sociological Review* 25 (October 1960): 645–54. See p. 647.

PSATHAS, GEORGE. "Ethnicity, Social Class and Adolescent Independence from Parental Control." *American Sociological Review* 22 (August 1957): 415–23. See p. 417.

ROSEN, BERNARD C. "The Achievement Syndrome: A Psychocultural Dimension of Social Stratification." *American Sociological Review* 21 (April 1956): 203–11. See p. 204.

————. "Race, Ethnicity, and the Achievement Syndrome." *American Sociological Review* 24 (February 1959): 47–60. See p. 48.

————. "Family Structure and Achievement Motivation." *American Sociological Review* 26 (August 1961): 574–85. See p. 576.

————. "Socialization and Achievement Motivation in Brazil." *American Sociological Review* 27 (October 1962): 612–24. See p. 613.

————. "The Achievement Syndrome and Economic Growth in Brazil." *Social Forces* 42 (March 1964): 341–54. See p. 345.

————, and D'ANDRADE, ROY. "The Psychosocial Origins of Achievement Motivation." *Sociometry* 22 (September 1959): 185–218. See p. 189.

SMITH, BULKELEY, JR. "The Differential Residential Segregation of Working Class Negroes in New Haven." *American Sociological Review* 24 (August 1959): 529–33. See p. 530.

STRODTBECK, FRED L.; MCDONALD, MARGARET R.; and ROSEN, BERNARD C. "Evaluation of Occupations: A Reflection of Jewish and Italian Mobility Differences." *American Sociological Review* 22 (October 1957): 546–53. See p. 547.

WECHSLER, HENRY. "Community Growth, Depressive Disorders, and Suicide." *American Journal of Sociology* 67 (July 1961): 9–16. See p. 15.

YARROW, MARIAN R.; SCOTT, PHYLLIS; deLEEUW, LOUISE; and HEINIG, CHRISTINE. "Child-Rearing in Families of Working and Nonworking Mothers." *Sociometry* 25 (June 1962): 122–40. See p. 124.

For more recent use see all references in the period 1965–74 in the *American Sociological Review Inventory* under Hollingshead Two Factor Index of Social Position in Section 4.M.1, p. 497 and pp. 505–506.

HOLLINGSHEAD'S TWO FACTOR INDEX OF SOCIAL POSITION

*1. The Occupational Scale**

    1. *Higher Executives of Large Concerns, Proprietors, and Major Professionals*

A. *Higher Executives* (Value of corporation $500,000 and above as rated by Dun and Bradstreet)

Bank	Business
Presidents	Vice-Presidents
Vice-Presidents	Assistant vice-presidents
Assistant vice-presidents	Executive secretaries
Business	Research directors
Directors	Treasurers
Presidents	

B. *Proprietors* (Value over $100,000 by Dun and Bradstreet)

Brokers	Farmers
Contractors	Lumber dealers
Dairy owners	

C. *Major Professionals*

Accountants (CPA)	Architects
Actuaries	Artists, portrait
Agronomists	Astronomers

Auditors
Bacteriologists
Chemical engineers
Chemists
Clergymen (professional trained)
Dentists
Economists
Engineers (college graduates)
Foresters
Geologists
Judges (superior courts)
Lawyers
Metallurgists

Military: commissioned officers,
    major and above
Officials of the executive branch of
    government, federal, state, local:
    e.g., Mayor, City manager, City plan
    director, Internal Revenue director
Physicians
Physicists, research
Psychologists, practicing
Symphony conductor
Teachers, university, college
Veterinarians (veterinary surgeons)

2. *Business Managers, Proprietors of Medium-Sized Businesses, and Lesser Professionals*

A. *Business Managers in Large Concerns* (Value $500,000)

Advertising directors
Branch managers
Brokerage salesmen
Directors of purchasing
District managers
Executive assistants
Export managers, international
    concerns
Government officials, minor, e.g.,
    Internal Revenue agents

Manufacturer's representatives
Office managers
Personnel managers
Police chief; Sheriff
Postmaster
Production managers
Sales engineers
Sales managers, national concerns
Store managers

B. *Proprietors of Medium Businesses* (Value $35,000–$100,000)

Advertising
Clothing store
Contractors
Express company
Farm owners
Fruits, wholesale
Furniture business

Jewelers
Poultry business
Real estate brokers
Rug business
Store
Theater

C. *Lesser Professionals*

Accountants (not CPA)
Chiropodists
Chiropractors
Correction officers
Director of Community House
Engineers (not college graduate)
Finance writers
Health educators
Labor relations consultants
Librarians

Military: commissioned officers,
    lieutenant, captain
Musicians (symphony orchestra)
Nurses
Opticians
Optometrists, D.O.
Pharmacists
Public health officers (MPH)
Research assistants, university
    (full-time)
Social workers

3. *Administrative Personnel, Owners of Small Businesses, and Minor Professionals*

A. *Administrative Personnel*

Advertising agents
Chief clerks

Credit managers
Insurance agents

Managers, departments
Passenger agents, railroad
Private secretaries
Purchasing agents
Sales representatives
Section heads, federal, state and local governmental offices

Section heads, large businesses and industries
Service managers
Shop managers
Store managers (chain)
Traffic managers

B. *Small Business Owners* ($6,000–$35,000)

Art gallery
Auto accessories
Awnings
Bakery
Beauty shop
Boatyard
Brokerage, insurance
Car dealers
Cattle dealers
Cigarette machines
Cleaning shops
Clothing
Coal businesses
Contracting businesses
Convalescent homes
Decorating
Dog supplies
Dry goods
Engraving business
Feed
Finance companies, local
Fire extinguishers
Five and dime
Florist
Food equipment
Food products
Foundry
Funeral directors

Furniture
Garage
Gas station
Glassware
Grocery, general
Hotel protection
Jewelry
Machinery brokers
Manufacturing
Monuments
Music
Package stores (liquor)
Paint contracting
Poultry
Real estate
Records and radios
Restaurant
Roofing contractor
Shoe
Signs
Tavern
Taxi company
Tire shop
Trucking
Trucks and tractors
Upholstery
Wholesale outlets
Window shades

C. *Semiprofessionals*

Actors and showmen
Army, master sargeant
Artists, commercial
Appraisers (estimators)
Clergymen (not professionally trained)
Concern managers
Deputy sheriffs
Dispatchers, railroad
Interior decorators
Interpreters, courts
Laboratory assistants
Landscape planners
Morticians

Navy, chief petty officer
Oral hygienists
Physiotherapists
Piano teachers
Publicity and public relations
Radio, TV announcers
Reporters, court
Reporters, newspapers
Surveyors
Title searchers
Tool designs
Travel agents
Yard masters, railroad

D. *Farmers*

Farm owners ($20,000–$35,000)

4. *Clerical and Sales Workers, Technicians, and Owners of Little Businesses*
(Value under $6,000)

A. *Clerical and Sales Workers*

Bank clerks and tellers
Bill collectors
Bookkeepers
Business machine operators,
    offices
Claims examiners
Clerical or stenographic
Conductors, railroad
Factory storekeepers

Factory supervisors
Post Office clerks
Route managers
Sales clerks
Sergeants and petty officers, military
    services
Shipping clerks
Supervisors, utilities, factories
Supervisors, toll stations

B. *Technicians*

Dental technicians
Draftsmen
Driving teachers
Expeditor, factory
Experimental tester
Instructors, telephone company,
    factory
Inspectors, weights, sanitary,
    railroad, factory
Investigators
Laboratory technicians

Locomotive engineers
Operators, PBX
Proofreaders
Safety supervisors
Supervisors of maintenance
Technical assistants
Telephone company supervisors
Timekeepers
Tower operators, railroad
Truck dispatchers
Window trimmers (stores)

C. *Owners of Little Businesses* ($3,000–$6,000)

Flower shop
Grocery

Newsstand
Tailor shop

D. *Farmers*

Owners (Value $10,000–$20,000)

5. *Skilled Manual Employees*

Auto body repairers
Bakers
Barbers
Blacksmiths
Bookbinders
Boilermakers
Brakemen, railroad
Brewers
Bulldozer operators
Butchers
Cabinet makers
Cable splicers
Carpenters
Casters (founders)
Cement finishers
Cheese makers
Chefs
Compositors
Diemakers
Diesel engine repair and
    maintenance (trained)
Diesel shovel operators

Electricians
Engravers
Exterminators
Firemen, city
Firemen, railroad
Fitters, gas, steam
Foremen, construction, dairy
Gardeners, landscape (trained)
Glass blowers
Glaziers
Gunsmiths
Gauge makers
Hair stylists
Heat treaters
Horticulturists
Linemen, utility
Linotype operators
Lithographers
Locksmiths
Loom fixers
Machinists (trained)
Maintenance foremen

Linoleum layers (trained)
Masons
Masseurs
Mechanics (trained)
Millwrights
Moulders (trained)
Painters
Paperhangers
Patrolmen, railroad
Pattern and model makers
Piano builders
Piano tuners
Plumbers
Policemen, city
Postmen
Printers
Radio, television maintenance
Repairmen, home appliances
Small farmers
Owners (Value under $10,000)

Rope splicers
Sheetmetal workers (trained)
Shipsmiths
Shoe repairmen (trained)
Stationery engineers (licensed)
Stewards, club
Switchmen, railroad
Tailors (trained)
Teletype operators
Tool makers
Track supervisors, railroad
Tractor-trailer trans.
Typographers
Upholsters (trained)
Watchmakers
Weavers
Welders
Yard supervisors, railroad

Tenants who own farm equipment

6. *Machine Operators and Semiskilled Employees*

Aides, hospital
Apprentices, electricians, printers,
    steam fitters, toolmakers
Assembly line workers
Bartenders
Bingo tenders
Bridge tenders
Building superintendents
    (construction)
Bus drivers
Checkers
Coin machine fillers
Cooks, short order
Deliverymen
Dressmakers, machine
Elevator operators
Enlisted men, military services
Filers, sanders, buffers
Foundry workers
Garage and gas station attendants
Greenhouse workers
Guards, doorkeepers, watchmen
Hairdressers
Housekeepers
Meat cutters and packers
Meter readers
Operators, factory machines
Oilers, railroad
Farmers
Smaller tenants who own little equipment

Practical nurses
Pressers, clothing
Pump operators
Receivers and checkers
Roofers
Setup men, factories
Shapers
Signalmen, railroad
Solderers, factory
Sprayers, paint
Steelworkers (not skilled)
Standers, wire machines
Strippers, rubber factory
Taxi drivers
Testers
Timers
Tire moulders
Trainmen, railroad
Truck drivers, general
Waiters-waitresses ("better places")
Weighers
Welders, spot
Winders, machine
Wiredrawers, machine
Wine bottlers
Wood workers, machine
Wrappers, stores and factories

7. *Unskilled Employees*

Amusement park workers
  (bowling alleys, pool rooms)
Ash removers
Attendants, parking lots
Cafeteria workers
Car cleaners, railroad
Carriers, coal
Countermen
Dairy workers
Deck hands
Domestics
Farm helpers
Fishermen (clam diggers)
Freight handlers
Garbage collectors
Gravediggers
Hod carriers
Hog killers
Hospital workers, unspecified
Hostlers, railroad
Janitors (sweepers)
Laborers, construction
Farmers
Sharecroppers

Laborers, unspecified
Laundry workers
Messengers
Platform men, railroad
Peddlers
Porters
Relief, public, private
Roofer's helpers
Shirt folders
Shoe shiners
Sorters, rag and salvage
Stage hands
Stevedores
Stock handlers
Street cleaners
Struckmen, railroad
Unemployed (no occupation)
Unskilled factory workers
Waitresses ("hash houses")
Washers, cars
Window cleaners
Woodchoppers

2. The Educational Scale

The educational scale is premised upon the assumption that men and women who possess similar educations will tend to have similar tastes and similar attitudes, and they will also tend to exhibit similar behavior patterns.

The educational scale is divided into seven positions:

1. Graduate professional training: Persons who completed a recognized professional course that led to the receipt of a graduate degree were given scores of 1.
2. Standard college or university graduation: All individuals who had completed a four-year college or university course leading to a recognized college degree were assigned the same scores. No differentiation was made between state universities or private colleges.
3. Partial college training: Individuals who had completed at least one year but not a full college course were assigned this position.
4. High school graduation: All secondary school graduates whether from a private preparatory school, public high school, trade school, or parochial school were given this score.
5. Partial high school: Individuals who had completed the tenth or eleventh grades, but had not completed high school were given this score.
6. Junior high school: Individuals who had completed the seventh grade through the ninth grade were given this position.
7. Less than seven years of school: Individuals who had not completed the seventh grade were given the same scores irrespective of the amount of education they had received.

REVISED OCCUPATIONAL RATING SCALE FROM W. L. WARNER, M. MEEKER, AND K. EELLS' INDEX OF STATUS CHARACTERISTICS

4.A.7

VARIABLE MEASURED: Social class position according to a seven-point rating.

DESCRIPTION: The rating of occupations is one measure included in the Index of Status Characteristics. The index is composed of four status characteristics: occupation, source of income, house type, and dwelling area. Each of these is rated on a seven-point scale, and this rating is then weighted according to its separate contributions to the total index. The weighted ratings are totaled to yield the scores that are appropriate to the various classes. The scores on the Index of Status Characteristics range from 12 to 84. The ranges are calculated by validating preliminary scores using the Evaluated Participation Method of determining social-class position. Occupation is the single measure most highly correlated with class position.

WHERE PUBLISHED: W. Lloyd Warner, Marcia, Meeker, and Kenneth Eells, *Social Class in America* (Chicago: Science Research Associates, 1949), pp. 121–59. The occupational rating scale is shown on pp. 140–41.

VALIDITY OF INDEX OF STATUS CHARACTERISTICS:

1. Accuracy in prediction: 85 percent of the Old Americans in *Yankee City* were placed correctly or within one point. Not as valid for ethnics.
2. Correlation with the Evaluative Participation Method as reported by Warner et al. on p. 168.

Occupation	$r = .91$
Source of Income	$r = .85$
House Type	$r = .85$
Dwelling Area	$r = .82$
I.S.C. (all four measures)	$r = .97$

3. Comparative Study by John L. Haer.
    Five indexes of social stratification were compared and evaluated by examining their capacities for predicting variables shown in previous studies to be related to measures of stratification. These five indexes include Center's class identification question, an open-ended question, occupation, education, and Warner's Index of Status Characteristics. An overall comparison reveals that coefficients are higher for the Index of Status Characteristics than for other indexes in 18 out of 22 comparisons. Its greater efficiency may be due to the fact that it is a composite index that provides a continuous series of ranks. These features make it possible to discern minute variations in relation to other variables. John L. Haer, "Predictive Utility of Five Indices of Social Stratification," *American Sociological Review* 22 (October 1957): 541–46.

VALIDITY OF THE OCCUPATION SCALE: Joseph A. Kahl and James A. Davis selected 19 single measures of socioeconomic status and measured their intercorrelations. They report a product moment correlation of .74 between occupation (Warner) and status of friends—". . . our data agree with Warner's that occupation (as he measures it) is the best predictor of either

Warner, Meeker, Eells' Revised Scale for Rating Occupation

Rating assigned to occupation	Professionals	Proprietors and managers	Businessmen	Clerks and kindred workers, etc.	Manual workers	Protective and service workers	Farmers
1	Lawyers, doctors, dentists, engineers, judges, high-school superintendents, veterinarians, ministers (graduated from divinity school), chemists, etc., with postgraduate training, architects	Businesses valued at $75,000 and over	Regional and divisional managers of large financial and industrial enterprises	Certified Public Accountants			Gentlemen farmers
2	High-school teachers, trained nurses, chiropractors, undertakers, ministers (some training), newspaper editors, librarians (graduate)	Businesses valued at $20,000 to $75,000	Assistant managers and office and department managers of large businesses, assistants to executives, etc.	Accountants, salesmen of real estate and insurance, postmasters			Large farm owners, farm owners
3	Social workers, grade-school teachers, optometrists, librarians (not graduate), undertaker's assistants, ministers (no training)	Businesses valued at $5,000 to $20,000	All minor officials of businesses	Auto salesmen, bank clerks and cashiers, postal clerks, secretaries to executives, supervisors of railroad, telephone, etc., justices of the peace	Contractors		

4	Businesses valued at $2,000 to $5,000	Stenographers, bookkeepers, rural mail clerks, railroad ticket agents, sales people in dry goods stores, etc.	Factory foreman, electricians, plumbers, carpenters, watchmakers (own business)	Dry cleaners, butchers, sheriffs, railroad engineers and conductors	Tenant farmers
5	Businesses valued at $500 to $2,000	Dime store clerks, hardware salesmen, beauty operators, telephone operators	Carpenters, plumbers, electricians (apprentice), timekeepers, linemen, telephone or telegraph, radio repairmen, medium skilled workers	Barbers, firemen, butcher's apprentices, practical nurses, policemen, seamstresses, cooks in restaurant, bartenders	
6	Businesses valued at less than $500		Moulders, semi-skilled workers, assistants to carpenter, etc.	Baggage men, night policemen and watchmen, taxi and truck drivers, gas station attendants, waitresses in restaurants	Small tenant farmers, laborers
7		Heavy labor, migrant work, odd-job men, miners		Janitors, scrubwomen, newsboys	Migrant farm laborers

social participation or the whole socioeconomic cluster represented by the general factor identified by factor analysis." "A comparison of Indexes of Socio-Economic Status," *American Sociological Review* 20 (June 1955): 317–25.

Stanley A. Hetzler reports the following coefficients between seven rating scales and ratings of social class and social position.

Rating Scales	Social Class	Social Position
Occupational prestige	.69	.57
Residential area	.54	.46
Family background	.53	.48
Personal influence	.49	.52
Dwelling unit	.47	.39
Family wealth	.45	.45
Personal income	.34	.44

The four rating scales showing the highest coefficients were occupational prestige, family background, residential area, and personal influence. The multiple correlation of these four scales with social class is .75; with social position it is .68. "An Investigation of the Distinctiveness of Social Classes," *American Sociological Review* 18 (October 1953): 493–97. See also J. L. Haer, "A Test of the Unidimensionality of the Index of Status Characteristics," *Social Forces* 34 (1955): 56–58.

UTILITY: The Index of Status Characteristics presents a comparatively objective means of determining social-class position. The limits defined for the various seven-point ratings are sufficiently precise to eliminate to a great degree any subjective judgment. All one needs to know is a person's name, occupation, and address; the source of income can generally be derived from the occupation, and the house type and dwelling area can be evaluated through the address. This eliminates extensive, time-consuming interviewing.

The Occupation Scale is the best single predictor of social-class position within a seven-point range. The high correlation it exhibits with the evaluative participative method of social-class position ($r = .91$) commends occupation as a single dimension. Researchers will achieve a high degree of predictive efficiency by use of the one scale. Robinson and his co-workers call Warner's index "the most sophisticated short classification of occupational status available." See John B. Robinson, Robert Athanasiou, and Kendra B. Head, *Measures of Occupational Attitudes and Occupational Characteristics,* Institute of Social Research, University of Michigan, Ann Arbor, 1969, p. 338 and pp. 362–66.

RESEARCH APPLICATIONS:

FREEMAN, HOWARD E., and SIMMONS, OZZIE G. "Social Class and Post-Hospital Performance Levels." *American Sociological Review* 24 (1959): 345–51.

GOFFMAN, IRWIN W. "Status Consistency and Preference for Change in Power Distribution." *American Sociological Review* 22 (June 1957): 275–81. See p. 277.

KANIN, EUGENE, JR., and HOWARD, DAVID H. "Postmarital Consequences of Premarital Sex Adjustments." *American Sociological Review* 23 (October 1958): 556–62. See p. 557.

HAVIGHURST, ROBERT J., and DAVIS, ALLISON. "A Comparison of the Chicago and Harvard Studies of Social Class Differences in Child Rearing." *American Sociological Review* 20 (August 1955): 438–42. See p. 439.

LAWSON, EDWIN D., and BOCK, WALTER E. "Correlations of Indexes of Families' Socioeconomic Status." *Social Forces* 39 (December 1960): 149–52.

LITTMAN, RICHARD A.; MOORE, ROBERT C. A.; and PIERCE-JONES, JOHN. "Social Class Differences in Child-Rearing: A Third Community for Comparison with Chicago and Newton." *American Sociological Review* 22 (December 1957): 694–704. See p. 695.

MORLAND, J. KENNETH. "Racial Recognition by Nursery School Children in Lynchburg, Virginia." *Social Forces* 37 (December 1958): 132–41. See p. 132.

———. "Educational and Occupational Aspirations of Mill and Town School Children in a Southern Community." *Social Forces* 39 (December 1960): 169–75.

SALISBURY, W. SEWARD. "Religion and Secularization." *Social Forces* 36 (March 1958): 197–205. See p. 198.

SCUDDER, RICHARD, and ANDERSON, C. ARNOLD. "Range of Acquaintance and of Repute as Factors in Prestige Rating Methods of Studying Social Status." *Social Forces* 32 (March 1954): 248–53. See p. 252.

———. "Migration and Vertical Occupational Mobility." *American Sociological Review* 19 (June 1954): 329–34. See p. 330.

STONE, GREGORY P., and FORM, WILLIAM H. "Instabilities in Status: The Problem of Hierarchy in the Community Study of Status Arrangements." *American Sociological Review* 18 (April 1953): 149–62.

———. "The Local Community Clothing Market: A Study of the Social and Social Psychological Contexts of Shipping." Technical Bulletin No. 247. East Lansing, Mich.: Michigan State University, June 1955.

SWINEHART, JAMES W. "Socioeconomic Level, Status Aspiration, and Maternal Role." *American Sociological Review* 28 (June 1963): 391–99.

WARNER, W. LLOYD, et al. *Democracy in Jonesville.* New York: Harper & Brothers, 1949.

WESTIE, FRANK R., and HOWARD, DAVID H. "Social Status Differentials and the Race Attitudes of Negroes." *American Sociological Review* 19 (October 1954): 584–91. See p. 587.

WHITE, MARTHA STURM. "Social Class, Child Rearing Practices and Child Behavior." *American Sociological Review* 22 (December 1957): 704–712.

For more recent research use see the *American Sociological Review Inventory,* 4, M.1.

ALBA M. EDWARDS' SOCIAL-ECONOMIC GROUPING OF OCCUPATIONS
4.A.8

VARIABLE MEASURED: Socioeconomic position.

DESCRIPTION: Occupations are classified into six major groups with each group purported to have a somewhat distinct economic standard of life and to exhibit intellectual and social similarities. The two major dimensions for the ranking order are income and education.

WHERE PUBLISHED: Alba M. Edwards, *Comparative Occupation Statistics for the United States* (Washington, D.C.: U.S. Government Printing Office,

1934), pp. 164–69; U.S. Bureau of the Census, *1960 Census of Population, Classified Index of Occupations and Industries* (Washington, D.C.: U.S. Government Printing Office, 1960).

RELIABILITY: Occupational grouping shows high comparability with similar occupational ranking systems such as Barr-Taussig, Beckman Goodenough and Anderson, Centers, etc.

VALIDITY: Major occupational groups can be ranked on the two dimensions of income and education with relatively high correspondence as shown for the following occupational groups.

Occupational Group	Men		Women	
	Mean School Years Completed 25 years & Over (1970)[a]	Mean Earnings 25-64 years (1969)[b]	Mean School Years Completed 25 years & Over 1970[a]	Mean Earnings 25-64 years 1969[b]
Professional, technical, and kindred workers	16.5	$16,007	16.1	$6,366
Managers and administrative workers, except farm	12.9	13,733	12.5	6,430
Sales workers	12.8	11,537	12.2	3,290
Clerical and kindred workers	12.5	8,461	12.5	4,605
Craftsman, foremen, and kindred workers	11.8	8,749	11.8	5,048
Operatives and kindred workers	10.7	7,376	10.3	3,810
Laborers, except farm and mine	9.3	6,089	10.6	3,466

[a]1970 U.S. Census of Population. *Educational Attainment.* PC (2)-5B (Washington, D.C.: U.S. Government Printing Office, March 1973). table 11, pp. 213-14.

[b]1970 U.S. Census of Population. *Earnings by Occupation and Education.* PC (2)-8B (Washington, D.C.: U.S. Government Printing Office, January 1973), tables 1 and 7.

UTILITY: This has been a widely used scale of social-economic groupings of gainful workers in the United States. It is the basis on which the U.S. Census has grouped workers since 1930 in the decennial census.

The universe of gainful workers is fully enumerated every ten years. Any research worker can check his sample against enumeration parameters and can draw generalizations with high confidence.

RESEARCH APPLICATIONS:

ANDERSON, H. DEWEY, and DAVIDSON, PERCY E. *Occupational Trends in the United States.* Stanford: Stanford University Press, 1940.

———. *Occupational Mobility in an American Community.* Stanford: Stanford University Press, 1937.

BLAU, PETER M., and DUNCAN, OTIS D. *The American Occupational Structure in the United States.* New York: Wiley, 1967.

DAVIDSON, PERCY E., and ANDERSON, DEWEY. *Ballots and the Democratic Class Struggle.* Stanford: Stanford University Press, 1943.

GLENN, NORVAL D., and ALSTON, JOHN P. "Cultural Distances Among Occupational Categories." *American Sociological Review* 33 (June 1968): 365–82.

JAFFE, A. J., and CARLETON, R. O. *Occupational Mobility in the United States, 1930–1960.* New York: Columbia University Press, 1954.

LIPSET, SEYMOUR MARTIN, and BENDIX, REINHARD. *Social Mobility and Industrial Society.* Berkeley: University of California Press, 1959.

TAUSSIG, F. W., and JOSLYN, C. S. *American Business Leaders.* New York: Macmillan, 1932.

WARNER, W. LLOYD, and ABEGGLEN, JAMES C. *Occupational Mobility in American Business and Industry, 1928–1952.* Minneapolis: University of Minnesota Press, 1955.

For an extensive list of applications, see Charles M. Bonjean, Richard J. Hill, and S. Dale McLemore, *Sociological Measurement* (San Francisco: Chandler, 1967), pp. 423–37.

Social-Economic Grouping of Occupations (After Alba M. Edwards)

Present U.S. Census Classification of Occupational Groups:

1. Professional, technical and kindred workers
2. Business managers, officials, and proprieters
    a. Nonfarm managers, officials, and proprietors
    b. Farm owners and managers
3. Clerical and sales workers
    a. Clerical and kindred workers
    b. Sales workers
4. Craftsmen, foremen and kindred workers
5. Operatives and kindred workers
6. Unskilled, service, and domestic workers
a. Private household workers
b. Service workers, except private household
c. Farm laborers, unpaid family workers
d. Laborers, except farm and mine

Group Structure and Dynamics

This section contains five scales, each of which measures a different variable relating to group structure and dynamics. Hemphill's Index of Group Dimensions, which ascertains thirteen dimensions of a group, is the most ambitious attempt to measure the structural properties of groups. Bale's International Process Analysis is a nominal scale, widely used to assess the characteristics of personal interaction in problem-solving groups. Seashore's Group Cohesiveness Index provides a measure of the strength of a group to maintain its identity and to persist. The Sociometry Scales of Sociometric Choice and Sociometric Preference reveal the interpersonal attractions of members in groups. These scales may be widely adapted to suit many different situations. They are useful not only to a researcher seeking basic relationships but also to the action researcher or social worker. New groupings of individuals can be quickly arranged and new measurements of morale or productivity can be made. The Bogardus Social Distance Scale may also be adapted to many different purposes. The social distance between two persons, between person and group, or between groups can be measured in such diverse situations as that involving an outgroup member and a country, a community, or an organization.

4.B.1 HEMPHILL'S INDEX OF GROUP DIMENSIONS

VARIABLE MEASURED: The index is designed to measure group dimensions or characteristics.

DESCRIPTION: The index is built upon 13 comparatively independent group dimensions: autonomy, control, flexibility, hedonic tone, homogeneity, intimacy, participation, permeability, polarization, potency, stability, stratification, and viscidity. The 150 items are answered on a five-point scale. The dimensions were selected from a list of group adjectives used by authorities. Items were suggested from a free-response type questionnaire administered to 500 individuals, and 5 judges then put the items into the dimensional categories.

WHERE PUBLISHED: John K. Hemphill, *Group Dimensions: A Manual for Their Measurement,* Research Monograph No. 87 (Columbus, Ohio: Bureau of Business Research, Ohio State University, 1956).

RELIABILITY: Split-half reliabilities range from .59 to .87. The relationship between an item and high-low categories ranges from .03 to .78 with a median of .36 on the keyed items and from .01 to .36 with a median of .12 on the randomly selected items. Intercorrelation of dimension scores ranges from −.54 to .81, with most within +.29 (which has a .01 significance level). Agreement between different reporters of the same group ranges from .53 to .74.

VALIDITY: The dimension scores describing the characteristics of two quite different groups vary accordingly, while those describing the characteristics of two similar groups are quite similar. A careful critique of reliability and validity is available in Dale G. Lake, Mathew B. Miles, and Ralph B. Earle, Jr., *Measuring Human Behavior* (New York: Teachers College Press, 1973), p. 91.

UTILITY: The index can be useful in studying the relationships between the behavior of leaders and characteristics of groups in which they function. Although fairly long, it is comparatively easy to administer and score.

RESEARCH APPLICATIONS: Validation and reliability studies on 200 descriptions of 35 groups.

BENTZ, V. J. "Leadership: A Study of Social Interaction." Unpublished report, Bureau of Business Research, Ohio State University.

HEMPHILL, JOHN K., and WESTIE, CHARLES M. "The Measurement of Group Dimensions." *Journal of Psychology* 29 (April 1950): 325–42.

———. "The Measurement of Group Dimensions," in *The Language of Social Research,* edited by Paul F. Lazarsfeld and Morris Rosenberg. Rev. ed., Glencoe, Ill.: Free Press, 1975.

GROUP DIMENSIONS DESCRIPTIONS QUESTIONNAIRE

Directions:

Record your answer to each of the items on the answer sheet for the group you are describing. Make no marks on the question booklet itself.

In considering each item go through the following steps:

1. Read the item carefully.
2. Think about how well the item tells something about the group you are describing.
3. Find the number on the answer sheet that corresponds with the number of the item you are considering.
4. After each number on the answer sheet you will find five pairs of dotted lines lettered A, B, C, D, or E.

   If the item you are considering tells something about the group that is definitely true, blacken the space between the pair of dotted lines headed by A.

If the item you are considering tells something that is mostly true, blacken the space between the pair of lines headed by B.

If the item tells something that is to an equal degree both true and false, or you are undecided about whether it is true or false, blacken the space between the pair of lines headed by C.

If the item you are considering tells something that is mostly false, blacken the space between the pair of lines headed by D.

If the item you are considering tells something about the group that is definitely false, blacken the space between the pair of dotted lines headed by E.

5. When blackening the space between a pair of lines, fill in all the space with a heavy black line. If you should make an error in marking your answer, erase thoroughly the mark you made and then indicate the correct answer.

6. In rare cases where you believe that an item does not apply at all to the group or you feel that you do not have sufficient information to make any judgment concerning what the item tells about the group, leave that item blank.

7. After you have completed one item, proceed to the next one in order. You may have as long as you need to complete your description. Be sure the number on the answer sheet corresponds with the number of the item being answered in the booklet.

Questions:

The questions that follow make it possible to describe objectively certain characteristics of social groups. The items simply describe characteristics of groups; they do not judge whether the characteristic is desirable or undesirable. Therefore, in no way are the questions to be considered a "test" either of the groups or of the person answering the questions. We simply want an objective description of what the group is like.

1. The group has well understood but unwritten rules concerning member conduct.
2. Members fear to express their real opinions.
3. The only way a member may leave the group is to be expelled.
4. No explanation need be given by a member wishing to be absent from the group.
5. An individual's membership can be dropped should he fail to live up to the standards of the group.
6. Members of the group work under close supervision.
7. Only certain kinds of ideas may be expressed freely within the group.
8. A member may leave the group by resigning at any time he wishes.
9. A request made by a member to leave the group can be refused.
10. A member has to think twice before speaking in the group's meetings.
11. Members are occasionally forced to resign.
12. The members of the group are subject to strict discipline.
13. The group is rapidly increasing in size.
14. Members are constantly leaving the group.
15. There is a large turnover of members within the group.
16. Members are constantly dropping out of the group but new members replace them.
17. During the entire time of the group's existence no member has left.
18. Each member's personal life is known to other members of the group.
19. Members of the group lend each other money.
20. A member has the chance to get to know all other members of the group.

21. Members are not in close enough contact to develop likes or dislikes for one another.
22. Members of the group do small favors for one another.
23. All members know each other very well.
24. Each member of the group knows all other members by their first names.
25. Members are in daily contact either outside or within the group.
26. Members of the group are personal friends.
27. Certain members discuss personal affairs among themselves.
28. Members of the group know the family backgrounds of other members of the group.
29. Members address each other by their first names.
30. The group is made up of individuals who do not know each other well.
31. The opinions of all members are considered as equal.
32. The group's officers hold a higher status in the group than other members.
33. The older members of the group are granted special privileges.
34. The group is controlled by the actions of a few members.
35. Every member of the group enjoys the same group privileges.
36. Experienced members are in charge of the group.
37. Certain problems are discussed only among the group's officers.
38. Certain members have more influence on the group than others.
39. Each member of the group has as much power as any other member.
40. An individual's standing in the group is determined only by how much he gets done.
41. Certain members of the group hold definite office in the group.
42. The original members of the group are given special privileges.
43. Personal dissatisfaction with the group is too small to be brought up.
44. Members continually grumble about the work they do for the group.
45. The group does its work with no great vim, vigor, or pleasure.
46. A feeling of failure prevails in the group.
47. There are frequent intervals of laughter during group meetings.
48. The group works independently of other groups.
49. The group has support from outside.
50. The group is an active representative of a larger group.
51. The group's activities are influenced by a larger group of which it is part.
52. People outside the group decide on what work the group is to do.
53. The group follows the examples set by other groups.
54. The group is one of many similar groups that form one large organization.
55. The things the group does are approved by a group higher up.
56. The group joins with other groups in carrying out its activities.
57. The group is a small part of a larger group.
58. The group is under outside pressure.
59. Members are disciplined by an outside group.
60. Plans of the group are made by other groups above it.
61. The members allow nothing to interfere with the progress of the group.
62. Members gain a feeling of being honored by being recognized as one of the group.
63. Membership in the group is a way of acquiring general social status.
64. Failure of the group would mean little to individual members.
65. The activities of the group take up less than ten percent of each member's waking time.
66. Members gain in prestige among outsiders by joining the group.
67. A mistake by one member of the group might result in hardship for all.
68. The activities of the group take up over ninety percent of each member's waking time.

69. Membership in the group serves as an aid to vocational advancement.
70. Failure of the group would mean nothing to most members.
71. Each member would lose his self-respect if the group should fail.
72. Membership in the group gives members a feeling of superiority.
73. The activities of the group take up over half the time each member is awake.
74. Failure of the group would lead to embarrassment for members.
75. Members are not rewarded for effort put out for the group.
76. There are two or three members of the group who generally take the same side on any group issue.
77. Certain members are hostile to other members.
78. There is constant bickering among members of the group.
79. Members know that each one looks out for the other one as well as for himself.
80. Certain members of the group have no respect for other members.
81. Certain members of the group are considered uncooperative.
82. There is a constant tendency toward conniving against one another among parts of the group.
83. Members of the group work together as a team.
84. Certain members of the group are responsible for petty quarrels and some animosity among other members.
85. There are tensions among subgroups that tend to interfere with the group's activities.
86. Certain members appear to be incapable of working as part of the group.
87. There is an undercurrent of feeling among members that tends to pull the group apart.
88. Anyone who has sufficient interest in the group to attend its meetings is considered a member.
89. The group engages in membership drives.
90. New members are welcomed to the group on the basis "the more the merrier."
91. A new member may join only after an old member resigns.
92. A college degree is required for membership in the group.
93. A person may enter the group by expressing a desire to join.
94. Anyone desiring to enter the group is welcome.
95. Membership is open to anyone willing to further the purpose of the group.
96. Prospective members are carefully examined before they enter the group.
97. No applicants for membership in the group are turned down.
98. No special training is required for membership in the group.
99. Membership depends upon the amount of education an individual has.
100. People interested in joining the group are asked to submit references which are checked.
101. There is a high degree of participation on the part of members.
102. If a member of the group is not productive he is not encouraged to remain.
103. Work of the group is left to those who are considered most capable for the job.
104. Members are interested in the group but not all of them want to work.
105. The group has a reputation for not getting much done.
106. Each member of the group is on one or more active committees.
107. The work of the group is well divided among members.
108. Every member of the group does not have a job to do.
109. The work of the group is frequently interrupted by having nothing to do.
110. There are long periods during which the group does nothing.
111. The group is directed toward one particular goal.
112. The group divides its efforts among several purposes.
113. The group operates with sets of conflicting plans.

114. The group has only one main purpose.

115. The group knows exactly what it has to get done.

116. The group is working toward many different goals.

117. The group does many things that are not directly related to its main purpose.

118. Each member of the group has a clear idea of the group's goals.

119. The objective of the group is specific.

120. Certain members meet for one thing and others for a different thing.

121. The group has major purposes which to some degree are in conflict.

122. The objectives of the group have never been clearly recognized.

123. The group is very informal.

124. A list of rules and regulations is given to each member.

125. The group has meetings at regularly scheduled times.

126. The group is organized along semimilitary lines.

127. The group's meetings are not planned or organized.

128. The group has an organization chart.

129. The group has rules to guide its activities.

130. The group is staffed according to a table of organization.

131. The group keeps a list of names of members.

132. Group meetings are conducted according to "Robert's Rules of Order."

133. There is a recognized right and wrong way of going about group activities.

134. Most matters that come up before the group are voted upon.

135. The group meets at any place that happens to be handy.

136. The members of the group vary in amount of ambition.

137. Members of the group are from the same social class.

138. Some members are interested in altogether different things than other members.

139. The group contains members with widely varying backgrounds.

140. The group contains whites and Negroes.

141. Members of the group are all about the same ages.

142. A few members of the group have greater ability than others.

143. A number of religious beliefs are represented by members of the group.

144. Members of the group vary greatly in social background.

145. All members of the group are of the same sex.

146. The ages of members range over a period of at least 20 years.

147. Members come into the group with quite different family backgrounds.

148. Members of the group vary widely in amount of experience.

149. Members vary in the number of years they have been in the group.

150. The group includes members of different races.

Scoring Key and Directions for Scoring

A subject's score for a particular dimension is the sum of the item scores for that dimension. For example, the raw score for the dimension "Control" is the sum of the scores for items 1 to 12 inclusive. The total (raw) score for this dimension can range from 12 to 60.

Occasionally a respondent may fail to indicate his answer. Such omissions are scored as C responses (neither true nor false). However, if the number of omitted items exceeds half the total number of items assigned to a given dimension, no score for that dimension is assigned. In general, experience has shown that few respondents deliberately omit items.

The answers are marked on a separate answer sheet (IBM Answer Sheet No. 1100 A 3870). A separate blank answer sheet may be used for preparing a scoring key for each dimension.

Scoring Keys

Control	A	B	C	D	E	Stratification	A	B	C	D	E
1	5	4	3	2	1	39	1	2	3	4	5
2	5	4	3	2	1	40	5	4	3	2	1
3	5	4	3	2	1	41	5	4	3	2	1
4	1	2	3	4	5	42	5	4	3	2	1
5	5	4	3	2	1						
6	5	4	3	2	1	**Hedonic tone**	A	B	C	D	E
7	5	4	3	2	1	43	5	4	3	2	1
8	1	2	3	4	5	44	1	2	3	4	5
9	5	4	3	2	1	45	1	2	3	4	5
10	5	4	3	2	1	46	1	2	3	4	5
11	5	4	3	2	1	47	5	4	3	2	1
12	5	4	3	2	1						
Stability	A	B	C	D	E	**Autonomy**	A	B	C	D	E
13	1	2	3	4	5	48	5	4	3	2	1
14	1	2	3	4	5	49	1	2	3	4	5
15	1	2	3	4	5	50	1	2	3	4	5
16	1	2	3	4	5	51	1	2	3	4	5
17	5	4	3	2	1	52	1	2	3	4	5
						53	1	2	3	4	5
Intimacy	A	B	C	D	E	54	1	2	3	4	5
18	5	4	3	2	1	55	1	2	3	4	5
19	5	4	3	2	1	56	1	2	3	4	5
20	5	4	3	2	1	57	1	2	3	4	5
21	1	2	3	4	5	58	1	2	3	4	5
22	5	4	3	2	1	59	1	2	3	4	5
23	5	4	3	2	1	60	1	2	3	4	5
24	5	4	3	2	1						
25	5	4	3	2	1	**Potency**	A	B	C	D	E
26	5	4	3	2	1	61	5	4	3	2	1
27	5	4	3	2	1	62	5	4	3	2	1
28	5	4	3	2	1	63	5	4	3	2	1
29	5	4	3	2	1	64	1	2	3	4	5
30	1	2	3	4	5	65	1	2	3	4	5
						66	5	4	3	2	1
Stratification	A	B	C	D	E	67	5	4	3	2	1
31	1	2	3	4	5	68	5	4	3	2	1
32	5	4	3	2	1	69	5	4	3	2	1
33	5	4	3	2	1	70	1	2	3	4	5
34	5	4	3	2	1	71	5	4	3	2	1
35	1	2	3	4	5	72	5	4	3	2	1
36	5	4	3	2	1	73	5	4	3	2	1
37	5	4	3	2	1	74	5	4	3	2	1
38	5	4	3	2	1	75	1	2	3	4	5

Viscidity	A	B	C	D	E
76	1	2	3	4	5
77	1	2	3	4	5
78	1	2	3	4	5
79	5	4	3	2	1
80	1	2	3	4	5
81	1	2	3	4	5
82	1	2	3	4	5
83	5	4	3	2	1
84	1	2	3	4	5
85	1	2	3	4	5
86	1	2	3	4	5
87	1	2	3	4	5

Permeability	A	B	C	D	E
88	5	4	3	2	1
89	5	4	3	2	1
90	5	4	3	2	1
91	1	2	3	4	5
92	1	2	3	4	5
93	5	4	3	2	1
94	5	4	3	2	1
95	5	4	3	2	1
96	1	2	3	4	5
97	5	4	3	2	1
98	5	4	3	2	1
99	1	2	3	4	5
100	1	2	3	4	5

Participation	A	B	C	D	E
101	5	4	3	2	1
102	5	4	3	2	1
103	1	2	3	4	5
104	1	2	3	4	5
105	1	2	3	4	5
106	5	4	3	2	1
107	5	4	3	2	1
108	1	2	3	4	5
109	1	2	3	4	5
110	1	2	3	4	5

Polarization	A	B	C	D	E
111	5	4	3	2	1
112	1	2	3	4	5
113	1	2	3	4	5
114	5	4	3	2	1
115	5	4	3	2	1
116	1	2	3	4	5
117	1	2	3	4	5
118	5	4	3	2	1
119	5	4	3	2	1
120	1	2	3	4	5
121	1	2	3	4	5
122	1	2	3	4	5

Flexibility	A	B	C	D	E
123	5	4	3	2	1
124	1	2	3	4	5
125	1	2	3	4	5
126	1	2	3	4	5
127	5	4	3	2	1
128	1	2	3	4	5
129	1	2	3	4	5
130	1	2	3	4	5
131	1	2	3	4	5
132	1	2	3	4	5
133	1	2	3	4	5
134	1	2	3	4	5
135	5	4	3	2	1

Homogeneity	A	B	C	D	E
136	5	4	3	2	1
137	1	2	3	4	5
138	1	2	3	4	5
139	1	2	3	4	5
140	1	2	3	4	5
141	5	4	3	2	1
142	1	2	3	4	5
143	1	2	3	4	5
144	1	2	3	4	5
145	5	4	3	2	1
146	1	2	3	4	5
147	1	2	3	4	5
148	1	2	3	4	5
149	1	2	3	4	5
150	1	2	3	4	5

Group Dimensions Profile and Face Sheet

Name _____ Age _____ Date _____

Name of group _____

Length of your membership _____ No. of group members _____

General purpose of the group _____

Dimension	Stanine score

		1	2	3	4	5	6	7	8	9
A	Autonomy	.	.	.	.	.	.	.	.	.
B	Control	.	.	.	.	.	.	.	.	.
C	Flexibility	.	.	.	.	.	.	.	.	.
D	Hedonic Tone	.	.	.	.	.	.	.	.	.
E	Homogeneity	.	.	.	.	.	.	.	.	.
F	Intimacy	.	.	.	.	.	.	.	.	.
G	Participation	.	.	.	.	.	.	.	.	.
H	Permeability	.	.	.	.	.	.	.	.	.
I	Polarization	.	.	.	.	.	.	.	.	.
J	Potency	.	.	.	.	.	.	.	.	.
K	Stability	.	.	.	.	.	.	.	.	.
L	Stratification	.	.	.	.	.	.	.	.	.
M	Viscidity	.	.	.	.	.	.	.	.	.

4.B.2 BALES'S INTERACTION PROCESS ANALYSIS

VARIABLE MEASURED: Group interaction.

DESCRIPTION: This index consists of twelve categories—shows solidarity, shows tension release, agrees, gives suggestion, gives opinion, gives orientation, asks for orientation, asks for opinion, asks for suggestion, disagrees, shows tension, shows antagonism. Scoring is made by designating each person in the group with a number. All interaction is analyzed according to the category and marked in the fashion of 1–5 or 1–0 as the interaction takes place. After observation, a summary or profile can be constructed and inferences made to describe the underlying workings of the group.

A slightly revised version of the categories has been developed by Bales and is presented in R. F. Bales, *Personality and Interpersonal Behavior* (New York: Holt, Rinehart & Winston, 1970). See Appendix 4 for description of the changes. A new interpersonal behavior rating system is organized around the dimensions of "up/down," "forward/back," and "positive/negative."

Category 1 is now labeled "Seems Friendly" and category 12 "Seems Unfriendly"; category 2 is now "Dramatizes," and categories 6 and 7 are "Gives Information" and "Asks for Information." Content of other categories (except 3, 8, and 10) have also been changed.

While the Bales's scheme is not widely used today in its original form, it remains the model in its field. It did much to aid early development of small-group analysis. The new form is somewhat simpler and easier to use. New norms are not available, but Bales provides estimates of how the changes may influence percentage distributions.

WHERE PUBLISHED: R. F. Bales, *Interaction Process Analysis: A Method for the Study of Small Groups* (Cambridge, Mass.: Addison-Wesley, 1950). Cf. John Madge, *The Origins of Scientific Sociology* (New York: Free Press, 1967), pp. 424–77.

RELIABILITY: With competent and trained observers an inter-observer correlation of between .75 and .95 can be obtained.

VALIDITY: Face validity. Consult critique of Dale G. Lake, Mathew B. Miles, and Ralph B. Earle, *Measuring Human Behavior* (New York: Teachers College Press, 1973).

UTILITY: A general purpose, standard set of categories well suited for the observation and analysis of small groups. The chief disadvantage is that the training of observers requires long practice. Frequent retraining is also necessary.

RESEARCH APPLICATIONS:

BALES, ROBERT F. *Personality and Interpersonal Behavior.* New York: Holt, Rinehart, & Winston, 1970. See Bibliography, pp. 532–42.

BURKE, PETER J. "Participation and Leadership in Small Groups." *American Sociological Review* 39 (December 1974): 832–43.

HARE, PAUL A. *Handbook of Small Group Research.* Second ed. Glencoe, Ill.: Free Press, 1975.

———; BORGATTA, EDGAR F.; and BALES, ROBERT F., eds. *Small Groups: Studies in Social Interaction.* Rev. ed. New York: Knopf, 1965. See the bibliography of small-group research.

SMITH, H. W. "Some Developmental Interpersonal Dynamics Through Childhood." *American Sociological Review* 38 (October 1973): 543–52.

For additional references check *Social Psychology Quarterly,* published by American Sociological Association.

1 SHOWS SOLIDARITY, raises others' status, gives help, reward:					
2 SHOWS TENSION RELEASE, jokes, laughs, shows satisfaction:					
3 AGREES, shows passive acceptance, understands, concurs, complies:					
4 GIVES SUGGESTION, direction, implying autonomy for other:					
5 GIVES OPINION, evaluation, analysis, expresses feeling, wish:					
6 GIVES ORIENTATION, information, repeats, clarifies, confirms:					

7 ASKS FOR ORIENTATION, information, repetition, confirmation:						
8 ASKS FOR OPINION, evaluation, analysis, expression of feeling:						
9 ASKS FOR SUGGESTION, direction, possible ways of action:						
10 DISAGREES, shows passive rejection, formality, withholds help:						
11 SHOWS TENSION, asks for help, withdraws "Out of Field":						
12 SHOWS ANTAGONISM, deflates other's status, defends or asserts self:						

PERCENT: 0

Prepared for use with Interaction Process Analysis by Robert F. Bales. Printed in U.S.A.
INTERACTION SCORING FORM Published by Addison-Wesley Publishing Co., Reading, Mass. 01867.

4.B.3   SEASHORE'S GROUP COHESIVENESS INDEX

VARIABLE MEASURED: The index measures group cohesiveness, defined as attraction to the group or resistance to leaving.

DESCRIPTION: The test consists of three questions: "Do you feel that you are really a part of your work group?" "If you had a chance to do the same kind of work for the same pay, in another work group, how would you feel about moving?" and "How does your work group compare with other work groups at Midwest on each of the following points?"—The way people get along together, the way people stick together, and the way people help each other on the job. The first two questions can be answered by five degrees, while the three items of the third question are answered by four degrees.

WHERE PUBLISHED: Stanley E. Seashore, *Group Cohesiveness in the Industrial Work Group* (Ann Arbor: Survey Research Center, Institute for Social Research, University of Michigan, 1954).

RELIABILITY: Intercorrelations among mean scale values for the groups on scales comprising the index of cohesiveness ranged from .15 to .70.

VALIDITY: The variance found between groups on this scale was significant beyond the .001 level.

UTILITY: As the questions are phrased, the index is especially set up for an industrial situation. It can probably, with a few changes, be adapted to almost any situation where an index of group cohesiveness is required. The test takes very little time to administer. The subject should be assured that his replies will be kept confidential.

RESEARCH APPLICATIONS: The study of 228 section-shift groups in a company manufacturing heavy machinery, described in the aforementioned Seashore article.

Index of Group Cohesiveness

"Do you feel that you are really a part of your work group?"

☐ Really a part of my work group
☐ Included in most ways
☐ Included in some ways, but not in others
☐ Don't feel I really belong
☐ Don't work with any one group of people
☐ Not ascertained

"If you had a chance to do the same kind of work for the same pay, in another work group, how would you feel about moving?"

☐ Would want very much to move
☐ Would rather move than stay where I am
☐ Would make no difference to me
☐ Would rather stay where I am than move
☐ Would want very much to stay where I am
☐ Not ascertained

"How does your work group compare with other work groups at Midwest on each of the following points?"

	Better than most	About the same as most	Not as good as most	Not ascertained
The way people get along together	☐	☐	☐	☐
The way people stick together	☐	☐	☐	☐
The way people help one another on the job	☐	☐	☐	☐

SOCIOMETRY SCALES OF SPONTANEOUS CHOICE AND SOCIOMETRIC PREFERENCE

4.B.4

VARIABLE MEASURED: The degree to which individuals are accepted in a group, interpersonal relationships that exist among individuals, and structure of the group.

DESCRIPTION: Results are most satisfactory for small cohesive groups. The sociometric technique consists of asking each individual in a group to state with whom among the members of the group he would prefer to associate for specific activities or in particular situations. Criteria (selected areas that should include different aspects of possible association: work, play, visiting) range in number from 1 to 8 or more; and choices, from 1 to as many as desired by the researcher.

WHERE PUBLISHED: J. L. Moreno, *Who Shall Survive?* (Beacon, N.Y.: Beacon House, 1934).

RELIABILITY:

Loeb's correlation between odd-even items	$r = .65$ to $.85$
Loeb's correlation between split-halves	$r = .53$ to $.85$
Mary L. Northway between general criteria	$r = .64$ to $.84$
Mary L. Northway between skill criteria	$r = .37$ to $.50$
Correlations between scores on tests given at different times	$r = .74$
Constancy of choice (actual preference on 1st test repeated later on)	$r = .69$

VALIDITY: Eugene Byrd comparison of sociometric choice with actual choice and then an 8-week interval retest shows $r = .76, .80, .89$. See Eugene Byrd, "A Study of Validity and Constancy of Choices in a Sociometric Test," *Sociometry* 9 (1946): 21.

N. Gronlund comparison of judgment of teachers vs. testing shows $r = .59$. See N. Gronlund, *Accuracies of Teachers' Judgments Concerning the Sociometric Status of Sixth Grade Pupils,* Sociometry Monograph No. 25 (Beacon, N.Y.: Beacon House, 1951).

For discussion of reliability and validity, see Mary L. Northway, *A Primer of Sociometry* (Toronto: University of Toronto, 1952), pp. 16–20. Also cf. Merl E. Bonney, "A Study of Constancy of Sociometric Ranks Among College Students Over a Two-Year Period," *Sociometry* 18 (December 1955): 531–42.

STANDARD SCORES: None.

RESEARCH APPLICATIONS:

BRONFENBRENNER, URIE. *The Measurement of Sociometric Status, Structure and Development.* Sociometry Monograph No. 6. Beacon, N.Y.: Beacon House, 1945.

HOLLAND, PAUL W., and LEINHARDT, SAMUEL. "A Method of Detecting Structure in Sociometric Data." *American Journal of Sociology* 76, no. 3 (November 1970): 492–513.

JACOBS, JOHN H. "The Application of Sociometry to Industry." *Sociometry* 8 (May 1945): 181–98.

JENNINGS, HELEN H. *Leadership and Isolation: A Study of Personality in Interpersonal Relations.* 2nd ed. New York: McKay, 1950.

LEINHARDT, SAMUEL. "Developmental Change in the Sentiment Structure of Children's Groups." *American Sociological Review* 37 (April 1972): 202–12.

LUNDBERG, GEORGE A., and DICKSON, LENORE. "Inter-Ethnic Relations in a High School Population." *American Journal of Sociology* 57 (July 1952): 1–10.

MASSARIK, FRED; TANNENBAUM, ROBERT; RAHANE, MURRAY; and WESCHLER, IRVING. "Sociometric Choice and Organizational Effectiveness: A Multi-Relational Approach." *Sociometry* (August 1953): 211–38. Or see MASSARIK, FRED, et al. *Leadership and Organization.* New York: McGraw-Hill, 1961. Pp. 346–70.

MORENO, J. L. *Who Shall Survive? A New Approach to the Problem of Human Relation-*

ships. Beacon, N.Y.: Beacon House, 1934. See also MORENO, J. L. *Sociometry and the Science of Man.* Beacon, N.Y.: Beacon House, 1956.

WHITE, HARRISON. "Management Conflict and Sociometric Structure." *American Journal of Sociology* 67 (September 1961): 185–99.

ZELENY, LESLIE D. "Selection of Compatible Flying Partners." *American Journal of Sociology* 52 (March 1947): 424–31.

For an excellent review of the literature on "Measures of Sociometric Structure" see M. Glanzer and R. Glaser, "Techniques for the Study of Group Structure and Behavior: I. Analysis of Structure," *Psychological Bulletin* 56 (September 1959): 317–32. Cf. J. L. Moreno, "Contributions of Sociometry to Research Methodology in Sociology," *American Sociological Review* 12 (June 1947): 287–92; Jacob L. Moreno et al., *The Sociometry Reader* (Glencoe, Ill.: Free Press, 1959). For more recent work check the *Social Psychology Quarterly.*

Spontaneous Choice Test

Opposite each name check how you feel about persons in your group.

	Like	Dislike	Indifferent
Mary J.			
James F.			
John J.			
Etc.			

Sociometric Preference Test

Choose five persons you would most like to work with. Mark 1st, 2nd, 3rd, 4th, 5th choice.

Mary J.	
James F.	
John J.	
Sam E.	
Etc.	

*Many criteria may be employed. For example, to have in a discussion group, to have in your neighborhood, to play bridge with, to work on a project with, etc.

BOGARDUS' SOCIAL-DISTANCE SCALE   *4.B.5*

VARIABLE MEASURED: The social distance or degree of social acceptance that exists between given persons and certain social groups. The scale may be adapted to measure the social distance between two persons or between two or more social groups. The method has been applied to racial distance, regional distance, sex distance, age distance, parent-child distance, educational distance, class distance, occupational distance, religious distance, international distance.

DESCRIPTION: Typically, a group of persons is asked to rank a series of social types with respect to the degrees of social distance on seven attributes starting with *acceptance to close kinship by marriage* and concluding with *would exclude from my country.* One hundred persons acting as judges have identified these seven attributes among 60 as those ordered on a continuant of social distance.

WHERE PUBLISHED: Best source is Emory S. Bogardus, *Social Distance* (Yellow Springs, Ohio: Antioch Press, 1959); Emory S. Bogardus, *Immigration and Race Attitudes* (Boston: Heath, 1928); E. S. Bogardus, "A Social Distance Scale," *Sociology and Social Research* 17 (January–February 1933): 265–71. Excellent instructions may be found in William J. Goode and Paul K. Hatt, *Methods in Social Research* (New York: McGraw-Hill, 1952), pp. 26, 245–49.

RELIABILITY: Split-half reliability coefficient reported at .90 or higher in repeated tests by Eugene L. Hartley and Ruth E. Hartley.

VALIDITY: Theodore Newcomb reports high validity if we use "agreement with other scales that in certain particulars are more exact." Application of the known-group method is advocated in determination of validity. This involves finding groups known to be favorable toward some of the ethnic types and unfavorable toward others. If the responses of these groups fit the requisite pattern, evidence for validity may be accepted. For full discussion see E. S. Bogardus, *Social Distance* (Yellow Springs, Ohio: Antioch Press, 1959), pp. 92–95.

SCORING: A variety of scoring methods has been used. A simple method that has been found to be as reliable as the more complex ones is that of counting the numbers of the "nearest column" that is checked. That is, if the racial distance quotient, *RDQ,* of a number of persons is desired, then the arithmetic mean of the total number of the "nearest columns" that are checked by all the subjects for each race is obtained. If the *RDQ* of a person is sought, then the arithmetic mean of the total numbers of the "nearest column" for each race is obtained.

STANDARD SCORES: Racial Distance Quotients Given Racial Groups in 1956 by 2053 selected persons throughout the United States.

1.	Americans (U.S. White)	1.08
2.	Canadians	1.16
3.	English	1.23
4.	French	1.47
5.	Irish	1.56
6.	Swedish	1.57
7.	Scots	1.60
8.	Germans	1.61
9.	Hollanders	1.63
10.	Norwegians	1.56
11.	Finns	1.80

12. Italians	1.89
13. Poles	2.07
14. Spanish	2.08
15. Greeks	2.09
16. Jews	2.15
17. Czechs	2.22
18. Armenians	2.33
19. Japanese Americans	2.34
20. Indians (American)	2.35
21. Filipinos	2.46
22. Mexican Americans	2.51
23. Turks	2.52
24. Russians	2.56
25. Chinese	2.68
26. Japanese	2.70
27. Negroes	2.74
28. Mexicans	2.79
29. Indians (from India)	2.80
30. Koreans	2.83

Arithmetic Mean of 61,590 Racial Reactions: 2.08.

UTILITY: The Bogardus Scale may be used to estimate the amount of potential and real conflict existing between any cultural groups, anywhere in the industrial, political, racial, religious, and other phases of life. It also helps to determine the extent of the trend toward conflict or toward cooperation between groups. The test is easy to administer and to score. It can be adapted easily to other problems of social distance.

A good illustration of such an adaptation is to be found in the Mock Table for a Scale to Measure the Attractiveness of Different Communities. See William J. Goode and Paul K. Hatt, *Methods in Social Research* (New York: McGraw-Hill, 1952), p. 248. The fullest description of applications is to be found in Emory S. Bogardus, *Social Distance* (Yellow Springs, Ohio: Antioch Press, 1959).

RESEARCH APPLICATIONS:

BARBER, BERNARD. *Social Stratification.* New York: Harcourt, Brace, 1957.

BARDIS, PANOS D. "Social Distance among Foreign Students." *Sociology and Social Research* 41:112–15.

———. "Social Distance in a Greek Metropolitan City." *Social Science* 37 (April 1962): 108–11.

BEST, W. H., and SOHNER, C. P. "Social Distance Methodology in the Measurement of Political Attitudes." *Sociology and Social Research* 40: 266–70.

———. "Social Distance and Politics," *Sociology and Social Research* 40: 339–42.

BIESANZ, J., and BIESANZ, M. "Social Distance in the Youth Hostel Movement." *Sociology and Social Research* 25: 237–45.

BINNEWIES, W. G. "A Method of Studying Rural Social Distance." *Sociology and Social Research* 10: 239–42.

BOGARDUS, EMORY S. *Sociometry* 10: 306–11; *International Journal of Opinion and Attitude Research* 1: 55–62; *American Sociological Review* 16: 48–53; *Journal of Educational Sociology* 3: 497–502; *Survey Graphic* 9: 169–70, 206, 208; *Journal of Applied Sociology* 9: 216–26; *Sociology and Social Research* 12: 173–78; 13:

73–81; 13: 171–75; 14: 174–80; 17: 167–73; 17: 265–61; 18: 67–73; 20: 473–77; 22: 462–76; 24: 69–75; 32: 723–27; 32: 798–802; 32: 882–87; 33: 291–95; 36: 40–47; 43: 439–41; *The Urban Community,* edited by E. W. Burgess. Chicago: University of Chicago Press, 1927. Pp. 48–54.

BRADWAY, JOHN S. "Social Distance Between Lawyers and Social Workers." *Sociology and Social Research* 14: 516–24.

BRIGGS, ARTHUR E. "Social Distance Between Layers and Doctors." *Sociology and Social Research* 13: 156–63.

BROOKS, LEE M. "Racial Distance as Affected by Education." *Sociology and Social Research* 21: 128–33.

CAMPBELL, DONALD T. "The Bogardus Social Distance Scale." *Sociology and Social Research* 36: 322–25.

CATAPUSAN, BENICIO T. "Social Distance in the Phillippines." *Sociology and Social Research* 38: 309–12.

DODD, STUART C. "A Social Distance Test in the Near East." *American Journal of Sociology* 41 (September 1935): 194–204.

———, and NEHNEVAJSA, J. "Physical Dimensions of Social Distance," *Sociology and Social Research* 38: 287–92.

DUNCAN, W. L. "Parent-Child Isolations." *The Family* 10: 115–18.

DUVALL, EVERETT W. "Child-Parent Social Distance." *Sociology and Social Research* 21: 458–63.

EISENSTADT, S. N. *From Generation to Generation: Age Groups and the Social Structure,* Glencoe, Ill.: Free Press, 1956.

ELLEFSEN, J. B. "Social Distance Attitudes of Negro College Students." *Phylon* 17: 79–83.

ELLIS, ROBERT A. "Social Status and Social Distance." *Sociology and Social Research* 40: 240–46.

FRANKLIN, CLAY. "The Effect of the Format Upon the Scale Values of the Bogardus Social Distance Scale." *Research Studies of the State College of Washington* 18: 117–20.

GLEASON, GEORGE. "Social Distance in Russia," *Sociology and Social Research* 17: 37–43.

GRACE, H. A., and NEUHAUS, J. O. "Information and Social Distance as Predictors of Hostility Toward Nations." *Journal of Abnormal and Social Psychology* 47 (1952): 540–45.

GREIFER, JULIAN L. "Attitudes to the Stranger." *American Sociological Review* 10 (December 1945): 739–45.

GURNEE, H., and BAKER, E. "Social Distances of Some Common Social Relationships." *Journal of Abnormal and Social Psychology* 33 (1938): 265–69.

HALBWACHS, M. *The Psychology of Social Classes.* Glencoe, Ill.: Free Press, 1958.

HAMREN, VANDYCE. "Social Farness Between the A.F. of L. and the C.I.O." *Sociology and Social Research* 24: 442–52.

———. "Social Nearness Between the A.F. of L. and the C.I.O." *Sociology and Social Research* 26: 232–40.

HARTLEY, EUGENE L. *Problems in Prejudice.* New York: Columbia University Press, 1946.

———, and HARTLEY, RUTH E. *Fundamentals of Social Psychology.* New York: Knopf, 1952. Pp. 431–43.

HUNT, CHESTER L. "Social Distance in the Philippines." *Sociology and Social Research* 40: 253–60.

HYPES, E. L. "The Social Distance Score Card as a Teaching Device." *Social Forces* 7 (December 1928): 234–37.

JAMESON, S. H. "Social Distance between Welfare Organizations." *Sociology and Social Research* 5: 230–43.

———. "Social Nearness among Welfare Organizations." *Sociology and Social Research* 15: 322–33.

KAHL, JOSEPH A. *The American Class Structure.* New York: Rinehart, 1957.

KOCH, H. L. "Study of Some Factors Conditioning the Social Distance between the Sexes." *Journal of Social Psychology* 20: 79–107.

KROUT, M. H. "Periodic Change in Social Distance; A Study in the Shifting Bases of Perception." *Sociology and Social Research* 27: 339–51.

LAMBERT, W. E. "Comparison of French and American Modes of Response to the Bogardus Social Distance Scale." *Social Forces* 31: 155–60.

McDONAGH, EDWARD C. "Social Distance between China and Japan." *Sociology and Social Research* 22: 131–36.

———. "Asiatic Stereotypes and National Distance." *Sociology and Social Research* 22: 474–78.

———. "Military Social Distance." *Sociology and Social Research* 29: 289–96.

McKENZIE, R. D. "Spatial Distance and Community Organization Pattern." *Social Forces* 5: 623–27.

———. "Spatial Distance," *Sociology and Social Research* 13: 536–44.

McMATH, ELLA M. "A Girl without a Country." *Journal of Applied Sociology* 11: 65–71.

MARTIN, R. R. "Sudden Change in Social Distance." *Sociology and Social Research* 22: 53–56.

MITCHELL, ROY. "An Ethnic Distance Study in Buffalo." *Sociology and Social Research* 40: 35–40.

MOWRER, E. R. *Domestic Discord.* Chicago: University of Chicago Press, 1928. Chap. 3.

NEPRASH, J. A. "Minority Group Contacts and Social Distance." *Phylon* 14: 207–12.

NEWCOMB, THEODORE M. *Social Psychology.* Rev. ed. New York: Holt, Rinehart & Winston, 1955. Pp. 154–75.

NIMKOFF, M. F. "Parent-Child Conflict." *Sociology and Social Research* 12: 446–58.

———. "Parent-Child Conflict." *Sociology and Social Research* 14: 135–50.

NORTH, C. C. *Social Differentiation.* Chapel Hill: University of North Carolina Press, 1926.

OWEN, JOHN E. "Social Distance in England." *Sociology and Social Research* 30: 460–65.

PARISH, HELEN R. "Social Nearness between Latin America and the United States." *Sociology and Social Research* 19: 253–58.

PARK, R. E. "The Concept of Social Distance." *Journal of Applied Sociology* 8: 339–44.

PETTIGREW, THOMAS F. "Social Distance Attitudes of South African Students." *Social Forces* 38 (March 1960): 246–53.

POOLE, W. C., JR. "Distance in Sociology." *American Journal of Sociology* 33: 99–104.

———. "Social Distance and Social Pathology." *Sociology and Social Research* 12: 268–72.

———. "Social Distance and Personal Distance." *Journal of Applied Sociology* 11: 114–20.

———. "The Social Distance Margin Reviewed." *Sociology and Social Research* 13: 49–54.

————, and POOLE, HARRIET K. "Laws of Social Distance." *Journal of Applied Sociology* 11: 365–69.

PROTHRO, E. T., and MILES, O. K. "Social Distance in the Deep South as Measured by a Revised Bogardus Scale." *Journal of Social Psychology* 37: 171–74.

RUNNER, JESSIE R. "Social Distance in Adolescent Relationships." *American Journal of Sociology* 43: 428–39.

SARTAIN, A. I., and BELL, HAROLD V., JR. "An Evaluation of the Bogardus Scale of Social Distance by the Method of Equal-Appearing Intervals." *Journal of Social Psychology* 29: 85–91.

SARVIS, GUY W. "Social Distance in Religion." *Christian Century* 49: 1331–33.

SCHENK, Q. F., and ROMNEY, A. K. "Some Differential Attitudes among Adolescent Groups as Revealed by Bogardus' Social Distance Scale." *Sociology and Social Research* 35: 38–45.

SCHNETZ, ALFRED. "The Stranger." *American Journal of Sociology* 49: 499–508.

SCHROFF, RUTH. "Charting Social Distance." *Sociology and Social Research* 14: 567–70.

SEYMOUR, J. G. "Rural Social Distance of Normal School Students." *Sociology and Social Research* 14: 238–48.

SHERIF, MUZAFER, and SHERIF, CAROLYN W. *An Outline of Social Psychology.* New York: Harper & Brothers, 1956. Pp. 659–78.

SHIDELER, ERNEST. "The Social Distance Margin." *Sociology and Social Research* 12: 243–52.

SOROKIN, P. *Social Mobility.* New York: Harper & Brothers, 1927. Chap. 6, "Occupational Stratification."

STEPHENSON, C. M., and WILCOX, CAROL G. "Social Distance Variations of College Students," *Sociology and Social Research* 39: 240–41.

TURBEVILLE, GUS. "A Social Distance Study of Duluth, Minnesota." *Sociology and Social Research* 18: 420–30.

VAN DER BERGHE, PIERRE L. "Distance Mechanisms of Stratification." *Sociology and Social Research* 44 (January–February 1960): 155–64.

WESTIE, F. R. "Negro-White Status Differentials and Social Distance," *American Sociological Review* 17 (October 1952): 550–58.

————, and WESTIE, MARGARET L. "The Social Distance Pyramid: Relationships between Caste and Class." *American Journal of Sociology* 63 (September 1957): 190–96.

————. "Social Distance Scales, a Tool for the Study of Stratification." *Sociology and Social Research* 43: 251–58.

WOOD, MARGARET MARY. *Paths of Loneliness.* New York: Columbia University Press, 1953.

ZELIGS, ROSE, and HENDRICKSON, G. "Checking the Social Distance Technique through Personal Interviews." *Sociology and Social Research* 18: 420–30.

ZIEGLER, GEORGE H. "Social Farness between Hindus and Moslems." *Sociology and Social Research* 33: 188–95.

Interesting adaptations of the social distance scale are found in:

DEFLEUR, M. L., and WESTIE, FRANK R. "Verbal Attitudes and Overt Acts: An Experiment on the Salience of Attitudes." *American Sociological Review* 23 (December 1958): 667–73.

JACKSON, ELTON F. "Status Consistency and Symptoms of Stress." *American Sociological Review* 27 (August 1962): 469–80.

LONGWORTHY, RUSSELL L. "Community Status and Influence in a High School." *American Sociological Review* 24 (August 1959): 537–39.

MARTIN, JAMES G., and WESTIE, FRANK R. "The Tolerant Personality." *American Sociological Review* 24 (August 1959): 521–28.

PHOTIADIS, JOHN D., and BIGGAR, JEANNE. "Religiosity, Education, and Ethnic Distance." *American Journal of Sociology* 67 (May 1962): 666–73.

PHOTIADIS, JOHN D., and JOHNSON, ARTHUR L. "Orthodoxy, Church Participation, and Authoritarianism." *American Journal of Sociology* 69 (November 1963): 244–48.

WESTIE, FRANK R. "A Technique for the Measurement of Race Attitudes." *American Sociological Review* 18 (February 1953): 73–78. See his "Note to Prospective Users of the Summated Differences Technique," in *Sociological Measurement,* ed. Charles M. Bonjean, Richard J. Hill, and Dale McLemore (San Francisco: Chandler, 1976), p. 158–162.

BOGARDUS' RACIAL-DISTANCE SCALE

(Race is defined here largely as a cultural group.)

1. Remember to give your *first feeling reactions* in every case.
2. Give your reactions to each race as a *group.* Do not give your reactions to the best or to the worst members that you have known, but think of the picture or stereotype that you have of the whole race.
3. Put a cross after each race in as many of the seven rows as your feeling dictate.

Category	English	Swedes	Poles	Koreans	Etc.
1. To close kinship by marriage					
2. To my club as personal chums					
3. To my street as neighbors					
4. To employment in my occupation					
5. To citizenship in my country					
6. As visitors only to my country					
7. Would exclude from my country					

HAGOEL'S FRIENDSHIP VALUE SCALES   *4.B.6*

VARIABLE MEASURED: This instrument measures four dimensions of friendship: (1) intensity—feeling of closeness, sharing secrets; (2) homophily—similarity of background with items for religious, ethnic, racial background, political views, marital status, age differences; (3) emotionality-instrumentality—tests polar concepts: friendship as an emotional, affectional experience or friendship as important in gaining personal goals; (4) intimacy—sharing of intimate personal information about oneself and others.

DESCRIPTION: The four dimensional scales were developed to measure the values people attach to friendship relations in general and to their friends in particular. The friendship relation is shown to be multidimensional; the dimensions can be distinguished from one another, and they vary at different rates. The four scales are made up of 32 items. Statements are presented in random order. There is no mention of number or nature of the four dimensions when the scales are administered. A scoring code for the researcher follows the presentation of the scales.

WHERE PUBLISHED: Lee Hagoel, "Friendship Values and Intimacy Patterns in an Urban Community" (paper presented at the annual meeting of the American Sociological Association, New York, August 1980); Lee Hagoel, "Qualitative and Quantitative Aspects of Primary-Relations in an Urban Community Context" (Ph.D. dissertation, Library of the University of Minnesota, Minneapolis, 1980).

RELIABILITY: Alpha scores on the reliability test are as follows: Intensity, 6 items, .736; Homophily, 12 items, .850; Emotionality/Instrumentality, 8 items, .680; Intimacy, 6 items, .587.

VALIDITY: Factor analysis indicates that the four dimensions are not directly related to one another. The internal consistency of each dimension has been demonstrated. The scales were applied in a study of dyad relations among residents in a suburban area of the Minneapolis-St. Paul metropolitan area (the South Dale Cluster). Friendship patterns characterized the entire sample (in a cosmopolitan type of interaction), while friendship values significantly distinguished among subgroups by age and sex in the same sample.

STANDARD SCORES: Scores of the 57 residents in the South Dale study for the four dimensions of the friendship scale are as follows:

Dimension	Score range	Mean score	Standard deviation
A. Intensity	6–36	17.82	3.12
B. Homophily	12–72	55.74	6.65
C. Emotionality/Instrumentability	8–14	17.84	4.00
D. Intimacy	6–36	20.14	2.78

FRIENDSHIP VALUE SCALES

The following is a copy of the scales as they were applied in the study. Note that statements are presented in random order. There is no mention of number or nature of the four dimensions nor of the scales. Respondents are presented with this instrument as a single scale.

DIRECTIONS: The following statements are meant to explore some of your feelings toward friends and friendships. There are no right or wrong answers.

We are interested in what *you* think. Please read each item carefully and decide whether you agree or disagree with the view expressed, then circle the intensity of your agreement or disagreement with the view expressed. Please use the following code for your answers:

Very strongly agree (VSA)	Strongly agree (SA)	Agree (A)	Disagree (D)	Strongly disagree (SD)	Very strongly disagree (VSD)

1. Friends ought to know what one another is doing most of the time. (VSA) (SA) (A) (D) (SD) (VSD)
2. Friends are important because one can borrow money from them. (VSA) (SA) (A) (D) (SD) (VSD)
3. The understanding of my friends is more important to me than their material help. (VSA) (SA) (A) (D) (SD) (VSD)
4. Friends ought to help and support one another in bad times. (VSA) (SA) (A) (D) (SD) (VSD)
5. Friends are people we feel very close to. (VSA) (SA) (A) (D) (SD) (VSD)
6. I would like to have friendships last a life-time. (VSA) (SA) (A) (D) (SD) (VSD)
7. I would never make friends with people of different religious beliefs than mine. (VSA) (SA) (A) (D) (SD) (VSD)
8. Friends ought to know as much as possible about one another's past lives. (VSA) (SA) (A) (D) (SD) (VSD)
9. Good friends do not necessarily have to feel close. (VSA) (SA) (A) (D) (SD) (VSD)
10. I want to feel close to my friends. (VSA) (SA) (A) (D) (SD) (VSD)
11. I would not like to make friends with people who are much older than I am. (VSA) (SA) (A) (D) (SD) (VSD)
12. I want my friends to feel close to me. (VSA) (SA) (A) (D) (SD) (VSD)
13. I feel that friends should know as much about each other's lives as possible. (VSA) (SA) (A) (D) (SD) (VSD)
14. Single people cannot be good friends with married people. (VSA) (SA) (A) (D) (SD) (VSD)
15. Friends should share their secrets with me. (VSA) (SA) (A) (D) (SD) (VSD)
16. A good friend is someone who understands my problems. (VSA) (SA) (A) (D) (SD) (VSD)
17. Blacks and whites do not make the best of friends. (VSA) (SA) (A) (D) (SD) (VSD)
18. I won't be friends with people who don't return favors. (VSA) (SA) (A) (D) (SD) (VSD)
19. Close friends should probably be of the same religious belief. (VSA) (SA) (A) (D) (SD) (VSD)
20. Friendships exist in the here and now, and have no reference to the past or future. (VSA) (SA) (A) (D) (SD) (VSD)
21. I could not make friends with people of different political views than mine. (VSA) (SA) (A) (D) (SD) (VSD)
22. A good friend will provide me with advice when I need it. (VSA) (SA) (A) (D) (SD) (VSD)
23. A man and a woman can be good friends. (VSA) (SA) (A) (D) (SD) (VSD)
24. An important thing about friends is that they can relax in each other's company. (VSA) (SA) (A) (D) (SD) (VSD)
25. Whether or not a friend is married is unimportant. (VSA) (SA) (A) (D) (SD) (VSD)
26. Friends are important because of the "connections" they provide. (VSA) (SA) (A) (D) (SD) (VSD)
27. I would not like to make friends with people who are much younger than I am. (VSA) (SA) (A) (D) (SD) (VSD)
28. Friends ought to have a pretty clear idea of one another's plans for the future. (VSA) (SA) (A) (D) (SD) (VSD)
29. Good friends should hold the same political views. (VSA) (SA) (A) (D) (SD) (VSD)
30. Blacks and whites should not be friends. (VSA) (SA) (A) (D) (SD) (VSD)
31. Good friends can be of different ethnic (national) backgrounds. (VSA) (SA) (A) (D) (SD) (VSD)
32. I expect my friends to return the favors I've done for them as soon as they possible can. (VSA) (SA) (A) (D) (SD) (VSD)

RESEARCHER'S SCORING CODE

A. The scoring of each statement.
B. Summation—by dimension (scale) only.

A. The following statements (numbers match the form used in data collection)—
1,3,4,5,6,7,8,10,11,12,13,14,15,16,17,19,21,22,24,27,28,29,30—are scored in this
way:

Very strongly agree   = 1
Strongly agree   = 2
Agree   = 3
Disagree   = 4
Strongly disagree   = 5
Very strongly disagree = 6

The following statements (numbers match the form used in data collection)—
2,9,18,20,23,25,26,31,32—are scored in this way:

Very strongly agree   = 6
Strongly agree   = 5
Agree   = 4
Disagree   = 3
Strongly disagree   = 2
Very strongly disagree = 1

B. Summation is done for all the statements in a *given dimension*. Thus, each
respondent has 4 scores.

The code for the statements in each dimension is as follows:

Dimension *A* (Intensity) consists of these statements: 9,10,12,15,16,22.
Dimension *B* (Homophily) consists of these statements: 7,11,14,17,19,21,23,25,27,29,30.
Dimension *C* (Instrumentality/Emotionality) consists of these statements:
2,3,4,5,18,24,26,32.
Dimension *D* ("completeness") consists of these statements: 1,6,8,13,20,28.

section C

Social Indicators

The role of social indicators known as Social Reporting, Social Systems Accounting, and Social Intelligence is set forth in the following definition: Social indicators—statistics, statistical series, and all other forms of evidence—are summary measures that enable policy and decision makers to assess various social aspects of an ongoing society and to evaluate specific programs and determine their impact. Social indicators help experts and lay persons alike to better understand their own and other societies with respect to values and goals and the nature of social change. Stuart Rice has provided a most compact statement:

> Social Indicators, the tools, are needed to find pathways through the maze of society's interconnections. They delineate *social states,* define *social problems,* and trace *social trends,* which by *social engineering* may hopefully be guided toward *social goals* formulated by *social planning.* [1]

The potential scope of social indicators is very broad. The question of goals must be resolved before the appropriate scope can be determined. The final answer may best be given by the needs of a society and the requests of policy makers for information about problems they must meet and solve. On February 17, 1974, the U.S. Office of Management and Budget released a pioneering study in the field of social reporting: *Social Indicators, 1973.* This study began by identifying widely held basic social objectives: good health and long life, freedom from crime and the fear of crime, sufficient education to take part in society and make the most of one's abilities, the opportunity to work at a job that is satisfying and rewarding, income sufficient to cover the necessities of life with opportunities for improving one's income, housing that is comfortable within a congenial environment, and time and opportunity for discretionary activities. For each identified social concern, one or more indicators—statistical measures of important aspects of the concerns—was identified.

In 1977 *Social Indicators II* appeared,[2] and this was followed in December 1980 by *Social Indicators III.* Like its predecessors, *Social Indicators III* is restricted almost entirely to data about objective conditions. It details both the current status of American society and some of the trends and developments that may presage the nature of changes to come. Eleven major subject

339

areas are treated in separate chapters. The indicators are primarily time series showing national totals. The list of the indicators is reproduced on the following pages and may be compared with the Economic Indicators that follow in 4.C.2. Social indicators have not yet been institutionalized as have economic indicators, which were mandated by the Employment Act of 1946. The legislation necessary to enact the development of a social report was first presented in 1967 and called for a Council of Social Advisers and the publication of an annual social report. Senator Walter Mondale of Minnesota was not able to muster sufficient votes for its enactment, but the idea has been planted. Meanwhile, research on and use of social indicators continue to be vigorous, as can be seen by the abundant bibliographies in *Social Indicators III.*

Notes

1. Stuart A. Rice, "Social Accounting and Statistics for the Great Society," *Public Administration Review* 27 (June 1967): 173.
2. *Social Indicators II* included three new areas; family, social welfare and security, and social mobility and stratification.

4.C. 1   NATIONAL SOCIAL INDICATORS, 1980*

Introduction

    Quality of life in the United States: An Overview
A. Evaluations of Qualities of a Happy Life: 1978
B. Feelings about Present Life: 1971 and 1978
C. Domain Satisfaction Measures: 1971 and 1978
D. Satisfaction with Selected Life Domains: 1973–1980
E. Evaluations of Personal Financial Situation, Selected Years: 1956–1980
F. Indicators of Alienation: 1978
G. Experience of Traumatic Events: 1978
H. Personal and National Ladder Ratings, Selected Years: 1959–1979
I. Confidence in Leaders of Specified Institutions: 1973–1980
J. Evaluation of Spending on National Priorities: 1971–1980
K. Evaluation of Life in the United States: 1971 and 1978
L. Economic Expectations, Selected Countries: 1977 and 1980

1. Population and the family

Public perceptions
1/1   Lifetime Births Expected by Wives 18 to 34 Years Old, by Race, Selected Years: 1967–1978
1/2   Satisfaction with Family Life and Attitudes Toward Older Persons Sharing Home with Their Grown Children, Marital Happiness, and Ease of Divorce: 1973–1978

Population growth and composition
1/3a   Population Growth, Selected Years: 1790–2040
1/3b   Average Annual Rate of Population Change, Selected Years: 1790–2040

* Contents pages from *Social Indicators III: Selected Data on Social Conditions and Trends in the United States.* (Washington, D.C.: U.S. Government Printing Office, December, 1980). The information in each chapter is presented in three parts: text, charts, and statistical tables.

1/4   Population, by Sex and Age: 1890, 1950, and 2010
1/5   Population, by Race and Age: 1920, 1960, and 2000
1/6   Components of Population Change, Selected Years: 1930–2000
1/7a   Fertility Rates, by Age of Mother: 1940–1977
1/7b   Cumulative Fertility Rates for Selected Cohort Groups: 1942–1977
1/8   Immigrants Admitted, by Major Occupation Group, Selected Years: 1900–1977
1/9a   Average Annual Migration Rate, by Metropolitan Status: 1960–1970 and 1970–1976
1/9b   Average Annual Migration Rate in Counties Not Adjacent to SMSA's, by Population Density: 1960–1970 and 1970–1976

Family size and composition
1/10a   Families, by Type, Selected Years: 1955–1978
1/10b   Average Size of Families, by Age of Members, Selected Years: 1950–1978
1/11a   Families, by Type and Race: 1960, 1970, and 1978
1/11b   Marital Status of Women Maintaining Families with No Husband Present, by Race: 1960, 1970, and 1978
1/11c   Families, by Number of Own Children Under 18 Years Old and Race: 1960, 1970, and 1978
1/11d   Families, by Size and Race: 1960, 1970, and 1978

Living arrangements
1/12   Family Status of Persons, by Age and Sex: 1960, 1970, and 1978
1/13   Living Arrangements of Unrelated Individuals, by Age and Sex: 1960, 1970, and 1978
1/14   Children Under 18 Years Old in Families, by Presence of Parents and Race of Children: 1960, 1970, and 1978

Marital status and stability
1/15   Marital Status of the Population 14 Years Old and Over, by Sex, Selected Years: 1950–1978
1/16   Married Women 14 Years Old and Over, by Selected Age Group, Selected Years: 1950–1978
1/17   First Marriages, Divorces, and Remarriages of Women: 1950–1977
1/18   Divorced Persons per 1,000 Married Persons with Spouse Present, by Race, Sex, and Age, Selected Years: 1950–1978
1/19   Divorce Decrees Involving Children, by Number of Children Involved: 1960–1976
1/20   Marital Dissolution Based on Divorce and Death Rates: 1969
1/21   Divorce Rates for First and Second Marriages, by Sex and Selected Cohort Groups: 1975

International comparisons
1/22a   Population Growth, by Region of the World: 1950–1960, 1960–1970, and 1970–1977
1/22b   Years Required to Double Population, by Region of the World
1/22c   Population Growth, Selected Countries: 1950–1960, 1960–1970, and 1970–1977
1/22d   Years Required to Double Population, Selected Countries
1/23a   Total Fertility Rate for Selected Countries, Selected Years: 1969–1976
1/23b   Index of Aging and Dependency Ratio, by Region of the World: 1975
1/23c   Index of Aging and Dependency Ratio for Selected Countries, Selected Years: 1969–1976

2. Health and nutrition

Public perceptions
2/1   Self-Assessment of Health, by Age and Income: 1976–1977
2/2   Selected Opinion Items Relating to the Health Area: 1973–1978

Health resources, utilization, and costs
2/3   Primary Care Physicians, 1973, and Practicing Dentists, 1974, by Location
2/4   Visits to Physicians and Dentists, by Sex, Age, and Family Income of Patients: 1975 and 1977
2/5   Discharges from Short-Stay Hospitals and Average Length of Stay, by Age, Sex, and Family Income of Patients: 1976 and 1977
2/6   Inpatient and Outpatient Care Episodes in Mental Health Facilities: 1955 and 1975
2/7   New Admissions to State and County Mental Hospitals, by Primary Diagnosis and Sex of Patients: 1975
2/8   Admissions to Outpatient Mental Health Services, by Primary Diagnosis, and Race and Sex of Patients: 1975
2/9   National and Personal Expenditures for Health Care, by Source of Payment, Selected Years: 1950–1977
2/10   Consumer Price Indexes for Selected Medical Care Expenses, Selected Years: 1950–1979

Life chances
2/11   Life Expectancy at Birth, by Race and Sex: 1900–1977
2/12   Life Expectancy at Ages 20 and 65, by Race and Sex: 1900–1977
2/13   Death Rates Due to Heart Disease and Malignant Neoplasm, Persons 50 Years Old and Over, Selected Years: 1950–1976
2/14   Death Rates for Children and Teenagers, Selected Causes and Years: 1950–1977
2/15   Infant Mortality Rates, by Race: 1960–1977

Health status
2/16   Days of Disability, by Type, and by Sex and Family Income of Patient, Selected Years: 1965–1978
2/17   Prevalence of Selected Chronic Diseases, by Selected Population Characteristics: 1972, 1973, and 1976
2/18a   Adults Who Have Had Hypertension, by Sex, Race, and Age: 1974
2/18b   Adults Who Had a Blood Pressure Check Within the Past Year, by Sex, Race, and Age: 1974

Prevention and nutrition
2/19   Children 1 to 4 Years Old Immunized Against Measles, Rubella, DPT, and Polio, by Race: 1970–1977
2/20   Persons Who Smoke, by Sex, Race, and Selected Age Group, Selected Years: 1965–1979
2/21   Average Daily Consumption of 0.501 Oz. or More of Absolute Alcohol by Persons 18 Years Old or Over, by Selected Characteristics: 1975
2/22   Persons 20 to 74 Years Old Who Were Determined by Skinfold Measurement To Be Obese, by Sex, Race, Age, and Poverty Status: 1971–1974
2/23   Persons 17 Years Old and Over Who Assessed Themselves as Overweight, by Sex: 1974
2/24   Persons 12 to 74 Years Old on Diets for Weight Reduction, by Selected Characteristics: 1971–1975
2/25   Mean Iron Intake of Persons, by Sex, Race, Poverty Level and Age: 1971–1974

NATIONAL ECONOMIC INDICATORS

4.C.2

Monthly Report Prepared for the Joint Economic Committee by the Council of Economic Advisers

CONTENTS

Total Output, Income, and Spending
  The Nation's Income, Expenditure, and Saving
  Gross National Product or Expenditure
  National Income
  Sources of Personal Income
  Disposition of Personal Income
  Farm Income
  Corporate Profits
  Gross Private Domestic Investment
  Expenditures for New Plant and Equipment
Employment, Unemployment, and Wages
  Status of the Labor Force
  Selected Measures of Unemployment and Part-Time Employment
  Unemployment Insurance Programs
  Nonagricultural Employment
  Weekly Hours of Work—Selected Industries
  Average Hourly and Weekly Earnings—Selected Industries
Production and Business Activity
  Industrial Production
  Production of Selected Manufactures
  Weekly Indicators of Production
  New Construction
  New Housing Starts and Applications for Financing
  Business Sales and Inventories—Total and Trade
  Manufacturers' Shipments, Inventories, and New Orders
  Merchandise Exports and Imports
  U.S. Balances on Goods, Services, and Transfers
  U.S. Overall Balances on International Transactions

Prices
  Consumer Prices
  Wholesale Prices
  Prices Received and Paid by Farmers
Money, Credit, and Security Markets
  Money Stock
  Private Liquid Asset Holdings—Nonfinancial Investors
  Bank Loans, Investments, Debits, and Reserves
  Consumer and Real Estate Credit
  Bond Yields and Interest Rates
  Common Stock Prices, Yield, and Earnings
Federal Finance
  Federal Budget Receipts and Outlays and Debt
  Federal Budget Receipts by Source and Outlays by Function
  Federal Sector, National Income Accounts Basis

4.C.3   SOCIAL INDICATORS AT THE STATE LEVEL

The social-indicator movement has not neglected the state level. The U.S. Department of Labor has developed state economic and social indicators. The public welfare load, infant mortality, crime, and educational deficiency are cited as problem areas to provide the clues to social problems requiring social action to resolve. Indicators are presented under education, aid to families with dependent children, infant mortality rates under one year, and crime rates.

The Midwest Research Institute has devised a Social-Economics-Political Scale which measures "the good life" of a state. The S-E-P index is designed to reflect both a state's general economic health and its willingness to provide services essential to continual well-being. The study uses nine areas for measurement.

1. Status of the individual: enhancing personal dignity and widening areas of choice
2. Equality: efforts to end discrimination
3. Democratic process: informed and involved citizenry, good public administration
4. Education: improving quantity and quality of education at all levels
5. Economic growth: public capital investment, improved standard of living, education for a better-trained work force
6. Technological change: research and availability of manpower and facilities for economic growth
7. Agriculture: seeking efficient-size farm sector and helping excess farm workers relocate
8. Living conditions: alleviation of poverty and improvement of decayed urban areas
9. Health and welfare: improving level of welfare assistance, vocational rehabilitation, and provision of good public and private medical services[1]

California ranks first and Mississippi fiftieth on the S-E-P index.[2]

Notes

1. U.S. Department of Labor, *State Economic and Social Indicators,* Bulletin No. 328 (Washington, D.C.: U.S. Government Printing Office, 1973). $1 per copy.
2. Other publications providing information about quality-of-life indicators for the states developed by the Midwest Research Institute include the following: Ben-Chieh Liu, *The Quality of Life in the United States, 1970: Index, Rating and Statistics* (Kansas City: Midwest Research Institute, November 1973); idem, "Variations in the Quality of Life in the United States by State, 1970," *Review of Social Economy* 32, no. 2 (October 1974): 131–47; idem, "Quality of Life: Concept, Measure and Results," *American Journal of Economics and Sociology* 34, no. 1 (January 1975): 1–13; idem, *Quality of Life Indicators in U.S. Metropolitan Areas, 1970: A Summary* (Kansas City: Midwest Research Institute, May 1975); idem, *Quality of Life Indicators in U.S. Metropolitan Areas: A Statistical Analysis* (New York: Praeger, 1976).

4.C.4   SOCIAL INDICATORS AT THE COMMUNITY LEVEL

Community social indicators should meet the same criteria as do national and state indicators. They should demonstrate *measureability, tap social importance and shared goals,* have *policy importance,* and *fit into a model* that explicates the most important relationships between the indicator and empirically associated variables.[1]

Clark suggests a focus on policy outputs and policy impact as the two types of phenomena important for an understanding of community dynamics. He indicates that development of community indicators is at an early stage but suggests that policy outputs may be measured by fiscal indicators such as "funds spent for given activities" and by performance indicators such as "tons of refuse collected." A comparative measure of policy outputs in various communities would allow a community on a relative basis to evaluate the services it is getting.

Policy outputs can be contrasted with *policy impacts.* Policy impacts are "changes resulting in a social system as a consequence of policy outputs." Policy impacts can be considered in terms of these criteria on: (1) citizen preferences, (2) community leader preferences, (3) extra-community actor preferences, (4) professional criteria, and (5) social scientific criteria. Suggestions for indicators are developed in the cited article.

Clark and his co-workers have completed a study of 54 American cities ranking them on 29 fiscal strain indicators. Factors associated with fiscal strain have been identified and policy recommendations have been set forth.[2]

A tested community indicator is an index called Social Vulnerability developed by John C. Maloney, Community Service Council of Metropolitan Indianapolis, Inc. (July 1973).[3] This index was constructed "to measure the relative extent to which persons residing in specified geographic areas of the community were vulnerable to experiencing adverse social and physical strains beyond their ability to cope without help." It consists of eight sufficient but not exhaustive variables determined by factor analysis: (1) median family income, (2) percent of families below poverty level, (3) percent of families with both husband and wife, (4) percent of housing without some or all plumbing facilities, (5) percent of the civilian labor force unemployed, (6) percent of households lacking an available automobile, (7) rate of ambulance runs per 1000 population, and (8) rate of tuberculosis per 1000 population.

This index has identified areas in Marion County "most urgently requiring the investment of both human and capital social resources" in order to mitigate adverse conditions. Scores are available for all census tracts of Marion County. Listing of the scores for each census tract are shown on each of the eight variables listed above.

For the student or researcher who wishes to examine the use of social indicators in other cities, the excellent bibliography on pages xxxii–xxxiv in *Social Indicators III* provides extensive formation. Among the cities using social indicators are Albuquerque, Kansas City, Charlotte, New York City, Denver, San Diego, Austin, Detroit, Baltimore, Tampa, Phoenix, and Washington, D.C.

Notes

1. Terry N. Clark, "Community Social Indicators: From Analytical Models and Policy Applications," *Urban Affairs Quarterly,* September 1973, pp. 5–7. Cf. Peter H. Rossi, "Community Social Indicators," in *The Human Meaning of Social Change,* ed. A. Campbell and P. E. Converse (New York: Russell Sage, 1972), pp. 87–126.
2. Terry N. Clark, Irene S. Rubin, Lynne C. Pettler, and Erwin Zimmerman, "How Many

New Yorks? The New York Fiscal Crisis in Comparative Perspective" (Research report No. 72 of the Comparative Study of Community Decision Making, Sociology Department, University of Chicago, Chicago, Ill., 1976).

3. For further information write Research Department, Community Service Council of Metropolitan Indianapolis, Inc., 615 N. Alabama Street, Indianapolis, IN 46204.

4.C.5   RANGE OF SOCIAL INDICATORS AND CURRENT DEVELOPMENTS

The number of social indicators that are currently available to measure social trends is large. The potential is huge. Scholars and decision makers differ on their choices of important social areas or facets of society. In the comparative table below, three writers exhibit social areas in which they suggest a broad range of indicators. Their ideas can be compared with the indicators in the latest (1980) national edition of *Social Indicators.*

Comparative List of Social Areas with Compilation of Indicators

O. D. Duncan[a]	U.S. Department of Health Education, and Welfare[b]	Raymond A. Bauer[c]	*Social Indicators III*[d]
1. Occupational changes	1. Health and illness	1. Population	1. Population and the family
2. Conditional probabilities for attending college (SES and mental ability)	2. Social mobility	2. Technological advances	2. Health and nutrition
3. Air-pollution index	3. Physical environment	3. Education	3. Housing and the environment
4. Incidence of victimization by criminal acts	4. Income and property	4. Military appropriations	4. Transportation
5. Educational opportunity	5. Public order and safety	5. Utilities and transportation	5. Public safety
6. Political participation	6. Learning, science, and art	6. Governmental growth	6. Education and training
7. Voluntary association membership	7. Participation and alienation	7. Natural resources	7. Work
8. Tolerance of political dissent		8. Welfare	8. Social security and welfare
9. Mental health			9. Income and productivity
10. Alienation			10. Social participation
11. Time budgets			11. Culture, leisure, and use of time
12. Income and assets			
13. Value change			
14. Religious affiliation and belief			

[a] Otis Dudley Duncan, *Toward Social Reporting: Next Steps* (New York: Russell Sage Foundation, 1969).
[b] U.S. Department of Health, Education, and Welfare (now the Department of Health and Human Welfare), *Toward a Social Report* (Ann Arbor: University of Michigan Press, 1970).
[c] Raymond A. Bauer, ed., *Social Indicators* (Cambridge, Mass.: MIT Press, 1969).
[d] U.S. Bureau of the Census, *Social Indicators III* (Washington, D.C.: U.S. Government Printing Office, 1980).

Current Development in Social-Indicator Research

IN THE UNITED STATES:

Russell Sage Foundation. This foundation has had a long interest in social indicators as a part of its study on social change. It has supported research on indicators of social trends by developing a general orientation as shown by *Indicators of Social Change: Concepts and Measurements,* ed. Eleanor B. Sheldon and Wilbert E. Moore (1968). A number of specific research volumes published by Russell Sage are listed in the bibliography of social indicators (p. 355).

Social Science Research Council. This is an interdisciplinary organization that maintains several research committees. One of these is the Committee on Social Indicators. The Social Science Research Council's Center for Social Indicators has added a planning staff to the program it has had in place since 1972. In October 1977 the Center was urged by a site visit team appointed by the National Science Foundation (NSF) to prepare explicit guidelines for research on social indicators for the United States over the next decade. In 1979 the Center began full-scale work on this project, with support from the NSF. Over the next few years, SSRC's Advisory and Planning Committee on Social Indicators, which provides intellectual guidance for the Center, will be seeking the views of a wide community of scholars, staff in statistical agencies and research institutes, and others who have an interest in the future of social indicators.*

During the 1970s much was accomplished by the replication of selected existing studies. These include:

A project at the University of Wisconsin to produce public use samples from the U.S. Censuses of 1940 and 1950 that will afford researchers a decennial series of public use samples from 1940 through 1980.

The 1962 Occupational Changes in a Generation Study was replicated in 1973.

The cohorts of the National Longitudinal Survey of Labor Market Experience have been refreshed by the addition of cohorts of men and women aged 14–21 in 1978, and by a new longitudinal study, "High School and Beyond," which was fielded in 1980 to follow that year's sophomore and senior classes.

In addition to development of the data base, both substantive research and methodology advanced in the 1970s in ways that have contributed to fundamental research on social change. There have been important analytical advances in the study of longitudinal data including log-linear models for the analysis of categorical data and solutions (e.g., maximum likelihood) for systems of linear structural equations. These latter methods are proving especially important because they permit the researcher to bring a theory of measurement and a concern for error structures to the final stages of statistical analysis. Journal articles frequently report quantitative studies of social change, many of which use social indicators time series. People involved in this research are to be found in disciplines as varied as historical demography, life-span developmental psychology, labor economics, social history, and sociology.

Considerable effort is being made to identify some of the issues that should

---

* For a more complete description see *Footnotes* of the American Sociological Association, April 1981, p. 3.

be the foci of planning for social indicators in the 1980s. Central to the planning effort is an assessment of the condition of social measurement in the United States—what is going well, where some revision is needed, and where no measurement work is being undertaken. Linked to this interest in the improvement of measurement is a concern with ensuring the integrity of the time series that are fundamental to social indicators research. The integrity of these time series is problematic due to a basic tension between the desire to maintain continuity and the need to respond to opportunities for improvement and innovation.

One area in which innovation may be called for concerns social indicators of change in social organization, structure, conflict, and integration. The majority of social indicators are derived from survey observations of individual behavior or attitudes, while much of the theoretical emphasis of the social sciences has been at collective levels of social organization, culture, and conflict. It is clear that many central research questions cannot be addressed by today's data base. The planning report will outline ways in which to broaden the content of social indicators beyond the present focus on the individual and family.

The Center issues a *Social Indicators Newsletter* on research in the field and via its library is assisting the new journal called *Social Indicator Research.* Communications may be sent to the Center at 1785 Massachusetts Avenue N.W., Washington, DC 20036.

National Science Foundation (NSF). The NSF's major role in current activities is the funding of research projects in various social-indicator-oriented areas, such as objective measurement of social and urban conditions; developing goals accounting systems; and trend analyses of political, economic, and social changes. Although funds have been cut since 1981, the NSF continues to give high priority to measurement methods and data resources. Support for the NORC General Social Survey (National Opinion Research Center, Illinois) and for the Center for Coordination of Research on Social Indicators (Social Science Research Council, New York) has been steady over the last ten years.

U.S. Bureau of the Census. The Center for Demographic Studies in the Census Bureau published *Social Indicators III* in December 1980. This continues the pioneer efforts of 1973 and 1976 in providing a comprehensive overview of current social conditions and trends in the United States.

U.S. Department of Labor. In 1974 the U.S. Department of Labor organized a Working Group on Indicators of the Quality of Employment. This group has been clarifying conceptual issues involved in developing measures of the quality of employment to be used in an accounting system of national social indicators. See the bibliography (p. 355) for published work.

Institute for Social Research, University of Michigan. On a general level, the Institute is continuing its wide interest in social indicators. It has done several studies to measure social changes in consumer behavior, economic well-being, youth in transition, residential mobility, and early retirement. Studies of attitudes and values have included such areas as drugs, violence, racial behavior, and discrimination. Note the work of Angus Campbell and his associates shown in the accompanying bibliography on the Quality of Life in the United States.

Survey Research Center, University of California (Berkeley), Bank of Amer-

ica, General Motors, State and Local Governments, et al. Numerous organizations are active in social indicator research as part of long-range planning programs. Each accumulates data and is concerned with social indicator research generally in order to make comparisons useful to their specific goals.

ON THE INTERNATIONAL LEVEL:

Organization for Economic Cooperation and Development. This is an international program consisting of 15 member states concerned with developing measurement instruments related to the quality of living across several countries. The program is designed to last several years, looking at such "agreed-upon" primary goal areas as personal health and safety; time and leisure; and the physical, social, and political environments.

United States Research Institute for Social Development. This institute has been established as a result of government grants from both the United States and the Netherlands. The UN agency is concerned with studying problems from an international viewpoint, one not often examined by national universities and institutes. Some of its activity areas are the "quantitative analysis of socio-economic development, methods of decision-making, preparation of the child for economic and technological modernization and measurement of real progress at the local level" (UNRISD 1971).

SELECTED BIBLIOGRAPHY STRESSING HISTORY, THEORY, AND ROLE OF SOCIAL INDICATORS

4.C.6

Annals of the American Academy of Political and Social Science 453 (January 1981). Special Issue: *Social Indicators: American Society in the Eighties.*

BAUER, RAYMOND A., ed. *Social Indicators.* Cambridge, Mass.: MIT Press, 1966.

CARLEY, MICHAEL. *Rational Techniques in Policy Analysis.* London: Heinemann Educational Books, 1980.

———. *Social Measurement and Social Indicators.* London: Allen & Unwin, 1981.

DUNCAN, OTIS DUDLEY. *Toward Social Reporting: Next Steps.* New York: Russell Sage Foundation, 1969.

FOX, KARL A. *Social Indicators and Social Theory, Elements of an Operational System.* New York: Wiley, 1974.

JUSTER, E. THOMAS, and LAND, KENNETH C., eds. *Social Accounting Systems: Essays on the State of the Art.* New York: Academic Press, 1981.

LAND, KENNETH C., and SPILERMAN, SEYMOUR, eds. *Social Indicator Models.* New York: Russell Sage Foundation, 1975.

NEUFVILLE, JUDITH INNES DE. *Social Indicators and Public Policy.* New York: Elsevier, 1975.

Bibliography of Special Indicators

BIDERMAN, ALBERT D., and DRURY, THOMAS F., eds. "The Quality of Employment Indicators." *American Behavioral Scientist* 17 (January–February 1975): 299–432.

The volume includes the following papers: "Introduction" by Albert D. Biderman; "The Role of Quality Employment Indicators in General Social Reporting Systems" by Kenneth C. Land; "Job Satisfaction Indicators and Their Correlates" by Stanley E. Seashore and Thomas D. Taber; "Going Beyond Current Income: A Preliminary Appraisal" by E. Thomas Juster and Greg Duncan; "Equity Concepts and the World of Work" by Lester Thurow; "Evaluating Changes in the Occupational Distribution and the Occupational System" by Arthur L. Stinchcombe.

———. *Measuring Work Quality for Social Reporting.* New York: Wiley, 1976.

> A collection of papers dealing with problems of matching concepts and indicators of work in relation to health criteria, psychic values, general well-being, life careers, positive and negative aspects of job mobility, social and moral qualities of jobs, responsiveness to workers of employment systems, and the dynamics of the occupational system.

CAMPBELL, ANGUS. *The Sense of Well-Being in America: Recent Patterns and Trends.* New York: McGraw-Hill, 1981.
———; CONVERSE, PHILIP E.; and RODGERS, WILLARD L. *The Quality of American Life: Perceptions, Evaluations, and Satisfactions.* New York: Russell Sage Foundation, 1976.
CONVERSE, PHILIP E.; DOTSON, JEAN D.; HOAG, WENDY J.; and McGEE, WILLIAM H. III. *American Social Attitudes Data Sourcebook, 1947–1978.* Cambridge, Mass.: Harvard University Press, 1980.

> Selected attitudinal data gathered from 1947 to 1978 to generate a portfolio of long-term indicators of the nature and quality of American life. Areas covered include attitudes toward self and others, blacks and whites, women, family living, work and retirement, personal economic outlook, national economic outlook, and government spending.

DAVIS, LOUISE E., and CHERNS, ALBERT B. *The Quality of Working Life,* vol. 1. New York: Free Press, 1975.

> See especially chapter 2, Defining and Measuring the Overall Quality of Working Life.

FERRISS, ABBOTT L. *Indicators of Trends in American Education; Indicators of Change in the American Family; Indicators of Trends in the Status of American Women,* 3 vols, New York: Russell Sage Foundation, 1970, 1971.
STRUMPEL, BURKHARD. *Economic Means for Human Needs: Social Indicators of Well-Being and Discontent.* Ann Arbor: Institute of Social Research, University of Michigan, 1976.
United Nations. *Social Indicators for Housing and Urban Development.* New York: UNIPUB, 1973.

A Comprehensive Annotated Bibliography

GILMARTIN, KEVIN J., et al. *Social Indicators—An Annotated Bibliography of Current Literature.* New York: Garland, 1979.
WILCOX, LESLIE D., et al. *Social Indicators and Societal Monitoring: An Annotated Bibliography.* New York: Elsevier, 1974.

A Handbook of Social Indicators

ROSSI, ROBERT J., and GILMARTIN, KEVIN J. *The Handbook of Social Indicators: Sources, Characteristics, and Analysis.* New York: Garland STPM Press, 1980.

A Specialized Research Journal

NICHALOS, ALEX C. *Social Indicators Research: An International and Interdisciplinary Journal for Quality of Life Measurement.* Established 1974. University of Guelph, Department of Philosophy, Guelph, Ontario, Canada. Publisher: D. Reidel Publishing, Dordrecht, Netherlands.

Measures of Organizational Structure

There are a number of basic facts about organizational measurement:

1. A very large number of structural attributes and interpersonal relationships exist within the same and different organizations.
2. The development of organizational measurement has come a long way in recent years, but serious shortcomings remain.
3. There is little standardization of the measures used in studying organizations. The lack of standardization hinders the development of organizational theory; it forces the researcher to use a high degree of judgment in selecting an organizational measure.
4. While the measurement and description of structure is an interesting process and exercise in its own right, important research problems are centered about the correlation of various structural arrangements in organizations.
5. Correlates will range from such internal factors as morale and decision making to the impact of structure on external relationships such as cooperative, defensive, and competitive postures vis-à-vis other organizations. Interrelationships of structural relationships themselves reveal a great deal about the character of the organization as a collective unit.
6. Some consensus about the most important structural variables is emerging. These include Size, Formalization, and Centralization. Whatever else may be of interest, these variables usually cannot be ignored in research designs.
7. There is high interest in many other variables including Absenteeism, Administrative Staff, Alienation, Autonomy, Communication, Complexity, Consensus, Coordination, Dispersion, Distributive Justice, Effectiveness, Innovation, Mechanization, Motivation, Bases of Power, Routinization, Satisfaction, Span of Control, Specialization, and Succession.
8. Two different sets of measures exist to assess many of these variables. One set represents the institutional approach, which relies on documents and informants; the other set relies on the survey approach, which is characterized by the use of questionnaire and interview schedules.
9. The best available guide for the selection of an organizational measure is James L. Price, *Handbook of Organizational Measurement* (Lexington, Mass.: Heath, 1972). The researcher will save time by using it for immediate reference. For research design, see Victor H. Vroom, ed., *Methods of Organizational Research*

(Pittsburgh: University of Pittsburgh Press, 1967); and James D. Thompson, ed., *Approaches to Organizational Design* (Pittsburgh: University of Pittsburgh Press, 1966). For a comprehensive survey of contemporary developments in the field of organizational studies, see David Dunkerley and Graeme Salaman, eds., *The International Yearbook of Organizational Studies 1979* (Boston: Routledge & Kegan Paul, 1979), which is described as the first volume in a series to portray developments in organizational research.

10. Measures for the three variables believed most important in analyzing correlates between themselves and other variables—Size, Formalization, and Centralization—are selected and reproduced. One social psychological measure, Index of Job-Related Tensions in Organizations, is also introduced.

4.D.1   SIZE

DEFINITION: Size is the scale of operations of an organization. A measure of size might be the number of personnel, the amount of assets, and the degree of expenditures. In organizational research, size is generally expressed as the number of employees, even though the number of employees is not necessarily the best way to measure the scale of operations. A firm may be quite large, but because of a very high degree of mechanization it may have relatively few personnel. Still, as an operating index the number of employees remains the most common measure.

MEASUREMENT: Advice to a researcher about the measurement of size would be conditioned by the design of the research. Will it involve few or many organizations? Will these organizations be small, intermediate, or large in size? What breakdowns will you need? by department, division, by total organization? What sensitivity about the data may be involved by the nature of the organizations to be studied—health, governmental, industrial, etc. What resources do you have? Only funds to write? or telephone? Funds to make a personal interview?

Organizations do not usually give out information casually. They make some information public as a matter of custom or law. It is suggested that the data may be available from the last annual report of the organization. Try this first if you need only total employment.

The number of employees for industrial and commercial organizations is found in the following volumes: *Standard and Poor's Register of Corporations, Directors, and Executives* (Dun and Bradstreet): vol. 1, *Million Dollar Directory,* vol. 2, *Middle Market Directory;* and *Moody's Industrial Manuals.*

If not available publicly, a letter, telephone call, or visit should be directed to the industrial relations director or personnel director stating the needs, reasons, and sponsorship of the research. The officials may be able to provide what you need as expressed in department and division breakdown. (Be sure to indicate what you can do with their data that may be useful to them.)

You will probably find that the employment department stores personal records and the payroll department has an official payroll printout. The latter record may be the more accurate. Of course, payrolls (and employment) often fluctuate greatly during the course of the year. It is important to indicate how your computations take this fact into account.

Validity of Size as an Independent Factor in Organization Structuring and Dynamics

A summary of research on size and its correlates is provided by Richard H. Hall in his *Organizations: Structures and Process* (Englewood Cliffs, N.J.: Prentice-Hall, 1972), pp. 112–39. This summary points out that the size factor has led to rather contradictory conclusions in the determination of the form of the organization. There is, however, growing consensus that larger organizations tend to have more specialization, more standardization, and more formalization than smaller organizations. But a lack of relationship between size and the remaining structural dimensions, i.e., concentration of authority and line control of work flows is equally striking. Hall, Haas, and Johnson, using data on 75 North American organizations, report on the conclusions of their findings:

> The most immediate implication of these findings is that neither complexity nor formalization can be implied from organizational size. A social scientist conducting research in a large organization would do well to question the frequent assumption that the organization under study is necessarily highly complex and formalized. . . . He will need to examine empirically, for each organization, the level of complexity and formalization extant at that time.[1]

Pugh and his associates used size as a "contextual variable" relating it to various aspects of organizational structure in 46 English organizations. Their conclusions are generally supportive of the consensus reported above.[2]

In Hall's review of research on size, conclusions are drawn about correlates with technology, professionalization, work flow, administrative components, the individual, organization, and society. The most important conclusions may be stated:[3]

1. The size factor is greatly modified by the technology or technologies employed by the organization.
2. The administrative component in relation to overall size of the organization displays a curvilinear relationship: the administrative component tends to decrease in size as organizational size increases; however, in very large organizations the relative size of the administrative component again increases with overall size.
3. Large size has an impact on the individuals in the organization. There is more stress, and the depersonalization process can lead to a great deal of discomfort for many members. Negative consequences are partially alleviated by the presence of informal friendship groups found in all organizations.
4. Large size creates difficulties in organizational control, coordination, and communications; at the same time it gives the organization more power over its environment, more resources for planning, and less dependence on particular individuals.
5. The concentration of power in large organizations may concentrate power in the society with threats to democratic processes.

Notes

1. Richard H. Hall, J. Eugene Haas, and Norman J. Johnson, "Organizational Size, Complexity, and Formalization," *American Sociological Review* 32, no. 6 (December 1967): 111.
2. D. S. Pugh, D. J. Hickson, C. R. Hinings, and C. Turner, "The Context of Organizational Structure," *Administrative Science Quarterly* 14, no. 1 (March 1969): 98.
3. Hall et al., "Organizational Size," p. 138.

4.D.2 FORMALIZATION

DEFINITION: Formalization represents the use of rules in an organization. Some organizations carefully describe the specific authority, responsibility, duties, and procedures to be followed in every job and then supervise job occupants to ensure conformity to the job definitions. A penalty system may be spelled out in writing for impartial monitoring of discipline for infractions. Other organizations have loosely defined jobs and do not carefully control work behavior.

The two dimensions of formalization may be specified as job codification, the degree of work standardization; and rule leniency, the measure of the latitude of behavior that is tolerated from standards.

MEASUREMENT: Extensive research on formalization has been done by Aiken and Hage, Richard Hall and his associates, and by Pugh-Hickson and their colleagues. Aiken and Hage have relied on the traditional type of survey. Both Hall and Pugh have relied more on documentary data. Both approaches are recommended, but for economy the Aiken-Hage measure is reproduced.

Hage and Aiken Formalization Inventory*

The data are collected by means of interviews. Fifteen questions are used.

"I'm going to read a series of statements that may or may not be true for your job in [name of organization]. For each item I read, please answer as it applies to you and your organization; using the answer categories on this card.

1. Definitely true
2. More true than false
3. More false than true
4. Definitely false"

	Definitely true	More true than false	More false than true	Definitely false
1. First, I feel that I am my own boss in most matters.	____	____	____	____
2. A person can make his own decisions here without checking with anybody else.	____	____	____	____
3. How things are done around here is left pretty much up to the person doing the work.	____	____	____	____
4. People here are allowed to do almost as they please.	____	____	____	____
5. Most people here make their own rules on the job.	____	____	____	____

* A minor adaptation has been made by James L. Price. Used with permission.

360

	Definitely true	More true than false	More false than true	Definitely false
6. The employees are constantly being checked on for rule violations.	___	___	___	___
7. People here feel as though they are constantly being watched to see that they obey all the rules.	___	___	___	___
8. There is no rules manual.	___	___	___	___
9. There is a complete written job description for my job.	___	___	___	___
10. Whatever situation arises, we have procedures to follow in dealing with it.	___	___	___	___
11. Everyone has a specific job to do.	___	___	___	___
12. Going through the proper channels is constantly stressed.	___	___	___	___
13. The organization keeps a written record of everyone's job performance.	___	___	___	___
14. We are to follow strict operating procedures at all times.	___	___	___	___
15. Whenever we have a problem we are supposed to go to the same person for an answer.	___	___	___	___

COMPUTATION. The five following measures are constructed from the 15 questions: job codification (questions 1–5), rule observation (questions 6–7), rule manual (question 8), job descriptions (question 9), specificity of job descriptions (questions 10–15). Replies to these 15 questions are scored from 1 (definitely true) to 4 (definitely false). A mean is constructed for each respondent for each of the five measures of formalization. The higher the mean (4 is the highest mean), the higher the formalization. The researchers report no ranges for the means of the five measures. Each respondent is then classified by "social position," and based on the first mean, a second mean is computed for each social position in the organization for each of the five measures. A social position is defined by the level or stratum in the organization, and the department or type of professional activity. For example, if an agency's professional staff consists of psychiatrists and social workers, each divided into the hierarchical levels, the agency has four social positions: supervisory psychiatrists, psychiatrists, supervisory social workers, and social workers. The organizational scores for each of the five measures are determined by computing an average of all social position means in the organization.

WHERE PUBLISHED: Michael Aiken and Jerald Hage, "Organizational Alienation," *American Sociological Review* 31 (August 1966): 497–507. Scale and data on reliability and validity reproduced in James L. Price, *Handbook of Organizational Measurement* (Lexington, Mass.: Heath, 1972) pp. 108–11.

RELIABILITY: The study contains no data relevant to reliability.

VALIDITY: Formalization is positively related to alienation. The greater the degree of formalization in the organization, the greater the likelihood of alienation from work. There is great dissatisfaction with work in those organizations in which jobs are rigidly structured. Strict enforcement of rules was strongly related to work dissatisfaction; social relations are also disturbed when rules are strictly enforced. Significant positive relationships are found between routine work and rule manual, job description, and specificity of job descriptions.

UTILITY: The interview can be conducted in less than five minutes in most cases.

RESEARCH APPLICATIONS:

AIKEN, MICHAEL, and HAGE, JERALD. "Organizational Alienation." *American Sociological Review* 31 (August 1966): 497–507.

HAGE, JERALD, and AIKEN, MICHAEL. "Program Change and Organizational Properties." *American Journal of Sociology* 72 (March 1967): 503–19.

———. "Relationship of Centralization to Other Structural Properties." *Administrative Science Quarterly* 12 (June 1967): 72–92.

———. *Social Change in Complex Organizations.* New York: Random House, 1970.

DOCUMENTARY MEASURES OF FORMALIZATION:

The measures developed by Hall and his associates may be found in Richard H. Hall, J. Eugene Haas, and Norman J. Johnson, "Organizational Size, Complexity, and Formalization," *American Sociological Review* 32, no. 6 (December 1967).

The measures developed by Inkson, Pugh, and Hickson may be found in J. H. K. Inkson, D. S. Pugh, and D. J. Hickson, "Organization Context and Structure: An Abbreviated Replication," *Administrative Science Quarterly* 15 (September 1970): 318–29. The measure and data on reliability and validity are reproduced in James L. Price, *Handbook of Organizational Measurement* (Lexington, Mass.: Heath, 1972), pp. 111–15.

The serious researcher will examine each of these excellent measures and choose the one that best fits his research design.

4.D.3 CENTRALIZATION

DEFINITION: Centralization is the degree to which power is concentrated in an organization.

Power is an important component in every organization. The distribution of power has major consequences for the performance of an organization and the behavior of its members.

An important consideration in dealing with power is the manner in which it is distributed. The maximum degree of centralization would exist if all power were exercised by a single individual; the minimum degree of centralization would exist if all power were exercised equally by all members of the organization. Most organizations fall between these two extremes.

Various problems are generated by the degree of centralized power and the manner in which actors wield their power and influence over superordinate, coordinate, and subordinate members of the organization. The following topics are commonly generated by problems of power stratification: participation-management, industrial democracy, group decision making, employee representation, collective bargaining, alienation, and organizational conflict.

MEASUREMENT: As with most measures, centralization may be assessed by the institutional approach using documents and informants or by the use of the survey approach with questionnaires and interview schedules as the principal instruments.

Pugh and his associates rely on data that are obtained by interviewing one or a few top executives and from documents which organizations (24 manufacturing and 16 services) made available to the researchers. Aiken and Hage collected all their data on centralization by interviewing executive directors, department heads, and staff members in 16 social welfare and health organizations.

Johannes Pennings has submitted the measures used by these researchers to validity tests. He contrasts the two research approaches as shown below:

Institutional approach
A₁. Centralization

Autonomy: This scale consists of 23 issues to measure whether decisions on these issues are made inside or outside the organization (Pugh et al. 1968, pp. 102–4).

Chief executive span of control: This indicates the number of subordinates who report directly to the chief executive, regardless of the hierarchical position of the subordinates (Pugh et al. 1968, p. 104).

Worker/supervisory ratio: This value indicates the number of subordinates in production departments per first-line supervisor (Pugh et al. 1968, p. 104).

Number of direct supervisors (%): This indicates the number of first-line supervisors in production departments, including the assistants and deputies (Pugh et al. 1968, p. 104).

Questionnaire approach
A₂. Centralization

Personal participation in decision making. This is a Likert scale measuring how much the individual participates in decisions about the allocation of resources and the determination of organizational policies (Hage and Aiken 1967, p. 78).

Hierarchy of authority: This scale measures the degree to which the organization member participates in decisions involving the tasks associated with his position (Hage and Aiken 1967, pp. 78–79).

Departmental participation in decision making: This Likert scale measures how much an individual "and his colleagues" participate in decisions involving their work and work environment (personal communication).

The organizational researcher should examine these measures carefully in choosing those most suitable to his design. Again for economy, only Aiken and Hage's scales of *personal participation in decision making and hierarchy of authority* are reproduced.

Aiken and Hage Scale of Personal Participation in Decision Making and Hierarchy of Authority*

The questions for the index of actual participation are as follows:

1. How frequently do you usually participate in the decision to hire new staff?

            ____ Never   ____ Often
            ____ Seldom   ____ Always
            ____ Sometimes

2. How frequently do you usually participate in the decisions on the promotion of any of the professional staff?
3. How frequently do you participate in decisions on the adoptions of new policies?
4. How frequently do you participate in the decisions on the adoptions of new programs?

The questions for the scale of hierarchy of authority are as follows:

1. There can be little action taken here until a supervisor approves a decision.

            ____ Definitely false   ____ True
            ____ False   ____ Definitely true

2. A person who wants to make his or her own decisions would be quickly discouraged here.
3. Even small matters have to be referred to someone higher up for a final decision.
4. I have to ask my boss before I do almost anything.
5. Any decision I make has to have my boss' approval.

COMPUTATION: The computations differ for the two types of decisions. For the index of actual participation, the five responses are assigned numbers from 1 (low participation) to 5 (high participation). A "Never" response receives 1; at the other extreme, an "Always" response receives 5. An average score on these five questions is computed for each respondent. Each respondent is then classified by "social position" and a second mean computed for each social position in the organization. "A social position," according to Aiken and Hage, "is defined by the level or stratum in the organization and the department or type of professional activity. For example, if an agency's professional staff consists of psychiatrists and social workers, each divided into two hierarchical levels, the agency has four social positions: supervisory psychiatrists, psychiatrists, supervisory social workers, and social workers." The organizational score is determined by computing the average of all social position means in the organization.

Computations for the hierarchy of authority scale are similar to those for the index of actual participation. The responses are assigned numbers from 1 (definitely false) to 4 (definitely true). As with the index of actual participation, the organizational score for the hierarchy of authority scale is based on social position means, which in turn are based on the means for each respondent.

* Used with permission.

WHERE PUBLISHED: M. Aiken and J. Hage, "Organizational Interdependence and Intraorganizational Structure," *American Sociological Review* 33, no. 6 (1968): 912–30. Scales are described in footnotes 6 and 7, p. 924. For measures used by Pugh and associates, see D. S. Pugh, D. J. Hickson, C. R. Hinings, and C. Turner, "Dimensions of Organization Structure," *Administrative Science Quarterly* 13, no. 1 (1968): 65–105; J. H. K. Inkson, D. S. Pugh, and D. J. Hickson, "Organization Context and Structure: A Replication Study," *Administrative Science Quarterly* 15, no. 3 (1970): 318–29.

RELIABILITY: No relevant data provided by Aiken and Hage.

VALIDITY: Organizations in which the decisions were made by only a few people at the top relied on rules and close supervision as a means of ensuring consistent performance by the workers. These organizations were also characterized by a less professional staff. The presence of a well-trained staff is related to a reduced need for extensive rules. Penning reports that organizations that are highly autonomous tend to have a nonparticipative internal decision structure. The greater the autonomy, the larger the executive's span of control.[1]

RESEARCH APPLICATIONS:

AIKEN, MICHAEL, and HAGE, JERALD. "Organizational Alienation." *American Sociological Review* 31 (August 1966): 497–507.

HAGE, JERALD, and AIKEN, MICHAEL. "Program Change and Organizational Properties." *American Journal of Sociology* 72 (March 1967): 503–19.

———. "Relationship of Centralization to Other Structural Properties." *Administrative Science Quarterly* 12 (June 1967): 72–92.

———. *Social Change in Complex Organization.* New York: Random House, 1970.

HALL, RICHARD H. "An Empirical Study of Bureaucratic Dimensions and Their Relation to Other Organizational Characteristics." Ph.D. dissertation, Columbus, The Ohio State University, 1961.

———. "The Concept of Bureaucracy: An Empirical Assessment." *American Journal of Sociology* 69 (July 1963): 32–40.

SMITH, CLAGETT G., and TANNENBAUM, ARNOLD S. "Organization Control Structure: A Comparative Analysis." *Human Relations* 16 (1963): 299–316. For a critique of the Tannenbaum Organizational Control Questionnaire see Lake, Miles, and Earle, Jr., *Measuring Human Behavior.* New York: Teachers College Press, 1973. Pp. 214–19.

For more recent research, see all references in section 4.M.1. Under Group Structures and Dynamics. *American Sociological Review,* 1965–80. Also check *Administrative Science Quarterly.*

Notes

1. Johannes Pennings, "Measures of Organizational Structures: A Methodological Note," *American Journal of Sociology* 79, no. 3 (November 1973): 688–89.

VARIABLE MEASURED: This index purports to measure the amount of tension experienced as a result of one's job.

DESCRIPTION: The index consists of 15 statements describing what the authors judge to be symptoms of conflict or ambiguity. Respondents are asked to estimate how often they are bothered by each type of symptom on a 5-point Likert scale.

WHERE PUBLISHED: Robert L. Kahn et. al., *Organizational Stress* (New York: Wiley, 1964, pp. 424–25.

RELIABILITY: No test-retest reliability is indicated, but an intercorrelation analysis of the items was performed on a national sample of 725 employed adults; in addition, an intensive survey was taken of 53 supervisory personnel. On the whole the average inter-item correlation appears to be in the middle .70s. The intercorrelation matrix figures for the intensive sample are quite close to those found in the national sample.

VALIDITY: The survey utilized an open-ended question to elicit information about the number, content, and intensity of job-related worries. These were shown to be closely related to the tension index. Some indirect relationships between tension and satisfaction were found.

UTILITY: Time required for test administration is estimated at less than 15 minutes. The scale is equally applicable to employees and supervisory personnel. It is a diagnostic instrument as well as a measurement index. The Handbook author believes that the diagnostic capacity of the index in identifying major tensions may be its most significant attribute.

SCORING: Respondent answers each item by choosing one of six fixed alternative responses: Never bothered; Rarely bothered; Sometimes bothered; Bothered rather often; Bothered nearly all the time; Does not apply. Scores of 1 to 5 are assigned to the first five responses. Respondent's total score is his average score over all the items *except* those to which he responded "Does not apply." A range of scores between 0 and 5 is indicated.

RESEARCH APPLICATION:
DUNCAN, ROBERT B. "The Effects of Mobility Orientation on the Manager's Perception of Role Pressure in an Industrial Work Organization." M.A. thesis, Indiana University, 1966.

Index of Job-Related Tensions in Organizations*

All of us occasionally feel bothered by certain kinds of things in our work. I am going to read a list of things that sometimes bother people, and I would like you to tell me how frequently you feel bothered by each of them. You are to indicate your response by choosing one of the six alternative answers provided each item.

1. Feeling that you have too little authority to carry out the responsibilities assigned to you.
   1. Never bothered
   2. Rarely bothered
   3. Sometimes bothered
   4. Bothered rather often
   5. Bothered nearly all the time
   6. Does not apply

2. Being unclear on just what the scope and responsibilities of your job are.
   1. Never bothered
   2. Rarely bothered
   3. Sometimes bothered
   4. Bothered rather often
   5. Bothered nearly all the time
   6. Does not apply

3. Not knowing what opportunities for advancement or promotion exist for you.
   1. Never bothered
   2. Rarely bothered
   3. Sometimes bothered
   4. Bothered rather often
   5. Bothered nearly all the time
   6. Does not apply

4. Feeling that you have too heavy a work load, one that you can't possibly finish during an ordinary workday.
   1. Never bothered
   2. Rarely bothered
   3. Sometimes bothered
   4. Bothered rather often
   5. Bothered nearly all the time
   6. Does not apply

5. Thinking that you'll not be able to satisfy the conflicting demands of various people over you.
   1. Never bothered
   2. Rarely bothered
   3. Sometimes bothered
   4. Bothered rather often
   5. Bothered nearly all the time
   6. Does not apply

6. Feeling that you're not fully qualified to handle your job.
   1. Never bothered
   2. Rarely bothered
   3. Sometimes bothered
   4. Bothered rather often
   5. Bothered nearly all the time
   6. Does not apply

7. Not knowing what your supervisor thinks of you, how he evaluates your performance.
   1. Never bothered
   2. Rarely bothered
   3. Sometimes bothered
   4. Bothered rather often
   5. Bothered nearly all the time
   6. Does not apply

8. The fact that you can't get information needed to carry out your job.
   1. Never bothered
   2. Rarely bothered

3. Sometimes bothered
4. Bothered rather often
5. Bothered nearly all the time
6. Does not apply

9. Having to decide things that affect the lives of individuals, people that you know.
    1. Never bothered
    2. Rarely bothered
    3. Sometimes bothered
    4. Bothered rather often
    5. Bothered nearly all the time
    6. Does not apply

10. Feeling that you may not be liked and accepted by the people you work with.
    1. Never bothered
    2. Rarely bothered
    3. Sometimes bothered
    4. Bothered rather often
    5. Bothered nearly all the time
    6. Does not apply

11. Feeling unable to influence your immediate supervisor's decisions and actions that affect you.
    1. Never bothered
    2. Rarely bothered
    3. Sometimes bothered
    4. Bothered rather often
    5. Bothered nearly all the time
    6. Does not apply

12. Not knowing just what the people you work with expect of you.
    1. Never bothered
    2. Rarely bothered
    3. Sometimes bothered
    4. Bothered rather often
    5. Bothered nearly all the time
    6. Does not apply

13. Thinking that the amount of work you have to do may interfere with how well it gets done.
    1. Never bothered
    2. Rarely bothered
    3. Sometimes bothered
    4. Bothered rather often
    5. Bothered nearly all the time
    6. Does not apply

14. Feeling that you have to do things on the job that are against your better judgment.
    1. Never bothered
    2. Rarely bothered
    3. Sometimes bothered
    4. Bothered rather often
    5. Bothered nearly all the time
    6. Does not apply

15. Feeling that your job tends to interfere with your family life.
    1. Never bothered
    2. Rarely bothered
    3. Sometimes bothered
    4. Bothered rather often
    5. Bothered nearly all the time
    6. Does not apply

---

* Reprinted by permission.

Evaluation Research and Organizational Effectiveness

EVALUATION RESEARCH AS A PROCESS

Every attempt to reduce or eliminate a social problem involves a theory, a program, and usually a large amount of money. The effectiveness of programs to reduce crime and delinquency, combat drug addiction, conquer health problems, improve neighborhoods and communities and the quality of life generally—all pose problems of evaluation. Because these problems are so important to national and community life and are so costly, evaluation has been given a high priority and evaluation research is increasing.

Edward Suchman wrote:

It may be helpful to visualize the evaluation process as a circular one, stemming from and returning to the formation of value, as shown in figure 1.*

Figure 1. Evaluation Process

* From *Evaluative Research, Principles and Practice in Public Service and Social Action Programs,* by Edward A. Suchman. © 1967 by Russell Sage Foundation. Reprinted with permission.

Evaluation always starts with some value, either explicit or implicit—for example, it is good to live a long time; then a goal is formulated derived from this value. The selection of goals is usually preceded by or concurrent with *"value formation."* An example of *"goal-setting"* would be the statement that fewer people should develop coronary disease, or that not so many people should die from cancer. Goal-setting forces are always in competition with each other for money, resources, and effort.

There next has to be some way of *"measuring goal attainment."* If we set as our goal that fewer people should die from cancer, then we need some means of discovering how many are presently dying from cancer (for example, vital statistics). The nature of the evaluation will depend largely on the type of measure we have available to determine the attainment of our objective.

The next step in the process is the identification of some kind of "goal-attaining activity." In the case of cancer, for example, a program of cancer-detecting activities aimed at early detection and treatment might be considered. Then the goal-attaining activity is put into operation. Diagnostic centers are set up and people urged to come in for check-ups.

Then, at some point, we have the *assessment* of this goal-directed operation. This stage includes the evaluation of the degree to which the operating program has achieved the predetermined objectives. As stated previously, this assessment may be scientifically done or it may not.

Finally, on the basis of the assessment, a *judgment* is made as to whether the goal-directed activity was worthwhile. This brings us back to value formation. Someone now may say that it is "good" to have cancer diagnostic centers. At the end of the evaluation process, we may get a new value, or we may reaffirm, reassess, or redefine an old value. For example, if the old value was "It is good to live a long time," the new value might be, "It is good to live until 100 if you remain healthy; but if you can't remain healthy it's better not to live past eighty."

In actuality, when the evaluation process begins, activities may be, and usually are, already going on. The evaluator may come in at any point. A crucial question in evaluative research is, "What do we mean by a successful result?" All programs will have some effects, but how do we measure these effects and how do we determine whether they are the particular effects we are interested in producing? As in the case of the independent program variables, we note a multiplicity and interdependence of effect variables. Again, our main problem is one of selecting from among the myriad of possible effects, those most relevant to our objectives.

We have already noted five major criteria for determining relevance: (1) effort or activity; (2) performance or accomplishment; (3) adequacy or impact; (4) efficiency or output relative to input; and (5) process or specification of conditions of effectiveness. In a sense we may classify the first two criteria as *evaluative*, that is, concerned with the determination of the relationship between activities and effects; the second two as *administrative*, dealing with a judgment about the size and cost of the effort relative to the effects; while the last one is really a *research* criterion, concerned with increased knowledge or understanding irrespective of effect.

Indices for the first two, effort and performance, are likely to be defined by the public service worker in terms of professional standards; the next two, adequacy and efficiency, are more likely to be determined by the administrator in terms of basic knowledge. To a large extent, the formulation of the objectives and design of an evaluative research project will depend upon who is conducting the project and what use will be made of the results.

Evaluation: How to Do It

Sage Publications of Beverly Hills, California, has made a very active publication effort in the field of evaluation with coverage of theory, method, and utilization. Sage has three major programs addressed to researchers who wish to learn how to do evaluation research. The reader will find (1) *A Program Evaluation Kit* (described below), (2) *Evaluation Primer* and *Workbooks,* and (3) *A Progress Series in Evaluation* that addresses specific problems in evaluation. The student or researcher interested in the operational aspects should first examine these three programs, then continue reading this section for other selected examples of evaluation research focused on specific problems. The concluding *general research* references are directed to the student who seeks a fuller understanding of theory, method, and research advances. The interest in evaluation is exploding in scope and publication.

PROGRAM EVALUATION KIT

Lynn Lyons Morris, Carol Taylor Fitz-Gibbon, and Marlene E. Henerson

The 8-volume Program Evaluation Kit is a step-by-step procedural guide that enables even a novice evaluator to plan and manage an evaluation. Clearly written, eminently practical, the Kit has been field tested at over 150 sites and is an outstanding resource for teachers and consultants, as well as those who have never given a test, written a report, or computed a mean.

EVALUATOR'S HANDBOOK. Lynn Morris and Carol Fitz-Gibbon. 136 pages.
HOW TO DEAL WITH GOALS AND OBJECTIVES. Lynn Morris and Carol Fitz-Gibbon. 80 pages.
HOW TO DESIGN A PROGRAM EVALUATION. Lynn Morris and Carol Fitz-Gibbon. 164 pages.
HOW TO MEASURE PROGRAM IMPLEMENTATION. Lynn Morris and Carol Fitz-Gibbon. 140 pages.
HOW TO MEASURE ATTITUDES. Marlene Henerson, Lynn Morris, and Carol Fitz-Gibbon. 184 pages.
HOW TO MEASURE ACHIEVEMENT. Lynn Morris and Carol Fitz-Gibbon. 160 pages.
HOW TO CALCULATE STATISTICS. Carol Fitz-Gibbon and Lynn Morris. 144 pages.
HOW TO PRESENT AN EVALUATION REPORT. Lynn Morris and Carol Fitz-Gibbon. 80 pages.

Evaluation Primer and Workbooks

An Evaluation Primer takes the reader—student, human services practitioner, or program administrator—step by step through the process of designing, implementing, and reporting an evaluation. The Primer is supplemented by two Workbooks—Practical Exercise for Health Professionals and Practical Exercises for Educators—that make the set ideal for use both as a classroom text and as a self-teaching tool for the evaluator of small-scale community programs. The Primer and the Workbook that is right for your needs as a health professional or as an educator will provide you with an invaluable resource to demystify the evaluation process, focusing on these crucial steps:

Formulating credible evaluation questions
Constructing evaluation designs
Planning and collecting evaluation information
Planning and conducting information analysis activities
Reporting evaluation information
Managing an evaluation

AN EVALUATION PRIMER. Arlene Fink and Jacqueline Kosecoff. Forewords by Charles E. Lewis and Wilson Riles. 1980.

AN EVALUATION PRIMER WORKBOOK: PRACTICAL EXERCISES FOR EDUCATORS. Arlene Fink and Jacqueline Kosecoff. 1980.

Sage Research Progress Series in Evaluation

UTILIZING EVALUATION: CONCEPTS AND MEASUREMENT TECHNIQUES. Edited by James A. Ciarlo, Mental Health Systems, Evaluation Project and Department of Psychology, University of Denver. 1981.

QUALITATIVE AND QUANTITATIVE METHODS IN EVALUATION RESEARCH. Edited by Thomas D. Cook, Northwestern University, and Charles S. Reichardt, University of Denver. 1979.

EVALUATOR INTERVENTION PROS AND CONS. Edited by Robert Perloff, Graduate School of Business, University of Pittsburgh. 1979.

TRANSLATING EVALUATION INTO POLICY. Edited by Robert F. Rich, Woodrow Wilson School of Public and International Affairs, Princeton University. 1979.

EVALUATING VICTIM SERVICES. Edited by Susan E. Salasin, Chief, Research Diffusion and Utilization Section, Mental Health Services Development Branch, National Institute of Mental Health. 1981.

THE EVALUATION AND MANAGEMENT. Edited by Herbert C. Schulberg and Jeanette M. Jerrell, both at Western Psychiatric Institute and Clinic, University of Pittsburgh School of Medicine. 1979.

METHODS FOR EVALUATING HEALTH SERVICES. Edited by Paul M. Wortman, School of Public Health, University of Michigan. 1981.

EVALUATION IN LEGISLATION. Edited by Franklin M. Zweig, Committee on Human Resources, U.S. Senate. Foreword by Senator Harrison A. Williams, Jr. 1979.

EDUCATING POLICYMAKERS FOR EVALUATION: LEGISLATION. Edited by Franklin M. Zweig, Director, Center for Public Services, University of Rhode Island, and Keith E. Marvin, Associate Director, Institute for Program Evaluation, U.S. General Accounting Office. 1981.

Selected Examples of Evaluation Research

ABT, CLARK C., ed. *The Evaluation of Social Programs.* Beverly Hills, Calif.: Sage, 1977.

ABT, WENDY PETER, and MAGIDSON, JAY. *Reforming Schools: Problems in Program Implementation and Evaluation.* Beverly Hills, Calif.: Sage, 1980.

ALKIN, MARVIN C.; DAILLAK, RICHARD; and WHITE, PETER. *Using Evaluations: Does Evaluation Make a Difference?* Beverly Hills, Calif.: Sage, 1979.

ARGYRIS, CHRIS. *Diagnosing Human Relations in Organizations: A Case Study of a Hospital.* New Haven: Yale University Press, 1956.

COMREY, A. L.; PFIFNER, J. M.; and BEEM, H. P. *Studies in Organizational Effectiveness I.* Los Angeles: U.S. Forest Survey, University of California, 1951.

FILSINGER, ERIK E., and LEWIS, ROBERT A. *Assessing Marriage: New Behavioral Approaches.* Beverly Hills, Calif.: Sage, 1981.

HAMILTON, WILLIAM L. *A Social Experiment in Program Administration: The Housing Allowance Administrative Agency Experiment.* Cambridge, Mass.: ABT Books, 1979.

KATZ, DANIEL; GUTEK, BARBARA A.; KAHN, ROBERT L.; and BARTON, EUGENIA. *Bureaucratic Encounters, A Pilot Study in the Evaluation of Government Services.* Ann Arbor: Institute for Social Research, University of Michigan, 1975.

KATZER, JEFFREY; COOK, KENNETH H.; and CROUCH, WAYNE W. *Evaluating Information: A Guide to Users of Social Science Research.* Reading, Mass.: Addison-Wesley, 1978.

LIPTON, DOUGLAS; MARTINSON, ROBERT; and WILKS, JUDITH. *The Effectiveness of Correctional Treatment: A Survey of Evaluation Treatment Studies.* 2 vols. New York: Praeger, 1975.

MEYER, HENRY J., and BORGATTA, EDGAR F. *An Experiment in Mental Patient Rehabilitation.* New York: Russell Sage Foundation, 1959.

ROBINS, PHILIP K.; SPIEGELMAN, ROBERT G.; and WEINER, SAMUEL, eds. *A Guaranteed Annual Income: Evidence from a Social Experiment.* New York: Academic Press, 1980.

ROTHMAN, JACK. *Using Research in Organizations: A Guide to Successful Application.* Beverly Hills, Calif.: Sage, 1980.

RUTMAN, LEONARD, ed. *Evaluation Research Methods: A Basic Guide.* Beverly Hills, Calif.: Sage, 1977.

SCHIERER, MARY ANN. *Program Implementation: The Organizational Context.* Beverly Hills, Calif.: Sage 1981.

STERN, PAUL C. *Evaluating Social Science Research.* New York: Oxford University Press, 1979.

WILLIAMS, WALTER, and ELMORE, RICHARD F., eds. *Social Programs Implementation.* New York: Academic Press, 1976.

WILNER, DANIEL M.; WALKLEY, ROSABELLE P.; PINKERTON, THOMAS C.; and TAYBACK, MATTHEW. *The Housing Environment and Family Life.* Baltimore: Johns Hopkins University Press, 1962.

WORTMAN, PAUL, ed. *Methods for Evaluating Health Services.* Beverly Hills, Calif.: Sage, 1981.

WRIGHT, JAMES D.; ROSSI, PETER H.; and WRIGHT, SONIA R. *After the Clean Up: Long Range Effects of Natural Disasters.* Beverly Hills, Calif.: Sage, 1979.

ZUSMAN, JACK. *Program Evaluation: Alcohol, Drug Abuse, and Mental Health Services.* Lexington, Mass.: Lexington Books, 1975.

General References to Evaluation Research

ABERT, JAMES G., and KAMRASS, MURRAY, eds. *Social Experiments and Social Program Evaluation.* Cambridge, Mass.: Ballinger, 1974.

BERNSTEIN, ILENE N., and FREEMAN, HOWARD E. *Academic and Entrepreneurial Research: The Consequences of Diversity in Federal Evaluation Studies.* New York: Russell Sage Foundation, 1975.

   Provides data about "high" and "low" quality evaluation research and contains recommendations for restructuring the entire evaluation research enterprise.

BERNSTEIN, ILENE N., ed. *Validity Issues in Evaluative Research.* Sage Contemporary Social Science Issues, No. 23. Beverly Hills, Calif.: Sage, August 1975.

CONNER, ROSS F., ed. *Methodological Advances in Evaluation Research.* Beverly Hills, Calif.: Sage 1981.

DOLBEARE, KENNETH M., ed. *Public Policy Evaluation.* Beverly Hills, Calif.: Sage 1975.

>   See especially chapter 1 by James S. Coleman, "Problems of Studying Policy Impacts."

EPSTEIN, IRWIN, and TRIPODI, TONY, *Research Techniques for Program Planning, Monitoring, and Evaluation.* New York: Columbia University Press, 1977.

FRANKLIN, JACK L., and THRASHER, JEAN H. *Introduction to Program Evaluation.* New York: Wiley Interscience, 1976.

GUTTENTAG, MARCIA, and STRUENING, ELMER L., eds. *Handbook of Evaluation Research.* 2 vol. Beverly Hills, Calif.: Sage, 1975.

LEVINE, ROBERT A.; SOLOMON, MARIAN A.; HELLSTERN, GERD-MICHAEL; and WALLMAN, HELMUT. *Evaluation Research and Practice: Comparative and International Perspectives.* Beverly Hills, Calif.: Sage, 1980.

LIVINGSTONE, JOHN LESLIE, and GUNN, SANFORD C. *Accounting for Social Goals: Budgeting and Analysis of Non-Market Projects.* New York: Harper & Row, 1974.

MOOS, RUDOLF H. *Evaluating Treatment Environments: A Social Ecological Approach.* New York: Wiley-Interscience, 1974.

>   Compares and evaluates treatment milieus in hospital-based and community based programs.

MOREHOUSE, THOMAS A. *The Problem of Measuring the Impacts of Social-Action Programs.* Fairbanks, Alaska: Institute of Social Economic and Government Research, 1972.

MOURSUND, JANET. *Evaluation: An Introduction to Research Design.* Monterey, Calif.: Brooks/Cole, 1973.

National Research Council. *Policy and Program Research in a University Setting: A Case Study Report.* Washington, D.C.: National Academy of Sciences, 1971.

RIECKEN, HENRY W., and BORUCH, ROBERT F. *Social Experimentation: A Method for Planning and Evaluating Social Intervention.* New York: Academic Press, 1974.

RIVLIN, ALICE M. *Systematic Thinking for Social Action.* Washington, D.C.: Brookings Institution, 1971.

ROESCH, RONALD, and CORRADO, RAYMOND H. *Evaluation and Criminal Justice Policy.* Beverly Hills, Calif.: Sage 1981.

ROSSI, PETER H.; FREEMAN, HOWARD E.; and WRIGHT, SONIA R. *Evaluation: A Systematic Approach.* Beverly Hills, Calif.: Sage, 1979.

SMITH, NICK L., ed. *New Techniques for Evaluation.* Beverly Hills, Calif.: Sage, 1981.

Symposium Proceedings at Fordham University. *Evaluation of Social Intervention.* San Francisco: Jossey-Bass, 1972.

>   The most comprehensive survey available for the entire evaluation process. A panel of 50 expert consultants offer guidance on program types and content, strategies and methods of evaluation, reviews of relevant literature, data aggregation across program parameters, determination of program effects, obstacles, and errors.

WEISS, CAROL H. *Evaluation Research: Methods for Assessing Program Effectiveness.* Englewood Cliffs, N.J.: Prentice-Hall, 1972.

———, comp. *Evaluating Action Programs: Readings in Social Action and Education.* Boston: Allyn & Bacon, 1972.

WILLIAMS, WALTER. *The Capacity of Social Science Organizations to Perform Large Scale Evaluative Research.* Seattle: Institute of Governmental Research, 1971.

———. *Social Policy Research and Analysis: The Experience in the Federal Agencies.* New York: Elsevier, 1971.

Analyzes use of policy research to improve antipoverty and equal-opportunity programs.

An Annotated Bibliography

FRANKLIN, JEROME L. *Organization Development: An Annotated Bibliography.* Ann Arbor: Institute of Social Research, University of Michigan, 1974.

Abstracts of books and articles that focus on the improvement of organizational performance. Each abstract contains a summary description of the major ideas, a listing of major topics, a table of contents, and a list of contributing authors.

The Exploding Research Frontier of Evaluation: For the Researcher Who Tries to Keep Up with Contemporary Developments

Evaluation Studies Review Annuals (Sage Publications, Beverly Hills, Calif.) have traced the dramatic growth in the concerns of the evaluation specialist from the beginning to the issues of today: integration rather than production of data, the validity of data aggregations, and the utilization of evaluation research in policy decisions. The 189 ground-breaking articles contained in these volumes were prepared by an interdisciplinary editorial board drawn from universities, government agencies, and independent research firms. In addition to studies on evaluation method and theory, there are included articles on evaluation research in the fields of education, mental health and public health services, welfare and social services, and criminal justice.

Volume 1 edited by Gene V. Glass. 1976. 704 pages.
Volume 2 edited by Marcia Guttentag with Shalom Saar. 1977. 736 pages.
Volume 3 edited by Thomas D. Cook and Associates. 1978. 783 pages.
Volume 4 edited by Lee Sechrest and Associates. 1979. 768 pages.
Volume 5 edited by Ernst W. Stromsdorfer and George Farkas. 1980. 800 pages.
Volume 6 edited by Howard E. Freeman, University of California, Los Angeles, and Marian A. Solomon, System Development Corporation. 1981. 769 pages.

Drawing on the rich and varied literature on evaluation that appeared in 1980, the editors of volume 6 present a book that focuses on the emerging issues of the decade: the increasing concerns with pre- and postevaluation processes (with evaluability assessment or exploratory evaluations on the one hand and utilization on the other); the challenges (and uncertainties) evaluators will face in an era of budgetary restraint; the attempts to bring evaluation efforts closer to operational activities and policy decision-making through a greater emphasis on implementation and via the growing sophistication in both the procurement and monitoring of evaluation research. These concerns are illustrated in the areas of education, human resources, social services, law, public safety, health, mental health, and substance abuse.

A Specialized Research Journal

Evaluation Review: A Journal of Applied Social Research. 1977. Quarterly. Editors: Richard A. Berk, Department of Sociology, University of California at Santa Barbara;

Howard E. Freeman, Institute for Social Research, University of California, Los Angeles.

Provides a forum for planners, researchers, evaluators, and policy makers engaged in the development, implementation, and utilization of evaluation research.

EFFECTIVENESS INDICES AS EVALUATIVE RESEARCH CRITERIA

Effectiveness may be defined as the degree to which a social system achieves its goals. For example, a drug addiction center that has a therapeutic goal that successfully reduces addiction in a high proportion of its treatment population would be considered an effective center.

Effectiveness must be distinguished from efficiency. Efficiency is mainly concerned with cost relative to output. Effectiveness is directly concerned with goal attainments. The social researcher may be asked to make a cost/benefit analysis, but such a request would be supplementary to any effectiveness assessment.

Organizational effectiveness is the task best performed by sociological or social-psychological researchers. Economists are best prepared to provide cost/benefit analyses.

The organizational goals most commonly set by their leaders are high productivity and employee will to work. How these goals are translated within different organizations varies greatly. Organizations functioning in the market sector must achieve a level of productivity sufficient to maintain profitability. Those private and public organizations that dispense services must maintain a level of efficiency that continues to attract funds from their contributors (donors or taxpayers). In all cases the quality of the good or service must satisfy the needs of the consumer.

A general appraisal of an organization is based on some concept of the interaction of employees with the organization. The most commonly accepted assumption is that effective teamwork is related to productivity and morale and that both goals should be appraised. Two superior efforts are represented in Rensis Likert, *The Human Organization* (New York: McGraw-Hill, 1967), and E. Wight Bakke, *Bonds of Organization* (New York: Harper & Row, 1950).

Likert describes many years of research conducted at the Institute of Social Research of the University of Michigan on the effect of performance of four management systems. He calls these (1) exploitive-authoritative, (2) benevolent-authoritative, (3) consultative, and (4) participative group. Each refers to a cluster of motivating and decision-making beliefs and behaviors. He demonstrates that as management systems move from (1) to (4), they demonstrate higher productivity, lower costs, more favorable attitudes, and excellent labor relations.

Bakke, in his appraisal of effective teamwork, assesses the adequacy of five elements that he regards as most important in achieving high productivity and will to work. They are *functional specifications,* which weld men together as partners in production; *the status system,* as directors and directed employees; *the communication system,* as givers and receivers of information; *the reward and penalty system,* as agents of reward and penalty; *the organizational charter,* as sharers of a conception of the organization as a whole.

The researcher seeking general criteria for assessment of organizational effectiveness will find yardsticks in both these books that may be applied to almost any organization, private or public. Likert's Profile of Organizational Characteristics is reproduced in section 4.E.1. It is a well-tested set of rating scales that may be applied to probe the motivating facets of the relevant organizational variables. Productivity measures themselves must usually be devised by operating officials in the given organization. Appraisals have been conducted in many different kinds of organizations: hospitals, schools, government agencies, banks, voluntary organizations, and the like. Special criteria have been formulated to deal with the different qualities of these organizations. A selected bibliography is appended to provide suggestions to the researcher.

Researchers may wish to compare the Profile of Organizational Characteristics with the *Survey of Organizations* by James C. Taylor and David G. Bowers (Ann Arbor: Institute of Social Research, University of Michigan, 1974). This is a machine-scored questionnaire that taps certain critical dimensions of organizational climate, managerial leadership, peer behavior, group processes, and satisfaction. The manual traces the origin, concepts, development, methodology, and administrative procedure of the survey. The 1970 questionnaire is composed of 92 items, about half of which probe attitudes using the Likert scale response set. The items are drawn from numerous studies made at the Institute including many from the Profile of Organizational Characteristics. The survey has been administered to more than 20,000 respondents in many different organizations. It takes from 30 to 45 minutes to complete. Numerous tests of reliability and validity are reported. For further information, write Organizational Development Research Program, Institute for Social Research, P.O. Box 1248, Ann Arbor, MI 48106.

The Profile of Organizational Characteristics on pages 378–85 is a set of rating scales used in interviewing managers in the organization. They are applicable for any group of supervisory heads in any organization. The form can be used to measure the management system of any unit within an organization, as well as that of the total organization.

Data gathered by the researcher through observation and records may be assembled, if desired, to validate further the dominant system of the organization as exploitive-authoritative, benevolent-authoritative, consultative, or participative group. Likert has prepared a chart of the Organizational and Performance Characteristics of Different Management Systems Based on a Comparative Analysis (see *The Human Organization,* pp. 14–24; or see Rensis Likert, *New Patterns of Management* [New York: McGraw-Hill, 1961]). Responses to the profile indicate that leadership styles and related organizational characteristics display a remarkably consistent set of interrelationships. In Appendix I of *The Human Organization,* Pearsonian coefficients of correlation are shown that measure the extent to which answers to one item are consistent with answers to the other. Apart from the performance items, all correlations between an item and the total score are greater than +.73. (For the validation of the high relationship between productivity and the consultative and participative group systems, see the results reported on the Weldon Plant, Plant L, and Company H. For an excellent critique, see Dale G. Lake et al., *Measuring Human Behavior* (New York: Teachers College Press, 1973), pp. 262–64.

4.E.2 PROFILE OF ORGANIZATIONAL CHARACTERISTICS*

Instructions (for managers to be interviewed)

1. On the lines below each organizational variable (item), please place an *n* at the point which, *in your experience*, describes your organization at the present time (*n* = now). Treat each item as a continuous variable from the extreme at one end to that at the other.
2. In addition, if you have been in your organization one or more years, please also place a *p* on each line at the point which, *in your experience*, describes your organization as it was one to two years ago (*p* = previously).
3. If you were not in your organization one or more years ago, please check here _____ and answer as of the present time, i.e., answer only with an *n*.

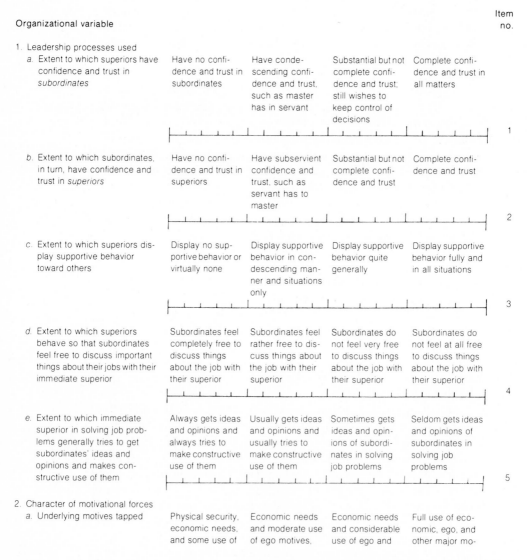

Organizational variable					Item no.
1. Leadership processes used					
a. Extent to which superiors have confidence and trust in *subordinates*	Have no confidence and trust in subordinates	Have condescending confidence and trust, such as master has in servant	Substantial but not complete confidence and trust; still wishes to keep control of decisions	Complete confidence and trust in all matters	1
b. Extent to which subordinates, in turn, have confidence and trust in *superiors*	Have no confidence and trust in superiors	Have subservient confidence and trust, such as servant has to master	Substantial but not complete confidence and trust	Complete confidence and trust	2
c. Extent to which superiors display supportive behavior toward others	Display no supportive behavior or virtually none	Display supportive behavior in condescending manner and situations only	Display supportive behavior quite generally	Display supportive behavior fully and in all situations	3
d. Extent to which superiors behave so that subordinates feel free to discuss important things about their jobs with their immediate superior	Subordinates feel completely free to discuss things about the job with their superior	Subordinates feel rather free to discuss things about the job with their superior	Subordinates do not feel very free to discuss things about the job with their superior	Subordinates do not feel at all free to discuss things about the job with their superior	4
e. Extent to which immediate superior in solving job problems generally tries to get subordinates' ideas and opinions and makes constructive use of them	Always gets ideas and opinions and always tries to make constructive use of them	Usually gets ideas and opinions and usually tries to make constructive use of them	Sometimes gets ideas and opinions of subordinates in solving job problems	Seldom gets ideas and opinions of subordinates in solving job problems	5
2. Character of motivational forces					
a. Underlying motives tapped	Physical security, economic needs, and some use of	Economic needs and moderate use of ego motives,	Economic needs and considerable use of ego and	Full use of economic, ego, and other major mo-	

*Reprinted from Rensis Likert, *The Human Organization.* Copyright © 1967 by McGraw-Hill, Inc. Used with permission of McGraw-Hill Book Co.

Organizational variable

Organizational variable					Item no.
	the desire for status	e.g., desire for status, affiliation, and achievement	other major motives, e.g., desire for new experiences	tives, as, for example, motivational forces arising from group goals	6
b. Manner in which motives are used	Fear, threats, punishment, and occasional rewards	Rewards and some actual or potential punishment	Rewards, occasional punishment, and some involvement	Economic rewards based on compensation system developed through participation; group participation and involvement in setting goals, improving methods, appraising progress toward goals, etc.	7
c. Kinds of attitudes developed toward organization and its goals	Attitudes are strongly favorable and provide powerful stimulation to behavior implementing organization's goals	Attitudes usually are favorable and support behavior implementing organization's goals	Attitudes are sometimes hostile and counter to organization's goals and are sometimes favorrable to the organization's goals and support the behavior necessary to achieve them	Attitudes usually are hostile and counter to organization's goals	8
d. Extent to which motivational forces conflict with or reinforce one another	Marked conflict of forces substantially reducing those motivational forces leading to behavior in support of the organization's goals	Conflict often exists; occasionally forces will reinforce each other, at least partially	Some conflict, but often motivational forces will reinforce each other	Motivational forces generally reinforce each other in a substantial and cumulative manner	9
e. Amount of responsibility felt by each member of organization for achieving organization's goals	Personnel at all levels feel real responsibility for organization's goals and behave in ways to implement them	Substantial proportion of personnel, especially at higher levels, feel responsibility and generally behave in ways to achieve the organization's goals	Managerial personnel usually feel responsibility; rank and file usually feel relatively little responsibility for achieving organization's goals	High levels of management feel responsibility; lower levels feel less; rank and file feel little and often welcome opportunity to behave in ways to defeat organization's goals	10
f. Attitudes toward other members of the organization	Favorable, cooperative attitudes throughout the	Cooperative, reasonable favorable attitudes toward	Subservient attitudes toward superiors; compe-	Subservient attitudes toward superiors coupled	

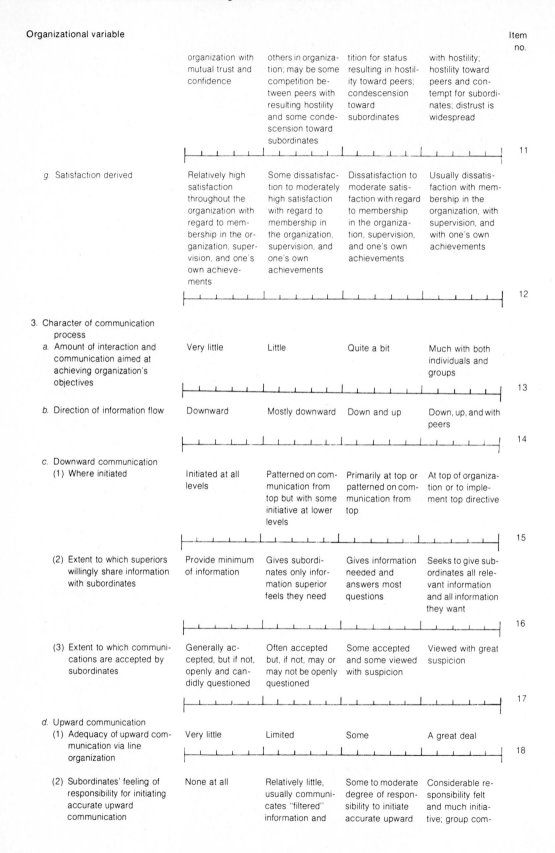

Organizational variable						Item no.

Organizational variable

organization with mutual trust and confidence | others in organization; may be some competition between peers with resulting hostility and some condescension toward subordinates | tition for status resulting in hostility toward peers; condescension toward subordinates | with hostility; hostility toward peers and contempt for subordinates; distrust is widespread

Item no. 11

g. Satisfaction derived — Relatively high satisfaction throughout the organization with regard to membership in the organization, supervision, and one's own achievements | Some dissatisfaction to moderately high satisfaction with regard to membership in the organization, supervision, and one's own achievements | Dissatisfaction to moderate satisfaction with regard to membership in the organization, supervision, and one's own achievements | Usually dissatisfaction with membership in the organization, with supervision, and with one's own achievements

Item no. 12

3. Character of communication process
 a. Amount of interaction and communication aimed at achieving organization's objectives — Very little | Little | Quite a bit | Much with both individuals and groups

Item no. 13

 b. Direction of information flow — Downward | Mostly downward | Down and up | Down, up, and with peers

Item no. 14

 c. Downward communication
  (1) Where initiated — Initiated at all levels | Patterned on communication from top but with some initiative at lower levels | Primarily at top or patterned on communication from top | At top of organization or to implement top directive

Item no. 15

  (2) Extent to which superiors willingly share information with subordinates — Provide minimum of information | Gives subordinates only information superior feels they need | Gives information needed and answers most questions | Seeks to give subordinates all relevant information and all information they want

Item no. 16

  (3) Extent to which communications are accepted by subordinates — Generally accepted, but if not, openly and candidly questioned | Often accepted but, if not, may or may not be openly questioned | Some accepted and some viewed with suspicion | Viewed with great suspicion

Item no. 17

 d. Upward communication
  (1) Adequacy of upward communication via line organization — Very little | Limited | Some | A great deal

Item no. 18

  (2) Subordinates' feeling of responsibility for initiating accurate upward communication — None at all | Relatively little, usually communicates "filtered" information and | Some to moderate degree of responsibility to initiate accurate upward | Considerable responsibility felt and much initiative; group com-

Organizational variable				Item no.

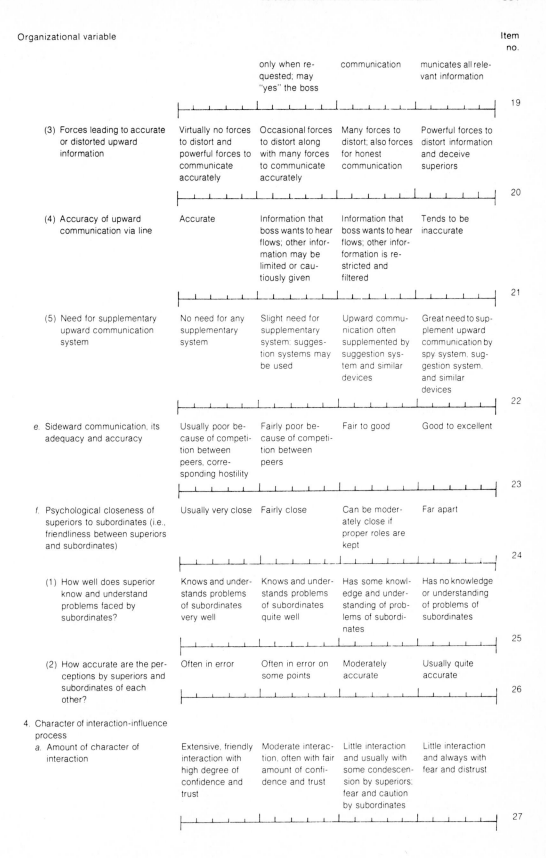

		only when requested; may "yes" the boss	communication	municates all relevant information	
					19
(3) Forces leading to accurate or distorted upward information	Virtually no forces to distort and powerful forces to communicate accurately	Occasional forces to distort along with many forces to communicate accurately	Many forces to distort; also forces for honest communication	Powerful forces to distort information and deceive superiors	
					20
(4) Accuracy of upward communication via line	Accurate	Information that boss wants to hear flows; other information may be limited or cautiously given	Information that boss wants to hear flows; other information is restricted and filtered	Tends to be inaccurate	
					21
(5) Need for supplementary upward communication system	No need for any supplementary system	Slight need for supplementary system; suggestion systems may be used	Upward communication often supplemented by suggestion system and similar devices	Great need to supplement upward communication by spy system, suggestion system, and similar devices	
					22
e. Sideward communication, its adequacy and accuracy	Usually poor because of competition between peers, corresponding hostility	Fairly poor because of competition between peers	Fair to good	Good to excellent	
					23
f. Psychological closeness of superiors to subordinates (i.e., friendliness between superiors and subordinates)	Usually very close	Fairly close	Can be moderately close if proper roles are kept	Far apart	
					24
(1) How well does superior know and understand problems faced by subordinates?	Knows and understands problems of subordinates very well	Knows and understands problems of subordinates quite well	Has some knowledge and understanding of problems of subordinates	Has no knowledge or understanding of problems of subordinates	
					25
(2) How accurate are the perceptions by superiors and subordinates of each other?	Often in error	Often in error on some points	Moderately accurate	Usually quite accurate	
					26
4. Character of interaction-influence process					
a. Amount of character of interaction	Extensive, friendly interaction with high degree of confidence and trust	Moderate interaction, often with fair amount of confidence and trust	Little interaction and usually with some condescension by superiors; fear and caution by subordinates	Little interaction and always with fear and distrust	
					27

Organizational variable

Item no.

b. Amount of cooperative team-work present

| Very substantial amount through-out the organization | A moderate amount | Relatively little | None |

28

c. Extent to which subordinates can influence the goals, meth-ods, and activity of their units and departments
  (1) As seen by superiors

| None | Virtually none | Moderate amount | A great deal |

29

  (2) As seen by subordinates

| None except through "informal organization" or via unionization | Little except through "informal organization" or via unionization | Moderate amount both directly and via unionization (where it exists) | Substantial amount both directly and via unionization (where it exists) |

30

d. Amount of actual influence which superiors can exercise over the goals, activity, and methods of their units and departments

| Believed to be substantial but actually moderate unless capacity to exercise severe punishment is present | Moderate to somewhat more than moderate, especially for higher levels in organization | Moderate to sub-tantial, especially for higher levels in organization | Substantial but often done indi-rectly, as, for ex-ample, by superior building effective interaction-influence system |

31

e. Extent to which an effective structure exists enabling one part of organization to exert influence upon other parts

| Highly effective structure exists enabling exercise of influence in all directions | Moderately effec-tive structure exists; influence exerted largely through vertical lines | Limited capacity exists; influence exerted largely via vertical lines and primarily downward | Effective structure virtually not present |

32

5. Character of decision-making process
  a. At what level in organization are decisions formally made?

| Bulk of decisions at top of organization | Policy at top, many decisions within prescribed frame-work made at lower levels but usually checked with top before action | Broad policy deci-sions at top, more specific decisions at lower levels | Decision making widely done throughout or-ganization, al-though well inte-grated through linking process provided by over-lapping groups |

33

  b. How adequate and accurate is the information available for decision making at *the place where the decisions are made?*

| Information is generally inade-quate and inaccurate | Information is often somewhat inadequate and inaccurate | Reasonably ade-quate and accu-rate information available | Relatively com-plete and accu-rate information available based both on measure-ments and effi-cient flow of infor-mation in organization |

34

  c. To what extent are decision makers aware of problems, particularly those at lower levels in the organization

| Generally quite well aware of problems | Moderately aware of problems | Aware of some, unaware of others | Often are unaware or only partially aware |

35

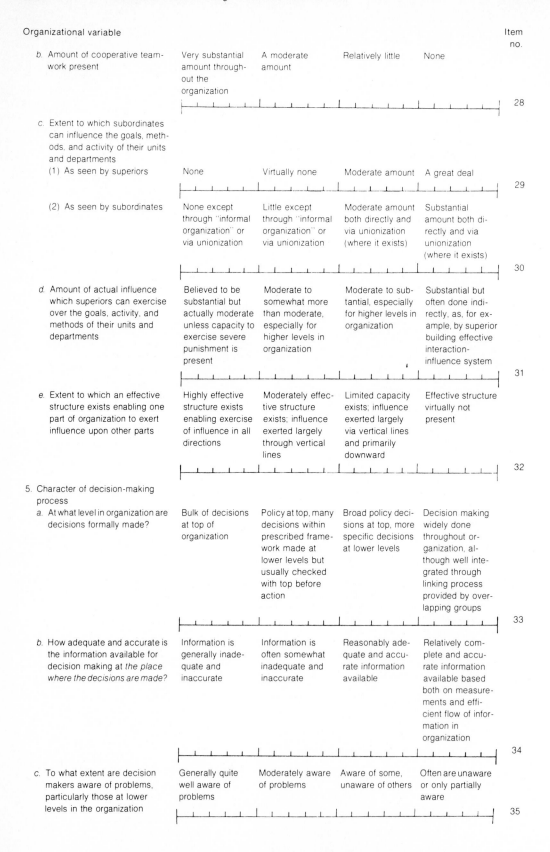

Organizational variable					Item no.
d. Extent to which technical and professional knowledge is used in decision making	Used only if possessed at higher levels	Much of what is available in higher and middle levels is used	Much of what is available in higher, middle, and lower levels is used	Most of what is available anywhere within the organization is used	36
e. Are decisions made at the best level in the organization as far as					
(1) Availability of the most adequate and accurate information bearing on the decision	Overlapping groups and group decision processes tend to push decisions to point where information is most adequate or to pass the relevant information to the decision-making point	Some tendency for decisions to be made at higher levels than where most adequate and accurate information exists	Decisions often made at levels appreciably higher than levels where most adequate and accurate information exists	Decisions usually made at levels appreciably higher than levels where most adequate and accurate information exists	37
(2) The motivational consequences (i.e., does the decision-making process help to create the necessary motivations in those persons who have to carry out the decision?)	Substantial contribution by decision-making processes to motivation to implement	Some contribution by decision making to motivation to implement	Decision making contributes relatively little motivation	Decision making contributes little or nothing to the motivation to implement the decision, usually yields adverse motivation	38
f. To what extent are subordinates involved in decisions related to their work?	Not at all	Never involved in decisions; occasionally consulted	Usually are consulted but ordinarily not involved in the decision making	Are involved fully in all decisions related to their work	39
g. Is decision making based on man-to-man or group pattern of operation? Does it encourage or discourage teamwork?	Man-to-man only, discourages teamwork	Man-to-man almost entirely, discourages teamwork	Both man-to-man and group, partially encourages teamwork	Largely based on group pattern, encourages teamwork	40
6. Character of goal setting or ordering					
a. Manner in which usually done	Except in emergencies, goals are usually established by means of group participation	Goals are set or orders issued after discussion with subordinates of problems and planned action	Orders issued, opportunity to comment may or may not exist	Orders issued	41
b. To what extent do the different hierarchial levels tend to strive for high performance goals?	High goals sought by all levels, with lower levels sometimes pressing for higher goals than top levels	High goals sought by higher levels but with occasional resistance by lower levels	High goals sought by top and often resisted moderately by subordinates	High goals pressed by top, generally resisted by subordinates	42

Organizational variable					Item no.
c. Are there forces to accept, resist, or reject goals?	Goals are overtly accepted but are covertly resisted strongly	Goals are overtly accepted but often covertly resisted to at least a moderate degree	Goals are overtly accepted but at times with some covert resistance	Goals are fully accepted both overtly and covertly	43
7. Character of control processes a. At what hierarchial levels in organization does major or primary concern exist with regard to the performance of the control function?	At the very top only	Primarily or largely at the top	Primarily at the top but some shared feeling of responsibility felt at middle and to a lesser extent at lower levels	Concern for performance of control functions likely to be felt throughout organization	44
b. How accurate are the measurements and information used to guide and perform the control function, and to what extent do forces exist in the organization to distort and falsify this information?	Strong pressures to obtain complete and accurate information to guide own behavior and behavior of own and related work groups; hence information and measurements tend to be complete and accurate	Some pressure to protect self and colleagues and hence some pressures to distort; information is only moderately complete and contains some inaccuracies	Fairly strong forces exist to distort and falsify; hence measurements and information are often incomplete and inaccurate	Very strong forces exist to distort and falsify; as a consequence, measurements and information are usually incomplete and often inaccurate	45
c. Extent to which the review and control functions are concentrated	Highly concentrated in top management	Relatively highly concentrated, with some delegated control to middle and lower levels	Moderate downward delegation of review and control processes; lower as well as higher levels perform these tasks	Review and control done at all levels with lower units at times imposing more vigorous reviews and tighter controls than top management	46
d. Extent to which there is an informal organization present and supporting or opposing goals of formal organization	Informal organization present and opposing goals of formal organization	Informal organization usually present and partially resisting goals	Informal organization may be present and may either support or partially resist goals of formal organization	Informal and formal organization are one and the same; hence all social forces support efforts to achieve organization's goals	47
e. Extent to which control data (e.g., accounting, productivity, cost, etc.) are used for self-guidance or group problem solving by managers and nonsupervisory employees, or used by superiors in a punitive, policing manner	Used for policing and in punitive manner	Used for policing coupled with reward and punishment, sometimes punitively; used somewhat for guidance but in accord with orders	Used for policing with emphasis usually on reward but with some punishment; used for guidance in accord with orders; some use also for self-guidance	Used for self-guidance and for coordinated problem solving and guidance; not used punitively	48

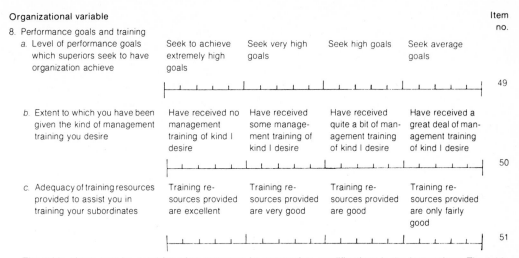

Organizational variable					Item no.
8. Performance goals and training					
a. Level of performance goals which superiors seek to have organization achieve	Seek to achieve extremely high goals	Seek very high goals	Seek high goals	Seek average goals	49
b. Extent to which you have been given the kind of management training you desire	Have received no management training of kind I desire	Have received some management training of kind I desire	Have received quite a bit of management training of kind I desire	Have received a great deal of management training of kind I desire	50
c. Adequacy of training resources provided to assist you in training your subordinates	Training resources provided are excellent	Training resources provided are very good	Training resources provided are good	Training resources provided are only fairly good	51

The table above can be used for other purposes by appropriate modifications in the instructions. The table was used to obtain from managers their descriptions of particularly high- and low-producing organizations. The directions below indicate other uses:

Form S Instructions

On the line below each organizational variable (item), please indicate the kind of organization you are trying to create by the management you are providing. Treat each item as a continuous variable from the extreme at one end to that at the other. Place a check mark on each line to show the kind of management you are using and the kind of organization you are creating.

Form D Instructions

On the line below each organizational variable (item), please indicate by a check mark where you would *like* to have your organization fall with regard to that item. Treat each item as a continuous variable from the extreme at one end to that at the other.

SELECTED REFERENCES TO ASSESSMENT OF ORGANIZATIONAL EFFECTIVENESS   *4.E.3*

THE AMERICAN INSTITUTE FOR RESEARCH. *Evaluating the Performance of Research Personnel.* University of Pittsburgh, 1951.

ANDREWS, FRED M., ed. *Scientific Productivity: The Effectiveness of Research Groups in Six Countries.* New York: Cambridge University Press and UNESCO, 1979.

ARGYRIS, CHRIS. *Organization of a Bank.* New Haven: Labor and Management Center, Yale University, 1954.

BAKKE, E. WIGHT. *Bonds of Organization.* New York: Harper & Row, 1950.

BECKER, SELWYN W., and NEUHAUSER, DUNCAN. *The Efficient Organization.* New York: Elsevier, 1975.

CORSON, JOHN T., and STEINER, GEORGE A. *Measuring Business Social Performance: The Corporate Social Audit.* New York: Committee for Economic Development, 1974.

CUMMINGS, LARRY L., and SCHWAB, DONALD P. *Performance in Organizations: Determinants and Appraisal.* Glenview, Ill.: Scott, Foresman, 1973.

GEORGOPOULOS, BASIL S., and MANN, FLOYD C. *The Community General Hospital.* New York: Macmillan, 1962.

GHORPADE, JAISINGH, ed. *Assessment of Organizational Effectiveness: Issue, Analysis, and Readings.* Pacific Palisades, Calif.: Goodyear, 1971.

Articles by A. W. Gouldner, A. Etzioni, D. Katz and R. L. Kahn, B. S. Georgopoulos, and A. S. Tannenbaum et al.

LAWLER, EDWARD E. III; NADLER, DAVID; and CAMMAN, CORTLANDT. *Organizational Assessment: Perspectives on the Measurement of Organizational Behavior* and *Quality of Working Life.* New York: Wiley-Interscience, 1980.

LIKERT, RENSIS. *The Human Organization: Its Management and Value.* New York: McGraw-Hill, 1967.

LUCK, THOMAS J. *Personnel Audit and Appraisal.* New York: McGraw-Hill, 1955.

Office of Personnel Management. *Measuring Federal Productivity.* Washington, D.C.: U.S. Government Printing Office, 1978.

MUNDAY, LEO A. *Toward a Social Audit of Colleges: An Examination of College Student Outcomes in Terms of Admission Information.* ACT Research Report No. 75. Iowa City, Iowa: Research and Development Division, American College Testing Program, 1976.

PRICE, JAMES . *Organizational Effectiveness; An Inventory of Propositions.* Homewood, Ill.: Irwin, 1968.

ROSSI, PETER H.; FREEMAN, HOWARD E.; and WRIGHT, SONIA R. *Evaluation: A Systematic Approach.* Beverly Hills: Sage, 1979.

See especially chapter 8 on measuring efficiency, an excellent summary of cost-benefit and cost-effectiveness analysis.

WICKERT, FREDERICK R., and McFARLAND, DALTON E., eds. *Measuring Executive Effectiveness.* New York: Appleton-Century-Crofts, 1967.

section **F**

Community

Measures of community variables are limited. One of the first attempts to secure measures of the "goodness" of a city was made by E. L. Thorndike. His research monograph, *Our City* (New York: Harcourt, Brace, 1939), provided the first careful attempt to evaluate the quality of American cities. Ratings of 310 American cities with over 30,000 population were made. In his *144 Smaller Cities,* Thorndike applied his "goodness" rating to cities with between 20,000 and 30,000 population. The method requires the gathering of statistics on factors not too easily obtained. Paul B. Gillen in his *The Distribution of Occupations as a City Yardstick* (New York: Columbia University Press, 1951) presents a shorter technique based on the occupational distribution of the city.

Over the past fifteen years there has been a growing interest in what is now called quality of life, or well-being. Numerous researchers and research organizations are seeking to measure quality of life in different communities. Part of this interest reflects the importance of attracting industry to a community by the local chamber of commerce, the state's Economic Development Agency, and numerous other interested parties. Local pride alone is sufficient to provide impetus to the measurement of community achievements. To observe this activity, note the selected bibliography that follows.

FLAX, MICHAEL J. "A Study in Comparative Urban Indicators: Conditions in 18 Large Metropolitan Areas." Washington, D.C.: Urban Institute, April 1972.

GODFREY, JAN, and WEAVER, JIM. *Community Indicators for Your City.* Austin, Tex.: Lyndon B. Johnson School of Public Affairs, University of Texas, 1975.

HUGHES, JAMES. *Urban Indicators, Metropolitan Evaluation and Public Policy.* New Brunswick, N.J.: Rutgers University, Center for Urban Policy Research, 1973.

JOHNSON, WILLARD. *An Index of Life Quality: How Does Your Community Stand in Relation to Other Cities of Its Size in the USA?* San Diego, Calif.: San Diego Urban Observatory, December 1973.

LIU, BEN-CHIEH. *Quality of Life Indicators in U.S. Metropolitan Areas.* New York: Praeger, 1976.

NATIONAL URBAN COALITION. *City Profiles: A Statistical Profile of Selected Cities.* 3 vols. Washington, D.C., March 1977.

ONTELL, ROBERT. *"The Quality of Life in Eight American Cities: Selected Indicators of Urban Conditions and Trends."* NTIS: PB-245 255/5ST. Washington, D.C.: National League of Cities, Urban Observatory Program, March 1975.

SMITH, DAVID M. *The Geography of Social Well-Being in the United States: An Introduction to Territorial Social Indicators.* New York: McGraw-Hill, 1973.

WHORTON, JOSEPH W., JR., and MORGAN, DAVID R. *Measuring Community Performance: A Handbook of Indicators.* Norman, Okla.: University of Oklahoma, Bureau of Government Research, 1975.

ZEHNER, ROBERT B. *Indicators of the Quality of Life in New Communities.* Cambridge, Mass.: Ballinger, 1977.

The measurement of quality of life in communities, comparative evaluations, and trend patterns represents an excellent area for applied sociology. The potential enlargement of this area is promising.

Indeed, the scales chosen for this section are chosen for more diagnostic research within a given community. Bosworth's Community Attitude Scale is designed to assess the degree of progressive attitude evidenced by members of a community. Fessler's Community Solidarity Index purports to measure community member solidarity. This scale is useful in determining relationships between community progress and solidarity. The Community Rating Schedule is a useful rating device in ascertaining the different views of such groups as businessmen, labor leaders, ministers, teachers, welfare workers, and so on. The Scorecard for Community Services Activity can be used to assess participation in the community services activity of the community. The relationship of community member progressiveness and community service activity might be fruitfully explored. Each scale opens possibilities of studying the impact of such background factors as occupation, social class, education, age, sex, and marital status on community participation and progress.

4.F.1   COMMUNITY ATTITUDE SCALE

VARIABLE MEASURED: The degree of progressive attitude evidenced on such areas of community life as (1) general community improvement, (2) living conditions, (3) business and industry, (4) health and recreation, (5) education, (6) religion, (7) youth programs, (8) utilities, and (9) communications.

DESCRIPTION: A cross section of a wide range of groups in various communities defined the meaning of progress by submitting a number of statements that they designated as progressive and unprogressive. These statements provided 364 items that were placed in a five point Likert-type format. A representative panel of leaders independently designated each item as progressive or unprogressive. Various tests showed that 60 items were most discriminating. These 60 items were compiled into three subscales with 20 items each. These scales are identified as Community Integration, Community Services, and Civic Responsibilities.

WHERE PUBLISHED: A Ph.D. dissertation by Claud A. Bosworth, submitted to the University of Michigan, 1954.

RELIABILITY: 60 items scale, $r = .56$.

VALIDITY: Total mean scores discriminated significantly between a progressive and an unprogressive group at the .025 level. It was also found that those citizens who positively endorsed the scale items designed to measure attitudes toward other phases of community progress also voted for the sewer extension plan.

UTILITY: The scale is easily administered either in an interview or by questionnaire. Approximate time required is 20 minutes.

COMMUNITY ATTITUDE SCALE

Claud A. Bosworth

(Community Services Subscale)	St. Agree	Agree	?	Dis- agree	St. Dis.
1. The school should stick to the 3 R's and forget about most of the other courses being offered today.	___	___	___	___	___
2. Most communities are good enough as they are without starting any new community improvement programs.	___	___	___	___	___
3. Every community should encourage more music and lecture programs.	___	___	___	___	___
4. This used to be a better community to live in.	___	___	___	___	___
5. Long term progress is more important than immediate benefits.	___	___	___	___	___
6. We have too many organizations for doing good in the community.	___	___	___	___	___
7. The home and the church should have all the responsibility for preparing young people for marriage and parenthood.	___	___	___	___	___
8. The responsibility for older people should be confined to themselves and their families instead of the community.	___	___	___	___	___
9. Communities have too many youth programs.	___	___	___	___	___
10. Schools are good enough as they are in most communities.	___	___	___	___	___
11. Too much times is usually spent on the planning phases of community projects.	___	___	___	___	___
12. Adult education should be an essential part of the local school program.	___	___	___	___	___
13. Only the doctors should have the responsibility for the health program in the community.	___	___	___	___	___
14. Mental illness is not a responsibility of the whole community.	___	___	___	___	___
15. A modern community should have the services of social agencies.	___	___	___	___	___

(Community Services Subscale)	St. Agree	Agree	?	Dis-agree	St. Dis.
16. The spiritual needs of the citizens are adequately met by the churches.	____	____	____	____	____
17. In order to grow, a community must provide additional recreation facilities.	____	____	____	____	____
18. In general, church members are better citizens.	____	____	____	____	____
19. The social needs of the citizens are the responsibility of themselves and their families and not of the community.	____	____	____	____	____
20. Churches should be expanded and located in accordance with population growth.	____	____	____	____	____
(Community Integration Subscale)					
21. No community improvement program should be carried on that is injurious to a business.	____	____	____	____	____
22. Industrial development should include the interest in assisting local industry.	____	____	____	____	____
23. The first and major responsibility of each citizen should be to earn dollars for his own pocket.	____	____	____	____	____
24. More industry in town lowers the living standards.	____	____	____	____	____
25. The responsibility of citizens who are not actively participating in a community improvement program is to criticize those who are active.	____	____	____	____	____
26. What is good for the community is good for me.	____	____	____	____	____
27. Each one should handle his own business as he pleases and let the other businessmen handle theirs as they please.	____	____	____	____	____
28. A strong Chamber of Commerce is beneficial to any community.	____	____	____	____	____
29. Leaders of the Chamber of Commerce are against the welfare of the majority of the citizens in the community.	____	____	____	____	____
30. A community would get along better if each one would mind his own business and others take care of theirs.	____	____	____	____	____
31. Members of any community organization should be expected to attend only those meetings that affect him personally.	____	____	____	____	____
32. Each of us can make real progress only when the group as a whole makes progress.	____	____	____	____	____
33. The person who pays no attention to the complaints of the persons working for him is a poor citizen.	____	____	____	____	____

(Community Integration Subscale)	St. Agree	Agree	?	Dis- agree	St. Dis.
34. It would be better if we would have the farmer look after his own business and we look after ours.	___	___	___	___	___
35. All unions are full of Communists.	___	___	___	___	___
36. The good citizens encourage the wide-spread circulation of all news including that which may be unfavorable to them and their organizations.	___	___	___	___	___
37. The good citizen should help minority groups with their problems.	___	___	___	___	___
38. The farmer has too prominent a place in our society.	___	___	___	___	___
39. A citizen should join only those organizations that will promote his own interests.	___	___	___	___	___
40. Everyone is out for himself at the expense of everyone else.					

(Civic Responsibilities Subscale)

	St. Agree	Agree	?	Dis- agree	St. Dis.
41. Busy people should not have the responsibility for civic programs.	___	___	___	___	___
42. The main responsibility for keeping the community clean is up to the city officials.	___	___	___	___	___
43. Community improvements are fine if they don't increase taxes.	___	___	___	___	___
44. The younger element have too much to say about our community affairs.	___	___	___	___	___
45. A progressive community must provide adequate parking facilities.	___	___	___	___	___
46. Government officials should get public sentiment before acting on major municipal projects.	___	___	___	___	___
47. A good citizen should be willing to assume leadership in a civic improvement organization.	___	___	___	___	___
48. Progress can best be accomplished by having only a few people involved.	___	___	___	___	___
49. Community improvement should be the concern of only a few leaders in the community.	___	___	___	___	___
50. A community would be better if less people would spend time on community improvement projects.	___	___	___	___	___
51. Only those who have the most time should assume the responsibility for civic programs.	___	___	___	___	___
52. Living conditions in a community should be improved.	___	___	___	___	___

(Community Integration Subscale)	St. Agree	Agree	?	Dis-agree	St. Dis.
53. A good citizen should sign petitions for community improvement.	——	——	——	——	——
54. Improving slum areas is a waste of money.	——	——	——	——	——
55. The police force should be especially strict with outsiders.	——	——	——	——	——
56. The paved streets and roads in most communities are good enough.	——	——	——	——	——
57. The sewage system of a community must be expanded as it grows even though it is necessary to increase taxes.	——	——	——	——	——
58. Some people just want to live in slum areas.	——	——	——	——	——
59. The main problem we face is high taxes.	——	——	——	——	——
60. Modern methods and equipment should be provided for all phases of city government.	——	——	——	——	——

4.F.2 COMMUNITY SOLIDARITY INDEX

VARIABLE MEASURED: Amount of consensus among members of primary rural communities (250–2000 pop.).

DESCRIPTION: Eight major areas of community behavior are examined:

1. community spirit
2. interpersonal relations
3. family responsibility toward the community
4. schools
5. churches
6. economic behavior
7. local government
8. tension areas

These eight areas are covered in a series of 40 statements that are rated by the respondent on a five-item scale according to his judgment of how the statements apply to his community. The items range from "very true" to "definitely untrue" with scores ranging from 5 for the "very true" response to 1 for the "definitely untrue" response. The standard deviation of the scores of all the schedules for the community is taken as a measure of the degree of consensus and, therefore, of solidarity in the community. The smaller the S, the greater the solidarity is assumed to be. The mean of the total score is considered to be an index of the members' opinion of the quality of the community. For comparison with other communities an octagonal profile may be used.

WHERE PUBLISHED: Donald R. Fessler, "The Development of a Scale for Measuring Community Solidarity," *Rural Sociology* 17 (1952): 144–52.

RELIABILITY: Split-half *r* was described as being high but not given.

VALIDITY: Face validity.

UTILITY: This index measures an important community variable. When relationships are examined between community action programs and community solidarity, this measure may be highly predictive of the success or failure of community efforts.

RESEARCH APPLICATIONS: Other scales and efforts to measure community attachment and identification include:

ANDERSON, C. ARNOLD. "Community Chest Campaigns as an Index of Community Integration." *Social Forces* 33 (October 1954): 76–81.

FANELLI, A. ALEXANDER. "Extensiveness of Communication Contacts and Perceptions of the Community." *American Sociological Review* 21 (August 1956): 439–45.

KASARDA, JOHN D., and JANOWITZ, M. "Community Attachment in Mass Society." *American Sociological Review* 39 (June 1974): 328–39.

WILENSKY, HAROLD L. "Mass Society and Mass Culture: Interdependence or Independence?" *American Sociological Review* 29 (April 1964): 173–97.

ANGELL, ROBERT C. "The Social Integration of Selected American Cities," *American Journal of Sociology,* 47 (January 1942), 575–92.

COMMUNITY SOLIDARITY INDEX SCHEDULE

Name _____ Community _____

Occupation _____ Married _____ Single _____

If married, number of children in school, if any _____

boys _____ girls _____, number of children out of school _____

Number of years resident in community _____. Location of residence:

in town _____ outside of town _____ how far _____ miles?

Think of each of the statements below as relating to the people of this entire community both in town and on neighboring farms. If you think the statement fits this community very well, after the statement circle *vt* (for very true); if it applies only partially, circle *t* (for true); if you cannot see how it relates one way or another to this particular community, circle *nd* (for not decided); if you think it is not true, circle *u* (for untrue); and if it definitely is not true, circle *du* (for definitely untrue). PLEASE RECORD THE IMPRESSION THAT FIRST OCCURS TO YOU. Do not go back and change your answers.

1. Real friends are hard to find in this community. *vt t nd u du* (2)*
2. Our schools do a poor job of preparing young people for life. *vt t nd u du* (4)
3. Local concerns deal fairly and squarely with everyone. *vt t nd u du* (6)
4. The community is very peaceful and orderly. *vt t nd u du* (8)
5. A lot of people here think they are too nice for you. *vt t nd u du* (1)
6. Families in this community keep their children under control. *vt t nd u du* (3)

* The number in parentheses indicates the area to which the statement belongs.

7. The different churches here cooperate well with one another. *vt t nd u du* (5)
8. Some people here "get by with murder" while others take the rap for any little misdeed. *vt t nd u du* (7)
9. Almost everyone is polite and courteous to you. *vt t nd u du* (2)
10. Our schools do a good job of preparing students for college. *vt t nd u du* (4)
11. Everyone here tries to take advantage of you. *vt t nd u du* (6)
12. People around here show good judgment. *vt t nd u du* (8)
13. People won't work together to get things done for the community. *vt t nd u du* (1)
14. Parents teach their children to respect other people's rights and property. *vt t nd u du* (3)
15. Most of our church people forget the meaning of the word brotherhood when they get out of church. *vt t nd u du* (5)
16. This community lacks real leaders. *vt t nd u du* (7)
17. People give you a bad name if you insist on being different. *vt t nd u du* (2)
18. Our high-school graduates take an active interest in making their community a better place in which to live. *vt t nd u du* (4)
19. A few people here make all the dough. *vt t nd u du* (6)
20. Too many young people get into sex difficulties. *vt t nd u du* (8)
21. The community tries hard to help its young people along. *vt t nd u du* (1)
22. Folks are unconcerned about what their kids do so long as they keep out of trouble. *vt t nd u du* (3)
23. The churches are a constructive factor for better community life. *vt t nd u du* (5)
24. The mayor and councilmen run the town to suit themselves. *vt t nd u du* (7)
25. I feel very much that I belong here. *vt t nd u du* (2)
26. Many young people in the community do not finish high school. *vt t nd u du* (4)
27. The people here are all penny pinchers. *vt t nd u du* (6)
28. You must spend lots of money to be accepted here. *vt t nd u du* (8)
29. The people as a whole mind their own business. *vt t nd u du* (1)
30. Most people get their families to Sunday School or church on Sunday. *vt t nd u du* (3)
31. Every church wants to be the biggest and the most impressive. *vt t nd u du* (5)
32. A few have the town politics well sewed up. *vt t nd u du* (7)
33. Most of the students here learn to read and write well. *vt t nd u du* (4)
34. People are generally critical of others. *vt t nd u du* (2)
35. Local concerns expect their help to live on low wages. *vt t nd u du* (6)
36. You are out of luck here if you happen to be of the wrong nationality. *vt t nd u du* (8)
37. No one seems to care much how the community looks. *vt t nd u du* (1)
38. If their children keep out of the way, parents are satisfied to let them do whatever they want to do. *vt t nd u du* (3)
39. Most of our churchgoers do not practice what they preach. *vt t nd u du* (5)
40. The town council gets very little done. *vt t nd u du* (7)

4.F.3   COMMUNITY RATING SCHEDULE

VARIABLE MEASURED: The quality of community life, of "goodness" of the community, is assessed.

DESCRIPTION: Ten institutional areas of community life are rated as good, fair, or poor. The areas selected include education, housing and planning, religion, equality of opportunity, economic development, cultural opportunities, recreation, health and welfare, government, and community organization. Scores range from 0–100.

WHERE PUBLISHED: New York State Citizen's Council, *Adult Leadership* 1, No. 5 (October 1952): 19.

RELIABILITY: Not known.

VALIDITY: Rests upon face validity.

STANDARD SCORES:

> Good communities = 90–100
> Fair communities = 70–89
> Poor communities = 0–69

UTILITY: The schedule is easy to administer; the time required is about 10 minutes. Raters often have difficulty in making a general judgment and express qualifications. These should be expected. The special advantage of this index is that it permits analysis of individual raters. Individual raters from business, labor, welfare, education, and religion often differ widely in their assessments of the same community.

RESEARCH APPLICATIONS: No reported studies. However, the index opens possibilities of examining the patterns of new industrial locations with quality of the community. The relationship of leadership to community quality is an important area that should be explored.

COMMUNITY RATING SCHEDULE*

Ask respondent to rate community as good, fair, or poor as judged by similar communities in the United States.

	Good	Fair	Poor
Standard No. 1 Education Modern education available for every child, youth and adult. Uncrowded, properly equipped schools in good physical conditions. Highly qualified, well paid teachers.			
Standard No. 2 Housing and Planning Every family decently housed. Continuous planning for improvement of residential areas, parks, highways, and other community essentials. Parking, traffic, and transportation problems under control.			

* Prepared by New York State Citizen's Council; Reprinted in *Adult Leadership* 1, no. 5 (October 1952): 19.

	Good	Fair	Poor

Standard No. 3 Religion

Full opportunity for religious expression accorded to every individual—churches strong and well supported.

Standard No. 4 Equality of Opportunity

People of different races, religions, and nationalities have full chance for employment and for taking part in community life. Dangerous tensions kept at minimum by avoidance of discrimination and injustices.

Standard No. 5 Economic Development

Good jobs available. Labor, industry, agriculture, and government work together to insure sound economic growth.

Standard No. 6 Cultural Opportunities

Citizens' lives strengthened by ample occasion to enjoy music, art, and dramatics. A professionally administered library service benefits people of all ages. Newspapers and radio carefully review community affairs.

Standard No. 7 Recreation

Enough supervised playgrounds and facilities for outdoor activities. Full opportunity to take part in arts and crafts, photography, and other hobbies.

Standard No. 8 Health and Welfare

Positive approach to improving health of entire community. Medical care and hospitalization readily available. Provision made for underprivileged children, the aged, and the handicapped. Families in trouble can secure needed assistance.

Standard No. 9 Government

Capable citizens seek public office. Officials concerned above all with community betterment. Controversy stems from honest differences of opinion, not from squabbles over privilege.

Standard No. 10 Community Organizations

An organization-community forum, citizen's council, or community federation-representative of entire town is working for advancement of the whole community. Citizens have opportunity to learn about and take part in local affairs. There is an organized, community-wide discussion program. Specialized organizations give vigorous attention to each important civic need.

Total Score for your Town   Good _____   10 points for each item _____

Fair _____   5 points for each item _____

Poor _____   no points

Total _____

VARIABLE MEASURED: Individual participation in community services.

DESCRIPTION: The scorecard is an arbitrary index to assess individual participation in community services. Fifteen possible behavioral items are presented as those that compose bulk of community service activity. Scores of 0–15 may be recorded as each item participation is given a weight of one.

WHERE PUBLISHED: Unpublished.

RELIABILITY: No tests have been made.

VALIDITY: Rests on face validity.

STANDARD SCORES:

> 10–15　outstanding community member
> 6–9　　an average member
> 0–5　　low participating member

Cutting points were based upon a random sample of 100 adults in a middle-class community.

UTILITY: Administration of the scorecard takes less than four minutes. It provides for both individual and group assessment.

RESEARCH APPLICATIONS: None reported. However, the index opens possibilities of exploring important facets of citizenship including the importance of background factors such as age, sex, education, race, and social class. The relation between community service activity, community solidarity, and community rating is a challenging research endeavor.

SCORECARD FOR COMMUNITY SERVICES ACTIVITY

Constructed by Delbert C. Miller

(*Score one point for each "yes")

FINANCIAL SUPPORT—Did you, in the past year,
_____ Contribute money to a community chest campaign?
_____ Contribute money to a church?
_____ Contribute money for other charitable purposes?

GENERAL ACTIVITY—Did you, in the past year,
_____ Serve on any board responsible for civic programs?
_____ Serve on any committee working to improve civic life?
_____ Assume leadership of any civic action program?

COMMUNITY ISSUES AND PROBLEMS—Did you, in the past year,
_____ Inform yourself about civic issues and problems?

_____ Discuss civic problems frequently with more than one person?
_____ Persuade others to take a particular position?
_____ Get advice from others?
_____ Speak to key leaders about problems?
_____ Visit community organizations or board meetings to inform yourself?
_____ Write letters, or circulate literature, or hold home meetings?

GROUP ACTION—Did you, in the past year,
_____ Belong to one or more organizations that takes stands on community issues
and problems?
_____ Make group visits or invite visits of community officials to your
organization?
_____ Total Score

   * 10–15 points—An outstanding community member
      6–9   points—An average member
      0–5   points—A low participating member

4.F.5   **HUNTER'S COMMUNITY LEADERSHIP INDEX**

VARIABLE MEASURED: The index measures with some accuracy the power position of individuals within a local community.

DESCRIPTION: Hunter has developed an index as a developmental effort. He seeks to establish a scale that should reflect the normal power position of an individual in community ratings. The information about a given leader may be drawn from anyone who knows this particular individual well, thus making it unnecessary to interview a whole panel of knowledgeables. Hunter believes that if this index seems to have value, others will develop the scale so that it is enhanced with greater rigor and validity.

In its present stage it will readily be seen that the index is more comprehensive in its coverage of factors than the usual device of judging a person to be powerful by naming one or two factors (e.g., mere fame or fortune). It allows for points in relation to business, politics, and professions singly or in combinations. It includes facets of activity and passivity, giving weight or demerit as the case might be. One may use the scale to measure his own power against that of his contemporaries in the same community.

WHERE PUBLISHED: Floyd Hunter, *Community Power Succession: Atlanta's Policy-Makers Revisited* (Chapel Hill: University of North Carolina Press, 1980).

RELIABILITY: Unknown.

VALIDITY: Validity rests in part on the completeness of the factors assembled to capture the power roles and role performances of leaders who influence community issues and projects. Scoring presents evidence of high validity. Significant scores obtained on Atlanta Leaders are as follows:

1. Average score of all Atlanta leaders nominated by others as top power leaders = 94.

2. Range of scores: 30–144.
3. Scores of leaders above 80 include a wide variety of business and political background but dominated by the banking interests.
4. White politicians' average score = 72.
5. Black politicians' average score = 56.
   Black businessmen's average score = 58.
   Black professionals' average score = 43.
6. Regional managers likely to be moved from the city by national businesses: average score = 54.
7. Civic lay leaders' average score = 45.
8. Civic professionals' average score = 39.

Other tests made include a comparison of scaled ratings of power structure members with assessments of highly knowledgeable informants; an assessment of the interrelationships between power structure nominees. These tests demonstrate a high validity of the scale scores.

UTILITY: The index promises to reduce the number of interviews needed to establish the power positions of community leaders and to improve the precision of their identity.

RESEARCH APPLICATIONS: Hunter's monograph, *Community Power Succession,* represents the first application. A careful reading will reveal application to problems of leadership continuity and succession. Applications have been made to private power; to political perspective; and to many projects, issues, and policies. An interesting description of leadership in the black community provides a comparative base of community power.

HUNTER'S COMMUNITY LEADERSHIP INDEX

Applicable items are graded +1 to +4 or −1 to −4.

---

1. Rating as a local power (weight by reputation)
2. Independent judgment as member, leading corporation
3. Independent judgment as executive, leading corporation
4. Will to exercise power (public/private)
5. Interest in general policy matters beyond own organization
6. Consulted on policy in own organization
7. Consulted on policy outside own organization
8. Leader recent project affecting body politic
9. Member other recent policy-making committees
10. Member prestige association(s)
11. Officer prestige association(s) or committee(s)
12. Member corporate board(s)
13. Officer corporate board(s)
14. Member prestige club(s)
15. Officer prestige club(s)
16. If extraordinary, institutional rating (education, church, family, welfare)
17. Bridging cultural leader
18. Policy-maker beyond local: state to national or multinational

19. Personal qualities:
    Peer acceptance
    Prime age
    Who's Who listing
    Society book listing
    Status schools
    Church prestige (local standard)
    Area residence
    Interaction with others
    2d, 3d generation
    2d, 3d generation ownership establishment
20. Media relations
21. Occupational quarters
22. Wealth:

moderate means	1
$10 million	2
$10 to $100 million	3
above $100 million	4

23. Uses wealth politically
24. Community residence:

relative newcomer	1
long residence	2
most of life	3
life	4

25. If corporate affiliate control of business

outside owned	1
local and outside	2
local owned	3
local owned and managed	4

26. If corporate affiliate, size of corporation (*Fortune 500* = very large)

small	1
medium	2
large	3
very large	4

27. Family succession in business organization or profession (if yes, +1 to +4)
28. Corporate chain "nomad" (if yes, +1 to +4)
29. Control corporation expenditures
30. Number employees under direction:

under 100	1
100 to 500	2
500 to 1,000	3
over 1,000	4

31. Professional status (besides business/industry)
32. Control finances beyond own organization
33. Run for public office

successful	+1 to +4
unsuccessful	−1 to −4

34. Recent political appointive office, by prestige
35. Political participation party politics (nonprofessional) (+1 to +4 or −1 to −4)
36. Political popularity (if professional politician in office)
37. Party affiliation by local majority or minority
38. Broker politics/business
39. Other items, by positive or negative weight points

ANGELL, ROBERT C. "Moral Integration of Cities." *American Journal of Sociology* 57, pt. 2 (July 1951).

BERRY, BRIAN, and SMITH, KATHERINE. *City Classification Handbook: Methods and Applications.* New York: Wiley-Interscience, 1972.

DOMHOFF, G. WILLIAM, ed. *Power Structure Research.* Beverly Hills, Calif.: Sage, 1980.

FORM, WILLIAM H., and MILLER, DELBERT C. *Industry, Labor, and Community.* New York: Harper & Brothers, 1960.

> Provides field study guides for assessing industry-community relations, community power structure, and community leadership. Discusses research problems of industry-community relations.

GIBBS, JACK P., ed. *Urban Research Methods.* Princeton, N.J.: Van Nostrand, 1961.

GRIMES, MICHAEL D.; BONJEAN, CHARLES M.; LYON, J. LARRY; and LINEBERRY, ROBERT L. "Community Structure and Leadership Arrangements: A Multidimensional Analysis." *American Sociological Review* 41 (August 1976) 706–25.

JONASSEN, CHRISTIAN T. *The Measurement of Community Dimensions and Elements.* Columbus: Center for Educational Administration, Ohio State University, 1959.

> Cf. his "Functional Unities in Eighty-eight Community Systems," *American Sociological Review* 26 (June 1961): 399–407.

KANTNER, ROSEBETH MOSS. *Commitment and Community.* Cambridge, Mass.: Harvard University Press, 1972.

LEVY, FRANK S.; MELTSNER, ARNOLD J.; and WILDAVSKY, AARON. *Urban Outcomes: Schools, Streets, and Libraries.* Berkeley: University of California Press, 1974.

> Provides analysis and measurement of outcomes in Oakland, California, as basis for policy analysis and new ways of understanding decisions that affect cities.

MILLER, DELBERT C. *International Community Power Structures.* Bloomington, Ind.: Indiana University Press. 1970

——. *Leadership and Power in BOS-WASH Megalopolis: Environment, Ecology, and Urban Organization.* New York: Wiley, 1975.

SHEVKY, ERSHREF, and BELL, WENDELL. *Social Area Analysis.* Stanford: Stanford University Press, 1955.

> Contains indexes of social rank, urbanization, and segregation. Cf. Robert C. Tryon, *Identification of Social Areas by Cluster Analysis* (Berkeley: University of California, 1955).

STEIN, BARRY A. *Size, Efficiency, Community Enterprise.* Cambridge, Mass.: Center for Community Economic Development, 1976.

SUTTLES, GERALD D. *The Social Construction of Communities.* Chicago: University of Chicago Press, 1972.

For measurement of occupational, ethnic, and social-class segregation, see the work of TAEUBER, KARL E., and TAEUBER, ALMA F. *Negroes in Cities.* Chicago: Aldine, 1965. Pp. 195–245.

> Cf. also Donald O. Cowgill, "Segregation Scores for Metropolitan Areas," *American Sociological Review* 27 (June 1962): 400–402; Otis D. Duncan and Beverly Duncan, "Measuring Segregation," *American Sociological Review* 28 (February 1963): 133; Julius Jahn and Calvin F. Schmid, "The Measurement of Ecological Segregation," *American Sociological Review* 12 (June 1947): 293–303; Theodore R. Anderson and Lee L. Bean, "The Shevky-Bell Social Areas: Confirmation of Results and a Rein-

terpretation," *Social Forces* 40 (December 1961): 119–24; and Gerald T. Slatin, "Ecological Analysis of Delinquency: Aggregation Effect" *American Sociological Review* 34 (December 1969): 894–907. For comprehensive research information on urban problems, see *Index to Current Urban Documents,* a quarterly index to documents from over 200 American and Canadian cities. Greenwood Press, 51 Riverside Avenue, Westport, CT 06880.

Researchers can keep in contact with many new research advances by using *Comparative Urban Research,* a journal of news and ideas devoted to rapid communication among scholars and others interested in the comparative study of urban areas throughout the world. Sponsored by the City University of New York's Comparative Urban Studies, it is the official newsletter of the Comparative Urban Studies Committee of the American Society for Public Administration's Comparative Administration Group and the Committee for Community Research of the International Sociological Association.

Social Participation

This section includes Chapin's Social Participation Scale. It is a general scale of participation in voluntary organizations of all kinds—professional, civic, and social. It is used when the total participation pattern is an important variable. The Leisure Participation and Enjoyment Scale enables the researcher to get a detailed picture of leisure patterns and also to get a score for each respondent on both participation and enjoyment.

A measure of neighborhood participation is included. Wallin's Women's Neighborliness Scale is a Guttman-type scale that has exhibited unidimensionality on the samples of respondents that have been tested. It is designed to be answered by women respondent only.

The Citizen Political Action Schedule is a scorecard for political behavior reported by a community resident. If the respondent reports accurately, the scale can reveal the behavioral acts in the political sphere.

CHAPIN'S SOCIAL PARTICIPATION SCALE, 1952 EDITION *4.G.1*

VARIABLE MEASURED: Degree of a person's or family's participation in community groups and institutions.

DESCRIPTION: This is a Guttman-type scale with reproducibility coefficients of .92 or .97 for groups of leaders. High scores of 18 and over represent titular leader achievement. The five components are (1) member, (2) attendance, (3) financial contributions, (4) member of committees, (5) offices held. These components measure different dimensions: intensity of participation by 2, 3, 4, and 5; extensity by 1. Also, rejection-acceptance in formal groups is measured by 1, 4, and 5, for which the intercorrelations are found to be of the order of $r_{14} = .53$ to $.58$; $r_{15} = .36$ to $.40$; $r_{45} = .36$ to $.40$. Social participation is measured by 2 and 3 with intercorrelations of $r_{23} = .80$ to $.89$. Other intercorrelations among the components have been found to be of the order of $r_{12} = .88$; $r_{13} = .89$; $r_{24} = .60$; $r_{34} = .40$; $r_{35} = .35$; and $r_{45} = .50$ to $.58$.

WHERE PUBLISHED: F. Stuart Chapin, *Experimental Designs in Sociological Research* (New York: Harper, 1955), Appendix B, pp. 275–78.

RELIABILITY: $r = .89$ to $.95$.

VALIDITY:

With Chapin's social status scale scores	$r = .62$ to $.66$
With income class	$r = .52$
With occupational groups	$r = .63$
With years of formal education	$r = .54$
Between husband and wife	$r = .76$

STANDARD SCORES: Mean scores for occupational groups are as follows:

I. Professional, 20.
II. Managerial and Proprietary, 20.
III. Clerical, 16.
IV. Skilled, 12.
V. Semiskilled, 8.
VI. Unskilled, 4.

UTILITY: One sheet is used for entries on each group affiliation of subject recorded in five entries under five columns by the visitor in reply to questions answered by the subject. It takes 10 to 15 minutes to fill in the subject's answers.

The scale may also be self-administered.

RESEARCH APPLICATIONS:

CHAPIN, F. S. "The Effects of Slum Clearance on Family and Community Relationships in Minneapolis in 1935–1936." *American Journal of Sociology* 43 (March 1938): 744–63.

———. "Social Participation and Social Intelligence." *American Sociological Review* 4 (April 1939): 157–66.

ERBE, WILLIAM M. "Social Involvement and Political Activity: A Replication and Elaboration." *American Sociological Review* 29 (April 1964): 198–215.

EVAN, WILLIAM M. "Dimensions of Participation on Voluntary Associations." *Social Forces* 35 (December 1957): 148–53.

LUNDBERG, G. A., and LANSING, MARGARET. "The Sociography of Some Community Relations." *American Sociological Review* 2 (June 1937): 318–28.

MARTIN, WALTER T. "A Consideration of Differences in the Extent and Location of the Formal Associational Activities of Rural-Urban Fringe Residents." *American Sociological Review* 17 (December 1952): 687–94.

NELSON, JOEL I. "Participation and Integration: The Case of the Small Businessman." *American Sociological Review* 33 (June 1968): 427–38.

SOCIAL PARTICIPATION SCALE, 1952 EDITION*

F. Stuart Chapin

Directions

1. List by name the organizations with which the husband and wife are affiliated (at the present time) as indicated by the five types of participation No. 1 to No. 5 across the top of the schedule.

* University of Minnesota Press, Minneapolis. Copyright 1938 by the University of Minnesota.

It is not necessary to enter the date at which the person became a member of the organization. It is important to enter L if the membership is in a purely local group, and to enter N if the membership is in a local unit of some state or national organization.

2. An organization means some active and organized grouping, usually but not necessarily in the community or neighborhood of residence, such as club, lodge, business or political or professional or religious organization, labor union, etc.; subgroups of a church or other institution are to be included separately *provided they are organized* as more or less independent entities.

3. Record under attendance the mere fact of attendance or nonattendance without regard to the number of meetings attended (corrections for the number attended *have not* been found to influence the final score sufficiently to justify such labor).

4. Record under contributions the mere fact of financial contributions or absence of contributions, and *not the amount* (corrections for amount of contributions *have not* been found to influence the final score sufficiently to justify such labor).

5. Previous memberships, committee work, offices held, etc., should *not be* counted or recorded or used in computing the final score.

6. Final score is computed by counting each membership as 1, each attended as 2, each contributed to as 3, each committee membership as 4, and each office held as 5. If both parents are living regularly in the home, add their total scores and divide the sum by two. The result is the mean social participation score of the family. In case only one parent lives in the home, as widow, widower, etc., the sum of that one person's participation is the score for the family (unless it is desired to obtain scores on children also).

Social Participation Scale

Address _____   Case No. _____

Husband

Age _____ Education _____ Race or Nationality _____

Occupation _____ Income _____

Name of organization	1. Member[a]	2. Attendance	3. Financial contributions	4. Member of committees (not name)	5. Offices held
1.					
2.					
3.					
4.					
5.					
6.					
7.					
8.					
9.					
10.					
Totals					

Wife

Age _____ Education _____

Occupation _____

Race or Nationality _____

Income _____

Name of organization	1. Member[a]	2. Attendance	3. Financial contributions	4. Member of committees (not name)	5. Offices held
1.					
2.					
3.					
4.					
5.					
6.					
7.					
8.					
9.					
10.					
Totals					

Date _____   Investigator _____

[a]Enter *L* if purely local group; enter *N* if a local unit of a state or national organization.
Distribution of total scores from a representative sample of an urban population, a *J*-curve; skewed to higher scores of 100 and over; mode at 0 to 11 points.

4.G.2 LEISURE PARTICIPATION AND ENJOYMENT

VARIABLE MEASURED: The customary use of and degree of enjoyment of leisure time.

DESCRIPTION: The scale includes 47 items that are activities in which one might be expected to participate. Each item is ranked on two five-point scales. Leisure participation is scaled according to frequency of participation (1. Never, 2. Rarely, 3. Occasionally, 4. Fairly Often, 5. Frequently), and leisure enjoyment is scaled according to likes (1. Dislike very much, 2. Dislike, 3. Indifferent, 4. Like, 5. Like very much). The appropriate degree on each scale is circled for each item. No ranking on the like-dislike scale is given for those items in which the individual never participates.

WHERE PUBLISHED: C. R. Pace, *They Went to College* (Minneapolis: University of Minnesota, 1941). Copyright 1941 by the University of Minnesota.

RELIABILITY: Not known.

VALIDITY: Leisure participation

With income	$r = .019$
With sociocivic activities scale	$r = .40$
With cultural status	$r = .039$

STANDARD SCORES: A summary of responses to the questionnaire on the Minnesota study is included on pages 142–45 of the Pace Book.

	1924–25		1928–29	
	Grads.	Nongrads.	Grads.	Nongrads.
Median leisure participation for men	125.00	123.24	132.29	131.72
Median leisure enjoyment for men	169.83	167.53	171.67	170.65
Median leisure participation for women	139.80	137.90	137.50	133.97
Median leisure enjoyment for women	177.73	178.75	180.38	176.87

UTILITY: This scale is easily administered and may be self-administered. It is equally easy to score. It takes little time to administer. Both leisure participation and leisure enjoyment scores are derived and can be compared.

RESEARCH APPLICATIONS: Comparative study of 951 graduates and nongraduates of the University of Minnesota (C. R. Pace, *They Went to College*).

YOUR LEISURE-TIME ACTIVITIES

The use of leisure time is supposed to be an increasingly important social problem. We want to know how people usually spend their leisure time. Here is a list of activities. On the left side of the page put a circle around the number that tells how often you do these things now, using the key at the top of the column. On the right side of the page put a circle around the number that tells how well you like these things, using the key at the top of the column. If you never do the activity mentioned, circle number one in the left column to indicate no participation, and circle no number on the right side of the page. Try not to skip any item.

How Often Do You Do These Things

1. Never
2. Rarely
3. Occasionally
4. Fairly often
5. Frequently

How Well Do You Like These Things

1. Dislike very much
2. Dislike
3. Indifferent
4. Like
5. Like very much

How Often		Activity	How Well
1 2 3 4 5	1.	Amateur dramatics	1 2 3 4 5
1 2 3 4 5	2.	Amusement parks and halls	1 2 3 4 5
1 2 3 4 5	3.	Art work (individual)	1 2 3 4 5
1 2 3 4 5	4.	Attending large social functions (balls, benefit bridge, etc.)	1 2 3 4 5
1 2 3 4 5	5.	Attending small social entertainments (dinner parties, etc.)	1 2 3 4 5
1 2 3 4 5	6.	Book reading for pleasure	1 2 3 4 5
1 2 3 4 5	7.	Conventions	1 2 3 4 5
1 2 3 4 5	8.	Conversation with family	1 2 3 4 5
1 2 3 4 5	9.	Card playing	1 2 3 4 5
1 2 3 4 5	10.	Church and related organizations	1 2 3 4 5
1 2 3 4 5	11.	Dancing	1 2 3 4 5
1 2 3 4 5	12.	Dates	1 2 3 4 5
1 2 3 4 5	13.	Entertaining at home	1 2 3 4 5
1 2 3 4 5	14.	Fairs, exhibitions, etc.	1 2 3 4 5
1 2 3 4 5	15.	Informal contacts with friends	1 2 3 4 5
1 2 3 4 5	16.	Informal discussions, e.g., "bull sessions"	1 2 3 4 5
1 2 3 4 5	17.	Indoor team recreation or sports—basketball, volleyball	1 2 3 4 5
1 2 3 4 5	18.	Indoor individual recreation or sports—bowling, gym, pool, billiards, handball	1 2 3 4 5
1 2 3 4 5	19.	Knitting, sewing, crocheting, etc.	1 2 3 4 5
1 2 3 4 5	20.	Lectures (not class)	1 2 3 4 5
1 2 3 4 5	21.	Listening to radio or TV	1 2 3 4 5
1 2 3 4 5	22.	Literary writing—poetry, essays, stories, etc.	1 2 3 4 5
1 2 3 4 5	23.	Magazine reading (for pleasure)	1 2 3 4 5
1 2 3 4 5	24.	Movies	1 2 3 4 5
1 2 3 4 5	25.	Newspaper reading	1 2 3 4 5
1 2 3 4 5	26.	Odd jobs at home	1 2 3 4 5

1 2 3 4 5	27. Organizations or club meetings as a member	1 2 3 4 5
1 2 3 4 5	28. Organizations or club meetings as a leader (as for younger groups)	1 2 3 4 5
1 2 3 4 5	29. Outdoor individual sports—golf, riding, skating, hiking, tennis	1 2 3 4 5
1 2 3 4 5	30. Outdoor team sports—hockey, baseball, etc.	1 2 3 4 5
1 2 3 4 5	31. Picnics	1 2 3 4 5
1 2 3 4 5	32. Playing musical instrument or singing	1 2 3 4 5
1 2 3 4 5	33. Shopping	1 2 3 4 5
1 2 3 4 5	34. Sitting and thinking	1 2 3 4 5
1 2 3 4 5	35. Spectator of sports	1 2 3 4 5
1 2 3 4 5	36. Symphony or concerts	1 2 3 4 5
1 2 3 4 5	37. Telephone visiting	1 2 3 4 5
1 2 3 4 5	38. Theater attendance	1 2 3 4 5
1 2 3 4 5	39. Traveling or touring	1 2 3 4 5
1 2 3 4 5	40. Using public library	1 2 3 4 5
1 2 3 4 5	41. Visiting museums, art galleries, etc.	1 2 3 4 5
1 2 3 4 5	42. Volunteer work—social service, etc.	1 2 3 4 5
1 2 3 4 5	43. Writing personal letters	1 2 3 4 5
1 2 3 4 5	44. Special hobbies—stamps, photography, shop work, gardening, and others not included above	1 2 3 4 5
1 2 3 4 5	45. Fishing or hunting	1 2 3 4 5
1 2 3 4 5	46. Camping	1 2 3 4 5
1 2 3 4 5	47. Developing and printing pictures	1 2 3 4 5

4.G.3 WALLIN'S SCALE FOR MEASURING WOMEN'S NEIGHBORLINESS

VARIABLE MEASURED: The neighborliness of women under sixty years of age.

DESCRIPTION: This instrument is a unidimensional Guttman scale consisting of twelve items. The scale items can be simply scored for any sample by counting each *GN* (greater neighborliness) answer as 1 and each *LN* (lesser neighborliness) as 0. The possible range of scores is 12 to 0.

WHERE PUBLISHED: Paul Wallin, "A Guttman Scale for Measuring Women's Neighborliness," *The American Journal of Sociology* 59 (1953): 243–46. Copyright 1953 by the University of Chicago.

RELIABILITY: The coefficient of reproducibility of the scale from two samples of women was .920 and .924.

VALIDITY: Face validity.

UTILITY: A short, easy-to-administer scale that may be used for investigating factors accounting for individual differences in neighborliness. The scale also can be used for testing hypotheses as to intracommunity and intercommunity difference in neighborliness.

RESEARCH APPLICATIONS:

EDELSTEIN, ALEX S., and LARSEN, OTTO N. "The Weekly Press's Contribution to a Sense of Urban Community." *Journalism Quarterly* (Autumn 1960): 489–98.

FAVA, SYLVA F. "Suburbanism as a Way of Life." *American Sociological Review* 21 (1956): 34–37.

GREER, SCOTT. "Urbanism Reconsidered: A Comparative Study of Local Areas in a Metropolis." *American Sociological Review* 21 (1956): 19–25.

LARSEN, OTTO N., and EDELSTEIN, ALEX S. "Communication, Consensus and the Community Involvement of Urban Husbands and Wives." *Acta Sociologia* (Copenhagen) 5 (1960): 15–30.

For some related research on neighborhood satisfaction and integration see:

FELLIN, PHILLIP, and LITWAK, EUGENE. "Neighborhood Cohesion under Conditions of Mobility." *American Sociological Review* 28 (June 1963): 364–76.

FISHMAN, JOSHUA. "A Sociolinguistic Census of a Bilingual Neighborhood." *American Journal of Sociology* 75 (November 1969): 323–39.

LITWAK, EUGENE. "Voluntary Associations and Neighborhood Cohesion." *American Sociological Review* 26 (April 1961): 258–71.

OLSEN, MARVIN E. "Social Participation and Voting Turnout." *American Sociological Review* 37 (June 1972): 317–33.

SEWELL, WILLIAM H. and ARMER, J. MICHAEL. "Neighborhood Context and College Plans." *American Sociological Review* 31 (April 1966): 159–68.

STUCKERT, ROBERT P. "Occupational Mobility and Family Relationships. *Social Forces* 41 (March 1963): 301–7.

SWINEHART, JAMES W. "Socio-Economic Level, Status Aspiration, and Maternal Role." *American Sociological Review* 28 (June 1963): 391–99.

WALLIN'S SCALE FOR MEASURING WOMEN'S NEIGHBORLINESS

1. How many of your best friends who live in your neighborhood did you get to know since you or they moved into the neighborhood? Two or more (*GN*); one or none (*LN*).

2. Do you and any of your neighbors go to movies, picnics, or other things like that together? Often or sometimes (*GN*); rarely or never (*LN*).

3. Do you and your neighbors entertain one another? Often or sometimes (*GN*); rarely or never (*LN*).

4. If you were holding a party or tea for an out-of-town visitor, how many of your neighbors would you invite? Two or more (*GN*); one or none (*LN*).

5. How many of your neighbors have ever talked to you about their problems when they were worried or asked you for advice or help? One or more (*GN*); none (*LN*).

6. How many of your neighbors' homes have you ever been in? Four or more (*GN*); three or less (*LN*).

7. Do you and your neighbors exchange or borrow things from one another such as books, magazines, dishes, tools, recipes, preserves, or garden vegetables? Often, sometimes, or rarely (*GN*); none (*LN*).

8. About how many of the people in your neighborhood would you recognize by sight if you saw them in a large crowd? About half or more (*GN*); a few or none (*LN*).
9. With how many of your neighbors do you have a friendly talk fairly frequently? Two or more (*GN*); one or none (*LN*).
10. About how many of the people in your neighborhood do you say "Hello" or "Good morning" to when you meet on the street? Six or more (*GN*); five or less (*LN*).
11. How many of the names of the families in your neighborhood do you know? Four or more (2); one to three (1); none (0).
12. How often do you have a talk with any of your neighbors? Often or sometimes (*GN*); rarely or never (*LN*).

4.G.4 CITIZEN POLITICAL ACTION SCHEDULE

VARIABLE MEASURED: Individual participation in citizen political action.

DESCRIPTION: This is an arbitrary index to assess individual participation in community services. Twelve possible behavioral items are presented as those that compose bulk of citizen political activity. Scores of 0–12 may be recorded as each item participation is given a weight of one.

WHERE PUBLISHED: League of Women Voters of Pennsylvania, Publication No. 101, Philadelphia, Pa.

RELIABILITY: No tests have been made.

VALIDITY: Face validity.

STANDARD SCORES:

> 10–12 an outstanding citizen!
> 6–9 an average citizen.
> 0–5 a citizen?

UTILITY: May be administered in less than four minutes. It provides a measure suitable for both individual and group assessment.

RESEARCH APPLICATION: None reported. However, index opens possibilities of exploring important facets of political behavior including the importance of background factors of age, sex, education, race, and social class. For selection of alternate scales and related research, see John P. Robinson et al., *Measures of Political Attitudes* (Ann Arbor, Mich.: Institute of Social Research, University of Michigan, 1968), pp. 427–35.

SCORECARD FOR CITIZEN POLITICAL ACTION

Published by the League of Women Voters of Pennsylvania, Publication No. 101

(*Score one point for each "yes")

VOTING—Did you vote

—Once in the last four years?   ＿＿＿

—Two to five time?   ＿＿＿

—Six or more times?   ＿＿＿

PUBLIC ISSUES—Do you

—Inform yourself from more than one
source on public issues?   ＿＿＿

—Discuss public issues frequently with
more than one person?   ＿＿＿

INDIVIDUAL ACTION ON PUBLIC ISSUES—
Did you

—Write or talk to your Congressman
or any other public official—local,
state or national—to express your
views once in the past year?   ＿＿＿

—Two or more times?   ＿＿＿

GROUP ACTION ON PUBLIC ISSUES—Do
you

—Belong to one or more organizations
that take stands on public issues?   ＿＿＿

PRIMARY ELECTION ACTIVITY—Did you

—Discuss the qualifications needed for
the offices on the ballot?   ＿＿＿

—Work for the nomination of a candidate before the primary election once
in the last four years?   ＿＿＿

GENERAL OR MUNICIPAL ELECTION
ACTIVITY—Did you

—Work for the election of a candidate
once in the last four years?   ＿＿＿

FINANCIAL SUPPORT—Did you

—Contribute money to a party or
candidate once in the last four years?   ＿＿＿

TOTAL SCORE   ＿＿＿＿

*10-12 points—An outstanding citizen!
  6-9   points—An average citizen.
  5-0   points—a citizen?

Leadership in the Work Organization

This section contains two leadership scales that may be widely used in work organizations. The first scale, the Leadership Opinion Questionnaire, is designed to find answers to the question, "What *should you* as a supervisor do?" The second scale, the Supervisory Behavior Description, is designed to find answers to the question, "What does *your own supervisor* actually do?" Note that these two scales make it possible to get measures of two levels of leadership in an organization. The relation of a supervisor to his immediate superior has been shown to be a very important one. The use of both questionnaires makes it possible to secure a comparison between the two levels. However, each scale may be used for the specific purpose for which it was designed. Use the Leadership Opinion Questionnaire whenever a measure of a leader's personal orientation is desired. Use the Supervisory Behavior Description when it is desirable to get the perceptions of a supervisor by those who report to him. This scale can be given to employees or any group of supervisors or managers. These two scales have been subjected to repeated refinement and may be considered highly reliable and valid in terms of present progress in scale construction.

The Work Pattern Profile is an analysis form, which permits a description of work activity patterns. This schedule has its greatest worth as a diagnostic instrument. The relation of the work pattern profile to the leadership orientation of initiation and consideration offer interesting research problems.

Many measures of organizational performance might be included. Space prevents their addition, but the following measures are annotated for the consideration of the organizational researcher:

Executive Position Description. This description contains 191 items to determine the basic characteristics of executive positions in business and industry. Part 1 covers Position Activities; part 2, Position Responsibilities; part 3, Position Demands and Restrictions; part 4, Position Characteristics. See John K. Hemphill, *Dimensions of Executive Positions* (Columbus: Ohio State University Bureau of Business Research, 1960).

Responsibility, Authority, and Delegation Scales. These scales were designed to measure different degrees of perceived responsibility, authority, and delegation as exhibited by individuals who occupy administrative or supervisory positions. See Ralph M. Stogdill and Carroll L. Shartle, *Methods in the Study of Administrative Leadership* (Columbus: Ohio State University Bureau of Business Research, 1955), pp. 33–43.

Multirelational Sociometric Survey. This survey measures interpersonal variables surrounding work activities. Five dimensions are included: the prescribed, the perceived, the actual, the desired, and the rejected. See Robert Tannenbaum, Irving W. Weschler, and Fred Massarik, *Leadership and Organization: A Behavioral Science Approach* (New York: McGraw-Hill, 1961), pp. 346–70.

A Method for the Analysis of the Structure of Complex Organizations. This is an application of sociometric analysis based on work contacts. The method enables the researcher to depict the organization coordination structure as established through the activities of liaison persons and the existence of the contacts between groups. See Robert S. Weiss and Eugene Jacobson, "A Method for the Analysis of the Structure of Complex Organizations," *American Sociological Review* 20 (December 1955): 661–68. Cf. with Ralph M. Stogdill and Carroll L. Shartle, *Methods in the Study of Administrative Leadership* (Columbus: Ohio State University Bureau of Business Research, 1955), pp. 18–32. For a review of Leadership Theory and Research see Ralph M. Stogdill, *Handbook of Leadership* (Riverside, N.J.: The Free Press, 1974).

RELIABILITY: Test-retest coefficients *for 31 foremen* after a 3-month interval show

---

LEADERSHIP OPINION QUESTIONNAIRE

4.H.1

VARIABLE MEASURED: The questionnaire measures leader's orientation around two major factors, *Structure* and *Consideration*.

Structure (S): Reflects the extent to which an individual is likely to define and structure his own role and those of his subordinates toward goal attainment. A high score on this dimension characterizes individuals who play a more active role in directing group activities through planning, communicating information, scheduling, trying out new ideas, etc.

Consideration (C): Reflects the extent to which an individual is likely to have job relationships characterized by mutual trust, respect for subordinate's ideas, and consideration of their feelings. A high score is indicative of a climate of good rapport and two-way communication. A low score indicates the superior is likely to be more impersonal in his relations with group members.

DESCRIPTION: This is a 40-item questionnaire divided into the two factors *Structure* and *Consideration.* Each factor is tested by 20 items. The items are presented with a five-point continuum with scoring weights of zero to four depending on item's orientation to total dimension.

WHERE PUBLISHED: Copyright © 1960, Science Research Associates, Inc., Chicago, Illinois. Scale is sold as Leadership Opinion Questionnaire by Edwin A. Fleishman. It was first presented to social scientists in Ralph M. Stogdill and Alvin E. Coons, eds., *Leader Behavior: Its Description and Measurement* (Columbus: Ohio State University Bureau of Business Research, 1957), pp. 120–33.

$r = .80$ on Consideration,
$r = .74$ on Initiating Structure;

for 24 Air Force NCO's

$r = .77$ on Consideration,
$r = .67$ on Initiating Structure.

Split-half reliability estimates for the Consideration and Initiating Structure were found to be .69 and .73, respectively.

VALIDITY: Validity was evaluated through correlations with independent leadership measures, such as merit rating by supervisors, peer ratings, forced choice performance reports by management, and leaderless group situation tests. Relatively low validities were found for the particular criteria employed, although a few statistically significant correlations were found. Correlations with other measures revealed that scores on the Leadership Opinion Questionnaire were independent of the "intelligence" of the supervisor, an advantage not achieved by other available leadership attitude questionnaires.

The questionnaire scores have been found to be sensitive for discriminating reliably between leadership attitudes in different situations as well as for evaluating the effects of leadership training.

Science Research Associates has compiled evidence for validity from recent studies in many different organizational settings. It has been used in a test battery to ascertain effectiveness of sales supervisors. It has been administered to foremen in a large wholesale pharmaceutical company, to first line supervisors in a large petrochemical refinery, to department managers in a large shoe manufacturing company, and to bank managers. In all instances, significant correlations between the questionnaire and proficiency have been shown. The Leadership Opinion Questionnaire has also shown that leadership patterns are directly related to organizational stress and effectiveness in three hospitals.

STANDARDIZED SCORES: Published in Edwin A. Fleishman, "The Measurement of Leadership Attitudes in Industry," *Journal of Applied Psychology* (June 1953): 156.

Dimension	Level in Organization	Mean	S.D.
Consideration	Superintendents (N = 13)	52.6	8.1
	General Foremen (N = 30)	53.2	7.1
	Foremen (N = 122)	53.9	7.2
	Workers (N = 394)		
Structure	Superintendents (N = 13)	55.5	5.7
	General Foremen (N = 30)	53.6	6.9
	Foremen (N = 122)	53.3	7.8
	Workers (N = 394)	44.2	3.9

UTILITY: Easily administered and scored. Time of administration, 10–15 minutes. See Edwin A. Fleishman, *A Manual for Administering the Leadership Opinion Questionnaire* (Chicago: Science Research Associates, 1960).

RESEARCH APPLICATIONS:

BASS, B. M. "Leadership Opinions as Forecasters of Supervisory Success," *Journal of Applied Psychology* (1956): 345–46.

FLEISHMAN, E. A. *Leadership Climate and Supervisory Behavior.* Columbus: Ohio State University Personnel Research Board, 1951.

———. "The Measurement of Leadership Attitudes in Industry." *Journal of Applied Psychology* (June 1953): 153–58.

———. "Leadership Climate, Human Relations Training, and Supervisory Behavior." *Personnel Psychology* 6 (1953): 205–22.

———, HARRIS, E. F., and BURTT, H. E. *Leadership and Supervision in Industry.* Columbus: Ohio State University, Bureau of Educational Research.

HEMPHILL, J. K. *Leader Behavior Description.* Columbus: Personnel Research Board, Ohio State University, 1950.

SEEMAN, MELVIN. "Social Mobility and Administrative Behavior." *American Sociological Review* 23 (December 1958): 633–42.

For a critique of reliability and validity and additional research references, see Dale G. Lake, Mathew B. Miles, and Ralph B. Earle, Jr., *Measuring Human Behavior* (New York: Teachers College Press, 1972).

LEADERSHIP OPINION QUESTIONNAIRE*

This questionnaire contains 40 items when presented as a complete scale. The items that follow exemplify the type found in the longer questionnaire. They are presented here so that the researcher may evaluate them for his possible use of the complete scale.

Structure

ASSIGN PEOPLE IN THE WORK GROUP TO PARTICULAR TASKS.
   1. Always   2. Often   3. Occasionally   4. Seldom   5. Never
STRESS BEING AHEAD OF COMPETING WORK GROUPS.
   1. A great deal   2. Fairly much   3. To some degree
   4. Comparatively little   5. Not at all
CRITICIZE POOR WORK.
   1. Always   2. Often   3. Occasionally   4. Seldom   5. Never
EMPHASIZE MEETING OF DEADLINES.
   1. A great deal   2. Fairly much   3. To some degree
   4. Comparatively little   5. Not at all

Consideration

PUT SUGGESTIONS MADE BY PEOPLE IN THE WORK GROUP INTO OPERATION.
   1. Always   2. Often   3. Occasionally   4. Seldom   5. Never

HELP PEOPLE IN THE WORK GROUP WITH THEIR PERSONAL PROB-
LEMS.
   1. Often   2. Fairly often   3. Occasionally   4. Once in a while
   5. Seldom
GET THE APPROVAL OF THE WORK GROUP ON IMPORTANT MATTERS
BEFORE GOING AHEAD.
   1. Always   2. Often   3. Occasionally   4. Seldom   5. Never

---

4.H.2   SUPERVISORY BEHAVIOR DESCRIPTION

VARIABLE MEASURED: Perceptions of subordinates of the leadership behavior
demonstrated by their immediate superior. Factor analysis revealed that "Initiating Structure" and "Consideration" items are the most significant factors
in distinguishing leadership performance. "Initiating Structure" reflects the
extent to which the supervisor facilitates group interaction toward goal attainment; "Consideration" reflects the extent to which the supervisor is consider-
ate of the feelings of those under him. All questions are worded in terms
of "What does your own supervisor actually do?"

DESCRIPTION: This is a 48-item questionnaire divided into two independent
areas of leadership called "Initiating Structure" and "Consideration." The
first area includes 20 items and the second is made up of 28 items. The
items were presented with a five-point continuum answer scale that has scoring
weights of zero to four depending on the item orientation to the total dimension. Highest possible score was 112 on "Consideration" and 80 for "Initiation."

WHERE PUBLISHED: Edwin A. Fleishman, "A Leader Behavior Description
for Industry," in *Leader Behavior: Its Description and Measurement,* ed. Ralph
M. Stogdill and Alvin E. Coons (Columbus: Ohio State University Bureau
of Business Research, 1957), pp. 103–19.

RELIABILITY: Test-retest reliability coefficients based on numerous samples
range from .46 to .87.
  Split-half reliabilities are reported for samples as between .68 to .98.

		Dimension	
Sample	Time Between Administration	Consideration *r*	Initiating Structure *r*
Workers describing 18 foremen	11 months	.87	.75
Workers describing 59 foremen	11 months	.58	.46
Workers describing 31 foremen	3 weeks	.56	.53

VALIDITY: The correlation between "Consideration" and "Initiating Structure" was found to be $-.02$ when based on replies of 122 foremen. The
intercorrelation was shown to be $-.33$ when administered to 394 workers

who described the 122 foremen. The correlation between the two scales was shown to be −.05 when administered to 176 Air Force and Army ROTC students who described their superior officers. The independence of the two factors appears to be confirmed.

Correlations have been obtained between descriptions of foremen behavior and independent indexes of accident rates, absenteeism, grievances, and turnover among the foreman's own work groups. In production departments, high scores on the "Consideration" scale were predictive of low ratings of proficiency by the foreman's supervisor, but low absenteeism among the workers. A high score on "Initiating Structure" was predictive of a high proficiency rating, but high absenteeism and labor grievances as well.

STANDARD SCORES:

Means and Standard Deviations of Supervisory Behavior Description Scores

	Dimension			
	Consideration		Initiating Structure	
Sample	*M*	*SD*	*M*	*SD*
Descriptions of 122 foremen	79.8	14.5	41.5	7.6
Descriptions of 31 foremen	71.5	13.2	37.5	6.3
Descriptions of 31 foremen	73.0	12.7	40.7	7.3
Descriptions of 8 civil service supervisors	75.1	17.6	37.3	9.6
Descriptions of 60 general foremen	82.3	15.5	51.5	8.8

UTILITY: The questionnaire may be administered in a 10–15 minute period. When used in group applications, it is very efficient. By using this questionnaire in conjunction with the Leader Behavior Description, it is possible to get a view of how a supervisor thinks he should lead and compare this view with an assessment by his subordinates of his actual leadership performance.

RESEARCH APPLICATIONS: The best summary of research is found in the monograph cited in the aforementioned. Other references may be found in the publications cited under the Leadership Opinion Questionnaire. Most of the research has been done by E. A. Fleishman in the plants of the International Harvester Company.

Revised Form of the Supervisory Behavior Description

Item Number	Item*

Consideration: revised key

1. He refuses to give in when people disagree with him.
2. He does personal favors for the foremen under him.
3. He expresses appreciation when one of us does a good job.
4. He is easy to understand.
5. He demands more than we can do.

*Most items were answered as: 1. always; 2. often; 3. occasionally; 4. seldom; 5. never.

Item Number	Item*

6. He helps his foremen with their personal problems.
7. He criticizes his foremen in front of others.
8. He stands up for his foremen even though it makes him unpopular.
9. He insists that everything be done his way.
10. He sees that a foreman is rewarded for a job well done.
11. He rejects suggestions for changes.
12. He changes the duties of people under him without first talking it over with them.
13. He treats people under him without considering their feelings.
14. He tries to keep the foremen under him in good standing with those in higher authority.
15. He resists changes in ways of doing things.
16. He "rides" the foreman who makes a mistake.
17. He refuses to explain his actions.
18. He acts without consulting his foreman first.
19. He stresses the importance of high morale among those under him.
20. He backs up his foremen in their actions.
21. He is slow to accept new ideas.
22. He treats all his foremen as his equal.
23. He criticizes a specific act rather than a particular individual.
24. He is willing to make changes.
25. He makes those under him feel at ease when talking with him.
26. He is friendly and can be easily approached.
27. He puts suggestions that are made by foremen under him into operation.
28. He gets the approval of his foremen on important matters before going ahead.

Initiating structure: revised key

1. He encourages overtime work.
2. He tries out his new ideas.
3. He rules with an iron hand.
4. He criticizes poor work.
5. He talks about how much should be done.
6. He encourages slow-working foremen to greater effort.
7. He waits for his foremen to push new ideas before he does.
8. He assigns people under him to particular tasks.
9. He asks for sacrifices from his foremen for the good of the entire department.
10. He insists that his foremen follow standard ways of doing things in every detail.
11. He sees to it that people under him are working up to their limits.
12. He offers new approaches to problems.
13. He insists that he be informed on decisions made by foremen under him.
14. He lets others do their work the way they think best.
15. He stresses being ahead of competing work groups.
16. He "needles" foremen under him for greater effort.
17. He decides in detail what shall be done and how it shall be done.
18. He emphasizes meeting of deadlines.
19. He asks foremen who have slow groups to get more out of their groups.
20. He emphasizes the quantity of work.

4.H.3   WORK PATTERNS PROFILE

VARIABLE MEASURED: The roles in the organization as composed of certain activities.

DESCRIPTION: The profile includes fourteen descriptions of leadership functions that have been found within leadership jobs. These include inspection of the organization; investigation and research; planning; preparation of procedures and methods; coordination; evaluation; interpretation of plans and procedures; supervision of technical operations; personnel activities; public relations; professional consultation; negotiations; scheduling, routing, and dispatching; technical and professional operations. By using questionnaire and interview methods, each person studied in the organization indicates the proportion of time spent on each activity.

WHERE PUBLISHED: Ralph M. Stogdill and Carroll L. Shartle, *Methods in the Study of Administrative Leadership* (Columbus: Ohio State University Bureau of Business Research, 1955), pp. 44–53; also Carroll L. Shartle, *Executive Performance and Leadership* (Englewood Cliffs, N.J.: Prentice-Hall, 1956), pp. 81–93.

RELIABILITY: Forms were administered to 32 officers in a Naval District Command Staff. One month later, the forms were administered again to the same officers. Test-retest coefficients are shown for the fourteen major responsibilities.

Inspection	.51
Research	.59
Planning	.49
Preparing procedures	.55
Coordination	.60
Evaluation	.58
Interpretation	.18
Supervision	.03
Personal functions	.46
Professional consultation	.61
Public relations	.83
Negotiations	.83
Scheduling	.38
Technical and professional performance	.59

VALIDITY: In a study of a Naval Air Station, 34 officers kept a log of work performance for a period of three days. Results suggest that there is a fairly high degree of correspondence between logged time and estimated time for objectively observable performances. More subjective, less observable performances, such as planning and reflection, are not estimated in terms that correspond highly with time recorded on the log. A number of officers expressed the feeling that their estimates of time spent in planning were more accurate than the log, for the reason that they were not always aware at the moment that what they were doing constituted planning.

STANDARD SCORES: The fourteen activities are plotted in percent of time spent in the activities. No standard scores have been developed since many roles must first be analyzed.

UTILITY: This instrument will make it possible to compare patterns of performance. Therefore, executive selection may be made more appropriately in relation to the role as defined in the organization.

RESEARCH APPLICATIONS:

STOGDILL, RALPH M.; SHARTLE, CARROLL L.; COONS, ALVIN E.; and JANES, WILLIAM E. *A Predictive Study of Administrative Work Patterns.* Columbus: Ohio State University Bureau of Business Research, 1956.

————, and others. *Patterns of Administrative Performance.* Columbus: Ohio State University Bureau of Business Research, 1956. Chap. 4.

WORK PATTERNS PROFILE

The Ohio State University Personnel Research Board

The purpose of this analysis is to determine the relative proportion of your time devoted to major administrative and operative responsibilities, disregarding the methods of accomplishment.

Please consider your entire range of responsibilities from day to day. Attempt to account as accurately as possible for the relative percentage of time devoted to various administrative and technical functions.

Before each item below, please write the approximate percentage of time spent in the responsibility described.

(%)   1. *Inspection of the Organization*—Direct observation and personal inspection of installations, buildings, equipment, facilities, operations, services or personnel—for the purpose of determining conditions and keeping informed.

(%)   2. *Investigation and Research*—Acts involving the accumulation and preparation of information and data. (Usually prepared and presented in the form of written reports.)

(%)   3. *Planning*—Preparing for and making decisions that will affect the aims or future activities of the organization as to volume or quality of business or service. (Including thinking, reflection, and reading, as well as consultations and conferences with persons relative to short-term and long-range plans.)

(%)   4. *Preparation of Procedures and Methods*—Acts involving the mapping of procedures and methods for putting new plans into effect, as well as devising new methods for the performance of operations under existing plans.

(%)   5. *Coordination*—Acts and decisions designed to integrate and coordinate the activities of units within the organization or of persons within units, so as to achieve the maximal overall efficiency, economy, and control of operations.

(%)   6. *Evaluation*—Acts involving the consideration and evaluation of reports, correspondence, data, plans, divisions, or performances in relation to the aims, policies, and standards of the organization.

(%)   7. *Interpretation of Plans and Procedures*—Acts involving the interpretation and clarification for assistants and other personnel of directives, regulations, practices, and procedures.

(%)   8. *Supervision of Technical Operations*—Acts involving the direct supervision of personnel in the performance of duties.

(%)   9. *Personnel Activities*—Acts involving the selection, training, evaluation, motivation or disciplining of individuals, as well as acts designed to affect the morale, motivation, loyalty, or harmonious cooperation of personnel.

(%)   10. *Public Relations*—Acts designed to inform outside persons, regarding the program and functions of the organization, to obtain information regarding public sentiment, or to create a favorable attitude toward the organization.

(%)   11. *Professional Consultation*—Giving professional advice and specialized assistance on problems of a specific or technical nature to persons within or outside the organization. (Other than technical supervision and guidance of own staff personnel.)

(%)   12. *Negotiations*—Purchasing, selling, negotiating contracts or agreements, settling claims, etc.

(%)   13. *Scheduling, Routing, and Dispatching*—Initiating action and determining the time, place, and sequence of operations.

(%)   14. *Technical and Professional Operations*—The performance of duties specific to a specialized profession (e.g., practice of medicine, conducting religious services, classroom teaching, auditing records, operating machines, or equipment).

(100%)   Total time spend in major responsibilities.

Morale and Job Satisfaction

Morale has been viewed as a global concept and also as a set of specific dimensions. The Minnesota (Rundquist-Sletto) Survey of Opinions (General Adjustment and Morale Scales) is a Likert-type scale that was carefully constructed to tap a general variable. Use the Short Form of the Minnesota Scale of General Adjustment and Morale when the problem calls for an overall assessment of morale. Use the Long Form to assess specific attitudes toward personal inferiority, family, law, conservatism, and education, in addition to morale and general adjustment.

Many social scientists believe that morale is a meaningful concept only when the separate dimensions of morale have been identified. Scale analysis has shown repeatedly that morale is composed of many dimensions. The SRA Employee Morale Inventory is a diagnostic tool that was constructed by including dimensions of job morale. This is the most widely used instrument for diagnosis of employee morale problems. Item analysis was used in its construction. Use the SRA Employee Morale Inventory if you are seeking to diagnose morale problems in work organizations. Norms are available that make possible departmental and interorganizational comparisons. This is probably the best standardized of all sociometric scales.

Nancy Morse and associates have constructed a set of subscales to measure intrinsic job satisfaction, pride in performance, company involvement, and financial and job status. Use the Morse Scales if short scales are needed to tap these dimensions. For a critical review of general job satisfaction scales, see John P. Robinson & Associates, *Measures of Occupational Attitudes and Occupational Characteristics.* Ann Arbor: Institute of Social Research 1969, pp. 99–103.

For more information on the reliability and validity of specific questionnaire items, the serious researcher will consult *Some Questionnaire Measures of Employee Motivation and Morale: A Report on their Reliability and Validity* by Martin Patchen, with Donald C. Pelz and Craig W. Allen (Ann Arbor: Institute of Social Research, University of Michigan, 1966):

> This monograph evaluates the reliability and validity of questionnaire items associated with job motivation, interest in work innovation, willingness to express disagreement with supervisors, attitude toward changes in the job situation, and identification with the work organization.

The Brayfield and Rothe Index of Job Satisfaction has been constructed by applying Thurstone's Method of Equal-Appearing Intervals and combining

Likert's scoring system that gives an intensity measure. This scale fits two important criteria: a continuum of interval measures and an intensity measure. Use the Brayfield and Rothe Index when a precise general measure of job satisfaction is desired.

SHORT FORM OF THE MINNESOTA SURVEY OF OPINIONS (GENERAL ADJUSTMENT AND MORALE SCALES)   *4.I. 1*

VARIABLE MEASURED: Individual morale and general adjustment.

DESCRIPTION: This short form is taken from the Minnesota Scale for the Survey of Opinions that consists of 132 items. The short form consists of only 31 of the most discriminating items. These items are taken from seven scales that make up the Minnesota Scale for the Survey of Opinions. These scales are the morale scale, the general adjustment scale, inferiority scale, family scale, law scale, conservatism, and education scale.

WHERE PUBLISHED: Edward A. Rundquist and Raymond F. Sletto, *Personality in the Depression,* Child Welfare Monograph Series No. 12 (Minneapolis: University of Minnesota). Copyright 1936 by the University of Minnesota.

RELIABILITY: Split-half reliability in the .80s may be expected for the adjustment *score* and the total morale *score.* Split-half reliability coefficients for the general adjustment *scale* range from .686 to .821 with high school seniors as the lowest correlation and an all male group as the highest correlation. The females on the same basis range from .686 to .836. Reliability of actual scores from test to retest was measured over a sixty-day period. The average changes were 4.03 for 68 General College men and 5.03 for 68 General College women. Test-retest r's are .793 for men and .668 for women.

VALIDITY: Validity for the general adjustment scale was determined by two general methods: (1) relating it to those outside variables that imply maladjustment and (2) relating it to scores on the other six scales. An extensive report of validity is included in Rundquist and Sletto, *Personality in the Depression,* pp. 226–41.

Karl Schuessler and Larry Freshnock have analyzed 31 separate tests of morale and similar concepts (e.g., anomie, alienation, life satisfaction, social isolation, etc.). Their factor analysis reveals seven different factors operating within their universe of selected items. They call these factors pessimism, depression, cynicism, anxiety, fatalism, job morale, life satisfaction, and personal morale. A relatively high correlation ($r = .682$) was found between the factor score on "pessimism" or "anomie" and the test scores shown for selected items of the Rundquist-Sletto morale scale. It can be said that the Rundquist-Sletto morale scale compares favorably with such scales as Srole's Anomia and the Struening-Richardson measure of Alienation via Rejection. Karl Schuessler and Larry Freshnock, "Measuring Attitudes Toward Self and Others in Society: State of the Art," *Social Forces* 56 (June 1978): 1228–1234. Researchers should compare the 12 new scales to measure social life feelings presented by Karl Schuessler in *Measuring Social Life Feelings* (San Francisco: Jossey-Bass, 1982).

UTILITY: This short form is presented to assist those who may wish to obtain a measure of general adjustment and morale without administering the entire survey. It consists of only 31 items in the questionnaire and can be administered in 15 to 20 minutes. There are 16 items in the general adjustment scale and 22 items in the morale scale, both scales included in the 31 item survey. The Long Form of the Survey takes 30 to 40 minutes.

RESEARCH APPLICATIONS:

CHAPIN, F. STUART. "The Effects of Slum Clearance and Rehousing on Family and Community Relationships in Minneapolis." *American Journal of Sociology* 43 (March 1938): 744–63.

———, and JAHN, JULIUS. "The Advantages of Work Relief over Direct Relief in Maintaining Morale in St. Paul in 1939." *American Journal of Sociology* 46 (July 1940): 13–22.

MILLER, D. C. "Morale of College Trained Adults." *American Sociological Review* 5 (December 1940): 880–89.

———. "Economic Factors in the Morale of College Trained Adults." *American Journal of Sociology* 47 (September 1941): 139–57.

SCORING INSTRUCTIONS FOR THE SHORT FORM MINNESOTA SCALE FOR THE SURVEY OF OPINIONS

Administration

The survey requires between 15 and 20 minutes for all to complete it. Although the printed directions on the survey are self-explanatory, it is advisable to read the directions aloud while the subjects are reading them silently. To secure frankness and cooperation, it is well to assure the group that their opinions are valued, will be held in complete confidence, and will not affect their grades in any course or their standing with their employers or other persons of responsibility. They may be directed to fill in all the information items (name, age, sex, etc.) or to omit those that the examiner does not require for research or counseling purposes.

Scoring

The five alternative responses to each item are weighted from 1 to 5 in scoring. The sum of the scores in the extreme lefthand column is the adjustment score; the sum of the next column is the score on the acceptable morale items; the sum of the next is the score on the unacceptable morale items. To obtain the total morale score, add the total scores on acceptable and unacceptable items.

Norms

The scoring norms in the table permit conversion of raw scores into standard scores. These norms are based on the scores of 1000 young people, 500 of each sex. The standardization group included 400 college students, 200 high school seniors, and 400 youth employed and unemployed persons in continuation classes at high school level. The distribution of paternal occupation for the standardization group approximates the census distribution of occupations and indicates that it is composed of a fairly representative sample of young persons between the ages of sixteen and twenty-five years. No significant differences between the scores of high school and college students were found, and the norms are adequate for both groups.

The standard scores given in the table were obtained by the McCall T-Score technique, which expresses scores in tenths of standard deviation units from the mean score for the standardization group. *The mean raw score of the standardization group becomes the standard score of 50.* A standard score of 60 is one standard deviation higher than the mean; a standard score of 40 is one standard deviation below the mean. Response weights to items have been so assigned that a high standard score is unfavorable.

To illustrate the use of the table, suppose an individual makes the same raw scores—say 57—on the morale, economic conservatism, and education scales. We find 57 in the raw score column. Reading to the right, we observe that the individual's standard scores are 50 on the morale scale, 40 on the economic conservatism scale, and 60 on the education scale. These scores indicate that the individual is average, that he is conservative in his economic views (one standard deviation below the mean), and that his estimate of the value of education is relatively unfavorable (one standard deviation above the mean).

Standard Score Equivalents for Raw Scores
(Based on Standardization Group of 1000)

Raw Score	Standard Score Equivalents*							Raw Score	Standard Score Equivalents						
	M	I	F	L	EC	E	GA		M	I	F	L	EC	E	GA
110								62	55	46	55	53	45	65	78
109				91				61	54	45	54	52	44	64	77
108				90				60	53	44	53	51	43	63	76
107				89											
106				88				59	52	43	52	50	42	62	74
105				87				58	51	42	51	49	41	61	73
104				86				57	50	41	51	48	40	60	72
103				85				56	49	40	50	47	39	59	70
102			92	84				55	48	39	49	46	38	58	69
101		86	91	83				54	47	37	48	45	37	57	68
100		85	90	82				53	46	36	47	44	36	56	66
								52	45	35	46	43	35	55	65
99		84	89	81				51	43	34	45	42	34	54	64
98		83	88	80				50	42	33	44	41	33	53	62
97		82	87	79											
96		81	86	78				49	41	32	43	39	32	52	61
95	90	80	85	77				48	40	31	42	38	31	51	60
94	89	79	84	76				47	39	30	41	37	30	49	58
93	88	78	84	75				46	38	29	40	36	29	48	57
92	87	77	83	74				45	37	28	40	35	28	47	56
91	86	76	82	73	96			44	36	27	39	34	27	46	54
90	85	75	81	84	72	95		43	35	26	38	33	26	45	53
								42	34	25	37	32	25	44	52

Standard Score Equivalents for Raw Scores (Continued)
(Based on Standardization Group of 1000)

Raw Score	Standard Score Equivalents*							Raw Score	Standard Score Equivalents						
	M	I	F	L	EC	E	GA		M	I	F	L	EC	E	GA
89	83	74	80	82	71	94		41	33	24	36	31	24	43	50
88	82	73	79	81	70	93		40	32	23	35	30	23	42	49
87	81	72	78	80	69	92									
86	80	71	77	79	68	90		39	31	22	34	29	22	41	48
85	79	70	76	78	67	89		38	30	21	33	28	21	40	47
84	78	68	75	77	66	88		37	29	20	32	27	20	39	45
83	77	67	74	76	65	87		36	28	19	31	26	19	38	44
82	76	66	73	75	64	86		35	27	18	30	24	18	37	43
81	75	65	73	74	63	85		34	26	17	29	23	17	36	41
80	74	64	72	73	62	84		33	25	16	29	22	16	35	40
								32	23	15	28	21	15	34	39
79	73	63	71	72	61	83		31	22	14	27	20	14	33	37
78	72	62	70	71	60	82		30	21	13	26	19	13	32	36
77	71	61	69	70	59	81									
76	70	60	68	69	58	80		29	20	12	25	18	12	31	35
75	69	59	67	67	57	79		28	19	11	24	17	11	30	33
74	68	58	66	66	56	78		27	18	10	23	16	10	28	32
73	67	57	65	65	56	77		26	17	9	22	15	9	27	31
72	66	56	64	64	55	76		25						26	29
71	65	55	63	63	54	75		24						25	28
70	63	54	62	62	53	74	89	23						24	27
								22						23	25
69	62	53	62	61	52	73	87	21							24
68	61	52	61	60	51	72	86	20							23
67	60	51	60	59	50	71	85								
66	59	50	59	58	49	69	83	19							21
65	58	49	58	57	48	68	82	18							20
64	57	48	57	56	47	67	81	17							19
63	56	47	56	55	46	66	79	16							17

*M—Morale; I—Inferiority; F—Family; L—Law; EC—Economic Conservatism; E—; GA—General Adjustment.

4.I.1.a. MINNESOTA SURVEY OF OPINION (SHORT FORM)

E. A. Rundquist and R. F. Sletto

Name _____ Age _____ Sex _____ Date _____
        (Last)   (First)

The following pages contain a number of statements about which there is no general agreement. People differ widely in the way they feel about each item. There are no right answers. The purpose of the survey is to see how different groups feel about each item. We should like your honest opinion on each of these statements.

READ EACH ITEM CAREFULLY AND UNDERLINE QUICKLY THE PHRASE THAT BEST EXPRESSES YOUR FEELING ABOUT THE STATEMENT. Wherever possible, let your own personal experience determine your answer.

Do not spend much time on any item. If in doubt, underline the phrase that seems most nearly to express your present feeling about the statement. WORK RAPIDLY. Be sure to answer every item.

1. TIMES ARE GETTING BETTER.
Strongly agree[1]   Agree[2]   Undecided[3]
Disagree[4]   Strongly disagree[5]

_____   _____

2. ANY MAN WITH ABILITY AND WILLING-NESS TO WORK HARD HAS A GOOD CHANCE OF BEING SUCCESSFUL.
Strongly agree[1]   Agree[2]   Undecided[3]
Disagree[4]   Strongly disagree[5]

_____

3. IT IS DIFFICULT TO SAY THE RIGHT THING AT THE RIGHT TIME.
Strongly agree[5]   Agree[4]   Undecided[3]
Disagree[2]   Strongly disagree[1]

_____

4. MOST PEOPLE CAN BE TRUSTED.
Strongly agree[1]   Agree[2]   Undecided[3]
Disagree[4]   Strongly disagree[5]

_____

5. HIGH SCHOOLS ARE TOO IMPRACTICAL.
Strongly agree[5]   Agree[4]   Undecided[3]
Disagree[2]   Strongly disagree[1]

_____

6. A PERSON CAN PLAN HIS FUTURE SO THAT EVERYTHING WILL COME OUT ALL RIGHT IN THE LONG RUN.
Strongly agree[1]   Agree[2]   Undecided[3]
Disagree[4]   Strongly disagree[1]

_____

7. NO ONE CARES MUCH WHAT HAPPENS TO YOU.
Strongly agree[5]   Agree[4]   Undecided[3]
Disagree[2]   Strongly disagree[1]

_____   _____

8. SUCCESS IS MORE DEPENDENT ON LUCK THAN ON REAL ABILITY.
Strongly agree[5]   Agree[4]   Undecided[3]
Disagree[2]   Strongly disagree[1]

_____

9. IF OUR ECONOMIC SYSTEM WERE JUST, THERE WOULD BE MUCH LESS CRIME.
Strongly agree[5]   Agree[4]   Undecided[3]
Disagree[2]   Strongly disagree[1]

_____

10. A MAN DOES NOT HAVE TO PRETEND HE IS SMARTER THAN HE REALLY IS TO "GET BY."
Strongly agree[1]   Agree[2]   Undecided[3]
Disagree[4]   Strongly disagree[5]

_____

11. LAWS ARE SO OFTEN MADE FOR THE BENE-FIT OF SMALL SELFISH GROUPS THAT A MAN CANNOT RESPECT THE LAW.
Strongly agree[5]   Agree[4]   Undecided[3]
Disagree[2]   Strongly disagree[1]

_____

12. ONE SELDOM WORRIES SO MUCH AS
    TO BECOME VERY MISERABLE.
    Strongly agree[1] Agree[2] Undecided[3]
    Disagree[4] Strongly disagree[5]
    _____

13. THE FUTURE LOOKS VERY BLACK.
    Strongly agree[5] Agree[4] Undecided[3]
    Disagree[2] Strongly disagree[1]
    _____   _____

14. REAL FRIENDS ARE AS EASY TO FIND AS
    EVER.
    Strongly agree[1] Agree[2] Undecided[3]
    Disagree[4] Strongly disagree[5]
    _____

15. POVERTY IS CHIEFLY A RESULT OF INJUS-
    TICE IN THE DISTRIBUTION OF WEALTH.
    Strongly agree[5] Agree[4] Undecided[3]
    Disagree[2] Strongly disagree[1]
    _____

16. IS IT DIFFICULT TO THINK CLEARLY THESE
    DAYS.
    Strongly agree[5] Agree[4] Undecided[3]
    Disagree[2] Strongly disagree[1]
    _____

17. THERE IS LITTLE CHANCE FOR ADVANCE-
    MENT IN INDUSTRY AND BUSINESS UNLESS
    A MAN HAS UNFAIR PULL.
    Strongly agree[5] Agree[4] Undecided[3]
    Disagree[2] Strongly disagree[1]
    _____   _____

18. IT DOES NOT TAKE LONG TO GET OVER
    FEELING GLOOMY.
    Strongly agree[1] Agree[2] Undecided[3]
    Disagree[4] Strongly disagree[5]
    _____

19. THE YOUNG MAN OF TODAY CAN EXPECT
    MUCH OF THE FUTURE.
    Strongly agree[1] Agree[2] Undecided[3]
    Disagree[4] Strongly disagree[5]
    _____   _____

20. IT IS GREAT TO BE LIVING IN THESE EXCIT-
    ING TIMES.
    Strongly agree[1] Agree[2] Undecided[3]
    Disagree[4] Strongly disagree[5]
    _____

21. LIFE IS JUST ONE WORRY AFTER ANOTHER.
    Strongly agree[5] Agree[4] Undecided[3]
    Disagree[2] Strongly disagree[1]
    _____   _____

22. THE DAY IS NOT LONG ENOUGH TO DO
    ONE'S WORK WELL AND HAVE ANY TIME
    FOR FUN.
    Strongly agree[5] Agree[4] Undecided[3]
    Disagree[2] Strongly disagree[1]
    _____

23. A MAN CAN LEARN MORE BY WORKING
    FOUR YEARS THAN BY GOING TO HIGH
    SCHOOL.

Strongly agree[5] Agree[4] Undecided[3]
Disagree[2] Strongly disagree[1]

_____

24. THIS GENERATION WILL PROBABLY NEVER SEE SUCH HARD TIMES AGAIN.
Strongly agree[1] Agree[2] Undecided[3]
Disagree[4] Strongly disagree[5]

_____

25. ONE CANNOT FIND AS MUCH UNDER-STANDING AT HOME AS ELSEWHERE.
Strongly agree[5] Agree[4] Undecided[3]
Disagree[2] Strongly disagree[1]

_____

26. THESE DAYS ONE IS INCLINED TO GIVE UP HOPE OF AMOUNTING TO SOMETHING.
Strongly agree[5] Agree[4] Undecided[3]
Disagree[2] Strongly disagree[1]

_____

27. EDUCATION IS OF NO HELP IN GETTING A JOB TODAY.
Strongly agree[5] Agree[4] Undecided[3]
Disagree[2] Strongly disagree[1]

_____

28. THERE IS REALLY NO POINT IN LIVING.
Strongly agree[5] Agree[4] Undecided[3]
Disagree[2] Strongly disagree[1]

_____

29. MOST PEOPLE JUST PRETEND THAT THEY LIKE YOU.
Strongly agree[5] Agree[4] Undecided[3]
Disagree[2] Strongly disagree[1]

_____

30. THE FUTURE IS TOO UNCERTAIN FOR A PERSON TO PLAN ON MARRYING.
Strongly agree[5] Agree[4] Undecided[3]
Disagree[2] Strongly disagree[1]

_____

31. LIFE IS JUST A SERIES OF DISAPPOINT-MENTS.
Strongly agree[5] Agree[4] Undecided[3]
Disagree[2] Strongly disagree[1]

_____   _____

GA	Ma	Mu	Ma + Mu = Total Morale Score

4.I.1.b. LONG FORM OF THE MINNESOTA SURVEY OF OPINIONS*

Directions

READ EACH ITEM CAREFULLY AND UNDERLINE QUICKLY THE PHRASE THAT BEST EXPRESSES YOUR FEELING ABOUT THE STATE-MENT. WORK RAPIDLY. BE SURE TO ANSWER EVERY ITEM.

* Containing the Scales of General Adjustment, Morale, Inferiority, Family, Law, Conservatism, and Education. For scoring, see Rundquist and Sletto, *Personality in the Depression,* p. 385. Add numbers given by response. Norms are shown above. Items marked *M* are in Morale Scale; *I* items are in Inferiority Scale; *F* items, Family Scale; *L* items, Law Scale; *EC,* Economic Conservatism Scale; *E,* Education Scale.

1. THE FUTURE IS TOO UNCERTAIN FOR A PERSON TO PLAN ON MARRYING.
Strongly agree[5] Agree[4] Undecided[3] Disagree[2]
Strongly disagree[1] (M)

2. AFTER BEING CAUGHT IN A MISTAKE, IT IS HARD TO DO GOOD WORK FOR A WHILE.
Strongly agree[5] Agree[4] Undecided[3] Disagree[2]
Strongly disagree[1] (I)

3. HOME IS THE MOST PLEASANT PLACE IN THE WORLD.
Strongly agree[1] Agree[2] Undecided[3] Disagree[4]
Strongly disagree[5] (F)

4. THE LAW PROTECTS PROPERTY RIGHTS AT THE EXPENSE OF HUMAN RIGHTS.
Strongly agree[5] Agree[4] Undecided[3] Disagree[2]
Strongly disagree[1] (L)

5. THE GOVERNMENT SHOULD TAKE OVER ALL LARGE INDUSTRIES.
Strongly agree[5] Agree[4] Undecided[3] Disagree[2]
Strongly disagree[1] (EC)

6. A MAN CAN LEARN MORE BY WORKING FOUR YEARS THAN BY GOING TO HIGH SCHOOL.
Strongly agree[5] Agree[4] Undecided[3] Disagree[2]
Strongly disagree[1] (E)

7. IT IS DIFFICULT TO THINK CLEARLY THESE DAYS.
Strongly agree[5] Agree[4] Undecided[3] Disagree[2]
Strongly disagree[1] (M)

8. IT IS EASY TO EXPRESS ONE'S IDEAS.
Strongly agree[1] Agree[2] Undecided[3] Disagree[4]
Strongly disagree[5] (I)

9. PARENTS EXPECT TOO MUCH FROM THEIR CHILDREN.
Strongly agree[5] Agree[4] Undecided[3] Disagree[2]
Strongly disagree[1] (F)

10. A PERSON SHOULD OBEY ONLY THOSE LAWS THAT SEEM REASONABLE.
Strongly agree[5] Agree[4] Undecided[3] Disagree[2]
Strongly disagree[1] (L)

11. LABOR SHOULD OBEY ONLY THOSE LAWS THAT SEEM REASONABLE.
Strongly agree[5] Agree[4] Undecided[3] Disagree[2] Strongly disagree[1] (EC)

12. THE MORE EDUCATION A MAN HAS THE BETTER HE IS ABLE TO ENJOY LIFE.
Strongly agree[1] Agree[2] Undecided[3] Disagree[4]
Strongly disagree[5] (E)

13. THE FUTURE LOOKS VERY BLACK.
Strongly agree[5] Agree[4] Undecided[3] Disagree[2]
Strongly disagree[1] (M)

14. IT IS DIFFICULT TO SAY THE RIGHT THING AT THE RIGHT TIME.
Strongly agree[5] Agree[4] Undecided[3] Disagree[2]
Strongly disagree[1]   (I)

15. ONE OUGHT TO DISCUSS IMPORTANT PLANS WITH MEMBERS OF HIS FAMILY.
Strongly agree[1] Agree[2] Undecided[3] Disagree[4]
Strongly disagree[5]   (F)

16. IT IS ALL RIGHT TO EVADE THE LAW IF YOU DO NOT ACTUALLY VIOLATE IT.
Strongly agree[5] Agree[4] Undecided[3] Disagree[2]
Strongly disagree[1]   (L)

17. LEGISLATURES ARE TOO READY TO PASS LAWS TO CURB BUSINESS FREEDOM.
Strongly agree[1] Agree[2] Undecided[3] Disagree[4]
Strongly disagree[5]   (EC)

18. EDUCATION HELPS A PERSON TO USE HIS LEISURE TIME TO BETTER ADVANTAGE.
Strongly agree[1] Agree[2] Undecided[3] Disagree[4]
Strongly disagree[5]   (E)

19. LIFE IS JUST ONE WORRY AFTER ANOTHER.
Strongly agree[5] Agree[4] Undecided[3] Disagree[2]
Strongly disagree[1]   (M)

20. ONE CAN USUALLY KEEP COOL IN IMPORTANT SITUATIONS.
Strongly agree[1] Agree[2] Undecided[3] Disagree[4]
Strongly disagree[5]   (I)

21. IN PLANS FOR THE FUTURE, PARENTS SHOULD BE GIVEN FIRST CONSIDERATION.
Strongly agree[1] Agree[2] Undecided[3] Disagree[4]
Strongly disagree[5]   (F)

22. THE SENTENCES OF JUDGES IN COURTS ARE DETERMINED BY THEIR PREJUDICES.
Strongly agree[5] Agree[4] Undecided[3] Disagree[2]
Strongly disagree[1]   (L)

23. FOR MEN TO DO THEIR BEST, THERE MUST BE THE POSSIBILITY OF UNLIMITED PROFIT.
Strongly agree[1] Agree[2] Undecided[3] Disagree[4]
Strongly disagree[5]   (EC)

24. A GOOD EDUCATION IS A GREAT COMFORT TO A MAN OUT OF WORK.
Strongly agree[1] Agree[2] Undecided[3] Disagree[4]
Strongly disagree[5]   (E)

25. MOST PEOPLE CAN BE TRUSTED.
Strongly agree[1] Agree[2] Undecided[3] Disagree[4]
Strongly disagree[5]   (M)

26. IT IS EASY TO GET ONE'S OWN WAY IN MOST SITUATIONS.
Strongly agree[1] Agree[2] Undecided[3] Disagree[4]
Strongly disagree[5]   (I)

27. A MAN SHOULD BE WILLING TO SACRIFICE EVERYTHING FOR HIS FAMILY.
    Strongly agree[1]   Agree[2]   Undecided[3]   Disagree[4]
    Strongly disagree[5]   (F)

28. ON THE WHOLE, JUDGES ARE HONEST.
    Strongly agree[1]   Agree[2]   Undecided[3]   Disagree[4]
    Strongly disagree[5]   (L)

29. POVERTY IS CHIEFLY A RESULT OF INJUSTICE IN THE DISTRIBU-TION OF WEALTH.
    Strongly agree[5]   Agree[4]   Undecided[3]   Disagree[2]
    Strongly disagree[1]   (EC)

30. ONLY SUBJECTS LIKE READING, WRITING, AND ARITHMETIC SHOULD BE TAUGHT AT PUBLIC EXPENSE.
    Strongly agree[5]   Agree[4]   Undecided[3]   Disagree[2]
    Strongly disagree[1]   (E)

31. TIMES ARE GETTING BETTER.
    Strongly agree[1]   Agree[2]   Undecided[3]   Disagree[4]
    Strongly disagree[5]   (M)

32. IT IS EASY TO HAVE A GOOD TIME AT A PARTY.
    Strongly agree[1]   Agree[2]   Undecided[3]   Disagree[4]
    Strongly disagree[5]   (I)

33. PARENTS TOO OFTEN EXPECT THEIR GROWN-UP CHILDREN TO OBEY THEM.
    Strongly agree[5]   Agree[4]   Undecided[3]   Disagree[2]
    Strongly disagree[1]   (F)

34. JURIES SELDOM UNDERSTAND A CASE WELL ENOUGH TO MAKE A REALLY JUST DECISION.
    Strongly agree[5]   Agree[4]   Undecided[3]   Disagree[2]
    Strongly disagree[1]   (L)

35. THE GOVERNMENT SHOULD NOT ATTEMPT TO LIMIT PROFITS.
    Strongly agree[1]   Agree[2]   Undecided[3]   Disagree[4]
    Strongly disagree[5]   (EC)

36. EDUCATION IS OF NO HELP IN GETTING A JOB TODAY.
    Strongly agree[5]   Agree[4]   Undecided[3]   Disagree[2]
    Strongly disagree[1]   (E)

37. IT DOES NOT TAKE LONG TO GET OVER FEELING GLOOMY.
    Strongly agree[1]   Agree[2]   Undecided[3]   Disagree[4]
    Strongly disagree[5]   (M)

38. MEETING NEW PEOPLE IS USUALLY EMBARRASSING.
    Strongly agree[5]   Agree[4]   Undecided[3]   Disagree[2]
    Strongly disagree[1]   (I)

39. ONE CANNOT FIND AS MUCH UNDERSTANDING AT HOME AS ELSEWHERE.
    Strongly agree[5]   Agree[4]   Undecided[3]   Disagree[2]
    Strongly disagree[1]   (F)

40. ON THE WHOLE, POLICEMEN ARE HONEST.
Strongly agree[1] Agree[2] Undecided[3] Disagree[4]
Strongly disagree[5]   (L)

41. THE MORE A MAN LEARNS ABOUT OUR ECONOMIC SYSTEM, THE LESS WILLING HE IS TO SEE CHANGES MADE.
Strongly agree[1] Agree[2] Undecided[3] Disagree[4]
Strongly disagree[5]

42. MOST YOUNG PEOPLE ARE GETTING TOO MUCH EDUCATION.
Strongly agree[5] Agree[4] Undecided[3] Disagree[2]
Strongly disagree[1]   (E)

43. THE DAY IS NOT LONG ENOUGH TO DO ONE'S WORK WELL AND HAVE ANY TIME FOR FUN.
Strongly agree[5] Agree[4] Undecided[3] Disagree[2]
Strongly disagree[1]   (M)

44. IT IS EASY TO KEEP UP ONE'S COURAGE.
Strongly agree[1] Agree[2] Undecided[3] Disagree[4]
Strongly disagree[5]   (I)

45. ONE OWES HIS GREATEST OBLIGATION TO HIS FAMILY.
Strongly agree[1] Agree[2] Undecided[3] Disagree[4]
Strongly disagree[5]   (F)

46. A MAN SHOULD OBEY THE LAWS NO MATTER HOW MUCH THEY INTERFERE WITH HIS PERSONAL AMBITIONS.
Strongly agree[1] Agree[2] Undecided[3] Disagree[4]
Strongly disagree[5]   (L)

47. THE GOVERNMENT OUGHT TO GUARANTEE A LIVING TO THOSE WHO CANNOT FIND WORK.
Strongly agree[5] Agree[4] Undecided[3] Disagree[2]
Strongly disagree[1]   (EC)

48. A HIGH SCHOOL EDUCATION IS WORTH ALL THE TIME AND EFFORT IT REQUIRES.
Strongly agree[1] Agree[2] Undecided[3] Disagree[4]
Strongly disagree[5]   (E)

49. NO ONE CARES MUCH WHAT HAPPENS TO YOU.
Strongly agree[5] Agree[4] Undecided[3] Disagree[2]
Strongly disagree[1]   (M)

50. IT IS EASY TO IGNORE CRITICISM.
Strongly agree[1] Agree[2] Undecided[3] Disagree[4]
Strongly disagree[5]   (I)

51. IT IS HARD TO KEEP A PLEASANT DISPOSITION AT HOME.
Strongly agree[5] Agree[4] Undecided[3] Disagree[2]
Strongly disagree[1]   (F)

52. COURT DECISIONS ARE ALMOST ALWAYS JUST.
Strongly agree[1] Agree[2] Undecided[3] Disagree[4]
Strongly disagree[5]   (L)

53. LARGE INCOMES SHOULD BE TAXED MUCH MORE THAN THEY ARE NOW.
Strongly agree⁵ Agree⁴ Undecided³ Disagree²
Strongly disagree¹   (EC)

54. OUR SCHOOLS ENCOURAGE AN INDIVIDUAL TO THINK FOR HIMSELF.
Strongly agree¹ Agree² Undecided³ Disagree⁴
Strongly disagree⁵   (E)

55. ANY MAN WITH ABILITY AND WILLINGNESS TO WORK HARD HAS A GOOD CHANCE OF BEING SUCCESSFUL.
Strongly agree¹ Agree² Undecided³ Disagree⁴
Strongly disagree⁵   (M)

56. IT IS EASY TO ACT NATURALLY IN A GROUP.
Strongly agree¹ Agree² Undecided³ Disagree⁴
Strongly disagree⁵   (I)

57. PEOPLE IN THE FAMILY CAN BE TRUSTED COMPLETELY.
Strongly agree¹ Agree² Undecided³ Disagree⁴
Strongly disagree⁵   (F)

58. IN THE COURTS A POOR MAN WILL RECEIVE AS FAIR TREATMENT AS A MILLIONAIRE.
Strongly agree¹ Agree² Undecided³ Disagree⁴
Strongly disagree⁵   (L)

59. MEN WOULD NOT DO THEIR BEST, IF GOVERNMENT OWNED ALL INDUSTRY.
Strongly agree¹ Agree² Undecided³ Disagree⁴
Strongly disagree⁵   (EC)

60. THERE ARE TOO MANY FADS AND FRILLS IN MODERN EDUCATION.
Strongly agree⁵ Agree⁴ Undecided³ Disagree²
Strongly disagree¹   (E)

61. IT IS GREAT TO BE LIVING IN THESE EXCITING TIMES.
Strongly agree¹ Agree² Undecided³ Disagree⁴
Strongly disagree⁵   (M)

62. IT IS HARD TO BRING ONESELF TO CONFIDE IN OTHERS.
Strongly agree¹ Agree² Undecided³ Disagree⁴
Strongly disagree⁵   (I)

63. ONE BECOMES NERVOUS AT HOME.
Strongly agree⁵ Agree⁴ Undecided³ Disagree²
Strongly disagree¹   (F)

64. PERSONAL CIRCUMSTANCES SHOULD NEVER BE CONSIDERED AN EXCUSE FOR LAWBREAKING.
Strongly agree¹ Agree² Undecided³ Disagree⁴
Strongly disagree⁵   (L)

65. MOST GREAT FORTUNES ARE MADE HONESTLY.
Strongly agree¹ Agree² Undecided³ Disagree⁴
Strongly disagree⁵   (EC)

66. EDUCATION ONLY MAKES A PERSON DISCONTENTED.
Strongly agree[5] Agree[4] Undecided[3] Disagree[2]
Strongly disagree[1]   (E)

67. THESE DAYS ONE IS INCLINED TO GIVE UP HOPE OF AMOUNTING
TO SOMETHING.
Strongly agree[5] Agree[4] Undecided[3] Disagree[2]
Strongly disagree[1]   (M)

68. IT IS HARD TO DO YOUR BEST WHEN PEOPLE ARE WATCHING
YOU.
Strongly agree[5] Agree[4] Undecided[3] Disagree[2]
Strongly disagree[1]   (I)

69. THE JOYS OF FAMILY LIFE ARE MUCH OVERRATED.
Strongly agree[5] Agree[4] Undecided[3] Disagree[2]
Strongly disagree[1]   (F)

70. A MAN SHOULD TELL THE TRUTH IN COURT, REGARDLESS OF
CONSEQUENCES.
Strongly agree[1] Agree[2] Undecided[3] Disagree[4]
Strongly disagree[5]   (L)

71. PRIVATE OWNERSHIP OF PROPERTY IS NECESSARY FOR ECO-
NOMIC PROGRESS.
Strongly agree[1] Agree[2] Undecided[3] Disagree[4]
Strongly disagree[5]   (EC)

72. SCHOOL TRAINING IS OF LITTLE HELP IN MEETING THE PROB-
LEMS OF REAL LIFE.
Strongly agree[5] Agree[4] Undecided[3] Disagree[2]
Strongly disagree[1]   (E)

73. THERE IS LITTLE CHANCE FOR ADVANCEMENT IN INDUSTRY
AND BUSINESS UNLESS A MAN HAS UNFAIR PULL.
Strongly agree[5] Agree[4] Undecided[3] Disagree[2]
Strongly disagree[1]   (M)

74. IT IS EASY TO GET ALONG WITH PEOPLE.
Strongly agree[1] Agree[2] Undecided[3] Disagree[4]
Strongly disagree[5]   (I)

75. ONE'S PARENTS USUALLY TREAT HIM FAIRLY AND SENSIBLY.
Strongly agree[1] Agree[2] Undecided[3] Disagree[4]
Strongly disagree[5]   (F)

76. A PERSON WHO REPORTS MINOR LAW VIOLATIONS IS ONLY A
TROUBLEMAKER.
Strongly agree[5] Agree[4] Undecided[3] Disagree[2]
Strongly disagree[1]   (L)

77. WITHOUT SWEEPING CHANGES IN OUR ECONOMIC SYSTEM, LIT-
TLE PROGRESS CAN BE MADE IN THE SOLUTION OF SOCIAL PROB-
LEMS.
Strongly agree[5] Agree[4] Undecided[3] Disagree[2]
Strongly disagree[1]   (EC)

78. EDUCATION TENDS TO MAKE AN INDIVIDUAL LESS CONCEITED.
Strongly agree[1] Agree[2] Undecided[3] Disagree[4]
Strongly disagree[5]   (E)

79. THE YOUNG MAN OF TODAY CAN EXPECT MUCH OF THE FUTURE.
Strongly agree[1] Agree[2] Undecided[3] Disagree[4]
Strongly disagree[5]   (M)

80. IT IS EASY TO FEEL AS THOUGH YOU HAD A WORLD OF SELF-CONFIDENCE.
Strongly agree[1] Agree[2] Undecided[3] Disagree[4]
Strongly disagree[5]   (I)

81. ONE SHOULD CONFIDE MORE FULLY IN MEMBERS OF HIS FAMILY.
Strongly agree[1] Agree[2] Undecided[3] Disagree[4]
Strongly disagree[5]   (F)

82. A PERSON IS JUSTIFIED IN GIVING FALSE TESTIMONY TO PROTECT A FRIEND ON TRIAL.
Strongly agree[5] Agree[4] Undecided[3] Disagree[2]
Strongly disagree[1]   (L)

83. ON THE WHOLE, OUR ECONOMIC SYSTEM IS JUST AND WISE.
Strongly agree[1] Agree[2] Undecided[3] Disagree[4]
Strongly disagree[5]   (EC)

84. SOLUTION OF THE WORLD'S PROBLEMS WILL COME THROUGH EDUCATION.
Strongly agree[1] Agree[2] Undecided[3] Disagree[4]
Strongly disagree[5]   (E)

85. THIS GENERATION WILL PROBABLY NEVER SEE SUCH HARD TIMES AGAIN.
Strongly agree[1] Agree[2] Undecided[3] Disagree[4]
Strongly disagree[5]   (M)

86. MOST PEOPLE JUST PRETEND THAT THEY LIKE YOU.
Strongly agree[5] Agree[4] Undecided[3] Disagree[2]
Strongly disagree[1]   (I)

87. ONE FEELS MOST CONTENTED AT HOME.
Strongly agree[1] Agree[2] Undecided[3] Disagree[4]
Strongly disagree[5]   (F)

88. A HUNGRY MAN HAS A RIGHT TO STEAL.
Strongly agree[5] Agree[4] Undecided[3] Disagree[2]
Strongly disagree[1]   (L)

89. LABOR DOES NOT GET ITS FAIR SHARE OF WHAT IT PRODUCES.
Strongly agree[5] Agree[4] Undecided[3] Disagree[2]
Strongly disagree[1]   (EC)

90. HIGH SCHOOL COURSES ARE TOO IMPRACTICAL.
Strongly agree[5] Agree[4] Undecided[3] Disagree[2]
Strongly disagree[1]   (E)

91. REAL FRIENDS ARE AS EASY TO FIND AS EVER.
Strongly agree[1] Agree[2] Undecided[3] Disagree[4]
Strongly disagree[5]   (M)

92. SO MANY PEOPLE DO THINGS WELL THAT IT IS EASY TO BECOME DISCOURAGED.
Strongly agree⁵ Agree⁴ Undecided³ Disagree²
Strongly disagree¹ (I)

93. FAMILY TIES ARE STRENGTHENED WHEN TIMES ARE HARD.
Strongly agree¹ Agree² Undecided³ Disagree⁴
Strongly disagree⁵ (F)

94. ALL LAWS SHOULD BE STRICTLY OBEYED BECAUSE THEY *ARE* LAWS.
Strongly agree¹ Agree² Undecided³ Disagree⁴
Strongly disagree⁵ (L)

95. WHEN A RICH MAN DIES, MOST OF HIS PROPERTY SHOULD GO TO THE STATE.
Strongly agree⁵ Agree⁴ Undecided³ Disagree²
Strongly disagree¹ (EC)

96. A MAN IS FOOLISH TO KEEP ON GOING TO SCHOOL IF HE CAN GET A JOB.
Strongly agree⁵ Agree⁴ Undecided³ Disagree²
Strongly disagree¹ (E)

97. LIFE IS JUST A SERIES OF DISAPPOINTMENTS.
Strongly agree⁵ Agree⁴ Undecided³ Disagree²
Strongly disagree¹ (M)

98. IT IS HARD NOT TO BE SELF-CONSCIOUS.
Strongly agree⁵ Agree⁴ Undecided³ Disagree²
Strongly disagree¹ (I)

99. PARENTS ARE INCLINED TO BE TOO OLD-FASHIONED IN THEIR IDEAS.
Strongly agree⁵ Agree⁴ Undecided³ Disagree²
Strongly disagree¹ (F)

100. LAWS ARE SO OFTEN MADE FOR THE BENEFIT OF SMALL SELFISH GROUPS THAT A MAN CANNOT RESPECT THE LAW.
Strongly agree⁵ Agree⁴ Undecided³ Disagree²
Strongly disagree¹ (L)

101. IF OUR ECONOMIC SYSTEM WERE JUST, THERE WOULD BE MUCH LESS CRIME.
Strongly agree⁵ Agree⁴ Undecided³ Disagree²
Strongly disagree¹ (EC)

102. SAVINGS SPENT ON EDUCATION ARE WISELY INVESTED.
Strongly agree¹ Agree² Undecided³ Disagree⁴
Strongly disagree⁵ (E)

103. ONE SELDOM WORRIES SO MUCH AS TO BECOME VERY MISERABLE.
Strongly agree¹ Agree² Undecided³ Disagree⁴
Strongly disagree⁵ (M)

104. IT IS NO TRICK TO BE THE LIFE OF THE PARTY.
Strongly agree¹ Agree² Undecided³ Disagree⁴
Strongly disagree⁵ (I)

105. MEMBERS OF THE FAMILY ARE TOO CURIOUS ABOUT ONE'S PERSONAL AFFAIRS.
Strongly agree⁵ Agree⁴ Undecided³ Disagree²
Strongly disagree¹ (F)

106. ALMOST ANYTHING CAN BE FIXED UP IN THE COURTS IF YOU HAVE ENOUGH MONEY.
Strongly agree⁵ Agree⁴ Undecided³ Disagree²
Strongly disagree¹ (L)

107. THE INCOMES OF MOST PEOPLE ARE A FAIR MEASURE OF THEIR CONTRIBUTION TO HUMAN WELFARE.
Strongly agree¹ Agree² Undecided³ Disagree⁴
Strongly disagree⁵ (EC)

108. AN EDUCATED MAN CAN ADVANCE MORE RAPIDLY IN BUSINESS AND INDUSTRY.
Strongly agree¹ Agree² Undecided³ Disagree⁴
Strongly disagree⁵ (E)

109. A MAN DOES NOT HAVE TO PRETEND HE IS SMARTER THAN HE REALLY IS TO "GET BY."
Strongly agree¹ Agree² Undecided³ Disagree⁴
Strongly disagree⁵ (M)

110. IT IS EASY TO KEEP PEOPLE FROM TAKING ADVANTAGE OF YOU.
Strongly agree¹ Agree² Undecided³ Disagree⁴
Strongly disagree⁵ (I)

111. PARENTS KEEP FAITH IN THEIR CHILDREN EVEN THOUGH THEY CANNOT FIND WORK.
Strongly agree¹ Agree² Undecided³ Disagree⁴
Strongly disagree⁵ (F)

112. IT IS DIFFICULT TO BREAK THE LAW AND KEEP ONE'S SELF-RESPECT.
Strongly agree¹ Agree² Undecided³ Disagree⁴
Strongly disagree⁵ (L)

113. A MAN SHOULD STRIKE IN ORDER TO SECURE GREATER RETURNS TO LABOR.
Strongly agree⁵ Agree⁴ Undecided³ Disagree²
Strongly disagree¹ (EC)

114. PARENTS SHOULD NOT BE COMPELLED TO SEND THEIR CHILDREN TO SCHOOL.
Strongly agree⁵ Agree⁴ Undecided³ Disagree²
Strongly disagree¹ (E)

115. SUCCESS IS MORE DEPENDENT ON LUCK THAN ON REAL ABILITY.
Strongly agree⁵ Agree⁴ Undecided³ Disagree²
Strongly disagree¹ (M)

116. MOST PEOPLE ARE TOO CRITICAL OF ONE'S BEHAVIOR.
Strongly agree⁵ Agree⁴ Undecided³ Disagree²
Strongly disagree¹ (I)

117. PARENTS ARE TOO PARTICULAR ABOUT THE KIND OF COMPANY
ONE KEEPS.
Strongly agree⁵ Agree⁴ Undecided³ Disagree²
Strongly disagree¹ (F)

118. ON THE WHOLE, LAWYERS ARE HONEST.
Strongly agree¹ Agree² Undecided³ Disagree⁴
Strongly disagree⁵ (L)

119. A MAN SHOULD BE ALLOWED TO KEEP AS LARGE AN INCOME
AS HE CAN GET.
Strongly agree¹ Agree² Undecided³ Disagree⁴
Strongly disagree⁵ (EC)

120. EDUCATION IS MORE VALUABLE THAN MOST PEOPLE THINK.
Strongly agree¹ Agree² Undecided³ Disagree⁴
Strongly disagree⁵ (E)

121. A PERSON CAN PLAN HIS FUTURE SO THAT EVERYTHING WILL
COME OUT ALL RIGHT IN THE LONG RUN.
Strongly agree¹ Agree² Undecided³ Disagree⁴
Strongly disagree⁵ (M)

122. FEAR OF SOCIAL BLUNDERS KEEPS ONE FROM HAVING A GOOD
TIME AT A PARTY.
Strongly agree⁵ Agree⁴ Undecided³ Disagree²
Strongly disagree¹ (I)

123. OBLIGATIONS TO ONE'S FAMILY ARE A GREAT HANDICAP TO A
YOUNG MAN TODAY.
Strongly agree⁵ Agree⁴ Undecided³ Disagree²
Strongly disagree¹ (F)

124. VIOLATORS OF THE LAW ARE NEARLY ALWAYS DETECTED AND
PUNISHED.
Strongly agree¹ Agree² Undecided³ Disagree⁴
Strongly disagree⁵ (L)

125. MONEY SHOULD BE TAKEN FROM THE RICH AND GIVEN TO THE
POOR DURING HARD TIMES.
Strongly agree⁵ Agree⁴ Undecided³ Disagree²
Strongly disagree¹ (EC)

126. A HIGH SCHOOL EDUCATION MAKES A MAN A BETTER CITIZEN.
Strongly agree¹ Agree² Undecided³ Disagree⁴
Strongly disagree⁵ (E)

127. THERE IS REALLY NO POINT IN LIVING.
Strongly agree⁵ Agree⁴ Undecided³ Disagree²
Strongly disagree¹ (M)

128. IT IS EASY TO LOSE CONFIDENCE IN ONESELF.
Strongly agree⁵ Agree⁴ Undecided³ Disagree²
Strongly disagree¹ (I)

129. SO FAR AS IDEAS ARE CONCERNED, PARENTS AND CHILDREN
LIVE IN DIFFERENT WORLDS.
Strongly agree⁵ Agree⁴ Undecided³ Disagree²
Strongly disagree¹ (F)

130. IT IS ALL RIGHT FOR A PERSON TO BREAK THE LAW IF HE DOESN'T GET CAUGHT.
Strongly agree[5]   Agree[4]   Undecided[3]   Disagree[2]
Strongly disagree[1]   (L)

131. OUR ECONOMIC SYSTEM IS CRITICIZED TOO MUCH.
Strongly agree[1]   Agree[2]   Undecided[3]   Disagree[4]
Strongly disagree[5]   (EC)

132. PUBLIC MONEY SPENT ON EDUCATION FOR THE PAST FEW YEARS COULD HAVE BEEN USED MORE WISELY FOR OTHER PURPOSES.
Strongly agree[5]   Agree[4]   Undecided[3]   Disagree[2]
Strongly disagree[1]   (E)

4.1.2   **THE SCIENCE RESEARCH ASSOCIATES ATTITUDE SURVEY**

VARIABLE MEASURED: The SRA Attitude Survey provides a measure of employee attitudes toward the work environment. It is a diagnostic instrument identifying attitudinal levels for individuals and groups in such areas as job demands, working conditions, pay, employee benefits, friendliness and cooperation of fellow employees, supervisor-employee interpersonal relations, confidence in management, technical competence of supervision, effectiveness of administration, adequacy of communication, security of job and work relations, status and recognition, identification with the company, opportunity for growth and advancement, and finally reactions to the inventory itself. See Zile S. Dabas, "The Dimensions of Morale: An Item Factorization of the SRA Inventory," *Personnel Psychology* 11 (Summer 1958): 217–34.

DESCRIPTION: The inventory is not just an opinion survey. It is a kind of "morale audit" for work organizations that provides standard scores in each category based upon more than one million employees in a wide variety of business firms. Practical uses include assessing the general level of morale in an organization, locating the problem departments in the organization, determining satisfactions and dissatisfactions among employees, evaluating supervisory and executive training needs, and providing material for supervisory training programs.

WHERE PUBLISHED: Science Research Associates, Inc., 259 East Erie Street, Chicago, IL 60611. Copyright, 1952, by the Industrial Relations Center of the University of Chicago. All rights reserved. Authors of the survey include Robert K. Burns, L. L. Thurstone, David G. Moore, and Melony E. Baehr.

RELIABILITY: Both individual and group reliability have been determined by the test-retest method with an interval of one week between the test administrations. A sample of 134 employees shows a product moment correlation of .89. Group reliabilities range from .96 to .99 with reliability greater for groups of 50 or more employees.

VALIDITY: Good correspondence was found to exist between the inventory results and the considered judgments of experienced observers. In three of the companies surveyed, validity was established by conducting nondirective interviews among a cross section of the employees. Cf. Robert J. Wherry, "Factor Analysis of Morale Data: Reliability and Validity," *Personnel Psychology* 11 (Spring 1958): 78–89.

STANDARD SCORES: Well standardized scores are available for comparative analysis of attitude levels in similar business firms and within similar departments. National, industrial, and occupational norms were checked and revised in 1970.

Science Research Associates

SRA Attitude Survey   *Instructions*   *Form A*

Purpose of the Survey

Your company would like to know what you think about your job, your pay, your boss, and the community in general. This inventory is designed to help you tell us your ideas and opinions quickly and easily without signing your name. This booklet contains a number of statements. All you have to do is to mark a cross by each statement to show how you feel. It is easy to do and you can be completely frank in your answers.

How to fill in the Survey

Read each statement carefully and decide how you feel about it. You will agree with some statements, and you will disagree with others. You may be undecided about some. To help you express your opinion, three possible answers have been placed beside each statement:

	AGREE	?	DISAGREE
I would rather work in a large city than in a small town	☐	☐	☐

Choose the answer most like your own opinion and mark a cross in the box under it.

For example:

This person feels he wants to work in a large city:

	AGREE	?	DISAGREE
I would rather work in a large city than in a small town	☐	☐	☐

This person wants to work in a small town:

	AGREE	?	DISAGREE
I would rather work in a large city than in a small town	☐	☐	☐

This person can't decide between a large city and a small town:

	AGREE	?	DISAGREE
I would rather work in a large city than in a small town	☐	☐	☐

This is not a test

There are no "right" answers and no "wrong" answers. It is your own, honest opinion that we want.

Work rapidly but answer all statements

Do *not* spend too much time on any one statement. If you cannot decide about a statement, mark the "?" box, and go on to the next statement. If you make a mistake, erase your mark, or fill in the box completely. Then mark a cross in the correct box.

General information

Do *not* sign your name on the booklet. Be *sure* to fill in the blanks for general information such as age, sex, department, etc., that will be asked of you. This information will be used only to make the results more meaningful. It will not be used to identify you in any way.

When you have finished

When you have finished filling out the questionnaire, check to see that you have marked every statement. Then turn to last page where you will find the space to write your comments. In this space we would like you to write anything about your job or the company that is important to you. If something is irritating or trying for you, please comment on it. If something is pleasing or satisfying, please comment on that also. Or if you have a suggestion to help your job or the company, write that also.

PART I. THE CORE SURVEY

1. The hours of work here are O.K.. . . . .   AGREE ☐   ? ☐   DISAGREE ☐

2. Management does everything possible to prevent accidents in our work . . . .   AGREE ☐   ? ☐   DISAGREE ☐

3. Management is doing its best to give us good working conditions .   AGREE ☐   ? ☐   DISAGREE ☐

4. In my opinion, the pay here is lower than in other companies . . .   AGREE ☐   ? ☐   DISAGREE ☐

5. They should do a better job of handling pay matters here . . . . .   AGREE ☐   ? ☐   DISAGREE ☐

6. I understand what the company benefit program provides for employees . . . .   AGREE ☐   ? ☐   DISAGREE ☐

7. The people I work with help each other out when someone falls behind or gets in a tight spot . . . .   AGREE ☐   ? ☐   DISAGREE ☐

8. My boss is too interested in his own success to care about the needs of employees . . . .   AGREE ☐   ? ☐   DISAGREE ☐

9. My boss is always breathing down our necks; he watches us to closely . . . .   AGREE ☐   ? ☐   DISAGREE ☐

10. My boss gives us credit and praise for work well done. . . . .   AGREE ☐   ? ☐   DISAGREE ☐

11. Management here does everything it can to see that employees get a fair break on the job . . . .   AGREE ☐   ? ☐   DISAGREE ☐

12. If I have a complaint to make, I feel free to talk to someone up-the-line . . . .   AGREE ☐   ? ☐   DISAGREE ☐

13. My boss sees that employees are properly trained for their jobs . . . .   AGREE ☐   ? ☐   DISAGREE ☐

14. My boss sees that we have the things we need to do our jobs . . . .   AGREE ☐   ? ☐   DISAGREE ☐

15. Management here is really trying to build the organization and make it successful . . . .   AGREE ☐   ? ☐   DISAGREE ☐

16. Management here sees to it that there is cooperation between departments . . . .   AGREE ☐   ? ☐   DISAGREE ☐

17. Management tells employees about company plans and developments. . . . .   AGREE ☐   ? ☐   DISAGREE ☐

18. They encourage us to make suggestions for improvements here . . . .   AGREE ☐   ? ☐   DISAGREE ☐

19. I am often bothered by sudden speedups or unexpected slack periods in my work . . . .
    AGREE ? DISAGREE

20. Changes are made here with little regard for the welfare of employees . . . .
    AGREE ? DISAGREE

21. Compared with other employees, we get very little attention from management . . . .
    AGREE ? DISAGREE

22. Sometimes I feel that my job counts for very little in this organization . . . .
    AGREE ? DISAGREE

23. The longer you work for this company the more you feel you belong. . . . .
    AGREE ? DISAGREE

24. I have a great deal of interest in this company and its future . . . .
    AGREE ? DISAGREE

25. I have little opportunity to use my abilities in this organization . . . .
    AGREE ? DISAGREE

26. There are plenty of good jobs here for those who want to get ahead . . . .
    AGREE ? DISAGREE

27. I often feel worn out and tired on my job . . . .
    AGREE ? DISAGREE

28. They expect too much work from us around here. . . . .
    AGREE ? DISAGREE

29. Poor working conditions keep me from doing my best in my work . . . .
    AGREE ? DISAGREE

30. For my kind of job, the working conditions are O.K. . . . .
    AGREE ? DISAGREE

31. I'm paid fairly compared with other employees . . . .
    AGREE ? DISAGREE

32. Compared with other companies, employee benefits here are good. . . . .
    AGREE ? DISAGREE

33. A few of the people I work with think they run the place . . . . .
    AGREE ? DISAGREE

34. The people I work with get along well together . . . .
    AGREE ? DISAGREE

35. My boss has always been fair in his dealings with me . . . .
    AGREE ? DISAGREE

36. My boss gets employees to work together as a team. . . . .
    AGREE ? DISAGREE

37. I have confidence in the fairness and honesty of management . . . .
    AGREE ? DISAGREE

38. Management here is really interested in the welfare of employees . . . .
    AGREE ? DISAGREE

39. Most of the higher-ups are friendly toward employees . . . .
    AGREE ? DISAGREE

40. My boss keeps putting things off; he just lets things ride . . . . . .
    AGREE ? DISAGREE

41. My boss lets us know exactly what is expected of us . . . .
    AGREE ? DISAGREE

42. Management fails to give clear-cut orders and instructions. . . . .
    AGREE ? DISAGREE

	AGREE	?	DISAGREE
43. I know how my job fits in with other work in this organization	☐	☐	☐
44. Management keeps us in the dark about things we ought to know.	☐	☐	☐
45. Long service means something in this organization	☐	☐	☐
46. You can get fired around here without much cause	☐	☐	☐
47. I can be sure of my job as long as I do good work	☐	☐	☐
48. I have plenty of freedom on the job to use my own judgment	☐	☐	☐
49. Everybody in this organization tries to boss us around	☐	☐	☐
50. I really feel part of this organization	☐	☐	☐
51. The people who get promotions around here usually deserve them.	☐	☐	☐
52. I can learn a great deal on my present job	☐	☐	☐
53. My job is often dull and monotonous	☐	☐	☐
54. There is too much pressure on my job	☐	☐	☐
55. Some of the working conditions here are annoying	☐	☐	☐
56. I have the right equipment to do my work	☐	☐	☐
57. My pay is enough to live on comfortably	☐	☐	☐
58. I'm satisfied with the way employee benefits are handled here	☐	☐	☐
59. The company's employee benefit program is O.K.	☐	☐	☐
60. The people I work with are very friendly	☐	☐	☐
61. My boss really tries to get our ideas about things	☐	☐	☐
62. My boss ought to be friendlier toward employees	☐	☐	☐
63. My boss lives up to his promises	☐	☐	☐
64. Management here has a very good personnel policy	☐	☐	☐
65. Management ignores our suggestions and complaints	☐	☐	☐
66. My boss knows very little about his job	☐	☐	☐

		AGREE	?	DISAGREE
67.	My boss has the work well organized.	☐	☐	☐
68.	This company operates efficiently and smoothly	☐	☐	☐
69.	Management really knows its job	☐	☐	☐
70.	They have a poor way of handling employee complaints here	☐	☐	☐
71.	You can say what you think around here.	☐	☐	☐
72.	You always know where you stand with this company	☐	☐	☐
73.	When layoffs are necessary, they are handled fairly	☐	☐	☐
74.	I am very much underpaid for the work that I do	☐	☐	☐
75.	I'm really doing something worthwhile in my job	☐	☐	☐
76.	I'm proud to work for this company	☐	☐	☐
77.	Filling in this Inventory is a good way to let management know what employees think.	☐	☐	☐
78.	I think some good may come out of filling in an Inventory like this one	☐	☐	☐

PART II. CUSTOM-BUILT SURVEY

This survey consists of up to 21 items designed especially for the client with the advice and assistance of SRA professionals. Responses to these items enable management to learn what needs to be known about situations specific to that company alone. SRA reproduces and collates this set of questions along with the other survey parts to be administered. A few sample items might be:

		STRONGLY AGREE	AGREE	?	DISAGREE	STRONGLY AGREE
79.	Our hospital-surgical-medical plan provides good protection	☐	☐	☐	☐	☐
80.	My best source of information concerning company plans is through the "grapevine."	☐	☐	☐	☐	☐

General information

1	2	3
4	5	6

PART III. ANONYMOUS COMMENTS

Employees are urged to express feelings on subjects they find most important to them.

UTILITY: Inexpensive, easily interpreted, quickly scored, and permits use in all kinds of work organizations. Comparative analysis is facilitated by available standard scores. There are two different supplemental surveys available, one for supervisors and one for salesmen.

RESEARCH APPLICATIONS:

ASH, PHILIP. "The SRA Employee Inventory—A Statistical Analysis." *Personnel Psychology* 7 (Autumn 1954): 337–63.

MOORE, DAVID G., and BURNS, ROBERT K. "How Good Is Good Morale?" *Factory* (February 1956): 130–36.

The *SRA Attitude Survey* (originally called *Employee Inventory*) was prepared by the Employee Attitude Research Group of the Industrial Relations Center, University of Chicago. This group has members from both the University and industry. Thus, both the theoretical and practical aspects are well represented in all development work. Further details are given in the *Manual*.

The researcher may wish to compare the *SRA Attitude Survey* with the newer *Survey of Organizations* by James C. Taylor and David G. Bowers (Ann Arbor: Institute of Social Research, University of Michigan, 1974). The Survey is described on page 000 of the Handbook.

4.1.3 MORSE INDEXES OF EMPLOYEE SATISFACTION

VARIABLE MEASURED: The degree of satisfaction that individuals obtain from the various roles they play in an organization; specifically (1) satisfaction with doing the actual content of the work, (2) satisfaction with being in the work group, (3) satisfaction with working in the company, (4) satisfaction with pay and job status.

DESCRIPTION: These are indexes of employee satisfaction, each of which contains four items developed through a combined logical and empirical method. The items were initially selected from an employee interview on the basis of the definitions of each area of employee satisfaction. Intercorrelations were then computed among all items that logically appeared to belong in each area. Items that showed very low correlations were removed. The items making up each index were not differentially weighed, but were added with unit weights to give a single measure of each type of employee satisfaction. The four indexes are called *intrinsic job satisfaction, company involvement, financial and job status satisfaction,* and *pride in group performance.* Each index has four items that are answered on a five-point scale ranging from strong like to strong dislike. This gives a range of scores from 4–20 on each index.

WHERE PUBLISHED: Nancy C. Morse, *Satisfactions in the White Collar Job* (Ann Arbor: University of Michigan, Institute for Social Research, 1953).

RELIABILITY: No split half or test-retest reliabilities are reported. Internal consistency of the scales is attested by the average intercorrelations of items:

Intrinsic job satisfaction	$r = .50$
Company involvement	$r = .45$
Financial and job status satisfaction	$r = .52$
Pride in group performance	$r = .39$

VALIDITY: The intrinsic job satisfaction, company involvement, and financial job status indexes, both from the intercorrelations of the total index scores and from the item analysis, appear to be significantly interrelated (intercorrelations ranging from $r = .35$ to $r = .43$). These three areas can be used to represent a general morale factor. This factor predicts the individual's desire to stay in the company rather than his productivity.

Pride in group performance (and its subitems) is, with few exceptions, not significantly related to the items of the other indexes or to the indexes themselves. It must be treated as an independent factor. This index was related to the amount of voluntary help given by members to one another, friendliness in interpersonal relations, and the absence of antiproductivity group norms. It was also correlated with supervisor's identification with employees.

STANDARD SCORES:

		Range	N
Intrinsic Job Satisfaction	High Group	04–07	(717)
	Medium Group	08–11	(222)
	Low Group	12–20	(181)
Financial and Job Status Satisfaction	High Group	04–08	(160)
	Medium Group	09–12	(227)
	Low Group	13–20	(248)
Company Involvement	High Group	04–08	(250)
	Medium Group	09–12	(255)
	Low Group	13–20	(165)
Pride in Group Performance	High Group	04–08	(227)
	Medium Group	09–10	(264)
	Low Group	11–20	(251)

UTILITY: The indexes consist of easily administered questionnaire items. The time required is about 10 minutes for the administration of all four indexes.

RESEARCH APPLICATIONS: Morse reports relationships between the indexes and various supervisory practices, working conditions, and various background factors such as sex, age, length of service, and education. See Morse, *Satisfactions in the White Collar Job.*

Company Involvement Index

1. "How do you like working here?"
   code: Five-point scale ranging from strong like, complete satisfaction to strong dislike.
2. "Would you advise a friend to come to work for the Company?"
   code: Three-point scale including: yes, pro-con, and no.

3. An overall coder rating of the employee's feelings about the fairness of the company, based on answers to questions throughout the interview.
   code: Three-point scale including: feels company fair and generous, feels company fair but very exacting, feels company unfair.
4. An overall coder rating of the employee's degree of identification with the company based on answers to questions throughout the interview.
   code: Three-point scale including: strong identification, some identification, and no identification.

Financial and Job Status Index

1. "How well satisfied are you with your salary?"
   code: Five-point scale ranging from very well satisfied to very dissatisfied.
2. "How satisfied are you with your chances of getting more pay?"
   code: Five-point scale ranging from very satisfied to very dissatisfied.
3. "How about your own case, how satisfied are you with the way things have been working out for you?" (This question was preceded by two questions on "getting ahead here at the Company" and was answered in that context.)
   code: Five-point scale ranging from very satisfied to very dissatisfied.
4. Coder overall rating of degree of frustration evidenced by respondent in advancing in his job or in his main vocational objectives. Answers to questions throughout the interview were used to measure the degree to which employee felt his vocational desires were blocked.
   code: Five-point scale ranging from strong frustration to high adjustment, no frustration.

Intrinsic Job Satisfaction Index

1. "How well do you like the sort of work you are doing?"
   code: Five-point scale varying from strong like to strong dislike.
2. "Does your job give you a chance to do things you feel you do best?"
   code: Five-point scale varying from yes (strong) to no (strong).
3. "Do you get any feeling of accomplishment from the work you are doing?"
   code: Five-point scale varying from strong sense of task completion to no sense of task completion.
4. "How do you feel about your work, does it rate as an important job with you?"
   code: Five-point scale varying from very important to of no importance.

Pride-in-Group-Performance Index

1. "How well do you think your section compares with other sections in the Company in getting a job done?"
   code: Five-point scale ranging from very good, one of best in company, to very poor, one of worst in company.
2. Answers to the section comparison question were also coded on the degree of emotional identification with the section that employee showed. (The use of "we" as opposed to "it" or "they" was one of the indications to the coder of identification.)
   code: Three-point scale: strong identification, mild identification, indifference or lack of identification.
3. "How well do you think your division compares with other divisions in the Company in getting a job done?"
   code: Five-point scale ranging from very good, one of best in company, to very poor, one of worst in company.

4. Answers to the division comparison question were also coded on degree of emotional identification with the division the employee showed.
code: Three-point scale: strong identification, mild identification, indifference or lack of identification.

BRAYFIELD AND ROTHE'S INDEX OF JOB SATISFACTION $4.1.4$

VARIABLE MEASURED: General measure of job satisfaction.

WHERE PUBLISHED: Arthur H. Brayfield and Harold F. Rothe, "An Index of Job Satisfaction." *Journal of Applied Psychology* 35 (October 1951): 307–11.

CONSTRUCTION: As a working approach for this study it was assumed that job satisfaction could be inferred from the individual's attitude toward his work. This approach dictated the methodology of attitude scaling. The following requirements were formulated as desirable attributes of an attitude scale designed to provide a useful index of job satisfaction: (1) it should give an index of "overall" job satisfaction rather than specific aspects of job satisfaction; (2) it should be applicable to a wide variety of jobs; (3) it should be sensitive to variations in attitude; (4) the items should be of such a nature (interesting, realistic, and varied) that the scale would evoke cooperation from both management and employees; (5) it should yield a reliable index; (6) it should yield a valid index; (7) it should be brief and easily scored.

The construction of this scale was made a class project in Personnel Psychology for members of an Army Specialized Training Program in personnel psychology at the University of Minnesota in the summer and fall of 1943. Seventy-seven men cooperated. Items referring to specific aspects of a job were eliminated since an "overall" attitudinal factor was desired.

The present index contains 18 items with Thurstone scale values ranging from 1.2 to 10.0 with approximately .5 step intervals. The items are not arranged in the order of magnitude of scale values. The Likert scoring system consisting of five categories of agreement-disagreement was applied to each item, and the Thurstone scoring system of five categories is applied to the items. The Thurstone scale value gives the direction of scoring method so that a low total score would represent the dissatisfied end of the scale and a high total score the satisfied end. The items are selected so that the satisfied end of the scale was indicated by *Strongly agree* and *Agree,* and *Disagree* and *Strongly disagree* for the other half. The neutral response is *Undecided.* The Likert scoring weights for each item range from 1 to 5, and the range of possible total scores is 18 to 90 with 54 (Undecided) the neutral point.

RELIABILITY: The revised scale (which is the present one) was administered as part of a study of 231 female office employees. The blanks were signed along with other tests. One of the investigators personally administered the tests to employees in small groups. The range of job satisfaction scores for this sample was 35–87. The mean score was 63.8 with an S. D. of 9.4. The odd-even product moment reliability coefficient computed for this sample was .77, which was corrected by the Spearman-Brown formula to a reliability coefficient of .87.

VALIDITY: Evidence for the high validity of the blank rests upon the nature of the items, the method of construction, and its differentiating power when applied to two groups that could reasonably be assumed to differ in job satisfaction. The nature of the individual items is partial, although not crucial, evidence for the validity of the scale. This is an appeal to "face" validity. Additional evidence is furnished by the method of construction. The attitude variable of job satisfaction is inferred from verbal reactions to a job expressed along a favorable-unfavorable continuum.

The job satisfaction blank was administered to 91 adult night school students in classes in Personnel Psychology at the University of Minnesota during 1945 and 1946. The range of job satisfaction scores for this sample was 29–89. The mean score was 70.4 with an S. D. of 13.2. The assumption was made that those persons employed in occupations appropriate to their expressed interest should, on the average, be more satisfied with their jobs than those members of the class employed in occupations inappropriate to their expressed interest in personnel work. The 91 persons accordingly were divided into two groups (personnel and nonpersonnel) with respect to their employment in a position identified by payroll title as a personnel function. The mean of the personnel group was 76.9 with an S. D. of 8.6 as compared to a mean of 65.4 with an S. D. of 14.02 for the nonpersonnel group. This difference of 11.5 points is significant at the 1 percent level; the difference between the variances also is significant at the 1 percent level. It might also be mentioned that scores on this index correlated .92 with scores on the Hoppock job satisfaction scale. See review of James L. Price, *Handbook of Organizational Measurement* (New York: Heath, 1972), pp. 156–73.

RESEARCH APPLICATIONS:

BRAYFIELD, ARTHUR H.; WELLS, RICHARD V.; and STRATE, MARVIN W. "Interrelationships Among Measures of Job Satisfaction and General Satisfaction." *Journal of Applied Psychology* 41 (August 1957): 201–5.

EWEN, ROBERT B. "Weighting Components of Job Satisfaction." *Journal of Applied Psychology* 51 (February 1967): 68–73.

AN INDEX OF JOB SATISFACTION*†

Some jobs are more interesting and satisfying than others. We want to know how people feel about different jobs. This blank contains 18 statements about jobs. You are to cross out the phrase below each statement that has best

* Arthur H. Brayfield and Harold F. Rothe, *Journal of Applied Psychology* 35, no. 5 (October 1951): 307–11.

† This blank containing 18 items with Thurstone scale values ranging from 1.2 to 10.0 with approximately .5 step intervals is not arranged in order of magnitude of scale values. The Likert scoring system of five categories is applied to each item. Thurstone scale values give the direction of scoring method. Likert scoring weights range for each item 1 to 5. The range of possible total scores became 18 to 90 with the undecided or neutral point at 54.

described how you feel about your present job. There are no right or wrong answers. We should like your honest opinion on each one of the statements. Work out the sample item numbered (0).

0. There are some conditions concerning my job that could be improved.
   Strongly agree, agree, undecided, disagree, strongly disagree.
1. My job is like a hobby to me.
   Strongly agree, agree, undecided, disagree, strongly disagree.
2. My job is usually interesting enough to keep me from getting bored.
   Strongly agree, agree, undecided, disagree, strongly disagree.
3. It seems that my friends are more interested in their jobs.
   Strongly agree, agree, undecided, disagree, strongly disagree.
4. I consider my job rather unpleasant.
   Strongly agree, agree, undecided, disagree, strongly disagree.
5. I enjoy my work more than my leisure time.
   Strongly agree, agree, undecided, disagree, strongly disagree.
6. I am often bored with my job.
   Strongly agree, agree, undecided, disagree, strongly disagree.
7. I feel fairly well satisfied with my job.
   Strongly agree, agree, undecided, disagree, strongly disagree.
8. Most of the time I have to force myself to go to work.
   Strongly agree, agree, undecided, disagree, strongly disagree.
9. I am satisfied with my job for the time being.
   Strongly agree, agree, undecided, disagree, strongly disagree.
10. I feel that my job is no more interesting than others I could get.
    Strongly agree, agree, undecided, disagree, strongly disagree.
11. I definitely dislike my work.
    Strongly agree, agree, undecided, disagree, strongly disagree.
12. I feel that I am happier in my work than most other people.
    Strongly agree, agree, undecided, disagree, strongly disagree.
13. Most days I am enthusiastic about my work.
    Strongly agree, agree, undecided, disagree, strongly disagree.
14. Each day of work seems like it will never end.
    Strongly agree, agree, undecided, disagree, strongly disagree.
15. I like my job better than the average worker does.
    Strongly agree, agree, undecided, disagree, strongly disagree.
16. My job is pretty uninteresting.
    Strongly agree, agree, undecided, disagree, strongly disagree.
17. I find real enjoyment in my work.
    Strongly agree, agree, undecided, disagree, strongly disagree.
18. I am disappointed that I ever took this job.
    Strongly agree, agree, undecided, disagree, strongly disagree.

Scales of Attitudes, Values, and Norms

This section includes selected attitude and value scales that revolve around current interests and concerns. In the 1960s and early 70s, as the countercultural movement gained momentum, much attention was focused on *alienation*. Sociologists responded to demand and research interest increased—using the Srole Anomia Scale, the Neal and Seeman Powerless Scale, the Dean Alienation Scale, and many others. Although the interest in alienation has lessened, related feelings of *powerlessness* remain as big government, big business, big religion, big labor, and big cities seem to dominate human life. For this reason, the Neal and Seaman Powerless Scale has been selected as representative of one of the dimensions in the alienation of persons and groups from major social institutions.

Achievement orientation has commanded considerable attention. Kahl's scale has been selected because of its special application to underdeveloped as well as developed societies. The researcher interested in the general factor of aspiration should examine carefully the excellent occupational aspiration scale by Archibald Haller and Irwin Miller listed in the references below.

The measurement of international patterns and norms relates to the growing interest in comparative studies. The author's Battery of Rating Scales is included for such measurements.

Innumerable attitude scales are in existence. If you are looking for more information on these scales, check the content tables of *Occupational Attitudes and Characteristics, Political Attitudes,* and *Social-Psychological Attitudes* by John P. Robinson and his co-workers as shown in section 4.M.5. Note also the Shaw and Wright Compilation of Scales for the Measurement of Attitudes in section 4.M.6. Other sources are listed under All-Inclusive and Special Compilation in section 4.M.4. Review the attitudes used in the *American Sociological Review,* 1964–80, in section 4.M.1.

If you are looking for a sourcebook on Attitudes that displays trend patterns, see Philip E. Converse, Jean D. Dotson, Wendy J. Hoag, and William H. McGee III, *American Social Attitudes Data Sourcebook, 1947–78* (Cambridge, Mass.: Harvard University Press, 1980). Cf. Elizabeth Martin and

Diana McDuffee, *A Sourcebook of Harris National Surveys: Repeated Questions, 1963–76* (Chapel Hill: Institute for Research in Social Science, University of North Carolina, 1981). This is a compilation of all repeated questions from 121 national surveys conducted by Louis Harris and Associates and achieved at the Louis Harris Data Center at North Carolina. Almost 14,000 questions are arranged by topic and identified by survey and date.

Interest in the measurement of values is growing. Some important sources of information on this topic are:

ALLPORT, GORDON W.; VERNON, PHILLIP E.; and LINDZEY, GARDNER. *Study of Values.* Boston: Houghton Mifflin, 1950.

ALMOND, GABRIEL A., and VERBA, SIDNEY. *The Civic Culture.* Boston: Little, Brown, 1963.

CANTRIL, HADLEY. *The Pattern of Human Concerns.* New Brunswick, N.J.: Rutgers University Press, 1965.

CARTER, ROY E. "An Experiment in Value Measurement." *American Sociological Review* 21 (April 1956): 156–63.

DODD, STUART C. "Ascertaining National Goals: Project Aimscales." *American Behavioral Scientist* 4 (March 1961): 11–15.

FALLDING, HAROLD. "A Proposal for the Empirical Study of Values." *American Sociological Review* 30 (April 1965): 223–33.

FAVE, L. RICHARD DELLS. "Success Values: Are They Universal or Class Differentiated?" *American Journal of Sociology* 80 (July 1974): 153–69.

HALLER, ARCHIBALD O., and MILLER, IRWIN W. *The Occupational Aspiration Scale: Theory, Structure and Correlates.* 2nd ed. Cambridge, Mass.: Schenkman, 1971.

NEAL, SISTER MARIE AUGUSTA. *Values and Interest in Social Change.* Englewood Cliffs, N.J.: Prentice-Hall, 1965.

ROKEACH, M. *Belief, Attitudes, and Values: A Theory of Organization and Change.* San Francisco: Jossey-Bass, 1968.

———. *The Nature of Human Values.* New York: Free Press, 1973.

SCOTT, WILLIAM A. *Values and Organizations.* Chicago: Rand McNally, 1965.

———. "Empirical Assessment of Values and Ideologies." *American Sociological Review* 24 (June 1959): 299–310.

THURSTONE, L. L. *The Measurement of Values.* Chicago: University of Chicago Press, 1959.

VICKERS, SIR GEOFFREY, *Value Systems and Social Processes.* New York: Basic Books, 1968.

WILSON, WILLIAM J., and NYE, F. IVAN. *Some Methodological Problems in the Empirical Study of Values.* Washington Agricultural Experiment Station Bulletin No. 672. Pullman: Washington State University, July 1966.

YANKELOVICH, D. *The Changing Values on Campus.* New York: John D. Rockefeller III Fund, 1972.

THE MEASUREMENT OF ALIENATION AND ANOMIE

The "rediscovery of alienation," as Daniel Bell puts it, has encouraged scientists to develop scales to measure these phenomena.[1] The research has been demonstrating that a number of independent factors may be identified. In 1959 Melvin Seeman set forth a fivefold classification: powerlessness, meaninglessness, normlessness, isolation, and self-estrangement.[2] The scales which have been produced have sought to isolate such factors and measure them. The first element, powerlessness, was suggested by Hegel, Marx, and Weber in their discussions of the workers' "separation" from effective control over their economic destiny; of their helplessness; of their being used for purposes other than their own. Weber argued that in the industrial society, the scientist, the civil servant, the professor is likewise "separated from control over his work."

The first scale presented is the Neal and Seeman Powerlessness Scale. It is especially useful for the measurement of worker alienation.[3] Other applications in the hospital, reformatory, and ghetto are cited in Research Applications of the scale. Other scales have sought to tap such variables as anomie or normlessness.

The loss or absence of social norms is seen to bring personal insecurity, the loss of intrinsic values that might give purpose or direction to life. Leo Srole has sought to isolate this variable by measuring self-to-others sense of belonging. His scale consists of five items, each one measuring one aspect of anomie. The unidimensionality of the anomia scale was assessed by the procedures of latent structure analysis and found to satisfy the criteria. It has been found that the anomia scale satisfies the requirements of a Guttman-type scale. The scale has had an extensive application to research problems.

Dwight Dean has developed three subscales to measure powerlessness, normlessness, and social isolation. He combined the three subscales to make up an alienation scale. He believes that the pattern of intercorrelations demonstrates that alienation may be treated as a composite concept, but "there appears to be enough independence among the subscales to warrant treating them as independent variables." Neal and Rettig, using factor analysis, have found empirical evidence for the structural independence of powerlessness, normlessness, and Srole's Anomia Scale. At this time, the subscales should be utilized when the greatest precision is desired. There is great variety in the scales being used and consensus is low.[4]

The researcher wishing to consult the Srole and Dean scales should see Leo Srole, "Social Integration and Certain Corollaries: An Exploratory Study," *American Sociological Review* 21 (December 1956): 709–16; and Dwight G. Dean, "Alienation: Its Meaning and Measurement," *American Sociological Review* 26 (October 1961): 753–58. The researcher may wish to examine other scales purporting to measure alienation and anomie. These include Herbert McClosky and John H. Schaar, "Psychological Dimensions of Anomie," *American Sociological Review* 30 (February 1965): 14–40; and Gwynn Nettler, "A Measure of Alienation," *American Sociological Review* 22 (December 1957): 670–77.

For a more thorough listing and appraisal, see John P. Robinson and Phillip R. Shaver, *Measures of Social Psychological Attitudes,* rev. ed. (Ann Arbor: Institute of Social Research, University of Michigan, 1973), pp. 254–94.

Notes

1. See, for example, Allan H. Roberts and Milton Rokeach, "Anomie, Authoritarianism, and Prejudice: A Replication," *American Journal of Sociology* 61 (January 1956): 355–58; Gwynn Nettler, "A Measure of Alienation," *American Sociological Review* 22 (December 1957): 670–77; and Leo Srole, "Social Integration and Certain Corollaries:

An Exploratory Study," *American Sociological Review* 21 (December 1956): 709–16. The concepts of alienation and anomie have not only become widely used but also misused terms of our times. Researchers need to be especially cautious in estimating the size of the alienated segment of the population when using the scales.

2. Melvin Seeman, "On the Meaning of Alienation," *American Sociological Review* 24 (December 1959): 783–91.

3. Arthur G. Neal and Solomon Rettig, "Dimensions of Alienation among Manual and Non-Manual Workers," *American Sociological Review* 26 (August 1963): 599–608.

4. Cf. J. L. Simmons, "Some Inter-correlations Among 'Alienation' Measures," *Social Forces* 44 (March 1966): 370–72

NEAL AND SEEMAN'S POWERLESSNESS SCALE   *4.J.1*

VARIABLE MEASURED: The authors define powerlessness as "low expectancies for control of events" as lack of control over the political system, the industrial economy, and international affairs. Basically measures the subjectively held probabilities that the outcome of political and economic events cannot be adequately controlled by oneself or collectively by persons like oneself.

DESCRIPTION: This instrument is a unidimensional 7-item scale that presents a choice between mastery and powerlessness.

The scale, as most of the powerlessness scales, is an adaptation of the forced-choice instrument developed by the late Professor Shephard Liverant and his colleagues at the Ohio State University. For further description of this method see Julian B. Rotter, Melvin Seeman, and Shephard Liverant, "Internal vs. External Control of Reinforcements: A Major Variable in Behavior Theory," in *Decisions, Values and Groups,* ed. Norman E. Washburne, vol. 2 (London: Pergamon, 1962), pp. 473–516.

WHERE PUBLISHED: Arthur G. Neal and Melvin Seeman, "Organizations and Powerlessness: A Test of the Mediation Hypothesis," *American Sociological Review* 29 (April 1964): 216–26.

RELIABILITY: The seven items yielded a reproducibility coefficient of .87 on the sample used by Neal and Seeman. An early version of the scale shows that the split-half reliability coefficient was .70. See Melvin Seeman and John Evans, "Alienation in a Hospital Setting," *American Sociological Review* 27 (December 1962): 772–82.

VALIDITY: The mean difference of alienation scores of organized and unorganized workers is significant at the .01 level. The difference of means for mobility-oriented and nonmobility-oriented nonmanual workers is significant at the .001 level. Correlation between anomie and powerlessness $r = .33$. M. Seeman and J. Evans found a negative relation between powerlessness and objective information concerning nature of illness among patients in hospital settings.

M. Seeman and J. Evans, "On the Personal Consequences of Alienation in Work," *American Sociological Review* 32 (April 1967): 273–85, report the following correlation between powerlessness and anomie for nonmanual workers and manual workers in Sweden:

	Manual workers	Nonmanual workers
Anomie	$.37P < .01$	$.39P < .01$
Expert Orientation	$.13P < .05$	$.29P < .01$
Mobility Attitude	$.15P < .05$	$.14$
Prejudice	$.24P < .01$	$.29P < .01$

Each of the seven items is scored dichotomously and the scores are summed. The powerlessness response is scored as "1" and the alternate response is scored as "0." A reproducibility coefficient of .87 (Guttman Scalogram Technique) was obtained for a community-wide sample (Columbus, Ohio) of 604 respondents.

RESEARCH APPLICATIONS:

BULLOUGH, BONNIE. "Alienation in the Ghetto." *American Journal of Sociology* 72 (March 1967): 469.

GROAT, THEODORE, and NEAL, ARTHUR G. "Social Psychological Correlates of Urban Fertility," *American Sociological Review* 32 (December 1967): 945–49.

NEAL, ARTHUR G. "Stratification Concomitants of Powerlessness and Normlessness: A Study of Political and Economic Alienation." Ph.D. dissertation, Ohio State University, Columbus, 1959.

———, and RETTIG, SOLOMON. "Dimensions of Alienation Among Manual and Non-Manual Workers." *American Sociological Review* 28 (August 1963): 599–608.

———. "On the MultiDimensionality of Alienation." *American Sociological Review* 32 (February 1967): 54–63.

SEEMAN, MELVIN. "On the Personal Consequences of Alienation in Work." *American Sociological Review* 32 (April 1967): 273–85.

———. "Alienation and Social Learning in a Reformatory." *American Journal of Sociology* 69 (November 1963): 270–84.

———, and EVANS, JOHN. "Alienation and Learning in a Hospital Setting." *American Sociological Review* 27 (December 1962): 772–82.

THE POWERLESSNESS SCALE*

(Respondent chooses between the 7 pairs of statements)

1. _____ I think we have adequate means for preventing runaway inflation.
    _____ There's very little we can do to keep prices from going higher.

2. _____ Persons like myself have little chance of protecting our personal interests when they conflict with those of strong pressure groups.
    _____ I feel that we have adequate ways of coping with pressure groups.

3. _____ A lasting world peace can be achieved by those of us who work toward it.
    _____ There's very little we can do to bring about a permanent world peace.

---

* These seven items were derived from a larger "internal-external control" scale by Neal and Seeman; cf. J. B. Rotter, "Generalized Expectancies for Internal vs. External Control of Reinforcements," *Psychological Monographs* 80, no. 1 (Whole #609, 1966): 1–28.

4. _____ There's very little persons like myself can do to improve world opinion of the United States.

_____ I think each of us can do a great deal to improve world opinion of the United States.

5. _____ This world is run by the few people in power, and there is not much the little guy can do about it.

_____ The average citizen can have an influence on government decisions.

6. _____ It is only wishful thinking to believe that one can really influence what happens to society at large.

_____ People like me can change the course of world events if we make ourselves heard.

7. _____ More and more, I feel helpless in the face of what's happening in the world today.

_____ I sometimes feel personally to blame for the sad state of affairs in our government.

KAHL'S ACHIEVEMENT ORIENTATION SCALE 4.J.2

VARIABLE MEASURED: "It is an index of a generalized motivation to do well, to excell in a variety of tasks."

DESCRIPTION: It is composed of four scales derived through the use of factor analysis from a series of studies in the United States, Mexico, and Brazil. The four scales were: (1) Occupational primacy, "occupational success [is placed] ahead of alternative possibilities." In Mexico and Brazil this scale was used with three items. (2) Trust, "belief in the stability of life and the trustworthiness of people." Composed of six items. (3) Activism, "emphasizes planning for a controllable future." Composed of seven items. (4) Integration with relatives, "loyalty to parents instead of to self or to career." Composed of three items.

WHERE PUBLISHED: Joseph A. Kahl, "Some Measurements of Achievement Orientation," *American Journal of Sociology* 70 (May 1965): 669–81; and his book, *The Measurement of Modernism: A Study of Values in Brazil and Mexico* (Austin, Texas: University of Texas Press, 1968).

RELIABILITY: Not known from the original study, but inferred from Michael A. LaSorte's Ph.D. dissertation, which used similar scales. Applying the Spearman-Brown prophecy formula for correction, the reliability coefficients were occupational primacy, .81, trust, .94, mastery (activism), .94, and familism (which departs significantly from the integration with relatives), .86.

VALIDITY: Trust, activism, and independence from family scales are positively correlated with an index of socioeconomic status (based on occupation, education, and self-identification); occupational primacy is negatively correlated with the others and with status:

	Brazil	Mexico
Trust	.30	.26
Activism	.42	.49
Occupational (primacy)	−.20	−.09
Integration with relatives	−.30	−.46

ADMINISTRATION OF THE SCALE: Positive and negative items should be intermingled to avoid "halo" or "acquiescence effects."

UTILITY: Can be administered in 15 minutes. Although Kahl constructed the scale for use in developing countries, it may be applied widely in developed countries with many different age or minority groups

SCORING: All questions have four possible answers as stated on the scale form when administered: These are: Agree very much; Agree a little; Disagree a little; Disagree very much. Each of the answers is scored in the order shown as 4, 3, 2, 1 whenever a factor loading is positive (e.g., by items 4, 12, 13, 14, 15, 16, 17, 18, 19, 20). The scoring is reversed to 1, 2, 3, 4 when factor loadings are negative (e.g., items 1, 2, 3, 5, 6, 7, 8, 9, 10, 11).

Each number is weighted by the loading shown by the factor analysis for that particular scale. This gives the most weight to the "best" items— those most closely related to the underlying dimension. In *The Measurement of Modernism* (pp. 29–35) Kahl reports that *unweighted scores would not change* the rank order of respondents by much.

RESEARCH APPLICATIONS:

Cox, Henrietta. "Study of Social Class Variations in Value Orientations in Selected Areas of Mother-Child Behavior." Ph.D. dissertation, Washington University, St. Louis, 1964.

Kahl, Joseph A. "Urbanizacão e Mudancas Occupacionais no Brasil." *America Latina* 5 (October 1962): 21–30.

———. "Some Measurements of Achievement Orientation." *American Journal of Sociology* 70 (May 1965): 669–81.

LaSorte, Michael Antonio. "Achievement Orientation and Community of Orientation." Ph.D. dissertation, Indiana University, Bloomington, 1967.

Scanzoni, John. "Socialization, Achievement, and Achievement Values." *American Sociological Review* 32 (June 1967): 449–56.

Sewell, William H.; Hauser, Robert M.; Featherman, David L., eds. *Schooling and Achievement in American Society.* New York: Academic Press, 1976.

The serious student should read the communication between Wallace D. Loh, Harry J. Crockett, Jr., Clyde Z. Nunn, and John Scanzoni over the relation of socialization practices and occupational achievement values. See *American Sociological Review* 33 (April 1968): 284–91.

For another important scale that incorporates occupational aspiration, see David Horton Smith and Alex Inkeles, "The OM Scale: A Comparative Socio-Psychological Measure of Individual Modernity," *Sociometry* 29 (December 1966): 353–77. Cf. A. O. Haller and I. W. Miller, *The Occupational Aspiration Scale: Theory, Structure, and Correlates* (2nd ed.; Cambridge, Mass.: Schenkman, 1971). See also Murray A. Straus, "Deferred Gratification, Social Class, and the Achievement Syndrome," *American Sociological Review* 27 (April 1962): 552–53.

KAHL'S INDEX OF ACHIEVEMENT ORIENTATION

(Scale Items Show Factor Loadings)

TRUST

	Mexico	Brazil	
1.	−.66	−.78	It is not good to let your relatives know everything about your life, for they might take advantage of you.
2.	−.71	−.74	It is not good to let your friends know everything about your life, for they might take advantage of you.
3.	−.67	−.55	Most people will repay your kindness with ingratitude.
4.	+.38		Most people are fair and do not try to get away with something.
5.	−.62		People help persons who have helped them not so much because it is right but because it is good business.
6.	−.40		You can only trust people whom you know well.

ACTIVISM

	Mexico	Brazil	
7.	−.63	−.74	Making plans only brings unhappiness because the plans are hard to fulfill.
8.	−.58	−.65	It doesn't make much difference if the people elect one or another candidate for nothing will change.
9.	−.67	−.63	With things as they are today an intelligent person ought to think only about the present, without worrying about what is going to happen tomorrow.
10.	−.54	−.57	We Brazilians (Mexicans) dream big dreams, but in reality we are inefficient with modern industry.
11.	−.61	−.47	The secret of happiness is not expecting too much out of life, and being content with what comes your way.
12.	+.46		It is important to make plans for one's life and not just accept what comes.
13.	+.41		How important is it to know clearly in advance your plans for the future? (*Very important* is coded positively.)

OCCUPATIONAL PRIMACY

	Mexico	Brazil	
14.	+.59	+.69	The job should come first, even if it means sacrificing time from recreation.
15.	+.64	+.59	The best way to judge a man is by his success in his occupation.
16.	+.80	+.62	The most important qualities of a real man are determination and driving ambition.
17.		+.46	The most important thing for a parent to do is to help his children get further ahead in the world than he did.

INTEGRATION WITH RELATIVES

	Mexico	Brazil	
18.	+.73	+.76	When looking for a job, a person ought to find a position in a place located near his parents, even if that means losing a good opportunity elsewhere.
19.	+.78	+.75	When you are in trouble, only a relative can be depended upon to help you out.
20.	+.65	+.64	If you have the chance to hire an assistant in your work, it is always better to hire a relative than a stranger.

4.J.3 MILLER'S SCALE BATTERY OF INTERNATIONAL PATTERNS AND NORMS

VARIABLE MEASURED: Norms and patterns of national cultures.

DESCRIPTION: It consists of a scale battery of twenty rating scales to ascertain important norms and patterns within national cultures: (1) social acceptance; (2) standards of personal and community health; (3) concern for and trust of others; (4) confidence in personal security and protection of property; (5) family solidarity; (6) independence of the child; (7) moral code and role definitions of men and women; (8) definition of religion and moral conduct; (9) class structure and class consciousness; (10) consensus on general philosophy and objectives of the society; (11) labor's orientation to the prevailing economic and social system; (12) belief in democratic political system; (13) definition of work and individual achievement; (14) civic participation and voluntary activity; (15) definition of the role of private and public ownership of property. Five more scales are under development with tests in United States, England, and Spain already completed. All rating scales have six positions ranging between two contrasting poles.

WHERE PUBLISHED: Delbert C. Miller, "The Measurement of International Patterns and Norms: A Tool for Comparative Research," *Southwestern Social Science Quarterly* 48 (March 1968): 531–47; Delbert C. Miller, "Measuring Cross National Norms: Methodological Problems in Identifying Patterns in Latin American and Anglo-Saxon Cultures," *International Journal of Comparative Sociology* 13, nos. 3–4 (September–December 1972): 201–16. See also D. C. Miller, *International Community Power Structures, Comparative Studies of Four World Cities* (Bloomington: Indiana University, 1970).

RELIABILITY: Test-retest correlations for the fifteen scales range from .74 to .97 as tested in the United States and Peru. Most scales have reliabilities of .90 and above.

VALIDITY: Three criteria for validity have been met. These are: (1) the mean difference on each rating scale is 2.00 or more when the United States and Peru are rated and compared; (2) average deviation of each scale shows a dispersion less than 1.00 when United States and Peru are rated; (3) judges' rankings permit a structuring of significant variations in the social patterning of the United States and Peru. Extended research in Argentina, Spain, England, and the United States reinforces these tests of validity.

UTILITY: Scales are rated by qualified judges who have experience in two or more national cultures. The rating requires approximately 30 minutes. The scales may be applied to numerous problems of cross-cultural research including the impact of a foreign culture on the stranger. The use of foreign and native judges rating the same two national cultures in which they have both had extensive experience reveals the significance of cross-cultural differences. Ratings can be made of national cultures by raters who had had no previous experience to examine stereotyping. The relation of the class position of the respondent offers the possibility of revealing international differences when viewed from varying class or racial positions occupied by the respondent in the national society.

COMPARATIVE SCORES: The mean scores shown for the rating scales on the seven samples may be used for comparative study.

RESEARCH APPLICATIONS: Delbert C. Miller, *International Community Power Structures, Comparative Studies of Four World Cities* (Bloomington: Indiana University Press, 1970), pp. 228–56. Chapter 14, "The Role of Values in International Decision Making: Anglo-American vs. Latin American Differences," reports on a test of the hypothesis that respondent exposure to any two countries in Latin America are more alike in cultural patterning than any Latin American country compared with the United States. Comparisons with samples in Spain and England are also reported to establish identity of Anglo-Saxon and Ibero-Latin American cultures. Ratings were made using panels of judges, both foreign and native, in Peru, Argentina, United States, Spain, and England. Studies have been made also with American university students who go abroad to study. Before-and-after ratings of their own country and the host country have been secured.

Teresa Camacho de Pinto has completed research on Colombia; her report of respondent ratings is shown in table 1. Paul D. Starr has completed a study in Lebanon to provide a valuable Middle East comparison and perspective. See "Social Patterns and Norms in Lebanon and the United States," *Human Relations* 26, no. 4 (1976): 357–66.

New scales have been added to the original fifteen to include: (1) degree of honesty and integrity in government; (2) degree of nepotism in business, governmental and organizational life generally; (3) degree of expected reciprocity in favors and rewards; (4) encouragement of foreign enterprise; (5) degree to which foreign enterprise is believed to influence the host government. The scales and scores are shown for the United States and Spain in the following test battery.

Applying Scales: Instructions to the Judge

(A qualified judge is a college graduate, especially trained to appraise his own country and with six months or more consecutive experience with the host country. He must be able to read and speak the language of the host country.)

Each characteristic has been placed on a scale of six points. The descriptions defining the scale are shown at 1 and 2, 3 and 4, and 5 and 6. Thus, the first characteristic, social acceptance, attributes highest social acceptance to number 1 position and lowest social acceptance to the number 6 position. The range between represents a continuum of different degrees of the characteristic.

Task 1. Establish anchor points for each scale by selecting countries from anywhere in the world that reflect the extreme positions of the scale for social acceptance. These countries may or may not be known to you personally. In making a selection *think of the way the pattern appears on the average*

Table 1

Scale of International Patterns and Norms	U.S.[a] (1966) N = 21	U.S.[b] (1968) N = 32	Spain[c] (1968) N = 17	Argen-tina[d] (1967) N = 15	Peru[e] (1966) N = 21	England[f] (1968) N = 15	Colom-bia[g] (1969) N = 10
1. Social Acceptance	1.7	1.6	3.1	3.2	4.5	4.0	4.2
2. Personal and Community Health	1.4	1.9	3.2	2.9	4.7	3.1	4.4
3. Concern and Trust of Others	1.8	2.7	4.1	3.3	4.9	2.0	4.3
4. Personal Security and Protection of Property	2.3	3.7	2.2	3.5	5.0	2.1	5.7
5. Family Solidarity	5.4	4.0	2.3	2.7	1.9	2.9	1.8
6. Independence of the Child	1.3	2.1	4.5	2.8	4.4	2.1	4.4
7. Moral Code and Role Definition	2.0	2.3	4.6	2.8	4.9	3.4	4.9
8. Religion and Moral Conduct	4.6	4.3	2.6	3.7	2.1	4.6	2.6
9. Class Structure and Consciousness	5.0	4.9	2.1	3.1	1.4	3.1	1.8
10. Societal Consensus	1.6	2.1	5.0	3.9	4.6	2.1	3.9
11. Labor's Orientation	5.3	5.4	2.3	2.7	3.1	4.0	2.7
12. Democratic Belief	1.4	1.8	4.6	2.8	3.7	2.1	3.8
13. Work and Achievement	1.5	2.1	4.0	3.1	4.8	3.1	4.2
14. Civic Participation	1.2	1.9	4.8	3.6	4.8	3.1	4.2
15. Role of Property	1.2	1.7	3.1	3.6	3.3	3.3	2.7
16. Honesty of Government Officials		1.8	3.5			1.3	
17. Political Influence of Foreign Enterprise		5.2	3.8			5.3	
18. Encouragement of Foreign Enterprise		2.2	2.5			2.3	
19. Nepotism in Organizations		4.8	1.5			4.0	
20. Reciprocity of Favors		3.9	1.5			5.0	

[a] American raters.
[b] American raters.
[c] Spanish raters in Madrid, Barcelona, and Seville.
[d] Argentine raters. (Data gathered by Judson Yearwood.)
[e] American raters living in Peru.
[f] Englishmen living in London, Liverpool, and Bristol, England.
[g] Colombian raters. (Data gathered by Dr. Teresa Camacho de Pinto.)

throughout the country and as it is experienced by a person in the middle sector of society—i.e., omitting the very rich and the very poor. When the selection has been made, write the names of the countries in the answer sheets. Proceed to select countries representing the extremes of all 19 remaining characteristics—i.e., standards of health, standards of personal and community health, etc. Write the names on the answer sheets.

Task 2. Now place the two countries in their proper positions on all 20 characteristics. Again, think of the pattern as it appears on the average throughout the country and as it is experienced by a person in the middle sector of society—i.e., omitting the very rich and the very poor. Write answers on answer sheet.

Task 3. Place a third country on the scale if you have lived six months or more within it. Write answers on answer sheet.

MILLER'S SCALE BATTERY OF INTERNATIONAL PATTERNS AND NORMS

Delbert C. Miller

Respondent: Kindly check if you are male or female and indicate years lived in native country and in other countries. Sign your name and give your address if you wish a final report. Read the accompanying directions carefully before you begin. Thank you.

Check: Male ___ Female ___

Years lived in:

Native Country _____

Other Countries _____

_____

_____

(Optional)

Name: _____

Address: _____

_____

_____

1. Social acceptance

1	2	3	4	5	6

High social acceptance. Social contacts open and nonrestrictive. Introductions not needed for social contacts. Short acquaintance provides entry into the home and social organizations.	Medium social acceptance. Ready acceptance in neighborhood and in community organizations but not in family and social life. Friendly in business and other public contacts.	Low social acceptance. Acceptance in specifically designated groups in which membership has been validated. Sponsored introduction is needed for social contacts in all parts of community life.

2. Standards of personal and community health

1	2	3	4	5	6

High standards of personal and community hygiene. Hygienic habits valued in all parts of society.	Varied. High community standards for water and sewage. Personal habits and community standards for cleanliness and hygiene vary widely across the community.	Personal and community standards of hygiene are not valued highly.

3. Concern for and trust of others

1	2	3	4	5	6

High concern for others. Respect for the motives and integrity of others. Mutual trust prevails.	Moderate or uneven pattern of concern for and trust of others.	Lack of concern for others and lack of trust.

4. Confidence in personal security and protection of property

1	2	3	4	5	6

High confidence in personal security. Free movement, night and day, for both sexes. High sense of security of property. Locking of homes is optional.	Moderate confidence in personal security. Confidence of men is high in personal security but women are warned to take precautions. Movements of women restricted to daytime. Simple property precautions essential.	Low confidence in both personal security and protection of property. Men and women restrict all movement at night to predetermined precautions. Many property precautions obligatory. Extensive use of locks, dogs, and guards.

5. Family solidarity

1	2	3	4	5	6

High solidarity with many obligations of kinship relations within large, extended family system.	Relations of solidarity within a limited kinship circle with specified obligations only.	Small, loosely integrated, independent family with highly specific individual relations.

6. Independence of the child

1	2	3	4	5	6

Child is raised to be self-reliant and independent in both thought and action.	Child is given specified areas of independence only.	Child is raised to be highly dependent and docile.

7. Moral code and role definitions of men and women

1	2	3	4	5	6

Single code of morality prevails for men and women. Separate occupational and social roles are not defined for men and women. Similar amounts and standards of education prevail.	Variations between moral definitions for men and women exist for certain specified behaviors. Occupational and social role definitions vary in degree. Varying educational provisions for the sexes.	Double code of morality prevails. Separate occupational and social roles for men and women exist and are sharply defined. Amount and standards of education vary widely between the sexes.

8. Definition of religion and moral conduct

1	2	3	4	5	6

Belief in the sacred interpretation of life as primary explanation of purpose of life and role of death. Emphasis is placed on importance of worshiper role in fulfilling spiritual obligations and duties.	Belief in supreme being a sacred purpose for life. Emphasis is placed on secular interpretation of moral values and importance of applying them to daily conduct.	Belief in secular interpretation of life. Emphasis on importance of achieving the good society for achieving the good life. Moral values prescribed by social and scientific definitions of human well being in the society. Emphasis on social conduct as moral conduct.

9. Class structure and class consciousness

1	2	3	4	5	6

Highly conscious of class differences. Extensive use of status symbols. Social classes and social circles rigidly defined. Very small upward class movement. Contacts between classes limited by social distinctions. Private schools predominate for upper social groups.	Class consciousness prevails moderately. Upward class movement occurs but definite characteristics mark off and limit contact between classes.	Class consciousness low. Class differences devalued. Minimal use of status symbols. Considerable upward class movement. Relatively free social contacts between social classes. Public schools dominate for all social classes.

10. Consensus over general philosophy and objectives of the society

1	2	3	4	5	6

High consensus over philosophy and objectives of the society as achieved either through evolution or revolution. Competition and conflict between parties takes place within generally accepted goals of the society. Stable governments usually prevail.	Consensus is partial. Differing ideological systems conflict. Stable government may be maintained but under threat of overthrow.	Absence of consensus (or very low) over philosophy and objectives of the society. Conflicting and splinter parties may represent the divergent ideologies and cleavages. Unstable governments prevail.

11. *Labor's orientation to the prevailing economic and social system*

1	2	3	4	5	6

Highly alienated. Ideologically opposed to the prevailing economic and social system. Revolutionary in orientation.

Antagonistic. Partly alienated with some unions ideologically in support and some in opposition to prevailing economic and social system.

Highly assimilated. Ideologically in agreement with prevailing economic and social system. Labor disputes over distribution shares of goods and services to working people but accepts on-going system.

12. *Belief in democratic political system*

1	2	3	4	5	6

Strongly committed. Deep and persistent belief in the democratic processes regardless of problems or crisis.

Reserved commitment. Belief in democracy as process requiring careful control against mass abuse. Accepts necessity of dictatorial intervention in crisis situations or special safeguard such as one-party systems, relinquishing freedoms in internal crises, etc.

Lack of belief in democracy as political system. Regarded as weak and ineffectual in the solving of problems and improving the lot of the average man. Generally regarded as dangerous because it exposes government to mob psychology.

13. *Definition of work and individual achievement*

1	2	3	4	5	6

A belief in hard work as obligation to self, employer, and God. Efficiency values accepted. Individual is expected to progress in his work life.

Work is important to the advancement of self and family. Efficiency values accepted. Achievement expectations vary.

Lack of belief in hard work. Work is regarded as necessary, but involves no obligation beyond delivery of minimum services. Efficiency values rejected. Individual is expected only to maintain family status at his inherited level.

14. *Civic participation and voluntary activity*

1	2	3	4	5	6

High civic activity. People work together to get things done for the community. High identity with volunteer groups. Civic participation and volunteer activity in groups is an important source of social prestige. Moral and altruistic motives are important sources of motivation.

Moderate activity in special areas. Organized participation exists for economic or political self-interest but often is lacking for a general community need.

Low civic activity, often deliberately avoided with no social sanctions. Low identity with volunteer groups. Civic participation is not an important source of prestige. Mistrust of motives is common since self-interest is generally assumed as the principle motivation for all persons.

15. *Definition of the role of private and public ownership of property*

1	2	3	4	5	6

Strong belief in the right of private property for all persons in all types of goods. Private ownership and control of means of production is accepted for all industries and services except for a few natural monopolies (i.e., water, post office, etc.)

Belief in the wide mixture of private ownership and public ownership in all industries and services. Public ownership of large basic industries (steel, coal, electricity, etc.) and services (transport and communication) is especially common.

Strong belief in the public ownership and governmental controls of all industries and services except for small enterprises. Private ownership accepted in the ownership of personal goods.

16. Standards of honesty and integrity of government officials

1	2	3	4	5	6

Government officials at all levels have a high standard of honesty and integrity. Violations are prosecuted vigorously and punished with appropriate penalties.

Government officials are generally honest but there are differences in the honesty of officials at different levels. Violations do occur and are prosecuted. The certainty of detection and the severity of penalty varies according to differing practices.

Government officials at all levels commonly engage in various kinds of corrupt practices. Most violations are seldom prosecuted. Occasionally token prosecutions are made when abuse becomes excessive.

17. Political influence of foreign enterprise on host government

1	2	3	4	5	6

Foreign enterprise has marked political influence on major economic and political policies of the nation. It can resist attempted nationalization of its own enterprises and enforce favorable trade and political relations.

Foreign enterprise does have significant political influence over certain economic conditions of its special concern, but it has no real influence over political policy and process within the host country.

Foreign enterprise has no real influence over national policies—economic or political. Host government may enforce strict control over all foreign enterprise but often permits foreign enterprise to operate within same set of guidelines as domestic firms.

18. Encouragement of foreign enterprise

1	2	3	4	5	6

All foreign enterprise is strongly encouraged to invest and operate business of all kinds throughout the country.

Selected forms of foreign investment are encouraged. Use of foreign management personnel may be discouraged.

Foreign investment and operation of enterprise is discouraged by official and unofficial means.

19. Degree of nepotism in organizational life

1	2	3	4	5	6

Family members of owners, managers, clerical, and manual workers are given preferential and sometimes privileged opportunities for employment in all types of organizations.

Family members of owners, managers, and professionals are given priority within organizations owned or managed by their relatives.

Merit and training is the sole basis for selection of all persons in all types of organizations.

20. Degree of expected reciprocity in favors and rewards

1	2	3	4	5	6

Pattern of expected reciprocity in favors prevails in regard to economic or political support given to individual or group. Personal basis of contact is encouraged and reciprocity is expected by a returned favor (or gift) in near future.

Reciprocity is expected only in specific situations when both parties have a written an oral agreement to exchange political and social support for services rendered.

No pattern of expected reciprocity prevails in economic or political life. Favors or special gifts for service and business rendered is regarded as self-serving and "wrong."

Family and Marriage

The Marriage-Prediction Schedule and the Marriage-Adjustment Schedule are products of intensive research efforts led by Ernest W. Burgess and his associates and aided by many social researchers who have been seeking factors associated with success or failure in marriage.

The Marriage-Prediction Schedule is used in assessing the probabilities of engaged couples to be able to establish happy marital adjustment if they should marry.

The Marriage-Adjustment Schedule is for married couples. It can be used as a diagnostic instrument to help the marriage counselor detect the social areas where difficulties exist. The researcher may use it to assess new relationships such as the role of parent-child relations and marital adjustment.

MARRIAGE-PREDICTION SCHEDULE AND MARRIAGE-ADJUSTMENT SCHEDULE

4.K.1

VARIABLE MEASURED: The marital prediction schedule predicts the statistical probabilities of success in marriage; the marriage adjustment schedule is predictive of adjustment in marriage.

DESCRIPTION: The marital adjustment schedule was the first schedule developed. Five hundred twenty-six Illinois couples who had been married one to six years were studied. Marital adjustment was defined as (1) agreement between husband and wife upon matters that might be made critical issues; (2) common interests and joint activities; (3) frequent overt demonstrations of affection and mutual confidence; (4) few complaints; (5) few reports of feeling lonely, miserable, irritable, and so on. Items classified under these five headings serve as indicators of marital adjustment. Each of the items shows a measurable relationship to the ratings given by the couples to their expressed happiness rating of their marriage. For the development of the marital adjustment schedule see E. W. Burgess and Leonard S. Cottrell, *Predicting Success or Failure in Marriage* (Englewood Cliffs, N.J.: Prentice-Hall, 1939). Cf. Nathan Hurvitz, "The Measurement of Marital Strain," *American Journal of Sociology* 65 (May 1960): 610–15.

The marital prediction schedule was developed by seeking items predictive of marriage adjustment among 1000 engaged couples. Selected background items significantly associated with marital adjustment were combined into an expectancy table for premarital prediction of success in marriage. For the development of the marital prediction schedule see Ernest W. Burgess and Paul Wallin, *Engagement and Marriage* (Philadelphia: Lippincott, 1953).

WHERE PUBLISHED: Ernest W. Burgess and Harvey J. Locke, *The Family,* 2nd ed. (New York: American Book, 1960), pp. 693–716. Contains the refined version of the schedules based upon approximately 25 years of research.)

RELIABILITY: Husband-wife adjustment scores correlated with $r = .88$. ($N = 526$ couples.)

VALIDITY:
Happiness ratings and adjustment scores correlated .92. ($N = 526$ couples.)
Second sample of 63 cases showed correlation between happiness ratings and adjustment scores of .95.
Correlation between happiness ratings and absence of marital disorganization, divorce, separation, and contemplation of divorce or separation. $r = .89$.
Harvey Locke computed Burgess-Cottrell Adjustment scores for divorced men, divorced women, happily married men, and happily married women. Correlations between scores attained in this way and scores from the 29 questions in his test were respectively, .83, .87, .85, and .88.
Burgess and Wallin gave an adjustment test to 1000 engaged couples, and then, three years after marriage, gave a marital adjustment test to as many couples as could be contacted. Correlation between adjustment scores of engaged couples was .57; three years after marriage, marital adjustment scores of 505 husbands and wives correlated .41. See Lewis M. Terman and Paul Wallin, "The Validity of Marriage Prediction and Marital Adjustment Tests," *American Sociological Review* 14 (August 1949): 497–504; Harvey J. Locke and Robert G. Williamson, "Marriage Adjustment: A Factor Analysis Study," *American Sociological Review* 23 (October 1958): 562–69.

Scoring the Marriage-Prediction and Marriage-Adjustment Schedules

The narrow columns at the right side of each page of the Marriage-Prediction Schedule and the Marriage-Adjustment Schedule are provided for scoring the replies to the questions. The score values assigned are arbitrary in the sense that usually each gradation in reply differs by one point. Although arbitrary, the score values are in general conformity with the findings of the studies in this field, particularly those of E. W. Burgess and L. S. Cottrell, *Predicting Success or Failure in Marriage;* L. M. Terman and Others, *Psychological Factors in Marital Happiness;* E. W. Burgess and Paul Wallin, *Engagement and Marriage;* and Harvey J. Locke, *Predicting Adjustment in Marriage: A Comparison of a Divorced and a Happily Married Group.*
   The two-digit numbers after each subdivision of the questions provide the code for scoring the replies. The score value of each response is obtained simply by adding together the two digits in the number that is a subscript

under the last letter of the final word of the response that has been checked. For example, if you have checked a response numbered 42, your score for that item is $4 + 2 = 6$. To obtain your total score, follow these steps:

1. For each item, enter in Column 1 at the right-hand side of each page the two-digit number that appears as a subscript under the last letter of the final word of the answers to each question. An example is: What is your present state of health? chronic ill-health (13) _____ ; temporary ill-health (23) _____ ; average health (15) _____ ; healthy (25) _____ ; very healthy (17) _____ . If your answer to this question is "average health," then write 15 in Column 1.

   In Part Two of the Marriage-Prediction Schedule, put only the score of your fiancé(e) in the blank on the right-hand margin.

2. Enter in Column 2 the sum of the two digits appearing in Column 1 for each item. For each part of the questionnaire, compute the total of the values appearing in Column 2, and enter that figure in the space provided at the end of that section.

3. In scoring Part Two of the Marriage-Adjustment Schedule, multiply the total number of check marks in each of the four columns as follows:

Column A by 6	Column C by 4
Column B by 5	Column D by 6

   Add together the four figures obtained in the four columns. This sum equals your total score for Part Two.

4. Enter the total score for each part in the spaces provided at the end of the questionnaire. Your total score on the inventory equals the sum of the total scores of the separate parts and is your marriage-adjustment score.

Standard Scores

A. Marriage-Prediction Schedule

High scores on the Marriage-Prediction Schedule, those above 630, are favorable for marital adjustment, as indicated by research findings that approximately 75 percent of persons with these scores in the engagement period are well adjusted in their marriages. Low scores, or those below 567, are much less favorable for happiness in marriage, as shown by the probability that only 25 percent of persons with these scores will be well adjusted in married life. Scores between 567 and 630 indicate that there is about a 50 percent change for marital success and about a 50 percent chance for marital failure.

The prediction score of a person and his corresponding matrimonial-risk-group assignment should be interpreted with extreme caution. The following points should be kept in mind:

1. The prediction does not apply directly to the individual. It states the statistical probabilities of marital success for a group of persons of which the individual is one. If he belongs to the lower risk group, in which 75 percent of the marriages turn out unhappily, there is no way of telling by this statistical prediction whether he falls in the 25 percent of the marriages with varying degrees of happiness or in the 75 percent of unhappy unions.

2. The prediction is for an individual's general matrimonial risk irrespective of the particular person to whom he is engaged. The individual's specific matrimonial

risk for marriage to a given person is much more valuable but also more complicated, and therefore not suited for self-scoring.

3. In the majority of cases the specific matrimonial risk of a couple may be roughly estimated from the two general matrimonial-risk groups to which the two persons are assigned. An average of the two scores will generally be close to what may be expected from a specific matrimonial-risk-group assignment.

4. With the aforementioned reservations in mind, a low prediction score should not be taken as indicating lack of suitability for marriage. It should, however, be helpful to the person in stimulating him to secure adequate preparation for marriage, to be more careful in the selection of a marriage partner, and to give attention to the solving of any difficulties in the relation before, rather than after, the marriage.

B. Marriage-Adjustment Schedule

In evaluating the total score secured on the Marriage-Adjustment Schedule, see the following table:

Marriage-Adjustment Scores as Indicative of Adjustment in Marriage

Marital-adjustment scores	Adjustment in marriage
720 and over	Extremely well adjusted
700 to 719	Decidedly well adjusted
680 to 699	Fairly adjusted
660 to 679	Somewhat adjusted
640 to 659	Indifferently adjusted
620 to 639	Somewhat unadjusted
600 to 619	Unadjusted
580 to 599	Decidedly unadjusted
579 and under	Extremely unadjusted

UTILITY: Each form may be filled out in approximately 30 minutes. The measure may be used for both research and counseling purposes. Short marital-adjustment and prediction tests are now available. It is claimed that "with the short tests, measurement or prediction can be accomplished with approximately the same accuracy in a few minutes as ordinarily would require an hour or more with the longer ones." Harvey J. Locke and Karl M. Wallace, "Short Marital-Adjustment and Prediction Tests: Their Reliability and Validity," *Marriage and Family Living* 21 (August 1959): 251–55.

RESEARCH APPLICATIONS:

BOWERMAN, CHARLES. "Adjustment in Marriage, Overall and in Specific Areas." *Sociology and Social Research* 41 (March–April 1957): 257–63.

BURGESS, E. W., and WALLIN, PAUL. "Predicting Adjustment in Marriage from Adjustment in Engagement." *American Journal of Sociology* 49 (1944): 324–30.

HURVITZ, NATHAN. "The Measurement of Marital Strain." *American Journal of Sociology* 65 (May 1960): 610–15.

KARLSSON, GEORG. *Adaptability and Communication in Marriage: A Swedish Predictive Study of Marital Satisfaction.* Uppsala, Sweden: Almquist & Wiksell, 1951.

KING, CHARLES. "The Burgess-Cottrell Method of Measuring Marital Adjustment Applied to a Non-White Southern Urban Population." *Marriage and Family Living* 14 (November 1952): 280–85.

LOCKE, HARVEY J. *Predicting Adjustment in Marriage: A Comparison of a Divorced and a Happily Married Group.* New York: Henry Holt, 1951

———, and KARLSSON, GEORG. "Marital Adjustment and Prediction in Sweden and the United States." *American Sociological Review* 17 (February 1952): 10–17.

———, and KLAUSNER, WILLIAM J. "Marital Adjustment of Divorced Persons in Subsequent Marriages." *Sociology and Social Research* 33 (1948): 97–101.

———, and MACKEPRANG, MURIEL. "Marital Adjustment and the Employed Wife." *American Journal of Sociology* 54 (1949): 536–38.

———, and SNOWBARGER, VERNON A. "Marital Adjustment and Predictors in Sweden." *American Journal of Sociology* 60 (July 1954): 51–53.

———, and WILLIAMSON, ROBERT C. "Marital Adjustment: A Factor Analysis Study." *American Sociological Review* 23 (October 1958): 562–69.

LUCKEY, ELEANORE BRAUN. "Marital Satisfaction and Congruent Self-Spouse Concepts." *Social Forces* 39 (December 1960): 153–57.

NIMKOFF, MEYER F., and GRIGG, C. M. "Values and Marital Adjustment of Nurses." *Social Forces* 37 (October 1958): 67–70.

SCHNEPP, GERALD J. "Do Religious Factors Have Predictive Value?" *Marriage and Family Living* 14 (1952): 301–4.

WILLIAMSON, ROBERT C. "Socio-Economic Factors and Marital Adjustment in an Urban Setting." *American Sociological Review* 19 (April 1954): 213–16.

WINCH, ROBERT F. "Personality Characteristics of Engaged and Married Couples." *American Journal of Sociology* 46 (1941): 686–97.

SCHEDULES FOR THE PREDICTION AND MEASUREMENT OF MARRIAGE ADJUSTMENT

I. Marriage-Prediction Schedule*

Please Read Carefully Before and After Filling Out Schedule.

This schedule is prepared for persons who are seriously considering marriage. Although designed for couples who are engaged or who have a private understanding to be married, it can also be filled out by other persons who would like to know their probability of success in marriage. The value of the findings of the schedule depends upon your frankness in answering the questions.

The following points should be kept in mind in filling out the schedule:

1. Be sure to answer every question.
2. Do not leave a blank to mean a "no" answer.
3. The word "fiancé(e)" will be used to refer to the person to whom you are engaged or are considering as a possible marriage partner.
4. Do not confer with your fiancé(e) on any of these questions.

---

* Reproduced by permission of Ernest W. Burgess, Leonard S. Cottrell, Paul Wallin, and Harvey J. Locke.

	1	2

Part One

1. What is your present state of health? chronic ill-health (13)_____; temporary ill-health (23)_____; average health (15)_____; healthy (25)_____; very healthy (17)_____

2. Give your present marital status: single (35)_____; widowed (43)_____; separated (41)_____; divorced (31)_____

3. Total number of years of schooling completed at present time:

   Grades (22)   High School (32)   College (15)
   1_2_3_4_5_6_7_8_;   1_2_3_4_;   1_2_3_4_;
   graduate of college (25); number of years beyond college in graduate work or professional training (35)_____

4. Work record: regularly employed (17)_____; worked only during vacations and/or only part time while in school (34)_____; none because in school or at home (24)_____; always employed but continually changing jobs (32)_____; irregularly employed (13)_____

5. Are you a church member? yes (16)_____; no (23)_____
   Your activity in church: never attend (40)_____; attend less than once a month (23)_____; once or twice a month (33)_____; three times a month (16)_____; four times a month (26)_____

6. At what age did you stop attending Sunday school or other religious school for children and young people? never attended (31)_____; before 10 years old (23)_____; 11–18 years (42)_____; 19 and over (16)_____; still attending (35)_____

7. How many organizations do you belong to or attend regularly, such as church club, athletic club, social club, luncheon club (like the Rotary, Kiwanis, Lions), fraternal order, college fraternity, college sorority, civic organization, music society, patriotic organization, Y.W.C.A., Y.M.C.A., C.Y.O., Y.M.H.A.? none (22)_____; one (32)_____; two (15)_____; three or more (25)_____

8. What do you consider to have been the economic status of your parents during your adolescence? well-to-do (34)_____; wealthy (43)_____; comfortable (15)_____; meager (32)_____; poor (40)_____

9. What do you consider to be the social status of your parents in their own community? one of the leading families (26)_____; upper class (16)_____; upper-middle class (42)_____; middle class (32)_____; lower-middle class (40)_____; lower class (21)_____; no status as they are dead (33)_____

10. Marital status of your parents: married (both living) (24)_____; separated (41)_____; divorced (31)_____; both dead (15)_____; one dead (specifiy which one) (33)_____

11. Your appraisal of the happiness of your parents' marriage; very happy (36)_____; happy (16)_____; average (24)_____; unhappy (41)_____; very unhappy (31)_____

12. Indicate your attitudes toward your parents on the following scales:
    (1) Your attitude toward your father when you were a child; very strong attachment (35)_____; considerable attachment (25)_____; mild attachment (41)_____; mild hostility (13)_____; considerable hostility (30)_____; very strong hostility (21)_____
    (2) Your present attitude toward your father: very strong attachment (44)_____; considerable attachment (16)_____; mild attachment (23)_____; mild hostility (22)_____; considerable hostility (12)_____; very strong hostility (21)_____; no attitude as he is dead (24)_____

	1	2

(3) Your attitude toward your mother when you were a child: very strong attachment (26)____; considerable attachment (34)____; mild attachment (14)____; mild hostility (31)____; considerable hostility (30)____; very strong hostility (12)____

(4) Your present attitude toward your mother: very strong attachment (17)____; considerable attachment (43)____; mild attachment (32)____; mild hostility (13)____; considerable hostility (21)____; very strong hostility (30)____; no attitude as she is dead (15)____

13. Rate your parents' appraisal of the happiness of their marriage. Write *M* for mother's rating; *F* for father's rating; extraordinarily happy (27)____; decidedly happy (25)____; happy (41)____; somewhat happy (30)____; average (30)____; somewhat unhappy (12)____; unhappy (21)____; decidedly unhappy (30)____; extremely unhappy (12)____

14. Outside your family and kin, how many separated and divorced people do you know personally? none (26)____; one (43)____; two (23)____; three (40)____; four (30)____; five (12)____; six or more (21)____

15. How do you rate your first information about sex? wholesome (16) ____; unwholesome (23)____

Where did you get your first information about sex? from parent (35)____; from wholesome reading (16)____; brother (41)____; sister (41)____; other relative (41)____; other adult or teacher (24) ____; other children (31)____; from pernicious reading (12)____; other (specify) (15)____

Do you consider your present knowledge of sex adequate for marriage? yes (34)____; no (14)____; doubtful (42)____

16. Do you smoke? not at all (26)____; rarely (15)____; occasionally (32)____; often (22)____

17. Do you drink? not at all (35)____; rarely (42)____; occasionally (33)____; often (31)____

(Side column markers for items 13: *M*, *F*; bottom: *T*)

Part Two

Rate the following personality traits of yourself, your fiancé(e), your father, your mother. Write *F* for father, *M* for mother, *S* for fiancé(e), and *Y* for yourself. If either of your parents is dead, rate as remembered. Be sure to rate your father, your mother, your fiancé(e), and yourself on each trait.

Trait	Very much so	Con- siderably	Some- what	A little	Not at all	1	2
Willingly takes responsibility	26	16	6	23	13		
Dominating	13	23	33	16	44		
Irritable	40	14	24	25	17		
Punctual	35	25	15	14	13		
Moody	22	41	51	43	35		
Angers easily	40	50	60	34	26		
Ambitious	13	23	33	25	44		

			1	2

Trait	Very much so	Con- siderably	Some- what	A little	Not at all	1	2
Jealous	31	41	15	16	26		
Sympathetic	17	16	24	32	4		
Easygoing	44	43	42	14	22		
Stubborn	22	14	24	25	17		
Sense of duty	26	25	15	41	31		
Sense of humor	35	34	24	23	22		
Easily hurt	31	23	51	52	35		
Self-confident	44	16	15	14	13		
Selfish	22	23	33	43	44		
Nervous	22	23	24	25	35		
Likes belonging to organizations	26	16	33	41	13		
Impractical	40	14	6	34	17		
Easily depressed	13	5	42	16	26		
Easily excited	31	32	24	7	44		
					T		

Part Three

	1	2

1. What is the attitude of your closest friend or friends to your fiancé(e)? approve highly (25)____; approve with qualification (15)____; are resigned (32)____; disapprove mildly (13)____; disapprove seriously (31)____

2. How many of your present men and women friends are also friends of your fiancé(e)? all (17)____; most of them (25)____; a few (23)____; none (13)____

3. How would you rate the physical appearance of your fiancé(e)? very good looking (35)____; good looking (25)____; fairly good looking (41)____; plain looking (22)____; very plain looking (31)____

4. Do you think your fiancé(e) is spending a disproportionate amount of present income on any of the following (check only one)? clothes (or other personal ornamentation) (13)____; recreation (41)____; hobbies (22)____; food (24)____; rent (33)____; education (16)____; do not think so (35)____

5. With how many of the opposite sex, other than your fiancé(e), have you gone steadily? none (25)____; one (42)____; two (24)____; three or more (15)____

6. Defining friends as something more than mere acquaintances but not necessarily as always having been boon companions, give an estimate of the number of your men friends before going steadily with your fiancé(e): none (31)____; few (14)____; several (24)____; many (34)____; (in round numbers, how many? ____)

7. Estimate the number of your women friends before going steadily with your fiancé(e): none (4)____; few (32)____; several (33)____; many (16)____; (in round numbers, how many? ____)

	1	2

8. Have you ever been engaged before (or had any previous informal understanding that you were to be married)? never (35)____; once (42)____; twice (14)____; three or more times (31)____

9. Give the attitude of your father and mother toward your marriage: both approve (26)____; both disapprove (31)____; one disapproves: (your father (22)____, your mother (31)____)

10. What is your attitude toward your future father-in-law? like him very much (25)____; like him considerably (15)____; like him mildly (32)____; mild dislike (40)____; considerable dislike (12)____; very strong dislike (30)____; no attitude, as he is dead (42)____
mother-in-law: like her very much (34)____; like her considerably (24)____; like her mildly (41)____; mild dislike (22)____; considerable dislike (21)____; very strong dislike (12)____; no attitude, as she is dead (24)____

11. How long have you been keeping company with your fiancé(e)? less than 3 months (13)____; 3 to 5 months (32)____; 6 to 11 months (24)____; 12 to 17 months (25)____; 18 to 23 months (35)____; 24 to 35 months (17)____; 36 months or more (44)____

12. How many months will elapse between your engagement (or time at which you both had a definite understanding that you were to be married) and the date selected for your marriage? less than 3 months (40)____; 3 to 5 months (14)____; 6 to 11 months (33)____; 12 to 17 months (25)____; 18 to 23 months (35)____; 24 or more months (44)____

Part Four

1. Do you and your fiancé(e) engage in interests and activities together? all of them (43)____; most of them (15)____; some of them (23)____; a few of them (31)____; none of them (22)____

2. Is there any interest vital to you in which your fiancé(e) does not engage? yes (31)____; no (43)____

3. Do you confide in your fiancé(e)? about everything (36)____; about most things (16)____; about some things (23)____; about a few things (22)____; about nothing (30)____

4. Does your fiancé(e) confide in you? about everything (27)____; about most things (25)____; about some things (41)____; about a few things (31)____; about nothing (12)____

5. What is the frequency of demonstrations of affection you show your fiancé(e) (kissing, embracing, etc.)? occupies practically all of the time you are alone together (18)____; very frequent (26)____; occasional (14)____; rare (31)____; almost never (12)____

6. Who generally takes the initiative in the demonstration of affection? mutual (26)____; you (23)____; your fiancé(e) (41)____

7. Are you satisfied with the amount of demonstration of affection? yes (35)____; (no: desire less (30)____; desire more (12)____)

8. Is your fiancé(e) satisfied with the amount of demonstration of affection? yes (44)____; (no : desires less (3)____; desires more (30)____)

9. In leisure-time activities: we both prefer to stay at home (26)____; we both prefer to be "on the go" (14)____; one prefers to stay at home and the other to be "on the go" (40)____

10. State the present approximate agreement or disagreement with your fiancé(e) on the following items. Please place a check in the proper column opposite every item.

								1	2
Check one column for each item below	Always agree (35)	Almost always agree (16)	Occa-sionally dis-agree (42)	Fre-quently dis-agree (14)	Almost always dis-agree (22)	Always dis-agree (30)	Never dis-cussed (15)		
Money matters									
Matters of recreation									
Religious matters									
Demonstrations of affection									
Friends									
Table manners									
Matters of conventionality									
Philosophy of life									
Ways of dealing with your families									
Arrangements for your marriage									
Dates with one another									

11. When disagreements arise between you and your fiancé(e) they usually result in: agreement by mutual give and take (53)_____; your giving in (16)_____; your fiancé(e) giving in (30)_____; neither giving in (21)_____

12. Do you ever wish you had not become engaged? never (44)_____; once (14)_____; occasionally (13)_____; frequently (40) _____

13. Have you ever contemplated breaking your engagement? never (35) _____; once (41)_____; occasionally (31)_____; frequently (40)_____

14. Has your steady relationship with your fiancé(e) ever been broken off temporarily? never (61)_____; once (23)_____; twice (40)_____; three or more times (13)_____

15. How confident are you that your marriage will be a happy one? very confident (25)_____; confident (33)_____; a little uncertain (14)_____; very uncertain (40)_____

Part Five

	1	2

1. Where do you plan to be married? at church (35)_____; at home (16) _____; elsewhere (32)_____

2. By whom do you plan to be married? minister, priest, or rabbi (16) _____; other person (14)_____

3. Where do you plan to live after marriage? private house (26)_____; small apartment building (52)_____; large apartment building (15)_____; apartment hotel (41)_____; hotel (22)_____; rooming house (30)_____

	1	2

4. Have bought a home (44)____; plan to buy a home (25)____; plan to rent a home (14)____

5. Population of city or town where you plan to live: open country (27) ____; 2,500 or under (35)____; 2,500 to 10,000 (16)____; 10,000 to 50,000 (42)____; 50,000 to 100,000 (32)____; 100,000 to 500,000 (4)____; over 500,000 (30)____; suburb (17)____

6. After marriage where do you plan to live? in own home (53)____; with your parents (13)____; with parents-in-law (30)____; with other relatives (21)____; with relatives-in-law (3)____; with other persons (12) ____

7. What is your attitude toward having children? desire children very much (25)____; mildly desire them (41)____; mild objection to them (31) ____; object very much to having them (13)____

8. How many children would you like to have? four or more (17)____; three (52)____; two (33)____; one (41)____; none (13)____

9. What is your fiancé(e)'s attitude toward having children? desires children very much (43)____; mildly desires them (14)____; mild objection to them (40)____; objects very much to having them (31)____

(T)

Part I ____, Part II ____, Part III ____, Part IV ____, Part V ____, Total ____

II. Marriage-Adjustment Schedule*

To be Filled Out by Married Persons

This schedule may be filled out by either the husband or the wife. Frank and sincere replies are of the highest importance if the findings are to be of value to the person filling it out or for research purposes. There are no right or wrong answers.

The following points are to be kept in mind in filling out the schedule:

1. Be sure to answer all questions.
2. Do not leave any blanks, as is sometimes done, to signify a "no" reply.
3. The word spouse is used to refer to your husband or wife.
4. Do not confer with your spouse in answering these questions or show your answers to your spouse.

Your Present Marital Status

1. Are you now (check): married____? divorced____? separated____? widowed____?
2. If divorced or separated, how long have you been separated? months____ (If you are divorced or separated, answer the questions as of the time of your separation.)

---

* Reproduced by permission of Ernest W. Burgess, Leonard S. Cottrell, Paul Wallin, and Harvey J. Locke.

Part One

	1	2

1. Present occupation of husband (be as specific as possible) _____
   _____ If unemployed, check here _____
   How satisfied are you, on the whole, with present occupation of husband? If unemployed, answer this question about his usual occupation:
   extremely satisfied (26)_____; very much satisfied (34)_____; satisfied
   (14)_____; somewhat satisfied (40)_____; somewhat dissatisfied (3)_____;
   dissatisfied (21)_____; very much dissatisfied (30)_____; extremely
   dissatisfied (12)_____

2. To what extent were you in love with your spouse before marriage?
   "head over heels" (17)_____; very much (25)_____; somewhat (32)
   _____; a little (22)_____; not at all (13)_____

3. To what extent was your spouse in love with you before your marriage?
   "head over heels" (26)_____; very much (43)_____; somewhat (23)
   _____; a little (40)_____; not at all (22)_____

4. How much conflict (arguments, etc.) was there between you before
   your marriage? none at all (35)_____; a little (43)_____; some (5)_____;
   considerable (31)_____; very much (13)_____

5. To what extent do you think you knew your spouse's faults and weak
   points before your marriage? not at all (44)_____; a little (52)_____;
   somewhat (32)_____; considerably (40)_____; very much (4)_____

6. To what extent do you think your spouse knew your faults and weaknesses before your marriage? not at all (17)_____; a little (43)_____;
   somewhat (41)_____; considerably (22)_____; very much (13)_____

7. What is your attitude toward your father-in-law? like him very much
   (61)_____; considerably (15)_____; somewhat (50)_____; a little (4)_____;
   dislike him a little (30)_____; dislike him somewhat (12)_____; dislike
   him considerably (3)_____; dislike him very much (21)_____; no attitude, as he is dead (24)_____

8. What is your attitude toward your mother-in-law? like her very much
   (25)_____; like her considerably (42)_____; like her somewhat (32)_____;
   like her a little (22)_____; dislike her a little (12)_____; dislike her somewhat (30)_____; dislike her considerably (3)_____; dislike her very much
   (21)_____; no attitude, as she is dead (51)_____

9. What is your attitude to having children? desire children very much
   (16)_____; desire children a good deal (62)_____; desire children somewhat (33)_____; desire children a little (5)_____; desire no children
   (31)_____

10. If children have been born to you, what effect have they had on your
    happiness? added to it very much (27)_____; added to it considerably
    (61)_____; added to it somewhat (14)_____; added to it a little (40)
    _____; have had no effect (30)_____; have decreased it a little (12)_____;
    have decreased it somewhat (21)_____; have decreased it considerably
    (3)_____; have decreased it very much (30)_____; no children (24)_____

11. In leisure-time activities: we both prefer to stay at home (26)_____;
    we both prefer to be "on the go" (41)_____; one prefers to be "on the
    go" and the other to stay at home (22)_____

12. Do you and your spouse engage in outside interests together? all of
    them (44)_____; most of them (51)_____; some of them (14)_____; a
    few of them (40)_____; none of them (22)_____

13. Do you kiss your spouse? every day (62)_____; almost every day (70)
    _____; quite frequently (24)_____; occasionally (32)_____; rarely (13)
    _____; almost never (40)_____

	1	2

14. Do you confide in your spouse? about everything (17)_____; about most things (52)_____; about some things (5)_____; about a few things (13) _____; about nothing (40)_____

15. Does your spouse confide in you? about everything (26)_____; about most things (52)_____; about some things (41)_____; about a few things (4)_____; about nothing (31)_____

16. Are you satisfied with the amount of demonstration of affection in your marriage? yes (25)_____; no: (desire less (22)_____; desire more (13) _____)

17. Is your spouse satisfied with the amount of demonstration of affection? yes (16)_____; no: (desires less (40)_____; desires more (31)_____)

18. How frequently do you "humor" your spouse? frequently (4)_____; occasionally (32)_____; rarely (51)_____; never (16)_____

19. Has your spouse ever failed to tell you the truth? often (22)_____; a few times (14)_____; once (33)_____; never (25)_____

20. If until now your marriage has been at all unhappy, how confident are you that it will work out all right in the future? very confident (32) _____; confident (13)_____; somewhat uncertain (21)_____; very uncertain (30)_____; marriage has not been at all unhappy (15)_____

21. Everything considered, how happy has your marriage been for you? extraordinarily happy (45)_____; decidedly happy (16)_____; happy (50)_____; somewhat happy (13)_____; average (31)_____; somewhat unhappy (3)_____; unhappy (12)_____; decidedly unhappy (30)_____; extremely unhappy (21)_____

22. If your marriage is now at all unhappy, how long has it been so (in months)? less than 3 (23)_____; 3 to 11 (31)_____; 12 or more (12)_____; marriage has not been at all unhappy (33)_____

23. Everything considered, how happy has your marriage been for your spouse? extraordinarily happy (36)_____; decidedly happy (43)_____; happy (32)_____; somewhat happy (4)_____; average (21)_____; somewhat unhappy (30)_____; unhappy (12)_____; decidedly unhappy (3)_____; extremely unhappy (21)_____

24. Indicate your approximate agreement or disagreement with your spouse on the following things. Do this for each item by putting a check in the column that shows extent of your agreement or disagreement.

Check one column for each item below	Always agree (35)	Almost always agree (16)	Occa-sionally dis-agree (42)	Fre-quently dis-agree (23)	Almost always dis-agree (22)	Always dis-agree (12)		
Handling family finances								
Matters of recreation								
Religious matters								
Demonstration of affection								
Friends								
Table manners								

Check one column for each item below	Always agree (35)	Almost always agree (16)	Occasionally disagree (42)	Frequently disagree (23)	Almost always disagree 22)	Always disagree (12)		
Matters of conventionality								
Philosophy of life								
Ways of dealing with your families								
Wife's working								
Intimate relations								
Caring for the baby								
Sharing of household tasks								
Politics								

25. When disagreements arise between you and your spouse they usually result in: agreement by mutual give and take (44)____; your giving in (52)____; your spouse giving in (33)____; neither giving in (40)____

26. Have you ever considered either separating from or divorcing your spouse? have never consider it (26)____; not seriously (61)____; somewhat seriously (40)____; seriously (22)____

27. How many serious quarrels or arguments have you had with your spouse in the past twelve months? none (27)____; one (42)____; two (32)____; three (13)____; four or more (30)____

28. Indicate to what extent you are in love with your spouse by placing a check in one square on the boxed line below, which ranges from extraordinarily in love to somewhat in love:

Extraordinarily in love	A	B	C	D	E	F	G	H	I	J	Somewhat in love
	36	17	25	43	15	33	23	41	40	13	

Indicate by a cross in the above scale the extent to which you think your spouse is in love with you.

29. How does your present love for your spouse compare with your love before marriage? very much stronger (27)____; considerably stronger (52)____; somewhat stronger (24)____; a little stronger (14)____; a little weaker (30)____; somewhat weaker (12)____; considerably weaker (3)____; very much weaker (21)____

30. If you had your life to live over, what do you think you would do? marry the same person: (certainly (35)____; possibly (41)____;) marry a different person (22)____; not marry at all (31)____

31. If your spouse could do it over again, do you think your spouse would marry you? (certainly (44)____; possibly (50)____); marry a different person (13)____; not marry at all (40)____

32. How satisfied, on the whole, are you with your marriage? entirely satisfied (18)____; very much satisfied (52)____; satisfied (23)____; somewhat satisfied (31)____; somewhat dissatisfied (3)____; dissatisfied (12)____; very much dissatisfied (30)____; entirely dissatisfied (21) ____

	1	2
T		

33. How satisfied, on the whole, is your spouse with your marriage? entirely satisfied (45)____; very much satisfied (34)____; satisfied (41)____; somewhat satisfied (22) ____; somewhat dissatisfied (21)____; dissatisfied (30)____; very much dissatisfied (12)____; entirely dissatisfied (3)____

34. Have you ever been ashamed of your spouse? never (44)____; once (14)____; a few times (31)____; often (40)____

35. Even if satisfied with your spouse, have you ever felt that you might have been at all happier if married to another type of person? never (26)____; rarely (41)____; occasionally (22)____; frequently (13)____

36. Do you ever regret your marriage? never (17)____; rarely (50)____; occasionally (13)____; frequently (40)____

Part Two

In responding to the following items, place a check in the appropriate column to the right of each item below.

Check Column A to indicate the things that have occurred in your marriage but have not interfered with your happiness.

Check Column B to indicate those things that have made your marriage less happy than it should have been.

Check Column C to indicate those things that have done most to make your marriage unhappy.

Check Column D if the item was not present in your marriage.

For the husband or wife to fill out	A	B	C	D
	24	32	13	33
Insufficient income				
Poor management of income				
Lack of freedom due to marriage				
Spouse considerably older than I				
Spouse considerably younger than I				
Matters relating to in-laws				
My spouse and I differ in: Education				
Intellectual interests				
Religious beliefs				
Choice of friends				
Preferences for amusements and recreation				
Attitude toward drinking				
Tastes in food				
Respect for conventions				
My spouse: is argumentative				

For the husband or wife to fill out	A	B	C	D
	24	32	13	33
My spouse: is not affectionate				
is narrow-minded				
is not faithful to me				
complains too much				
is lazy				
is quick-tempered				
criticizes me				
spoils the children				
is untruthful				
is conceited				
is easily influenced by others				
is jealous				
is selfish and inconsiderate				
is too talkative				
smokes				
drinks				
swears				

For the husband to fill out (cont.)	A 24	B 32	C 13	D 33
For the husband to fill out				
My wife:				
is slovenly in appearance				
has had much poor health				
is interested in other men				
is nervous or emotional				
neglects the children				
My wife:				
is a poor housekeeper				
is not interested in my business				
is extravagant				
lets her feelings be hurt too easily				
is too interested in social affairs				
has annoying habits and mannerisms				
is a poor cook				
interferes with my business				
For the wife to fill out				
My husband:				
pays attention to other women				
is nervous or impatient				
takes no interest in the children				
is untidy				
is always wrapped up in his business				
gambles				
is touchy				
is not interested in the home				
has vulgar habits				
dislikes to go out with me evenings				
is late to meals				
is harsh with the children				
has poor table manners				

For the husband to fill out (cont.)	A 24	B 32	C 13	D 33
For the husband to fill out				
My wife:				
wants to visit or entertain a lot				
does not have meals ready on time				
interferes if I discipline the children				
tries to improve me				
My wife:				
is a social climber				
is too interested in clothes				
is insincere				
gossips indiscreetly				
nags me				
interferes with my hobbies				
works outside the home				
is fussy about keeping the house neat				
For the wife to fill out				
My husband:				
is tight with money				
has no backbone				
does not talk things over freely				
is rude				
is bored if I tell him of the things that happen in my everyday life				
is unsuccessful in his business				
does not show his affection for me				
gets angry easily				
drinks too much				
has friends I do not approve of				
is constantly nagging and bickering				
lacks ambition				
T				

Part I _____, Part II _____, Total _____

Personality Measurements

Of the hundreds of personality inventories, only two are selected for presentation. These two measures are probably the most widely used personality measures in research today. The Minnesota Multiphasic Personality Inventory is described but not reproduced. It is a battery of scales containing 550 statements. It is thorough and so well constructed that it has generally won the confidence of researchers as the best scale to probe the personality. The research applications included in the description of the instrument attest to its use.[1]

The California F-Scale to measure the authoritarian personality has won high acceptance and has stimulated wide research application.[2]

Of all the personality measures, it was believed the social researcher might find these two scales to be the most useful for his purpose. For a compilation of other measures of personality the following might be consulted:

ANDERSON, HAROLD H., and ANDERSON, GLADYS L. *An Introduction to Projective Techniques and Other Devices for Understanding the Dynamics of Human Behavior.* Englewood Cliffs, N.J.: Prentice-Hall, 1951.

CATTELL, R. B. *Personality and Motivation Structure and Measurement.* New York: World Book, 1957.

GREENE, EDWARD B. *Measurements of Human Behavior.* Rev. ed. New York: Odyssey Press, 1952.

KRECH, DAVID; CRUTCHFIELD, RICHARD S.; and BALACHEY, EGERTON L. *Individual in Society.* New York: McGraw-Hill, 1962.

MEGAREE, E. I. *The California Psychological Inventory Handbook.* San Francisco: Jossey-Bass, 1972.

The Psychological Corporation has a catalog of personality and other psychological tests. This organization distributes such widely used tests as the Minnesota Multiphasic Personality Inventory, California Psychological Inventory, Edward's Personal Preference Schedule; Bernreuter Personality Inventory; Allport, Vernon, and Lindzey's Study of Values; Rorschach Technique; and Murray's Thematic Apperception Test. For a catalog of the Test Division, write The Psychological Corporation, 304 East 45 Street, New York, NY 10017.

Also consult section 4.M.4 for encyclopedic sources of psychological tests.

FOR GENERAL COMPILATIONS OF MMPI

HEDLUND, D. E. "A Review of the MMPI in Industry." *Psychological Reports* 17 (1965): 875–89.

KLEINNUNTZ, B. "Annotated Bibliography of MMPI Research Among College Populations." *Journal of Counseling Psychology* 9 (1962): 373–96.

SWENSON, W. M.; PEARSON, J. S.; and OSBORNE, D. *An MMPI Source Book: Basic Items, Scale, and Pattern Data on 50,000 Medical Patients.* Minneapolis: University of Minnesota Press, 1973.

FOR CROSS CULTURAL MMPI RESEARCH

BUTCHER, JAMES N., and PANCHERI, PAOLO. *A Handbook of Cross-National MMPI Research.* Minneapolis: University of Minnesota, 1976.

Report of extensive international research using the MMPI. The authors discuss basic issues in cross-national research, the adaptation of objective personality instruments for such research, and the cross-national validation of the MMPI. For an extensive bibliography of MMPI research, see pp. 415–51.

NEWER DEVELOPMENTS:

BUTCHER, J. N., ed. *MMPI: Research Developments and Clinical Applications.* New York: McGraw-Hill, 1969.

CARKHUFF, R. R.; BARNETT, L. JR.; and MCCALL, J. N. *The Counselor's Handbook: Scale and Profile Interpretation of the MMPI.* Urbana, Ill.: Parkinson, 1965.

CARSON, R. C. "Interpretative Manual to the MMPI." In *MMPI: Research Developments and Clinical Applications,* edited by J. N. Butcher. New York. McGraw-Hill, 1969.

DAHLSTROM, W. G.; WELSH, G. S.; and DAHLSTROM, L. E. *An MMPI Handbook.* Vol. 2: *Research Applications.* Minneapolis: University of Minnesota Press, 1975.

DUCKWORTH, JANE. *MMPI: Interpretation Manual for Counselors and Clinicians.* 2nd ed. Muncie, Ind.: Accelerated Development, 1979.

Notes

1. Another excellent option is the California Psychological Inventory by Harrison G. Gough, which is sold by Consulting Psychologists Press, Inc., 577 College Avenue, Palo Alto, CA 94306. Convincing evidence exists to validate each of the 18 scales. The CPI has been carefully standardized. It stresses social functioning in contrast to the greater clinical tone of the Minnesota Multiphasic Personality Inventory. For a critique of CPI see Dale G. Lake, Mathew B. Miles, and Ralph B. Earle, Jr., eds., *Measuring Human Behavior* (New York: Teachers College Press, Columbia University, 1973), pp. 37–40.

2. Many researchers prefer the Dogmatism Scale by Milton Rokeach; see his *The Open and Closed Mind* (New York: Basic Books, 1960). Rokeach has sought to devise a measure of general authoritarianism (regardless of ideological content) and general intolerance of those with differing belief systems. The scale has good validity and moderate reliability. It can be recommended for nonclinical use. See Lake et al. *Measuring Human Behavior,* pp. 63–68.

VARIABLE MEASURED: Measures twenty-six areas of personality traits and attitudes.

DESCRIPTION: The MMPI is primarily designed to provide, in a single test, scores on all the more clinically important phases of personality. The instrument itself comprises 550 statements covering a wide range of subject matter, from the physical condition of the individual being tested to his morale and social attitude. For administration of the inventory the subject is asked to respond to all statements, which are in the first person, as True, False, or Cannot Say. The MMPI yields scores on nine scales of personality characteristics indicative of clinical syndromes.

WHERE PUBLISHED: Starke R. Hathaway, *The Minnesota Multiphasic Personality Inventory* (Minneapolis: University of Minnesota, 1942); Starke R. Hathaway and J. Charnley McKinley, *Manual for the Minnesota Multiphasic Personality Inventory,* rev. ed. (New York: Psychological Corporation, 1951); W. Grant Dahlstrom and George Schlager Welsh, *An MMPI Handbook: A Guide to Use in Clinical Practice and Research* (Minneapolis: University of Minnesota, 1960).

RELIABILITY: $r = .71$ to .83. See Starke R. Hathaway and J. Charnley McKinley, *Manual for the Minnesota Multiphasic Personality Inventory,* rev. ed. (New York: The Psychological Corporation, 1951).

See also Harrison G. Gough, "Simulated Patterns on the Minnesota Multiphasic Personality Inventory," *Journal of Abnormal and Social Psychology* 42 (April 1947): 215–25; Charles A. Weisgerber, "The Predictive Value of the Minnesota Multiphasic Personality Inventory with Student Nurses," *Journal of Social Psychology* 33 (February 1951): 3–11.

VALIDITY: Hathaway and McKinley maintain, ". . . the chief criterion of excellence has been the valid prediction of clinical cases against the neuro-psychiatric staff diagnosis, rather than statistical measures of reliability and validity." Hathaway and McKinley, *Manual for the Minnesota Multiphasic Personality Inventory.*

See also:

ALTUS, W. D., and TAFEJIAN, T. T. "MMPI Correlates of the California E-F Scale." *Journal of Social Psychology* 38 (August 1953): 145–49.

BENTON, A. L., and PROBST, K. A. "A Comparison of Psychiatric Ratings with Minnesota Multiphasic Personality Inventory Scores." *Journal of Abnormal and Social Psychology* 41 (January 1946): 75–78.

ELLIS, A. "The Validity of Personality Questionnaires." *Psychological Bulletin* 43 (September 1946): 385–440.

LOUGH, ORPHA M., and GREEN, MARY E. "Comparison of the Minnesota Multiphasic Personality Inventory and the Washburne S-A Inventory as Measures of Personality of College Women." *Journal of Social Psychology* 32 (August 1950): 23–30.

MEEHL, PAUL E., and HATHAWAY, STARKE R. "The K Factor as a Suppressor

Variable in the Minnesota Multiphasic Personality Inventory." *Journal of Applied Psychology* 30 (1946): 525–64.

UTILITY: The inventory is easily administered. The time required varies from 30 to 90 minutes. No supervision is needed beyond that required for the subject to understand clearly the nature of his task and to assure his optimal cooperation.

RESEARCH APPLICATIONS:

ALTUS, WILLIAM D. "A College Achiever and Non-Achiever Scale for the Minnesota Multiphasic Personality Inventory." *Journal of Applied Psychology* 32 (August 1948): 385–97.

———, and TAFEJIAN, T. T. "MMPI Correlates of the California E-F Scale." *Journal of Social Psychology* 38 (August 1953): 145–49.

BENTON, ARTHUR L., and PROBST, KATHRYN A. "A Comparison of Psychiatric Ratings with Minnesota Multiphasic Personality Inventory Scores." *Journal of Abnormal and Social Psychology* 41 (January 1946): 75–78.

BROWER, DANIEL. "The Relation Between Intelligence and Minnesota Multiphasic Personality Inventory Scores." *Journal of Social Psychology* 25 (May 1947): 243–45.

———. "The Relations Between Minnesota Multiphasic Personality Inventory Scores and Cardio-Vascular Measures Before and After Experimentally Induced Visuo-Motor Conflict." *Journal of Social Psychology* 26 (August 1947): 55–60.

BURTON, ARTHUR. "The Use of the Masculinity-Femininity Scale of the Minnesota Multiphasic Personality Inventory as an Aid in the Diagnosis of Sexual Inversion." *Journal of Psychology* 24 (July 1947): 161–64.

CARP, ABRAHAM. "MMPI Performance and Insulin Shock Therapy." *Journal of Abnormal and Social Psychology* 45 (October 1950): 721–26.

CARPENTER, LEWIS G., JR. "An Experimental Test of an Hypothesis for Predicting Outcome with Electroshock Therapy." *Journal of Psychology* 36 (July 1953): 131–35.

CLARK, JERRY H. "Application of the *MMPI* in Differentiating A.W.O.L. Recidivists from Non-Recidivists." *Journal of Psychology* 26 (July 1948): 229–34.

CLARK, J. H. "Grade Achievement of Female College Students in Relation to Non-Intellective Factors: MMPI Items." *Journal of Social Psychology* 37 (May 1953): 275–81.

COFER, C. N.; CHANCE, JUNE; and JUDSON, A. J. "A Study of Malingering on the Minnesota Multiphasic Personality Inventory." *Journal of Psychology* 27 (April 1949): 491–99.

COOK, ELLSWORTH B., and WHERRY, ROBERT J. "A Factor Analysis of MMPI and Aptitude Test Data." *Journal of Applied Psychology* 34 (August 1950): 260–66.

COTTLE, WILLIAM C. "Card Versus Booklet Forms of the MMPI." *Journal of Applied Psychology* 34 (August 1950): 255–59.

DANIELS, E. E., and HUNTER, W. A. "MMPI Personality Patterns for Various Occupations." *Journal of Applied Psychology* 33 (December 1949): 559–65.

DRAKE, LEWIS E. "A Social *I.E.* Scale for the Minnesota Multiphasic Personality Inventory." *Journal of Applied Psychology* 30 (1946): 51–54.

———. "Differential Sex Responses to Items of the MMPI." *Journal of Applied Psychology* 37 (February 1953): 46.

ENGELHARDT, OLGA E. DE C., and ORBISON, WILLIAM D. "Comparison of the Terman-Miles M-F Test and the Mf Scale of the MMPI." *Journal of Applied Psychology* 34 (October 1950): 338–42.

FRY, FRANKLIN D. "A Normative Study of the Reactions Manifested by College Students and by State Prison Inmates in Response to the Minnesota Multiphasic Personality Inventory, the Rozenweig Picture-Frustration Study, and the Thematic Apperception Test." *Journal of Psychology* 34 (July 1952): 27–30.

———. "A Study of the Personality Traits of College Students and of State Prison Inmates as Measured by the Minnesota Multiphasic Personality Inventory." *Journal of Psychology* 28 (October 1949): 439–49.

GOUGH, HARRISON. "A New Dimension of Status: I. The Development of a Personality Scale." *American Sociological Review* 13 (August 1948): 401–9.

———. "A New Dimension of Status: II. Relationship of the *St* Scale to Other Variables." *American Sociological Review* 13 (October 1948): 534–37.

———. "A New Dimension of Status: III. Discrepancies Between the *St* Scale and 'Objective' Status." *American Sociological Review* 14 (April 1949): 275–81.

———. "Simulated Patterns on the Minnesota Multiphasic Personality Inventory." *Journal of Abnormal and Social Psychology* 42 (April 1947): 215–25.

GREENBERG, PAUL, and GILLILAND, A. R. "The Relationship Between Basal Metabolism and Personality." *Journal of Social Psychology* 35 (February 1952): 3–7.

GUTHRIE, GEORGE M. "Six MMPI Diagnostic Profile Patterns." *Journal of Psychology* 30 (October 1950): 317–23.

HAMPTON, PETER J. "The Minnesota Multiphasic Personality Inventory as a Psychometric Tool for Diagnosing Personality Disorders among College Students." *Journal of Social Psychology* 26 (August 1947): 99–108.

HARMON, LINDSEY R., and WIENER, DANIEL N. "Use of the Minnesota Multiphasic Personality Inventory in Vocational Advisement." *Journal of Applied Psychology* 29 (April 1945): 132–41.

HATHAWAY, STARKE R., and MONACHESI, ELIO D. *Analyzing and Predicting Juvenile Delinquency with the MMPI.* Minneapolis: University of Minnesota Press, 1953.

———. "The Minnesota Multiphasic Personality Inventory in the Study of Juvenile Delinquents." *American Sociological Review* 17 (December 1952): 704–10.

LOUGH, ORPHA M. "Teachers College Students and the Minnesota Multiphasic Personality Inventory," *Journal of Applied Psychology* 30 (June 1946): 241–47.

———. "Women Students in Liberal Arts, Nursing, and Teacher Training Curricula and the Minnesota Multiphasic Personality Inventory." *Journal of Applied Psychology* 31 (August 1947): 437–45.

———, and GREEN, MARY E. "Comparison of the Minnesota Multiphasic Personality Inventory and the Washburne S-A Inventory as Measures of Personality of College Women." *Journal of Social Psychology* 32 (August 1950): 23–30.

MACLEAN, A. G., et al. "F Minus K Index on the MMPI." *Journal of Applied Psychology* 37 (August 1953): 315–16.

MASLOW, A. H., et al. "A Clinically Derived Test for Measuring Psychological Security-Insecurity." *Journal of General Psychology* 33 (1945): 21–41.

MEEHL, PAUL E., and HATHAWAY, STARKE R. "The *K* Factor as a Suppressor Variable in the Minnesota Multiphasic Personality Inventory." *Journal of Applied Psychology* 30 (1946): 525–64.

MICHAELIS, JOHN U., and TYLER, FRED T. "MMPI and Student Teaching." *Journal of Applied Psychology* 35 (April 1951): 122–24.

MONACHESI, ELIO D. "Some Personality Characteristics of Delinquents and Non-Delinquents." *Journal of Criminal Law and Criminology* 37 (January-February 1948): 487–500.

NORMAN, RALPH D., and REDLO, MIRIAM. "MMPI Personality Patterns for Various College Major Groups." *Journal of Applied Psychology* 36 (December 1952): 404–9.

SCHMIDT, HERMANN O. "Test Profiles as a Diagnostic Aid: The Minnesota Multiphasic Inventory." *Journal of Applied Psychology* 29 (April 1945): 115–31.

SCHOFIELD, WILLIAM. "A Further Study of the Effects of Therapies on MMPI Responses." *Journal of Abnormal and Social Psychology* 48 (January 1953): 67–77.
———. "A Study of Medical Students with the MMPI: I. Scale Norms and Profile Patterns." *Journal of Psychology* 36 (July 1953): 59–65.
———. "A Study of Medical Students with the MMPI: II. Group and Individual Changes after Two Years." *Journal of Psychology* 36 (July 1953): 137–41.
———. "A Study of Medical Students with the MMPI: III. Personality and Academic Success." *Journal of Applied Psychology* 37 (February 1953): 47–52.
SOPCHACK, ANDREW L. "Parental 'Identification' and 'Tendency Toward Disorders' as Measured by the Minnesota Multiphasic Personality Inventory," *Journal of Abnormal and Social Psychology* 47 (April 1952): 159–65.
TYDLASKA, M., and MENGEL, R. "Scale for Measuring Work Attitude for the MMPI." *Journal of Applied Psychology* 37 (December 1953): 474–77.
TYLER, FRED T., and MICHAELIS, JOHN U. "Comparison of Manual and College Norms for the MMPI." *Journal of Applied Psychology* 37 (August 1953): 273–75.
VERNIAUD, WILLIE MAUDE. "Occupational Differences in the Minnesota Multiphasic Personality Inventory." *Journal of Applied Psychology* 30 (December 1946): 604–13.
WEISGERBER, CHARLES A. "The Predictive Value of the Minnesota Multiphasic Personality Inventory with Student Nurses." *Journal of Social Psychology* 33 (February 1951): 3–11.
WINFIELD, DON L. "The Relationship between IQ Scores and Minnesota Multiphasic Personality Inventory Scores." *Journal of Social Psychology* 38 (November 1953): 299–300.

For a few more recent applications, see section 4.M.1.

Contents of Minnesota Multiphasic Personality Inventory (MMPI)*

1. General health (9 items)
2. General neurologic (19 items)
3. Cranial nerves (11 items)
4. Motility and coordination (6 items)
5. Sensibility (5 items)
6. Vasomotor, trophic, speech, secretory (10 items)
7. Cardio-respiratory system (5 items)
8. Gastro-intestinal system (11 items)
9. Genito-urinary system (5 items)
10. Habits (19 items)
11. Family and marital (26 items)
12. Occupational (18 items)
13. Educational (12 items)
14. Sexual attitudes (16 items)
15. Religious attitudes (19 items)
16. Political attitudes—law and order (46 items)
17. Social attitudes (72 items)
18. Affect, depressive (32 items)
19. Affect, manic (24 items)
20. Obsessive and compulsive states (15 items)
21. Delusions, hallucinations, illusions, ideas of reference (31 items)
22. Phobias (29 items)

* By permission of Hathaway and McKinley and the University of Minnesota Press.

23. Sadistic, masochistic trends (7 items)
24. Morale (33 items)
25. Item primarily related to masculinity-femininity (55 items)
26. Items to indicate whether the individual is trying to place himself in an acceptable light (15 items)

AUTHORITARIAN PERSONALITY (F) SCALE, FORMS 45 AND 40   *4.L.2*

VARIABLE MEASURED: "Authoritarianism" or antidemocratic potential.

DESCRIPTION: The scale consists of thirty items grouped into nine attitudinal categories considered as variables in a personality syndrome. The items are rated on a seven-point scale, from $+3$ to -3, according to the subjects' agreement or disagreement with the statement.

WHERE PUBLISHED: T. W. Adorno, Else Frenkel-Brunswik, D. J. Levinson, and R. N. Sanford, *The Authoritarian Personality* (New York: Harper, 1950).

RELIABILITY: Authors' report on studies—mean $r = .90$, range .81 to .97.
Correlation with Ethnocentrism Scale—mean $r = .75$ with a range from $r = .59$ to $r = .87$.
Using Fisher's Z_r, each item was correlated with every other item—mean $r = .13$ and the range was from $r = -.05$ to $r = .44$.
In addition, each item was correlated with the remainder of the scale, the mean r being .33, the range .15 to .52.
See also:

CHRISTIE, RICHARD; HAVEL, JOAN; SEIDENBERG, BERNARD. "Is the *F* Scale Irreversible?" *Journal of Abnormal and Social Psychology* 56 (1958): 143–59.
———, and JAHODA, MARIE, eds. *Studies in the Scope and Method of "The Authoritarian Personality."* Glencoe, Ill.: Free Press, 1954.

VALIDITY: The authors used the case study method to validate the scale. The scale has been correlated with the Campbell Xenophobia: $r = .60$.
See also:
BASS, BERNARD M. "Authoritarianism or Acquiescence?" *Journal of Abnormal and Social Psychology* 51 (November 1955): 616–23.
CAMILLERI, SANTO F. "A Factor Analysis of the *F*-Scale." *Social Forces* 37 (May 1959): 316–23.
CHRISTIE, RICHARD, and JAHODA, MARIE, eds. *Studies in the Scope and Method of "The Authoritarian Personality."* Glencoe, Ill.: Free Press, 1954.
HIMMELHOCH, JEROME. "Tolerance and Personality Needs: A Study of the Liberalization of Ethnic Attitudes among Minority Group College Students." *American Sociological Review* 15 (February 1950): 79–88.
KIRSCHT, J. P., and DILLEHAY, R. C. *Dimensions of Authoritarianism: A Review of Research and Theory.* Lexington: University of Kentucky Press, 1967.
PROTHRO, E. TERRY, and MELIKIAN, LEVON. "The California Public Opinion Scale in an Authoritarian Culture." *Public Opinion Quarterly* 17 (1953): 115–35.

UTILITY: The test may be administered either in interviews or by questionnaire.

RESEARCH APPLICATIONS:

ADELSON, JOSEPH. "A Study of Minority Group Authoritarianism." *Journal of Abnormal and Social Psychology* 48 (October 1953): 477–85.

BASS, BERNARD M. "Authoritarianism or Acquiescence?" *Journal of Abnormal and Social Psychology* 51 (November 1955): 616–23.

BROWN, ROGER W. "A Determinant of the Relationship Between Rigidity and Authoritarianism." *Journal of Abnormal and Social Psychology* 48 (October 1953): 469–76.

CAMILLERI, SANTO F. "A Factor Analysis of the *F*-Scale." *Social Forces* 37 (May 1959): 316–23.

CAMPBELL, DONALD T., and McCORMACK, THELMA H. "Military Experience and Attitudes Toward Authority." *American Journal of Sociology* 62 (March 1957): 482–90.

CHRISTIE, RICHARD. "Changes in Authoritarianism as Related to Situational Factors." *American Psychologist* 8 (1952): 307–8.

———, and COOK, PEGGY. "Guide to Published Literature Relating to the Authoritarian Personality." *Journal of Psychology* 45 (1958): 171–99 (bibliography).

———, and GARCIA, JOHN. "Subcultural Variation in Authoritarian Personality." *Journal of Abnormal and Social Psychology* 46 (October 1951): 457–69.

———; HAVEL, JOAN; and SEIDENBERG, BERNARD. "Is the *F*-Scale Irreversible?" *Journal of Abnormal and Social Psychology* 56 (1958): 143–59.

———, and JAHODA, MARIE, eds. *Studies in the Scope and Method of "The Authoritarian Personality."* Glencoe, Ill.: Free Press, 1954.

DAVIDS, ANTHONY. "Some Personality and Intellectual Correlates of Intolerance of Ambiguity." *Journal of Abnormal and Social Psychology* 51 (November 1955): 415–20.

GELBMANN, FREDERICK JOHN. *Authoritarianism and Temperament.* Washington, D.C.: Catholic University of America Press, 1958.

GOUGH, HARRISON G. "Studies of Social Intolerance: I. Some Psychological and Sociological Correlates of Anti-Semitism." *Journal of Social Psychology* 33 (May 1951): 237–46.

———. "Studies of Social Intolerance: II. A Personality Scale for Anti-Semitism." *Journal of Social Psychology* 33 (May 1951): 247–55.

———. "Studies of Social Intolerance: III. Relationship of the *Pr* Scale to Other Variables." *Journal of Social Psychology* 33 (May 1951): 257–62.

GREENBERG, HERBERT, and HUTTO, DOLORES. "The Attitudes of West Texas College Students Toward School Integration." *Journal of Applied Psychology* 42 (October 1958): 301–4.

HAYTHORN, WILLIAM; COUCH, ARTHUR; FAEFNER, DONALD; LANGHAM, PETER; and CARTER, LAUNOR F. "The Behavior of Authoritarian and Equalitarian Personalities in Groups." *Human Relations* 9 (February 1956): 57–73.

HIMMELHOCH, JEROME. "Tolerance and Personality Needs: A Study of the Liberalization of Ethnic Attitudes among Minority Group College Students." *American Sociological Review* 15 (February 1950): 79–88.

JONES, EDWARD E. "Authoritarianism as a Determinant of First-Impression Formation." *Journal of Personality* 23 (September 1954): 107–27.

KATES, SOLIS L. "First-Impression Formation and Authoritarianism." *Human Relations* 12 (August 1959): 277–85.

———, and DIAB, LUFTY N. "Authoritarian Ideology and Attitudes on Parent-Child Relationships." *Journal of Abnormal and Social Psychology* 51 (July 1955): 13–16.

KAUFMAN, WALTER C. "Status, Authoritarianism, and Anti-Semitism." *American Journal of Sociology* 62 (January 1957): 379–82.

MacKINNON, WILLIAM J., and CENTERS, RICHARD. "Authoritarianism and Urban Stratification." *American Journal of Sociology* 61 (May 1956): 610–20.

MARTIN, JAMES G., and WESTIE, FRANK R. "The Tolerant Personality." *American Sociological Review* 24 (August 1959): 521–28.

MEER, SAMUEL J. "Authoritarianism Attitudes and Dreams." *Journal of Abnormal and Social Psychology* 51 (July 1955): 74–78.

MISHLER, ELLIOT G. "Personality Characteristics and the Resolution of Role Conflicts." *Public Opinion Quarterly* 17, no. 1 (1953): 115–35.

O'NEIL, WILLIAM M., and LEVINSON, DANIEL J. "A Factorial Exploration of Authoritarianism and Some of Its Ideological Concomitants." *Journal of Personality* 22 (June 1954): 449–63.

PROTHRO, E. TERRY, and MELIKIAN, LEVON. "The California Public Opinion Scale in an Authoritarian Culture." *Public Opinion Quarterly* 17, no. 3 (1953): 353–62.

ROBERTS, ALAN H., and ROKEACH, MILTON. "Anomie, Authoritarianism, and Prejudice: A Replication." *American Journal of Sociology* 61 (January 1956): 355–58.

SANFORD, NEVITT. "Recent Developments in Connection with the Investigation of the Authoritarian Personality." *Sociological Review* 2 (July 1954): 11–33.

SCODEL, ALVIN, and MUSSEN, PAUL. "Social Perceptions of Authoritarians and Nonauthoritarians." *Journal of Abnormal and Social Psychology* 48 (April 1953): 181–84.

SMITH, CHARLES U., and PROTHRO, JAMES W. "Ethnic Differences in Authoritarian Personality." *Social Forces* 35 (May 1957): 334–38.

SROLE, LEO. "Social Integration and Certain Corollaries: An Exploratory Study." *American Sociological Review* 21 (December 1956): 709–16.

THIBAUT, JOHN W., and RIECKEN, HENRY W. "Authoritarianism, Status, and the Communication of Aggression." *Human Relations* 8 (May 1955): 95–120.

For a few more recent applications, see section 4.M.1.

F-SCALE CLUSTERS: FORMS 45 AND 40*

A. Conventionalism: Rigid adherence to conventional, middle-class values.
  1. Obedience and respect for authority are the most important virtues children should learn.
  12. A person who has bad manners, habits, and breeding can hardly expect to get along with decent people.
  37. If people would talk less and work more, everybody would be better off.
  41. The businessman and the manufacturer are much more important to society than the artist and the professor.

B. Authoritarian Submission: Submissive, uncritical attitude toward idealized moral authorities of the ingroup.
  1. Obedience and respect for authority are the most important virtues children should learn.
  4. Science has its place, but there are many important things that can never possibly be understood by the human mind.
  8. Every person should have complete faith in some supernatural power whose decisions he obeys without question.
  21. Young people sometimes get rebellious ideas, but as they grow up they ought to get over them and settle down.
  23. What this country needs most, more than laws and political programs, is a few courageous, tireless, devoted leaders in whom the people can put their faith.

* From T. W. Adorno et al., "F-Scale Clusters: Forms 45 and 40," *The Authoritarian Personality* (New York: Harper, 1950).

42. No sane, normal, decent person could ever think of hurting a close friend or relative.
44. Nobody ever learned anything really important except through suffering.

C. Authoritarian Aggression: Tendency to be on the lookout for, and to condemn, reject, and punish, people who violate conventional values.

12. A person who has bad manners, habits, and breeding can hardly expect to get along with decent people.
13. What youth needs most is strict discipline, rugged determination, and the will to work and fight for family and country.
19. An insult to our honor should always be punished.
25. Sex crimes, such as rape and attacks on children, deserve more than mere imprisonment; such criminals ought to be publicly whipped, or worse.
27. There is hardly anything lower than a person who does not feel a great love, gratitude, and respect for his parents.
34. Most of our social problems would be solved if we could somehow get rid of the immoral, crooked, and feebleminded people.
37. If people would talk less and work more, everybody would be better off.
39. Homosexuals are hardly better than criminals and ought to be severely punished.

D. Anti-intraception: Opposition to the subjective, the imaginative, and tender-minded.

9. When a person has a problem or worry, it is best for him not to think about it, but to keep busy with more cheerful things.
31. Nowadays more and more people are prying into matters that should remain personal and private.
37. If people would talk less and work more, everybody would be better off.
41. The businessman and the manufacturer are much more important to society than the artist and the professor.

E. Superstition and Stereotypy: The belief in mystical determinants of the individual's fate; the disposition to think in rigid categories.

4. Science has its place, but there are many important things that can never possibly be understood by the human mind.
8. Every person should have complete faith in some supernatural power whose decisions he obeys without question.
16. Some people are born with an urge to jump from high places.
26. People can be divided into two distinct classes: the weak and the strong.
29. Some day it will probably be shown that astrology can explain a lot of things.
33. Wars and social troubles may someday be ended by an earthquake or flood that will destroy the whole world.

F. Power and "Toughness": Preoccupation with the dominance-submission, strong-weak, leader-follower dimension; identification with power figures; overemphasis upon the conventionalized attributes of the ego; exaggerated assertion of strength and toughness.

2. No weakness or difficulty can hold us back if we have enough willpower.
13. What youth needs most is strict discipline, rugged determination, and the will to work and fight for family and country.
19. An insult to our honor should always be punished.
22. It is best to use some prewar authorities in Germany to keep order and prevent chaos.
23. What this country needs most, more than laws and political programs, is a few courageous, tireless, devoted leaders in whom the people can put their faith.
26. People can be divided into two distinct classes: the weak and the strong.

38. Most people don't realize how much our lives are controlled by plots hatched in secret places.

G. Destructiveness and Cynicism: Generalized hostility, vilification of the human.
  6. Human nature being what it is, there will always be war and conflict.
  43. Familiarity breeds contempt.

H. Projectivity: The deposition to believe that wild and dangerous things go on in the world; the projection outwards of unconscious emotional impulses.
  18. Nowadays when so many different kinds of people move around and mix together so much, a person has to protect himself especially carefully against catching an infection or disease from them.
  31. Nowadays more and more people are prying into matters that should remain personal and private.
  33. Wars and social troubles may someday be ended by an earthquake or flood that will destroy the whole world.
  35. The wild sex life of the old Greeks and Romans was tame compared to some of the goings-on in this country, even in places where people might least expect it.
  38. Most people don't realize how much our lives are controlled by plots hatched in secret places.

I. Sex: Exaggerated concern with sexual "goings-on."
  25. Sex crimes, such as rape and attacks on children, deserve more than mere imprisonment; such criminals ought to be publicly whipped, or worse.
  35. The wild sex life of the old Greeks and Romans was tame compared to some of the goings-on in this country, even in places where people might least expect it.
  39. Homosexuals are hardly better than criminals and ought to be severely punished.

Inventories of Sociometric and Attitude Scales and Evaluation of Research Continuity

4.M   AN INVENTORY OF MEASURES UTILIZED IN THE *AMERICAN SOCIOLOGICAL REVIEW*, 1965–80

Instructions for Use of 4.M

A researcher who has not found scales in the Handbook to fit his particular problem should carry out the following search:

First, review the inventories of the *American Sociological Review* 1965–68, 1969–74, and 1975–80 to check on scales and related research. This journal is widely believed to set the highest standards for sociological research. The overall inventory has been deliberately broken into three parts so that the researcher can examine any trend patterns of scale use. He should evaluate carefully because instrument development and standardization are relatively rare; simple indices are being constructed de novo for the problem, while scales with far more validity and stability languish unused. The disappointing fact is that few researchers are willing to search for and to examine measuring instruments that are essential to scientific cumulation of knowledge. It is apparent that editors everywhere are failing to establish these requirements for acceptance of research. This does not relieve the researcher of the responsibility to use standardized instruments with demonstrated reliability and validity if he wishes his work to establish a place in cumulative knowledge. He now has a wealth of information on scales if he will only *search*. The researcher who does not find a scale suitable in the ASR Inventory should continue to examine the various compilations that follow. They report on a great number of scales and, in most instances, offer evaluations to aid in selection.

INVENTORY FOR 1965–68

Scales for Measuring Social Status

Duncan's Index of Socioeconomic Status	Bruce K. Eckland, "Academic Ability, Higher Education and Occupational Mobility," 30 (October 1965): 735–46.
	Ira L. Reiss, "Social Class and Premarital Sexual Permissiveness: A Reconsideration," 30 (October 1965): 747–56.
	Edward O. Laumann and Louis Guttman, "The Relative Associational Contiguity of Occupations in an Urban Setting," 31 (April 1966): 169–78.
	Peter M. Blau, "The Flow of Occupational Supply and Recruitment," 30 (August 1965): 475–90.
	Carolyn Cummings Perrucci, "Social Origins, Mobility Patterns and Fertility," 32 (August 1967): 615–25.
	Margaret A. Parman and Jack Sawyer, "Dimensions of Ethnic Intermarriage in Hawaii," 32 (August 1967): 593–607.
Occupational Prestige Scores; 1964 Study by National Opinion Research Center	Robert Hodge and Donald J. Treiman, "Social Participation and Social Status," 33 (October 1968): 722–40.
Ellis and Lane Index of Class Position for College Populations	Robert Ellis and W. Clayton Lane, "Social Mobility and Social Isolation: A Test of Sorokin's Dissociate Hypotheses," 32 (April 1967): 237–53.
Hollingshead Two-Factor Index of Social Position	R. Jay Turner and Morton O. Wagenfeld, "Occupational Mobility and Schizophrenia: An Assessment of the Social Causation and Social Selection Hypothesis," 32 (February 1967): 104–12.
Author Constructed Index That Includes Measure of Father's Educational Level, Mother's Educational Level, an Estimate of the Funds the Family Could Provide if the Student Were to Attend College, the Degree of Sacrifice This Would Entail for the Family, and the Approximate Wealth and Income Status of Student's Family	William H. Sewell and Michel Armer, "Neighborhood Context and College Plans," 31 (April 1966): 159–68.
Census "Index of Socioeconomic Status"	Charles B. Nam and Mary G. Powers, "Variations in Socioeconomic Structure By Race, Residence, and the Life Cycle," 30 (February 1965): 81–96.

Scales for Measuring Group Structures and Dynamics

Intergroup Hostility Scale for Measuring Hostility Toward Negroes, Americans, Estonians, Jews, and Gypsies. Based on Bogardus-Type Social Distance Scale

Melvin Seeman, "On the Personal Consequences of Alienation in Work," 32 (April 1967): 273–85.

Social Distance Scale for Measuring the Willingness to Accept Ex-Mental-Hospital-Patient; Author Constructed

Bruce P. Dohrenwend and Edwin Chin-Song, "Social Status and Attitudes Toward Psychological Disorder: The Problem of Tolerance of Deviance," (June 1967): 417–33.

Degree of Bureaucratization Scale Measuring Six Dimensions: Hierarchy of Authority, Division of Labor, Rules, Procedures, Impersonality, Technical Competence; Author Constructed Scale, Likert-Type

Richard Hall, "Professionalization and Bureaucratization," 33 (February 1968): 92–104.

Social Distance Scale for Measuring Reactions to Physical Handicaps; Author Constructed

Victor Matthews and Charles Westie, "A Preferred Method for Obtaining Rankings Reactions to Physical Handicaps," 31 (December 1966): 851–54.

Scales for Measuring Community Factors

Rancorous Conflict Index

William Gamson, "Rancorous Conflict in Community Politics," 31 (February 1966): 71–81.

Index of Occupational Community Involvement of Professional Workers; Author Constructed Index

Harold Wilensky and Jack Ladinsky, "From Religious Community to Occupational Group: Structural Assimilation Among Professors, Lawyers, and Engineers," 32 (August 1967): 541.

Scales for Measuring Social Participation and Alienation

Kuznets Index of Inequality for Measuring the Distribution of Material Rewards Within Nations

Phillips Cutright, "Inequality: A Cross-National Analysis," 32 (August 1967): 562.

Index of Religious Community Involvement of Professional Worker; Author Constructed Index

Harold Wilensky and Jack Ladinsky, "From Religious Community to Occupational Group: Structural Assimilation Among Professors, Lawyers, and Engineers," 32 (August 1967): 451.

Glock's Index of Religiosity Which Measures Several Dimensions of Religious Involvement

Gary T. Marx, "Religion: Opiate or Inspiration of Civil Rights Militancy Among Negroes," 37 (February 1967): 64–72.

Powerlessness Scale, Based on Arthur G. Neal and Salomon Rettig Scale

Theodore Groat and Arthur G. Neal, "Social Psychological Correlates of Urban Fertility," 32 (December 1967): 945–59.

Social Isolation Scale; Modified Version of Dwight Dean Scale

Theodore Groat and Arthur G. Neal, "Social Psychological Correlates of Urban Fertility," 32 (December 1967): 945–59.

Anomie Scale to Measure Feelings of Normlessness; Author Constructed

Herbert McClosky and John H. Scharr, "Psychological Dimensions of Anomy," 30 (February 1965): 14–40. See application of Robert C. Atchley and M. Patrick McCabe, "Socialization in Correctional Communities: A Replication," 35 (October 1968): 784.

Work Alienation Scale (Guttman-Type) of Five Items; Three Were Developed by the Author and Two by N. Morse

George Miller, "Professionals in Bureaucracy: Alienation Among Industrial Scientists and Engineers," 32 (October 1967): 755–68.

Author Constructed Index of Alienation from Work and from Expressive Relations; Based on a Selection from Thirteen Items of the Neal Gross, M. Mason, and H. McEachern Scales

Michael Aiken and Jerald Hage, "Organizational Alienation: A Comparative Analysis," 31 (August 1966): 497–507.

L. Pearlin's Alienation from Work Scale, Guttman-Type

Louis A. Zurcher, Jr., Arnold Meadow, and Susan Lee Zurcher, "Value Orientation, Role Conflict and Alienation from Work: A Cross-Cultural Study," 30 (August 1965): 539–48.

Marcus R-Scale for Measurement of Union Homogeneity (Guttman-Type)

Philip M. Marcus, "Union Conventions and Executive Boards: A Formal Analysis of Organizational Structure," 31 (February 1966): 61–70.

Author Constructed Index of Hierarchy of Authority and of Participation in Decision Making as Measure of Organizational Centralization

Michael Aiken and Jerald Hage, "Organizational Alienation: A Comparative Analysis," 31 (August 1966): 497–507.

Strole's Anomia Scale; Swedish Translated

Melvin Seeman, "On the Personal Consequences of Alienation in Work," 32 (April 1967): 273–85.

Neal and Seeman Powerlessness Scale

Melvin Seeman, "On the Personal Consequences of Alienation in Work," 32 (April 1967): 273–85.

Meaninglessness Scale; Author Constructed

Theodore Groat and Arthur G. Neal, "Social Psychological Correlates of Urban Fertility," 32 (December 1967): 945–59.

Normlessness Scale; Author Constructed

Theodore Groat and Arthur G. Neal, "Social Psychological Correlates of Urban Fertility," 32 (December 1967): 945–59.

Index of Work Alienation, Based on Blauner's Index

Melvin Seeman, "On the Personal Consequences of Alienation in Work," 32 (April 1967): 273–85.

Scales to Measure Leadership

Scale of Supervisory Responsibility; Author Constructed	Carolyn Cummings Perrucci, "Social Origins, Mobility Patterns and Fertility," 32 (August 1967): 615–25.
Measure of Political Involvement and Political Cleavages	Robert R. Alford and Harry M. Scoble, "Community Leadership, Education, and Political Behavior," 33 (April 1968): 259–71.
Technical Responsibility Scale; Author Constructed	Carolyn Cummings Perrucci, "Social Origins, Mobility Patterns and Fertility," 32 (August 1967): 615–25.

Scales to Measure Attitudes and Values

Racial Attitude Scale; Author Constructed	James M. Fendrich, "Perceived Reference Group Support: Racial Attitudes and Overt Behavior," 32 (December 1967): 960–70.
Degree of Professionalization Scale Measuring Four Additional Dimensions: Belief in Self-Regulation, Belief in Service to Public, Sense of Calling to Field and Reference; Author Constructed Scale; Likert-Type	Richard Hall, "Professionalization and Bureaucratization," 33 (February 1968): 92–104.
Mobility Orientation Scale for Measuring the Degree to Which the Respondent Placed the Value of Occupational Mobility Above Other Values in His Hierarchy of Goals	Melvin Seeman, "On the Personal Consequences of Alienation in Work," 32 (April 1967): 273–85.
University Student Political Attitudes and Behavior, Student Voice Factor Score	David Nasatir, "A Note on Contextual Effects and the Political Orientations of University Students," 33 (April 1968): 210–19.
Peer Value Teen-Age Index; Author Constructed	Paul Lerman, "Individual Values, Peer Values, and Sub-Cultural Delinquency," 33 (April 1968): 219–35.
Four Teen-Age Non-Conformity Scales: Ratfink, Ace-in-the-Hole, Sociability, and Deviance	LaMar T. Empey and Steven G. Lubeck, "Conformity and Deviance in the 'Situation of Company,'" 33 (October 1968): 760–74.
Measure of Political Attitude Toward the Cuban Revolution	Maurice Zeitlin, "Economic Insecurity and the Political Attitudes of Cuban Workers," 31 (February 1966): 35–51.
Rosenberg Attitudes Toward Work Scale for Measuring the Degree of Orientation Toward "Professional" or "Acquisitive" Values	John F. Marsh, Jr., and Frank P. Stafford, "The Effects of Values on Pecuniary Behavior: The Case of Academicians," 32 (October 1967): 740–54.
Orientation Toward Feminine Role Behavior; Author Constructed Scale, Guttman-Type	Kenneth C. Kammeyer, "Birth Order and the Feminine Sex Role Among College Women," 31 (August 1966): 508–15.

Measure of Political Liberalism: This Scale Includes Four Dimensions: Civil Rights, Civil Liberties, Internationalism, and Welfare, Each of Which Was Measured by a Guttman Scale Constructed by the Authors

K. Dennis Kelly and William J. Chambliss, "Status Consistency and Political Attitudes," 31 (June 1966): 375–82.

Pro-Integration Sentiments Scale Based on Favorable (Pro-Negro) Responses to Items Referring Largely to Interracial Contact; Author Constructed, Guttman-Type

Robert W. Hodge and Donald J. Treiman, "Occupational Mobility and Attitudes Toward Negroes," 31 (February 1966): 93–102.

Conformity Scale to Measure Attitudes Toward Conforming Behavior; the Scale Items Are from Four Sources: F. Baron, R. S. Crutchfield, M. L. Hoffman, and T. F. Pettigrew

Howard E. Freeman, J. Michael Ross, David J. Armor, and Thomas F. Pettigrew, "Color Gradation and Attitudes Among Middle Income Negroes," 31 (June 1966): 365–74.

Right-Wing Extremism Scale; Likert-Type, Author Constructed

Gary B. Rush, "Status Consistency and Right-Wing Extremism," 32 (February 1967): 86–92.

Anti-White Scale to Measure Resentment Against Caucasians; A Combination of Items from R. Johnson and G. A. Stedeler Scales

Howard E. Freeman, J. Michael Ross, David J. Armor, and Thomas F. Pettigrew, "Color Gradation and Attitudes Among Middle Income Negroes," 31 (June 1966): 365–74.

Career Orientation Anchorage Scale; Author Constructed

Curt Tausky and Robert Dubin, "Career Anchorage: Managerial Mobility Motivations," 30 (October 1965): 725–35.

Male and Female Premarital Sexual Permissiveness Scales; Author Constructed

Ira L. Reiss, "Social Class and Premarital Sexual Permissiveness: A Reexamination," 30 (October 1965): 747–56.

Mysticism Scale for Measuring Belief in Such Things as Spiritualism, Necromancy, and Astrology; Author Constructed

Herbert McClosky and John H. Scharr, "Psychological Dimensions of Anomy," 30 (February 1965): 14–40.

Scales Measuring Family and Marriage Factors

Index of Extended Familism Which Measures Four Dimensions: Intensity, Extensity, Interaction and Verba Cross-Cultural Study

Robert F. Winch, Scott Greer, and Rae L. Blumberg, "Ethnicity Familism in an Upper-Middle-Class Suburb," 32 (April 1967): 265–72.

Index of Parent-Youth Relations; Author Constructed Index Based on Items of Almond and Verba Cross-Cultural Study

Glen H. Elder, Jr., "Family Structure and Educational Attainment: A Cross-National Analysis," 30 (February 1965): 81–96.

Developmental Scale of Wife Independence; Author Constructed

Robert K. Leik and Merlyn Matthews, "A Scale for Developmental Processes," 33 (February 1968): 62–75.

Student Perception of Parenteral Encouragement Toward Attending College; Author Constructed Scale

William H. Sewell and Vimal P. Shah, "Parents, Education, and Children's Educational Aspirations and Achievements," 33 (April 1968): 191–209.

Index of Intermarriage Distance; Author Constructed

Margaret A. Parkman and Jack Sawyer, "Dimensions of Ethnic Intermarriage in Hawaii," 32 (August 1967): 593–607.

Measures of Personality Factors

Minnesota Multiphasic Personality Inventory

Bernard E. Segal, Robert J. Weiss, and Robert Sokol, "Emotional Adjustment, Social Organization and Psychiatric Treatment Rates," 30 (August 1965): 548–56.

Minnesota Multiphasic Personality Inventory Reports

Omer R. Galle and Karl E. Taeuber, "Metropolitan Migration and Intervening Opportunities," 31 (February 1966): 5–34.

United States Army Neuropsychiatric Screening Adjunct

Omer R. Galle and Karl E. Taeuber, "Metropolitan Migration and Intervening Opportunities," 31 (February 1966): 5–34.

Beliefs About Female Personality Traits; Author Constructed Scale, Likert-Type

Kenneth Kammeyer, "Birth Order and the Feminine Sex Role Among College Women," 31 (August 1966): 508–15.

Inflexibility Index; Author Constructed

Herbert McClosky and John H. Scharr, "Psychological Dimensions of Anomy," 30 (February 1965): 14–40.

Subjective Victimization Scale, Perceived Effects on Self of Racial Restrictions, A Reformulation of G. W. Allport and B. M. Kramer Scale

Howard E. Freeman, J. Michael Ross, David J. Armor, and Thomas F. Pettigrew, "Color Gradation and Attitudes Among Middle Income Negroes," 31 (June 1966): 365–74.

Authoritarianism Scale, The Authoritarian Personality Syndrome

Howard E. Freeman, J. Michael Ross, David J. Armor, and Thomas F. Pettigrew, "Color Gradation and Attitudes Among Middle Income Negroes," 31 (June 1966): 365–74.

Measures of Intelligence and Achievement

American Council on Education Psychological Examination

Bruce K. Eckland, "Academic Ability, Higher Education, and Occupational Mobility, 30 (October 1965): 735–46.

Hennon-Nelson Test of Mental Ability

William H. Sewell and Michael Armor, "Neighborhood Context and College Plans," 31 (April 1966): 159–68.

Measures of Identification

Peer-Value Index for Measuring Identification With Peer Groups; Author Constructed

Paul Lerman, "Argot, Symbolic Deviance and Subcultural Delinquency," 32 (April, 1967): 209–24.

Index of Religious Identification of Professional Workers; Author Constructed

Harold Wilensky and Jack Ladinsky, "From Religious Community to Occupational Group: Structural Assimilation Among Professors, Lawyers, and Engineers," 32 (August 1967): 541–61.

Wilensky Index of Professional Identification

Harold Wilensky and Jack Ladinsky, "From Religious Community to Occupational Group: Structural Assimilation Among Professors, Lawyers, and Engineers," 32 (August 1967): 541–61.

Miscellaneous Scales

Index of Professional Incentives; Author Constructed

George Miller, "Professionals in Bureaucracy: Alienation Among Industrial Scientists and Engineers," 32 (October 1967): 755–68.

Acquiescence Scale for Measuring the Consistency-Logicality Dimension of Cognitive Function; Author Constructed

Herbert McClosky and John H. Scharr, "Psychological Dimensions of Anomy," 30 (February, 1965): 14–40.

Reference Group Support Scale; Author Constructed

James M. Fendrich, "Perceived Reference Group Support: Racial Attitudes and Overt Behavior," 32 (December 1967): 960–70.

Index of Militancy, Measuring Several Dimensions of Racial Protest; Author Constructed

Gary T. Marx, "Religion: Opiate or Inspiration of Civil Rights Militancy Among Negroes," 32 (February 1967): 64–72.

Index of Perceived Legitimate Educational and Occupational Opportunities; Author Constructed

James F. Short, Jr., Ramon Rivera, and Ray A. Tennyson, "Perceived Opportunities, Gang Membership and Delinquency," 30 (February 1965): 56–67.

Stouffer-Toby Conflict Scale

Louis A. Zurcher, Jr., Arnold Meadow, and Susan Lee Zurcher, "Value Orientation, Role Conflict, and Alienation from Work: A Cross-Cultural Study," 30 (August 1965): 539–48.

Political Awareness Test for Measuring Degree of Information on Political Affairs; Author Constructed

Melvin Seeman, "On the Personal Consequences of Alienation in Work," 32 (April 1967): 273–85.

Social Indicators

Index of Political Representativeness for Measuring Degree of Political Organization and Constitutionalization; Author Constructed

Phillips Cutright, "Inequality: A Cross-National Analysis," 32 (August 1967): 562–78.

Index of Argot for Measuring Symbolic Deviance; Author Constructed

Paul Lerman, "Argot, Symbolic Deviance and Subcultural Delinquency," 32 (April 1967): 209–24.

Author Constructed Scale to Measure the Degree of Coercive vs. Persuasive Sanctions Toward Hospital Patients

Joseph Julian, "Compliance Patterns and Communication Blocks in Complex Organizations," 31 (June 1966): 382–89.

Index of Economic Development Based on Data From B. Russett et al., *World Handbook of Political and Social Indicators*

Phillips Cutright, "Inequality: A Cross-National Analysis," 32 (August 1967): 562–78.

Index of Democratic Political Enlightenment (Use of Moscos' items)

Arvin W. Murch, "Political Integration as an Alternative to Independence in the French Antilles," 33 (August 1968): 544–61.

Index of Governmental Reformism; Author Constructed

Terry N. Clark, "Community Structure, Decision Making, Budget Expenditures, and Urban Renewal in 51 American Communities," 33 (August 1968): 576–93.

INVENTORY FOR 1969–74

Scales for Measuring Social Status

Duncan's Index of Socioeconomic Status

Edward O. Laumann, "The Social Structure of Religious and Ethnoreligious Groups in a Metropolitan Community," 34 (April 1969): 186.

William A. Rushing, "Two Patterns in the Relationship Between Social Class and Mental Hospitalization," 34 (August 1969): 535.

Carolyn Cummings Perrucci and Robert Perrucci, "Social Origins, Educational Contexts, and Career Mobility," 35 (June 1970): 453.

William H. Sewell et al., "The Educational and Early Occupational Status Attainment Process: Replication and Revision," 35 (December 1970): 1017.

Reta D. Artz, Dianne Timbers Fairbank, Richard F. Curtis, and Elton F. Jackson, "Community Rank Stratification: A Factor Analysis," 36 (December 1971): 987.

Elton F. Jackson and Richard F. Curtis, "Effects of Vertical Mobility and Status Inconsistency: A Body of Negative Evidence," 37 (December 1972): 702.

Norvall D. Glenn, Adreain A. Ross, and Judy Corder Tully, "Patterns of Intergenerational Mobility of Females Through Marriage," 39 (August 1974): 688.

Archibald O. Haller, Luther B. Otto, Robert F. Meir, and George W. Ohlendorf, "Level of Occupational Aspiration: An Empirical Analysis," 39 (February 1974): 116.

Duane F. Alwin, "College Effects on Occupational Attainments," 39 (April 1974): 212–13.

Duncan SEI Used to Classify Head of Household, and to Derive Measures of Occupational Aspiration, Expectation, and Occupational Attainment

James N. Porter, "Race, Socialization and Mobility in Educational and Early Occupational Attainment," 39 (June 1974): 306–8.

Three Measures of Socioeconomic Status: Duncan SEI Scale, Education, and Subjective Social Class

David Knoke and Michael Hout, "Social and Demographic Factors in American Political Party Affiliations, 1952–72," 39 (August 1974): 702.

Charles W. Mueller, "City Effects on Socioeconomic Achievements: The Case of Large Cities," 39 (August 1974): 655–56.

Author Constructed Eight-Category SES Index Including Occupation of Head of Household (Coded by Duncan SES Index), Education of the Respondent, and Total Family Income

Marvin E. Olsen, "Social and Political Participation of Blacks," 35 (August 1970): 685.

Hollingshead's Two-Factor Index of Social Position

Melvin L. Kohn and Carmi Schooler, "Class, Occupation, and Orientation," 34 (October 1969): 660.

Gerald T. Slatin, "Ecological Analysis of Delinquency: Aggregation Effects," 34 (December 1969): 896.

Glen H. Elder, Jr., "Appearance and Education in Marriage Mobility," 34 (August 1969): 523.

Richard A. Rehberg, Walter E. Schafer, and Judie Sinclair, "Toward A Temporal Sequence of Adolescent Achievement Variables," 35 (February 1970): 34–37.

Roberta G. Simmons and Morris Rosenberg, "Functions of Children's Perceptions of the Stratification System," 30 (April 1971): 241.

Melvin L. Kohn, "Bureaucratic Man: A Portrait and an Interpretation," 36 (June 1971): 468.

Lloyd H. Rogler, "The Changing Role of a Political Boss in a Puerto Rican Migrant Community," 39 (February 1974): 63.

Hollingshead Index of Social Position, Use of Educational Seven Category Scale Only

Thomas Ewin Smith, "Foundations of Parental Influence upon Adolescents: An Application of Social Power Theory," 35 (October 1970): 864.

North-Hatt Scale of Occupational Prestige (NORC)

Roberta G. Simmons and Morris Rosenberg, "Functions of Children's Perceptions of the Stratification System," 30 (April 1971): 237.

Sanford Labovitz, "The Assignment of Numbers to Rank Order Categories," 35 (June 1970): 516–17.

C. Norman Alexander, Jr., "Status Perceptions," 37 (December 1972): 769.

Edwards Socio-Economic Grouping (U.S. Census)

Samuel H. Preston, "Differential Fertility, Unwanted Fertility, and Racial Trends in Occupational Achievement," 39 (August 1974): 498.

Classification of Occupations, London: Her Majesty's Stationery Office, 1966; for Study in England as Cited

John W. Loy, Jr., "Social Psychological Characteristics of Innovators," 34 (February 1969): 75.

Socioeconomic Status: Factor Weighted Combination of Education of Respondent's Father and Mother, Respondent's Perception of Economic Status of the Family, Respondent's Perception of Possible Parental Support Should He Go to College and Amount of Support, and Occupation of His Father; Author Constructed

William H. Sewell, Archibald O. Haller, and Alejandro Portes, "The Educational and Early Occupational Attainment Process," 34 (February 1969): 87.

Family Background Status: Mother's Education, Father's Education, Father's Occupational Status, and Acquisition Index; Author Constructed

Karl L. Alexander and Bruce K. Eckland, "Sex Differences in the Educational Attainment Process," 39 (August 1974): 672.

Status of High School: Author Constructed: Educational Status Index: Author Constructed

Joel I. Nelson, "High School Context and College Plans: The Impact of Social Structure on Aspirations," 37 (April 1972): 144.

Significance of External Status Characteristic in Small-Group Decision-Making

Joseph Berger, Bernard P. Cohen, and Morris Zelditch, Jr., "Status Conceptions and Social Interaction," 37 (June 1972): 249.

Socioeconomic Status Using Bogue Scale

H. Edward Ransford, "Blue Collar Anger: Reactions to Student and Black Protest," 37 (June 1972): 337–38.

Achieved Socioeconomic Status Index; Author Constructed
Ascribed Status; Author Constructed

Marvin E. Olsen and Judy Corder Tully, "Socioeconomic-Ethnic Status Inconsistency and Preference for Political Change," 37 (October 1972): 565.

Scales for Measuring Group Structures and Dynamics

Indicators of Organizational Interdependence, Complexity, Innovation, Internal Communication, Centralization, and Formalization; Author Constructed

Michael Aiken and Jerald Hage, "Organizational Interdependence and Intra-Organizational Structure," 33 (December 1968): 919, 921, 926.

Indices of Social Power: Coercive, Reward, Expert, Legitimate, and Referent

Donald I. Warren, "Power, Visibility, and Conformity in Formal Organizations," 33 (December 1968): 957.

Subscription to an Inmate Code, Inmate Cohesion, Criminal Subcultural Orientation, Disorganization of Social Background, Indicators of Contact; Author Constructed

Charles R. Little, "Inmate Organization: Sex Differentiation and the Influences of Criminal Subcultures," 34 (August 1969): 495–97.

Origin of Status Persistence; Author Constructed Index

Leo A. Goodman, "On the Measurement of Social Mobility: An Index of Status Persistence," 34 (December 1969): 938.

Indices of the Diversity of Institutions for Measurement of Social System Differentiation

Frank W. Young, "Reactive Subsystems," 35 (April 1970): 300.

Degrees of Status Crystallization; Author Constructed Index

Thomas S. Smith, "Structural Crystalization, Status Inconsistency, and Political Partisanship," 34 (December 1969): 915.

Indices of Organizational Size Consisting of Total Number of Employees in Organization Where Respondent Works and Size of Respondent's Immediate Work Group; Author Constructed

Carolyn Cummings Perrucci and Robert Perrucci, "Social Origins, Educational Contexts, and Career Mobility," 35 (June 1970): 453–54.

Index of Job Specificity in an Organization

Jerald Hage, Michael Aiken, and Cora Bagley Marrett, "Organization Structure and Communications," 36 (October 1971): 870.

Index of Participation in Organizational Decision-Making

Index of Regeneration for Social Organizations; Author Constructed

Kenneth McNeil and James D. Thompson, "The Regeneration of Social Organizations," 36 (August 1971): 625–26.

Index of Bureaucracy (Hierarchical Organization of Authority Dimension)

Melvin L. Kohn, "Bureaucratic Man: A Portrait and an Interpretation," 36 (June 1971): 462.

Index of Protest Definition; Author Constructed

Vincent Jeffries, Ralph H. Turner, and Richard T. Morris, "The Public Perception of the Watts Riot as Social Protest," 36 (June 1971): 443–45.

Industrial Conflict; Author Constructed

David Britt and Omer R. Gallo, "Industrial Conflict and Unionization," 37 (February 1972): 48.

Public Awareness of a Social Protest Incident; Author Constructed

David L. Altheide and Robert P. Gilmore, "The Credibility of Protest," 37 (February 1972): 102–3.

Sociomatrices of Children's Classroom Groups

Samuel Leinhardt, "Developmental Change in the Sentiment Structure of Children's Groups," 37 (April 1972): 203–5.

Index of Occupational Dispersion

David F. Sly, "Migration and the Ecological Complex," 37 (October 1972): 621.

Power and Prestige Order in Small Groups; Author Constructed

Elizabeth G. Cohen and Susan S. Roper, "Modification of Intersocial Interaction Disability: An Application of Status Characteristic Theory," 37 (December 1972): 647.

Organization Locus; Ownership, Bureaucratization, and Position in Supervisory Hierarchy; Author Constructed

Melvin L. Kohn and Carmi Schooler, "Occupational Experience and Psychological Functioning: An Assessment of Reciprocal Effects," 38 (February 1973): 103–4.

Visible and Legitimate Leadership in the Community

James M. Williams, "The Ecological Approach in Measuring Community Power Concentration: An Analysis of Hawley's MPO Ratio," 38 (April 1973): 235.

Bales' Interactional Process Analysis (Borgatta's Revision)

H. W. Smith, "Some Developmental Interpersonal Dynamics through Childhood," 38 (October 1973): 544.

Occupational Mobility; 12 Categories of Skill Histories; Author Constructed

Barbara Jackson and John M. Kendrick, "Education and Mobility: From Achievement to Ascription," 38 (August 1973): 446–47.

Measure of Managerial Component of Communal Units; Measure of Communicative Component of Communal Units; Measure of Professional and Technical Component of Communal units; All Scales Author Constructed

John D. Kasarda, "The Structural Implications of Social System Size: A Three Level Analysis," 39 (February 1974): 22.

Revivalism Measure; Author Constructed

John L. Hammond, "Revival Religion and Antislavery Politics," 39 (April 1974): 179.

Scales for Measuring Community Factors

National Headquarters Index of Extra-local Integration for 1960, Provided by National Headquarters of Voluntary Associations Found in *Encyclopedia of Associations* (1961)

Herman Turk, "Interorganizational Networks in Urban Society: Initial Perspectives and Comparative Research," 35 (February 1970): 1–5, 9–10, 10.

Community-Wide Association Index of Local Integration "taken to signify the presence of mechanisms for concerned action as well as the absence of highly organized cleavages within the city"

Municipal Revenue Index of Local Integration, Measuring Integration in

Terms of Control Exercised by the City's Government over the Communities' Affairs

Index of Interorganizational Activity Level Based on Per Capita Number of Poverty Dollars Flowing into a Particular City

Measures of Community Structure Compiled from *Municipal Year Books* ('63, '64), 1950 Census of Housing, and 1960 Census of Population

Michael Aiken and Robert R. Alford, "Community Structure and Innovation: The Case of Urban Renewal," 35 (August 1970): 652.

Measure of Community Innovation, i.e., Participation in Urban Renewal Program, compiled from *Urban Renewal Directory* (June 30, 1966, Department of Housing and Urban Development, U.S. Government, Washington, D.C.)

The Speed of Community Innovation Is Measured by Number of Years City Took to Enter Urban Renewal Program Either After 1944 or After State Enabling Legislation Was Enacted

Level of Community Output Measured by Number of Urban Renewal Dollars Reserved Per Capita as of June 30, 1966

Patterns of Vandalism; Author Constructed

Richard A. Berk and Howard E. Aldrich, "Patterns of Vandalism During Civil Disorders as an Indicator of Selection of Targets," 37 (October 1972): 538.

Reward Distribution in Kibbutz; Author Constructed

Ephraim Yuchtman, "Reward Distribution and Work-Role Attractiveness in the Kibbutz—Reflections on Equity Theory," 37 (October 1972): 584.

Community Elite Influence and Relationship of Pairs of Elite Members

Edward O. Laumann, Lois M. Verbrugge, and Franz U. Pappi, "A Causal Modeling Approach to the Study of a Community Elite's Influence Structure," 39 (April 1974): 163–66.

Community Attitudes and Sentiments; Friendship and Kinship Bonds in Local Community; Respondent's Participation in Formal Associations within the Local Community; Author Constructed

John D. Kasarda and Morris Janowitz, "Community Attachment in Mass Society," 39 (June 1974): 331.

Scales for Measuring Social Participation and Alienation

Index of Esteem (Evaluation of Others); Author Constructed

Rodolfo Alvarez, "Informal Reactions to Deviance in Simulated Work Organizations: A Laboratory Experiment," 33 (December 1968): 906.

Index of Relative Centrality in Group Association Based on Peer Nomination; Author Constructed

"Location and Innovativeness: Reformulation and Extension of the Diffusion Model," 35 (April 1970): 270.

Voluntary Association Participation Index; Political Organization Participation Index; Mass Media Exposure Index; Political News Exposure Index; Community Activities Index; Cultural Events Index; Church Participation Index; Friends Interaction Index; Relatives Interaction Index; Political Discussion Index; Registration and Voting Index; Partisan Political Activities Index; Partisan Political Involvement Index (All 12 Above Scales Author Constructed); Governmental Contacts Index

Marvin E. Olsen, "Social and Political Participation of Blacks," 35 (August 1970): 685, 686.

Index of Company Evaluation (5 Items) as Measure of Worker Integration; Author Constructed

Michael Fullan, "Industrial Technology and Worker Integration in the Organization," 35 (December 1970): 1035–36.

Integration Policy Strength Scale (10 Items), Guttman type; Author Constructed

James R. Wood, "Authority and Controversial Policy: The Churches and Civil Rights," 35 (December 1970): 1059–60.

Social Isolation Index (Geschwender et al.)

Clark McPhail, "Civil Disorder Participation: A Critical Examination of Recent Research," 36 (December 1971): 1069.

Index of Professional Activity

Jerald Hage, Michael Aiken, and Cora Bagley Marrett, "Organization Structure and Communications," 36 (October 1971): 870.

Index of Dissimilarity (ID) (Duncan and Duncan, 1955); Measure of Ghettoization (Taeuber and Taeuber, 1965)

Robert M. Jiobu and Harvey H. Marshall, Jr., "Urban Structure and the Differentiation Between Blacks and Whites," 36 (August 1971): 642, 643.

Strole Anomie Scale

Leslie G. Carr, "The Strole Items and Acquiescence," 36 (April 1971): 287–92.

Nominal Scale of Voluntary Associations; Author Constructed

Alan Booth, "Sex and Social Participation," 37 (April 1972): 188–89.

Social Participation; Author Constructed: (1) Voluntary Association Participation Index (2) Church Participation Index (3) Community Participation Index (4) Friends Interaction Index (5) Neighbors

Marvin E. Olsen, "Social Participation and Voting Turnout: A Multivariate Analysis," 37 (June 1972): 320–21.

Middleton Alienation Scale (1963), Internal-External Control (Powerlessness) Scale (Rotler 1966), Index of Work Alienation (Seeman 1967), Anomia Scale (Srole 1956)

Melvin Seeman, "The Signals of '68: Alienation in Pre-Crisis France," 37 (August 1972): 387, 391.

Formal Social Participation, Informal Social Participation, Anomia; Author Constructed

Elton F. Jackson and Richard F. Curtis, "Effects of Vertical Mobility and Status Inconsistency: A Body of Negative Evidence," 37 (December 1972): 707.

Orientation to Self and Society; Based on Factor Analysis of Fifty-Seven Questions; Author Constructed

Melvin L. Kohn and Carmi Schooler, "Occupational Experience and Psychological Functioning: An Assessment of Reciprocal Effects," 38 (February 1973): 100.

Rosenberg "Misanthropy" Scale (Variations of)

Claude S. Fisher, "On Urban Alienations and Anomie: Powerlessness and Social Isolation," 38 (June 1973): 311–26.

Membership and Participation in Voluntary Associations (Author Definition: average number of organizations belonged to by a particular population)

J. Allen Williams, Jr., and Nicholas Babchuk, "Voluntary Associations and Minority Status: A Comparative Analysis of Anglo, Black, and Mexican Americans," 38 (October 1973): 637–46.

Political Knowledge, Political Awareness, and Political Participation; Author Constructed

Anthony M. Orum and Roberta S. Cohen, "The Development of Political Orientations among Black and White Children," 38 (February 1973): 66.

Participation in Interpersonal Violence; Author Constructed

Sandra J. Ball-Rokeach, "Values and Violence: A Test of the Subculture of Violence Thesis," 38 (December 1973): 737–38.

Powerlessness Measured by Institute for Social Research: Personal Competency Scale of Robinson and Shaver

Claude S. Fisher, "On Urban Alienations and Anomie: Powerlessness and Social Isolation," 38 (June 1973): 313.

Occupational Self-Direction, Job Pressures and Uncertainties; Author Constructed

Melvin L. Kohn and Carmi Schooler, "Occupational Experience and Psychological Functioning: An Assessment of Reciprocal Effects," 38 (February 1973): 104–5.

Career Orientation Anchorage Scale (COAS) by Tausky and Dubin; Central Life Interest Instrument (CLI)

Daniel R. Goldman, "Managerial Mobility Motivations and Central Life Interests," 38 (February 1973): 120–21.

Measure of Professional Orientation Among Bureaucratic Managers; Author Constructed

William J. Haga, George Graen, and Fred Dansereau, Jr., "Professional and Role Making In a Service Organization: A Longitudinal Investigation," 39 (February 1974): 127.

Political Participation Scale; Political Discussion Scale (Designed for Children in Fourth Through Twelfth Grades)

Anthony M. Orum, Roberta S. Cohen, Sherri Grasmuck, and Amy W. Orum, "Sex, Socialization, and Politics," 39 (April 1974): 203.

Bales Interaction Process Analysis

Peter J. Burke, "Participation and Leadership in Small Groups," 39 (December 1974): 833.

Scales to Measure Leadership

Closeness of Supervision Index, Guttman Type (Kohn 1969)

Melvin L. Kohn, "Bureaucratic Man: A Portrait and an Interpretation," 36 (June 1971): 469.

Index of Relative Centrality in Group Association Based on Peer Nomination; Author Constructed

Marshall H. Becker, "Sociometric Location and Innovativeness: Reformulation and Extension of the Diffusion Model," 35 (April 1970): 270.

Scales to Measure Attitudes and Values

Index of Significant Other's Influence: Summated Score of Three Variables; Author Constructed

William H. Sewell, Archibald O. Haller, and Alejandro Portes, "The Educational and Early Occupational Attainment Process" (February 1969): 87.

Verbal Attitude Scale to Measure Prejudice toward Negroes; Author Constructed

Lyle G. Warner and Melvin L. DeFleur, "Attitude as an Interactional Concept: Social Constraint and Social Distance as Interviewing Variables between Attitudes and Action," 34 (April 1969): 156–57.

Commitment to Values Index: 20 Item Likert-Scale to Measure Commitment to a Specific Organization; Author Constructed

George Brager, "Commitment and Conflict in a Normative Organization," 34 (August 1969): 486.

Attractiveness: Scores on Selected Scales; Status Aspirations: Author Constructed; Aspiration for High Status: 101 Item California Q Set (Block 1961)

Glen H. Elder, Jr., "Appearance and Education in Marriage Mobility," 34 (August 1969): 522.

Indices of Parental Values, Values for Self, Social Orientation, Self-Conception; Author Constructed

Melvin L. Kohn and Carmi Schooler, "Class, Occupation, and Orientation," 34 (October 1969): 622–67.

Adolescent's Socio-Economic Level of Wish, Adolescent's Socioeconomic Level of Expectation; Author Constructed

Wan Sang Han, "Two Conflicting Themes: Common Values Versus Class Differential Values," 34 (October 1969): 681.

Author Constructed Index of Mobility Attitudes Including Six Factors: Educational Orientation, Person Orientation, Master Orientation, Occupational Primacy, Time Orientation, and Fatalism

Richard A. Rehberg, Walter E. Schafer, and Judie Sinclair, "Toward A Temporal Sequence of Adolescent Achievement Variables," 35 (February 1970): 36–37.

Scale of Occupational Values, Based on Six Characteristics Associated with Work Roles; Author Constructed

Carolyn Cummings Perrucci and Robert Perrucci, "Social Origins, Educational Contexts, and Career Mobility," 35 (June 1970): 453.

Level of Occupational Aspiration Determined by Assigning Duncan SES Index Scores to the Occupation Respondent Previously Indicated He Hoped to Enter in Future; Index of Significant Others Influence, Including Perceived

William H. Sewell et al., "The Educational and Early Occupational Status Attainment Process: Replication and Revision," 35 (December 1970): 1017.

Parental Encouragement to Attend College, Perceived Teacher Encouragement for College, and Friends' College Plans; Author Constructed

Indices of Attitudes Toward Negroes; Author Constructed

Vincent Jeffries, Ralph H. Turner, and Richard T. Morris, "The Public Perception of the Watts Riot as Social Protest," 36 (June 1971): 445–46.

Index of Values or Standards of Desirability (Kohn 1969); Indices of Social Orientation Including Authoritarian Conservatism, Criteria of Morality, and Stance Toward Change (Kohn 1969).

Melvin L. Kohn, "Bureaucratic Man: A Portrait and an Interpretation," 36 (June 1971): 463, 464.

Lenski's Index of Work Values

Howard Schuman, "The Religious Factor in Detroit: Review, Replication, and Reanalysis," 36 (February 1971): 33.

Occupational Aspiration Scale (Haller and Miller (1963); Occupational and Aspiration Scale (Haller and Woelfel 1969)

Joseph Woeffel and Archibald O. Haller, "Significant Others, The Self-Reflexive Act and the Attitude Formation Process," 36 (February 1971): 77.

Adolescent Conformity; Author Constructed

Darwin L. Thomas and Andrew J. Weigert, "Socialization and Adolescent Conformity to Significant Others: A Cross-National Analysis," 36 (October 1971): 839–40.

Indices of Leftist Radicalism; Author Constructed

Alejandro Portes, "Political Primitivism, Differential Socialization, and Lower-Class Leftist Radicalism," 36 (October 1971): 823.

Hall's Professionalism Scale (Attitude Scale)

William E. Snizek, "Hall's Professionalism Scale: An Empirical Reassessment," 37 (February 1972): 110.

Attitude Toward Work, Personal Satisfaction with Socioeconomic Attainment; Author Constructed

David L. Featherman, "Achievement Orientations and Socioeconomic Career Attainments," 37 (April 1972): 123, 133.

Individual Modernity: Compiled from Smith and Inkeles' 0-M6 Modernity Scale, Kahl's Modernity I and II Scales, Schnaiberg's Emancipation Scale, Armer's Individual Modernity Scale

Michael Armer and Allan Schnaiberg, "Measuring Individual Modernity: A Near Myth," 37 (June 1972): 304.

Hostility Demonstrated by Blue Collar Political and Social Attitudes and Values; Author Constructed

E. Edward Ransford, "Blue Collar Anger: Reactions to Student and Black Protest," 37 (June 1972): 338.

Preference for Political Change; Modified Likert Scale Items from Kelly and Chamblis

Marvin E. Olsen and Judy Corder Tully, "Socioeconomic-Ethnic Status Inconsistency and Preference for Political Change," 37 (October 1972): 563.

Work-Role Attractiveness (Thibant and Kelly 1959)	Ephraim Yuchtman, "Reward Distribution and Work-Role Attractiveness in the Kibbutz—Reflections on Equity Theory," 37 (October 1972): 585.
Five Scales of Race and Class Consciousness of Blacks; Author Constructed	Charles E. Hurst, "Race, Class and Consciousness," 37 (December 1972): 660–61.
Political Liberalism, Satisfaction and Symptoms of Stress, Intolerance, Aspirations for Son	Elton F. Jackson and Richard F. Curtis, "Effects of Vertical Mobility and Status Inconsistency: A Body of Negative Evidence," 37 (December 1972): 707.
Anti-Semitism Scale (Selznick and Steinberg)	Russell Middleton, "Do Christian Beliefs Cause Anti-Semitism?" 38 (February 1973): 39.
Political Cynicism, Government Benevolence, Favorable Image of the President; All Scales Author Constructed	Anthony M. Orum and Roberta S. Cohen, "The Development of Political Orientations Among Black and White Children," 38 (February 1973): 64, 65.
Occupational Commitment, Job Satisfaction, Valuation of Self-Direction or Conformity to External Authority	Melvin L. Kohn and Carmi Schooler, "Occupational Experience and Psychological Functioning: An Assessment of Reciprocal Effects," 38 (February 1973): 99–100.
Receptivity Toward Protest; Author Constructed	Hart M. Nelson, Raytha L. Yokley, and Thomas W. Madron, "Ministerial Roles and Social Actionist Stance: Protestant Clergy and Protest in the Sixties," 38 (June 1973): 377.
Self-Image Based on Four Guttman-Type Scales; Author Constructed	Roberta G. Simmons and Florence Rosenberg, "Disturbance in the Self-Image of Adolescence," 38 (October 1973): 566–67.
Attitude Toward Violence; Author Constructed; Rokeach Value Survey	Sandra J. Ball-Rokeach, "Values and Violence: A Test of the Subculture of Violence Thesis," 31 (December 1973): 736–49.
Occupational Aspiration Scale (Haller and Miller 1971)	Archibald O. Haller, Luther B. Otto, Robert F. Meir, and George W. Ohlendorf, "Level of Occupational Aspiration: An Empirical Analysis," 39 (February 1974): 116.
Image of the President Scale, Government Benevolence Scale, Political Cynicism Scale (Designed for Children in Fourth through Twelfth Grades); Author Constructed	Anthony M. Orum, Roberta S. Cohen, Sherri Grasmuck, and Amy W. Orum, "Sex, Socialization, and Politics," 39 (April 1974): 202–3.
Scales to Measure Inner-Directedness, Religious Experience, Modern Values, Loneliness, Work Satisfaction, Decision to Stay in the Public Ministry; Author Constructed	Richard A. Schoenherr and Andrew M. Greeley, "Role Commitment Processes and the American Catholic Priesthood," 39 (June 1974): 413.

Scales to Measure Academic Self-Concept, Educational Expectations, and Adult Influences; Author Constructed

Karl L. Alexander and Bruce K. Eckland, "Sex Differences in the Educational Attainment Process," 39 (October 1974): 673.

Scales Measuring Family and Marriage Factors

Index of Decision-Making in Marriages; Blood and Wolfe's Index of Most Valued Part of Marriage

Richard Centers, Bertram H. Raven, and Aroldo Rodrigues, "Conjugal Power Structure: A Re-examination," 36 (April 1971): 266, 267.

Cornell Parent Behavior Description Scale, Short Form

Darwin L. Thomas and Andrew J. Weigert, "Socialization and Adolescent Conformity to Significant Others: A Cross-National Analysis," 36 (October 1971): 839.

Indices of Family Stability Based on Current Marital Status, Family Types and Family Headship, Illegitimacy, and Changes in Living Arrangements of Young Children

Reynolds Farley and Albert I. Hermalin, "Family Stability: A Comparison of Trends Between Blacks and Whites," 36 (February 1971): 1–14.

Index of Marital Tension; Index of Husband-Wife Communication; Both Author Constructed

Robert Edward Mitchell, "Some Social Implications of High Density Housing," 36 (February 1971) 25.

Verbal and Nonverbal Family Interactional Analysis; Author Constructed

Bernard C. Rosen, "Social Change, Migration, and Family Interaction in Brazil," 38 (April 1973): 203.

Maternal Restrictions Scale, Guttman Type, White and Saltz; Husband Involvement Scale; Intramarital (Bargaining) Transactions.

Karen E. Paige and Jeffrey M. Paige, "The Politics of Birth Practices: A Strategic Analyis," 38 (December 1973): 671.

Indices of the Approval of Spanking Children; Author Constructed

Howard S. Erlanger, "Social Class and Corporal Punishment in Childrearing: A Reassessment," 39 (February 1974): 73.

Family Tension (Scale Range 1.0–5.0 Based on Items in NORC 1972 Report)

Richard A. Schoenherr and Andrew M. Greeley, "Role Commitment Processes and the American Catholic Priesthood," 39 (June 1974): 412.

Measures of Personality Factors

Minnesota Multiphasic Personality Inventory, IPAT Anxiety Scale (Cattell and Scheier 1963), Faith in People and Self-Esteem (Rosenberg Guttman-Type Scales)

Raymond J. Adamek and Edward Z. Dager, "Social Structure Identification and Change in a Treatment-Oriented Institution," 33 (December 1968): 935, 936.

Form A, Cattell's Sixteen Personality Factor Questionnaire

John W. Loy, Jr., "Social Psychological Characteristics of Innovators," 34 (February 1969): 75.

Mental Health Index Consisting of a 22-

Derek L. Phillips and Kevin J. Clancy,

Item Screening Inventory by Thomas S. Langner	"Response Biases in Field Studies of Mental Illness," 35 (June 1970): 504. See also D. L. Phillips and Bernard E. Segal, "Sexual Status and Psychiatric Symptoms," 34 (February 1969): 60.
California F-Scale Measuring Authoritarianism (Adorno et al. 1950); Rokeach's Dogmatism Scale	Walter Korpi, "Working Class Communism in Western Europe: Rational or Nonrational," 36 (December 1971): 975, 976.
Sanford and Older's 7-Item Scale of Authoritarianism Derived from Adorno's F-Scale; Douvan and Walker's Personal Competence Scale; Guttman Type	Richard Centers, Bertram H. Raven, and Aroldo Rodrigues, "Conjugal Power Structure: A Re-examination," 36 (April 1971): 266–67.
Srole Anomie Scale; Social Acquiescence Scale (Bass)	Leslie G. Carr, "The Srole Items and Acquiescences," 36 (April 1971): 288–90.
Indices of Emotional Strain Including Index of Superficial Levels of Strain, Index of Emotional Illness, Index of Hostility, Index of Behavioral Impairment, Index of Behavioral Withdrawal; Author Constructed	Robert Edward Mitchell, "Some Social Implications of High Density Housing," 36 (February 1971): 21–22.
Survey Research Center Index of Personal Effectiveness, Conceptualized as a Measure Tapping Seeman's Concept of Powerlessness	Bill Tudor, "A Specification of Relationships Between Job Complexity and Powerlessness," 37 (October 1972): 598.

Measures of Intelligence and Achievement

Henmon-Nelson Test of Mental Ability	William H. Sewell, Archibald O. Haller, and Alejandro Portes, "The Educational and Early Occupational Attainment Process," 34 (February 1969): 87.
Henmon-Nelson Test of Mental Ability	William H. Sewell et al., "The Educational and Early Occupational Status Attainment Process: Replication and Revision," 35 (December 1970): 1017.
California Test of Mental Maturity and Otis Quick Scoring Mental Ability, Beta Form	Richard A. Rehberg, Walter E. Schafer, and Judie Sinclair, "Toward a Temporal Sequence of Adolescent Achievement Variables," 35 (February 1970): 36–37.
Indices of Academic Achievement; Indices of Career Success; Both Author Constructed	Carolyn Cummings Perrucci and Robert Perrucci, "Social Origins, Educational Contexts, and Career Mobility," 35 (June 1970): 453, 454.
Indices of Intelligence; Author Constructed	Melvin L. Kohn, "Bureaucratic Man: A Portrait and an Interpretation," 36 (June 1971): 464–65.
Minnesota Scholastic Aptitude Test	Joel I. Nelson, "High School Context and College Plans: The Impact of Social Structure on Aspirations," 37 (April 1972): 145.

Measure of Intellectual Flexibility and Demands (Self-Imposed) on Intellectual Resources; Author Constructed

Melvin L. Kohn and Carmi Schooler, "Occupational Experience and Psychological Functioning: An Assessment of Reciprocal Effects," 38 (February 1973): 101.

Measure of Parents' Emphasis on Son's Achievement

Bernard C. Rosen, "Social Change, Migration, and Family Interaction in Brazil," 38 (April 1973): 198–212.

Science Citation Index

Paul D. Allison and John A. Stewart, "Productivity Differences Among Scientists: Evidence for Accumulative Advantage," 39 (August 1974): 599.

Science Citation Index

Warren O. Hagstrom, "Competition in Science," 39 (February 1974): 2, 5.

Measures of Identification

Identification with the Institution (for Delinquent Girls), 35-item Likert Scale

Raymond J. Adamek and Edward Z. Dager, "Social Structure Identification and Change in a Treatment-Oriented Institution," 33 (December 1968): 934.

Personal Integration into U.S. Culture, Six Indicators; Author Constructed

Alejandro Portes, "Dilemmas of a Golden Exile: Integration of Cuban Refugee Families in Milwaukee," 34 (August 1969): 508–9.

Gough's Masculinity-Femininity Scale of Sex Identity; Franck Drawing Completion Test of Sex Identity

William Bezdek and Fred L. Strodtbeck, "Sex-Role Identity and Pragmatic Action," 35 (June 1970): 494, 496.

Role-Taking; Author Constructed

Darwin L. Thomas, David D. Franks, and James M. Calonico, "Role-Taking and Power in Social Psychology," 37 (October 1972): 608.

Political Party Identification: Party Differences; Author Constructed

Anthony M. Orum and Roberta S. Cohen, "The Development of Political Orientations Among Black and White Children," 38 (February 1973): 68, 69.

Miscellaneous Scales

Author Constructed Measure of Educational Expectations—Considering Your Abilities, Grades, Financial Resources, etc., How Far Do You Actually Expect to Go in School?

Richard A. Rehberg, Walter E. Schafer, and Judie Sinclair, "Toward A Temporal Sequence of Adolescent Achievement Variables," 35 (February 1970): 36–37.

Mueller and Schuessler's Index of Qualitative Variation

Kathleen S. Crittenden and Richard J. Hill, "Coding Reliability and Validity of Interview Data," 36 (December 1971): 1075.

Featherman's Religio-Ethnic Categories Based on Nationality Background and Religious Affiliation

David L. Featherman, "The Socioeconomic Achievement of White Religio-Ethnic Subgroups: Social and Psychological Explanations," 36 (April 1971): 209.

Scientists' Analysis of Scientific Content of Various Fields, Behaviors and Attitudes; Author Constructed

Janice Beyer Lodahl and Gerald Gordon, "The Structure of Scientific Fields and the Functioning of University Graduate Departments," 37 (February 1972): 66–67.

Thirty-Seven Indicators of Institutional (High School and University) Innovations; Author Constructed

Ronald G. Corwin, "Strategies for Organizational Innovation: An Empirical Comparison," 37 (August 1972): 444.

Indices of Dissimilarity of Origins and of Occupational Destinations of Men and Women in Occupational Mobility

Andrea Tyree and Judith Treas, "The Occupational and Marital Mobility of Women," 39 (June 1974): 297.

Honoring of Accounts, Account Adequacy, Account Credibility, Demand Appropriateness, Demand Legitimacy, Offensiveness of Violation; Author Constructed

Philip W. Blumstein et al., "The Honoring of Accounts," 39 (August 1974): 555.

Social Indicators

Political Complexity Index, Social Differentiation Index; Author Constructed

Mark Abrahamson, "Correlates of Political Complexity," 34 (October 1969): 695.

"Multiversity" Index: Author Constructed

Joseph W. Scott and Mohamed El-Assal, "Multiversity Quality and Student Protest: An Empirical Study," 34 (October 1969): 704.

Index of Crime of Federal Bureau of Investigation

Edward Green, "Race, Social Status, and Criminal Arrest," 35 (June 1970): 476.

Indicators of Regional Integration Based on Urbanization, Industrialization, Occupational Redistribution, Income, and Education

John C. McKinney and Linda Brookover Bourque, "The Changing South: National Incorporation of a Region," 36 (June 1971): 400–407.

Index of Southerness; Author Constructed

Raymond D. Gastil, "Homicide and a Regional Culture of Violence," 36 (June 1971): 425–26.

Two Indices of National Economic Development; Author Constructed

Marion Blute, "The Growth of Science and Economic Development," 37 (August 1972): 457.

Social Insurance Program Experience (SIPE) Index; Author Adapted from Cutright

Robert W. Jackman, "Political Democracy and Social Equality: A Comparative Analysis," 39 (February 1974): 32–33, 33, 34.

Measurement of Income Inequality, Kuznets

Social Welfare Index; Author Adapted from Hibbs

Serious Ratings of 140 Criminal Offenses

Peter A. Rossi, Emily Waite, Christine E. Bose, and Richard E. Berk, "The Seriousness of Crimes: Normative Structure and Individual Differences," 39 (April 1974): 228–29.

Measure of "Best" Colleges	Duane F. Alwin, "College Effects on Educational and Occupational Attainments," 39 (April 1974): 213.
Index of Unionization	Richard Child Hill, "Unionization and Racial Income Inequality in the Metropolis," 39 (August 1974): 514.
Degree of Unionization, Index of Industrial Conflict	David W. Britt and Omer Galle, "Structural Antecedents of the Shape of Strikes: A Comparative Analysis," 39 (August 1974): 645.
Structural Poverty Index, Gini Index of Income Inequality	Colin Loftin and Robert H. Hill, "Regional Subculture and Homicide: An Examination of the Gastil-Hackney Thesis," 39 (October 1974): 719–20.
Sellin-Wolfgang Seriousness of Crime Index	Alfred Blumstein, "Seriousness Weights in an Index of Crime," 39 (December 1974): 854.

INVENTORY FOR 1975–80*

Scales for Measuring Social Status

Adaptation of Standard International Occupational Prestige Scale (Treiman)	Donald J. Treiman and Kermit Terrell, "Sex and the Process of Status and Attainment: A Comparison of Working Women and Men," 40 (April 1975): 174–200.
Social Status of Families: Husband's and Wife's Occupations, Husband's and Wife's Education, Race; Author Constructed	William A. Sampson and Peter H. Rossi, "Race and Family Social Standing," 40 (April 1975): 201–14.
Twelve Major Occupation Groups in 1960 Classification System of U.S. Bureau of the Census (Edwards)	Robert M. Hauser, John N. Koffel, Harry P. Travis, and Peter J. Dickinson, "Temporal Change in Occupational Mobility: Evidence for Men in the United States," 40 (June 1975): 279–97.
Occupational Prestige; Scores from 1964 Study NORC.	Angela Lane, "The Occupational Achievement Process, 1940–1949: A Cohort Analysis," 40 (August 1975): 472–82.
Occupational Status; Adaptation of Blau and Duncan 1967	Ivan D. Chase, "A Comparison of Men's and Women's Intergenerational Mobility in the United States," 40 (August 1975): 483–505.
Duncan's Index of Socioeconomic Status, Modified; Indexes of Occupational Mobility: Yasuda, Boudon, Author Constructed	Robert Hauser, Peter J. Dickinson, Harry P. Travis, and John N. Koffel, "Structural Changes in Occupational Mobility Among Men in the United States," 40 (October 1975): 585–98.

* I am indebted to Susan R. Cohen for assistance with the inventory for 1975–79.

Characteristics of Census Occupation Categories (Institute of Labor and Industrial Relations of Wayne State University and University of Michigan); Specific Vocational Preparation (Department of Labor Estimates of Years of Training Necessary for 4000 Jobs); Siegel's Prestige Scores

Ross M. Stozenberg, "Occupations, Labor Markets, and the Process of Wage Attainment," 40 (October 1975): 645–65.

Socioeconomic Status; Techniques developed by Nam and Powers and by U.S. Bureau of the Census

Theodore G. Chiricos and Gordon P. Waldo, "Socioeconomic Status and Criminal Sentencing: An Empirical Assessment of a Conflict Proposition," 40 (December 1975): 753–72.

Three Indicators of Socioeconomic Status Analyzed Separately: Educational Attainment, Occupational Status, and Income; Author Constructed

Charles W. Mueller and Weldon T. Johnson, "Socioeconomic Status and Religious Participation," 40 (Decemer 1975): 785–800.

Duncan's Socioeconomic Index

McKee J. McClendon, "The Occupational Status Attainment Processes of Males and Females," 41 (February 1976): 52–64.

Duncan's Socioeconomic Index

R. Paul Duncan and Carolyn Cummings Perrucci, "Dual Occupation Families and Migration," 41 (April 1976): 252–61.

Siegel (NORC) Occupational Prestige Scores

David Snyder and Paula M. Hudis, "Occupational Income and the Effects of Minority Competition and Segregation: A Reanalysis and Some New Evidence," 41 (April 1976): 209–34.

Occupational Categories Based on 1970 Census Occupation Code

John Angle, "Mainland Control of Manufacturing and Reward for Bilingualism in Puerto Rico," 41 (April 1976): 289–307.

Rate of Mobility Composed of Three Parts: Rate at Which People Quit; Rate at Which People Are Fired; residual, unexplained rate. Author Constructed

Nancy Brandon Tuma, "Rewards, Resources, and the Rate of Mobility: A Nonstationary Multivariate Stochastic Model," 41 (April 1976): 338–60.

Duncan's Socioeconomic Index

David L. Featherman and Robert M. Hauser, "Sexual Inequalities and Socioeconomic Achievement in the U.S., 1962–1973," 41 (June 1976): 462–83.

Duncan's Socioeconomic Index

Patricia Ann Taylor and Norval D. Glenn, "The Utility of Education and Attractiveness for Females' Status Attainment Through Marriage," 41 (June 1976): 484–98.

Occupational Mobility: Rate of Circulation of Talent and Skill (2 Author-Constructed Estimates, Deming-Stephan Technique Used); Measure Based on Nonmanual-Manual-Farm Classification

Lawrence E. Hazelrigg and Maurice A. Garnier, "Occupational Mobility in Industrial Societies: A Comparative Analysis of Differential Access to Occupational Ranks in Seventeen Countries," 41 (June 1976): 498–511.

Prestige of Postdoctoral Fellowships; Adaptation of Cole and Cole

Barbara F. Reskin, "Sex Differences in Status Attainment in Science: The Case of the Postdoctoral Fellowship," 41 (August 1976): 597–612.

Social Class: Educational Attainment, Occupational Prestige, Family Income, and Class Identification; Author Constructed; Edwards Occupational Categories

James D. Wright and Sonia R. Wright, "Social Class and Parental Values for Children: A Partial Replication and Extension of the Kohn Thesis," 41 (June 1976): 527–37.

Duncan Socioeconomic Index

John C. Heuretta and Richard T. Campbell, "Status Attainment and Status Maintenance: A Study of Stratification in Old Age," 41 (December 1976): 981–92.

Marxist Criteria of Class; Standard Duncan SEI Scores

Erik Olin Wright and Luca Perrone, "Marxist Class Categories and Income Inequality," 42 (February 1977): 32–55.

Duncan Socioeconomic Index

McKee J. McClendon, "Structural and Exchange Components of Vertical Mobility." 42 (February 1977): 56–74.

U.S. Census Score Developed by Nam

James M. Fendrich, "Keeping the Faith or Pursuing the Good Life," 42 (February 1977): 144–57.

Siegel (NORC) Prestige Index; Duncan Socioeconomic Index

Reeve Vanneman and Fred C. Pampel, "The American Perception of Class and Status," 42 (June 1977): 422–37.

Measures of Income Inequality (Lydall, Pryor, Paukert, Atkinson)

Christopher Hewitt, "The Effect of Political Democracy and Social Democracy on Equality in Industrial Societies: A Cross National Comparison," 42 (June 1977): 450–464.

Duncan Socioeconomic Index

Alan C. Kerckhoff, "The Realism of Educational Ambitions in England and the United States," 42 (August 1977): 563–71.

Objective and Status Subjective Class Measures: Duncan SEI, Education, Income; Respondents Place Selves in Lower, Working, Middle, or Upper Class; Respondents Indicate Class Placement of Their Occupation, Income, Way of Life, and Influence

James R. Kluegel, Royce Singleton, Jr., and Charles E. Starnes, "Subjective Class Identification A Multiple Indicator Approach," 42 (August 1977): 599–611.

Occupational Categories; Modified Edwards Used Because Author Believes Use of Prestige or Status Scores Hide Sex Differences in Occupational Location and Mobility Since Occupational Sex Segregation Does Not Follow Socioeconomic Lives Closely

Rachel A. Rosenfeld, "Women's Intergenerational Occupational Mobility," 43 (February 1978): 36–46.

Socioeconomic Status Based on Father's Education, Mother's Education, and Father's Occupation (Duncan SEI)

Karl L. Alexander, Martha Cook, and Edward L. McDill, "Curriculum Tracking and Educational Stratification: Some

Percentage of 16 to 20 Year Olds Attending School as Measure of Suburban Social Status.

Further Evidence," 43 (February 1978): 47–66.

Avery M. Guest, "Suburban Social Status: Persistence or Evolution?" 43 (April 1978): 251–64.

Measure of Socioeconomic Background Derived from Respondent Report on Father's Occupation, Father's Education, and Family Income (Age Adjusted in $1000 Units)

James R. Kluegel, "The Causes and Cost of Racial Exclusion from Job Authority," 43 (June 1978): 285–301.

Hollinghead's Seven Occupational Prestige Levels

R. Jay Turner and John W. Gartrell, "Social Factors in Psychiatric Outcome: Toward the Resolution of Interpretive Controversies," 43 (June 1978): 368–82.

Duncan's Socioeconomic Status Index

Ross M. Stolzenberg, "Bringing the Boss Back In: Employer Size, Employee Schooling, and Socioeconomic Achievement," 43 (December 1978): 813–28.

Duncan's Socioeconomic Status Index; Centers Class Identification; Fathers' Control of Means of Production Measure (NORC Surveys, 1974, '75, '76)

Robert V. Robinson and Jonathan Kelley, "Class as Conceived by Marx and Dahendorf: Effects and Income Inequality and Politics in the United States and Great Britain," 44 (February 1979): 38–57.

Siegel's (1971) Prestige Scores for Major Occupational Groups

Toby L. Parcel, "Race, Regional Labor Markets, and Earnings," 44 (April 1979): 262–79.

Measures of Three Dimensions of Vertical Differentiation of Occupations: Authority, Complexity, and Prestige; Author Constructed.

Joe L. Spaetti, "Vertical Differentiation Among Occupations," 44 (October 1979): 746–62.

Duncan's SEI Scores for Father's Occupation

Ronald R. Rindfuss, Larry Bumpass, and Craig St. John, "Education and Fertility: Implications for the Roles Women Occupy," 45 (June 1980): 431–47.

Scales for Measuring Group Structures and Dynamics

Measures re Popular Music Market: Level of Concentration (i.e., Oligopoly vs. High Degree of Competition; Homogeneity of Product; Author Constructed.

Richard A. Peterson and David G. Berger, "Cycles in Symbol Production: The Case of Popular Music," 40 (April 1975): 158–73.

"Direct" and "Supportive" Components of School Districts (Direct = Teachers; Supportive = Professional Staff, Administrators, and Nonprofessional Staff); Author Constructed

John Freeman and Michael T. Hannan, "Growth and Decline Processes in Organizations," 40 (April 1975): 215–28.

Measures of Labor Relations Contexts: Extent and Stability of Union Membership; National Political Position of Labor; Degree of Institutionalization of

David Snyder, "Institutional Setting and Industrial Conflict: Comparative Analyses of France, Italy and the United States," 40 (June 1975): 259–78.

Collective Bargaining; Author Constructed. Measures of Industrial Conflicts: Number of strikes beginning in the year and man-days lost. Data Adaptation.

Measures of Environmental Demand on Government Agencies; Author Constructed

Marshall W. Meyer, "Organizational Domains," 40 (October 1975): 599–615.

Measures of Productive Subsystem of Organization (P = Number of Production Employees; D = Number of Divisions That Functionally Differentiate Work Force); Measures of Administrative Subsystem of Organization (S = Number of Supervisory Employees; L = Number of Hierarchical Levels Over All Divisions); Author Constructed

Norman P. Hummon, Patrick Doreian, and Klaus Tueter, "A Structural Control Model of Organizational Change," 40 (December 1975): 813–24.

Task Variability: 4-Category Ordinal Scale Indicating Extent to Which Outputs Must Be Modified to Meet Customer Specifications; Automaticity: Extent to Which Machinery Replaces Manpower and Decision Making; Impersonal Rules and Procedures: Extent to Which Written Procedures Are Drawn Up in Advance to Serve as Integrative Mechanisms (Aston measure of formalization). First Two Measures Author Constructed

Phelps Tracy and Koya Azumi, "Determinants of Administrative Control: A Test of a Theory with Japanese Factories," 41 (February 1976): 80–94.

Index of Task Uncertainty (Author Constructed); Task Interdependence Index Based on Thompson Work Flow Interdependence Index and Mohr Task Interdependence Index.

Andrew H. Van de Ven, Andre L. Delbecq, and Richard Koenig, Jr., "Determinants of Coordination Modes Within Organizations," 41 (April 1976): 322–338.

Professional Stature of Social Scientists: Individual Professional Status (Author Constructed); and Department Professional Status (Roose and Anderson's "Quality of Graduate Faculty" Rating)

Michael Useem, "State Production of Social Knowledge: Patterns in Government Financing of Academic Social Research," 41 (August 1976): 613–29.

Differentiation: Gibbs-Martin D Adjusted for Maximum Value and Number of Occupations (Latter Author Constructed). Coordination: Proportion of Organizational Personnel in Administrative Intensity); Based on Author Constructed List of Hospital Occupations Judged as Performing Coordinative Functions

William A. Rushing, "Profit and Nonprofit Orientations and the Differentiations-Coordination Hypothesis for Organizations: A study of Small General Hospitals," 41 (August 1976): 676–91.

Measure of Group Participation; Author Constructed

Pat Lauderdale, "Deviance and Moral Boundaries," 41 (August 1976): 660–76.

Peer Characteristics: Friends' Academic

Karl L. Alexander and Edward L.

Aptitude, Socioeconomic Status, and Educational Expectations; Author Constructed

McDill, "Selection and Allocation Within Schools," 41 (December 1976): 963–80.

Problem Solving in Groups and Organization: Personal Influence Condition; Organizational Context Condition

Lynne G. Zucker, "The Role of Institutionalization in Cultural Persistence," 42 (October 1977): 726–43.

Measures of Organizational Structure in a Hospital (Author Constructed): Size and Structure, Degree of Specialization, Functional Differentiation, Centralization, and Innovation

Michael K. Moch and Edward V. Morse, "Size, Centralization, and Organizational Adoption of Innovations," 42 (October 1977): 716–25.

Measures of Structural Attributes of Bureaucratization (Frisbe 1975, Gibbs-Martin 1963, Labovitz and Gibbs 1964)

Fred C. Pampel, Kenneth C. Land, and Marcus Felson, "A Social Indicator Model of Changes in the Occupational Structure of the United States: 1947–1974," 42 (December 1977): 951–64.

Longitudinal Sociometric Measures of Friendship (Children Asked to Name Best Friends and Friends They Liked but Did Not Consider Best Friends); Data Collected at Seven Time Points During School Year

Donna Eder and Maureen T. Hallinan, "Sex Differences in Children's Friendships," 43 (April 1978): 237–49.

Complexity (Functional Differentiation) of Children's Play, Six Dimensions; Author Constructed

Janet Lever, "Sex Differences in the Complexity of Children's Play and Games," 43 (August 1978): 471–83.

Temporal Ordering of Events Marking the Passage to Adulthood; Author Constructed

Dennis P. Hogan, "The Variable Order of Events in the Life Course," 43 (August 1978): 573–86.

Aston Scales of Organizational Structure (Short Forms as Developed by Inkson)

James R. Lincoln, Jon Olson, and Mitsuyo Hanada, "Cultural Effects on Organizational Structure: The Case of Japanese Firms in the United States," 43 (December 1978): 829–47.

Roose and Anderson Departmental Bioscience Prestige Index: Publication Citation Index, Educational Experience Index, Professional Mentor Measure, and Austin's Indicator of Intelligence and Quality of Baccalaureate Education

J. Scott Long, "Productivity and Academic Position in the Scientific Career," 43 (December 1978): 889–908.

Authority in the Work Place (3 Items with Yes or No Answers Identified as Guttman-Type Variables); Author Constructed

Wendy C. Wolf and Neil D. Fligstein, "Sex and Authority in the Work Place: The Causes of Sexual Inequality" 44 (April 1979): 235–52.

Prestige of Doctoral Department as Measured by 3-Digit Rating of Faculty Quality (Carter)

J. Scott Long, Paul D. Allison, and Robert McGinnis, "Entrance into the Academic Career," 44 (October 1979): 816–30.

Measures of Primary Integration:

Larry Isaac, Elizabeth Mutran, and Shel-

Friends' Integration, Family Integration, and Neighborhood Integration; Four Observable Items in Each Scaled to Equal Intervals Ranging from Zero to One; Author Constructed. Measures of Relative Deprivation and Political Protest Orientations; Author Constructed. Exogenous Variable, Occupational Status, Measured by Duncan SEI

don Stryker, "Political Protest Orientations Among Black and White Adults," 45 (April 1980): 191–213.

Measures of Administrative Intensity, Interdepartmental Communication, and Decentralization of Decision Making; Author Constructed

James R. Lincoln and Gerald Zeitz, "Organizational Properties from Aggregate Data: Separating Individual and Structural Effects," 45 (June 1980): 391–408.

Marxist Class Categories, Average Income

Hagen Koo and Doo-Seung Hong, "Class and Income Inequality in Korea," 45 (August 1980): 610–26.

Corporate Directorate Ties (Data Adaptations)

Ronald S. Burt, Kenneth P. Christman, and Harold C. Kilburn, Jr., "Testing a Structural Theory of Corporate Cooptation: Interorganizational Directorate Ties as a Strategy for Avoiding Market Constraints on Profits," 45 (October 1980): 821–41.

Scales for Measuring Community Factors

Measures Amount of Policy Generated by Community: per Capita Expenditures by Municipal Government; Level of OEO Funding of Local Antipoverty projects; Index of Participation in Urban Renewal Programs (Similar to Hawley 1963 Index); Author Constructed

James R. Lincoln, "Power and Mobilization in the Urban Community: Reconsidering the Ecological Approach," 41 (February 1976): 1–15.

Local Community Reference Scale (scale items used by Dobriner 1968 and Dye 1963)

Wade Clark Roof, "Traditional Religion in Contemporary Society: A Theory of Local-Cosmopolitan Plausibility," 41 (April 1976): 195–208.

Duncan's Index of Dissimilarity Criticized and Revised

Charles F. Cortese, R. Frank Falk, and Jack K. Cohen, "Further Considerations on the Methodological Analysis of Segregation Indices," 41 (August 1976): 630–37.

Measure of Community Power: MPO Ratio (Hawley)

Richard A. Smith, "Community Power and Decision Making: A Replication and Extension of Hawley," 41 (August 1976): 691–705.

Local Facility Use Index; Informal Neighboring Index; Sense of Community Index (Foley 1952)

Albert Hunter, "The Loss of Community: An Empirical Test Through Replication," 40 (October 1975): 537–52.

Measures of Segregation: Index of Dissimilarity (Duncan and Duncan 1955); Index of Asymmetric Intergroup contact (Adapted from Proposal by Bell 1954 and Discussion by Lieberson 1969 and Farley and Taeuber 1968)

Brigitte Mack Erbe, "Race and Socioeconomic Segregation," 40 (December 1975): 801–12.

Seven Community Structure Factors, Indicators, and Weights (Bonjean, Browning, and Carter)

Michael D. Grimes, Charles M. Bonjean, J. Larry Lion, and Robert L. Lineberry, "Community Structure and Leadership Arrangements: A Multidimensional Analysis," 41 (August 1976): 706–25.

Conflict Intensity; Media Sensitively; Author Constructed

David Snyder and William R. Kelly, "Conflict Intensity, Media Sensitivity, and the Validity of Newspaper Data," 42 (February 1977): 105–23.

Residential Segregation Measured by Index of Dissimilarity (Duncan and Duncan 1955)

Albert A. Simkus, "Residential Segregation by Occupation and Race in Ten Urbanized Areas, 1950–1970," 43 (February 1978): 81–93.

Multiple Measures to Assess Community Structure: Gibbs and Martin Index; Absentee Ownership; Employment Concentration; Degree of Unionization; Union Concentration

James R. Lincoln, "Community Structure and Industrial Conflict: An Analysis of Strike Activity in SMSA's, 43 (April 1978): 199–220.

Measure of Suburban Status: Percent 16–20 Attend School 1920; Percent High School Graduates 1950; Percent High School Graduates 1970 (U.S. Bureau of Census Data)

Avery M. Guest, "Suburban Social Status: Persistence or Evolution," 43 (April 1978): 251–64.

Guttman Scale of Commercial Services, Index of Closure (Feldt 1965); Gini Index of Income Dissimilarity, Moral Integration (Augell 1951); Guttman Scale of Voluntary Organizations; Guttman Scales Author Constructed

Richard A. Smith, "Decision Making and Non-Decision Making in Cities: Some Implications for Community Structural Research," 44 (February 1979): 147–61.

Socioeconomic Status of American Suburbs, Data Adaptations

Andrew Collver and Moshe Semyonov, "Suburban Change and Persistence," 44 (June 1979): 480–86.

Network Characteristics of Collective Actors; Measures of Size, Density, Maximum Path Distance, and Average Path Distance

Edward O. Laumann and Peter V. Marsden, "The Analysis of Oppositional Structures in Political Elites: Identifying Collective Actors," 44 (October 1979): 713–32.

Economic Inequality of Metropolitan Areas (Data on Family Incomes); Police Strength (Number of Police per 100,000); Census Statistics on Unemployment, Data Adaptation

David Jacobs, "Inequality and Police Strength: Conflict Theory and Coercive Control in Metropolitan Areas," 44 (December 1979): 913–25.

Suburban Status Indicators: Percent of Population with twelve or More Years Education; Percentage in White Collar

John M. Stahura, "Suburban Status Evolution/Persistence: A Structural Model," 44 (December 1979): 937–47.

Jobs; percentage with Incomes of $10,000 or More ($15,000 or More in 1970) Data Adaptation

Probability Measures That Central-City Residents and Immigrants to Metropolitan Areas Settle in Suburbs

Harvey Marshall, "White Movement to the Suburbs: A Comparison of Explanations," 44 (December 1979): 975–94.

Six Indicators of Modernization, Data Adaptions

Francois Nielsen, "The Flemish Movement in Belgium After World War II: A Dynamic Analysis," 45 (February 1980): 76–94.

Community Involvement: Professional Practitioner Contact and Activism with Community Organizations; Author Constructed

Jon Miller, "Access to Interorganizational Networks as a Professional Resource," 45 (June 1980): 479–96.

Scales for Measuring Participation and Alienation

Measures of: Imprisonment, Relative Expected Value of Criminal Choice, and Probability of Future Criminal Behavior; Author Constructed

Anthony R. Harris, "Imprisonment and the Expected Value of Criminal Choice: A Specification and Test of Aspects of the Labeling Perspective," 40 (February 1975): 71–87.

Measures of Political Alienation 2 Items on Alienation Scale Used by University of Michigan Survey Research Center Are Valid Measures of Political Trust

James S. House and William M. Mason, "Political Alienation in America, 1952–1968," 40 (April 1975): 123–47.

Intensity of Peasant Rebellions Determined by Measuring Extent of Diffusion and Degree of Violence; Author Constructed

Daniel Chirot and Charles Ragin, "The Market, Tradition and Peasant Rebellion: The Case of Romania in 1907," 40 (August 1975): 428–44.

Measures of System Involvement (8 Measures Originally Used by Form 1973 reanalyzed)

Kenneth I. Spenner, "The Internal Stratification of the Working Class: A Reanalysis," 40 (August 1975): 513–20.

Measure of Participation in Organization Meetings; Author Constructed

Anne M. McMahon and Santo F. Camilleri, "Organizational Structure and Voluntary Participation in Collective-Good Decisions," 40 (October 1975): 616–44.

Measures of Powerlessness and Self-Estrangement; Adaption of Seeman 1972

Luther B. Otto and David L. Featherman, "Social Structure and Psychological Antecedents of Self-Estrangement and Powerlessness," 40 (December 1975): 701–19.

Church Attendance, Religious Organizations, and Congregational Friendships; Author Constructed

Wade Clark Roof, "Traditional Religion in Contemporary Society: A Theory of Local-Cosmopolitan Plausibility," 41 (April 1976): 195–208.

Instrumental commitment to criminal choice: Criminal Income and Relative Expected Value of Criminal Choice (Adaptation of Harris 1975 and Stradtbeck and Short 1964), Self-Typing: Criminal and "Straight" identity (Harris 1973)

Anthony R. Harris, "Race, Commitment to Deviance, and Spoiled identity," 41 (June 1976): 432–42.

Severity of Punishment Index, Certainty of Punishment Index, and Peer Involvement Index (all Waldo and Chiricos 1972); Criminal Involvement Index (adaptation of Waldo and Chiricos); Morality Index (Author Constructed)

Matthew Silberman, "Toward a Theory of Criminal Deterrence," 41 (June 1976): 442–61.

Riot severity scale; Adaptation of Downes

Seymour Spilerman, "Structural Characteristics of Cities and the Severity of Racial Disorders," 41 (October 1976): 771–93.

Lawyers Participations in Legal Services Program; Author Constructed

Howard S. Erlanger, "Social Reform Organizations and Subsequent Careers of Participants: A Follow-Up Study of Early Participants in the OEO Legal Services Programs," 42 (April 1977): 233–48.

Fifteen-Item Scale Referring to Traits of Practicing Physician Grouped into Three Basic Components of Medical Practice: People, Status, and Science; Scales Author Constructed

Israel Adler and Judith T. Shuval, "Cross Pressures during Socialization for Medicine," 43 (October 1978): 693–704.

Participation Scale: Measures Participation in Antibusing Activities and Groups; Author Constructed

Bert Useem, "Solidarity Model, Breakdown Model, and the Boston Anti-Busing Movement," 45 (June 1980): 357–369.

Scales to Measure Attitudes and Values

Scale Revealing Two Factors: Humanism/Materialism and Collectivism/Individualism (Respondents Rank-Order 16 value items; Similar to Rokeach Procedure but with Items Chosen to Reflect Above Dimensions)

Vern L. Bengtson, "Generation and Family Effects in Value Socialization," 40 (June 1975): 358–71.

Measure to Determine Conceptions of Mental Illness; Jum C. Nunnally's Information Questionnaire 1961

J. Marshall Townsend, "Cultural Conceptions, Mental Disorders, and Social Roles: A Comparison of Germany and America," 40 (December 1975): 739–52.

Anti-Black Prejudice Scale (Expansion of Selznick and Steinberg Index of Anti-Negro Prejudice); Anti-Semitic Beliefs Scale; Hostility Toward Jews Scale; All Author Constructed

Russell Middleton, "Regional Differences in Prejudice," 41 (February 1976): 94–117.

F Scale (Short-Form Adaptation of Adorno F Scale); Anomia Scale (Short-Form adaptation of Srole Scale); Psychic Distress Scale (Adaptation of Selznick and Steinberg Scale); Validity and Reliability Measures Given for All Scales

Doctrinal Orthodoxy: Responses about God, Jesus, Heaven and Hell, Bible;

Wade Clark Roof, "Traditional Religion in Contemporary Society: A Theory of

Devotionalism: Frequency of Personal Prayer and Bible Reading; Both Author Constructed

Work Attitudes: Beliefs about Benefits and Costs of Female Labor Force Participation (9 Likert-scale attitude questions); Author Constructed

Racial Prejudice Scale; Author; Class Prejudice Scale; Author Adaptation of Westie's Scale of Residential Social Distance

Political Perspective Scale; Author Constructed; Government Confidence Scale; Adaptation of Muller's Trust in Political Authorities Scale

Sex-Role Attitudes; 13 Items Drawn from 5 Previous Surveys

Self-Direction: Parental Values for Children; Adaptation of Kohn

Value Orientations: instrumental, expressive, political, other; Author Constructed

Job Satisfaction: 5-Item Scale with Reliability and Unidimensionality Measures; Author Constructed

Radicalism-Conservation Political Scale (Nettler and Huffman 1957); Occupational Values (Rosenberg 1957)

Semantic Differential Scales: Strong-Weak; Powerful-Powerless; Potent-Nonpotent; Dominant-Submissive; Valuable-Worthless; Important-Unimportant; Sought after–not sought after; desirable-undersirable. Adaptations from Previous Research

Push Buttons and Lights to Indicate Choices on "Variety of Tasks Under Individual and Team Conditions; Author Constructed

Twelve Exogenous and Three Endogamous Variables; One Endogamous

---

Local-Cosmopolitan Plausibility," 41 (April 1976): 195–208.

Linda J. Waite and Ross M. Stolzenberg, "Intended Childbearing and Labor Force Participation of Young Women: Insights from Nonrecursive Models," 41 (April 1976): 235–52.

Michael W. Giles, Douglas S. Gatlin, and Everett F. Cataldo, "Racial and Class Prejudice: Their Relative Effects on Protest against School Presegregation," 41 (April 1976): 280–88.

Michael Useem, "State Production of Social Knowledge: Patterns in Government Financing of Academic Research," 41 (August 1976): 613–29.

Karen Opperiheim Mason, John L. Czajka, and Sara Arber, "Change in U.S. Women's Sex-Role Attitudes," 41 (August 1976): 573–96.

James D. Wright and Sonia R. Wright, "Social Class and Parental Values for Children: A Partial Replication and Extension of the Kohn Thesis," 41 (June 1976): 527–37.

James L. Spates, "Counterculture and Dominant Culture Values: A Cross-National Analysis of the Underground Press and Dominant Culture Magazines," 41 (October 1976): 868–83.

Arne L. Kalleberg, "Work Values and Job Rewards," 42 (February 1977): 124–43.

James M. Fendrich, "Keeping the Faith or Pursuing the Good Life," 42 (February 1977): 144–57.

H. Andrew Michener, Eugene D. Cohen, and Aage D. Sorenson, "Social Exchange: Predicting Transactional Outcomes in Five-Event, Four-Person Systems," 42 (June 1977): 522–35.

Murray Webster, Jr., and James E. Driskell, Jr., "Status Generalization: A Review and Some New Data," 43 (April 1978): 220–36.

Lynn Smith-Lovin and Ann R. Tickamyer, "Nonrecursive Models of Labor

Variable in Sex-Role Attitudes Measured by 15-Item Likert-Type Scale Relating to Women's Roles; Author Constructed

Three Attitude Areas Explored by Likert and Open-Ended Questions Dealing with Respondent's Relation to: Sending Country, Receiving Country, and Relating to both countries; Author Constructed

Subjective Experience of Crowding Measured by Six Attitude Clusters (Factor Analysis): Lack of Privacy Scale; Felt Demands Scale; Physical Withdrawal; Psychological Withdrawal Scale; Lack of Planning Scale; Washed-out Scale; All Author Constructed

Mental health measures include: Psychiatric Symptom Scale (Gove and Geerken 1977); Positive Affect (Bradburn 1969); Mental Health Balance Scale; Nervous breakdown; Manifest irritation (Gove 1978); General Alienation Scale; Self-Esteem (Gove 1978)

Measures of Mental Health and Physical Health: 12-Item Scale to Measure Subjective Mental Health (Gove and Gerken 1977); 4-Item Scale to Measure Subjective Overall Health (Reynolds et al. 1974)

Use and Attitude Toward Marijuana; Author Constructed

Self-Esteem: 6-Item Guttman Scale Described by Rosenberg and Simmons

Srole Five-Item Anomie Scale

Support Scale; Attitudinal Support for Anti-Busing Movement; Author Constructed

Seven-Point Self-Rating Scales on Five Public Issues; Data from National Survey Panel Study, Institute for Social Research, University of Michigan

Force Participation, Fertility Behavior, and Sex Role Atitudes," 43 (August 1978): 541–57.

David E. Payne, "Cross-National Diffusion: The Effects of Canadian TV on Rural Minnesota Viewers," 43 (October 1978): 740–56.

Walter R. Gove, Michael Hughes, and Omer R. Galle, "Overcrowding in the Home: An Empirical Investigation of Its Pathological Consequences," 44 (February 1979): 59–80.

Walter R. Gove and Michael Hughes, "Possible Causes of Apparent Sex Differences in Physical Health: An Empirical Investigation," 44 (February 1979): 126–146.

Kenneth H. Andrews and Denise B. Kandell, "Attitude and Behavior: A Specification of the Contingent Consistency Hypothesis," 44 (April 1979): 288.

Roberta G. Simmons, Edward F. Von Clive, Dale A. Blyth, and Dave Mitsch Bush, "Entry into Early Adolescence: The Impact of School Structure, Puberty, and Early Dating on Self Esteem," 44 (December 1979): 948–67.

Mark Abrahamson, "Sudden Wealth, Gratification, and Attainment: Durkheim's Anomie of Influence Reconsidered," 45 (February 1980); 49–57.

Bert Useem "Solidarity Model, Breakdown Model, and the Boston Anti-Busing Movement," 45 (June 1980): 357–69.

Charles M. Judd and Michael A. Milburn, "The Structure of Attitude Systems in the General Public: Comparisons of a Structural Equation Model," 45 (August 1980): 627–43.

Numerous-Item Measures of Crime and Fear of Crime: Respondent's Perception of Ineffectiveness of Police; Perceived Crime Rate in County; Fear of Crime; Violent Attitudes; Racist attitudes (Survey Research Laboratory, University of Illinois); Overt Behavioral Measures include: Victimization Home Defense Measures, and Gun for Protection; Author Constructed

Alan J. Lizotte and David J. Bordua, "Firearms Ownership for Sport and Protection," 45 (April 1980): 229–44.

Scales Measuring Family and Marriage Factors

Measure of Society's Dependence on Five Major Subsistence Activities; Female Participation in Each Activity; Murdock 1957 and 1967, Modified by Author

Joel Aronoff and William D. Crano, "A Re-Examination of the Cross-Cultural Principles of Task Segregation and Sex Role Differentiation in the Family," 40 (February 1975): 12–20.

Measure of Status Background of Husband and Wife (Occupational Statuses of Respective Fathers Before Marriage); Measure of Stress in Marriage; Measure of Exchange in Marriage: Reciprocity, Expressiveness, Attention, and Affection Values; Author Constructed

Leonard I. Pearlin, "Status Inequality and Stress in Marriage," 40 (June 1975): 344–57.

Scale of Contraceptive Practice (Note: Measured Use and Kind of Contraception but Could *Not* Measure Faithfulness of Use, Probably Most Important Variant); Adaptation of Robert Potter et al. 1962

Linda J. Waite, "Working Wives: 1940–1960," 41 (February 1976): 65–80.

Measures of Crowding: People per Room, Households per Block, Household Objective, Household Subjective, Neighborhood Objective, and Neighborhood Subjective; last four Author Constructed. Measures of Family Relations: Index of Affection Between Spouses, Number of Disagreements Between Spouses, Threats to Leave, Cessation of Intercourse, Time Spent Playing with Children, Times Struck Children, and Number of Sibling Quarrels; Author Constructed

Alan Booth and John N. Edwards, "Crowding and Family Relations," 41 (April 1976): 308–21.

Work Attitudes; 9-Item Scale of Young Woman's Beliefs about Costs and Benefits of Labor Force Participation by Married Women; Likert type; Author Constructed

Ross M. Stolzenberg and Linda J. Waite, "Age, Fertility Expectations, and Plans for Employment," 42 (October 1977): 769–83.

Levels of Parental Involvement; Bairy and Paxon Cross-Cultural Codes

William D. Crano and Joel Aronoff, "A Cross-Cultural Study of Expressive and Instrumental Role Complementarity in the Family," 43 (August 1978): 463–71.

Six-Attribute Scale of Complexity of Children's Play; Author Constructed Based on Work of Etzioni, Blau, and Schoenheen

Janet Lever, "Sex Differences in the Complexity of Children's Play and Games," 43 (August 1978): 471–83.

Multivariable Path Analysis Study. Factors Transformed into Variables Include: Father's Education, Mother's Education, Father's Occupational Prestige (NORC Occupational Prestige Scores), Family Income, Number of Siblings, Measured Intelligence (Standard IQ Scales), Parental Encouragement to Go to College, Enrollment in a College Preparatory Curriculum, Friend's Educational Expectations, Academic Effort, Grade-Point Average, Participation in Extracurricular Activities, Adolescent Rebellion, Dating Frequency, Educational Expectations, Age at First Marriage, and Educational Attainment; Author Selected and Constructed)

Margaret Mooney Marini, "The Transition to Adulthood: Sex Differences in Educational Attainment and Age at Marriage," 43 (August 1978): 483–507.

Index of Constitutional Provisions Concerning Childhood (Childhood Index); Author Constructed

John Boli-Bennett and John W. Meyer, "The Ideology of Childhood and the State Rules Distinguishing Children in National Constitutions," 43 (December 1978): 797–812.

Orshansky Index of Poverty

Sandra L. Hofferth and Kristin A. Moore, "Early Childrearing and Later Economic Well-Being," 44 (October 1979): 784–815.

Indices of Fertility, Wife's Labor Force plans, and Expected Family size; Author Constructed

James C. Cramer, "Fertility and Female Employment: Problems of Causal Direction," 45 (April 1980); 167–90.

Fairness of Earnings Rating for Single and Married Males and Females; Author Constructed

Guillerma Jasso and Peter H. Rossi, "Distributive Justice and Earned Income," 42 (August 1977): 639–51.

Measures of Personality and Leadership Factors

Self-Esteem Index; Combination of Rosenberg Self-Esteem Scale and Cobb Self-Esteem Scale

Alejandro Portes and Kenneth L. Wilson, "Black-White Differences in Educational Attainment," 41 (June 1976): 414–31.

Self-Esteem (Adaptation of Rosenberg Index); Stability of Self-Imagery (Rosenberg); Personal Control (Based on Rotter 1966 and Gurin et al. 1969)

Anthony R. Harris, "Race, Commitment to Deviance, and Spoiled Identity," 41 (June): 432–42.

Dimensions of Leadership Structure: Legitimacy, Visibility, Scope of Influence, and Consensus; Bonjean and Olson 1964, Bonjean 1971, and Bonjean and Grimes 1974

Michael D. Grimes, Charles M. Bonjean, J. Larry Lyon, and Robert L. Lineberry, "Community Structure and Leadership Arrangements: A Multidimensional Analysis," 41 (August 1976): 706–25.

Occupational and Financial Stress

Carlton A. Horning, "Social Status, Status Inconsistency, and Psychological Stress," 42 (August 1977): 623–38.

Measure of Depression: Asks Respondents the Frequency with Which They Experience Each of Eleven Symptoms; Lipmon et al. 1971 and Derogatis et al. 1969

Leonard I. Pearlman and Joyce S. Johnson, "Marital Status, Life-Strains and Depression," 42 (October 1977): 704–15.

Five-Item Scale of Job Authority Developed in Author's Ph.D. Dissertation, Department of Sociology, University of Wisconsin, Madison, 1975

James R. Kluegal, "The Causes and Cost of Racial Exclusion from Job Authority," 43 (June 1978): 285–301.

Hogan Empathy Scale; Gough Socialization Scale; Identification with Criminal Others

D. A. Andrews, "Some Experimental Investigations of the Principles of Differential Association Through Deliberate Manipulations of the Structure of Service Systems," 45 (June 1980): 448–62.

Measures of Subjectively Experienced Mood Disorder; MacMillan's Symptom Check List as Modified by Gurin et al.

Ronald C. Kessler and Paul D. Cleary, "Social Class and Psychological Distress," 45 (June 1980): 463–78.

Measures of Intelligence and Achievement

Otis IQ Test

James E. Rosenbaum, "The Stratification of Socialization Processes," 40 (February 1975): 48–54.

Stanford Achievement Test; Iowa Test of Educational Development and Test of Academic Progress (results by grade level)

Charles E. Bidwell and John P. Kasarda, "School District Organization and Student Achievement," 40 (February 1975): 55–70.

Family Background Status: Mother's and Father's Education, Father's Occupational Status (Duncan's SEI Scale), and Acquisition Index (Maxwell's Weighing Scheme); Academic Aptitude (Educational Testing Service Test); Peer College Orientation Index; Sophomore and Senior Class Standing; Sophomore and Senior Curriculum Enrollment (College Prep vs. Other); Influence of Adult "Significant Others"; Academic Self-Concept; Educational Expectations; Educational Attainment; Author Constructed Unless Otherwise Noted

Karl Alexander and Bruce K. Eckland "Contextual Effects in the High School Attainment Process," 40 (June 1975): 402–16.

Occupational Aspirations; Adaptation of Duncan as Suggested by Yuchtman and Fishelson; Educational Aspirations; Author Constructed

Ephraim Yuchtman (Yaar) and Yitzhak Samuel, "Determinants of Career Plans: Institutional Versus Interpersonal Effects," 40 (August 1975): 521–31.

Mental Ability Measured by Weighted Combination of Three Tests: Quick Test of General Intelligence; GATB,

Alejandro Portes and Kenneth L. Wilson, "Black-White Differences in Educational Attainment," 41 (June 1976): 414–31.

part J-Test of Vocabulary Level; Gates
Reading Comprehension

Mental Ability Measured by Performance on Armed Forces Qualification Test (AFQT); Recoded by Author	John Sibley Butler, "Inequality in the Military: An Examination of Promotion Time for Black and White Enlisted Men," 41 (October 1976): 807–18.
Academic Attitudes (Dailey and Shaycraft); Mathematics Achievement (Project Talent); Academic Rank in Senior Class	Karl L. Alexander and Edward L. McDill, "Selection and Allocation Within Schools," 41 (December 1976): 963–980.
Educational Goal Orientations; Self-Conceptions of Academic Competence (Author Constructed); Intellectual Orientations (McDill and Rigsby)	
Productivity and Recognition Measures of 238 Doctoral Chemists in United States; Author Adaptation	Barbara F. Reskin, "Scientific Productivity and the Reward Structure of Science," 42 (June 1977): 491–504.
Measure of Status Achievement for Scientists: Year of Ph.D, Research Funding, Papers Published, and Citations Received; Author Adaptation	Nicholas C. Mullins, Lowell L. Hargens, Pamela K. Hecht, and Edward L. Kick, "The Group Structure of Co-Citation Clusters," 42 (August 1977): 552–62.
Lorge-Thorndike IQ Test	Alan C. Kerckhoff, "The Realism of Educational Ambitions in England and the United States," 42 (August 1977): 563–77.
Wechsler Adult Intelligence Scale	Sandra Scarr and Richard A. Weinberg, "The Inflence of Family Background on Intellectual Attainment," 43 (October 1978): 674–92.
Wechsler Intelligence Scale; Two of Twelve Tests Utilized	Lala Carr Steelman and James A. Mercy, "Unconfounding the Confluence Model: A Test of Sibship Size and Birth Order Effects on Intelligence," 45 (August 1980); 571–82.
Career Achievement Indexed by Socioeconomic Status (Duncan SEI 1961) and Hourly Earnings	Rachel A. Rosenfield, "Race and Sex Differences in in Career Dyanmics," 45 (August 1980): 583–609.

Miscellaneous Scales

Measures of Spanish Colonialism in Latin America: Colonial Penetration and Extraction of Wealth; Author Constructed	Phillips Cutright, Michael Hout, and David R. Johnson, "Structural Determinants of Fertility in Lain America: 1800–1970," 41 (June 1976): 511–27.
Measure of Households with Four Different Types of Structure; Author Constructed	Barbara Laslett, "Social Change and the Family: Los Angeles, California, 1850–1870," 42 (April 1977): 268–91.
Measures Related to Use and Nonuse of Marijuana; Author Constructed	Robert F. Meier and Weldon T. Johnson, "Deterrence as Social Control: The Legal and Extralegal Production of Conformity," 42 (April 1977): 292–304.

Index of Prior Convictions; Interval Scale with 71–36 Range; Author Constructed

Ilene Nagel Bernstein, William R. Kelly, and Patricia A. Doyle, "Societal Reaction to Deviants: The Case of Criminal Defendants," 42 (October 1977): 743–55.

Five-Item Index of Evaluated Equality; Author Constructed

Robert V. Robinson and Wendell Bell, "Equality, Success, and Social Justice in England and the United States," 43 (April 1978): 125–43.

Severity of Juvenile Court Dispositions; Author's Constructed Ordinal Scale

Lawrence E. Cohen and James R. Kluegel, "Determinants of Juvenile Court Dispositions: Ascriptive and Achieved Factors in Two Metropolitan Courts," 43 (April 1978): 162–76.

Index of Psychological Disorder

Blair Wheaton, "The Sociogenesis of Psychological Disorder: Re-examining the Causal Issues with Longitudinal Data," 43 (June 1978): 383–403.

Index of Promotion in the Foreign Service; Author Constructed to Measure Career Mobility of Cohorts

Theodore L. Reed, "Organizational Change in the American Foreign Service, 1925–1965," 43 (June 1978): 404–21.

Indices of Objective Health: Shared Index of Incapacity, Number of Chronic Illnesses, Hospitalization, and Confinement to Bed; Author Constructed

John F. Miles, "Institutionalization and Sick Role Identification Among the Elderly," 43 (August 1978): 508–21.

Indices Include: Socioeconomic Status (Education and Occupation), Level of Impairment, and Admission Diagnosis; Author Constructed

William A. Rushing. "Status Resources, Societal Reactions, and Type of Mental Hospital Admission," 43 (August 1978): 521–33.

Four Indicators of Occupational Task: Cognitive Skill and Physical Strength; Sex Typing by "Male" Occupations, "Female" Occupations, and "Mixed Type"; Hodge-Siegel-Ross: Index for 1970 Censensus Occupations; Author Selected and Constructed

Steven D. McLaughlin, "Occupational Sex Identification and the Assessment of Male and Female Earnings Inequality," 43 (December 1978): 909–21.

Discretionary Use of Health Services: Preventive Use, Initiation of Care, and Health-Related Attitudes of Respondent; Author Constructed

Diana B. Dutton, "Explaining the Low Use of Health Services by the Poor: Costs, Attitudes, or Delivery Systems?" 43 (June 1978): 348–68.

Capacity to Hold a Job (Modified Version of Myers and Bean Occupational-Adjustment Index); Severity and Psychopathology (Patient Rated by Psychiatrist on Eight Mental Status Dimensions and Assigned Overall Severity Rating; Measures Developed by Hetznecker et al.)

R. Jay Turner and John W. Gartrell, "Social Factors in Psychiatric Outcomes: Toward the Resolution of Interpretive Controversies," 43 (June 1978): 368–82.

Achievement Competence of Patient; Tumin and Feldman's Generational Occupational Mobility Score Coded in Hollingshead's Seven Occupational Categories

Sellin-Wolfgang 1964 Seriousness Scale of Crime Taking into Account Extent and Nature of Bodily Injury, Weapon Use, Intimidation, Forcible Sexual Intercourse, and Financial Loss

Michael R. Gottfredson and Michael J. Hindelang, "A Study of the Behavior of Law," 44 (February 1979): 3–18.

Abstinence-Use of Alcohol, Abstinence-Use of Marijuana; List of Social Learning Variables with 16 Scales; Author Constructed or Adopted

Ronald L. Akers, Marvin D. Krohn, Loun-Lanza-Kaduce, and Marcia Rudosevich, "Social Learning and Deviant Behavior: A Specific Test of a General Theory," 44 (August 1979): 636–648.

Measure of Priest Resignation. (Data Adaptation); Numerous Measures of Independent Variables

John Seidler, "Priest Resignations in a Lazy Monopoly," 44 (October 1979): 763–83.

Social Indicators

Content Analysis of Magazine Articles 1825–50: Examination of Power in Man-Woman Relationships, Romantic Love, Motivations for Marriage, and Advocated and Actual Sanctions Implemented Toward People Involved in Premarital or Extramarital Sexual Relationships; Author Constructed

Herman R. Lantz, Jane Keyes, and Martin Schultz, "The American Family in the Preindustrial Period: From Base Lines in History to Change," 40 (February 1975): 21–36.

Measure of Acceptance of Ghost Dance by American Indian Tribes, *ca.* 1889; Author Constructed Based on Information from Mooney

Michael P. Carroll, "Revitalization Movements and Social Structure: Some Quantitative Tests," 40 (June 1975): 389–401.

Association of Social Class with Vote; Alford's Index of Class Voting and Author Constructed Index

Rick Ogmundson, "Party Class Images and the Class Vote in Canada," 40 (August 1975): 506–12.

Economic Development: Log Gross National Product per Capita; Log Kilowatt Hours Electricity Consumer per capita; Percentage Male Labor force Not in Agriculture (these are conventional measures of aggregate economic development). Income Inequality: Individual and Household Income Inequality; Gini Index Gathered by Adelman and Morris and Improved by Paukert 1973

Christopher Chase-Dunn, "The Effects of Internatinal Economic Dependence on Development and Inequality: A Cross-National Study," 40 (December 1975): 720–38.

Index Sustenance Organization of Nonmetropolitan Counties; Author Constructed

W. Parker Frisbie and Dudley L. Poston, Jr., "Components of Sustenance Organization and Nonmetropolitan Population Change: A Human Ecological Problem," 40 (December 1975): 773–84.

Split Labor Market: Difference in Price of Labor Between Two or More Groups of Workers, Holding Constant ethnicity and Productivity; Author Constructed 1972

Edna Bonacich, "Advanced Capitalism and Black/White Race Relations in the United States: A Split Labor Market Interpretation," 41 (February 1976): 34–51.

Occupational Migration Potential; Measure of Migration Demands Inherent in Being Member of Particular Occupation; Author Constructed. Occupational Migration Compatibility; Amenability of Particular Occupation to Migration Demands from Outside Occupation Itself; Author Constructed

R. Paul Duncan and Carolyn Cummings Perrucci, "Dual Occupation Families and Migration," 41 (April 1976): 252–61.

Indicators Affecting Level of White Solidarity in South ca. 1890: Percent Black, Urbanization, and Religious Homogeneity; Indicators Reflecting Level of White Solidarity in South: Percent Democratic Vote 1892 Presidential Election, and Percent Democratic Vote 1896 Gubernatorial Election; Author Constructed

James M. Inverarity, "Populism and Lynching in Louisiana, 1889–1896: A Test of Erikson's Theory of the Relationship Between Boundary Crises and Repressive Justice," 41 (April 1976): 262–80.

White Male Gini Inequality Index

Albert Szymanski, "Racial Discrimination and White Gain," 41 (June 1976): 403–14.

Structural Modernization Indicators: Percent Literate, Percent in Cities, Life Expectancy, and Telephones per Capita; Author Constructed

Phillips Cutright, Michael Hout, and David R. Johnson, "Structural Determinants of Fertility in Latin America: 1800–1970," 41 (June 1976): 511–27.

Inequality in the Military Measured by Promotion Time; Author Constructed

John Sibley Butler, "Inequality in the Military: An Examination of Promotion Time for Black and White Enlisted Men," 41 (October 1976): 807–18.

Economic Development: Log Kilowatt Hours Consumed per Capita (Adaptation of Jackman); State strength: Government Revenue as Percent of Gross Domestic Product (Author Constructed) Social Insurance Program Experience (SIPE) (Cutright, Jackman) Direct Economic Penetration: Value on Debits of Investment Income; Author Constructed Economic Dependency on External Market: Exports and Imports as Percent of Gross Domestic Product; Author Constructed

Richard Rubinson, "The World-Economy and the Distribution of Income Within States: A Cross-National Test," 41 (August 1976): 638–59.

Religious Indicator; Modernization Trend Indicator; Countercultural Involvement Indicator; Author Constructed

Robert Wathnow, "Recent Pattern of Secularization: A Problem of Generations?" 41 (October 1976): 850–67.

Turner Index; Ratio of Percent of Nonwhites in "Good" Occupations Divided by Percent of Whites in "Good" Occupations (1951)

Ross M. Stolzenberg and Ronald J. D'Amico, "City Differences and Nondifferences in the Effect of Race and Sex on Occupational Distribution," 42 (December 1977): 937–50.

Index of Concentration; Index for Agricultural Knowledge; Index for Resource Capital; All by Gini

John W. Gartrell, "Status Inequality and Innovation: The Green Revolution in Andra Pradesh, India," 42 (April 1977): 318–37.

Indicators of Urban Dominance in the National, Regional, and Local Domains

"Mark Abrahamson and Michael A. DuBick, "Patterns of Urban Dominance: The U.S. in 1890," 42 (October 1977): 756–68.

Ecological Measures Related to Migration: 7 Indices Relating to Rate of Net Migration; Sly 1972

David F. Sly and Jeff Tayman, "Ecological Approach to Migration Reexamination," 42 (October 1977): 783–95.

Measures of Economic Growth; Data Adaptations

Jacques Delacroix, "The Export of Raw Materials and Economic Growth: A Cross National Study," 42 (October 1977): 795–808.

Reward, Responsibility, and Performance Measures; Data Adaptations by Author

Leonard Broom and Robert G. Cushing, "A Modest Test of an Immodest Theory: The Functional Theory of Stratification," 42 (February 1977): 157–69

Insurgency Measures; Author Constructed

J. Craig Jenkins and Charles Perron, "Insurgency of the Powerless: Farm Workers Movements 1946–1972," 42 (April 1977): 249–68.

Indexes of Educational Dissimilarity; Eight Categories; Author Constructed

Reynolds Farley, "Trends in Racial Inequalities: Have the Gains of the 1960s Disappeared in the 1970s?" 42 (April 1977): 189–208.

Witch-Hunting Dispersion Index; Adapted from Simpson's Index of Population Diversity

Albert James Bergesen, "Political Witch Hunts: The Sacred and the Subversive in Cross-National Perspective," 42 (April 1977): 220–33.

Broom and Halldorson State Redistribution Index; Measure of Extent to Which Total Spending and Taxing Activities of State Governments Progressively Redistribute Income to Poor Households; Author Selected

Alexander Hicks, Roger Friedland, and Edwin Johnson, "Class Power and State Policy: The Case of Large Business Corporations, Labor Unions, and Governmental Redistribution in the American States," 43 (June 1978): 302–15.

Factors Affecting Response Rates to Questionnaires; Ten Variable Models Predicting Final Response Rate; Author Selected

Thomas A. Heberlein and Robert Baumgartner, "Factors Affecting Response Rate to Model Questionnaires," 43 (August 1978): 444–62.

Percent Change in White Enrollment as Indicator of School Desegregation; Author Operational Measure

Michael W. Giles, "White Enrollment Stability and School Desegregation," 43 (December 1978): 848–64.

Gini Index of Inequality

Steven Stack, "The Effect of Direct Government Involvement in the Economy on the Degree of Income Inequality: A Cross-National Study," 43 (December 1978): 880–88.

Index of Size Administrative Component

Patrick D. Nolan "Size and Administra-

of Nation; System Size Operationalized by Use of Government Employment Data as Best Cross-National Indicator of Size of Government; Two Indicators of Technological Development: Percent of Total Employment Engaged in Agriculture and Measures of Population Size and Concentration

tive Intensity in Nations," 44 (February 1979): 110–25.

Indices of Urbanization, Economic Development, Agricultural Density, and Land Tenure; Adaptations from Other Researchers

Glen Firebaugh, "Structural Determinants of Urbanization in Asia and Latin America," 44 (April 1979): 199–215.

Index of Institutional Concentration; Author Constructed

William L. Yancey and Eugene P. Ericksen, "The Antecedents of Community: The Economic and Institutional Structure of Urban Neighborhoods," 44 (April 1979): 253–62.

Income Poverty Guidelines; Community Services Administration 1975

Steven L. Gortmaker, "Poverty and Infant Mortality in the United States," 44 (April 1979): 280–97.

Indices of Dissimilarity Between Groups; Gini Concentration Ratios

Stanley Lieberson and Donna K. Carter, "Making It in America: Differences Between Eminent Blacks and White Ethnic Groups," 44 (June 1979): 347–66.

Mobility Index and Indexes of Income Inequality; Data Adaptations

Andrea Tyree, Moshe Semyonov, and Robert W. Hodge, "Gaps and Glissandos: Inequality, Economic Development, and Social Mobility in 24 Countries," 44 (June 1979): 410–24.

Mobility Incidence Rate Among City Residents; Suburban Propensity Rate Among City Movers. Data Adaptation

William H. Frey, "Central City White Flight: Racial and Nonracial Causes," 44 (June 1979): 425–48.

Gini Index of Income Inequality

Volker Bornschier and Hans Huyen Ballmer-Cao, "Income Inequality: A Cross National Study of Relationships Between MNC-Penetration, Dimensions of the Power Structure, and Income Distribution," 44 (June 1979): 487–506.

Changes in Work Content: Dictionary of Occupational Titles; Levels of Involvement with People, Data, and Things

Kenneth I. Spenner, "Temporal Changes in Work Content," 44 (December 1979): 968–75.

Index of Status Persistence; Goodman 1969

Frank Newport, "The Religious Switches in the United States," 44 (August 1979): 528–52.

Political Democracy Index; Six Components Based on Previous Research Work; Author Constructed

Kenneth A. Bollen, "Political Democracy and the Timing of Development," 44 (August 1979): 572–87.

Three Tests of Ethnic Political Mobilization: Test of Development Perspective; Test of Reactive Ethnicity; Test of Ethnic Competition;

Charles C. Ragin, "Ethnic Political Mobilization: The Welsh Case," 44 (August 1978): 619–35.

New Self-Report Measure of 47 Items of Delinquent Behavior Believed to Be More Comprehensive and More Representative; Author Constructed

Delbert S. Elliott and Suzanne S. Ageton, "Reconciling Race and Class Differences in Self-Reported and Official Estimates of Delinquency," 45 (February 1980): 95–110.

Indicators of Distributive Justice; Theoretically Derived by Author

Guillermina Jasso, "A New Theory of Distributive Justice," 45 (February 1980): 3–32.

Femaleness of Occupational Structure; Industry's Preference for Females; Data Adaptions

William P. Bridges, "Industry Marginality and Female Employment," 45 (February 1980): 58–75.

Revised Political Democracy Index; Author Constructed

Kenneth A. Bollen, "Issues in the Comparative Measurement of Political Democracy," 45 (June 1980): 370–90.

Economic Power and Institutional Size; Measures of Banks, Bank Loan Capital, Networks of Economic Power, and Upper-Class Social Interaction; Data Adaptations

Richard E. Patcliff, "Banks and Corporate Lending: An Analysis of the Impact of the Internal Structure of the Capitalist Class on the Lending Behavior of Banks," 45 (August 1980): 553–70.

Gini Index of Income Inequality

Peter B. Evans and Michael Timberlake, "Dependence, Inequality, and the Growth of the Tertiary: A Comparative Analysis of Less Developed Countries," 45 (August 1980): 531–52.

Property Arrests of Criminals; Nonproperty Arrests; Number of Weeks Employed; Number of Weeks Incarcerated; Aid Payments; Data Adaptations

Richard A. Berk, Kenneth J. Lenihans, and Peter H. Rossi, "Crime and Poverty: Some Experimental Evidence from Ex-Offenders," 45 (October 1980): 766–86.

Sentence Severity of White-Collar Offenders: Efforts to Devise an Approximate Interval Scale; Based on Tiffany et al

John Hagan, Ilene H. Nagel, and Celesta Albonetti, "The Differential Sentencing of White-Collar Offenders in Ten Federal District Courts," 45 (October 1980): 802–20.

Nine Sequential Processing Decisions Involving Rape Suspects; Author Constructed

Gary D. Lafree, "The Effect of Sexual Stratification by Race on Official Reactions to Rape," 45 (October 1980): 842–54.

4.M.2   **A BRIEF HISTORY OF SOCIOLOGICAL MEASURES UTILIZED BY RESEARCHERS IN MAJOR JOURNALS**

Delbert C. Miller

The most thorough inventory of sociological measures was made between January 1954 and the end of 1965 by Charles M. Bonjean, Richard J. Hill, and S. Dale McLemore.[1] The *American Sociological Review, American Journal of Sociology, Social Forces,* and *Sociometry* (now *Social Psychology Quarterly*) were taken to be representative of the main research currents in American sociology. Every article and research note published in these four journals from 1954 through 1965 was examined carefully. For each article or research note the compilers listed: (1) a complete reference to the article in which the measure appeared, (2) the concept indicated by the measure employed, (3) the technique(s) of measurement employed, and (4) other uses and users of the same or similar techniques.

Table 1, which shows the most frequently used and cited measures, reveals the findings of the inventory. Note that the Socio-Economic Grouping of Occupations devised by Alba M. Edwards of the U.S. Census leads the list with 91 uses and citations. In addition to the use of the Edwards scale as a status measure it is used as a related measure (16 mentions) and in studies of occupational mobility (12 mentions). The North-Hall (NORC) prestige ratings of occupations has 53 mentions; it is also used as an occupational mobility measure (10 mentions).

The central importance of social status in sociological research is under-scored by the use of Hollingsheads' Index of Social Position (30 mentions); another of his measures of occupational status has 8 mentions. W. L. Warner's Index of Status Characteristics receives 27 mentions; another of Warner's status measures adds 16 mentions. Duncan's Occupational Status (SEI) is just beginning to receive recognition for his 1961 measure (9 mentions). In the four journals reviewed, 435 attempts to measure socioeconomic status were noted.

Measures that have won wide acceptance include the California F Scale; Shevky, Williams, and Bell's measures of Urban Rank, Urbanization, and Segregation; Burgess, Cottrell, and Locke's Marital Adjustment; Bogardus's Social Distance; and Chapin's Social Participation.

The repeated uses of these measures suggest that social researchers are using standard instruments in many replicated designs under controlled conditions. Unfortunately, the inventory does not reveal this most desired outcome. Indeed, the compilers report that "fragmentation, rather than continuity, is the important characteristic of measurement in social research: a comparison of the number of measures found for each conceptual class—indicates that *most measures* used and cited in the journals examined were developed or modified by the investigator for the specific research reported."[2] Continuity may be measured by the following data from the inventory:

1. 3609 attempts were made to measure various social variables. Of these, 2080 differ-ent measures were used. Only 589, or 28.3 percent, of the total number of scales and indices were used more than *once*.
2. Of the 2080 scales and indices appearing in the journals over the twelve-year period covered by the analysis, only 47, or 2.26 percent, were used more than five times.[3]
3. Continuity is most characteristic among investigations dealing with occupational status, authoritarianism, racial and ethnic stereotypes, community leadership, repu-tational status, and residential segregation.
4. Little or no continuity is observed in regard to the measurement of achievement, authority, community characteristics, attitudes toward and perceptions of complex organizations, concensus, and characteristics of education.[4]

Bonjean et al. explain that when the investigator tries to build continuity in his research, he is faced with a double difficulty: (1) So many different

Table 1. *Most Frequently Used and Cited Measures from All Articles and Research Notes in the* American Sociological Review, American Journal of Sociology, Social Forces, *and* Sociometry (*Now* Social Psychology Quarterly) from January 1954 through December 1965

Measure	Frequency of use and citations
1. Occupational Status (Census, Edwards)	91
2. California F Scale and Modifications	53
3. Occupational Prestige (North, Hatt)	53
4. Leadership (Reputational Approach)	35
5. Stereotype Check List (Katz, Braly)	33
6. Indexes of Social Position (Hollingshead)	30
7. Anomia (Srole)	28
8. Social Rank (Shevky, Williams, Bell)	28
9. Index of Status Characteristics (Warner)	27
10. Urbanization (Shevky, Williams, Bell)	26
11. Segregation (Shevky, Williams, Bell)	25
12. Sociometric Status and Structure (Various Measures)	19
13. Marital Adjustment (Burgess, Cottrell, Locke)	18
14. Social Distance (Bogardus)	18
15. Social Participation (Chapin)	17
16. Achievement Motivation (Murray, McClelland, Atkinson)	16
17. Occupational Status (Census, Edwards Related)	16
18. Occupational Status (Warner)	16
19. Ethnocentrism (California E Scale)	15
20. Segregation (Duncan, Duncan)	15
21. Occupational Mobility, Intergenerational (Census, Edwards Related)	12
22. Occupational Mobility, Intergenerational (North, Hatt Related)	10
23. Social Class: Judges or Informants	10
24. Occupational Status (Duncan)	9
25. Socioeconomic Status (Sewell)	8
26. American Council on Education Psychological Examination	8
27. Centralization	8
28. Consideration (Ohio State Leader Behavior Description Questionnaire and Related Measures)	8
29. Delinquency Proneness, Social Responsibility (Gough)	8
30. Initiating Structure (Ohio State Leader Description Questionnaire and Related Measures)	8
31. Occupational Status (Hollingshead)	8
32. Status Crystalization (Lenski)	8
33. Dogmatism (Rokeach)	7
34. Segregation (Cowgill, Cowgill)	7
35. Segregation (Jahn, Schmid, Schrag)	7
36. Social Distance, Summated Differences Technique (Westie)	7
37. Achievement Training (Winterbottom)	6
38. Administrative Rationality (Udy)	6
39. Alienation (Nettler)	6
40. Alienation, Powerlessness (Neal)	6
41. California Test of Personality (Tiegs, Clark, Thrope)	6
42. Conservatism (McClosky)	6
43. Delinquent Behavior Checklist (Nye, Short)	6
44. Edwards Personal Preference Schedule	6
45. Marital Satisfaction (Burgess, Wallin)	6
46. Religious Orthodoxy (Putney, Middleton)	6
47. Social-Emotional Reactions (Bales)	6

Table 1. (Continued)

Measure	Frequency of use and citations
48. Status Concern (Kaufman)	6
49. Urbanization (Davis)	6
50. Values (Allport, Vernon, Lindzey)	6

Source: Charles M. Bonjean, Richard J. Hill, and S. Dale McElmore, *Sociological Measurement: An Inventory of Scales and Indices* (San Francisco: Chandler, 1967), pp. 13–14.

measures are available for some phenomena that the selection of a scale or index may itself be a research problem of large magnitude; and (2) in other cases an extensive search through the literature may yield no scale or measure of the variable(s) that concerns the investigator.[5] But the writer believes that there are other, more important reasons for the lack of continuity in research. The further explanation awaits another query: What has happened since 1965? Has continuity increased or has fragmentation continued to dominate. A partial answer may be found by examining the summary review of articles in the *American Sociological Review* from 1965 through 1980.

The data on which to judge research continuity from 1965 through 1980 rest on a narrower base than the data from 1954 to 1965. The inventory is restricted to the *American Sociological Review.* However, it is probably the best single sociological journal that could be chosen. It is the official organ of the American Sociological Association. All members of the association receive it and with such a guaranteed audience, it becomes the most prestigious and sought-after publication source for sociologists. In 1980, 404 manuscripts were submitted. All papers were refereed. In 26 percent of reviews, three referees were involved; in 16 percent of reviews, four or more reviewers were required. In at least two cases, a manuscript was sent to seven different referees. The acceptance rate for 1980 was 15 percent; for 1979, 14 percent; and for 1978, 11 percent.[6]

A summary of measures most frequently used and cited in the *American Sociological Review* from 1965 through 1980 is shown in table 2. Again the high interest in social status is repeated with 59 measures used to measure the socioeconomic standing of persons in the various studies (see 1, 2, 3, 4, and 12). Duncan's Occupational Status measure (SEI) is easily the most frequent scale employed by social researchers.

After the social status measures are removed, the number of scales that appear two to five times is narrowed to only nine! What this means can be explained by the number of measures that are either author constructed or a data adaptation. Data adaptations refer to any use of data to express a factor or variable, such as percent of high school graduates, relative earnings of men compared with women, or education of the father. Author constructed scales are usually a selection of two to five items made by the author and scored to give an index value. Reliability and validity are rarely determined. Face validity is assumed.

Of 461 articles cited in the Miller 1965–1980 inventory (theoretical and opinion articles, research notes, and comments were not included), 267 were

Table 2. *Most Frequently Used and Cited Measures in the* American Sociological Review *1965–80*

	Frequency of use and citations
1. Occupational Status (SEI) (Duncan)	30
2. NORC 1964 Prestige Scores (Siegel)	9
3. Two Position Index of Social Position (Hollingshead)	9
4. Occupational Census Classifications (Edwards)	8
5. Anomie Scale (Srole)	5
6. Index of Income Inequality (Gini)	5
7. Self Esteem (Rosenberg & Simmons)	4
8. Index of Dissimilarity (Duncan & Duncan)	4
9. Powerless Scale (Neal and Seeman)	4
10. Occupational Aspiration Scale (Haller)	3
11. Minnesota Multiphasic Personality Inventory	3
12. Occupational Status (Nam and Powers Census Scores)	3
13. Interaction Categories (Bales)	2

Author constructed or data adaptation measures

	1965–68	1968–74	1975–80	1965–80
Number of author constructed	$N = 52$	$N = 88$	$N = 127$	$N = 267$
Total number of articles reviewed	$N = 83$	$N = 165$	$N = 213$	$N = 461$
Percentages of author constructed scales	61%	54%	60%	58%

author constructed or data defined (i.e., 58 percent were measures with no previous utilization). This figure underestimates the actual lack of continuity because at least another 15 percent represent measures in which the author selects a limited number of items that might serve his purpose from previous scales. It may be concluded that research built on established scales and indices is in the distinct minority—about 20 or 25 percent. On this basis the writer drew the conclusions in section 4.M.3.

Notes

1. Charles M. Bonjean, Richard J. Hill, and S. Dale McLemore, *Sociological Measurement: An Inventory of Scales and Indices* (San Francisco; Chandler, 1967), p. 4.
2. Ibid., p. 8.
3. Ibid., p. 9.
4. Ibid., pp. 7–8.
5. Ibid., p. 1.
6. William Form, editor, *American Sociological Review; Footnotes* of the American Sociological Association, March 1981, p. 14.

Delbert C. Miller

A. *Diagnosis*
  1. High attention is usually given to ties between theory and research methodology.
  2. High attention is given to cause-and-effect relationships with numerous applications of path analysis and structural equation models.
  3. High attention is given to methodological sophistication. There is an application of many new modeling and statistical techniques.
  4. Measures of dependent variables are usually self-constructed employing 1 to 5 items and showing little concern with the reliability and validity of the measures.
  5. The number of variables, dependent and independent, introduced into the design are increasing in number.
  6. Only a limited number of articles deal with the examination of social scales.
  7. Articles dealing solely with the accumulating evidence from other studies are almost nonexistent. One or two appear in a three-year period.
  8. The overall conclusion is that sociological research lacks the essential attributes of a science that is building cumulative evidence in spite of the significant methodological advances shown in almost all the articles employing quantitative analysis.
  9. Sociological research may be viewed as going through a transitional period when new methodology is being tested on social data. But utilization of scientific techniques does not alone build a science of society.
B. *Prognosis*
  1. The direction of sociological research toward a science of sociology will not take place until standard measures of important social variables are in place.
  2. This direction is not likely to be established until the accumulation of tested findings has been given the highest priority by scholars and students—and especially by publishers, editors, and reviewers, who determine what should be published.
C. *Action*
  1. To further the accumulation of social knowledge, many of the most prestigious researchers and their students will be replicating the best available research with the same design and standard measures on different populations, holding constant the conditions of prior research.
  2. Others will be giving increasing attention to prediction studies, social forecasting, and policy-making research to provide definitive tests against societal needs and demands.

I asked ten professors on the sociology faculty of Indiana University to comment on each statement. In general there was agreement on all conclusions, but there were some important reservations. A few stressed that the *American Sociological Review* is not necessarily a good testing standard because many subareas of sociology are not included in the journal in sufficient scope. Some stress that in an area like social stratification where standard measures have almost always been employed, cumulative research can be observed. Two reviewers said that measures of dependent variables should be judged according to the problem: "Most macro measures (e.g., percent urban, gross national product, literacy, do not need a lot of discussion. Attitudes, values, and other constructs in the 'black box' of social psychology are often self-constructed and are never again seen in the literature."

My conclusion that sociological research lacks the essential attribute of a science in building cumulative evidence (#8) received some objection; and conclusions 1, 2, and 3 were said to provide opposite evidence. All of these reservations deserve consideration before there is an acceptance of the conclusions. Yet it must be noted that all reviewers see that sociological research must face up to more stringent standards of continuity.[1]

Why has the present situation developed? It will be remembered that Bonjean and his co-workers say it is because of the dual problem: too many scales to choose from, and no scales available for many problems. The reasons go deeper than this. They begin with the lack of a professional research value structure that gives high priority to continuity and accumulation of consistent evidence for the validity of propositions. This lack of continuity values extends to most researchers, the referees of papers, and the editors who publish them. As one reviewer wrote: "Replicating the best available research would be good for sociology in general, but this is not high status seminal research. The reward structure discourages replications." It might follow that editors of journals and monographs are not receptive to publishing replications of research.

Ballen and Phillips have one of the few articles published as a *replication* in a major journal. They suggest that one reason why replication in sociology is "very rare" is because replication, like most research, is expensive. "This expense may not be justified unless the research to be replicated has substantial implications or produced counterintuitive results."[2]

Moreover, there is some evidence that the computer is now a tail that wags the sociologist. This powerful instrument can take large masses of data and analyze many factors and their various relationships and interrelationships. Secondary use of data gathered by agencies tends to replace the firsthand gathering of data with standard scales selected to fit the design the researcher has formulated. Well-designed quantitative studies developing large matrices of correlations appear to have some exceptional merit often not justified by their ability to build cumulative evidence affirming or rejecting general propositions.

This is the important story of the scales and the inventories. The published research cries out for researchers to build upon it, or failing that, to improve it with standardization of appropriate measures. One lesson is that the researcher should first *search* for the appropriate measures that have been previously developed. The storehouse is bulging with thousands of social and psychological measures, as the numerous compilations attest.

Notes

1. Cf. Chris Argyris, *Inner Contradictions of Rigorous Research.* (New York: Academic Press, 1980).
2. Kenneth A. Bollen and David P. Phillips, "Suicidal Motor Vehicle Fatalities in Detroit: A Replication," *American Journal of Sociology* 87 (September 1981): 404–12.

A listing of major sources for scale information and appraisal are shown:

ALL-INCLUSIVE COMPILATIONS

BONJEAN, CHARLES M.; HILL, RICHARD J.; and McLEMORE, S. DALE. *Sociological Measurement: An Inventory of Scales and Indices.* San Francisco: Chandler, 1967.

This book is essentially an extensive bibliography that references 3609 uses of citations of 2080 separate scales or indexes. Scales are not generally analyzed for reliability and validity. Although limited to research up to 1965, this is still the most comprehensive bibliography. Use this book to locate various scales and research in which the scale was used.

LAKE, DALE G.; MILES, MATTHEW B.; and EARLE, RALPH B., JR. *Measuring Human Behavior.* New York: Teachers College Press, 1973.

A selection of 84 different instruments meeting stringent criteria including reasonably current information on reliability and validity. Included are 38 measures of personal variables, 24 interpersonal, 10 group, and 12 organizational. Information is provided for availability, variables measured, description of the instrument, administration and scoring, development, critique, and general comment. Truly a model for scale evaluation!

SPECIAL COMPILATIONS

SHAW, MARVIN E., and WRIGHT, JACK W. *Scales for the Measurement of Attitudes.* New York: McGraw-Hill, 1967.

Thorough information on 176 attitude measures. Entries are reasonably complete with criticism of the adequacy of the scales. A bibliography of more than 600 attitude scales is appended. The list of attitude scales is appended in the latter part of this section for the researcher seeking a particular attitude scale in which he may be interested.

Occupational Attitudes and Characteristics

ROBINSON, JOHN P.; ATHANASIOU, ROBERT; and HEAD, KENDRA B. *Measures of Occupational Attitudes and Occupational Characteristics.* Ann Arbor: Institute for Social Research, University of Michigan, 1969.

Reviews a total of 77 test instruments and provides accurate assessments of the form and scope. The author's criteria include sample adequacy, norms, reliability, homogeneity, discrimination of known groups. Typical items and ease of administration and scoring are indicated. (Contents reproduced in section 4.M.5.a.)

Political Attitudes

ROBINSON, JOHN P.; RUSK, JERROLD G.; and HEAD, KENDRA B. *Measures of Political Attitudes.* Ann Arbor: Institute of Social Research, University of Michigan, 1969.

Ninety-five measures of political attitudes are reviewed with similar criteria to that of the companion volume cited above. Accurate assessments of the form and scope of each study are made. (Contents reproduced in section 4.M.5.b.)

Social-Psychological Attitudes

ROBINSON, JOHN P.; and SHAVER, PHILLIP R. *Measures of Social Psychological Attitudes.* Ann Arbor: Institute of Social Research, University of Michigan, 1969. Revised 1973, with expanded sections on internality-externality and self-esteem.

> One hundred six measures of social-psychological attitudes are reviewed. There is a long review of the major attempts to measure "life satisfaction" and "happiness" over the past 15 years. As with its companion volumes, accurate assessments are made using the criteria cited. (Contents reproduced in section 4.M.5.c.)

Family Measurement

STRAUS, MURRAY A. *Family Measurement Techniques.* Minneapolis: University of Minnesota Press, 1969. Up-dated to 1974. University of Minnesota Press, 1978.

> Abstracts of 319 instruments focusing on one or more of the following domains: adolescent, 20; child, 75; family, 63; parent, 129; premarital, 20; and spousal, 81. Criteria used include validity evidence, reliability, norms, availability, and references. Well-organized collection of measures. Discusses problems of scales with lack of reliability and validity—roughly 56 percent of measures abstracted.

Organizational Measurement

PRICE, JAMES L. *Handbook of Organizational Measurement.* Lexington, Mass.: Heath, 1972.

> Describes measures for 22 concepts about which there is the greatest agreement among organizational researchers. Selection of the measures was derived from seven criteria that include reliability, validity, ease of administration. Each measure is discussed under such headings as description, definition, data collection, computation, validity, reliability, comments, source, and further sources. Additional readings are appended. This is the book that organizational researchers should consult first in designing their research.

KEGAN, DANIEL L. *Scales/RIQS: An Inventory of Research Instruments.* Evanston, Ill.: Technological Institute, Northwestern University, 1970.

> This inventory contains 360 instruments measuring variables relevant to organizational theory. For each instrument the information is fully computer stored and retrievable. Requests from users can be handled without charge or at minimum cost. The following information is stored: author, reference, date, where instrument was used, reliability and validity, variables measured, comments by author or person depositing the item in *SCALES/RIQS.* Total length of entries is usually 100 to 150 words. A useful working tool for researchers prepared to make their own judgments of adequacy.

INDIK, B. P.; HOCKMEYER, M.; and CASTORE, C. *A Compendium of Measures of Individuals, Groups and Organizations Relevant to the Study of Organizational Behavior.* Technical Report No. 16, Nour-404. New Brunswick, N.J.: Rutgers, The State University, 1968.

> A file of several hundred measures can be assessed by writing Dr. Bernard P. Indik, Graduate School of Social Work, Rutgers University, New Brunswick, NJ 08903. A nominal fee is charged to cover xeroxing and other costs. The variables covered are reviewed in B. P. Indik and F. K. Berrien, *People, Groups, and Organizations* (New York: Teachers College Press, 1968).

Personality and Motivation

BUROS, OSCAR KRISEN. *The Eighth Mental Measurements Yearbook.* Highland Park, N.J.: Gryphon Press, 1978.

The Buros Series of Mental Measurements Yearbooks dates from 1938 and has become the reference work in the field. The reader with particular interest in personality measures should consult *Personality Tests and Review* (Highland Park, N.J.: Gryphon Press, 1970). It includes 513 personality measures. Each test is briefly described with a complete bibliography. A variety of supporting indexes makes the user's task easy. Historical trend data are provided showing numbers of published references for each test over the past thirty years.

Numerous other compendia of special instruments are described and analyzed by Dale G. Lake, Matthew B. Miles, and Ralph B. Earle, Jr., in *Measuring Human Begavior.* See pp. 341–87. These should be consulted especially by researchers in education and personality.

CHUN, KI-TAEK; COBB, SYDNEY; and FRENCH, JOHN R. P., JR. *Measures for Psychological Assessment: A Guide to 3000 Original Sources and Their Applications.* Ann Arbor: Institute of Social Research, University of Michigan, 1975.

Compilation of annotated references to social science measures. Work grew out of an effort to build a comprehensive, computerized national repository of social science measures. The first of the volume's two major sections lists the original sources for each of 3000 instruments of attitude measurement. The Applications section cites and annotates all studies in which each measure was subsequently used. The entries were obtained through a search of 26 measurement-related journals in psychology and sociology from the period 1960–70. Author and descriptor indices are included to facilitate the use of these major sections.

WEBB, EUGENE J.; CAMPBELL, DONALD T.; SCHWARTZ, RICHARD D.; and SECHREST, LEE. *Unobtrusive Measures: Nonreactive Research in the Social Sciences.* Chicago: Rand McNally and Company, 1966.

Discusses measures not obtained by interview or questionnaire. The measures are observational in nature which do not require the cooperation of a respondent and that do not themselves contaminate the response.

Child Development

JOHNSON, ORVAL G. *Tests and Measurements in Child Development.* Handbook II. San Francisco: Jossey-Bass, 1976.

Very Comprehensive (1327 pages) inventory of psychological tests for children.

WALKER, DEBORAH K. *Socioemotional Measures for Preschool and Kindergarten Children.* San Francisco: Jossey-Bass, 1973.

A specialized inventory of measures for children of kindergarten age and younger.

Mental Measures

BUROS, O. K. *Tests in Print II.* Highland Park: Gryphon Press, 1974.

A Comprehensive bibliography of tests for use in education, psychology, and industry. Updated from 1961 printing.

GOLDMAN, B. A., and BUSCH, J. C. *Directory and Unpublished Experimental Mental Measures.* Vol. 2. New York: Human Sciences Press, 1978.

Mental and Personality Tests with bibliographies for both. Updated from 1974 printing by Behavioral Publications, New York.

Gerontology

MANGEN, DAVID J., and PETERSON, WARREN A., eds. *Research Instruments in Social Gerontology.* Vol. 1, Clinical and Social Psychology; Vol. 2, Social Roles and Social Participation; Vol. 3, Health, Program Evaluation, and Demography. Minneapolis: University of Minnesota Press, 1982–83.
MARQUIS ACADEMIC MEDIA. *Sourcebook on Aging.* 2nd ed. Chicago: Marquis Who's Who, 1979.

Contains a wide range of source material.

Women and Women's Issues

BEERE, CAROLE A. *Women and Women's Issues: A Handbook of Tests and Measures.* San Francisco: Jossey-Bass, 1979.

The recent explosion of interest in the study of women and women's issues has produced literally hundreds of new tests and measures—instruments for investigating sex roles; sex sterotypes; women's roles as spouse, parent, and employee; attitudes toward women including equal rights, abortion, and sexuality. This encyclopedic handbook contains 235 tests selected for reliability, validity, extent of use, and ease of administration. Each test has the following description: title and author of the instrument year first published, what the instrument measures, with whom it can be used, sample items from the test, directions for administering and scoring, background or test development, data on reliability and validity, source from which the complete instrument is available, notes and comments by Beere on the use of the test, and bibliographic data on studies that have used the instrument.

4.M.5 CONTENT TABLES FOR MICHIGAN INSTITUTE OF SOCIAL RESEARCH ON OCCUPATIONAL, POLITICAL, AND SOCIAL PSYCHOLOGICAL SCALES

4.M.5.a CONTENTS OF JOHN P. ROBINSON, ROBERT ATHANASIOU, AND KENDRA HEAD, *MEASURES OF OCCUPATIONAL ATTITUDES AND OCCUPATIONAL CHARACTERISTICS**

CHAPTER

* Published by Institute for Social Research, University of Michigan, Ann Arbor, 1969.

4.M.5.b CONTENTS OF JOHN P. ROBINSON, JERROLD G. RUSK, AND KENDRA P. HEAD, *MEASURES OF POLITICAL ATTITUDES**

* Published by Institute for Social Research, University of Michigan, Ann Arbor, 1968.

4.M.5.C CONTENTS OF JOHN P. ROBINSON AND PHILLIP P. SHAVER, *MEASURES OF SOCIAL PSYCHOLOGICAL ATTITUDES**

* Published by Institute of Social Research, University of Michigan, Ann Arbor. Revised edition 1973.

4.M.6 **SHAW AND WRIGHT COMPILATION OF SCALES FOR THE MEASUREMENT OF ATTITUDES**

The following list of 175 attitude inventories and scales have been classified so that the researcher may examine such common areas of interest as Family and Child, Education, Work and Occupations, Economics, Religion, Welfare, Politics and Law, Nationalism and Internationalism, War, Mass Media, Race and Ethnicity, Health and Medicine, and Personal Interaction and Customary Behavior. All scales may be examined in Marvin E. Shaw and Jack M. Wright, *Scales for the Measurement of Attitudes* (New York: McGraw-Hill, 1967).

Family and Child

A Survey of Opinions Regarding the Bringing Up of Children (Itkin 1952)
A Survey of Opinions Regarding the Discipline of Children (Itkin 1952)
Attitude Toward Discipline Exercised by Parents (Itkin 1952)
Attitude Toward the Freedom of Children (Koch, Dentler, Dysart, and Streit 1934)
Attitude Toward Parental Control of Children's Activities (Stott 1940)
Attitude Toward Self-Reliance (Ojemann 1934)
Attitude Toward the Use of Fear as a Means of Controlling the Behavior of Children (Ackerley 1934)
Attitude Toward Parents Giving Sex Information to Children Between the Ages of Six and Twelve (Ackerley 1934)
Attitude Toward Older Children Telling Lies (Ackerley 1934)
The Traditional Family Ideology (TFI) Scale (Levinson and Huffman 1955)
Familism Scale (Bardis 1959)

The Family Scale (Rundquist and Sletto 1936)
Attitudes Toward Parents (Form F) (Itkin 1952)
Parents' Judgment Regarding a Particular Child (Itkin 1952)
Attitudes Toward Feminism Belief Patterns Scale (Kirkpatrick 1936)
The Open Subordination of Women (OSW) Scale (Nadler and Morrow 1959)
Attitude Toward Divorce (Thrustone 1929–34)
A Divorce Opinionnaire (Hardy 1957)
Attitude Toward Birth Control (Wang and Thurstone 1931)
Birth Control (Scale BC) Scale (Wilke 1934)
[Panos D. Bardis has constructed "A Pill Scale: A Technique for the Measurement of Attitudes Toward Oral Contraception," *Social Science* (January 1969): 35–42.]

Education

Attitude Toward Teaching (F. D. Miller 1934)
Attitude Toward Teaching as a Career (Merwin and DiVesta 1960)
Attitude Toward Physical Education as a Career for Women (Drinkwater 1960)
Attitude Toward Education (Mitchell 1941)
Opinionnaire on Attitudes Toward Education (Lindgren and Patton 1958)
Education Scale (Kerlinger and Kaya 1959)
Attitude Toward Intensive Competition in Team Games (McCue 1953)
Attitude Toward Intensive Competition for High School Girls (McGee 1956)
The Education Scale (Rundquist and Sletto 1936)
Attitude Toward Education (Glassey 1945)
Attitudes Toward Mathematics (Gladstone, Deal, and Drevdahl 1960)
Revised Math Attitude Scale (Aiken and Dreger 1961)
Physical Education Attitude Scale (Wear 1955)
Counseling Attitude Scale (Form 1955)
Problem-Solving Attitude Scale (Carey 1958)
High School Attitude Scale (Remmers 1960)
Knowledge About Psychology (KAP) Test (Costin 1963)
An Attitude Scale for Measuring Attitude Toward Any Teacher (Hoshaw 1935)
Attitude Toward Any School Subject (Silance and Temmers 1934)
A Scale to Study Attitudes Toward College Courses (Hand 1953)
Attitudes Toward School Integration (IA) Scale Form I (Greenberg, Chase, and Cannon 1957)
Faculty Morale Scale for Institutional Improvement (AAUP) 1963)
Attitude Toward College Fraternities (Banta 1961)

Work and Occupation

Attitude Toward Labor Scale (Newcomb 1939)
IRC (Industrial Relations Center) Union Attitude Questionnaire (Uphoff and Dunnette 1956)
Scale for Management Attitude Toward Union (Stagner, Chalmers, and Derber 1958)
About Your Company (Storey 1955)
Scales to Measure Attitudes Toward the Company, Its Policies, and Its Community Contributions (Riland 1959)
Attitude Toward Earning a Living (Hinckley and Hinckley 1939)
Attitude Toward Work Relief as a Solution to the Financial Depression (Hinckley and Hinckley 1939)
Attitude Toward Farming (Myster 1944)
Attitude Toward Any Practice (Bues 1934)

Attitude Toward Any Home-Making Activity (Kellar 1934)
Attitude Toward Any Occupation (H. E. Miller 1934)
Attitude Toward the Supervisor (AS) Scale (Schmid, Morsh, and Detter 1956)
The Superior-Subordinate (SS) Scale (Chapman and Campbell 1957)
Attitude Toward the Supervisor (Nagle 1953)
Attitude Toward Employment of Older People (Kirchner, Lindbom, and Patterson 1952)
The (Work Related) Change Scale (Trumbo 1961)
Attitudes Toward Dependability: Attitude Scale for Clerical Workers (Dudycha 1941)
Attitudes Toward Legal Agencies (Chapman 1953)
Older Workers Questionnaire (Tuckman and Lorge, 1952)

Economic

Attitude Toward the Tarifff (Thurstone 1929–34)
Distribution of the Wealth (DW) Scale (Wilke 1934)

Religion

Religionism Scale: Scale I (Ferguson 1944)
Belief Pattern Scale; Attitude of Religiosity (Kirkpatrick 1949)
Religious Ideology Scale (Putney and Middleton 1961)
The Religious Attitude Inventory (Ausubel and Schpoont 1957)
The Religion Scale (Bardis 1961)
Religious Belief Scale (Martin and Nichols 1962)
A Survey of Attitudes Toward Religion and Philosophy of Life (Funk 1958)
The Existence of God Scale (Scale G) (Wilke 1934)
Attitude Toward God: The Reality of God (Chave and Thurstone 1931)
Attitude Toward God: Influence on Conduct (Chave and Thurstone 1931)
Attitude Toward the Church (Thurstone 1931)
Attitudes and Beliefs of LDS Church Members Toward Their Church and Religion (Hardy 1940)
Attitude Toward Sunday Observance (Thurstone 1929–34)
An Attitude Scale Toward Church and Religious Practices (Dynes 1955)
Relation Between Religion and Psychiatry Scale (Webb and Kobler 1961)
Attitudes Toward Evolution (Thurstone 1931)
Death Attitudes Scale (Kalish 1963)

Welfare

Attitude Toward Receiving Relief (Hinckley and Hinckley 1939)
Humanitarianism Scale: Scale II (Ferguson 1944)
Belief Pattern Scale; Attitude of Humanitarianism (Kirkpatrick 1949)
Attitudes Toward Any Proposed Social Action (Remmers 1934)

Politics and Law

The Conservatism-Radicalism (C-R) Opinionnaire (Lentz 1935)
The Florida Scale of Civic Beliefs (Kimbrough and Hines 1963)
The Economic Conservatism Scale (Rundquist and Sletto 1936)
Questionnaire on Politico-Economic Attitudes (Sanai 1950)
Conservatism-Radicalism (C-R) Battery (Centers 1949, Case 1963)

Tulane Factors of Liberalism-Conservatism Attitude Value Profile (Kerr 1936)
The Social Attitudes Scale (Kerlinger 1965)
Political and Economic Progressivism (PAP) Scale (Newcomb 1943)
Public Opinion Questionnaire (Edwards 1941)
Attitude Toward the Law (Katz and Thurstone 1931)
The Law Scale (Rundquist and Sletto 1936)
The Ideological and Law-Abidingness Scales (Gregory 1939)
Attitudes Toward Law and Justice (Watt and Maher 1958)
Attitude Toward the Constitution of the United States (Rosander and Thurstone 1931)
Attitude Toward Capital Punishment (Balogh and Mueller 1960)
Attitude Toward Capital Punishment (Thurstone 1932)
Attitude Toward Punishment of Criminals (Wang and Thurstone 1931)
Attitude Toward the Police (Chapman 1953)
Attitude Toward Probation Officers (Chapman 1953)
Juvenile Deliquency Attitude (JDA) Scale (Alberts 1962)
The Academic Freedom Survey (Academic Freedom Committee, American Civil Liberties Union 1954)

Nationalism and Internationalism

Internationalism Scale (Likert 1932)
Nationalism Scale: Scale III (Ferguson 1942)
A Survey of Opinions and Beliefs about International Relations (Helfant 1952)
The Internationalism-Nationalism (IN) Scale (Levinson 1957)
The Worldmindedness Scale (Sampson and Smith, 1957)
The Patriotism (NP) Scale (Christiansen 1959)
Attitude Toward Patriotism Scale (Thurstone 1929–34)
Attitude Toward Communism Scale (Thurstone 1929–34)

War

The Peterson War Scale (Thurstone 1929–34)
A Scale of Militarism-Pacifism (Droba 1931)
Attitude Toward Defensive, Cooperative, and Aggressive War (Day and Quackenbush 1942)
Attitude Toward War (Scale W) (Wilke 1934)
A Scale for Measuring Attitude Toward War (Stagner 1942)
The M-P Opinion Scale (Gristle 1940)

Mass Media

Attitude Toward Newspapers (Rogers 1955)
Atttitude Toward Freedom of Information (Rogers 1955)
Attitude Toward Movies (Thurstone 1930)
Semantic Distance Questionnaire (Weaver 1959)

Race and Ethnicity

Attitude Toward the Negro (Hinckley 1932)
Attitude Toward Segregation Scale (Rosenbaum and Zimmerman 1959)
The Segregation Scale (Peak, Morrison, Spivak, and Zinnes 1956)

The Desegregation Scale (Kelly, Ferson, and Holtzman 1958)
Attitude Toward Accepting Negro Students in College (Grafton 1964)
Attitude Toward Negroes (Thurstone 1931)
Attitude Toward the Negro Scale (Likert 1932)
The Anti-Negro Scale (Steckler 1957)
Negro Behavior Attitude Scale (Rosander 1937)
Experiences with Negroes (Ford 1941)
The Social Situations Questionnaire (Kogan and Downey 1956)
The Anti-Semitism (A-S) Scale (Levinson and Sanford 1944)
Attitude Toward Jews Scale (Harlan 1942)
Opinions on the Jews (Eysenck and Crown 1949)
The Anti-White Scale (Steckler 1957)
Attitude Toward the German People (Thurstone 1931)
Attitude Toward the Chinese (Thurstone 1931)
A Survey of Opinions and Beliefs about Russia: The Soviet Union (Smith 1946)
Ethnocentrism Scale (Levinson 1949)
Intolerant-Tolerant (IT) Scale (Prentice 1956)
The Social Distance Scale (Bogardus 1925)
Scale to Measure Attitudes Toward Defined Groups (Grice 1935)

Health and Medicine

Attitudes Toward Physical Fitness and Exercise (Richardson 1960)
Opinions About Mental Illness (Cohen and Struening 1959)
The Socialized Medicine Attitude Scale (Mahler 1953)
Attitude Toward Censorship Scale (Rosander and Thurstone 1931)
Attitudes Toward Mentally Retarded People (Bartlett, Quay, and Wrightsman 1960)
The Custodial Mental Illness Ideology (CMI) Scale (Gilbert and Levinson 1956)
The Psychotherapy-Sociotherapy Ideology (PSI) Scale (Sharaf and Levinson 1957)
Medication Attitudes (Gorham and Sherman 1961)
Attitude to Blindness Scale (Cowen, Underberg, and Verrillo 1958)
Attitude Toward Disabled People (ATDP) Scale (Yuker, Block, and Campbell 1960)
Medical Information Test (Perricone 1964)
Attitude Toward Menstruation (McHugh and Wasser 1959)
The Vivisection Questionnaire (Molnar 1955)
Attitudes Toward Mental Hospitals (Souelem 1955)
Attitudes Relating to the State Hospital (Pratt, Giannitrapani, and Khanna 1960)

Personal Interaction and Customary Behavior

The Self-Others Questionnaire (Phillips 1951)
Acceptance of Self and Others (Berger 1952)
People in General (Banta 1961)
An Intimacy Permissiveness Scale (Christensen and Carpenter 1962)
Old People (OP) Scale (Kogan 1961)
The "CI" Attitude Scale (Khanna, Pratt, and Gardiner 1962)
The Chivalry (C) Scale (Nadler and Morrow 1959)
Attitudes Toward Old People (Tuckman and Lorge 1953)
Attitude Toward Any Institution (Kelley 1934)
Attitude Toward the Aesthetic Value (Cohen 1941)
The Competitive Attitude (CA) Scale (Lakie 1964)
The "Value Inventory" (Jarrett and Sherriffs 1953)
Attitude Toward Safe Driving: Siebrecht Attitude Scale (Siebrecht 1941)

One constructs a new scale if: (1) after a literature search, a scale is not found that fits the problem; or (2) the available scale is poorly constructed. Any constructed scale should be good enough to invite future researchers to use it in the ongoing process of accumulating research findings. Putting some items together and assigning arbitrary weights to them does not produce this kind of scale. The acceptable scale will cover an important theoretical construct and meet the following evaluative criteria:

Check List of Evaluative Criteria for Assessing a Scale*

I. Item Construction Criteria
 1. Selected items reflect accurately the universe of items encompassed by the variable to be measured.
 2. Items are simply worded so that they can be easily understood by the population to whom the scale is to be given.
 3. Item analysis demonstrates that each item is closely related to the selected variable.
 Techniques of item analysis include:
 a. Item-intercorrelation matrix.
 b. Factor analysis.
 c. Complex multidimensional analysis.
 d. Item correlation with external criteria.
 4. Pretest and eliminate or revise undersirable items.
II. Response Set Criteria
 1. Avoid response set due to acquiescence (subservient syndrome)
 Techniques:
 a. Discard simple affirmative items.
 b. Switch occasional response alternatives between positive and negative.
 c. Use "forceful choice" items: Two or more replies to a question are listed, and the respondent is asked to choose only one.
 2. Avoid response set due to social desirability (good impression syndrome)
 Techniques:
 a. Use forced-choice items in which the alternatives have been equated on the basis of social desirability ratings.
 b. Items are pretested in social desirability, and alternative pairings (or item pairings) that do not prove to be equated are dropped and revised.
 3. Analyze and eliminate efforts of respondents to fake responses according to some image that the respondent wishes to convey.
 4. Analyze and eliminate spurious replies due to respondent's wanting to appear too consistent, to use few or many categories in his replies, or to choose extreme alternatives.
III. Scale Metric Criteria
 1. Representative sampling: Sampling methods accurately produce a miniature population that reflects the universe under study.

---

* These criteria are drawn largely from John P. Robinson, Robert Athanasiou, and Kendra B. Head, *Measures of Occupational Attitudes and Occupational Characteristics* (Ann Arbor: Survey Research Center, University of Michigan, 1969), pp. 4–13.

2. Adequate normative information: To understand the meaning of responses secured in research the constructed scale should provide:

   a. Mean scale score and standard deviation for the sample on which it was constructed.

   b. Means and standard deviations for certain well-defined groups.

   c. Item means and standard deviations.

3. Reliability: A reliable scale measures consistently that which it is supposed to measure. The term refers to three major criteria: (1) the correlation between the same person's score on the same items at two separate points in time; (2) the correlation between two different sets of items at the same time (these sets may be presented as "parallel forms" with items in a separate format or as a "split half" when all items are presented together); (3) the correlation between the scale items for all people who answer the items.

   It is widely agreed by experts that the test-retest index is the best measure of reliability. Many insist that measures (2) and (3) are actually indices of homogeneity and not "reliability," which is commonly used in an ambiguous fashion. The test-retest reliability level may be approximately estimated from indices of homogeneity, but there is no substitute for actual test-retest data.

4. Homogeneity: A homogeneous scale "agrees with itself." The term refers to the internal consistency of a scale. This property is crucial in scale construction. Only a homogeneous scale presents a common attribute.

   Techniques:

   a. Split-half correlation.

   b. Parallel forms and inter-item indices of internal homogeneity (Cronbach's Alpha).

   c. Inter-item correlation matrix.

   d. Guttman Scaling Technique.

5. Validity: A valid scale measures that which it is supposed to measure. Validity implies a predictive power beyond the immediate range of factors in the scale. The best test is the correlation achieved with an external criterion.

   Techniques:

   1. Discrimination of known groups.

   2. Double cross-validation.

   3. Multitrait, multimethod matrix.

   4. Correlation of scale scores with one or more independent criteria of the phenomena being measured.

4.M.8   MODELS OF MASTER SCALE CONSTRUCTION

Bureau of the Census. *Methodology and Scores of Socioeconomic Status.* Working paper No. 15. Washington, D.C.: U.S. Government Printing Office, 1963.

BURGESS, E. W., and COTTRELL, LEONARD. *Predicting Success or Failure in Marriage.* Englewood Cliffs, N.J.: Prentice-Hall, 1939.

HALLER ARCHIBALD O., and MILLER, IRVING W. *The Occupational Aspiration Scale: Theory, Structure, and Correlates.* 2nd ed. Cambridge, Mass.: Schenkman, 1971.

HEMPHILL, JOHN K. *Group Dimensions: A Manual for Their Measurement.* Research Monograph No. 87, Bureau of Business Research. Columbus, Ohio: Ohio State University, 1956.

INKELES, ALEX, and MILLER, KAREN A. "Construction and Validation of a Cross-National Scale of Family Modernism." *International Journal of Sociology of the Family* 4 (August 1974): 127–47.

————, and SMITH, DAVID H. *Becoming Modern.* Cambridge, Mass.: Harvard University Press, 1974.

NEWCOMB, THEODORE M. *Personality and Social Change: Attitude Formation in a Student Community.* New York: Dryden Press, 1943.

REISS, ALBERT J., with DUNCAN, O. D.; HATT, PAUL K.; and NORTH, C. C. *Occupations and Social Status.* Glencoe, Ill.: Free Press, 1961.

RUNDQUIST, EDWARD A., and SLETTO, RAYMOND F. *Personality in the Depression.* Minneapolis: University of Minnesota Press, 1936.

SEWELL, WILLIAM H. *The Construction and Standardization of a Scale for the Measurement of the Socio-Economic Status of Oklahoma Farm Families.* Technical Bulletin No. 9, Agricultural Experiment Station. Stillwater, Okla.: Oklahoma A & M College, 1940.

SCHUESSLER, KARL. *Measuring Social Life Feelings.* San Francisco: Jossey-Bass, 1982.

THORNDIKE, E. L. *Your City.* New York: Harcourt, Brace, 1939.

TREIMAN, DONALD J. *Occupational Prestige in Comparative Perspective.* New York: Academic Press, 1977.

WARNER, W. LLOYD; MEEKER, MARCHIA; AND EELLS, KENNETH. *Social Class in America: A Manual of Procedure for the Measurement of Social Status.* Chicago: Science Research Associates, 1949.

part 5

Research Proposal, Funding, Costing, Reporting, and Utilization

T HE end product of research designing is a proposal. The student setting forth on his or her first independent research and the professional with a lifetime of research achievement both face the same requirement. They must produce an acceptable proposal. Other professionals will critically examine the proposal and decide if it is acceptable. The planning and submission of proposals may take up to a year or more—always longer than expected. The competition for funds is often intense. In general, more proposals are rejected than accepted because of the quality of the proposal or the limited amount of funds. The researcher must know where the money is and develop the skill of research negotiation.

Section A, *The Research Proposal,* describes the preliminary planning of a proposal and offers a few useful hints that are especially appropriate to the evaluations of judges. A general outline of a research proposal follows.

Section B, *Research Funding,* lists various guides to research agencies. B.1 is a list of major financing agencies of social science research and information providing guides to a search for research funding. B.2 is a description of current federal funding policy and behavioral science reactions. B.3 is a selected list of federal government and private organizations offering fellowships and grants, with sources of more comprehensive listings. B.4 describes programs of particular relevance including predoctoral and postdoctoral fellowships offered by the National Science Foundation, National Institute of Mental Health, Social Security Administration, and the U.S.

Office of Education. Aside from university fellowships, the National Science Foundation and the U.S. Department of Health and Human Services provide the major source of competitive fellowships in the social sciences.

Section C, *Research Costing,* discusses a difficult task. Most researchers have never had training in this aspect of research, and they acquire their knowledge by trial and error. Most researchers drastically underestimate the time and effort required to complete their proposals. There are many unforeseen handicaps and delays.

The Guide to Research Costing, C.1, requires detailed cost data before it can be used. The researcher must secure the going wage rate for interviewers, the cost of transportation, the rate for machine calculation, and so forth. These cannot be provided here since they vary by time and place. However, the guide alerts the social scientist to factors that must be taken into account in planning the cost of the research. It should be remembered that overhead costs are not shown. Universities usually demand substantial overhead costs ranging from 30 to 50 percent of the total contract.

Guides C.2 and C.3 provide costing estimates for the Mail Questionnaire, the Telephone Survey, and the Personal Interview.

The Guide to Research Budgeting, C.4, is the form used by the National Science Foundation. This guide provides all items in the budget that may be required in a research project. If the college or university has a contract research officer, seek his help. The researcher can easily overlook some important items or misjudge the expenditures required. Most universities have strict regulations governing all expenditures, and the researcher must learn about them and follow them.

Section D, *Research Reporting.* Finally, plans for the report must be made. This is the "payoff" for the researcher. Specifications for Sociological Report Rating, D.1, indicates criteria that judges will commonly use in appraising the publishing possibilities of the report. The Form for Sociological Report Rating, D.2, provides a final check on the research design at the point where it counts—transmission to the profession.

Generally, two or three professional examiners will be using similar criteria in determining upon their recommendation for acceptance or rejection of the research report. Recently the editors of the five journals sponsored by the American Sociological Association reported an average acceptance of 15 percent. Learning how to handle rejection, the most common experience, is never taught to researchers. It is probably one of the most significant adjustments they must make. They must learn to utilize the criticism of their work and try to meet objections if possible. Often what is needed is better writing. The best advice for all researchers is to rewrite and resubmit. There are scores of journals. Try to get in the best, but above all, try to get published.

John Pease and Joan (Rytina) Huber began a compilation of world sociological journals in 1967. Since then, Lawrence Rhoades has compiled an author's guide to selected sociological and related journals. This is Guide to Sociological Journals, D.3.

D.4 is devoted to publishing in books and journals. Norval Glenn lists the prestige accorded sixty-three journals used frequently by sociologists. D.5 describes how sociologists get published.

A professional research life includes professional communication and reporting to professional meetings. D.6, Professional Communication and Reporting, describes the leading sociological associations and the role they play in professional socialization.

D.7 is a calendar of annual meetings of various sociological societies and some related societies in the social sciences. Although these meetings change officers and meeting places each year, the national offices can supply current information. Common patterns of topical sections for sociology, psychology, and anthropology are shown.

Guides D.8 and D.9 list journals sponsored by the American Sociological Association and the American Psychological Association respectively.

D.10 through D.13 are Guides to Major Journals in Political Science and Public Administration, Anthropology, Education, Business and Journalism and Communication Researchers respectively.

Section E, *Knowledge Utilization,* describes the final act of research activity—research put into practice. Guide E.1 explains the role of Applied Sociology and Policy Making. A selected bibliography is appended. Guide E.2 provides guides to sociology job applicants and other behaviorial science applicants facing the job market.

The Research Grant Proposal

PRELIMINARY PLANNING

The purpose of a research proposal is to provide a statement establishing the objectives and scholarly significance of the proposed activity, the technical qualifications of the project director/principal investigator and his or her organization, and the level of funding required.

The proposal should contain sufficient information to persuade both the professional staff of the agency and members of the scholarly community that the proposed activity is sound and worthy of support under the agency's criteria for the selection of projects or under specific criteria specified in the applicable proposal-generating mechanism. The proposal should be both succinct and complete.

Writing a proposal, like writing any other request, is a challenge in effective persuasion. Every agency has its own method for selecting proposals it wants to fund. Whatever the method used, individuals at the agency will be reading the proposal to determine how it fits into their funding pattern and how cogently the applicant has presented it.

There are a few hints that are especially appropriate to the evaluations of judges:

1. A clearly written abstract is especially helpful. The review committee may be examining many proposals over a busy weekend. An abstract makes it possible to grasp, define, and retain the proposal for a comparative judgment.
2. A statement of previous work serves to validate the ability of the applicant to get into his or her research quickly without false starts and to carry out the proposed research successfully.
3. The availability of the research population is important. An indication from pretests that show that the population is responsive adds weight.
4. The availability of research facilities is also important. If matching funds or supporting facilities are needed, it is important for the committee to know that they are forthcoming.
5. Clear, professionally defined budgets over the time period are imperative. The committee must be convinced that the size of the grant is appropriate and that the money will be spent wisely. They want to know if the applicant is realistic.
6. Supporting evidence that convinces the committee the applicant is able and will

carry the research to completion is especially important. Such evidence may include a biographical sketch, a statement of ongoing research, current support letters of recommendation, and published material relevant to the proposal. (See Guide to Research Costing and Guide to Research Budgeting in section C.)

Each funding agency has its own rules for the applicant of a grant. Some seek very short statements, perhaps limited to five to ten pages; others prefer longer statements. Some provide forms that prescribe precisely what is wanted; others encourage latitude. The researcher must bend to meet the requirements.

Whatever the differences between agencies or foundations, all are greatly concerned with elements of the research design. In general, they include those shown in this handbook in section 1.1, "An Outline Guide for the Design of a Social Research Problem."

GUIDE FOR A RESEARCH GRANT PROPOSAL

Writing the Proposal

When an agency has a set of instructions and/or forms, use them and follow them rigorously. In the absence of any instructions, the general outline that follows may be helpful:

Parts of a proposal:

1. Title page
2. Abstract
3. Table of contents
4. Introduction
5. Background
6. Description of proposed research
7. Evaluation
8. Description of relevant institutional resources
9. List of references
10. Vitae
11. Personnel
12. Budget
13. Other items

1. Title Page. Many sponsoring agencies have their own format for a title, which is usually self-explanatory. In the absence of that requirement, the face page should include most of the following items: the agency to which the proposal is to be submitted; the name and address of the institution submitting the proposal; the title of the proposed work; the name, title, phone number, and address of the project director; the period of time; the requested amount; the date of the proposal and endorsements. Minimum endorsement should be arranged for signature of the project director and the authorizing official of the submitting institution.

2. Abstract. Though the abstract appears at the front of the proposal, it is written last, as a concise summary of the material presented in the proposal. The abstract usually includes the major objectives of the proposal and the procedures to be used to meet these objectives. These materials are condensed to a page or less (specific lengths are sometimes given in guidelines), and if the proposal is awarded, the abstract will be printed in national data banks. The abstract serves several purposes: (*a*) The reviewer usually reads it first to gain a perspective of the study and its expected significance; (*b*) the reviewer uses it as a reference to the nature of the study when the project comes up for discussion; (*c*) it will sometimes be the only part of the proposal that is ready by those reviewing a panel's recommendation or the field readers' consensus. With these many uses, it is important that the abstract be prepared with the utmost care and that objectives and procedures are paraphrased using general but precise statements. Key concepts presented in the body of the proposal are highlighted in the abstract to alert the reviewer to look for them in the body of the proposal.

3. Table of contents. Brief proposals do not necessarily need a table of contents. The convenience of the reader should be the guiding consideration. When included, the table of contents should list all major parts and divisions.

4. Introduction. The introduction should be clear to the layman, should give enough background to enable the reader to place the proposal in a context of common knowledge, and should show how the proposed activities will advance the field or be important to the solution of the problem.

5. Background. Information should be presented here to review what has been accomplished in the field, to demonstrate the faculty member's competence in connection with the problem, and to show what he or she will add to the existing field of knowledge.

6. Description of proposed research. The proposal should present a detailed description of the work to be undertaken. The objectives and significance should be clearly and specifically stated. Research methods or operating procedures should be detailed, and the general plan of work, including the broad design of experiments, should be outlined.

7. Evaluation. The proposal should provide an evaluation component designed to determine how effective the program is in reaching the objectives established and in solving the problems dealt with. If possible, the evaluation should also be designed to allow for appropriate changes and adjustments in a program as it proceeds.

8. Description of relevant institutional resources. Available facilities and major items of equipment especially adapted to the proposed project should be described. These facilities could include libraries, computer centers, other recognized centers, and any special but relevant equipment.

9. List of references. This list is desirable only if the proposal contains six or more references. Otherwise, references can be inserted in the text.

10. Vitae. Most sponsoring agencies require a curriculum vitae and list of publications for each faculty member and senior professional staff member in the project.

11. Personnel. All personnel who will participate in the proposed project should be identified by name, title, and the expected amount of time to be devoted to the project. Unfilled positions should be marked "vacant" or "to be selected." If the individuals involved have exceptional qualifications that would merit consideration in the evaluation of the proposal, this information should be included.

12. Budget. A checklist for budget items should include:*

* Office of Research and Graduate Development, *Research Policy Manual* Bloomington: Indiana University, July 1978.

Salaries and wages	Animals and animal supplies
Academic personnel during academic year	Xerox costs
	Office supplies
Academic personnel during summer	Film
Research associates	Travel
Research assistants	Domestic
Technicians	Foreign
Secretarial staff	Alterations and renovation
Hourly help	Other costs
Fringe benefits	Trainee costs
Consultants	Publication of reports
Fee	Telephone and telegraph
Travel expenses	Equipment rental
Equipment, including installation and freight	Data processing
	Postage
Supplies	Subcontracts
Chemicals and glassware	Indirect costs

For further assistance, see the Budget Time Schedule Guide and the NSF Research Grant Proposal Budget in section C.4.

If a Grant Research Officer is available in your organization, seek his help and counsel. The preparation of a budget requires all the planning skill that can be mustered. Nothing but problems await for failures at this phase of the research.

13. Other items. Space does not permit the publication of a complete proposal; however, the outline of a successful proposal to the National Science Foundation is appended. Those interested in more detailed advice on proposal writing are referred to D. R. Krathwohl, *How to Prepare a Research Proposal,* 2nd ed. (Syracuse, N.Y.: Syracuse University Book Store), 1977.

After you have written your proposal, imagine that you are a member of a review board. What questions would you have? Check carefully the Specifications for Sociological Report Rating on page 611. Will you receive a superior rating on all specifications? If not, start again.

PITFALLS AND WHAT YOU CAN DO ABOUT THEM

No one can foresee all the contingencies and conflicts that may arise in a research project. The sociology of research is a neglected area of study. There is not space in journals to detail all the problems encountered in each piece of published research. But it can be assumed that every researcher encounters unanticipated problems. Some problems can be so severe that it is not possible to complete the research. In other cases the end result is agonizing conflict until a resolution is reached. A few writings are now available to provide the kind of forewarnings that may be helpful.[1] And certain procedures can be followed to protect the researcher when dealing with a granting agency.

One important matter is the protection of the researcher against the claims of the granting or monitoring agent after the research is under way. For example, there is the confidentiality of the data. One researcher found himself pressed by a granting agency to display his data after he had promised complete confidentiality to his respondents. He will not accept future grants without an explicit legal statement on confidentiality.[2]

The use of respondents in the research design may cause special problems when the research calls for concealing from the respondents certain treatments needed to conduct a successful test of the hypotheses. This has usually emerged as a legal question in the last decade because of abuses with research on the physical and psychological effects of drugs. Even in sociological research, however, the question of psychological injury may arise in such areas as role playing, group dynamics, and stress research. Criminologists and educational sociologists are directly involved because of their work with special groups. Sex researchers are also on warning. The U.S. Department of Health and Human Services has expressed its concern with research on human subjects in areas involving their privacy; the need for informed consent; and protection against physical, psychological, sociological, or legal risks. If the grant proposal involves human subjects, the research applicant is required to do the following:

1. Describe the requirements for a subject population and explain the rationale for using in this population special groups such as prisoners, children, the mentally disabled, or groups whose ability to give voluntary informed consent may be in question.
2. Describe and assess any potential risks—physical, psychological, social, legal or other—and assess the likelihood and seriousness of such risks. If methods of research create potential risks, describe other methods, if any, that were considered and why they will not be used.
3. Describe consent procedures to be followed, including how and where informed consent will be obtained.
4. Describe procedures (including confidentiality safeguards) for protecting against or minimizing potential risks and an assessment of their likely effectiveness.
5. Assess the potential benefits to be gained by the individual subject, as well as benefits which may accrue to society in general as a result of the planned work.
6. Analyze the risk-benefit ratio.[3]

Statements submitted by the applicant are subject to review by the local organization's review committee. The responsibility then shifts to the organizational review committee and the HHS staff and advisory committees. Any changes in the researcher's procedures must be reported.[4]

Obviously, this means that all parties should get their agreements in hand so that no barriers can be thrown in the path of the researcher once the work is under way.

A guarantee of publication rights should be clearly spelled out. The problem can arise with any contract research agency of the federal government. Most applied-research contracts contain either a "rights in data" clause or a copyright clause. Two propositions, partially incompatible, must be reconciled. One states that everything done under a government contract belongs to the government, to do with as it sees fit. The second holds that the work done under a government contract should be freely available to the public. In actual practice this usually means that the government reserves exclusive license over the product of the study but interposes no objection to the publishing of results by the investigator as long as he or she *first secures the permission of the contracting officer.*

Academic researchers must recognize that a grant and a contract have two different sets of rules with respect to publication. The grant carries the right of publication; indeed, the National Science Foundation assures researchers that it encourages publication and distribution of the results of research conducted under its grants. Under contract research, the investigator cannot go off on his own and publish articles from the study.[5] Many applied-research agencies are uninterested in generating publications. Instead, the agency will insist upon reports that fit the specifications that meet its internal needs. It is up to the investigator to work out an understanding on publication rights. In dealing with a military funding agency, this is especially important; it is possible that the military will clamp a censorship or restraining order on research publication as the uncertain winds of military security blow across the Pentagon.

If none of the possible sources of conflict has frightened you against the research life, you are ready to enter or renew the exciting quest for knowledge. If you are the "academic man," you will probably seek "clean" money, i.e., a grant to do basic research with no strings attached. But you may find such a posture automatically removes you from many research opportunities. Basic research amounts to only about one-third of federal spending for applied research.[6]

Notes

1. Margaret Archer, ed., *Problems of Current Sociological Research*, vol. 22, *Current Sociology*, The Journal of the International Sociological Association (Beverly Hills, Calif.: Sage, 1974); Gunnar Boalt, *The Sociology of Research* (Carbondale: Southern Illinois University Press, 1969); Richard O'Toole, ed. *The Organization, Management, and Tactics of Social Research* (Cambridge, Mass.: Schenkman, 1971). Refer also to section 1.14 of this handbook, The Shaping of Research Design in Large-Scale Group Research.
2. Robert F. Boruch and Joe S. Cecil: *Assuring the Confidentiality of Social Research Data* (Philadelphia: University of Pennsylvania Press, 1979); Sandra C. Reese, "Retention of Raw Data: A Problem Revisited," *American Psychologist* (August 1973): 723; R. W. Johnson, "Retain the Original Data," *American Psychologist* 19 (1964): 350–51; L. Wolins, "Responsibility for Raw Data," *American Psychologist* 17 (1962): 657–58.
3. These regulations follow from sec. 212 of the National Research Act, Public Law 93–348, and were made effective July 1, 1974.
4. Robert T. Bower and Priscilla de Gasparis, *Ethics in Social Research: Protecting the Interests of Human Subjects* (Washington, D.C.: Bureau of Social Science Research, 1978); Paul Davidson Reynolds, *Ethical Dilemmas and Social Science Research: An Analysis of Moral Issues Confronting Investigators in Research Using Human Participants* (San Francisco: Jossey-Bass, 1979). Tom A. Beauchamp, Roth R. Faden, R. Jay Wallace, Jr., and LeRoy Walters, *Ethical Issues in Social Research* (Baltimore: The Johns Hopkins University Press, 1982).
5. Keith Baker, "A New Grantsmanship," *American Sociologist* 10 (10 November 1975): 212–13.
6. *Ibid.*, p. 206.

Research Funding

MAJOR FINANCING AGENCIES OF SOCIAL SCIENCE RESEARCH   *5.B.1*

1. U.S. Department of Health and Human Services
   National Institute of Mental Health
   5600 Fishers Lane
   Rockville, MD 20857

2. Department of Education
   400 Maryland Ave. S.W.
   Washington, DC 20202

3. National Science Foundation
   The Fellowship Office
   National Research Council
   1800 G. St. N.W.
   Washington, DC 20550

4. U.S. Department of Labor
   200 Constitution Ave. N.W.
   Washington, DC 20210

5. Social Science Research Council
   230 Park Avenue
   New York, NY 10017

6. Ford Foundation
   320 East 43 Street
   New York, NY 10017

7. Rockefeller Foundation
   1153 Ave. of the Americas
   New York, NY 10036

8. Carnegie Corporation of N.Y.
   437 Madison Ave.
   New York, NY 10022

9. Russell Sage Foundation
   633 Third Ave.
   New York, NY 10017

579

10. National Endowment for the Humanities
806 15 Street, N.W.
Washington, DC 20506
(Grants for humanistically oriented sociology projects)

Other grant organizations are listed in section 5A.2

For further information see *Annual Register of Grant Support* (current edition) Marquis Academic Media, subsidiary of Marquis Who's Who, Inc., which lists more than 1700 sources of nonrepayable funds.

Another way of conducting a research for research funding is to consult the information compiled by The Foundation Center on about 26,000 American foundations.

Information compiled by The Foundation Center is available to the public through national collections in three cities, regional collections in 39 states, publications and services, and membership in an associates program.

The national collections of source materials on the foundations and their grant-making activities includes the basic records filed by every private foundation with the Internal Revenue Service, annual reports, and the Center's standard reference works. Also available are books, reports, and guides relating to the foundation field.

The New York collection also includes reference materials on foundations in other countries, as well as information on the international activities of American foundations.

The national collections are located at the following addresses:

The Foundation Center, 888 Seventh Avenue, New York, NY 10019.

The Foundation Center, 1001 Connecticut Avenue, N.W., Washington, DC 20036.

Donors' Forum, 208 South LaSalle Street, Chicago, IL 60604.

In addition, 49 regional collections are located in 39 states. These collections contain the Center's standard reference works, some recent books and reports on foundations, foundation annual reports on film, and a smaller collection of foundation information returns limited usually to the state in which the collection is located. Selected computer listings of grants data on topics of broad general interest are available for consultation. A listing of the regional collections is available from the New York office.

Anyone who visits the national or regional collections may consult all of the published sources and film records, including subject lists of recent foundation grants, without charge. Reference staff is available to assist visitors.

In addition to the collections, The Foundation Center produces some publications which are most likely available in the reference section of a nearby college, university or public library. They may also be purchased from the Columbia University Press.

The publications are:

The Foundation Directory and *Supplements* which contain information on the 2533 largest foundations in the country. These foundations account for about 90 percent of all foundation assets and 80 percent of all grants given in this country.

The Center also plans to publish regional directories in order to provide information on the smaller foundations.

The Foundation Grants Index which is published bimonthly in *Foundation News.* The *Index* report grants by state in which foundation is located, by recipient and by subject matter.

Foundation News is published by the Council on Foundations, Inc., 1828 L St., Washington, DC 20036.

Several leaflets dealing with information sources to foundation facts, proposal writing, and evaluation of proposal are available for free from the Center.

Selected listings of grants made by the foundations in 1972 and 1973 may be purchased on microfiche for a nominal charge from the Center. The grants are grouped into 31 broad subject areas including psychology/sociology. Request order forms from the New York office.

Finally, the Center's Associates Program provides individuals and nonprofit organizations with telephone reference services, mail service, copying services, custom searches, library research service and custom computer searches. A membership fee is charged.

The Center is an educational corporation chartered in 1956 by the Board of Regents of the University of the State of New York and is governed by its own Board of Trustees. It has been supported principally by foundation grants.

Federal Government Contract Research

Any academic institution seriously interested in contract research should have somebody who reads *Commerce Business Daily* and refers relevant announcements to interested faculty immediately. Subscriptions to the *Commerce Business Daily* may be obtained from the Superintendent of Documents, U.S. Government Printing Office, Washington, DC 20402. The *Federal Register* is an excellent secondary resource.

The Art and Science of Grantsmanship

The procurement of grants and contracts is a game that many universities and research institutes play. For many of these organizations, research funding is big business amounting to millions of dollars yearly.[1] A large part of the funding of graduate students rests upon a steady flow of federal research grants.

"Grantsmanship" sometimes refers to a personality attribute (like showmanship): the ability to persuade and influence others to trade their research dollars for a promised performance. At other times, it refers to an elaborate institutional mechanism (Division of Research and Development) erected solely to influence the flow of research dollars to a given institution. Prestige and power are thrown into the operation in a competitive game to get more and more. Individual researchers who stay outside these contests often pay the price: underfunding. Those who get in pay another kind of price: large amounts of time and energy expended in cultivating contacts and writing proposals. It is also not commonly understood that the recipient of a large research grant is almost automatically converted from a research investigator to a research administrator. He or she gives up field research for the recruiting of personnel, drafting of reports, supervision of professional and staff members, and the endless flow of paper between the financial offices of the university and the granting agency. (Of course, well-funded researchers get the right people to assume much of the administrative responsibility.)

Since grantsmanship is part art and part management, no one can teach it with high efficiency. Experience is the best teacher. And it is necessary to have experience in both grants and contracts. Clive Veri provides experienced guidance for successful pursuance of grants.[2] Keith Baker describes how to get a contract that he calls "the new grantsmanship" and by which he means "contractmanship."[3] Dave Krathwohl and George R. Allen have detailed advice for proposal writing in general.[4] Smith and Skjei have a creative guide to the grants system promising how to find funders, write convincing proposals, and make your grants work.[5]

Notes

1. According to the National Science Foundation, federal spending in 1971 for applied research totaled $89,099,000 for Sociology, $49,855,000 for Economics, and $66,833,000 for Psychology. For current funding of basic research see 5.B.2.
2. Clive C. Veri, "How to Write a Proposal and Get It Funded," *Adult Leadership* 16, no. 9 (March 1968): 318–20; 343–44.
3. Keith Baker, "A New Grantsmanship," *American Sociologist* 10, no. 4 (November 1975): 206–18.
4. David R. Krathwohl, *How to Prepare a Research Proposal* 2nd ed. (Syracuse, N.Y.: Syracuse University Bookstore, 1977); George R. Allen, *The Graduate Student's Guide to Theses and Dissertations: A Political Manual for Writing and Research* (San Francisco: Jossey-Bass, 1973).
5. Craig W. Smith and Eric W. Skjei, *Getting Grants* (New York: Harper & Row, 1980). Other sources include: Marquis Media. *Grantsmanship: Money and How to Get It.* (Chicago: Marquis Academic Media, 1978); Virginia P. White, *Grants: How to Find Out About Them and What to Do Next.* (New York: Plenum Press, 1975).

5.B.2 FEDERAL FUNDING POLICY AND BEHAVIORAL SCIENCE REACTIONS

The Reagan administration has stated that it is pledged to "turning the national economy around." Budget cuts in social programs have not left research funding, especially for the social and economic sciences, in a protected position. Table 1 shows the changes in federal funding for basic behavioral and social science research from 1976 to the estimated budget for fiscal '82. Note that comparisons are made for fiscal years 1976–82 and 1980–82. The various declines in the social sciences are obvious; the social sciences overall are cut by 28.6 percent between 1980 and 1982. Sociology shows a decline of 31.2 percent for this period.

Social and economic sciences have been put on the defensive. The administration requires a reorientation to place stress on research directly related to productivity and innovation. The case being made by the Consortium of Social Science Associations (COSSA), which is composed of major social science associations, is to stress the importance of the social sciences in national affairs. COSSA has decided to center attention on the National Science Foundation, National Endowment for the Humanities, National Institutes of Education, and National Institutes of Mental Health.

The danger is twofold: a drastic reduction in budget for research activity and a reduction in funding for basic research. Applied research is in the saddle, and many researchers will be forced to formulate research proposals directed to productivity and innovation of the technology or go without funding. The American Sociological Association is fully aware of the need

Table 1 *Federal Support for Basic Research in Behavioral and Social Sciences, Fiscal Years 1976–82; Detailed Field of Science, Obligations in Constant (FY 1972) Dollars* (in millions of dollars)*

Field of science	1976	1977	1978	1979	1980	Est. 1981	Est. 1982	Percent difference FY 82/ FY 76	Percent difference FY 82/ FY 80
Psychology:									
Biological aspects	$14.0	$16.0	$25.3	$16.2	$17.1	$15.8	$14.9	+ 6.4%	−12.9%
Social aspects	10.8	13.2	15.6	18.4	17.7	15.6	17.5	+62.0%	− 1.1%
Other	7.6	8.8	12.8	9.0	12.9	13.7	14.4	+89.5%	+11.6%
Subtotal, Psych.	32.3	38.1	53.7	43.7	47.7	45.2	46.8	+44.9%	− 1.9%
Social sciences:									
Anthropology	4.9	5.7	8.0	7.7	8.0	6.9	7.1	+44.9%	−11.2%
Economics	19.4	20.7	22.3	20.1	22.6	21.1	16.8	−13.4%	−25.7%
Political science	2.3	1.8	2.1	2.5	4.2	2.4	1.1	−52.2%	−73.8%
Sociology	12.5	11.2	12.3	11.2	14.4	13.1	9.9	−20.8%	−31.2%
Soc. sci. not classified	26.4	28.4	38.0	38.1	34.1	31.1	24.6	− 6.8%	−27.9%
Subtot, soc. sci.	65.5	67.9	82.8	79.5	83.3	74.7	59.5	− 9.2%	−28.6%
Total, behavioral & social sciences	$97.8	$106.0	$136.5	$123.2	$131.0	$119.9	106.3	+8.7%	−18.9%
GNP implicit deflators	1.317	1.406	1.500	1.628	1.767	1.935	2.101		

* NOTE: Some columns do not add due to rounding.

Source: Otto N. Larsen, Director, Division of Social and Economic Science, National Science Foundation, *Statement before the Science, Research, and Technology Subcommittee of the House Committee on Science and Technology*, U.S. House of Representatives, September 10, 1981.

Comment: In constant FY 1972 dollars, federal support for basic research in the social and behavioral sciences peaked in FY 1978 and has declined since then. The change between FY 1980 funding and FY 1982 estimate is marked: Support for the social sciences decreased 28.6%; political science, which receives 90% of its support from NSF, declined by 73.8%; economics experienced a drop of 25%. Comparisons with FY 1976 funding show that anthropology and psychology received increased funding; research on the biological aspects of psychology increased only slightly over the FY 1976–82 period; support for other disciplines, especially political science and sociology, declined.

to reassess the capability of sociology to make knowledge available that relates to productive goals and to furnish knowledge valuable to evaluation and policy making. The ASA is sponsoring workshops on Directions in Applied Sociology. For eligibility standards, see specific programs.

A recent article describes the results of a questionnaire mailed to 119 American Ph.D.-granting departments in sociology.[1] A total of 89 departmental chairpersons responded to the question, *"In this decade what curriculum changes and/or requirements do you anticipate being introduced to make our Ph.d.'s more competitive for positions in the public and private sectors of our economy?"*

The results show the following:

N	Response[2]
55	Applied research training research
30	Evaluative analysis
15	Data and word processing skills
10	Interdiscipline outreach experience
8	Increased statistical sophistication
6	Field internships

The methodological training stresses skill in computer analysis with mastery of the required software necessary for treatment of data calculations. Evaluation and policy-making research will have high priority.[3]

It must be remembered that applied research training does not stand in opposition to basic research training. Quite the contrary—the best applied researcher will always possess basic research training. Essentially, the only difference is the goal orientation. Federal funding for the training of applied behavioral scientists and for applied research will get the major federal funding. It is hoped that a core of basic research funds will still come from federal funds and private foundations.

Notes

1. *Footnotes* (ASA) 9 (October 1981): 1.
2. Most respondents gave only one answer, a few gave more. See Edward C. McDonagh and Kent P. Schwirian, *Footnotes ASA* 9 (October 1981): 8.
3. Ibid.

5.B.3 SELECT LIST OF FEDERAL GOVERNMENT AGENCIES AND PRIVATE ORGANIZATIONS OFFERING FELLOWSHIPS AND GRANTS

American Council of Learned Societies, 800 Third Ave., New York, NY 10022.
Several categories of fellowships and grants for which scholars in various fields whose research programs have predominantly humanistic emphasis may apply.
American Philosophical Society, 104 South Fifth Street, Philadelphia, PA 19106.
Grants averaging $800 and not exceeding $2000 to individuals for expenses of research in all fields, including the social sciences. Awards made on the first Fridays of October, December, February, April, and June; applications due 8 weeks in advance; the Society does not offer fellowships or predoctoral grants.
Danforth Foundation, 222 South Central Avenue, St. Louis, MO 63105.

Several fellowship programs for men and women at various stages of graduate study. Applicants must be planning for careers in college teaching or administration; fields of study common to the undergraduate liberal arts curriculum in the United States.

The Ford Foundation. 1. Postdoctoral grants for research in Southeast Asia in the social sciences and humanities: address inquiries to Southeast Asia Regional Council, Box 17, 5828 South University Avenue, Chicago, IL 60637. 2. Graduate Fellowship Program for black Americans, Mexican-Americans, Native Americans (American Indians), and Puerto Ricans planning a career in higher education and enrolled in or planning to enter an accredited U.S. graduate school in the social sciences, natural sciences, or humanities: black American students address inquiries to Graduate Fellowships for Black Americans, National Fellowships Fund, 795 Peachtree Street, N.E., Suite 484, Atlanta, GA 30308; Mexican-American and Native American students address inquiries to Educational Testing Service, Box 200, Berkeley, CA 94704; Puerto Rican students address inquiries to Graduate Fellowships for Puerto Ricans, Educational Testing Service, Box 2822, Princeton, NJ 08540.

Japan Foundation, 1302 18th St. N.W., Suite 704, Washington, D.C. 20036. Postdoctoral grants and dissertation fellowships for research conducted in Japan in the social sciences, the humanities, and professional fields.

Fulbright-Hays and other U.S. Government awards for predoctoral study and postdoctoral research in certain foreign countries: address inquiries concerning predoctoral applications to Institute of International Education, 809 United Nations Plaza, New York, NY 10017; postdoctoral applications to Council for International Exchange of Scholars, 2101 Constitution Avenue, N.W., Washington, DC 20418.

John Simon Guggenheim Memorial Foundation, 90 Park Avenue, New York, NY 10016. Postdoctoral fellowships in social sciences and other fields.

National Endowment for the Humanities, 806 15 Street, N.W., Washington, DC 20506. Research grants and fellowships for humanists and certain social scientists whose projects will strengthen the humanistic aspects of a social science.

The National Institutes of Health offer research and research-training grants and awards in the biomedical and health-related sciences. For information, write Division of Research Grants, National Institutes of Health, Bethesda, MD 20014.

The National Institute of Mental Health. For information on research grants, address Social Sciences Section, Behavioral Sciences Research Branch, Division of Extramural Research Programs, NIMH, Parklawn Bldg., 5600 Fishers Lane, Rockville, MD 20852.

Other Agencies that offer grants for research relevant to their respective responsibilities are the following: Office of Education, Social Security Administration, Vocational Rehabilitation Administration, Welfare Administration.

National Science Foundation, 1800 G. St. N.W., Washington, DC 20550. Research grants and fellowships in anthropology, economics, geography, history and philosophy of science, linguistics, political science, psychology, and sociology. Also included are interdisciplinary areas composed of two or more overlapping fields, and work in the field of law which employs the methodology of the social sciences or which interrelates with research in the natural or social sciences and research on science policy. Not supported is research or study in business administration, clinical psychology, or social work. Predoctoral fellowships are open only to students who have completed not more than one year of graduate study. The NSF also administers NATO Postdoctoral and Senior Fellowships, in cooperation with the Department of State. Research grants are intended primarily for established scholars. A special program of doctoral dissertation research grants provides assistance toward the expenses of research but does not include a stipend.

Population Council, One Dag Hammarskjöld Plaza, New York, NY 10017. Fellowships and grants for training and research in demography and in family planning.

The Rockefeller Foundation, 1133 Avenue of the Americas, New York, NY 10036.
Several categories of research fellowships and grants including a fellowship program
in environmental affairs, fellowships in conflict in international relations, and the
Rockefeller Foundation and Ford Foundation program in support of population
policy research in the social sciences.

Social Science Research Council, 605 Third Avenue, New York, NY 10016. Several
categories of research fellowships and grants including (1) postdoctoral research
training fellowships, (2) grants to minority scholars for research on racism and
other social factors in mental health, (3) postdoctoral fellowships in criminal justice
indicators, (4) fellowships for international doctoral research, (5) postdoctoral grants
for research on foreign areas, (6) grant programs for training and travel in foreign
countries. Programs 4, 5, 6 sponsored jointed with American Council of Learned
Societies.

More comprehensive listings of other fellowship and grant opportunities may
be found in:

*A Selected List of Major Fellowship Opportunities and Aids to Advanced Education
for United States Citizens.* National Research Council, 2101 Constitution Avenue,
N.W., Washington, DC 20418.

Handbook on International Study for U.S. Nationals. Institute of International Education, 809 United Nations Plaza, New York, NY 10017.

Study Abroad. UNESCO, 75 Place de Fontenoy, Paris VII, France.

*A Guide to Selected Fellowships and Grants for Research on Latin America and the
Caribbean,* by Michael Potashnik. Social Science Research Council, 605 Third
Avenue, New York, NY 10016.

5.B.4 PROGRAMS OF PARTICULAR RELEVANCE INCLUDING PREDOCTORAL AND POSTDOCTORAL FELLOWSHIPS

National Science Foundation
Washington, DC 20550

Information may be obtained by writing to the foundation, and informal
communication with the foundation's staff is encouraged prior to formal
submission of a proposal. Among a variety of forms of foundation support,
the activities of greatest interest to sociologists are:

1. Grants for *basic scientific research,* or for related activities, such as research conferences, construction of specialized research facilities, and travel to selected meetings
of international scientific organizations of major importance. In addition, social
science dissertation research grants provide funds for research expenses (not stipends) in order to improve the quality and significance of dissertations and reduce
the time required for their completion. All of these programs seek basic scientific
understanding of behavioral and social processes and improved research methods.
Support is provided for research which seeks to discover and test scientific generalizations. Criteria for the selection of research projects as approved by the National
Science Board August 21, 1981, include: (*a*) competent performance of the research,
(*b*) intrinsic merit of the research, (*c*) utility or relevance of the research, and
(*d*) effect of the research on the infrastructure of science and engineering.

2. *Computer research* including theoretical computer science, software systems, intelligent systems, and societal issues in computer science including privacy and security,

social and economic impact, and new directions in computer science and applications.

3. *Measurement methods and data resources.* Survey operations research; methods and models for the quantitative analysis of social data; improvements in the scientific adequacy and accessibility of social statistical data, including those generated by government as well as the academic research community; development and testing of new social indicators.

4. *Institutional programs.* NSF programs include support of small college faculty in research at large institutions; support for research workshops, symposia, publications and monographs, conferences, the purchase of scientific equipment for research purposes, the operation of specialized research facilities, and the improvement of research collections. For the past seven years the Foundation has been encouraging working linkages between industry and universities in research activity (university cooperative research center).

5. *International cooperative research programs.* The areas of research supported are health sciences, natural sciences, energy, and social and behavioral sciences.

6. *Socioeconomic aspects of science and technology* are supported under the Division of Policy Research and Analysis. A special program of interest is Ethics and Values in Science and Technology (EVIST).

7. The status of *science and engineering education programs* for fiscal 1982 is not yet known and is not available in NSF Guide to Programs (1982). Individuals wishing to receive information about these programs when such information is available are advised to send their names and complete mailing addresses to: Directorate for Science and Engineering Education, National Science Foundation, Washington, DC 20550.

National Science Foundation Directorate for Biological, Behavioral, and Social Sciences; Division of Social and Economic Science

The Division of Social and Economic Science supports fundamental research in economics, geography and regional science, history and philosophy of science, law and social sciences, political science, sociology, and measurement methodology. Interdisciplinary studies also are eligible. The goal of the Division is to support research that will contribute to the basic understanding of how social organizations and institutions function and change and how human interaction and decision-making are influenced by social conditions and institutional arrangements.

Programs within the Division also consider proposals for doctoral dissertation support, research conferences, the acquisition of specialized research equipment, and data resource development.

The three programs of widest concern to social and behavioral scientists are:

The *Political Science Program* supports research designed to understand the political processes by which societies coordinate their activities through governments. Research areas supported include studies of governmental institutions and their effects on social life, investigations of the effects of structural factors on political participation and effectiveness, and explorations of how political processes are modified in response to economic and social change.

The *Sociology Program* supports research on problems of human social organization, demography, and the processes of institutional change. The program provides support for theoretical investigations aimed at improving the explanation of fundamental social processes. Included is research on decision-making, organization change, social movements, urban development, resource allocation, reward distribution, and the social construction of norms.

The *Measurement Methods and Data Resources Program* supports projects to improve the scientific adequacy and accessibility of social data, with emphasis on improving survey data and on increasing the research usefulness of Federal statistical data. Projects designed to enhance the reliability, validity, or accessibility of existing data sources, to develop and make available new data resources, and/or to create analytic tools of broad utility are considered. The program also includes measurement and data projects focused on the development of social indicators and systems of social accounts.

The *Division of Policy Research and Analysis* (PRA) at NSF is funding research on technological innovation in a wide variety of public and private settings addressing activities associated with development of advances in technology and with the diffusion and widespread utilization of technologically advanced products, processes, and services.

Formal application blanks are not used in the research grants program. However, a desired cover page is requested as given in Appendix I of the NSF *Guide to Grants for Scientific Research.* Information to be included:

1. Name and address of institution.
2. Name, address (if different), and department of principal investigator(s). Telephone numbers are helpful.
3. Title of proposed research project.
4. Desired starting date (the earliest date on which funds would be required).
5. Time period for which support is requested.
6. Abstract of description of proposed research project.
7. Description of proposed research project, including objectives and research design.
8. Bibliography of related research.
9. Description of facilities available for the research.
10. Biographical information for senior personnel, and for junior personnel when appropriate, including bibliographies.
11. Budget.
12. Statement of current support and pending applications for this and other research by the principal investigator(s).

Please use this as a check list when submitting an application. Twenty complete copies of the proposal are necessary. One copy should be signed by the principal investigator, by the department head, and by an official authorized to sign for the institution. For more complete information, see NSF 78–41A *Grants for Scientific Research.* Carefully check *What to Submit* and Appendices I, II, III, IV, V, and VI.

Proposals for research support may be submitted at any time. Reviewing and processing usually require six to eight months. Proposals are normally evaluated by ad hoc reviewers selected for their expertise from throughout the scientific community and by an advisory subcommittee that meets two or three times a year to discuss and make recommendations on proposals. Submission target dates vary for each program and are published in the *National Science Foundation Bulletin.* Further information on proposals, target dates, and review may be obtained from individual program staff listed below: For Sociology the target dates are February 1 and September 1 with the corresponding (possible) starting dates July/August and January/February.

Division Director	Dr. Otto N. Larsen	202/357–7966
Staff Associate	Ms. Sonja B. Sperlich	202/357–7967
Section Head	Dr. James H. Blackman	202/357–9674
Program Director, Economics	Dr. Daniel H. Newlon	202/357–9675
Program Director, Economics	Dr. Lynn A. Pollnow	202/357–7425
Acting Program Director, Geography & Regional Science	D. James H. Blackman	202/357–7326
Acting Program Director, Political Science	Dr. Frank P. Scioli, Jr.	202/357–7534
Section Head	Dr. Murray Aborn	202/357–7913
Program Director, Measurement Methods & Data Resources	Dr. Murray Aborn	202/357–7913
Staff Associate	Dr. Sara B. Nerlove	202/357–7969
Program Director, Law & Social Sciences	Dr. Felice J. Levine	202/357–9567
Program Director, Sociology	Dr. James J. Zuiches	202/357–7802
Program Director, History & Philosophy of Science	Dr. Ronald J. Overmann	202/357–7617

National Science Foundation Directorate for Biological, Behavioral, and Social Sciences, Division of Behavioral and Neural Sciences

SOCIAL AND DEVELOPMENTAL PSYCHOLOGY PROGRAM

The Social and Developmental Psychology Program supports laboratory and field research in all areas of human social behavior including social perception, attitude formation and change, and social influence. The Program includes research on developmental processes in children and adults, with emphasis on social, personality, and emotional development. Research to improve the conceptual and methodological base of social and developmental psychology is encouraged. Social and Developmental Psychology (Acting) Program Director: Dr. Richard T. Louttit (202) 357–7564.

FELLOWSHIPS AND OTHER NSF PROGRAMS

Graduate Fellowship Program

NSF Graduate Fellowships are awarded for study or work leading to master's or doctoral degrees in the mathematical, physical, biological, engineering, and social sciences; and in the history and philosophy of science. Awards are not made in law, education, or business fields; in history or social work; for work leading to medical, dental, or public health degrees; or for study in joint science-professional degree programs. Applications are encouraged from minorities, women, the physically handicapped, and members of other groups underrepresented in science and engineering.

NSF Graduate Fellowships are offered subject to the availability of funds. New fellowships offered in March 1982 are for maximum tenured periods of three years.

Graduate Fellowship stipends during 1982–83 for all new and continuing Fellows will be $6900 for 12-month tenures, prorated monthly at $575 for lesser periods. There are no dependency or travel allowances.

Minority Graduate Fellowships
New three-year Minority Graduate Fellowships are also being offered.

For a detailed deadline sheet for either of the above programs and additional information contact: Fellowship Office, National Research Council, 2101 Constitution Avenue, Washington, DC 20418. Telephone (202) 334–2872

National Science Foundation Directorate for Biological, Behavioral, and Social Sciences; Division of Environmental Biology, Division of Behavioral and Neural Sciences, and Division of Social and Economic Science

Grants are awarded in support of doctoral dissertation research in the environmental, behavioral, neural, and social sciences in order to improve the overall quality of dissertation research in these sciences. The grants allow doctoral candidates opportunities for greater creativity in the gathering and analyzing of data than would otherwise be possible. Proposals are judged on the basis of scientific content, importance, and originality. Dissertation proposals compete for research grant funds with proposals for regular research projects. Awards will be made only when it is clear that the dissertation to be produced will be of the highest scientific merit.

The grants are intended to provide funds for items not normally available from the student's university or other sources. Allowable items include travel to specialized facilities or field research locations, sample survey costs, specialized research equipment and services not otherwise available, supplies, microfilms and other forms of unique data, payments to subjects or informants, rental of environmental chambers or other research facilities, and computer time only when not available at the institution. A request for per diem allowance for time away from a home base to conduct research should be carefully justified in terms of living costs in excess of those in the vicinity of the home base.

Funds may not be used as a stipend for the student, for tuition, or for dependents of students. Textbooks and journals cannot be purchased with dissertation research grant funds, and funds may not be used for typing or reproduction of the student's dissertation. In special circumstances and with special justification, funds may be requested for research assistants.

Who May Submit:
A proposal should be submitted through regular university channels by the dissertation advisor on behalf of a graduate student who is at the point of initiating dissertation research. A proposal may be submitted while the student is completing other requirements for the doctorate. Only students enrolled at U.S. institutions are eligible. Academic departments should limit the applications submitted to outstanding dissertation proposals with unusual financial requirements that cannot be met by the university.

Contents of the Proposal:
The proposal should have the same format as proposals by faculty members for support of their own research (see *Grants for Scientific Research,* NSF 78–41). A 200-word project summary of the proposed research, suitable for publication, is required. The main body of the proposal should not exceed eight single-spaced typewritten pages and should include a: (a) description of the scientific significance of the work and the design of the project in sufficient detail to permit evaluation; (b) presentation and interpretation of progress to date if the research is already underway; (c) statement of the items for which funds are requested and their estimated costs with an explanation of their necessity for the research; and (d) schedule for the research including the date funds will be required.

Biographical data should be included for the student and the dissertation advisor, including educational background, training, and experience directly relevant to the dissertation, together with a list of other financial aid received, applied for, or anticipated during the award period. Transcripts are not required, but lists of relevant courses and grades may be included. Statements from faculty members or other references concerning the student are optional. If survey questionnaires or interviews are to be used, the proposal should contain a copy of the questionnaire, if available, or sample questions, and information on who will conduct the interviews.

Submission Procedures and Grant Administration:
Proposals should be submitted by the university to the Central Processing Section, National Science Foundation, Washington, DC 20550. Six copies of doctoral dissertation research proposals are necessary, one of which should be signed by the student, the dissertation advisor, and an official authorized to sign for the university. Formats for the cover page, project summary, and summary proposal budget are contained in the appendixes of *Grants for Scientific Research.* Proposals may be submitted at any time. Up to 6 months should be allowed for normal processing. The Foundation's decision will be announced as promptly as possible.

Awards will be made to the institution with the student's dissertation advisor designated as "project director." Grants will be awarded for periods up to 24 months. The grant is to be administered in accordance with the applicable policies and procedures contained in the NSF *Grant Policy Manual* (NSF 77–47). *Grants for Scientific Research* (NSF 78–41) summarizes the salient provisions of interest to the project director and to the student. A final project report (in the general format of Appendix VI to NSF 8–41) is required within 90 days after the expiration of the grant. A copy of the dissertation abstract or other publication deriving from it may be submitted with the final project report. NSF does not reimburse grantee institutions for the indirect costs associated with doctoral dissertation research and considers this as satisfaction of the cost-sharing requirement.

National Institute of Mental Health, 5600 Fishers Lane, Rockville, MD 20852

General Funding Statement, Research Support Programs (Catalog of Research Assistance No. 13.242). The Institute supports programs designed "to increase knowledge and improve research methods on mental and behavioral disorders; to generate information regarding basic biological and behavioral processes underlying these disorders and the maintenance of mental health; and to improve mental health services."

Availability of Funds. The amount budgeted for new and renewal research grants for 1982 is $39 million, up $4 million from the fiscal 1981 appropriation. One possible interpretation is that with the additional funds much social research will continue under the sponsorship of NIMH but that proposals will have to be more carefully written and targeted to specific "eligible" areas.

Limitations on Centers Supporting Sociological Research. There remains the question whether the divisions and centers within NIMH, which traditionally have supported the research of sociologists, will have budgets that are adequate for this in the future. For example, within the Division of Special Mental Health Programs, the Center for Minority Group Mental Health Programs, the Center for Studies of Crime and Delinquency, the Center for Studies of Work and Mental Health, and the National Center for the Prevention and Control of Rape have all been major supporters of social science research. Under early budget proposals, the amounts that they were to receive for new research grants were quite restricted.

Specific areas eligible for support	Specific areas NOT eligible for support
1. Studies employing a variety of research techniques and dealing with a wide range of populations are eligible for support. Specific areas for which supports is available are: neuro sciences, behavioral sciences, epidemiology, clinical assessment and etiological studies, treatment, prevention, and services research.	1. "Unless shown clearly relevant to mental illness and health, NIMH does not support studies of school achievement, artistic or literary accomplishment and/or occupational success, or the development of related psychometric instruments."
2. "Studies of personality, motivational and emotional processes, and problems relevant to issues of mental illness and health" will be supported.	2. Not to be supported, unless shown clearly relevant to mental health, are studies of "the measurement and enhancement of intelligence, artificial intelligence, school learning and educational processes, classical linguistics, language and speech processes not intimately related to significant cognitive operations, fundamental sensory processes, or responses to stimuli as a function of their physical characteristics."
3. Normative and developmental studies in areas of perception, information processing, learning, and memory that contribute to an understanding of mental illness and health will be supported.	3. "Unless explicitly focused on mental illness or mental health, NIMH does not support studies of large-scale social conditions or problems (e.g., poverty, unemployment, inadequate housing and slums, divorce, day care arrangements, accidents, and criminal behav-

Specific areas eligible for support	Specific areas NOT eligible for support
	ior); social classes and groups and their interrelations; the structure and functioning of groups, institutions, or societies; social roles and career determination."
4. "Psychosocial processes that contribute to an understanding of mental health and illness" are eligible for funding. This would include, for example, studies of the relationship of life events, including family processes and conditions, to mental illness; the influence of attitudes on mental health and health-related behavior; the influence of specific environmental factors on normal and abnormal behavior and mental processes; and the development and maintenance of personal networks and support systems as these affect individual and family functioning; cultural beliefs and values; the legal or educational systems; game theory and decision-making; sociolinguistics; and animal models of social structure and interactions."	**4.** Specify relevance. In a brief statement explaining the purpose of the document, NIMH Director Herbert Pardes points out that the absence of support for certain areas is due to "funding constraints, state of the field, or assessment of nonapplicability to mental health issues." His statement also indicates that if the mental health relevance of a proposal is not readily apparent, the applicant should indicate the mental health problems to which the proposal relates.

INFORMATION SOURCES

Persons interested in more information about the announcement and about the behavioral science research program at NIMH should contact: David Pearl, Ph.D., Chief, Behavioral Sciences Research Branch, Division of Extramural Research Programs; telephone number (301) 443–4524. The Director of Special Mental Health Programs is Juan Ramos, Ph.D.; (301) 443–3533. Letters should be addressed to them at: NIMH, Parklawn Building, 5600 Fishers Lane, Rockville, MD 20857.* Programs of particular relevance to sociologists include:

Behavioral Sciences Research Branch, Social Sciences Section. Chief: David Pearl, Ph.D. Research support is provided for projects with mental health relevance in anthropology, sociology, and social psychology in such areas as socialization process, the changing nature of family structure and function, sex-role behavior, social structure and dynamics, social change, group processes, social perception and attitudes, and belief systems.

Applied Research Branch. Chief: Edward J. Hynn. Program areas: Research on developmental problems focuses on affective development in infancy including hospital practices, maternal and paternal interaction, and early childrearing practices; preschool development in the home, nursery, day-care program; foster care, adoption,

---

* All information about NIMH has been drawn from *Footnotes* (American Sociological Association) 9 (November 1981): 1, 7.

and the impact of cultural enrichment programs on young children; transition to school and the interaction of home, school, and community; adjustment during the prepubertal and adolescent periods to home, school, and community; transition from school to employment or higher education; impact of changing value systems on attitudes and behavior, alternative life styles, social change; patterns of abuse during childhood or adolescence; patterns of segregation and discrimination in schools and other social institutions. Social problem research focuses family disruption as influenced by separation, divorce, remarriage, cultural and ethnic differences, and other significant variables; problems associated with sex roles including sex education and issues associated with human sexual development such as gender identity, values and mores, and homosexuality; the impact of abrupt or sustained social change resulting from such factors as poverty, natural disasters, migration, or cultural change; alternative life styles, such as the unmarried parent, single-parent family, contractual marriage, group living, and other options; adjustment patterns and problems in middle age and approaching retirement; intergenerational differences including value systems and cultural change or conflict; grief patterns and impact of the death of a spouse, child, or parent.

Center for Studies of Crime and Delinquency. Chief: Saleem A. Shah, Ph.D. Research program areas: Although some support is provided for basic research, the bulk of the Center's resources are directed to problem-oriented research in the following priority areas: 1. Development of new and improved community-based treatment models as alternatives to institutionalization of youth who persistently engage in delinquent and related problem behaviors; models currently being assessed include a community-based residential group home, a new type of inschool program, and parent-training programs. 2. Development of empirically based criteria for improved decision making in difficult and complex law and mental health issues. Research is addressed to determinations of competency to stand trial; dangerousness as related to confinement, treatment and release of mentally disordered offenders, sexual psychopaths, defective delinquents, and involuntarily committed mentally ill persons. 3. Studies designed to increase biomedical, behavioral, and social science knowledge with respect to family violence and individual violent behavior. This area includes the development of incidence data on occurrence and seriousness of family violence, and the evaluation of experimental treatment approaches for family/individual violent behavior. 4. Development of new knowledge on the etiology and epidemiology of criminal and delinquent behaviors. Of importance are longitudinal studies of factors underlying career patterns of young people who mature out of delinquent behaviors and those who persist in serious antisocial and delinquent behavior that can lead to adult criminal behavior.

Center for Studies of Metropolitan Problems. Chief: Elliot Liebow, Ph.D. Program objectives: The Center serves as a focal point for Institute activities concerned with the impact of urban life on mental health, well-being, and human behavior with emphasis on the relationship of contemporary social issues and social structure to individual, family, and community functioning. An additional objective is to provide policy makers with new approaches to social problems, based on scientific inquiry. The Center supports both training and research related to metropolitan mental health.

Other organized areas of specialized interest include *Demography and Social Studies Branch; National Center for Prevention and Control of Rape; Center for Studies of Mental Health of Aging; Center of Group Mental Health Programs.*

Assistance to Research Careers in Relation to Mental Health Problems is made through the *Research Scientist Development Section.* Chief: Leonard Lash, Ph.D. The Section is designed to support research investigators working on mental health problems. Its function is to develop and stabilize careers of research scientists and to ensure continuity of effort in research programs. Research Scientist Development Awards are made for five-year periods and may be renewed for one second term, following competitive review. Two types of awards are made: (*a*) for persons with research potential who require experience in a research environment, (*b*) for those who are functioning as independent investigators but need additional research experience to realize their full potential. Research Scientist Awards support senior scientists who are well qualified to conduct research independently and make significant contributions to the research programs of their sponsoring institutions. These awards are also made for a five-year period and may be renewed for five-year terms, with competitive review.

National Institute of Child Health and Human Development, Bethesda, MD 20014

Social and Behavioral Sciences Branch Center for Population Research. Sidney H. Newman, Ph.D., Behavior Scientist Administrator. Research problem areas: (1) Fertility of Human Population Groups; (2) Family Planning in Developed Societies; (3) Social Acceptability of Measures for the Biological Regulation of Human Fertility; (4) Household Formation, Family Structure, Fertility, and Migration; (5) Marriage, Divorce, and Fertility; (6) Age at Marriage, Child Spacing, Family Size and Fertility; (7) Status and Roles of Women in Relation to Fertility, with Special Reference to Implication for the U.S.; (8) Nutrition and Fertility; (9) Relation of Economic Development to Population Growth and Decline; (10) Antecedents and Consequences of Stability or Change in the Size of U.S. Population; (11) Population Modeling for the Projection and/or Prediction of Human Population change in the U.S.; (12) Migration of Human Population Groups; (13) Population re Distribution in the U.S.; (14) Human Population Density and Crowding as Factors in Population Change; (15) Population Composition and Structure in the U.S.; (16) Mortality of Human Population Groups.

Other outlines are available. Write for outlines on Demographic Effects and Psychological Aspects of Population. Outlines being developed include Population Sociology, Population Economics, Population Geography and Population Aspects of Political Science.

National Institutes of Health Pre- and Postdoctoral Fellowships

The National Research Service Award Act of 1974 (NRS) authorizes the National Institutes of Health (NIH) and the Alcohol, Drug Abuse, and Mental Health Administration (ADAMHA) to have predoctoral and postdoctoral research training programs—individual fellowships and institutional fellowships (training grants).

Although NIH has this authorization, it has been determined (new legislation pending) that individual support would be available only at the postdoctoral level and that predoctoral support would be available only through the institutional fellowship program. Some institutional support at this level may possibly be available through existing NIH training grants and inquiries concerning this kind of support should be directed to the Graduate or Medical Dean of the institution where you would like to study.

INSTITUTIONAL NATIONAL RESEARCH SERVICE AWARDS

A domestic public or nonprofit private institution may apply for a grant for a research training program in a specified area of research from which a number of awards will be made to individuals selected by the training program director at the institution. Grants may also be made to Federal institutions which are eligible under Section 507 of the Public Health Service Act. Support for both predoctoral and postdoctoral trainees may be requested. Each applicant institution must submit an application according to instructions, using forms provided by NIH or ADAMHA.

The applicant institution must have or be able to develop the staff and facilities required for the proposed program. The training program director at the institution will be responsible for the selection and appointment of trainees and the overall direction of the training program. In selecting trainees, the program director must make certain that individuals receiving support meet the eligibility requirements set forth in these guidelines (see pages 2 and 3) and that they will submit a signed Payback Agreement at the time of appointment and prior to receiving any stipend or other allowance from the grant.

The stipends for predoctoral and postdoctoral trainees are the same as for the individual award. In addition to stipends, the applicant institution may request and be provided with tuition, fees, and travel costs for predoctoral trainees; an allowance of up to $1000 for each postdoctoral (in lieu of tuition, fees, and travel); actual indirect costs or 8 percent of the total award for related institutional costs such as salaries, equipment, and supplies.

A Statement of Appointment form (PHS-2271) and a Payback Agreement signed by the trainee indicating his or her intent to meet the service or payback requirements must be submitted to the awarding unit at the time the training begins for each appointment or reappointment of a trainee on the grant. Subsequent changes in the terms and conditions of appointments will require amended appointment forms. Any change in training status that will affect the payback requirement must be reported to the awarding unit by the grantee institution.

Applications and Receipt

Application kits containing forms, instructions, and related information may be obtained from Grants Inquiries, Division of Research Grants, NIH, Bethesda, MD 20014; from NIMH or NIAA, Grants Management Branch, both located at 5600 Fishers Lane, Rockville, MD 20852; or NIDA Grants Management Branch, 11400 Rockville Pike, Rockville, MD 20852. Applicants are encouraged to submit applications well in advance of the published application receipt dates to allow awarding units sufficient time to request any supplemental information that may be required. Application receipt dates will be widely distributed in NIH and ADAMHA announcements. Applications received too late for one review will be considered at the next review cycle.

The Alcohol, Drug Abuse, and Mental Health Administration Pre- and Postdoctoral Fellowships

The Alcohol, Drug Abuse, and Mental Health Administration (ADAMHA) of HHS has *predoctoral* national research service awards available for behavioral research. Awards are made to individual applicants selected as a result of national competition.

To be eligible, one must be a U.S. citizen or a noncitizen national of the United States, or must have a permanent visa at the time of application. Further, one must have completed two or more years of graduate work as of the proposed activation date of the award and must have a doctoral prospectus.

The annual stipend for predoctoral individuals is $5040. Applications are processed according to the following schedule:

Receipt dates	Initial review group meeting	Earliest possible start date
February 1	June	September 1
June 1	November	February 1
October 1	March	June 1

Although fellowships are awarded for twelve-month periods, applicants may receive up to three years' support under the national research service award. Upon completion of the term, recipients are expected to engage in biomedical or behavioral research or to teach for a period equal to the period of support. Individuals who fail to fulfill this obligation may be required to pay back an amount of the stipend received plus interest. All applicants are alerted to this payback agreement.

Given the decreasing level of support for institutional-level training grants, graduate students are encouraged to consider the possibility of applying for these fellowships.

The Alcohol, Drug Abuse, and Mental Health Administration also has postdoctoral support available. The level of the stipend varies, depending upon the amount of relevant postdoctoral experience one has had. Table 1 gives these levels of stipend for years of relevant experience at entry and for the year of the award.

Table 1 *Postdoctoral Stipends*

Years of relevant postdoctoral experience	Amount of annual stipend
0	$13,380
1	14,040
2	14,736
3	15,468
4	16,236
5	17,040
6	17,892
7	18,780

Application forms are to be submitted to the Division of Research Grants, 5333 Westbard Avenue, Bethesda, MD 20205. Requests for application forms, program guidelines (i.e., "Guidelines for National Research Service Awards" and "NRSA Support and Payback Guidelines"), and other inquiries regarding the ADAMHA NRSA program should be addressed to the following individuals, whose mailing address is 5600 Fishers Lane, Rockville, MD 20857:

National Institute on Alcohol Abuse and Alcoholism	Grants Management Officer National Institute on Alcohol Abuse and Alcoholism
National Institute on Drug Abuse	Grants Management Officer National Institute on Drug Abuse
National Institute of Mental Health	Grants Management Officer National Institute of Mental Health

Requests for program information regarding ADAMHA National Research Service Awards for *individual fellowships* should be addressed to the following persons, whose mailing address is 5600 Fishers Lane, Rockville, MD 20857: National Institute on Alcohol Abuse and Alcoholism:

Biomedical Research	Dr. Kenneth R. Warren Park Building Room 127 (301) 443–4223
Psychosocial Research	Dr. E. Vanderveen Park Building Room 129 (301) 443–4223
National Institute on Drug Abuse	Mr. Edward Morgan Room 10A-46 (301) 443–6720
National Institute of Mental Health: Division of Biometry and Epidemiology, Mental Health Epidemiology & Biostatistics	Ms. Mildred Cannon Room 18C-05 (301) 443–3774
Division of Manpower and Training Programs: Research Fellowships	Dr. G. Peter Arnott Room 8C-02 (301) 443–3855
Division of Special Mental Health Programs: Center for Studies of Mental Health of the Aging	Dr. Barry Lebowitz Room 11A-16 (301) 443–1185
Center for Studies of Crime and Delinquency	Mr. Ecford Voit Room 7-103 (301) 443–3728
Center for Studies of Work and Mental Health	Dr. Herbert Vreeland 8Room 18-104 (301) 443–3373
Center for Minority Group Mental Health Problems	Dr. Freda Cheung Room 18C-04 (301) 443–3724
National Center for the Prevention and Control of Rape	Dr. Marvin Feuerberg Room 15-99 (301) 443–1910

Research Career Development Awards

Awards are made to institutions to increase the number of stable full-time career opportunities for scientists of superior potential and capability in the sciences related to health. Institutions may apply for awards on behalf of individuals who have had three or more years of relevant postdoctoral research or professional experience and who are in need of further research career development. Application material may be obtained by writing to: Office of Grants Inquiries, Division of Research Grants, National Institutes of Health, Bethesda, MD 20205. A self-addressed gummed mailing label accompanying the request will expedite handling.

U.S. Department of Labor, Employment and Training Administration

The Department of Labor has a number of research programs administered by its Office of Research and Development. These include Institutional Grants, Doctoral Disertation Fellowships, and Small-Grant Research Projects. The proposed projects should focus on potential solutions to significant employment and training problems. These programs are described in detail in U.S. Department of Labor, *Research and Development Projects,* 1980 ed. For information, write Employment and Training Administration, Office of Research and Development, Washington, DC 20213.

Social Security Administration

Funds are available from the Social Security Administration (SSA) for research on improving the Old-Age Survivors and Disability Insurance and Supplemental Security Income programs. The SSA is interested in research projects that develop and implement analytical models for comparing the merits of alternative methods for carrying out income security goals. Priority areas for research funding include (1) labor force participation of women; (2) factors that affect the social, psychological, occupational, and financial situations of the aged; (3) impacts of immigration and immigration policy on social security and related programs; (4) analysis of need for income support, health services, retraining or relocation assistance in relation to disability; (5) comparative studies and analysis of other countries' social security concepts and programs; (6) research that uses available SSA data bases such as the Retirement History Study.

Administration for Children, Youth, and Family

ACYF is accepting grant applications from social scientists undertaking studies that address: (1) child neglect, (2) adolescent maltreatment, and (3) secondary analysis of data collected in the National Study of the Incidence and Severity of Child Abuse and Neglect.

U.S. Department of Education

Organizational change is making it very difficult to describe the many programs offered by this department. A *Guide to Programs* is available for each fiscal year and is probably the best source of information. In the past the Office of Education administered funds for the support of educational research and development through its Bureau of Research. The Bureau is made up of five divisions that deal with elementary education, secondary and vocational education, higher education, information technology and dissemination, and research centers and regional laboratories. Each of the first four divisions handles basic research projects as well as those focused on the development of curricula, methods of teaching and learning, and organizational and administrative procedures in education.

The general purpose of basic research projects is to develop new knowledge about the educational process, thus providing a foundation for further developmental work. The content of basic studies draws primarily on the fields of psychology, for more information about learning and motivation; sociology and anthropology, to examine social and cultural factors related to education; and physiology, to explore the relationships between physical and mental functions.

The Bureau of Research identifies, develops, and programs funds for priority areas, but it is always in a position to receive unsolicited proposals, and funds are reserved for this purpose. Also, "guideline" statements pertaining to particular areas are sometimes made available to stimulate their development, and occasional requests for proposals are issued in selected areas. It is always useful for those interested in specific projects to contact appropriate members of the Bureau's staff before actually drafting a proposal in order to become acquainted with current directions as a guide to proposal development.

Persons interested in participating in the Department's research and development program should request a copy of the *Guide to Programs, Fiscal Year 1982* (as following). Write to: Henrietta Wexler, Office of the Public Affairs Staff, U.S. Department of Education, Washington, DC 20202.

The Bureau also operates the Educational Resources Information Center (ERIC), which provides direct access to research literature in behavioral sciences and education. Monthly issues of *Research in Education* (available from the Government Printing Office) abstract and index over 700 documents—the latter available from the ERIC Document Reproduction Service, National Cash Register Company, 4936 Fairmont Avenue, Bethesda, MD 20014.

Academic Research Support for Defense Program

The Defense Intelligence Agency is seeking statements of interest and qualification for academic research support to a program intended to increase the availability and quality of expertise on various world regions and their languages. Areas of specific interest are Africa, Southwest Asia, the Middle East, South and Southeast Asia, and Latin America. This is part of an effort to acquire more refined perspectives within the Defense Intelligence community. Both institutional and individual responses will be considered. Need may variously exist for (1) specialized language and area training for analysts; (2) applied, unclassified publishable research (including interdisciplinary research) in the fields of history, political science, economics, geography, linguistics, cultural anthropology, social-psychology, sociology, and the geophysical sciences. Direct inquiries to:

Ms. Loretta Komisar, Virginia Contracting Activity, Washington, DC 20301.

Research Costing

How much does it cost to conduct a research project? One writer says that such a question can no more be answered than a question about how much it costs to go on a vacation. One major cost can be the overhead charges of the sponsoring agency. The overhead or indirect costs charged by universities to grants (especially federal grants) are commonly in the 40 to 50 percent range of the total grant. Other major cost variables include the size of population or sample involved, the mode of collecting data, the amount of assistance required, and the size of salaries needed for the principal investigator(s) and assistants. The motivation and efficiency of each member of the research team is a hidden variable.

Frequently, when the cost question is asked, researchers want to know all costs for every single aspect of planning and conducting a project, analyzing the data, and writing a final report. In other instances, they assume that researchers' salaries, typewriters, clerical staff, and even the graphic illustrator are fixed costs of the sponsoring organization; their only interest is in the out-of-pocket costs that will be incurred for data collection. Sometimes even computer costs are underwritten by the sponsoring organization. It is not surprising, therefore, that costs reported by one researcher are likely to be double or triple those reported by another.

Our purpose here is to enable various researchers working under different conditions to make cost estimates that apply to their own designs. In this section the first guide is a general form to apply to any research project. The Guide to Research Costing (C.1) is a budget-time schedule summary setting forth all the major activities that are necessary and that will incur costs. To utilize this guide one of the principal needs is information about the costs associated with various modes of collecting data. The Guide to Costs of a Mail Questionnaire is presented in C.2. This is followed by the Guide to Comparative Costs of a Telephone Survey with the Personal Interview (C.3). A subsection devoted to research budgeting (C.4) places the cost data in the format of a research proposal.

5.C.1   GUIDE TO RESEARCH COSTING*†

Activity	Total	Week ending _____	Week ending _____	Week ending _____	_____

1. Total
   a) Man hours
   b) Cost ($)
   c) % of total completed					

2. Planning
   a) Man-hours
   b) Cost
   c) % completed					

3. Pilot Study and Pretests
   a) Man-hours
   b) Cost
   c) % completed					

4. Drawing Sample
   a) Man-hours
   b) Cost
   c) % completed					

5. Preparing Observational Materials
   a) Man-hours
   b) Cost
   c) % completed					

6. Selection and Training
   a) Man-hours
   b) Cost
   c) % completed					

7. Trial Run
   a) Man-hours
   b) Cost
   c) % completed					

8. Revising Plans
   a) Man-hours
   b) Cost
   c) % completed					

9. Collecting Data
   a) Man-hours
   b) Cost
   c) % completed					

10. Processing Data
   a) Man-hours
   b) Cost
   c) % completed					

*Source: Russell K. Ackoff, *Design for Social Research* (Chicago: University of Chicago, 1953), p. 347. By permission of the University of Chicago Press. Copyright 1953 by the University of Chicago.

†Suggested form for budget-time schedule summary. (There is nothing necessary or sufficient about this listing of activities, nor is the order absolute in any sense.)

GUIDE TO RESEARCH COSTING (*Continued*)

Activity	Total	Week ending ___	Week ending ___	Week ending ___	___

11. Preparing Final Report
   a) Man-hours
   b) Cost
   c) % completed					

GUIDE TO COSTS OF THE MAIL QUESTIONNAIRE

5.C.2

Dillman has studied mail questionnaire costs over a ten-year period. The minimum first-class mailing rate was 6 cents in 1970, 8 cents in 1971, 13 cents in 1977, 15 cents in 1980, and 20 cents in 1981— a 333 percent increase in just over a decade. Other costs continue to increase rapidly. Most research agencies are projecting a minimum 10 percent yearly increase in costs for the next few years. In this situation only a base date may be established; the researcher must make projections of cost from the base date.

Dillman has provided itemized costs for questionnaire surveys using his Total Design Method (see his article in Part 2 of this Handbook). The costs are shown for general public surveys of Washington residents in 1977 which have been updated to 1982. The cost specifications include:

Twelve-page questionnaires mailed for the minimum first-class postage in 1982 (20 cents).

No keypunching or computer processing costs included.

Labor costs calculated at the prevailing rate ($4.50 per hour) for part-time clerical help, the type of labor normally used in studies.

Professional supervision costs based on the number of hours actually spent by the principal investigator providing direct supervision of data collection activities.

Table 1 shows costs by general expenditure area followed by phases of the study. The reader will note that costs are shown for one large statewide survey of the general public (a sample of 4500) and one smaller statewide survey of the general public (450). The bottom line is a mean cost for each potential respondent of $4.33 for the larger sample and $6.86 for the smaller— a difference of $2.53.

Elimination of the cost for professional supervision (often considered a fixed cost) brings the difference down by 50 cents for the larger sample and $1.11 for the smaller; with free access to an existing clerical staff, the mean cost per interview drops to $1.85 and $2.81 for the two samples, respectively. Economies of scale make the difference; nearly all aspects of surveying can be achieved with lower cost as size increases. Getting both professional and clerical services free is seldom attained.

The variation in costs reported by different researchers can now be more fully understood. The costs shown in table 1 cannot be transferred to any other survey. Dillman reports TDM surveys cited by other researchers in which costs of $15 to $20 per potential respondent are given. In such cases the researcher felt that such things as consultant fees, expensive computer

Table 1. *Sample Budgets for TDM Mail Surveys**

	Large statewide survey of general public (N = 4500)	Small statewide survey of general public (N = 450)	Your survey?
General Costs			
Draw systematic sample from telephone directories or other sample source	$1350	$150	_____
Purchase mailout envelopes	210	40	_____
Purchase business reply envelopes	160	30	_____
Print questionnaires	775	275	_____
Graphics design for cover	125	125	_____
Telephone (toll charges)	200	20	_____
Supplies (miscellaneous)	400	60	_____
Type, proof, and store names in automatic typewriters	1500†	190†	_____
Sub-total	$3260	$665	_____
First Mailout			
Print cover letter	$ 150	$ 30	_____
Address letters and envelopes	1500†	165†	_____
Postage for mailout	910	95	_____
Prepare mailout packets	825†	115†	_____
Postage for returned questionnaires (business reply envelopes)	250	25	_____
Process and precode returns	375†	55†	_____
Sub-total	$4010	$485	_____
Postcard Follow-up			
Purchase postcards	$ 585	$ 60	_____
Print postcards	220	30	_____
Address postcards	675†	75†	_____
Prepare mailout	225†	30†	_____
Process and precode returns	375†	55†	_____
Postage for returned questionnaires (business reply envelopes)	250	25	_____
Sub-total	$2330	$275	_____
Third Mailout			
Print cover letter	$ 125	$ 25	_____
Address letters and envelopes	1425†	150†	_____
Prepare mailout packets	600†	75†	_____
Postage for mailout	500	50	_____
Process and precode returns	375†	50†	_____
Postage for returned questionnaires	170	17	_____
Sub-total	$3195	$367	_____

* Reprinted from Don A. Dillman, "Mail and Other Self-Administered Questionnaires," in *Handbook of Survey Research*, ed. Peter Rossi, James Wright and Andy Anderson (New York: Academic Press, in press), chap. 12.

† Costs calculated on 1977 bases of clerical labor at $4.50 per hour and first-class postage at 20 cents per ounce. (First-class postage was raised to 20 cents per ounce in November 1981.) All operations involving typing of names and addresses onto letters, envelopes, and postcards included an additional charge for use of memory typewriters.

Table 1. (*Cont.*)

	Large statewide survey of general public ($N = 4500$)	Small statewide survey of general public ($N = 450$)	Your survey?
Fourth Mailout			
Print cover letter	$ 75	$ 20	_____
Address letters and envelopes	375†	40†	_____
Prepare mailout packets	450†	50†	_____
Postage for mailout (certified)	1700	170	_____
Process and precode returns	225†	25†	_____
Postage for returned questionnaires	170	17	_____
Sub-total	$2995	$322	_____
Professional Supervision			
Clerical staff	$2250	$750	_____
Grand Total	$19,500	$3089	_____
Mean Cost/Potential Respondent	$4.33	$6.86	_____
Mean Cost, Omitting Professional Supervision	$3.83	$5.75	_____
Mean Cost Assuming Free Access to Existing Clerical Staff	$1.85	$2.81	_____

equipment, and professional time spent drafting and redrafting the questionnaire should be charged to the survey budget. It is not unusual for the computer cost of data analysis to far exceed that reported in the table for data collection alone.

The researcher seeking estimates for a proposed mail questionnaire survey can utilize the table shown by estimating the percent of expenditure required using the data given in the survey more nearly comparable to his or her own own sample. A determination of inflationary costs since 1982 must be projected to the year of administration selected.

Conclusion: Data collection by mail is relatively inexpensive; in general, costs will be substantially lower than those encountered for personal interview or telephone surveys.

COMPARATIVE COSTS OF THE TELEPHONE SURVEY AND PERSONAL INTERVIEW

5.C.3

Groves and Kahn of the Survey Research Center of the University of Michigan undertook a study in 1976 to identify certain basic characteristics of telephone surveys and compare them to corresponding features of personal interview surveys. A comparison of costs was an important objective.

The cost data shown in table 1 is based on two national surveys: a telephone survey sample of 1618 persons using random digit dialing, and a personal interview sample of 1548 persons. These surveys include the following cost items:

1. All cost factors in sampling, pretest, training of interviewers, materials, field salaries, field travel, communication costs, control functions, and postinterview activities (interview evaluation/debriefing, verification, and final report to respondents).
This is a cost package in which the salaries of a large staff is a sizable component
of the expense. But it still does not include various analyses made with the data
collected.

2. The overall expense of sampling and field costs for the telephone survey comes
to $37,939 and for the personal survey, $84,864. This makes the telephone survey
45 percent less expensive for a roughly similar size sample of personal interviews.

3. The per-completed-interview cost for sampling and fieldwork is $23 using telephone
interviews and $55 using personal interviews. This involves an average of 3.3 person-
hours per telephone interview and 8.7 person-hours per personal interview.

Dillman has conducted extensive studies of the comparative costs of mail
questionnaires and telephone surveys. [New York: Academic Press, 1978].
In responding to my request for his current experience with telephone survey
costs, he wrote on October 1, 1980: (See his *Mail and Telephone Survey.*)

> I have resorted to using a rule-of-thumb. There are two major costs components:
> toll charges and interviewer time. I multiply the average length of interview times
> the per minute telephone cost. On in-state surveys, we have a standard per minute
> rate, and it's quite simple. On national surveys, one has to do some rough estimates

Table 1 *A Comparative Summary of Costs for Two Large Sample Studies and a
Design Utilizing Telephone Survey and Personal Interview as Modes of Data Collection (1976)*[*]

Major Divison of Work	Telephone survey (N = 1618)		Personal interview (N = 1548)	
	$	%	$	%
1. Sampling costs	955.27	2.5	8,547.15	10.1
2. Pretesting	723.45	1.9	1,113.10	1.3
3. Training and prestudy work	2,066.34	5.4	9,523.61	11.2
4. Materials	1,374.96	3.6	3,660.15	4.3
5. Ann Arbor headquarters field office salaries: administrative and clerical (typing)	1,394.74	3.7	4,159.42	4.9
6. Field salaries: supervisory and interviewer	12,544.69	33.1	32,277.92	38.0
7. Field staff travel		0.0	16,815.11	19.8
8. Communications	15,793.60	41.6	5,980.31	7.0
9. Control function	1,202.55	3.2	883.22	1.0
10. Postinterview activities				
a. Interviewer evaluation/ debriefing	246.72	0.6	281.29	0.3
b. Verification	507.53	1.3	876.38	1.0
c. Report to respondents	1,129.94	3.0	746.26	0.9
Total	$37,929.79		$84,863.92	
Per interview costs	$ 23.45		$ 54.82	
Per interview average hours required	3.3		8.7	

[*] Adapted from Robert M. Groves and Robert L. Kahn, *Surveys by Telephone: A National Comparison with Personal Interviews* (New York: Academic Press, 1979), pp. 189, 193.

as to how many calls will be in each zone. I then increase that value by about 20 percent to cover call-backs, wrong numbers and other connections that do not result in interviews. The other major component of cost is interviewer time. Based on experience using my methods, I have concluded that the time required per completed interview is about twice the length of that interview. In other words, if my interviews are averaging 30 minutes, I allocate about 60 minutes of interviewer time per interview. The excess time is used for editing, coffee breaks, wrong numbers, callbacks, etc. To the minutes associated with each completed interview, I then allocate hourly wages. Adding together toll charges and interviewer costs give me most of the costs of doing the surveys. Using the methods outlined in the book, I usually end up with about $1.50 per interview of additional cost: e.g., supervision and paper. So for a 30-minute instate interview, I figure [30 mins. × .09¢ (current toll charge)] $1.20 + $4.00 for wages plus $1.50 for supervision = $9.40.

Costs vary tremendously depending upon geographic area, sampling method, and call-back requirements.

It is interesting to observe the difference between the $23.45 reported by Groves and Kahn per completed telephone interview and the $9.40 given by Dillman. These figures substantiate my earlier statement that great variation can be observed in the reports of different researchers.

Total costs for a completed study are subject to wide variation depending on the amount of developmental work and analysis performed. Here is where computer time and salaries can incur very large costs.

There is considerable variation in the costs of operating phases of the two modes. Five areas exhibit the largest differences. Table 1 shows these to be sampling, prestudy, training, travel, and communication costs.

Conclusion: The telephone survey is substantially less expensive in time and money than the personal interview.* Nevertheless, selection of the more appropriate mode depends on a total evaluation of the advantages and disadvantages. See section 2.14, Choosing between the Mail Questionnaire, Personal Interview, and Telephone Survey.

GUIDE TO RESEARCH BUDGETING

5.C.4

This guide includes all items that are required in the NSF Research Grant Proposal Budget.** If the researcher has carefully followed the Guide to Research Costing, the preparation of the Grant Proposal Budget will be more accurate.

* On August 30, 1982, Dillman wrote to me as follows:

In response to your question about shifting costs relative to mail and telephone, I think the gap has narrowed a bit, but telephone surveys remain considerably more expensive. The changes in postage and labor costs are the reasons. Comparing of mail and telephone costs is confounded by the different way that greater length affects cost. For telephone surveys, costs go up in fairly direct proportion to length. But for mail, the difference in cost between administering a four- and a twelve-page questionnaire is fairly insignificant. The first "jump" comes when one goes beyond the maximum weight for the 20-cent stamp, which for the TDM usually occurs after twelve pages.

** National Science Foundation, Grants for Scientific Research, NSF73-12, Appendix III, pp. 34–39. For a copy, write National Science Foundation, Washington, D.C. 20550.

Budget Format

Proposals for research grants should include budgets in the following format for each year of support requested. It is important to note the use of a budget summary does not eliminate the need for an itemized explanation of proposed costs when required in this booklet.

Research Grant Proposal Budget
Year Beginning _____

Budget Category	NSF funded Man-months			Proposed amount
	Cal	Acad	Sum	
A. Salaries and Wages				
1. Senior personnel				
a. (Co) Principal investigator (list by name)	___	___	___	___
b. Faculty associates (list by name)	___	___	___	___
Subtotal				___
2. Other personnel (nonfaculty)				
a. Research associates (postdoctoral) (list separately by name if available, otherwise give numbers)				
. . . .	___	___	___	___
. . . .	___	___	___	___
b. Nonfaculty professionals (list separately, by category, giving number, e.g., one computer programmer)				
. . . .	___	___	___	___
c. (number) Grad. students (Res. Asst.)				___
d. (number) Prebaccalaureate students				___
e. (number) Secretarial-clerical				___
f. (number) Technical, shop, and other				
Total salaries and wages				___
B. Staff Benefits				___
C. Total Salaries, wages and staff Benefits (A + B)				___
D. Permanent Equipment (list as required)				
1.				___
2.				___
Total permanent equipment				___
E. Expendable Supplies and Equipment . . .				
F. Travel				
1. Domestic.				___
2. Foreign (list as required)				___
Total travel				___
G. Publication Costs				___
H. Computer Costs (if charged as direct costs)				___
I. Other Costs (itemize by major type)				
1.				___
2.				___
3.				___
Total other costs				___
J. Total Direct Costs (C through I)				___
K. Indirect Costs				
1. On campus. . . . . .% of				___
2. Off campus . . . . .% of				___
Total indirect costs				___
L. Total Costs (J plus K)				___
M. Total Contributions from Other Sources				___
N. Total Estimated Project Cost				___

Research Reporting

Within the professional code, the reporting of research is one of the mores. Beyond the mundane pressures to publish, there is an underlying normative prescription: *Let the world know what you have found. Add to the storehouse of knowledge. Try to write so that you connect past research with your findings and so that other scholars may build upon your work in the future.*

In this section both oral and written reporting is described. Research reporting usually takes place in a rather closed world where professionals interact with one another either in professional meetings or through learned journals. Some important attributes of this subculture will be described.

This section has a varied selection of aids including:

Specifications for Sociological Report Rating
Form for Sociological Report Rating
Guide to Journals in Sociology and Related Fields; Research Annuals in Sociology and Related Fields; Current Information About Published Work
Where Sociologists Publish; Where Prestigious Sociologists Publish and Why
How Sociologists Get Published; How to Take Rejection
Professional Communication and Reporting
Annual Meetings Held by Various Sociological and Kindred Societies with Common Section Topics in Sociology, Psychology, and Anthropology
Guide to the Journals Sponsored by the American Sociological Association and the American Psychological Association
Guide to Major Journals in Political Science and Public Administration; Anthropology; Education; Organizational and Behavioral Researchers in Business; Journalism and Communication Researchers

SPECIFICATIONS FOR SOCIOLOGICAL REPORT RATING*

5.D.1

	Defective	Substandard	Standard	Superior
Statement of Problem:				
1. Clarity of Statement	Statement is ambiguous, unclear, biased, inconsistent, or irrelevant to the research.	Problem must be inferred from incomplete or unclear statement.	Statement is unambiguous and includes precise description of research objectives.	Statement is unambiguous and includes formal propositions, and specifications for testing them.
2. Significance of Problem	No problem stated, or problem is meaningless, unsolvable, or trivial.	Solution of the problem would be of interest to a few specialists.	Solution of the problem would be of interest to many sociologists.	Solution of the problem would be of interest to most sociologists.
3. Documentation	No documentation to earlier work, or documentation is incorrect.	Documentation to earlier work is incomplete or contains errors of citation or interpretation.	Documentation to earlier work is reasonably complete.	Documentation shows in detail the evolution of the research problem from previous research findings.
Description of Method:				
4. Appropriateness of Method	Problems cannot be solved by this method.	Only a partial or tentative solution can be obtained by this method.	Solution of the problem by this method is possible, but uncertain.	Problem is definitely solvable by this method.
5. Adequacy of Sample or Field	Sample is too small, or not suitable, or biased, or of unknown sampling characteristics.	The cases studied are meaningful, but findings can not be projected.	Findings are projectable, but with errors of considerable, or of unknown, magnitude.	Results are projectable with known small errors, or the entire universe has been enumerated.
6. Replicability	Not replicable.	Replicable in substance, but not in detail.	Replicable in detail with additional information from the author(s).	Replicable in detail from the information given.

*Source: Theodore Caplow designed this form. It was tested by the Committee on Research. American Sociological Review (December 1958), 704-11. Cf. Stuart C. Dodd and Louis N. Gray, "Scient-Scales for Measuring Methodology," Institute for Sociological Research, University of Washington, Seattle, 1962. Mimeograph copies available on request.

SPECIFICATIONS FOR SOCIOLOGICAL REPORT RATING* (Continued)

	Defective	Substandard	Standard	Superior
Presentation of Results:				
7. Completeness				
8. Comprehensibility	Results are incomprehensible, or enigmatic.	Comprehension of results requires special knowledge or skills.	Relevant results are presented, partly in detail, partly in summary form.	Relevant details are presented in detail.
9. Yield	No contribution to solution of problem.	Useful hints or suggestions toward solution of problem.	Tentative solution of problem.	Definitive solution of problem.
Interpretation:				
10. Accuracy	Errors of calculation, transcription, dictation, logic, or fact detected.	Errors likely with the procedures used. No major errors detected.	Errors unlikely with the procedures used. No errors detected.	Positive checks of accuracy included in the procedures.
11. Bias	Evident bias in presentation of results and in interpretation.	Some bias in interpretation, but not in presentation of results.	No evidence of bias.	Positive precautions against bias included in procedures.
12. Usefulness	Not useful.	Possible influence on some future work in this area.	Possible influence on some future work in this area.	Probable influence on all future work in this area.

FORM FOR SOCIOLOGICAL REPORT RATING*

5.D.2

Author _____

Title _____

Publication Reference _____

Rater _____

Date _____

Check (√) Appropriate Columns	Defective 0	Substandard 1	Standard 2	Superior 3
Statement of problem:				
1. Clarity of Statement	_____	_____	_____	_____
2. Significance of Problem	_____	_____	_____	_____
3. Documentation	_____	_____	_____	_____
Description of method:				
4. Appropriateness of Method	_____	_____	_____	_____
5. Adequacy of Sample or Field	_____	_____	_____	_____
6. Replicability	_____	_____	_____	_____
Presentation of results:				
7. Completeness	_____	_____	_____	_____
8. Comprehensibility	_____	_____	_____	_____
9. Yield	_____	_____	_____	_____
Interpretation:				
10. Accuracy	_____	_____	_____	_____
11. Bias	_____	_____	_____	_____
12. Usefulness	_____	_____	_____	_____

Enter number of checks in each column in appropriate blanks; weight as indicated, and add for Total Rating

_ X 0 = 0   _ X 1 = _   _ X 2 = _   _ X 3 = _

[*Total Rating*   ]
[   ]

*Theodore Caplow designed this rating form. Test reliabilities appear in "Official Reports and Proceedings," *American Sociological Review* 23 (December 1958): 704–11. See also the reports of the Educational Testing Service, Princeton, N.J., for ingenious rating scales on a large variety of subjects.

GUIDE TO SOCIOLOGICAL JOURNALS*

5.D.3

Acta Sociologica (Scandinavian Review of Sociology) Munksgaard, A.S. 47 Prags Boulevard, Copenhagen S., Denmark.

* This guide has been assembled from the work of Lawrence J. Rhoades, John Pease, and Joan Rytina Huber. When first published the guide was the revised work of John Pease. An earlier work was first presented by John Pease and Joan Rytina, "Sociological Journals," *American Sociologist* 3 (February 1968): 41–45. Lawrence Rhoades has now compiled *The Authors Guide to Selected Journals,* Professional Information Series No. 1 (1975), American Sociological Association, 1722 N Street N.W., Washington, DC 20036, $3 per copy. The published guide contains a much longer list because it includes all journals that expressed interest in receiving manuscripts from sociologists and social psychologists. Those journals not listed under this section are named in the section immediately following.

For the most recent compilation of sociological journals, see Marvin Sussman, *Author's Guide to Journals in Sociology and Related Fields* (New York: Haworth Press, 1978).

1955. Quarterly. Book reviews. Cumulative index for vols. 1–5. Text in English, French, German, and the Scandinavian languages.

The American Journal of Sociology. The University of Chicago Press, 5750 Ellis Avenue, Chicago, IL 60637.

1895. Bimonthly. Abstracts. Book reviews. Annual index. Cumulative index for vols. 1–70.

American Sociological Review. American Sociological Association, 1722 N Street N.W., Washington, DC 20036.

1936. Bimonthly. Abstracts. Book Reviews. Annual index. Cumulative index for vols. 1–25 and vols. 26–30. Official journal of the American Sociological Association and distributed free to members.

The American Sociologist. American Sociological Association, 1722 N Street N.W., Washington, DC 20036.

1966. Quarterly. Devoted primarily to discussion of professional concerns and includes employment bulletins and announcements of professional meetings. Official journal of the American Sociological Association and distributed free to members.

Annual Review of Sociology. American Sociological Association, 1722 N Street N.W., Washington, DC 20036

1975. Bimonthly. Progress reports of developments in various fields of sociology. Official journal of the American Sociological Association.

Archives Européens de Sociologie (European Journal of Sociology). Musée de l'Homme, Palais de Chaillot, F.-75, Paris XVI, France.

1960. Semiannually. Annual index. Text in English, French, and German.

Australian Journal of Social Issues. Australian Council of Social Services, P.O. Box 388, Haymarket 200, Sydney, Australia.

1961. Four issues per year. Significant issues of social welfare, public interest, and social change.

The Australian and New Zealand Journal of Sociology. Department of Social Studies, University of Melbourne, Parkville, N. 2, Victoria, Australia.

1965. Semiannually. Abstracts. Book reviews. Annual index. Official Journal of the Sociological Association of Australia and New Zealand.

Berkeley Journal of Sociology. 410 Barrows Hall, University of California, Berkeley, CA 94720.

1955–58, vols. 1–4 published as *Berkeley Publications in Society and Institutions.* 1959. Annually. Cumulative index for volumes 1–11. Official publication of the Graduate Sociology Club of the University of California at Berkeley.

The British Journal of Sociology. Routledge & Kegan Paul, Ltd., Broadway House, 68–74 Carter Lane, London E.C.4, England.

1950. Quarterly. Book reviews. Annual index. Cumulative index for volumes 1–10.

Canadian Journal of Sociology/Cahiers Canadiens de Sociologie. (Canadian Journal of Sociology), Department of Sociology, University of Alberta, Edmonton, Alberta, Canada T6G2H4.
Canadian Review of Sociology and Anthropology. Department of Sociology, University of Toronto, Toronto M5S 1A1, Ontario, Canada.

1965. Quarterly.

Case Western Reserve Journal of Sociology. Department of Sociology, Case Western Reserve University, Cleveland, OH 44106.

1967. Annually. Book reviews.

The Commonwealth Sociologist. Department of Sociology, Pennsylvania State University, 206 Liberal Arts Tower, University Park, PA 16802.

1970. Semiannually. Provides forums for superior undergraduate and graduate work as well as professional papers.

Contemporary Sociology: A Journal of Review. American Sociological Association. 1722 N Street N.W., Washington, DC 20036.

1972. Bimonthly. Book reviews. Book notes. Letters. Official journal of the American Sociological Association.

Contributions to Indian Sociology. Mouton & Company, Herderstraat 5, The Hague, Netherlands.

1957. Irregularly. Book reviews. Annual index.

The Cornell Journal of Social Relations. Sociology Department, Uris Hall, Cornell University, Ithaca, NY 14850.

1966. Semiannually. Publishes especially, but not exclusively, the work of young scholars.

Current Sociology. International Sociological Association. Publisher: Mouton and Company, 43 rue de Lille, Paris 7e, France. Business address: Department of Sociology, University of Warwick, Coventry, Warwickshire, England.

1952. Triannually. Each issue contains an analysis of trends in, and an annotated bibliography on, some aspect of sociology.

et al. Sociological Corporations. P.O. Box 77951, Los Angeles, CA 90007.

1967. Triannually. Each is primarily about a single topic.

European Journal of Sociology. Journal Department, Cambridge University Press, 32 East 57 Street, New York, NY 10022.
G.S.S. Journal. Columbia University Graduate Sociology Club, Department of Sociology, Columbia University, 605 West 115 Street, New York, NY 10025.

1961. Triannually. Official journal of the Columbia University Graduate Sociology Club and distributed free to members.

Ghana Journal of Sociology. Department of Sociology, University of Ghana, Legon, Ghana, West Africa.

1963. Semiannually. Book reviews. Official publication of the Ghana Sociological Association.

Graduate Sociology Journal. The Graduate Sociology Club, The University of Pennsylvania, Philadelphia, PA 19104.

1960. Annually. Official publication of the Graduate Sociology Club of the University of Pennsylvania and distributed free to members.

Indian Journal of Social Research. Singhal House, Shivaji Road, Meirut (U.P.), India.

1960. Triannually.

The Insurgent Sociologist. Department of Sociology, University of Oregon, Eugene, OR 97403.

1970. Quarterly. Devoted to development of new sociology with Marxist orientation.

International Journal of Comparative Sociology. E. J. Brill, Leiden, Netherlands, publisher. Manuscript address: Department of Sociology and Anthropology, York University, Downsview, Ontario M3J 1P3, Canada.

International Journal of Contemporary Sociology (Indian Sociological Bulletin). Rakesh Marg, Pili Kothi, G. T. Road, Ghaziabad, U.P., India.

1963. Quarterly. Book reviews. Annual index.

The International Journal of Critical Sociology. Editor: T. K. N. Unnithan, Department of Sociology, Jaipur, India.

1975. Biannual publication of Jaipur Institute of Sociology. Publishes articles critical of present type of sociology and critical appraisals of social issues and policies.

International Journal for the Sociology of Law. Editors: Maureen Cain, Department of Sociology, Brunel University, Uxbridge, England; Kit Carson, Department of Criminology, University of Edinburgh, Scotland; and Paul Wiles, Department of Law, University of Sheffield, England. Publisher: Academic Press, 111 Fifth Avenue, New York, NY 10003.

International Review of Modern Sociology. International Journals, Inc., Department of Sociology, Northern Illinois University, Dekalb, IL 60115.

1971. Semiannually.

The Jewish Journal of Sociology. 55 New Cavendish Street, London, W.I, England.

1959. Semiannually. Book reviews. Annual index.

Journal of Health and Social Behavior. American Sociological Association, 1722 N Street N.W., Washington, DC 20036.

1960–66 vols. 1–7 published as the *Journal of Health and Human Behavior.* 1967. Quarterly. Book reviews. Annual index. Official publication of the American Sociological Association.

Journal of the History of Sociology. Editor: J. N. Porter, 42 Englewood Avenue, Brookline, MA 02146.

Journal of Mathematical Sociology. Gordon and Breach, Science Publishers, Inc., Department of Social Relations, Carnegie-Mellon University, Pittsburgh, PA 15213.

1971. Biannually.

International Journal of Sociology. International Arts and Science Press, Inc., 901 N. Broadway, White Plains, NY 10603.

1971. Quarterly.

International Journal of Sociology of the Family. Department of Sociology, Northern Illinois University, DeKalb, IL 60115.

1971. Semiannually.

International Review of Modern Sociology. Department of Sociology, Northern Illinois University, DeKalb, IL 60115.

1971. Semiannually.

Journal of Political and Military Sociology. Department of Sociology, Northern Illinois University, DeKalb, IL 60115.

1972. Semiannually.

Journal of Sociology and Social Welfare. Department of Sociology, California State University, Northridge, CA 91324.

1973. Quarterly.

The Kansas Journal of Sociology. Department of Sociology, The University of Kansas, Lawrence, KS 66045.

The Pacific Sociological Review. Sage Publications with Pacific Sociological Association, 275 South Beverly Drive, Beverly Hills, CA 90212.

1958. Semiannually. Annual index. Cumulative index for vols 1–6. Official journal of the Pacific Sociological Association and distributed free to members.

Philippine Sociological Review. Philippine Sociological Society, Central Subscriptions Service, Box 655, Greenhills, Rizal D738, Philippines.

1953. Quarterly. Cumulative index for vols. 1–13. Official journal of the Philippine Sociological Society and distributed free to members.

The Polish Sociological Bulletin. RUCH Export and Import Enterprise, P.O. Box 154, Warsaw I, Poland.

1961. Semiannually. Official Publication of the Polish Sociological Association.

Qualitative Sociology. Editors: Barry Glassner and Derral Cheatwood. Publisher: Human Sciences Press, 72 Fifth Avenue, New York, NY 10011.

1977. Quarterly. Devoted to the qualitative interpretation of social life.

Rivista Di Sociologia. Instituto Di Sociologia, Libera Universita, Viale Pola, 12, Roma, Italy.

1963. Quarterly.

The Review of Social Theory. Department of Sociology, University of Missouri, Columbia, MO 65207.

1972. Semiannually.

Revista Latino Americana de Sociologia. Instituto Torcuato Di Tella, Virrey del Pino 3230, Buenos Aires, Argentina.

1970. Triannually.

Revista Mexicana de Sociologia. Facultad de Ciencias Politicas y Sociales, Ciudad Universitaria, Mexico 20, D.F.

1938. Quarterly.

Revista de Sociologia. Departmento de Sociologia de la Universidad Nacional Mayor de San Marcos de Lima, Lima, Peru.

1963. Biannually.

Revue Internationale de Sociologie (International Review of Sociology). Director: Vittorio Castellano (University of Rome).

1964. Triannually. Covers proceedings of International Institute of Sociology.

Romanian Journal of Sociology. Publishing House of the Romanian People's Republic, Cartimex, Str. 13 Decemvrie 3–5, P.O. Box 134135, Bucharest, Romania.

1962. Volume 1 published as *Rumanian Journal of Sociology.* 1963. Annually. Book reviews. Text in English, French, and Romanian.

Rural Sociology. 206 Weaver Building, Pennsylvania State University, University Park, PA 16802.

> 1936. Quarterly. Abstracts. Book reviews. Annual index. Cumulative indexes for vols. 1–20 and vols. 21–30. Official journal of Rural Sociological Society and distributed to members free.

Social Forces. University of North Carolina Press with Southern Sociological Society, 168 Hamilton Hall, University of North Carolina, Chapel Hill, NC 27514.

> 1922–25, vols. 1–3 published as the *Journal of Social Forces.* 1925. Quarterly. Abstracts. Book reviews. Annual index.

Social Problems. Post Office Box 190, Kalamazoo, MI 49005.

> 1953. Quarterly. Book reviews. Annual index. Official journal of the Society for the Study of Social Problems and distributed free to members.

Social Research. New School for Social Research, 65 Fifth Avenue, New York, NY 10003.

> 1953. Quarterly.

Social Science Research. Editors: Robert K. Leik and Peter H. Rossi, University of Massachusetts, Amherst. Publisher: Academic Press, 111 Fifth Avenue, New York, NY 10003.

> 1975. Quarterly. Multidisciplinary journal emphasizing quantitative and methodological techniques.

Social Studies: Irish Journal of Sociology. St. Patricks College, Maynooth, Co. Kildare, Ireland.

> 1972. Bimonthly.

Sociologia. Fundacao Escola de Sociologia e Politica, Rua General Jardin, 522 Sao Paulo, SP, Brazil.

> 1939. Quarterly. Abstracts. Book reviews. Annual index. Text in English and Portuguese.

Sociologia Internationalis. Verlagsbuchhandlung, Duncker and Humblot, 1000 Berlin 41 (Steglitz), Dietrich-Schäfer-Weg 9, Postfact 330, Germany.

> 1963. Semiannually. Book reviews. Text in English, French, German, and Spanish.

Sociologia Neerlandica. Royal VanGorcum, Limited, Assen, Netherlands.

> 1962. Semiannually. Book reviews. Official publication of the Netherlands Sociological Society.

Sociologia Ruralis. Royal VanGorcum, Limited, Assen, Netherlands.

> 1960. Quarterly. Abstracts. Book reviews. Annual index. Text in English, French, and German. Official journal of the European Society for Rural Sociology and distributed to members free.

Sociological Bulletin. Indian Sociological Society, Department of Sociology, Delhi School of Economics, University of Delhi, Delhi-7, India.

> 1952. Semiannually. Official publication of the Indian Sociological Society.

Sociological Focus. North Central Sociological Association, Department of Sociology, University of Akron, Akron, OH 44325.

1967. Quarterly. Official journal of the Ohio Valley Sociological Society and distributed free to members.

Sociological Inquiry. O.I.E.S., 252 Bloor Street West, Toronto, Ontario, Canada M56 1V6.

1930–60, vols. 1–30 published as *Alpha Kappa Deltan.* 1961. Semiannually. Annual index. Each issue devoted to a single topic. Official journal of Alpha Kappa Delta and distributed free to members for the first two years.

Sociological Methods and Research. Editors: Edgar F. Borgatta and George W. Bohrnstedt, Sage Publications, Inc., 275 South Beverly Drive, Beverly Hills, CA 90212.

1974. Quarterly. Devoted to sociology as a cumulative empirical science, focused on the assessment of the scientific status of sociology.

Sociological Practice. Editors: Donald E. Gelfand and Bernard Phillips. Publisher: Human Services Press, 72 Fifth Avenue, New York, NY 10011.
The Sociological Quarterly. 1004 Elm Street, Columbia, MO 65201.

1953. Quarterly. Book reviews. Annual index. Official journal of the Midwest Sociological Society and distributed free to members.

Sociological Review Monographs. University of Keele, Keele, Staffordshire ST5 5BG, England.

1958. Annually. Each issue is devoted to a single topic.

The Sociological Review. University of Keele, Keele, Staffordshire, ST5, 5BG, England.

1953. Triannually. Book reviews. Annual index.

Sociological Studies. Cambridge University Press, 32 East 57 Street, New York, NY 10022.

1968. Annually. Each issue is devoted to a single topic.

Sociologie et Societes. Department de Sociologie, Universite de Montreal, Montreal, Canada.

1969. Semiannually. Cross-cultural journals in sociology in French.

Sociological Symposium. Virginia Polytechnic Institute and State University, 660 McBridge Hall, Virginia Polytechnic and State University, Blacksburg, VA 24061.

1968. Semiannually. Each issue is devoted to a single topic.

Sociologiske Meddelelser. Sociological Institute, University of Copenhagen, Rosen-borggrade 15, Copenhagen K, Denmark.

1952. Semiannually. Book reviews. Annual index. Cumulative index for vols. 1–10. Text in Danish (and occasionally in other Scandinavian languages) and English.

Sociologus: New Series. Duncker and Humblot, Dietrich-Schäfer-Weg 9, Berlin 41, Germany.

1951. Semiannually. Abstracts. Book reviews. Text in English and German.

Sociology. British Sociological Association. Publisher: Oxford University Press, Press Road, Neasden, London N.W. 10, ODD, England.

1967. Triannually. Official publication of the British Sociological Association.

Sociology of Business Newsletter. Editor: J. N. Porter, 42 Englewood Avenue, Brookline, MA 02146.

Sociology of Leisure and Sports Abstracts. Elsevier Scientific Publishing Co., P.O. Box 211, 1000 AE Amsterdam, The Netherlands.

> Provides extensive summaries of between 1000 and 1200 recently published articles and books and bibliographies of sports and leisure.

Sociology: Reviews of New Books. Heldrex Publications, 4000 Albermarle Street, N.W., Washington, DC 20016.

> Provides rapid review of current work in sociology.

Sociology of Education. American Sociological Association, 1722 N Street N.W., Washington, DC 20036.

> 1927–62, vols. 1–36 published as the *Journal of Educational Sociology.* 1963. Quarterly. Abstracts. Annual index. Official publication of the American Sociological Association.

Sociology and Social Research. University of Southern California, 703 West 34 Street, Los Angeles, CA 90007.

> 1916–21, vols. 1–5 published as *Studies in Sociology;* 1921–27, volumes 6–11 published as *Journal of Applied Sociology.* 1927. Quarterly. Abstracts. Book reviews. Annual index. Cumulative index for volumes 1–30.

Sociology of Work and Occupations: An International Journal. Sage Publications, 275 South Beverly Drive, Beverly Hills, CA 90212.

> 1974. Quarterly.

Sociometry. American Sociological Association, 1722 N Street N.W., Washington, DC 20036.

> 1937. Quarterly. Abstracts. Annual index. Official publication of the American Sociological Association.

Soviet Sociology. International Arts and Sciences Press, 108 Grand Street, White Plains, NY 10701.

> 1962. Quarterly. Book reviews. Annual index. A journal of translations.

Summation. Department of Sociology, Michigan State University, East Lansing, MI 48824.

> 1968. Semiannually. Abstracts. Book reviews. Official journal of the Michigan State University Sociological Association and distributed free to members.

Teaching Sociology. Sage Publications, 275 South Beverly Drive, Beverly Hills, CA 90212.

> 1973. Semiannually.

Theory and Society. Elsevier Scientific Publishing Co., P.O. Box 330, Amsterdam, Netherlands. Renewal and critique in social theory. Editor: Alvin W. Gouldner, Sociologist Instituut, University van Amsterdam, Korte Spinhulsstegg 3, Amsterdam, Netherlands.

The West African Journal of Sociology and Political Science. Editor: Justin Labinjoh, University of Ibadan, Department of Sociology, Ibadan, Nigeria.

The Wisconsin Sociologist: New Series. Department of Sociology, University of Wisconsin-Milwaukee, Milwaukee, WI 53211.

1962. Quarterly. Book reviews. Official journal of the Wisconsin Sociological Association.

Guide to Related Sociological Journals

These journals were identified by Lawrence J. Rhoades as those expressing interest in receiving manuscripts from sociologists and social psychologists. See his *The Authors Guide to Selected Journals.* Cf. *Directory of Scholarly and Research Opportunities* (Los Angeles: Academic Media, 1975).

JOURNAL

Academy of Management Journal
Acta Criminologica
Administration & Society
Administration in Mental Health
Administrative Science Quarterly
Administrative Science Review
Adolescence
Africa Today
African Studies Review
Altered States of Consciousness
Journal of American Folklore
American Educational Research Journal
Journal of the American Geriatrics Society
Journal of the American Institute of Planners
American Journal of Economics and
  Sociology
American Journal of Political Science
American Journal of Psychology
American Psychologist
The American Statistician
Journal of Applied Communications Research
Journal of Applied Social Psychology
Asian Survey
AV Communication Review
Journal of Black Studies
Behavior Research Methods &
  Instrumentation
Behavior Science Research
Journal of Broadcasting
California Journal of Educational Research
Catalyst
Character Potential: A Record of Research
Child Care Quarterly
Child Psychiatry and Human Development
Child Welfare
The Cleveland State Law Review
Clinical Social Work Journal
Cognition
The Colorado Quarterly
Journal of Communication
Communication Research

Community College Social Science Quarterly
Journal of the Community Development
  Society
Community Mental Health Journal
Comparative Political Studies
Compensation Review
Journal of Conflict Resolution
Journal of Consumer Affairs
Journal of Criminal Law & Criminology
Criminology
Journal of Cross-Cultural Psychology
Cybernetica
Cycles
Day Care and Early Education
Demography
The Journal of Developing Areas
Drug Forum
Economic and Social Review
Education and Urban Society
Journal of Educational Psychology
Journal of Educational Thought
The Journal of Emotional Education
Environment and Behavior
et al.
ETC. A Review of General Semantics
The Journal of Ethnic Studies
European Journal of Social Psychology
Ethnicity
Evaluation
Exceptional Children
The Family Coordinator
Family Planning Digest
Family Planning Perspectives
Family Process
Federal Probation
The Futurist
The Journal of General Psychology
Georgia Social Science Journal
The Gerontologist
The Green Revolution
Group Psychotherapy & Psychodrama

Growth and Change
Handbook of International Sociometry
Harvard Business Review
Health Services Research
Journal of Higher Education
Journal of the Assoc. for the Study of
   Perception
Journal of Homosexuality
Hospital Administration
Milbank Memorial Fund Quarterly/Health
   and Society
Human Behavior Magazine
The Human Context
Human Mosaic
Journal of Human Resources
Human Resource Management
Humanitas
Improving College & University Teaching
The Indian Historian
Industrial and Labor Relations Review
Industrial Relations: A Jrnl. of Economy &
   Society
Intellect
Journal of Interamerican Studies & World
   Affairs
International Development Review
International Interactions
International Journal of the Addictions
International Journal of Cooperative
   Development
International Journal of Ethnic Studies
International Journal of Offender Therapy &
   Comparative Criminology
International Journal of Symbology
International Migration Review
International Review of Administrative
   Sciences
International Studies Quarterly
Issues in Criminology
Law & Society Review
Journal of Leisure Research
Suicide & Life-Threatening Behavior
Manpower
Journal of Marketing Research
Journal of Marriage and the Family
Methods of Information in Medicine
Multivariate Behavioral Research
Journal of Negro Education
The New Scholar
Opinion
Peace and Change, a Journal of Peace
   Research
People Watching

Journal of Personality & Social Psychology
Journal of Personality Assessment
Personnel
The Personnel Administrator
Personnel and Guidance Journal
Political Science Quarterly
Journal of Popular Culture
Population Review
Population Studies
Public Opinion Quarterly
The Prison Journal
Psychiatry
Psychological Bulletin
The Psychological Record
Psychological Review
Psychology
The Journal of Psychology
Psychometrika
Public Administration Review
Public Welfare
Quarterly Journal of Economics
Quarterly Journal of Speech
Race
Journal for the Scientific Study of Religion
Review of Religious Research
Religious Humanism
Journal of Research in Crime & Delinquency
Research on Consumer Behavior
Review of Educational Research
Review of Public Data Use
The Review of Social Theory
Rocky Mountain Social Science Journal
S.A.M. Advanced Management Journal
The Journal of Sex Research
Journal of School Psychology
Science & Society
Simulation and Games
Small Group Behavior
Social Action
Social Biology
Social Compass
Social Policy
Journal of Social Issues
Journal of Social Policy
The Journal of Social Psychology
Social Science Quarterly
Social Work
Journal of Socio-Economic Planning Sciences
Sociological Analysis
Soundings: An Interdisciplinary Journal
Southeastern Review
Southern Speech Communication Journal
Studies in Family Planning

Technology Assessment
Technology and Culture
Journal of Thought
Town Planning Review
Trans-Action
University of Chicago School Review
Urban Affairs Quarterly
Urban and Social Change Review

Urban Education
Urban Life and Culture
Journal of Vocational Behavior
War on Hunger
War/Peace Report
Women's Studies
World Politics
Youth and Society

Supplementary List of Related Sociological Journals

This is a list of journals that publish work of interest to sociologists who have specialized interests. Some are new in the last five to seven years and express increased concern with drugs, crime, family, health, and environmental problems. Even this supplementary list does not begin to exhaust the array of journals with some relationship to sociology. Many journals related to education, law, communication, politics, and the economy are not listed. Those that are listed fall most closely within the "sociological orbit."

Advances in Alcohol and Substance Abuse
Aging and Society
Alternative Higher Education
Armed Forces and Society
Behavior Today
The Behavioral and Brain Sciences
Bioethics Quarterly
Caribbean Review
Case Analysis
Comparative Education Review
Comparative Studies in Society and History
Contemporary Psychology
Current Anthropology
Decision Sciences
Economy and Society
Ethnic and Racial Studies
Evaluation: A Forum for Human Service Decision Centers
Evaluation Quarterly
Family Relations
Family Therapy
Focus on Poverty Research
Group
Health Policy Quarterly
Health and Social Work
Home Health Care Services Quarterly
Housing and Safety
Human Communication Research
Human Sexuality Update
Human Studies
International Journal of Aging and Human Development
International Journal of Health Services

International Journal of Urban and Regional Research
International Social Science Journal
International Quarterly of Community Health Education
Journal of American Statistical Association
Journal of Applied Behavioral Science
Journal of Business
Journal of Community Health
Journal of Comparative Health Studies
The Journal of Consumer Research
Journal of Divorce
Journal of Drug Education
Journal of Family History
Journal of the History of the Behavioral Sciences
Journal of Homosexuality
Journal of Housing for the Elderly
Journal of International and Comparative Social Welfare
Journal of Organizational Behavior and Performance Management
Journal of Nonverbal Behavior
Journal of Religion
Journal of Religion and Health
Journal of Research in Personality
Journal of Social Service Research
Language in Society
Marriage and Family Review
Merrill-Palmer Quarterly of Behavior and Development
Multivariate Behavioral Research
Offender Rehabilitation
Omega—Journal of Death and Dying

Organizational Behavior and Human Performance

Organizational Studies

New Human Services Review

Population: Behavioral, Social, and Environmental Issues

Population and Environment

Psychology of Women Quarterly

Quarterly Journal of Ideology

Social Analysis

Social Indicator Research

Social Service Review

Social Work in Health Care

Social Work Research and Abstracts

Society Magazine

Survey Research

Symbolic Interaction

Topics in Strategic Planning for Health Care

Women and Criminal Justice

Women and Health

Women and Politics

Women Studies Abstracts

Selected New Journals

Aging and Society. Editor: Malcolm L. Johnson, Policy Studies Institute, London. Publisher: Cambridge University Press, 12 East 59 Street, New York, NY 10022.

1981. Triannually.

Contemporary Crisis. Crime, Law, and Social Policy. Editor: William J. Chambliss, University of Delaware. Publisher: Elsevier Scientific Publishing Co., P. O. Box 211, Amsterdam, The Netherlands.

1977. Quarterly. International journal focused on crime, law, politics, social change, imperialism, women's struggles, rebellion and revolution.

Human Studies. A Journal for Philosophy and Social Sciences. Editor: George Psathas, Boston University. Publisher: Ablex Publishing Corporation, 335 Chestnut Street, Norwood, NJ 07648.

1978. Quarterly. Emphasizes relationships between philosophy and the social sciences. Problem-oriented rather than discipline-oriented.

Journal of Social and Biological Structures: Studies in Human Sociobiology. Editor: Harvey Wheeler. Publisher: Academic Press, 111 Fifth Avenue, New York, NY 10003.

1978. Quarterly.

Knowledge: Creation, Diffusion, Utilization. Editor: Robert F. Rich, Woodrow Wilson School, Princeton University. Princeton, NJ 08540 Publisher: Sage Publications, Inc., 275 Beverly Drive, Beverly Hills, CA 90212.

1979. Quarterly. An international journal committed to the creation, diffusion, and utilization of knowledge development. Researchers, policy makers, R&D managers, and practitioners are encouraged to submit manuscripts.

New Directions for Methodology of Behavioral Science. Editor: Donald W. Fiske. Publisher: Jossey-Bass, 433 California Street, San Francisco, CA 94104.

1979. Quarterly.

New Publications: Replications in Social Psychology. Editors: Keith E. Campbell and Thomas T. Jackson, Box 301, Fort Hays University, Hayes, KS 67601.

1978. Quarterly. Specifically publishes replicated research in social psychology.

Sociology of the Sciences. D. Reidel Publishing Co., Box 17, Dordrecht, Netherlands.

1977. Yearbook. Each volume is directed to a particular topic in the sociology of the sciences.

For all journals, sociological journals and related sociological journals, Sussman has assembled a large amount of information about each. *The Authors Guide to Journals in Sociology and Related Fields* by Marvin B. Sussman (New York: Haworth Press, 1977) is a comprehensive directory of over 400 English-language periodicals in sociology and related fields. It has much information for the writer not obtainable from any other source. For each of the journals there is information on:

Types of articles the journal usually accepts and usually rejects
Types of articles the journal usually recieves, but which are inappropriate
Correct manuscript submission address
Acceptance/rejection ratio
Publication lag time
Early publication options
Authorship restrictions, if any
Page charges, if any
Availability of style sheet from the editor
Review period lag time
Style requirements
Policies on publication of revised M.A./Ph.D. theses and student papers
Topics of particular interest to the journal
Topics frequently received but not published

Research Annuals in Sociology and Related Fields

The research annuals shown below are all new publications that have appeared since 1979. They are usually under the editorship of specialists who change with each issue. For current information, write the publisher, Jai Press, Inc., P. O. Box 1678, 165 W Putnam Avenue, Greenwich, CT 06830.

Advances in Early Education and Day Care
Advances in Special Education
Advances in Substance Abuse
Comparative Social Research
Contemporary Studies in Sociology
Current Perspectives in Social Theory
Political Power and Social Theory
Research in Community and Mental Health
Research in Economic Anthropology
Research in Law and Sociology
Research in Organizational Behavior
Research in Race and Ethnic Relations
Research in Social Movements, Conflict and Change
Research in Social Problems and Public Policy
Research in Social Stratification and Mobility
Research in Sociology of Education and Socialization
Research in Sociology of Knowledge, Sciences and Art
Research in the Interweave of Social Roles: Women and Men
Research in the Sociology of Health Care
Research in the Sociology of Work
Studies in Communication Research
Studies in Symbolic Interaction

Current Information about Published Work

Current Contents in the Social and Behavioral Sciences is a weekly listing of the contents of journals and some books in the social and behavioral sciences. It also includes an index by first author and principal words in the titles of articles.

The Educational Resources Information Center (ERIC) of the National Institute of Education (NIE) publishes a monthly abstract journal, *Resources in Education* (RIE), which announces research reports and other nonjournal literature of interest to the educational community. These documents are cataloged, abstracted, and indexed by subject, author or investigator, and responsible institution.

Resources in Education started publication in November 1966 and can be purchased in single copies or on subscription from the Superintendent of Documents, U.S. Government Printing Office, Washington, DC 20402. Annual cumulative sets have been reprinted and can be obtained from Macmillan Information, 216R Brown Street, Riverside, NJ 08075.

Macmillan Information also publishes *Current Index to Journals in Education* (CIJE), which indexes articles in over 700 journals. These journals represent the core of the periodical/serial literature in the field of education.

Individual monthly volumes and yearly cumulations of *Resources in Education* and *Current Index to Journals in Education* are available in many college and university libraries, as well as some special libraries. Most of these libraries are open to the public for on-site reference and many also have complete ERIC microfiche collections. *Resources in Education* is also available in the offices of many school systems at the state and local level. All routine searches for documentary material should begin with *Resources in Education.*

ERIC was originally conceived in the U.S. Office of Education in the mid-1960s as a system of providing ready access to recent educational research and other education related literature. The ERIC Processing and Reference Facility is a centralized information processing facility serving Central ERIC and sixteen decentralized clearinghouses, each specializing in a branch of knowledge. For further information, write ERIC Processing and Reference Facility, 4833 Rugby Avenue, Suite 303, Bethesda, MD 20014. Telephone (301) 656-9723.

5.D.4 WHERE SOCIOLOGISTS PUBLISH; WHERE PRESTIGIOUS SOCIOLOGISTS PUBLISH AND WHY

Sociologists publish research monographs with numerous publishing companies and university presses and research articles in 300 or more journals. A directory of publishers lists more than 260 publishing outlets in the United States. The *Guide to Sociological Journals* includes 72 journals and the list of *Related Sociological Journals* extends to almost 200. Other outlets include many well-known journals that print sociological articles including *Harpers Magazine, Atlantic Monthly, Commentary, New Republic,* and so on. Sociologists write in newspapers, prepare pamphlets, and distribute mimeograph and printed materials to selected audiences.[1] They write to secure tenure and promotion, gain merit increases, increase their status, and because they just like to write and "get their work out." They are driven by an ethic that impels them to "make their work known" so that their knowledge will be preserved and transmitted.

Of all the motives that drive the scholar to write, the most universal and persistent is the desire for status. This is expressed first as a desire to become "known" and then to rank even higher in prestige. It is appropriate therefore to find out which journals rank high in prestige.

Where Do the Prestigious Sociologists Publish and Why?

Ideally, every writer would be judged by the intrinsic worth of his research in whatever journal it appeared. In fact, no scholar, no matter how thorough, can read all or even a substantial part of the available journals. The result is that each sociologist who publishes is evaluated in part (in large part?) by the reputations of the journals in which he publishes. The degree to which most articles are noticed, read, and cited depends to a great extent on the kinds of journals in which the articles are published.

Norval D. Glenn undertook investigations of American sociologists' evaluations of 63 journals in which sociologists frequently publish.[2] In February 1970, he mailed a questionnaire to a randomly drawn sample of 250 professors and associate professors in departments with Sociology Ph.D. programs listed in the *Guide to Graduate Departments of Sociology, 1969.* He asked his respondents to assign weights to the list of 63 journals in accordance with their judgment of the average importance of their contributions to the field. They were asked to use articles in the *American Sociological Review* as a standard for reference, using a weight of 10 to an article in that journal.[3] A publication judged only half as important was to be assigned a weight of 5. Using relative weights in this manner, judges produce mean weights that are shown in table 1.

Glenn describes some of his conclusions to the findings as each column is analyzed:

"The data in the first column of table 1 indicate two major dimensions of the reputations of the journals. The mean weight is essentially an indicator of the *intensity* of prestige, whereas the number of respondents who assigned weights (shown in parentheses) is a rough indicator of how well the journal was known among the respondents, or of the *extensity* of the journal's prestige. The extent of being known and the extensity of prestige are not the same, of course, unless all of those who know an object grant it some prestige."[4]

"If the measure of extensity were exact, total prestige could be arrived at by multiplying the measure of extensity by the measure of intensity. However, since no measure of total prestige can be derived from the data at hand, and since the measures of intensity and extensity are imperfectly correlated ($r = +.73$), the journals can be only partially ordered as to their prestige."[5]

"The reader must be cautioned that citation data indicate that the prestige of the journals does not closely correspond with the average impact their articles have on the discipline. For instance, Lin and Nelson (1969) found substantial differences in the frequency of citation of articles in the *ASR,*

Table 1. *Means of the Weights Assigned to 63 Journals by a Sample of American Sociologists*

Journal	Mean weight	(N)	Standard deviation	Had published in journal		Relevant specialists[a]	
				Mean	(N)[b]	Mean	(N)[b]
American Sociological Review	10.0[c]	—	—	—	—		
American Journal of Sociology	9.6	(129)	1.2	9.6	(35)	—	—
Social Forces	8.1	(127)	1.9	8.1	(41)	—	—
Sociometry	7.8	(119)	2.2	8.6	(8)	8.1	(34)
British Journal of Sociology	7.8	(115)	2.1	—	—	—	—
American Anthropologist	7.7	(118)	2.3	—	—	—	—
Social Problems	7.6	(113)	2.2	8.7	(15)	—	—
American Political Science Review	7.5	(110)	2.2	—	—	8.0	(9)
Demography	7.4	(90)	2.2	8.8	(5)	9.1	(13)
Annals of the American Academy of Political and Social Science	7.2	(126)	2.3	8.1	(10)	—	—
Public Opinion Quarterly	7.1	(116)	2.1	7.4	(14)	7.2	(14)
American Economic Review	7.1	(99)	2.9	—	—	—	—
Journal of Personality and Social Science	7.1	(81)	2.2	—	—	7.1	(26)
European Journal of Sociology	6.9	(69)	2.4	—	—	—	—
Behavioral Science	6.8	(87)	2.3	—	—	—	—
Rural Sociology	6.7	(109)	2.2	7.2	(18)	7.8	(8)
Human Organization	6.7	(104)	2.0	7.4	(5)	—	—
Journal of Social Psychology	6.7	(102)	2.1	5.3	(6)	6.8	(33)
Administrative Science Quarterly	6.7	(98)	2.4	6.5	(5)	—	—
Milbank Memorial Fund Quarterly	6.7	(97)	2.4	—	—	7.1	(14)
International Journal of Comparative Sociology	6.7	(77)	2.4	—	—	—	—
American Behavioral Scientist	6.6	(110)	2.4	—	—	—	—
Journal of Social Issues	6.6	(108)	2.0	—	—	—	—
Social Research	6.6	(88)	2.2	—	—	—	—
Daedalus	6.5	(111)	2.8	—	—	—	—
Human Relations	6.5	(91)	2.2	6.4	(5)	—	—
Population Studies	6.5	(74)	2.2	—	—	7.3	(12)
Harvard Educational Review	6.4	(93)	2.9	—	—	6.0	(7)
Current Sociology	6.4	(78)	2.4	—	—	—	—
Canadian Review of Sociology and Anthropology	6.4	(77)	2.1	—	—	—	—
Sociological Review	6.3	(68)	2.0	—	—	—	—
International Social Science Journal	6.3	(65)	2.2	—	—	—	—
American Sociologist	6.2	(123)	2.4	7.9	(8)	—	—
Journal of Marriage and the Family	6.2	(108)	2.4	6.4	(14)	6.5	(21)
Journal of Conflict Resolution	6.2	(86)	2.6	—	—	—	—
Journal of Health and Social Behavior	6.2	(83)	2.4	8.8	(6)	8.3	(12)
Sociology of Education	6.1	(93)	2.0	6.4	(5)	6.1	(8)
Sociological Quarterly	6.1	(83)	1.9	6.6	(11)	—	—
Acta Sociologica	6.1	(71)	2.1	—	—	—	—
Social Science Quarterly	6.0	(64)	2.0	—	—	—	—
Southwestern Journal of Anthropology	6.0	(54)	2.2	—	—	—	—
Sociology and Social Research	5.9	(107)	1.9	6.0	(10)	—	—

Table 1. *Continued*

Journal	Mean weight	(N)	Standard deviation	Had published in journal		Relevant specialists[a]	
				Mean	(N)[b]	Mean	(N)[b]
Sociology	5.9	(33)	2.0	—	—	—	—
Sociological Inquiry	5.8	(86)	1.9	6.7	(13)	—	—
Transaction	5.7	(118)	2.7	5.0	(8)	—	—
Pacific Sociological Review	5.7	(94)	2.2	5.7	(7)	—	—
Law and Society Review	5.7	(62)	2.3	—	—	8.0	(5)
Sociological Analysis	5.7	(57)	1.7	6.2	(5)	5.7	(7)
Journal of Gerontology	5.4	(51)	2.2	6.5	(6)	—	—
Journal of Research in Crime and Delinquency	5.4	(46)	1.9	—	—	6.6	(14)
American Journal of Economics and Sociology	5.3	(96)	2.0	—	—	—	—
British Journal of Criminology	5.3	(61)	1.8	—	—	6.7	(14)
Gerontologist	5.3	(57)	2.1	—	—	—	—
Crime and Delinquency	5.2	(58)	1.9	—	—	5.6	(16)
Science and Society	5.2	(51)	2.1	—	—	—	—
Journal of Criminal Law, Criminology, and Police Science	5.1	(64)	1.9	—	—	5.9	(15)
Phylon	5.0	(82)	2.1	5.4	(8)	5.4	(12)
Eugenics Quarterly[d]	5.0	(51)	2.3	—	—	—	—
Jewish Journal of Sociology	4.9	(43)	1.8	—	—	—	—
American Journal of Correction	4.8	(73)	2.0	—	—	5.3	(15)
Eugenics Review	4.7	(41)	2.2	—	—	—	—
Journal of Negro Education	4.5	(57)	2.2	—	—	5.5	(11)
New Society	4.5	(37)	2.0	—	—	—	—
Federal Probation	3.8	(57)	1.8	—	—	4.5	(15)

Source: Norval D. Glenn, "American Sociologists Evaluation of 63 Journals," *TAS* 6 (November 1971): 300–301. Used with permission of American Sociological Association.

[a] The relevant specialists for a specialized journal are the respondents with a specialty in the same area as that of the old journal.
[b] Means are shown only where the N is five or more.
[c] The weight for the *ASR* was given on the questionnaire and was not assigned by the respondents.
[d] This journal is now called *Social Biology*.

the *AJS,* and *Social Forces;* yet my data indicate that those three journals were very similar in prestige. A major reason for this discrepancy may be that variation in circulation of the three journals (16,584 for the *ASR,* 9335 for the *AJS,* and about 4000 for *Social Forces* in 1969 and 1970); authors probably are more likely to cite an article if the journal is in their personal library."[6]

It is important to direct the reader's attention to the considerable dissensus in the evaluations of the journals, as roughly indicated by the standard deviations in table 1, column 2.

"These data, plus data not shown, make it clear that there is not a highly integrated system of prestige in sociology. Therefore, the best outlets for the writings of a particular sociologist depend on who are his or her significant others and who is likely to judge and reward him or her. Only the highest-prestige general journals seem to be very good outlets for almost any sociologist."[7]

One might suspect that a respondent would tend to overevaluate journals in which he had published or with which he was otherwise identified, but in the case of the general journals, the means of the weights given by respondents who had and who had not published in them were invariably similar and in some cases identical (table 1, column 3). There was, however, a tendency for persons to assign unusually high weights to the lower-prestige journals if they had published in them but not in the higher-prestige journals.

Although articles in prestigious journals rank high, the highest weights are given to Research and Theoretical Monographs (mean weight = 33.8), Textbooks (18.1), and Edited Books (11.2).[8]

Notes

1. For a comprehensive guide to publishing opportunities, see *Directory of Publishing Opportunities,* 3rd ed. (Chicago, Ill.: Marquis Who's Who, 1975).
2. Norval D. Glenn, "American Sociologists' Evaluations of Sixty-Three Journals," *American Sociologist* 6 (November 1971): 298–303.
3. The *American Sociological Review* is the official journal of the American Sociological Association and is received by all members.
4. Glenn, "American Sociologists' Evaluations of Sixty-Three Journals," p. 300.
5. Ibid., p. 301.
6. Ibid., p. 302.
7. Ibid.
8. Glenn and Villemez have derived a weighting scheme for the different types of publications. It yields a useful index of "importance to the discipline." The Glenn-Villemez Comprehensive Index (GUCI) generates six distinct indices of publication productivity: number of articles, number of books, total publications (articles plus books), article points, book points, and total points. See Norval D. Glenn and Wayne Villemez, "The Productivity of Sociologists at 45 American Universities," *American Sociologist* 5 (August 1970): 244–52.

5.D.5   **HOW SOCIOLOGISTS GET PUBLISHED; HOW TO TAKE REJECTION**

Few academics know all the ins and outs of publishing because the rules governing this activity are not a few, easily learned principles, but rather a multitude of various considerations any one of which can work for or against you. Each form of publishing has its own set of particular requirements.

Finding a Publisher for Articles

Each journal has its own goals and its own preferred style. It may have its own definition of "appropriate length." And most important will be the standards of quality that the editors impose upon their acceptance of articles received. The extent to which the writer gauges these considerations accurately, the greater will be his or her chance of acceptance. The way to gain such a background is to become thoroughly familiar with the journal in which you hope to publish. If you want to publish in the most prestigious journals you should not send them any work that fails to meet the standards exhibited in those journals. You must be aware that the competition is intense and that the acceptance rate ranges each year between 10 and 20 percent of the articles received. And this rate includes articles often rejected until substantial revisions have been made to meet editors' criticisms. Each article is read by two or more professional readers, whose evaluations are subsequently weighed by the editor.

The younger scholar might be advised to choose among journals where the competition is less intense. Specialized journals in the area of interest may more readily accept an article if it conforms to their interest pattern. Many journals look for theoretical or opinion material and do not impose patterns of design and statistical rigor. They are more interested in well-written material that treats of concerns to their journal readers.

The writer who gets published usually makes tentative drafts and asks for the advice of colleagues. He or she is willing to accept criticism and willing to rewrite, rewrite, and rewrite if necessary. The final draft is a perfect copy as far as possible. This means good paper, clear and correct typing, with footnoting and all style requirements matched against the format of the given journal.

Whatever the fate of the papers submitted, it must be remembered that writing is an art even for scientific work. The writer who wants to be published keeps writing and submitting work. There are numerous journals, and most work of reasonable quality can be published somewhere. This is a wonderful opportunity that is offered. In the exercise of the art the writer learns the ins and outs both of writing and the placement of work. If a writer seeks prestige, he or she will aim for the prestigeful journals only when the work merits it and when the writing commends it.[1]

Finding a Publisher for Books

It will be recalled that Norvall Glenn reported that "although articles in prestigious journals rank high, the highest weights are given to Research and Theoretical Monographs (mean weight = 33.8), Textbooks (18.1), and Edited Books (11.2)." In addition to gaining the writer higher prestige, books may make money. Royalties for best-selling texts and books of readings can be very rewarding. All books have the prospect of making some money, but research monographs ordinarily yield only prestige. But the monograph has a long and durable life, and the writer may be remembered for it long after his other writings are forgotten. The decision as to publishing monographs, texts, or readings is one that requires a balancing of motives and skills—all timed according to appropriate stages in the professional career. A few general rules for finding a publisher for books has been set forth by Carolyn Mullins:

When and How?

The ideal time to begin interesting publishers in a research monograph is when you begin the research or receive funds to support it. If a text or trade book is on your mind, start looking for a publisher as soon as you get the idea for it.

Texts are usually intended for classroom use only. Rarely do they have scholarly interest. Trade books—e.g., Vance Packard's books and Riesman's *The Lonely Crowd*—have a nonacademic market in addition to whatever student or professional market they may have. Monographs are usually intended for faculty use; many have some utility in graduate seminars, and a few are useful in advanced undergraduate courses. Publishers, naturally, are delighted when a genuine research monograph also has obvious text and/or trade markets. Publishers (some university presses excepted) usually show greater interest in texts and trade books than in monographs because the former are more likely to make money. It follows, then, that competition is more likely to develop if you are trying to interest publishers in a text or trade book than if a monograph is your intended product.

Edited collections—whether of previously published papers or of unpublished papers—can fall into any category. They present many different and specialized problems. These have to do with obtaining permissions, pricing, keeping them within reasonable size limits, getting several contributors to cooperate and meet deadlines, trying to set contract obligations and rewards equitably, and so forth. They are also less popular now than they used to be, partly because of the high permission cost that is often involved.[2]

Notes

1. For assistance, the following may prove helpful: Jacques Barzun and Henry F. Graff, *The Modern Researcher*, 3rd ed. (New York: Harcourt Brace Jovanovich, 1977); chap. 16, p. 326, is excellent for revising of writing. David W. Ewing, *Writing for Results in Business, Government, the Sciences, and the Professions*, 2nd ed. (New York: Wiley, 1979). Oliver Holmes, "Thesis to Book: What to Get Rid Of," *Scholarly Publishing* 5 (July 1974); 339–49. C. P. Lee, *Library Resources: How to Research and Write a Paper* (Englewood Cliffs, N.J.: Prentice-Hall, 1971).
2. Carolyn J. Mullins, "Everything You Always Wanted to Know About Book Publishing" (Paper given at Indiana University, February 1, 1975), pp. 2–3. Quote used by permission of author. Writing books and finding a publisher for monographs and textbooks is discussed more fully in C. J. Mullins, *Writing and Publishing in the Social and Behavioral Sciences* (New York: Wiley–Interscience, 1977).

HOW TO TAKE REJECTION

Rejection Comes Naturally

The probability is far higher that your learned paper will receive a rejection from a major journal than be awarded acceptance for publication. There are many reasons for this:

1. *Lack of space.* The *American Sociological Review* receives approximately 400 papers a year (1980); the *American Journal of Sociology,* 350. Even a specialized journal like *Social Psychological Quarterly* may get 200. Obviously, only a fraction of the submitted papers can be accepted. The four major journals in Sociology accept about 16 percent of the papers submitted to them.
2. *Errors of judgment made by competent reviewers and editors.* Let us assume that no biases exist in the review process and that the same level of measurement efficiency exists as in other measurement processes based on coding of qualitative materials. Given these assumptions, Stinchcombe and Ofshe estimate the validity of a judgment of article quality to be about .70. They then set forth a model providing an estimate of the proportion of acceptance of papers of different quality at the acceptance level of 16 percent. If the quality of the papers is approximately normal, we can say papers *judged* to be one standard deviation or more above the mean of the papers submitted will be accepted. For papers at different points

of *true quality,* the researchers calculate what proportion will be judged to be above the acceptance level of one standard deviation above the mean. They compute the conditional distribution of *judged* quality for a given value of *true* quality. They apply the resulting model to a random 100 papers submitted for publication with the following results: of 84 submitted papers that were truly below the acceptance level, 77 (92 percent) were rejected and only 7 (8 percent) were accepted. Of 16 papers truly above the cut-off point 9 (56 percent) were accepted and 7 (44 percent) were rejected. "In terms of numbers of papers, there are about equal numbers of distinguished papers mistakenly rejected and mediocre papers mistakenly accepted."[1]

Many editors would dispute this finding and would contend that good reviewers and editors are better judges than the validity coefficient (.70) allows. Stinchcombe and Ofshe contend that the virtue of their model does not "take a conspiracy theory of journal editing to account for the rejection of a great many good papers and the publishing of a large number of mediocre papers."[2] And of course, since the cut-off level is 16 percent, 84 out of every 100 papers are, on the average, rejected.

3. *Reviewer and editor incompetence and bias.* There is a widespread suspicion (but no proof) that considerable incompetence exists among referees and editors.[3] It is possible that such suspicion is based on the understandable reaction that "*my* paper was of such high quality that only poor reviewing failed to discern its merit." But wounded ego aside, it must be remembered that most reviewers are *volunteer workers* (the exceptions are paid editorial assistants when they exist) and that they sometimes give their valuable time grudgingly and unevenly. Almost none have been specifically trained to review. It is like college teaching; you are expected to learn this as a by-product of other training. Some reviewers get an "ego trip" by overcritical behavior; some just do a lazy "once over"; some are simply not competent to handle the paper. And some react with ideological or methodological bias rather than give a decision with balanced judgment.

It is up to the editor to "catch" this kind of crime, but editors, too, have human frailties. And as professionals, editors must budget their time. There is just so much time to give to the reviewing process of the journal. In defense of editors it may be said:

  a. The editor lacks information about many reviewers' work and lacks resources to identify the ablest reviewers.
  b. The editor must persuade busy professionals to give up valuable productive time in order to get the best reviews; failing to get the best, an editor often must take second or third best if a review is to be made at all.
  c. The editor cannot read every paper and every review if the journal commands a large number of papers.
  d. The editor is probably a specialist in a given field and cannot be expected to judge wisely on papers in a large number of fields.

4. *Inherent difficulty of judging social research.* Finally, for editor and reviewer alike, ascertaining the "quality" of a paper is more difficult in sociology and the other social sciences than in the physical sciences. Standards are difficult to apply. In the physical sciences criteria for quality can be established more easily, and rejection rates in physical science journals are proportionately much lower than in the major sociological journals.

Don't Blow Your Cool

There are sensitive egos in any profession. Professionals have worked many years and have surmounted many barriers to prove their right to hold degrees and to practice. Egos get a jolt when an "excellent" paper fares badly. The range of emotion runs from *disappointment and despondence to humiliation to anger and explosive vehemence.* One editor writes, "In my judgment, authors' distress with the review process is more a function of the rejection of submitted articles than the quality of reviews; the two are not necessarily related. . . . Nothing so infuriates an author as to be told that little fault can be found with an article but that it cannot be accepted for publication."[4] In the world of "publish or perish," with tenure, promotion, and merit increases at stake, there is ample impetus to raise both adrenaline and blood pressure in the human organism.

THE ADAPTIVE RESPONSE

You can "stew in your juice" or take a new look at your paper and at the reviews. (Ordinarily the editor will send copies of the review in whole or in part.) Maybe you will be asked to revise and resubmit. Now is the time to apply some social insight. What kind of reviewers did you have? A typology of reviewers is provided so that you can make a judgment.

Table 1   *A typology of reviewers*

Lazy reviewers	The ego aggrandizer	The ego projectionist	The competent	The compassionate
Gives the paper a hasty examination.	Wants to parade his critical and superior faculties.	Wants the author to write just as he, the reviewer, would do it.	Studies carefully and conscientiously prepares a balanced critique.	Does a competent review and takes added care in pointing out ways of improving the article.

Table 2   *Orientations of Reviewers*

Radical		Humanist			Positivist	
(personality & organizational change oriented)		(historical, theoretical, value, oriented)			(measurement oriented)	
Concern with rapid social change		Concern with current social problems			Concern with sociological problems	
Marxist ideologist.	Ideologically uncommitted but critical of established institutions.	Active intervention in social problems.	Monitoring of crisis.	Eschews any interest in applied work. Concerned only with theoretical and value implications.	Favors placing method secondary to the cumulation of new knowledge around central persistent sociological themes.	Favors rigorous empirical treatment with emphasis on sophisticated mathematical statistical methods.

This typology may give you some clues as to the quality of your reviewers and help you make up your mind as to the worth and future prospects for your paper. You may want to dig deeper into the motivations of the anonymous persons who judged your paper. To do this it is suggested that you examine some basic orientations of social researchers. This is the age of diversity and professionals come in all colors. Look at the classification in Table 2 and examine carefully the Radicals, the Humanists, and the Positivists. Did you get caught in an ideological bias that helped to reject your paper? Where do you fit in these orientations? What is the dominant orientation of the journal to which you offered your paper?

It is entirely possible that your reviewers may have "liked your paper but found weaknesses in your method." This may mean that their methodological biases are showing. A look at methodological bias is in order.

Table 3 *Methodological Predispositions of Reviewers*

Introspection	Theory	Observation	Measurement
Likes evidence of capable intuitive identification of personal and social processes.	Likes demonstration of interrelated theoretical propositions ranging from global to middle range according to reviewer's preference.	Gives special significance to the manner of observation ranging from 1. archival and documentary work 2. field work 3. laboratory work	Gives favor to the rigor of measurement ranging from 1. qualitative to 2. quantitative methodology

Make Decisions, Then Act

You are now ready to reevaluate your paper. Go over the reviewer's criticisms and look at your paper as if you are a critic.

Your choices are these:

1. Submit a revised version of your paper with an accompanying letter to the editor setting out your dispute with points used in the initial rejection. Ask the editor to bring your revised paper and notes to the attention of the previous reviewers in order to get a reappraisal.
2. Try another publication channel. They are numerous. Look at section 5.D.3, *Guide to Sociological and Related Journals,* which lists journals not only in sociology but also in related fields.[5] If your paper has something to offer, it will get published. Keep trying.
3. Have the guts to admit that the paper is seriously flawed and get on with new work.[6]

Notes

1. Arthur L. Stinchcombe and Richard Ofshe, "On Journal Editing as Probabilistic Process," *American Sociologist* 4 (May 1969): 116.
2. Ibid., p. 117. A symposium in *Contemporary Sociology* 8 (November 1979): 789–824 reviews in detail the *American Journal of Sociology, American Sociological Review,* and *Social Forces* for 1975–79. Discussions are by Jerry Gaston, Norbert Wiley, Walter

B. Gove, Everett K. Wilson, Morris Zelditch, Jr., James L. McCartney, Samuel A. Mueller, and Duncan Lindsey. Critiques and suggestions for improvement of the review process abound. This symposium is the most thorough analysis made to date.

3. Lee Freese, "On Changing Some Role Relationships in the Editorial Review Process," *American Sociologist* 14 (November 1979): 231–38.

4. Sheldon Stryker, "On the Editorial Review Process," *American Sociologist* 14 (November 1979); 238. See other comments by Rita James Simon, Duncan Lindsey, Helen MacGill Hughes, and George W. Bohrnstedt.

5. For a broader view, see Duncan Lindsey, *The Scientific Publication System in Social Science, A Study in the Operation of Leading Professional Journals in Psychology, Sociology and Social Work* (San Francisco: Jossey-Bass, 1978); John S. Harris and Reed H. Blake, *Technical Writing for Social Scientists* (Chicago: Nelson-Hall, 1979).

6. For a discussion of behavioral response to the failure, see Kathleen S. Crittenden and Mary G. Wiley, "Causal Attribution and Behavioral Response to Failure," *Social Psychology Quarterly* 43 (September 1980): 353–58. Authors' attributions to rejections in the referred journals *Sociology of Work* and *Sociological Quarterly* are studied using regression procedures. They find the behavioral response is directly influenced by past experience. It makes a difference in confidence whether one attributes the rejection to variable causes or to stable causes. Women, especially, are prone to attribute rejection to stable causes.

5.D.6 PROFESSIONAL COMMUNICATION AND REPORTING

A professional research life is an ongoing process of research investigation, reading research journals, preparing scientific papers and reading them before professional audiences of various learned societies, and finally publishing articles and monographs. In order to command attention, it is necessary for researchers to make themselves and their work known to colleagues in local, state, regional, national and international circles.

The North American sociologist who wishes to be known in national and international circles will join the American Sociological Association and may affiliate with one or both of the leading international sociological associations: International Sociological Association and Institut International de Sociologie.

Of all the many circles in which the researcher may move and find outlets, no forums are more important than reports at annual meetings of the American Sociological Association and publication in the *American Sociological Review.* If you are a young sociologist, you should join the American Sociological Association as soon as you make a commitment to professional life. You should begin reading the *ASR*, which will provide research examples of high-quality work as well as names of leaders in the field. For the aspiring sociologist, the *ASR* should stimulate participation in the annual meetings and encourage growth of research interests. One of the first steps to professionalization is to know the research in your fields of interest and the leading researchers who are at the cutting edge of the discipline. The second and most important step is to join this circle by participation, achievement, and recognition.

The American Sociological Association is a voluntary association of individual members. Many categories of membership exist. Full membership in the ASA requires the holding of a Ph.D. degree in sociology or in some related field, or the completion of three years of graduate study in such field. Students are encouraged to join as associates at low fees. There were 12,588 members of all categories in 1981; of this number, 9245 (74 percent) were full (voting) members. An earlier survey showed that eight out of ten members are employed in sociology departments in colleges and universities, another 12 percent have appointments in academic units outside of sociology, and 9 percent work in nonacademic settings. Of the total membership, 11,249 come from the 50 states of the United States and 1339 come from outside the United States. Approximately 30 percent of the members are women. The proportion of women has risen steadily over the last decade. The growth of the ASA is indicated by a membership of 115 in 1906, the year of founding, to membership of 12,588 in 1981.

Regional associations are part of the contact and communication pattern and often represent the first professional experience of the young scholar. Regional meetings are smaller, the competition for acceptance of papers is less intense. This is a good place for the young scholar to start becoming a professional. There are associations in every region; their names are listed in section 5.D.7.

ANNUAL MEETINGS HELD BY VARIOUS SOCIOLOGICAL AND KINDRED SOCIETIES WITH COMMON SECTION TOPICS IN SOCIOLOGY, PSYCHOLOGY, AND ANTHROPOLOGY

5.D.7

For information about annual meetings of the American Sociological Association and the other sociological societies write:

American Sociological Association
1722 N Street, N.W.
Washington, DC 20036
Telephone: 202/833-3410

Meetings of the American Sociological Association:

1982	San Francisco Hilton Hotel	Sept. 6–10
1983	Detroit Plaza Hotel	Aug. 31–Sept. 4
1984	San Antonio Convention Center	Aug. 27–31
1985	Washington, D.C., Hilton Hotel	Aug. 26–30

Other major sociological associations:

American Catholic Sociological Society
District of Columbia Sociological Society
Eastern Sociological Society
International Sociological Association
Institut International de Sociologie
Midwest Sociological Society
North Central Sociological Association
Pacific Sociological Association
Rural Sociological Society
Society for the Study of Social Problems
Southern Sociological Society
Southwestern Sociological Association

Annual meetings held by kindred social science and allied societies:

American Anthropological Association. Executive Offices, American Anthropological Association, 1703 New Hampshire Ave. N.W. Washington, D.C. 20009.

American Association for the Advancement of Science. American Association for the Advancement of Science, 1515 Massachusetts Avenue, N.W., Washington, DC 20005.

American Political Science Association. American Political Science Association, 1527 New Hampshire Avenue, N.W., Washington, DC 20036.

American Psychological Association. American Psychological Association, 1200 17th Street, N.W., Washington, DC 20036.

American Public Health Association. American Public Health Association, Inc., 1015 15th Street N.W., Washington, DC 20005.

American Statistical Association. Executive Director, American Statistical Association, 806 15th Street N.W., Suite 640, Washington, DC 20005.

Canadian Sociology and Anthropology Association. Canadian Sociology and Anthropology Association, Postal Box 878, Montreal, P.Q., Canada.

Population Association of America. Population Association of America, P.O. Box 14182, Benjamin Franklin Station, Washington, DC 20044.

Annual sociological meetings are commonly organized in sections around the following topics:

METHODOLOGY AND RESEARCH TECHNOLOGY
  Methodology (Social Science and Behavioral)
  Research Technology
  Statistical Methods
SOCIOLOGY: HISTORY AND THEORY
  Of Professional Interest
  History and Present State of Sociology
  Theories, Ideas and Systems
SOCIAL PSYCHOLOGY
  Personality and Culture
  Interaction Within (Small) Groups
  Leadership
GROUP INTERACTIONS
  Interaction Between (Large) Groups (Race Relations, Group Relations, etc.)
CULTURE AND SOCIAL STRUCTURE
  Social Organization
  Culture (Evolution)
  Social Anthropology (and Ethnology)
COMPLEX ORGANIZATIONS (MANAGEMENT)
  Industrial Sociology (Labor)
  Military Sociology
  Bureaucratic Structures
SOCIAL CHANGE AND ECONOMIC DEVELOPMENT
  Social Change and Economic Development

Market Structures and Consumer Behavior
MASS PHENOMENA
  Social Movements
  Public Opinion
  Communication
  Collective Behavior
  Sociology of Leisure
  Mass Culture
POLITICAL INTERACTIONS
  Interactions Between Societies, Nations and States
  Political Sociology
SOCIAL DIFFERENTIATION
  Social Stratification
  Sociology of Occupations and Professions
RURAL SOCIOLOGY AND AGRICULTURAL ECONOMICS
  Rural Sociology (Village, Agriculture)
URBAN STRUCTURES AND ECOLOGY
  Urban Sociology and Ecology
SOCIOLOGY OF THE ARTS
  Sociology of Language and Literature
  Sociology of Art (Creative and Performing)
SOCIOLOGY OF EDUCATION
  Sociology of Education
SOCIOLOGY OF RELIGION
  Sociology of Religion

SOCIAL CONTROL
  Sociology of Law
  Penology and Correctional Problems

SOCIOLOGY OF SCIENCE
  Sociology of Science and Technology

DEMOGRAPHY AND HUMAN
BIOLOGY
  Demography (Population Study)
  Human Biology

THE FAMILY AND
SOCIALIZATION
  Sociology of the Child and Socialization
  Adolescence and Youth
  Sociology of Sexual Behavior
  Sociology of the Family

SOCIOLOGY OF HEALTH AND
MEDICINE
  Sociology of Medicine (Public Health)
  Social Psychiatry (Mental Health)

SOCIAL PROBLEMS AND SOCIAL
WELFARE
  Social Gerontology
  Social Disorganization (Crime)
  Applied Sociology (Social Work)
  Delinquency

SOCIOLOGY OF KNOWLEDGE
  Sociology of Knowledge
  History of Ideas

COMMUNITY DEVELOPMENT
  Sociology of Communities and Regions

PLANNING, FORECASTING, AND
SPECULATION
  Planning, Forecasting, and Speculation

Meetings of the International Sociological Association are developed around 34 research committee sections. These divisions of interest represent a good statement of what modern sociologists are doing around the world.

01 Armed Forces and Society
02 Aspirations, Needs and Development
03 Community Research
04 Sociology of Education
05 Ethnic, Race and Minority Relations
06 Family Research
07 Futures Research
08 History of Sociology
09 Innovative Processes in Social Change
10 Sociology of International Relations
11 Sociology of Aging
12 Sociology of Law
13 Sociology of Leisure
14 Sociology of Mass Communications
15 Sociology of Medicine
16 Sociology of National Movements and Imperialism
17 Sociology of Organization
18 Political Sociology
19 Sociology of Poverty, Social Welfare and Social Policy
20 Sociology of Mental Health
21 Regional and Urban Development
22 Sociology of Religion
23 Sociology of Science
24 Social Ecology
25 Sociolinguistics
26 Sociotechnics
27 Sociology of Sport
28 Social Stratification
29 Deviance and Social Control
30 Sociology of Work

31   Sociology of Migration
32   Sex Roles in Society
33   Logic and Methodology in Sociology
34   Sociology of Youth

A series of sociological studies has recently been sponsored by the International Sociological Association (ISA). The series represents a collection of outstanding and original research in sociology that has emerged from presentations of World Congresses of Sociology held in Toronto (1974) and Uppsala (1978). They provide a forum for the intellectual exchange among internationally respected sociologists and demonstrate the intellectual frontiers, disciplinary challenges, and professional controversies with international perspectives. The Studies in International Sociology are published by Sage Publications, Inc., 275 South Beverly Drive, Beverly Hills, CA 90212. The current list includes:

Crisis and Contention in Sociology, edited by Tom Bottomore
The Military and the Problem of Legitimacy, edited by Gwyn Harries-Jenkins and Jacques van Doorn
Sociological Praxis, Current Roles and Settings, edited by Elisabeth Crawford and Stein Rokkan
Internal Migration: The New World and the Third World, edited by Anthony H. Richmond and Daniel Kubat
The Intelligentsia and the Intellectuals: Theory, Method and Case Study, edited by Aleksander Geila
Power and Control: Social Structures and Their Transformation, edited by Tom R. Burns and Walter Buckley
Beyond the Nuclear Family Model: Cross-Cultural Perspectives, edited by Luis Lenero-Otero
Scientific Technological Revolution: Social Aspects, by R. Dahrendorf et al.
Power, Paradigms, and Community Research, edited by Roland J. Liebert and Allen W. Imershein
Work and Technology, edited by Marie R. Haug and Jacques Dofny
Education in a Changing Society, edited by Antonina Kloskowska and Guido Martinotti
Organization and Environment: Theory, Issues and Reality, edited by Lucien Karpik
Disasters: Theory and Research, edited by E. L. Quarantelli
Social Policy and Sex Roles, edited by Jean Lipman-Blumen and Jessie Bernard
The Social Ecology of Change: From Equilibrium to Development, edited by Zdravko Mlinar and Henry Teune
Identity and Religion: International, Cross-Cultural Approaches, edited by Hans Mol

COMMON SECTION TOPICS FOR PSYCHOLOGY AND ANTHROPOLOGY AT ANNUAL MEETINGS*

PSYCHOLOGY

Clinical Psychology	Group therapy
Behavior problems	Individual diagnosis
Community mental health	Mental deficiency
Crime and delinquency	Objective tests
Experimental psychopathology	Projective techniques

* The classification shown is used by the National Science Foundation in its Register of Social Scientists.

Psychotherapy
Speech pathology
Counseling and Guidance
  Educational counseling
  Nondirective therapy
  Personal adjustment
  Rehabilitation
  Vocational counseling
Developmental Psychology
  Childhood and adolescence
  Infancy
  Maturity and old age
  Nursery and pre-school
Personality
  Development
  Measurement
  Personality and body
  Personality and learning
  Personality and perception
  Personality theory
  Structure and dynamics
School Psychology
  Anthropological linguistics
  Physical anthropology
  Social/Cultural anthropology
Specialities
  Anthropological folklore
  Cultural ecology
Educational Psychology
  Educational measurement
  Programmed learning
  School adjustment
  School learning

Special education
Student personnel
Teacher personnel
Engineering Psychology
General Psychology
  History and biography
  Theory and systems
Industrial and Personnel Psychology
  Employee and executive training and
    development
  Employee morale and attitudes
  Job analysis and position classification
  Labor-management relations
  Market research, advertising
  Organizational behavior
  Performance evaluation, criterion de-
    velopment
  Recruiting, selection, placement
  Safety research and training
  Salary and pay plans

ANTHROPOLOGY
Major Divisions
  Archeology
  Ethnology
  History of anthropology
  Methodology
  Economic anthropology
  Ethnomusicology
  Human paleontology
  Museology
  Primatology
  Psychological anthropology

GUIDE TO JOURNALS SPONSORED BY THE AMERICAN SOCIOLOGICAL ASSOCIATION

5.D.8

American Sociological Review is the official journal of the American Sociological Association publishing articles of major concern to social scientists. New trends and developments in theory and research are reported. Comments from readers and authors are printed relevant to articles previously published. The *Review* is sent to all members and is the journal most widely read by sociologists. Bimonthly.

Social Psychology Quarterly is a journal of research in social psychology. It is genuinely interdisciplinary in the publication of works by both sociologists and psychologists. Quarterly. Formerly called *Sociometry*.

Contemporary Sociology: A Journal of Reviews. This journal is devoted entirely to book reviews and is designed to give new thrust and style to book reviewing. Besides reviews of specific books it features survey essays, symposium essays, review essays, and letters. Bimonthly.

The American Sociologist contains major articles analyzing sociology as a profession and as a discipline. Included are reports on standards and practices in teaching, research, publication, and the application of sociological knowledge. Short notes and letters are accepted. Quarterly.

Journal of Health and Social Behavior is distinctive for a sociological approach to the definition and analysis of problems bearing on human welfare. Articles range from drugs and smoking to health care organizations and costs, professional and nonprofessional role conflicts, and various topics related to women. Bimonthly.

Sociology of Education is a forum for educators and social scientists seeking to advance sociological knowledge about education. The journal serves as a significant medium for the application of this knowledge to major issues of educational policy and practice. Quarterly.

Other Important Publications Issued Regularly

ASA Footnotes is the organ for the official reports and proceedings of the Association. It invites opinion on such matters as the state of undergraduate education, the future employment of sociologists, the status of women and minorities in sociology, the linkage of sociology to social policy, alternative modes of graduate training, broadening the world perspective of American sociology, and adding to the knowledge base of the discipline.

Arnold Rose Monograph Series provides an opportunity for members and student members of the ASA to publish short research monographs (100–300 typed pages) in any subject matter field in sociology that normally is beyond the scope of publication in regular academic journals. Numerous volumes have been published since its establishment in 1968.

Employment Bulletin is published monthly and contains current position vacancies.

Annual Review of Sociology summarizes progress of development in various fields, of sociology. Established in 1975.

ASA-Sponsored Publications Available from Other Sources

The following publications must be ordered directly from the publishers; do *not* send orders or payments to the ASA.

Sociological Methodology. Vols. 1970–77, 1978–79, and 1980. Publisher: Jossey-Bass, Inc., 433 California Street, San Francisco, CA 94104.

Issues and Trends Series. The Formal Organization, edited by Richard H. Hall; *Neighborhood and Ghetto,* edited by Scott Greer and Ann Lennarson Greer. Publisher: Basic Books, Inc., 10 East 53 Street, New York, NY 10022.

Social Policy and Sociology, edited by N. J. Damerath III, Karl F. Schuessler, and Otto N. Larsen. Publisher: Academic Press, 111 Fifth Avenue, New York, NY 10003.

Sociology and the Public Policy: The Case of the Presidential Commissions, edited by Mirra Komarovsky. Publisher: Elsevier Scientific Publishing Company, Inc., 52 Vanderbilt Avenue, New York, NY 10017.

Sociology and Rehabilitation, edited by Marvin E. Sussman. Publisher: University Microfilms, Books Editorial Department, 300 North Zeeb Road, Ann Arbor, MI 48106.

Presidential Series

The Presidential Series is an annual publication of addresses and other papers from the annual meetings of the American Sociological Association. The series is usually under the editorship of the current president of the Association. The series is published by The Free Press, 866 Third Avenue, New York, NY 10022. Listed here are recent issues:

Approaches to the Study of Social Structure, edited by Peter M. Blau
Conflict and Dissensus, edited by Lewis A. Coser and Otto N. Larsen
Major Social Issues: A Multidisciplinary View, edited by J. Milton Yinger
Societal Growth: Processes and Implications, edited by Amos H. Hawley
Sociological Theory and Research: A Critical Approach, edited by Hubert M. Blalock

ASA Publications

The list that follows includes publications of professional interest to sociologists and students majoring in sociology. All are available from the American Sociological Association, 1722 N. Street, N.W., Washington, DC 20036.

Majoring in Sociology: A Guide for Students
Careers in Sociology
Guidelines for Initial Appointments in Sociology
Sociologists in Non-Academic Employment
Report: Status of Women in Sociology, 1934–1977
Federal Funding Programs for Social Scientists
Directory of Members, 1980
Directory of Departments of Sociology, 1980
Guide to Graduate Departments of Sociology, 1980
Annual Meeting Proceedings

GUIDE TO JOURNALS SPONSORED BY THE AMERICAN PSYCHOLOGICAL ASSOCIATION

5.D.9

American Psychologist, the official journal of the American Psychological Association, publishes the official papers of the Association and substantive articles on psychology. Monthly.

Contemporary Psychology is a journal of reviews—critical reviews of books, films, and other material in the field of psychology. Monthly.

Journal of Abnormal Psychology is devoted to basic research and theory in the broad area of abnormal behavior. Bimonthly.

Journal of Applied Psychology gives primary consideration to original quantitative investigations of value to those people interested in the following broad areas: personnel research; industrial working conditions, research on opinion and morale factors; job analysis and classification research; marketing and advertising research; vocational and educational prognosis, diagnosis, and guidance at the secondary and college levels. Bimonthly.

Journal of Comparative and Physiological Psychology publishes original research reports in the field of comparative and physiological psychology, including animal learning, conditioning, and sensory processes. Bimonthly, 2 vols. per year.

Journal of Consulting and Clinical Psychology is devoted to the area of clinical psychology, both child and adult. Bimonthly.

Journal of Counseling Psychology serves as a primary publication medium for research on counseling theory and practice.

Journal of Educational Psychology publishes original investigations and theoretical papers dealing with problems of learning and teaching, and with the psychological development, relationships, and adjustment of the individual. Monthly, 3 vols. per year.

Journal of Personality and Social Psychology is devoted to basic research and theory in the broad areas of social interaction and group processes. Specifically, it deals with interpersonal perception and attitude change, the psychological aspects of formal social systems and less structured collective phenomena, the socialization process at both child and adult levels, social motivation and personality dynamics, the structure of personality, and the relation of personality to group process and social systems. Monthly, 3 vols. per year.

Psychological Abstracts publishes concise abstracts of the world's literature in psychology and pertinent allied subjects. All titles and abstracts of foreign material are translated into English. Monthly.

Psychological Bulletin is concerned with research reviews and methodological contributions in the field of psychology. One of the principal functions of this journal is to publish critical, evaluative summaries of research. The methodological articles are directed toward people who might or do make practical use of such information, and are intended to bridge the gap between the technical statistician and the typical research psychologist. Articles feature the application of new methodology as well as the creative application of more familiar methodology. Monthly, 2 vols. per year.

Psychological Review is the major psychological journal of articles of theoretical significance to any area of scientific endeavor in psychology. Bimonthly.

5.D.10   **GUIDE TO MAJOR JOURNALS IN POLITICAL SCIENCE AND PUBLIC ADMINISTRATION**

American Political Science Review. American Political Science Association, 1527 New Hampshire Avenue, N.W., Washington, DC 20036.

Official journal of the American Political Science Association. Offers scientific studies, essays, bibliographies, and news and notes on contemporary matters in the profession. Founded 1903.

Political Science Quarterly. Academy of Political Science, Fayerweather Hall, Columbia University, New York, NY 10027.

Studies in the field of political science and economics of interest to scholars and laymen. Founded 1886.

Annals of the American Academy of Political and Social Science, 3397 Chestnut Street, Philadelphia, PA 19104.

Founded 1890.

Journal of Politics. Southern Political Science Association, University of Florida, Gainesville, FL 32601.

Interpretative articles covering all of the various subfields of political science by leading United States and foreign scholars. Scholarly review of new publications. Founded 1938.

Midwest Journal of Political Science. Wayne State University Press, 5980 Cass Avenue, Detroit, MI 48202.

Scholarly publication of Midwest Conference of Political Science. Founded 1957.

Public Administration Review. American Society for Public Administration, 1225 Connecticut Ave., N.W., Washington, DC 20036.

Publishes material representative of all interests and opinions among practitioners, teachers, researchers, and students of public administration. Founded 1939. Bimonthly.

The Review of Politics. University of Notre Dame, Notre Dame, IN 46556.

Political theory, contemporary social movements, international relations, cultural developments, and politics. Founded 1939.

Foreign Affairs. Council on Foreign Relations, Inc., 58 East 68 Street, New York, NY 10021.

A nonpartisan review of current ideas and policies affecting United States relations in all parts of the world, including international, political, commercial, and business communities. Founded 1922.

Social Research. Graduate Faculty of New School for Social Research, 66 West 12 Street, New York, NY 10011.

International quarterly of political and social science. Founded 1934.

World Politics. Center of International Studies, Princeton University, Crown Hall, Princeton, NJ 08540.

Problems of international relations of a general and theoretical nature, emphasizing social change and employing multidisciplinary methods and concepts. Founded 1948.

Other journals to which political scientists contribute and read are the *Western Political Quarterly, Public Interest,* and *Commentary.* A great number of specialized journals exist.

GUIDE TO MAJOR JOURNALS IN ANTHROPOLOGY   *5.D.11*

There are many specialized fields and journals in anthropology to be found in physical anthropology, ethnology, archeology, and linguistics. The three journals of most general interest to social scientists generally are probably the following:

American Anthropologist. American Anthropological Association, 1530 P Street N.W., Washington, DC 20005.

Founded 1899.

Current Anthropology. University of Chicago Press, 5750 Ellis Avenue, Chicago, IL 60637.

Founded 1953.

Human Organization. Society for Applied Anthropology, Lafferty Hall, University of Kentucky, Lexington, KY 40506.

Founded 1941.

5.D.12 GUIDE TO MAJOR RESEARCH JOURNALS IN EDUCATION

Education represents a field of breadth and scope since it extends from nursery school to adult education and encompasses a wide variety of subject matter. The journals listed below are the research journals that have the broadest scope.

American Educational Research Journal
Journal of Experimental Education
Educational and Psychological Measurement
Journal of Educational Psychology
Review of Educational Research
Child Development
Journal of Educational Measurement

Other more specialized research journals include *Journal of Research in Science Teaching, American Journal of Mental Deficiency, Journal of Reading Behavior, Reading Research Quarterly, The Educational Psychologist.*

5.D.13 GUIDE TO MAJOR JOURNALS USED BY ORGANIZATIONAL AND BEHAVIORAL RESEARCHERS IN BUSINESS

Administrative Science Quarterly
Journal of Applied Psychology
Organizational Behavior and Human Performance
Academy of Management Journal
Organization and Administrative Sciences
Decision Sciences
Human Relations
Social Psychology Quarterly

5.D.14 GUIDE TO MAJOR JOURNALS USED BY JOURNALISM AND COMMUNICATION RESEARCHERS

Public Opinion Quarterly
Journalism Quarterly
Journal of Communication
Communication Research
Newspaper Research Journal

There are hundreds of journals in anthropology, economics, education, law, business, social work, etc. Directories of world journals include:

INTERNATIONAL COMMITTEE FOR SOCIAL SCIENCES: *Documentation in the Social Sciences: World List of Social Science Periodicals.* 5th ed. Paris: UNESCO, 1980.
The Standard Periodical Directory. 7th ed. New York: Oxbridge, 1980.

Knowledge Utilization

APPLIED SOCIOLOGY AND POLICY MAKING   *5.E.1*

Applied sociology has received greatly renewed interest because of the growth
of employment opportunities outside universities combined with a tight academic market. Moreover, over the past two decades social science has been
found to be increasingly useful in applied social science research in support
of social programs of a wide variety. Otto Larsen, director of Social and
Economic Sciences at the National Science Foundation, explains the role
of social scientists in policy making:

> Scientists do not make public policies, elected officials do. Research from social
> and behavioral research can and does inform the decision-making process through
> a variety of mechanisms. For example, the National Research Council of the Na-
> tional Academy of Sciences is regularly consulted for advice on policy matters.
> Its committees and panels draw heavily on the research of the social and behavioral
> sciences as they evaluate programs and deal with such concerns as energy, taxation,
> biomedical technologies, environmental monitoring, alcohol abuse, protection of
> individual privacy, aging, noise abatement, child development, and changes in fertil-
> ity and mortality. The same is true of the many Presidential Commissions such
> as those dealing with violence, obscenity, population, or crime. Organizations outside
> government also use social science data to inform and advise the policy process.
> For example, under the auspices of the Hoover Institution at Stanford University,
> a distinguished set of scholars, mainly economists and political scientists, provides
> a review and analysis of major domestic and international issues in a book, *The
> United States in the 1980's,* edited by Peter Duignan and Alvin Rabushka.[1]

Peter Rossi believes social science departments have a major opportunity
to serve as suppliers of social science expertise through bidding on applied
social science contracts. "As an organized discipline, we have to build linkages
to the applied social science world, apprising the contracting agencies and
the research industry that sociology has something to offer and to our own
colleagues and students that applied social research is a career that is exciting
and interesting."[2]

647

Writing as chairman of the Committee on Professional Opportunities in Applied Sociology (American Sociological Association), Howard E. Freeman points to the current status of applied sociology:

> Applied sociology has long roots in the discipline; certainly since the 1930's there have been numerous declarations by outstanding sociologists about the need to apply the findings of social research, conferences about the importance of applied work, and books documenting the utility of sociological studies. Further, applied sociology has been growing within the discipline as evidenced by the increase in extra university employment and career opportunities, possibilities for research support, and graduate training opportunities. The 1980 *Guide to Graduate Departments of Sociology* lists over 100 departments offering courses and special programs in applied sociology; some of the larger profit and non-profit research organizations employ more sociologists than many sociology departments; and Federal support for basic research is only a small fraction of current applied research funding.[3]

Notes

1. Otto Larsen "Need for Continuing Support for Social Sciences," *Footnotes of the American Sociological Association,* March 1981, p. 8.
2. *Footnotes,* August 1980, p. 20.
3. *Footnotes,* December 1980, p. 1. Cf. *Study Project on Social Research and Development,* vol. 1: *Study Project Report, The Federal Investment in Knowledge of Social Problems* (Washington, D.C.: National Academy of Sciences, 1978). See especially pp. 66–67 and the excellent bibliography.

Bibliography on Applied Sociology, Knowledge Utilization, and Policy Making

ABT, CLARK C., ed. *Perspectives on the Costs and Benefits of Applied Social Research.* Cambridge, Mass.: Abt Books, 1979.

> Over the last decade the United States has spent almost a billion dollars on applied social research. In this book, leading social researchers from government, academia, and the private research community examine the complex analytical problems and issues involved in effective cost-benefit measurement of their work.

ALLEN, T. HARRELL. *New Methods in Social Science Research, Policy Sciences and Futures Research.* New York: Praeger, 1978.

> Describes new methods of social science research suited to the analysis of complex problems. Argues that researchers have been relying on survey methods and that many new methods, which attack the whole system rather than its separate parts, are better suited to solving increasingly interrelated social issues. This approach is especially relevant to the fields of policy science and futures research. Case studies explain the methodologies.

ARROW, KENNETH; ABT, CLARK C.; and FITZSIMMONS, STEPHEN J., eds. *Applied Research for Social Policy: The United States and the Federal Republic of Germany Compared.* Cambridge, Mass.: Abt Books, 1979.

> A unique attempt on the part of leading German and American social scientists to exchange information, review major social science research efforts that have influenced political decision making in their countries, and define ways in which applied social research can contribute to better political decision making.

BRENNER, M. HARVEY. *Assessing the Contributions of the Social Sciences to Health.* Boulder, Colo.: Westview Press, 1980.

American Association for the Advancement of Science. AAAS selected symposium.

CHERNS, ALBERT. *Using the Social Sciences,* Boston: Routledge and Kegan Paul, 1979.

A collection of papers published over the past ten years that brings together the extraordinarily wide ranging contribution made by Albert Cherns to the study of the role of the social sciences in policy making.

DeNEAFVILLE, JUDITH INNES. *Social Indicators and Public Policy.* New York: Elsevier, 1975.

ETZIONI, AMATAI, ed. *Policy Research* Leiden: Brill, 1978.

Research papers and discussions of the application of the social sciences to policy.

HAVELOCK, RONALD G., et al. *Planning for Innovation Through Dissemination and Utilization of Knowledge.* Ann Arbor: Institute of Social Research, University of Michigan, 1969.

Provides an understanding of how knowledge is disseminated and utilized. Brings together the research and theory from over 1000 studies on the planning of change, the diffusion of innovations, and the transfer and utilization of scientific knowledge.

HOROWITZ, IRVING L. *Constructing Policy: Dialogues with Social Scientists in the National Political Arena.* New York: Praeger, 1979.

Perceptive, in-depth interviews with twelve of our nation's leading social science policy makers present insights into the ideological and intellectual stances of such important figures as Sar Levitan, Eli Ginsberg, Seymour Martin Lipset, and Frank Reissman. Thoughtful questions and comments by Dr. Horowitz bring forth each individual's premises, principles, expertise, orientation, and role, as well as wide-ranging discussions of his or her work, experiences, and views on historical events. From these interviews Dr. Horowitz ponders such areas of the social scientist policy-making process as expertise vs. political stance, success in government, and equity vs. equality.

————, and KATZ, JAMES E. *Social Science and Public Policy in the United States.* New York: Praeger, 1975.

A very worthwhile book about the interaction among social scientists, social science, public policy makers, and public policy in the United States.

JUDD, CHARLES M., and KENNY, DAVID A. *Estimating the Effects of Social Interventions.* New York: Cambridge University Press, 1981.

Methods for measuring the impact of social interventions of all sorts; the strengths and weaknesses of various research designs—experimental, quasi-experimental, and nonexperimental—with a systematic and critical review of statistical measures for analyzing data.

LEWIN, ARLE Y., and SHAKUN, MELVIN F. *Policy Sciences: Methodologies and Cases.* Oxford, England: Pergamon Press, 1976.

Presents a pragmatic, descriptive/normative methodology for policy analysis within which different disciplines can be integrated for policy analysis and formulation. Part 1 presents the framework within which components of policy science may be integrated and applied to real decision problems. Part 2 focuses on methodologies, and Part 3 presents a number of cases that apply methodologies to real-world problems. Designed as a text for courses in policy sciences and interorganizational decision making or for similar courses at the advanced undergraduate or graduate level, this book is also suitable as a basic reference for practicing policy scientists and policy makers.

LEWIS, MICHAEL. *Research in Social Problems and Policy: A Research Annual.* Greenwich, Conn.: JAI Press, 1979, 1981.

Presents original analyses of contemporary social issues and the policy responses they elicit. It is informed by an editorial philosophy which holds that the value of sociology must ultimately be measured by its power to provide an analytic basis for maximizing human serviceability in society. Each contribution was selected because it breaks new ground and promises to provide fresh premises for policy discourse. On the assumption that the nature of the problem to be studied should determine the method of its study, the papers appearing in this annual series will represent a variety of analytic approaches extant in contemporary society.

OLSEN, MARVIN E., and MICKLIN, MICHAEL. *Handbook of Applied Sociology, Frontiers of Contemporary Research.* New York: Praeger, 1981.

Five parts: Developing Applied Techniques, Improving Social Institutions, Reducing Social Inequities, Providing Human Services, and Ensuring Human Survival.

PRICE, RICHARD H., and POLITSER, PETER E. *Evaluation and Action in the Social Environment.* New York: Academic Press, 1980.

Begins with the presentation of a conceptual and methodological framework for doing evaluation and action research. Examples of evaluation and action strategies in a wide range of contexts are presented, including family settings, hospital settings, personal social networks, residential treatment settings, human service organizations, community groups, and architectural environments. Each chapter describes the relevant research literature, an analytical framework used to assess the setting, a rationale for translating the assessment into proposals for action, and a description of the evaluation method used to assess the impact of the change strategy. For further information, see section 4.E on Evaluation Research in this Handbook.

SAKS, MICHAEL J., and BARON, CHARLES H., eds. *The Use/Nonuse/Misuse of Applied Social Research in the Courts.* Cambridge, Mass.: Abt Books, 1980.

A significant step toward cooperation between the legal community and the social science community.

SCOTT, ROBERT A., and SHAW, ARNOLD. *Why Sociology Does Not Apply: A Study of the Use of Sociology in Public Policy.* N.Y.: Elsevier, 1979.

An analysis of problems in the application of sociology to public policy.

SEGALL, MARSHALL H. *Human Behavior and Public Policy: A Political Psychology.* Oxford, England: Pergamon Press, 1976.

Based on the conviction that existing knowledge of human behavior contains important lessons for policy makers, this book aims to demonstrate that important social and political implications are inherent in social psychological research findings. What social psychologists know, or know how to find out, is of crucial relevance to the real world. Knowledge as to why and under what conditions people behave as they do permits evaluation of social policy alternatives. Written primarily for undergraduates, the book contains illustrations of the implications of existing social psychological findings for such problems as intergroup relations, educational innovations, relations between the sexes, and the control of violence in a free society. The work contains most of what is included in a traditional social psychology course, but embeds it in a context of relevance.

Smithsonian Science Information Exchange. *Research Information Packages.* Washington, D.C.: Smithsonian Science Information Exchange, 1980.

The exchange is the national registry for providing current research information in all the sciences, including sociology, political science, and economics. Contains up-to-date knowledge about research in progress. Each package is a collection of one-page descriptions of social science projects relevant to the title. Classifications of packages include Criminology, Environmental Sociology, Medical Sociology, Political Economy of World Systems, Racial and Cultural Minorities, Rural Sociology, Social Indicators, Social Change, Social Psychology, Social Sciences Management and Methodology, Social Welfare, Sociology of Population, and Urban Sociology.

Study Project on Social Research and Development. *Assembly of Behavioral and Social Sciences.* 6 vols. Vol. 1, *Knowledge and Policy: The Uncertain Connection;* vol. 2, *The Funding of Social Knowledge Production and Application: A Survey of Federal Agencies;* vol. 3, *The Uses of Basic Research: Case Studies in Social Science;* vol. 4, *Studies in the Management of Social R&D: Selected Issues;* vol. 5, *Case Studies in the Management of Social R&D: Selected Policy Areas;* vol. 6, *Understanding Crime.* Washington, D.C.: National Academy of Sciences, 1977–80.

All of these volumes are concerned with social science and policy relevance. They explore means of improving the linkage between social research and public policy.

TROPMAN, JOHN E.; DLUHY, MILAN; VASEY, WAYNE; and CROXTON, TOM A., eds. *Strategic Perspectives in Social Policy.* Oxford, England: Pergamon Press, 1976.

The development of social policy by administrators requires an assessment of goals, elements of social change, and the politics of policy making. Emphasis is on the process of intervention in developing a policy for practical ends. Strategic points of intervention within the policy system are examined from the point of view of policy makers, policy conceptualizers, and students of government. Included are guides for both social policy and social program analyses of interest to students of public administration, policy science, social work, urban and regional planning, and political science.

WILDAVSKY, AARON. *Speaking Truth to Power: The Art and Craft of Policy Analysis.* Boston: Little, Brown, 1979.

A political scientist describes policy analysis in terms of political processes and procedures.

CAREERS FOR SOCIOLOGY DEGREE HOLDERS IN ACADEMIC AND NONACADEMIC MARKETS

5.E.2

Each of the three degrees in sociology—the B.A., the M.A., and the Ph.D.— offers a varying range of opportunities. Usually the Ph.D. degree is required for full-time teaching in a college or university. No degree holders can teach in public elementary or secondary schools without a degree in education and state certification.

Careers for Students with a B.A. Degree

The B.A. is not considered a professional degree in any of the social studies (history, political science, economics, human geography, social psychology, or social anthropology). The B.A. holder in sociology usually seeks entry-level jobs in social work; in nonprofit or religious organizations; in federal, local, or state government; or in business and industry. The American Sociological Association states in Careers in Sociology:

> There are still very few employers who are looking for sociology BA's in the same sense in which they might look for BA's in engineering, nursing, accounting, etc. Sociology BA's will often find themselves competing with other liberal arts students who have majored in English, history, psychology, etc. Here, a strong undergraduate program in sociology can conceivably produce a competitive advantage. For example, students interested in business careers after the BA might emphasize courses in industrial sociology and complex organization; students seeking work with public welfare agencies might concentrate their course work in areas such as stratification, race and ethnic relations, sociology of the family, and urban sociology.
>
> Regardless of one's special interests, many students would do well to emphasize research methods and statistics. It is precisely these courses that are cited as most valuable by persons already employed in non-academic jobs who are asked to reconsider their education with the wisdom of hindsight. Statistics is not as difficult as many students fear and it often provides the most valuable and marketable career skills. This is especially true for the student who plans to stop with the BA.[1]

Careers for Students Who Hold the M.A. Degree

The holder of an M.A. or M.S. degree in sociology often teaches in a junior or other two-year college. Thus educational background offers occupations with public agencies and private businesses. The M.A. is often sought for technical skill in social research.

Careers for Students Who Hold the Ph.D. Degree

The "best" jobs usually go to the holder of a Ph.D. in sociology. Teaching in the university is possible at undergraduate and graduate levels. Research and administration jobs at higher levels become available as experience is gained and competence is demonstrated. (This can be seen in table 3, which reports on the occupations of sociologists with earned doctorates.)

ROLES OF ACADEMIC AND NONACADEMIC MARKETS

The professional sociologist with a Ph.D. has usually trained for college or university teaching and hopes to find opportunity for his own research as a part of his total responsibilities. In fact, two out of three Ph.D.s (68.5 percent, according to table 3) do just that. Research and its publication actually becomes obligatory for tenure and promotions at major universities.

With teaching opportunities becoming increasingly restricted, the nonacademic market is an ever more important outlet. It is the nonacademic market that has provided most of the jobs for B.A. and M.A. degree holders in sociology. In terms of number, this is the major market. For this reason, the remainder of this section is devoted to it. A simple graph would depict

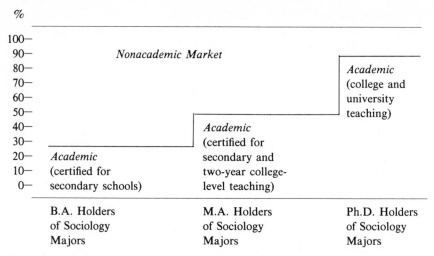

Figure 1 *The Academic and Nonacademic Markets for Sociology Degree Holders*

the relationship between the academic and nonacademic markets for the three degree holders as shown in figure 1.

Education That Facilitates Entry into the Nonacademic Market

1. *Master existing knowledge.* Acquire a substantial store of knowledge about social problems and theories. This is the resource that will provide your best source for attacking problems. Many nonacademic researchers are not scholars; some are little more than technicians. The majority of administrators in nonacademic institutions have limited opportunities to do systematic reading in the broad field of social knowledge. Someone who is able to provide needed knowledge may have an immediate value. The three degree holders—of the A.B., M.A., and Ph.D.— have opportunities for more important responsibilities.
2. Do everything possible to *improve your basic writing and quantitative skills.* Seeking opportunities to write papers for credit. Select courses in statistics and computer science that can give you marketable skills for many entry-level positions.
3. *Consider a double major* and interdisciplinary programs such as sociology and communications (or economics, urban planning, statistics, computer science, journalism, or business administration).
4. *Seek opportunities for student-originated research* at the undergraduate level and research support at the graduate level.
5. *Locate opportunities for internships and work experience.* Make your summer and college work count. If at all possible, find work that can be used later as "good experience for an entry-level job."
6. *Develop an understanding of the job market* in your college town as well as your home community. Talk with professionals about careers and technical expertise such as writing and editorial skills, experience in computer programming, statistical knowledge, graphic skills, and interviewing.
7. Remember, regardless of whether your degree is a B.A., M.A., or Ph.D., the nonacademic market has *not* been structured to fit your social science major. You must fit your major study to the market under whatever name you find a job related to your knowledge and skills.

Understanding the Nonacademic Job Market

A survey made in the mid-1970s of nonacademic sociologists showed that most of them were in research or administration. Table 1 shows the main work activity of men and women. The jobs include research, administration, consultation, program planning, writing and editing, counseling, and computer programming. Table 2 locates employers and lists them in order of frequency as nonprofit organizations, federal government, state or local government, self-employed, business and industry, and religious organizations.[2]

In early 1978 Doris Wilkinson of Howard University sought information from sociologists in business, industry, and government on positions held and tasks performed. Of those responding ($N = 191$), the majority held administrative positions (e.g., program manager, research director, chief of law enforcement); 46 percent of the males ($N = 133$) and nearly 30 percent of the females ($N = 58$) were in this general category. (It may be noted that this gives females a marked increase over the 14.3 percent shown in the 1975 report.)

The agencies in which these sociologists were employed as administrators/ managers included hospitals and health systems agencies, research councils, housing organizations, departments of corrections, state planning bureaus, and the federal government. The occupational group with the second largest number of respondents (males, 19.5 percent and females 36.3 percent) was that of researcher/research assistant (e.g., research analyst, public health analyst, behavioral research associate). Of those who held positions as sociologists, 12 percent were females and 4 percent were males. All others in the survey held job titles such as statistician/statistical analyst, consultant, Fellow, planner, clinical counselor, project director, equal opportunity specialist, higher education organizer, minister, community development specialist, consultant, and assistant representative to the U.N.

It should be noted here that not all respondents to this survey held doctorates.[3]

A third survey, made by the National Research Council, reveals the relationship of academic to nonacademic sociologists in 1977. In this survey,

Table 1   *Main Work Activity of Sociologists in Nonacademic Employment, 1975*

Nature of work	Total Frequency	%	Females Frequency	%	Males Frequency	%
Research	63	52.5	18	64.3	44	48.9
Administration	26	21.7	4	14.3	22	24.4
Consultation	11	9.2	3	10.7	7	7.8
Program planning	8	6.7	2	7.1	6	6.7
Writing and editing	6	5.0	1	3.6	5	5.6
Counseling	3	2.5	0	0.0	3	3.3
Training or teaching	0	0.0	0	0.0	0	0.0
Computer program-ming	1	.8	0	0.0	1	1.1
Public relations	0	0.0	0	0.0	0	0.0
Other	2	1.7	0	0.0	2	2.2
No information	1		3			
Totals	121		28		90	

Table 2 *Employers of Sociologists in Nonacademic Employment, 1975*

Employers	Total Frequency	%	Females Frequency	%	Males Frequency	%
Nonprofit organization (nonreligious)	51	42.5	15	53.6	36	40.0
Federal government agency	33	27.5	5	17.9	27	30.0
State, local government agency	13	10.8	2	7.1	10	11.1
Self-employed	11	9.2	3	10.7	8	8.9
Business and industry	6	5.0	1	3.6	5	5.6
Religious organization	4	3.3	1	3.6	3	3.3
Nonprofit organization, business and industry	2	1.7	1	3.6	1	1.1
No information	1		3			
Totals	121		28		90	

Table 3 *Primary Work Activities of Sociologists with Earned Doctorates, 1977*

Position	N	%
Management or administrative, R&D	210	2.7
Management or administrative, other than R&D	162	2.1
Management or administrative both	57	.7
Basic research	540	6.8
Applied research	718	9.1
Teaching	5409	68.5
Writing, editing	78	1.0
Consulting	37	.5
Professional services	64	.8
No report	625	7.9

Source: Report of National Research Council.

68.5 percent of sociologists with earned doctorates were in teaching, and 31.5 percent were in nonacademic positions.[4]

According to a 1978 report of the National Research Council, holders of doctorates are increasingly taking nonfaculty research positions. The single largest area of employment outside of teaching is applied research. (Research moneys are increasingly being shunted from basic research to applied research by federal agencies.) Note also that 5.5 percent of doctorate holders are in administration, management or management of research or operations positions where supervisory skills are needed. Most of the high-paying jobs are found in this classification.

Getting In and Staying In

Put your skills front and center. For the nonacademic market it is not sufficient to simply itemize areas of specialization. Employers want to know, What can a sociologist do? Applicants for positions must specify skills beyond those of subject-matter expertise. In the Wilkinson survey of nonacademic sociologists, the following skills were listed by practitioners:

advising, academic
advertising
community service
computer programming
consulting
counseling
curricula development
designing & conducting training pro-
    grams
developing & administering educational
    programs

directing & implementing research
    projects
editing
market research
policy administration & analysis
program evaluation
providing informed testimony
public opinion polling
reviewing grant proposals
survey design & research
technical writing
testing & measurement
urban planning[5]

Job Titles for Sociology Trainees

An academic degree holder enters the nonacademic market as an innocent. No matter the degree held, there is much to learn about the goals of the department and the distinctive cultural world in which the work is set.

A number of factors will determine whether you get the particular job you want. These factors include, among others, demand for applicant's skills and training, number of persons applying for the same position, qualifications of applicant, and applicant's success in the interviewing session. The list that follows is of selected positions for which the study of sociology, supplemented with relevant training, is useful. Most of the occupational titles are found in nonacademic outlets—business, industry, government—and do not carry the label "sociologist." Many of these jobs require advanced training and previous work experience. Each job seeker must inventory his or her skills objectively.

Admission Counselor/Director of Ad-
    missions
Affirmative Action Coordinator
Alumni Relations Coordinator
Audiovisual Supervisor/Specialist
Bank Teller
Book Salesperson
Boy Scouts Professional Worker
Camp Counselor
Card Punch Operator
College Placement Officer
Community Planner
Computer Aide/Programmer
Computer Analyst/Computer Specialist
Correctional Officer
Correctional Program Assistant
Counselor (alcoholism, career, drug
    abuse, handicapped)
Day Care Worker
Demographer
Department Store Manager
Editor/Editorial Assistant

Educational Therapist/Educational
    Therapy Assistant
Employment Counselor/Interviewer
Environmental Analyst/Planner
Equal Opportunity Specialist (Employ-
    ment)
Foreign Service Worker
Forestry Aide/Environmental Specialist
Girl Scouts Professional Worker
Grants Officer or Assistant
Group Worker (in social service agency
    or hospital)
Guidance Counselor
Health Planner
Hospital Aide/Hospital Director
Journalist/Reporter
Key Punch Operator
Labor Relations Specialist
Legal Assistant
Management Trainee (department stores
    and corporations have training pro-
    grams)

Marketing Researcher/Assistant
Medical Records Librarian/Medical
  Records Administrator/Assistant
Park & Recreation Program
  Planner
Peace Corp Volunteer
Personnel Management/Personnel Rela-
  tions Assistant
Photographer
Police Officer
Policy Analyst/Policy Evaluator
Probation Officer
Proofreader[6]
Program Analyst
Public Information Specialist
Public Relations Supervisor

Recreation Director/Aide
Red Cross Worker
Registrar
Rehabilitation Counselor
Research Analyst/Assistant
Resident Director
Salesperson (pharmaceutical, computer,
  etc.)
Social Science Analyst
Social Science Research Assistant
Social Service Worker or Aide
Statistician/Statistical Assistant
Urban Planner/Urban Analyst
Vocational Development Specialist
Writer/Editor
Writing Skills Teacher

The author has had the following nonacademic titles in his career: (1) *Supervisor of Supervisory Training* (Sperry Gyroscope Co.); (2) *Senior Economist and Policy Appraisal Specialist* (National War Labor Board); (3) *Labor Relations Consultant* (Fisher Flouring Mills, Boeing, and others); (4) *Supervisory Trainer Consultant* (Fort Benjamin Harrison Army Post, Wright Patterson Air Force Base, U.S. Chamber of Commerce, Yale University, and others); (5) *Labor Arbitrator* (American Arbitration Association, State of Indiana, Hoover Vacuum Sweeper Co., American Smelting and Refining Co., Indiana State Reformatory, and others); (6) *Wage Stabilization Commissioner* (Pacific Region); (7) *Labor Mediator* (Indiana Employment Relations Board); (8) *Public Relations Advisor* (American Public Relations Association). Of these positions, only two were full-time; all the others were practiced in tandem with full-time university teaching. They are cited here to call attention to the job variety. Note that not one job carries the title *Sociologist,* although my specialized area is industrial sociology.

Finding Where the Jobs Are

In the early stages of a career the applicant may have to search hard and long for jobs. Later, jobs may come to the experienced worker. It is entirely possible that the first job is the only one that must be seriously searched. For the young worker anxious for employment this is little consolation, but people are willing to help. The applicant must find these helpers and find the available jobs. What follows are some step-by-step hints.

Step 1. Use the resources of your college's sociology department. Provide faculty members with good résumés and ask their counsel.

Step 2. Use your college's employment office. Find out which interviewers are coming to the college and talk with as many as possible.

Step 3. Attend the annual meetings of your Regional Sociological Society and the American Sociological Association. All have employment services where registrants seeking jobs and employers seeking applicants can get together. The ASA has a nonacademic roster. Ask to see this, and use employed sociologists to assist you in locating jobs and arranging interviews. Try to get face-to-face contact with possible employers. Employers want to see you in person!

Step 4. Utilize any relevant job bank, information or employment services. Suggested options:

1. *Evaluation Research Society Job Bank.* The Society has established a job bank for individuals seeking new positions and employers looking for qualified job applicants in the fields of program evaluation, evaluation research, and applied social research. For further information, contact Dr. Ann Majchrzak, Chair, Employment Committee, Evaluation Research Society, c/o Westat, Inc., 11600 Nebel Street, Rockville, MD 20854. Phone: (301) 881-5310, ext. 245.

2. *Federal Employment Information Services of the U.S. Civil Service.* The Civil Service Commission offers federal employment information through a nationwide network of Federal Job Information Centers. For a directory of these centers, as well as for job announcements, write or phone the Civil Service Office in your area. The address for the U.S. Civil Service Commission in the District of Columbia is 1900 E Street, N.W., Washington, DC 20415.

3. *Register for International Service in Education* (RISE) is a computer-based referral service that matches teaching, research, and consulting assignments in other countries to the qualifications and interests of registered scholars. RISE is administered by the Institute of International Education (IIE). A $35 registration fee keeps your application active for two years. For more detailed information and registration forms, write RISE, Institute of International Education, 809 United Nations Plaza, New York, NY 10017.

4. *Occupational Outlook Handbook,* 1980–81 (Washington, D.C.: Bureau of Labor Statistics). Copies may be ordered from the U.S. Superintendent of Documents, Dept. 34, U.S. Government Printing Office, Washington, DC 20402. It provides excellent coverage of current occupational opportunities.

5. *Alternative Careers for Academics Bulletin.* According to Department of Labor projections, between 1972 and 1985, about 583,000 Ph.D.s will be granted in all fields. But 396,000 of these degree holders will not find academic employment. The *Alternative Careers Bulletin* is a monthly periodical that discusses openings suitable for professionals with advanced degrees. For example, a typical issue dealt with political action to create new jobs, discussed different government positions with hundreds of openings annually, described a career for which most sociologists would be eligible and in which experienced people average $44,000 a year, told where to apply for some excellent overseas posts, and suggested practical ways to start your own consulting or other business. Write: Creative Career Services, A Division of Intellect Corp., P. O. Box 6405-G2, Mobile, AL 36606.

6. Consult Ronald B. Uleck, *Social and Behavioral Sciences Jobs Handbook,* 1979. Write: R. B. Uleck, Box 3069, Diamond Farms Branch, Gaithersburg, MD 20760. Included in the book are:

   a. A Periodicals Matrix showing periodicals that contain job listings for the social and behavioral sciences. There is a description of each periodical stating address and type of job listings.

   b. A list of city newspapers with circulations over 100,000 that are the focus of activity in a state. Addresses are given.

   c. Placement services with addresses and statements of services rendered.

   d. Federal agencies with responsibility for activities in the social and behavioral sciences classified by subject focus: community development, culture and cultural exchange programs, etc. State and local agencies are also listed with their addresses.

    e. Consulting firms set out and classified by function.

    f. A description of professional help and various career guides.

7. *Consider a private employment agency.* Agencies work for you and in many cases charge a fee only if they find you a job. Make sure that you use an agency that has a good record for results and integrity.

8. *Try the Shotgun approach.* Write to any organization you would be willing to work for and state your assets in the best possible way. Learn to write a résumé that sells *you.* A book is available on *Resume Writing: A Comprehensive How-to-Do-It Guide* (New York: Wiley Interscience, 1976). It includes:

    a. How to prepare a résumé that will bring your goals, personality, and attributes to the fore and will make the most of your vocational experiences.

    b. When, how, and where to use your résumé for maximum effect; and what employers want to see in your résumé.

    c. A glossary of motivating words, phrases, sentences, and paragraphs; and instruction on items to omit from your resume.

    d. Valuable source lists of companies.

Staying in the Upstream

This discussion would require a book* and a self-analysis: How hard and how long are you willing to work? What kind of a record do you have? What references can you get? What creative skills do you have? What technical skills do you have? Are you keeping up with new developments? What human relations skills do you possess? Are you a good team worker? Have you political savvy? Can you play internal politics successfully? Have you developed a reputation for integrity and compassion? Have you an advancement plan with goals and targets? Are you willing to take risks—to move when opportunity knocks?

    You must find the answers to these questions. No one can make predictions without data. But keeping steady and on course should give you a marked advantage.

Evaluation Check List for University Faculty Job Seekers Who Make Research a High Priority

1. Research

    a. Research/teaching/service orientation of the department and the institution generally.

    b. Types and scopes of research encouraged.

    c. Research budget for department or division (dollars per faculty member).

    d. Assistance available in securing grants.

    e. Research facility—computer capabilities, editorial or computer assistance, a supportive institute of social research.

---

    * A good choice would be Jeanne Curran and Carol Telesky, *Up the Job Market: Controlling the Ascent.* It is available at ASA Teaching Resources Center, 1722 N Street, N.W., Washington, DC 20036. Chapter headings: The Array of Career Opportunities: Evaluating Trends in the Job Market; Social Problem Issues; Indicators of Job Market Trends; Penetrating Organizational Boundaries: Probing the Career Path; Organizational and Self-Identity; Individual Fit with the Organization: and Definition of Self and Career: Controlling the Social Context of Identity.

    f. Number of hours per week per professor of secretarial help. Research atmosphere implies great secretarial support.

    g. Reproduction support (access to machines, type and number of machines).

    h. Machine availability (dictating, electric typewriter, photocopy, computer type, and programming assistance).

    i. Number of research assistants (criteria for obtaining assistants).

    j. Grading help (number of hours per week per professor) Research atmosphere implies grading help.

    k. Relief time for research; sabbatical program.

    l. Teaching demands on time: class size to expect; number of preparations per term; number of *new* preparations per term; number of courses per term; summer course load; day/night schedule; travel time committed to teaching.

    m. Graduate program: seminar teaching opportunities; number and quality of graduate students.

    n. Fellow faculty members, especially in area of interest; research emphasis, compatibility, competence of faculty.

    o. Travel money for professional conferences.

2. Salary offered: Check bulletin of American Association of University Professors for most recent report on the economic status of the profession showing salary rating of the institution. Also check to see if they are among *Censured Institutions.*

    a. Summer salary available; moving expenses provided; life insurance; health insurance.

3. Faculty housing available; cost of housing and other living expenses in the area.

4. Office space and equipment.

5. Library facility; extent and quality of holdings.

6. Number of undergraduate and graduate majors in the department.

7. Tenure rules.

8. Promotion procedures.

9. Retirement program.

10. Morale of the Faculty; history of faculty mobility in the department.

11. Relationships across departments and schools.

12. Quality and character of the administration, especially the Chair of the Department and the Dean.

13. History and current status of the financing of the institution.

14. Faculty governance and rules (ask for faculty handbook).

Notes

1. *Careers in Sociology,* Washington, DC: American Sociological Association, p. 14.

2. Sharon K. Panian and Melvin L. De Fleur, *Sociologists in Non-Academic Employment* (Washington, D.C.: American Sociological Association, 1975), tables 6 and 7.

3. Doris Wilkinson, *"Skills Assessment: Market Our Assets," Footnotes* of the American Sociological Association, October 1980, p. 3.

4. *Footnotes* (ASA), May 1979, p. 3.

5. Wilkinson, "Skills Assessment," p. 3.

6. *Footnotes* (ASA), August 1978, p. 7.

Selected Bibliography of Nonacademic Careers

American Sociological Association. *Careers in Sociology,* Washington, D.C.: American Sociological Association, 1975.

FOOTE, NELSON. "Putting Sociologists to Work." *American Sociologist* 9 (August 1974): 125–34.

GELFAND, DONALD E. "The Challenge of Applied Sociology." *American Sociologist* 10 (February 1975): 13–18.

MONTOYA, MARCO. *The Sociologist in Government.* Resource Development Center, 1858 Quebec Street, Severn, MD 21144. 1976.

————. "The Federal Government: Getting In and Staying In." Paper presented at American Sociological Association, Chicago, September 6, 1977.

PANIAN, SHARON K., and DE FLEUR, MELVIN L. *Sociologists in Non-Academic Employment.* Washington, D.C.: American Sociological Association, 1975.

ROSSI, PETER H. "The Challenge and Opportunities of Applied Social Research." *American Sociological Review* 45 (December 1980): 889–904.

SCOTT, ROBERT A., and SHORE, ARNOLD. "Sociology and Policy Analysis." *American Sociologist* 9 (May 1974): 51–59.

TUCHFELD, BARRY S. "Putting Sociology to Work: An Insider's View." *American Sociologist* 11 (November 1976): 188–92.

Subject Guide

Part I

Part II

Part V

Index of Names